Business
Plans
Handbook

Business Plans Handbook

A COMPILATION OF BUSINESS PLANS DEVELOPED BY INDIVIDUALS THROUGHOUT NORTH AMERICA

VOLUME

19

**Lynn M. Pearce,
Project Editor**

GALE
CENGAGE Learning

Detroit • New York • San Francisco • New Haven, Conn • Waterville, Maine • London

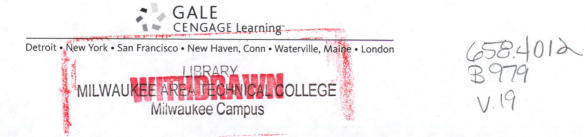

Business Plans Handbook, Volume 19

Project Editor: Lynn M. Pearce

Product Manager: Jenai Drouillard

Product Design: Jennifer Wahi

Composition and Electronic Prepress: Evi Seoud

Manufacturing: Rita Wimberley

For product information and technology assistance, contact us at
Gale Customer Support, 1-800-877-4253.
For permission to use material from this text or product,
submit all requests online at **www.cengage.com/permissions.**
Further permissions questions can be emailed to
permissionrequest@cengage.com

Gale, a part of Cengage Learning
27500 Drake Rd.
Farmington Hills, MI 48331-3535

ISBN-13: 978-1-4144-6831-8
ISBN-10: 1-4144-6831-8
1084-4473

Printed in Mexico
1 2 3 4 5 6 7 13 12 11 10

Contents

BUSINESS PLANS

CONTENTS

Highlights

Business Plans Handbook, Volume 19 (BPH-19) is a collection of business plans compiled by entrepreneurs seeking funding for small businesses throughout North America. For those looking for examples of how to approach, structure, and compose their own business plans, *BPH-19* presents 20 sample plans, including plans for the following businesses:

- Assisted Living Facility
- Auto Detailing
- Automotive Dealer
- Automotive Repair Service
- Bowling Alley
- Commodities Trading Firm
- Diaper Delivery Business
- Digital Presentations
- Farm
- Furniture Store
- Gas Station
- Ice Cream Shop
- Interior Decorator
- Interior Design Firm
- Laundry Mat
- Marina
- Mobile Pizza Kitchen Business
- Roller Skating Rink
- Stained Glass Business
- Web Design

FEATURES AND BENEFITS

BPH-19 offers many features not provided by other business planning references including:

- Twenty business plans, each of which represent an attempt at clarifying (for themselves and others) the reasons that the business should exist or expand and why a lender should fund the enterprise.
- Two fictional plans that are used by business counselors at a prominent small business development organization as examples for their clients. (You will find these in the Business Plan Template Appendix.)
- A directory section that includes: listings for venture capital and finance companies, which specialize in funding start-up and second-stage small business ventures, and a comprehensive

listing of Service Corps of Retired Executives (SCORE) offices. In addition, the Appendix also contains updated listings of all Small Business Development Centers (SBDCs); associations of interest to entrepreneurs; Small Business Administration (SBA) Regional Offices; and consultants specializing in small business planning and advice. It is strongly advised that you consult supporting organizations while planning your business, as they can provide a wealth of useful information.

- A Small Business Term Glossary to help you decipher the sometimes confusing terminology used by lenders and others in the financial and small business communities.

- A cumulative index, outlining each plan profiled in the complete *Business Plans Handbook* series.

- A Business Plan Template which serves as a model to help you construct your own business plan. This generic outline lists all the essential elements of a complete business plan and their components, including the Summary, Business History and Industry Outlook, Market Examination, Competition, Marketing, Administration and Management, Financial Information, and other key sections. Use this guide as a starting point for compiling your plan.

- Extensive financial documentation required to solicit funding from small business lenders. You will find examples of: Cash Flows, Balance Sheets, Income Projections, and other financial information included with the textual portions of the plan.

Introduction

Perhaps the most important aspect of business planning is simply doing it. More and more business owners are beginning to compile business plans even if they don't need a bank loan. Others discover the value of planning when they must provide a business plan for the bank. The sheer act of putting thoughts on paper seems to clarify priorities and provide focus. Sometimes business owners completely change strategies when compiling their plan, deciding on a different product mix or advertising scheme after finding that their assumptions were incorrect. This kind of healthy thinking and re-thinking via business planning is becoming the norm. The editors of *Business Plans Handbook, Volume 19 (BPH-19)* sincerely hope that this latest addition to the series is a helpful tool in the successful completion of your business plan, no matter what the reason for creating it.

This nineteenth volume, like each volume in the series, offers business plans used and created by real people. *BPH-19* provides 20 business plans. The business and personal names and addresses and general locations have been changed to protect the privacy of the plan authors.

NEW BUSINESS OPPORTUNITIES

As in other volumes in the series, *BPH-19* finds entrepreneurs engaged in a wide variety of creative endeavors. Examples include a proposal for an assisted living facility, a bowling alley, and an ice cream shop. In addition, several other plans are provided, including a commodities trading firm, a marina, and a roller rink, among others.

Comprehensive financial documentation has become increasingly important as today's entrepreneurs compete for the finite resources of business lenders. Our plans illustrate the financial data generally required of loan applicants, including Income Statements, Financial Projections, Cash Flows, and Balance Sheets.

ENHANCED APPENDIXES

In an effort to provide the most relevant and valuable information for our readers, we have updated the coverage of small business resources. For instance, you will find: a directory section, which includes listings of all of the Service Corps of Retired Executives (SCORE) offices; an informative glossary, which includes small business terms; and a cumulative index, outlining each plan profiled in the complete Business Plans Handbook series. In addition we have updated the list of Small Business Development Centers (SBDCs); Small Business Administration Regional Offices; venture capital and finance companies, which specialize in funding start-up and second-stage small business enterprises; associations of interest to entrepreneurs; and consultants, specializing in small business advice and planning. For your reference, we have also reprinted the business plan template, which provides a comprehensive overview of the essential components of a business plan and two fictional plans used by small business counselors.

SERIES INFORMATION

If you already have the first eighteen volumes of *BPH*, with this nineteenth volume, you will now have a collection of over 397 business plans (not including updated plans that originally appeared in earlier volumes); contact information for hundreds of organizations and agencies offering business expertise; a helpful business plan template; more than 1,500 citations to valuable small business development material; and a comprehensive glossary of terms to help the business planner navigate the sometimes confusing language of entrepreneurship.

ACKNOWLEDGEMENTS

The Editors wish to sincerely thank the contributors to *BPH-19*, including:

- BizPlanDB.com
- Heidi Denler
- Paul Greenland
- Kari Lucke

COMMENTS WELCOME

Your comments on *Business Plans Handbook* are appreciated. Please direct all correspondence, suggestions for future volumes of *BPH*, and other recommendations to the following:

Managing Editor, Business Product
Business Plans Handbook
Gale, a part of Cengage Learning
27500 Drake Rd.
Farmington Hills, MI 48331-3535
Phone: (248)699-4253
Fax: (248)699-8052
Toll-Free: 800-347-GALE
E-mail: BusinessProducts@gale.com

Assisted Living Facility
Home Again Assisted Living

2345 Houston Ave.
Bronx, NY 10468

BizPlanDB.com

Home Again Assisted Living is a New York based corporation that will provide assisted living services through its home-like facility to customers in its targeted market. The Company was founded in 2010 by Eloise Littleton.

1.0 EXECUTIVE SUMMARY

The purpose of this business plan is to raise $1,000,000 for the development of an assisted living facility while showcasing the expected financials and operations over the next three years. Home Again Assisted Living is a New York based corporation that will provide assisted living services through its home-like facility to customers in its targeted market. The Company was founded in 2010 by Eloise Littleton.

1.1 The Services

Home Again Assisted Living is in the business of providing compassionate assisted living services that will allow developmentally disabled people to live happy and productive lives while having direct access to assistance. The Company will also retain a number of healthcare professionals in the event that more significant treatment is needed or in the event of an emergency.

In addition to the assisted living services, the Company will have its aides take their patients out so that they are not constantly confined to the facility. This is especially true for people that are still mobile and active but no longer have the ability to operate a car.

The third section of the business plan will further describe the services offered by Home Again Assisted Living.

1.2 Financing

Ms. Littleton is seeking to raise $1,000,000 from as a bank loan. The interest rate and loan agreement are to be further discussed during negotiation. This business plan assumes that the business will receive a 30 year loan with a 7% fixed interest rate. The financing will be used for the following:

*   Development of the Company's Home Again Assisted Living location.

*   Financing for the first six months of operation.

*   Capital to purchase FF&E for the facility.

*   Capital for licensure and professional fees associated with the establishment of the assisted living facility location.

Ms. Littleton will contribute $100,000 to the venture.

1.3 Mission Statement

It is the goal of the Company to provide a caring environment for those that need assisted living and round the clock medical and living support. The Company is committed to providing a safe and secure home environment for patients. Management will also ensure that the facility complies with all local, state, and federal regulations concerning assisted living services.

1.4 Management Team

The Company was founded by Eloise Littleton. Ms. Littleton has more than 10 years of experience in the healthcare industry. Through her expertise, she will be able to bring the operations of the business to profitability within its first year of operations.

1.5 Sales Forecasts

Ms. Littleton expects a strong rate of growth at the start of operations. Below are the expected financials over the next three years.

Proforma profit and loss (yearly)

Year	1	2	3
Sales	$857,172	$917,174	$981,376
Operating costs	$463,583	$479,787	$496,628
EBITDA	$265,014	$299,811	$337,542
Taxes, interest, and depreciation	$237,026	$223,316	$237,166
Net profit	$ 27,987	$ 76,495	$100,376

Sales, operating costs, and profit forecast

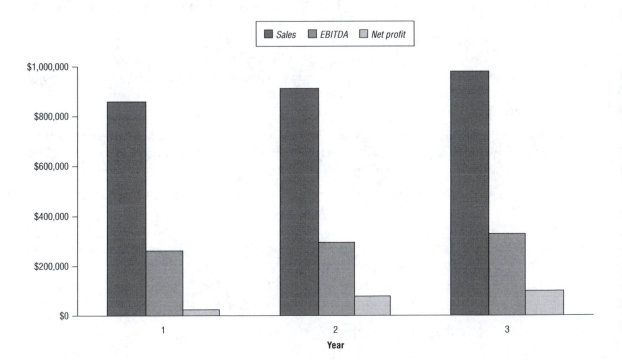

1.6 Expansion Plan

The Founder expects that the business will aggressively expand during the first three years of operation. Ms. Littleton intends to implement marketing campaigns that will effectively target families with individuals that require continued care and oversight within a compassionate assisted living facility.

2.0 COMPANY AND FINANCING SUMMARY

2.1 Registered Name and Corporate Structure

Home Again Assisted Living, Inc. is registered as a corporation in the State of New York.

2.2 Required Funds

At this time, Home Again Assisted Living requires $1,100,000 of debt funds. Below is a breakdown of how these funds will be used:

Projected startup costs

Facility acquisition	$ 550,000
Working capital	$ 165,000
FF&E	$ 75,000
Leasehold improvements	$ 80,000
Licensure	$ 25,000
Insurance	$ 30,000
Facility transportation vehicle	$ 65,000
Marketing budget	$ 35,000
Miscellaneous and unforeseen costs	$ 75,000
Total startup costs	**$1,100,000**

Use of funds

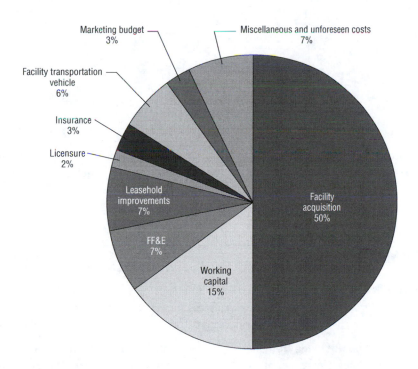

2.3 Investor Equity

Ms. Littleton is not seeking an investment from a third party at this time.

2.4 Management Equity

Eloise Littleton owns 100% of Home Again Assisted Living.

2.5 Exit Strategy

If the business is very successful, Ms. Littleton may seek to sell the business to a third party for a significant earnings multiple. Most likely, the Company will hire a qualified business broker to sell the business on behalf of Home Again Assisted Living. Based on historical numbers, the business could fetch a sales premium of up to 6 times earnings plus the value of the appreciated real estate owned by Home Again Assisted Living.

3.0 PRODUCTS AND SERVICES

Below is a description of the services offered by Home Again Assisted Living.

3.1 Assisted Living Facility Services

Home Again Assisted Living's business seeks to provide people with an alternative to the uncompassionate facilities of normal mental health institutions. Management will only hire nurses and assisted living aides that truly seek to improve the quality of life for the Company's clients. The staff will engage clients with many projects, activities, and trips that are not offered by institutional facilities.

Additionally, the business will have a number of specialty health professionals on retainer so that each of the Company's clients receives the highest level of medical service should the need arise. Management intends to have several specialty allied health professionals on retainer. These professionals include:

- Pharmacy Consultants
- Psychologists
- Physical Therapists
- Dieticians
- Speech Pathologists
- Physician Consultant
- Occupational Therapy Consultants

All billing will be administered by a third party processing agent. Using a third party billing agent will ensure that the specialty services administrated by the Company will be quickly reimbursed by the New York healthcare reimbursement programs.

4.0 STRATEGIC AND MARKET ANALYSIS

4.1 Economic Outlook

This section of the analysis will detail the economic climate, the assisted living facility industry, the customer profile, and the competition that the business will face as it progresses through its business operations.

Currently, the economic market condition in the United States is in recession. This slowdown in the economy has also greatly impacted real estate sales, which has halted to historical lows. Many economists expect that this recession will continue until mid-2010, at which point the economy will begin a prolonged recovery period. However, assisted living facilities typically operate with great economic stability as people will continue to require specialized medical care regardless of the general economic climate.

4.2 Industry Analysis

There are over 19,000 assisted living service companies in the United States. Each year, the industry generates over $49 billion dollars in billable revenue. The industry also employs more than 1,000,000 people, and provides average annual payrolls of over $22 billion dollars.

The assisted living industry has grown tremendously over the past fifteen years. According to the last economic census, the industry's five year growth rate is 31.3%. This exceptional growth is attributed to the general public's acceptance and compassion for developmentally disabled and elderly people. Large institutions that cater to the needs of the developmentally disabled are becoming less popular because of their cold nature. Developmentally disabled people and their primary caretakers are quickly adopting in-home assisted living services as an alternative to traditional institutional care.

4.3 Customer Profile

All of the Company's patients will be developmentally disabled that require full time assisted living services. Ms. Littleton expects that patients will have a range of developmental and old age disorders, but are able to live within a facility that provides a host of specialty physical and mental health care services. Management anticipates that the average client will be between the ages of 25 and 85.

Based on population information provided by the United States' Census, there are approximately 50,000 people that live within the Company's market that are in need of assisted living facility services. Among these residents, the annual household income is $35,000 with 70% of this income coming from pension and Social Security income distribution services.

4.4 Competition

In the Company's targeted area within the New York metropolitan area there are approximately 10 facilities that operate in a similar or identical capacity to that of the Company. The business does not necessarily need to provide a strong competitive advantage over these other competitors as many of these facilities are already filled to capacity. As such, once the business launches its operations, Management expects that maximum occupancy will occur within one year of establishing the business.

5.0 MARKETING PLAN

Home Again Assisted Living intends to maintain an extensive marketing campaign that will ensure maximum visibility for the business in its targeted market. Below is an overview of the marketing strategies and objectives of the Company.

5.1 Marketing Objectives

- Develop an online presence by developing a website and placing the Company's name and contact information with online directories.

- Implement a local campaign with the Company's targeted market via the use of local newspaper advertisements and word of mouth advertising.

- Establish relationships with doctors and mental health professionals that will refer business to Home Again Assisted Living.

5.2 Marketing Strategies

The Company intends to use a referral network from doctors, surgeons, hospitals, and post operative clinics in target area in order to generate a patient list. As such, it is imperative that the Company develop these relationships with medical professionals at the onset of operation. Many insurance carriers and Medicare/Medicaid require that a physician authorize the use of assisted living facility services.

The Company will use both traditional and experimental forms of marketing to inform, educate, and sell the Company's assisted living facility service. Traditional means of advertising will include print and media advertising within local newspapers in the target market.

Finally, the Company will develop an online website that will showcase the assisted living facility, its operations, its fees, and its commitment to compassionate care.

5.3 Pricing

On a monthly basis, Management anticipates that each patient of Home Again Assisted Living will generate approximately $3,000 to $5,000 for the business with the average patient generating revenues of $3,500. The exact pricing will depend on the level of care and medications required by each individual patient.

6.0 ORGANIZATIONAL PLAN AND PERSONNEL SUMMARY

6.1 Corporate Organization

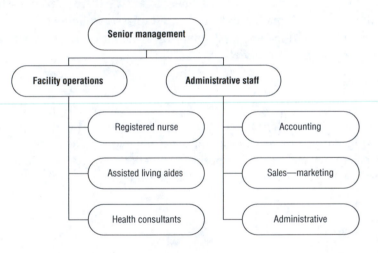

6.2 Organizational Budget

Personnel plan—yearly

Year	1	2	3
Owner	$ 50,000	$ 51,500	$ 53,045
Facility manager	$ 42,500	$ 43,775	$ 45,088
Registered nurse	$100,000	$103,000	$106,090
Assisted living aides	$116,000	$119,480	$123,064
Administrative and accounting	$ 21,000	$ 21,630	$ 22,279
Total	**$329,500**	**$339,385**	**$349,567**

Numbers of personnel

Owner	1	1	1
Facility manager	1	1	1
Registered nurse	2	2	2
Assisted living aides	4	4	4
Administrative and accounting	1	1	1
Totals	**9**	**9**	**9**

Personnel expense breakdown

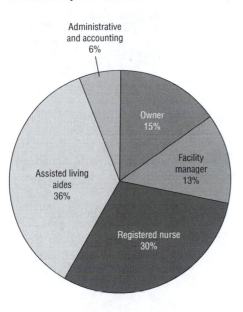

7.0 FINANCIAL PLAN

7.1 Underlying Assumptions

The Company has based its proforma financial statements on the following:

- Home Again Assisted Living will have an annual revenue growth rate of 7% per year.

- The Owner will acquire $1,000,000 of debt funds to develop the business.

- The loan will have a 30 year term with a 7% interest rate.

7.2 Sensitivity Analysis

Developmentally disabled and elderly people require assisted living services regardless of the overall economic climate. As such, the Company does not expect that economic recessions or downturns will affect the overall profitability of the Company. Additionally, much of the revenues generated from the Company will be paid for by public health systems. As this is a health and medical services related business, the Company is insulated from any changes in the economy.

7.3 Source of Funds

Financing

Equity contributions	
Management investment	$ 100,000.00
Total equity financing	**$ 100,000.00**
Banks and lenders	
Banks and lenders	$ 1,000,000.00
Total debt financing	**$ 1,000,000.00**
Total financing	**$ 1,100,000.00**

7.4 General Assumptions

General assumptions

Year	1	2	3
Short term interest rate	9.5%	9.5%	9.5%
Long term interest rate	10.0%	10.0%	10.0%
Federal tax rate	33.0%	33.0%	33.0%
State tax rate	5.0%	5.0%	5.0%
Personnel taxes	15.0%	15.0%	15.0%

7.5 Profit and Loss Statements

Proforma profit and loss (yearly)

Year	1	2	3
Sales	**$857,172**	**$917,174**	**$981,376**
Cost of goods sold	$128,576	$137,576	$147,206
Gross margin	85.00%	85.00%	85.00%
Operating income	**$728,596**	**$779,598**	**$834,170**
Expenses			
Payroll	$329,500	$339,385	$349,567
General and administrative	$ 25,200	$ 26,208	$ 27,256
Marketing expenses	$ 17,143	$ 18,343	$ 19,628
Professional fees and licensure	$ 5,219	$ 5,376	$ 5,537
Insurance costs	$ 1,987	$ 2,086	$ 2,191
Facility maintenance costs	$ 20,572	$ 22,012	$ 23,553
Rent and utilities	$ 4,250	$ 4,463	$ 4,686
Miscellaneous costs	$ 10,286	$ 11,006	$ 11,777
Payroll taxes	$ 49,425	$ 50,908	$ 52,435
Total operating costs	**$463,583**	**$479,787**	**$496,628**
EBITDA	**$265,014**	**$299,811**	**$337,542**
Federal income tax	$ 87,454	$ 76,186	$ 88,897
State income tax	$ 13,251	$ 11,543	$ 13,469
Interest expense	$ 69,678	$ 68,944	$ 68,156
Depreciation expenses	$ 66,643	$ 66,643	$ 66,643
Net profit	**$ 27,987**	**$ 76,495**	**$100,376**
Profit margin	**3.27%**	**8.34%**	**10.23%**

Sales, operating costs, and profit forecast

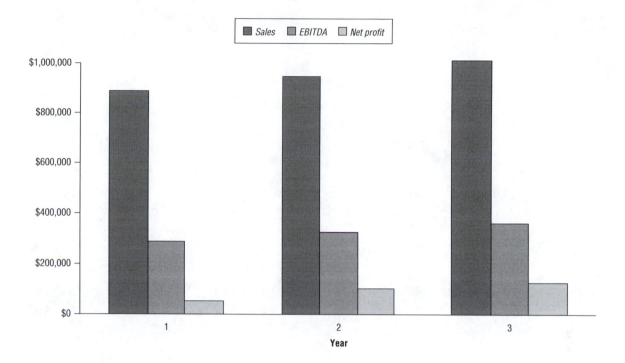

7.6 Cash Flow Analysis

Proforma cash flow analysis—yearly

Year	1	2	3
Cash from operations	$ 94,630	$143,138	$167,019
Cash from receivables	$ 0	$ 0	$ 0
Operating cash inflow	**$ 94,630**	**$143,138**	**$167,019**
Other cash inflows			
Equity investment	$ 100,000	$ 0	$ 0
Increased borrowings	$1,000,000	$ 0	$ 0
Sales of business assets	$ 0	$ 0	$ 0
A/P increases	$ 37,902	$ 43,587	$ 50,125
Total other cash inflows	**$1,137,902**	**$ 43,587**	**$ 50,125**
Total cash inflow	**$1,232,532**	**$186,725**	**$217,144**
Cash outflows			
Repayment of principal	$ 10,158	$ 10,892	$ 11,680
A/P decreases	$ 24,897	$ 29,876	$ 35,852
A/R increases	$ 0	$ 0	$ 0
Asset purchases	$ 900,000	$ 35,784	$ 41,755
Dividends	$ 56,778	$ 85,883	$100,211
Total cash outflows	**$ 991,833**	**$162,436**	**$189,498**
Net cash flow	**$ 240,699**	**$ 24,289**	**$ 27,647**
Cash balance	**$ 240,699**	**$264,988**	**$292,635**

Proforma cash flow (yearly)

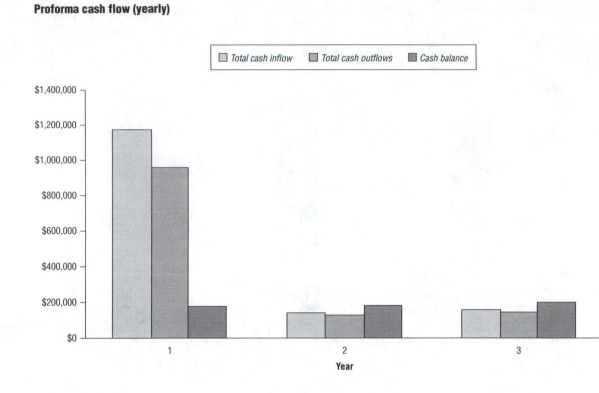

7.7 Balance Sheet

Proforma balance sheet—yearly

Year	1	2	3
Assets			
Cash	$ 240,699	$ 264,988	$ 292,635
Amortized development costs	$ 210,000	$ 213,578	$ 217,754
FF&E	$ 75,000	$ 101,838	$ 133,154
Vehicles	$ 65,000	$ 70,368	$ 76,631
Property	$ 583,000	$ 617,980	$ 655,059
Accumulated depreciation	($ 66,643)	($ 133,286)	($ 199,929)
Total assets	**$1,107,056**	**$1,135,467**	**$1,175,304**
Liabilities and equity			
Accounts payable	$ 13,005	$ 26,716	$ 40,990
Long term liabilities	$ 989,842	$ 978,949	$ 968,057
Other liabilities	$ 0	$ 0	$ 0
Total liabilities	**$1,002,847**	**$1,005,665**	**$1,009,047**
Net worth	**$ 104,209**	**$ 129,801**	**$ 166,258**
Total liabilities and equity	**$1,107,056**	**$1,135,467**	**$1,175,304**

Proforma balance sheet

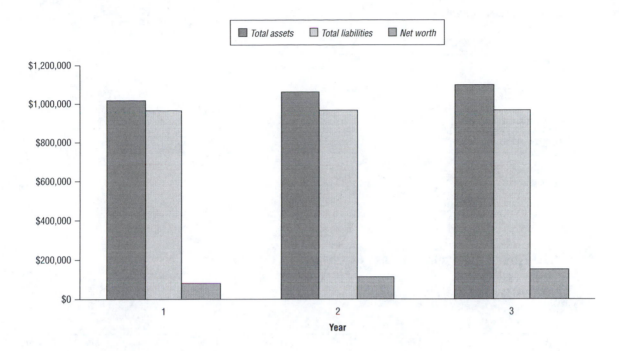

7.8 Breakeven Analysis

Monthly break even analysis

Year	1	2	3
Monthly revenue	$ 45,449	$ 47,038	$ 48,689
Yearly revenue	$545,391	$564,455	$584,268

Break even analysis

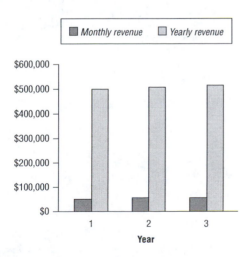

7.9 Business Ratios

Business ratios—yearly

Year	1	2	3
Sales			
Sales growth	0.0%	7.0%	7.0%
Gross margin	85.0%	85.0%	85.0%
Financials			
Profit margin	3.27%	8.34%	10.23%
Assets to liabilities	1.10	1.13	1.16
Equity to liabilities	0.10	0.13	0.16
Assets to equity	10.62	8.75	7.07
Liquidity			
Acid test	0.24	0.26	0.29
Cash to assets	0.22	0.23	0.25

7.10 Three Year Profit and Loss Statement

Profit and loss statement (first year)

Months	1	2	3	4	5	6	7
Sales	$70,760	$70,882	$71,004	$71,126	$71,248	$71,370	$71,492
Cost of goods sold	$10,614	$10,632	$10,651	$10,669	$10,687	$10,706	$10,724
Gross margin	85.0%	85.0%	85.0%	85.0%	85.0%	85.0%	85.0%
Operating income	**$60,146**	**$60,250**	**$60,353**	**$60,457**	**$60,561**	**$60,665**	**$60,768**
Expenses							
Payroll	$27,458	$27,458	$27,458	$27,458	$27,458	$27,458	$27,458
General and administrative	$ 2,100	$ 2,100	$ 2,100	$ 2,100	$ 2,100	$ 2,100	$ 2,100
Marketing expenses	$ 1,429	$ 1,429	$ 1,429	$ 1,429	$ 1,429	$ 1,429	$ 1,429
Professional fees and licensure	$ 435	$ 435	$ 435	$ 435	$ 435	$ 435	$ 435
Insurance costs	$ 166	$ 166	$ 166	$ 166	$ 166	$ 166	$ 166
Facility maintenance costs	$ 1,714	$ 1,714	$ 1,714	$ 1,714	$ 1,714	$ 1,714	$ 1,714
Rent and utilities	$ 354	$ 354	$ 354	$ 354	$ 354	$ 354	$ 354
Miscellaneous costs	$ 857	$ 857	$ 857	$ 857	$ 857	$ 857	$ 857
Payroll taxes	$ 4,119	$ 4,119	$ 4,119	$ 4,119	$ 4,119	$ 4,119	$ 4,119
Total operating costs	**$38,632**	**$38,632**	**$38,632**	**$38,632**	**$38,632**	**$38,632**	**$38,632**
EBITDA	**$21,514**	**$21,618**	**$21,722**	**$21,825**	**$21,929**	**$22,033**	**$22,136**
Federal income tax	$ 7,219	$ 7,232	$ 7,244	$ 7,257	$ 7,269	$ 7,282	$ 7,294
State income tax	$ 1,094	$ 1,096	$ 1,098	$ 1,100	$ 1,101	$ 1,103	$ 1,105
Interest expense	$ 5,833	$ 5,829	$ 5,824	$ 5,819	$ 5,814	$ 5,809	$ 5,804
Depreciation expense	$ 5,554	$ 5,554	$ 5,554	$ 5,554	$ 5,554	$ 5,554	$ 5,554
Net profit	**$ 1,814**	**$ 1,908**	**$ 2,002**	**$ 2,096**	**$ 2,191**	**$ 2,285**	**$ 2,379**

Profit and loss statement (first year cont.)

Month	8	9	10	11	12	Year 1
Sales	$71,614	$71,736	$71,858	$71,980	$72,102	$857,172
Cost of goods sold	$10,742	$10,760	$10,779	$10,797	$10,815	$128,576
Gross margin	85.0%	85.0%	85.0%	85.0%	85.0%	85.0%
Operating income	**$60,872**	**$60,976**	**$61,079**	**$61,183**	**$61,287**	**$728,596**
Expenses						
Payroll	$27,458	$27,458	$27,458	$27,458	$27,458	$329,500
General and administrative	$ 2,100	$ 2,100	$ 2,100	$ 2,100	$ 2,100	$ 25,200
Marketing expenses	$ 1,429	$ 1,429	$ 1,429	$ 1,429	$ 1,429	$ 17,143
Professional fees and licensure	$ 435	$ 435	$ 435	$ 435	$ 435	$ 5,219
Insurance costs	$ 166	$ 166	$ 166	$ 166	$ 166	$ 1,987
Facility maintenance costs	$ 1,714	$ 1,714	$ 1,714	$ 1,714	$ 1,714	$ 20,572
Rent and utilities	$ 354	$ 354	$ 354	$ 354	$ 354	$ 4,250
Miscellaneous costs	$ 857	$ 857	$ 857	$ 857	$ 857	$ 10,286
Payroll taxes	$ 4,119	$ 4,119	$ 4,119	$ 4,119	$ 4,119	$ 49,425
Total operating costs	**$38,632**	**$38,632**	**$38,632**	**$38,632**	**$38,632**	**$463,583**
EBITDA	**$22,240**	**$22,344**	**$22,447**	**$22,551**	**$22,655**	**$265,014**
Federal income tax	$ 7,307	$ 7,319	$ 7,331	$ 7,344	$ 7,356	$ 87,454
State income tax	$ 1,107	$ 1,109	$ 1,111	$ 1,113	$ 1,115	$ 13,251
Interest expense	$ 5,799	$ 5,794	$ 5,789	$ 5,784	$ 5,779	$ 69,678
Depreciation expense	$ 5,554	$ 5,554	$ 5,554	$ 5,554	$ 5,554	$ 66,643
Net profit	**$ 2,474**	**$ 2,568**	**$ 2,662**	**$ 2,757**	**$ 2,851**	**$ 27,987**

Profit and loss statement (second year)

Quarter	Q1	Q2	Q3	Q4	Year 2
Sales	$183,435	$229,294	$247,637	$256,809	$917,174
Cost of goods sold	$ 27,515	$ 34,394	$ 37,146	$ 38,521	$137,576
Gross margin	85.0%	85.0%	85.0%	85.0%	85.0%
Operating income	**$155,920**	**$194,899**	**$210,491**	**$218,287**	**$779,598**
Expenses					
Payroll	$ 67,877	$ 84,846	$ 91,634	$ 95,028	$339,385
General and administrative	$ 5,242	$ 6,552	$ 7,076	$ 7,338	$ 26,208
Marketing expenses	$ 3,669	$ 4,586	$ 4,953	$ 5,136	$ 18,343
Professional fees and licensure	$ 1,075	$ 1,344	$ 1,451	$ 1,505	$ 5,376
Insurance costs	$ 417	$ 522	$ 563	$ 584	$ 2,086
Facility maintenance costs	$ 4,402	$ 5,503	$ 5,943	$ 6,163	$ 22,012
Rent and utilities	$ 893	$ 1,116	$ 1,205	$ 1,250	$ 4,463
Miscellaneous costs	$ 2,201	$ 2,752	$ 2,972	$ 3,082	$ 11,006
Payroll taxes	$ 10,182	$ 12,727	$ 13,745	$ 14,254	$ 50,908
Total operating costs	**$ 95,957**	**$119,947**	**$129,542**	**$134,340**	**$479,787**
EBITDA	**$ 59,962**	**$ 74,953**	**$ 80,949**	**$ 83,947**	**$299,811**
Federal income tax	$ 15,237	$ 19,047	$ 20,570	$ 21,332	$ 76,186
State income tax	$ 2,309	$ 2,886	$ 3,117	$ 3,232	$ 11,543
Interest expense	$ 17,307	$ 17,260	$ 17,213	$ 17,164	$ 68,944
Depreciation expense	$ 16,661	$ 16,661	$ 16,661	$ 16,661	$ 66,643
Net profit	**$ 8,449**	**$ 19,100**	**$ 23,389**	**$ 25,558**	**$ 76,495**

Profit and loss statement (third year)

Quarter	Q1	Q2	Q3	Q4	Year 3
Sales	$196,275	$245,344	$264,972	$274,785	$981,376
Cost of goods sold	$ 29,441	$ 36,802	$ 39,746	$ 41,218	$147,206
Gross margin	85.0%	85.0%	85.0%	85.0%	85.0%
Operating income	**$166,834**	**$208,542**	**$225,226**	**$233,568**	**$834,170**
Expenses					
Payroll	$ 69,913	$ 87,392	$ 94,383	$ 97,879	$349,567
General and administrative	$ 5,451	$ 6,814	$ 7,359	$ 7,632	$ 27,256
Marketing expenses	$ 3,926	$ 4,907	$ 5,299	$ 5,496	$ 19,628
Professional fees and licensure	$ 1,107	$ 1,384	$ 1,495	$ 1,550	$ 5,537
Insurance costs	$ 438	$ 548	$ 591	$ 613	$ 2,191
Facility maintenance costs	$ 4,711	$ 5,888	$ 6,359	$ 6,595	$ 23,553
Rent and utilities	$ 937	$ 1,171	$ 1,265	$ 1,312	$ 4,686
Miscellaneous costs	$ 2,355	$ 2,944	$ 3,180	$ 3,297	$ 11,777
Payroll taxes	$ 10,487	$ 13,109	$ 14,157	$ 14,682	$ 52,435
Total operating costs	**$ 99,326**	**$124,157**	**$134,090**	**$139,056**	**$496,628**
EBITDA	**$ 67,508**	**$ 84,385**	**$ 91,136**	**$ 94,512**	**$337,542**
Federal income tax	$ 17,779	$ 22,224	$ 24,002	$ 24,891	$ 88,897
State income tax	$ 2,694	$ 3,367	$ 3,637	$ 3,771	$ 13,469
Interest expense	$ 17,115	$ 17,065	$ 17,014	$ 16,962	$ 68,156
Depreciation expense	$ 16,661	$ 16,661	$ 16,661	$ 16,661	$ 66,643
Net profit	**$ 13,259**	**$ 25,068**	**$ 29,823**	**$ 32,226**	**$100,376**

7.11 Three Year Cash Flow Analysis

Cash flow analysis (first year)

Month	1	2	3	4	5	6	7	8
Cash from operations	$ 7,368	$ 7,462	$ 7,556	$ 7,650	$ 7,744	$ 7,839	$ 7,933	$ 8,027
Cash from receivables	$ 0	$ 0	$ 0	$ 0	$ 0	$ 0	$ 0	$ 0
Operating cash inflow	**$ 7,368**	**$ 7,462**	**$ 7,556**	**$ 7,650**	**$ 7,744**	**$ 7,839**	**$ 7,933**	**$ 8,027**
Other cash inflows								
Equity investment	$ 100,000	$ 0	$ 0	$ 0	$ 0	$ 0	$ 0	$ 0
Increased borrowings	$1,000,000	$ 0	$ 0	$ 0	$ 0	$ 0	$ 0	$ 0
Sales of business assets	$ 0	$ 0	$ 0	$ 0	$ 0	$ 0	$ 0	$ 0
A/P increases	$ 3,159	$ 3,159	$ 3,159	$ 3,159	$ 3,159	$ 3,159	$ 3,159	$ 3,159
Total other cash inflows	**$1,103,159**	**$ 3,159**	**$ 3,159**	**$ 3,159**	**$ 3,159**	**$ 3,159**	**$ 3,159**	**$ 3,159**
Total cash inflow	**$1,110,526**	**$ 10,620**	**$ 10,714**	**$ 10,809**	**$ 10,903**	**$ 10,997**	**$ 11,091**	**$ 11,186**
Cash outflows								
Repayment of principal	$ 820	$ 824	$ 829	$ 834	$ 839	$ 844	$ 849	$ 854
A/P decreases	$ 2,075	$ 2,075	$ 2,075	$ 2,075	$ 2,075	$ 2,075	$ 2,075	$ 2,075
A/R increases	$ 0	$ 0	$ 0	$ 0	$ 0	$ 0	$ 0	$ 0
Asset purchases	$ 900,000	$ 0	$ 0	$ 0	$ 0	$ 0	$ 0	$ 0
Dividends	$ 0	$ 0	$ 0	$ 0	$ 0	$ 0	$ 0	$ 0
Total cash outflows	**$ 902,894**	**$ 2,899**	**$ 2,904**	**$ 2,909**	**$ 2,914**	**$ 2,919**	**$ 2,924**	**$ 2,929**
Net cash flow	**$ 207,632**	**$ 7,721**	**$ 7,810**	**$ 7,900**	**$ 7,989**	**$ 8,078**	**$ 8,168**	**$ 8,257**
Cash balance	**$ 207,632**	**$215,353**	**$223,163**	**$231,063**	**$239,052**	**$247,130**	**$255,298**	**$263,555**

Cash flow analysis (first year cont.)

Month	9	10	11	12	1
Cash from operations	$ 8,121	$ 8,216	$ 8,310	$ 8,405	$ 94,630
Cash from receivables	$ 0	$ 0	$ 0	$ 0	$ 0
Operating cash inflow	**$ 8,121**	**$ 8,216**	**$ 8,310**	**$ 8,405**	**$ 94,630**
Other cash inflows					
Equity investment	$ 0	$ 0	$ 0	$ 0	$ 100,000
Increased borrowings	$ 0	$ 0	$ 0	$ 0	$1,000,000
Sales of business assets	$ 0	$ 0	$ 0	$ 0	$ 0
A/P increases	$ 3,159	$ 3,159	$ 3,159	$ 3,159	$ 37,902
Total other cash inflows	**$ 3,159**	**$ 3,159**	**$ 3,159**	**$ 3,159**	**$1,137,902**
Total cash inflow	**$ 11,280**	**$ 11,374**	**$ 11,469**	**$ 11,563**	**$1,232,532**
Cash outflows					
Repayment of principal	$ 859	$ 864	$ 869	$ 874	$ 10,158
A/P decreases	$ 2,075	$ 2,075	$ 2,075	$ 2,075	$ 24,897
A/R increases	$ 0	$ 0	$ 0	$ 0	$ 0
Asset purchases	$ 0	$ 0	$ 0	$ 0	$ 900,000
Dividends	$ 0	$ 0	$ 0	$ 56,778	$ 56,778
Total cash outflows	**$ 2,933**	**$ 2,938**	**$ 2,944**	**$ 59,727**	**$ 991,833**
Net cash flow	**$ 8,347**	**$ 8,436**	**$ 8,525**	**−$ 48,163**	**$ 240,699**
Cash balance	**$271,901**	**$280,337**	**$288,863**	**$240,699**	**$ 240,699**

Cash flow analysis (second year)

Quarter	Q1	2	Q3	Q4	2
		Q2			
Cash from operations	$ 28,628	$ 35,784	$ 38,647	$ 40,079	$143,138
Cash from receivables	$ 0	$ 0	$ 0	$ 0	$ 0
Operating cash inflow	**$ 28,628**	**$ 35,784**	**$ 38,647**	**$ 40,079**	**$143,138**
Other cash inflows					
Equity investment	$ 0	$ 0	$ 0	$ 0	$ 0
Increased borrowings	$ 0	$ 0	$ 0	$ 0	$ 0
Sales of business assets	$ 0	$ 0	$ 0	$ 0	$ 0
A/P increases	$ 8,717	$ 10,897	$ 11,769	$ 12,204	$ 43,587
Total other cash inflows	**$ 8,717**	**$ 10,897**	**$ 11,769**	**$ 12,204**	**$ 43,587**
Total cash inflow	**$ 37,345**	**$ 46,681**	**$ 50,416**	**$ 52,283**	**$186,725**
Cash outflows					
Repayment of principal	$ 2,652	$ 2,699	$ 2,746	$ 2,795	$ 10,892
A/P decreases	$ 5,975	$ 7,469	$ 8,067	$ 8,365	$ 29,876
A/R increases	$ 0	$ 0	$ 0	$ 0	$ 0
Asset purchases	$ 7,157	$ 8,946	$ 9,662	$ 10,020	$ 35,784
Dividends	$ 17,177	$ 21,471	$ 23,188	$ 24,047	$ 85,883
Total cash outflows	**$ 32,961**	**$ 40,585**	**$ 43,663**	**$ 45,227**	**$162,436**
Net cash flow	**$ 4,384**	**$ 6,096**	**$ 6,753**	**$ 7,056**	**$ 24,289**
Cash balance	**$245,083**	**$251,179**	**$257,932**	**$264,988**	**$264,988**

ASSISTED LIVING FACILITY

Cash flow analysis (third year)

Quarter	Q1	3 Q2	Q3	Q4	3
Cash from operations	$ 33,404	$ 41,755	$ 45,095	$ 46,765	$167,019
Cash from receivables	$ 0	$ 0	$ 0	$ 0	$ 0
Operating cash inflow	**$ 33,404**	**$ 41,755**	**$ 45,095**	**$ 46,765**	**$167,019**
Other cash inflows					
Equity investment	$ 0	$ 0	$ 0	$ 0	$ 0
Increased borrowings	$ 0	$ 0	$ 0	$ 0	$ 0
Sales of business assets	$ 0	$ 0	$ 0	$ 0	$ 0
A/P increases	$ 10,025	$ 12,531	$ 13,534	$ 14,035	$ 50,125
Total other cash inflows	**$ 10,025**	**$ 12,531**	**$ 13,534**	**$ 14,035**	**$ 50,125**
Total cash inflow	**$ 43,429**	**$ 54,286**	**$ 58,629**	**$ 60,800**	**$217,144**
Cash outflows					
Repayment of principal	$ 2,844	$ 2,894	$ 2,945	$ 2,997	$ 11,680
A/P decreases	$ 7,170	$ 8,963	$ 9,680	$ 10,038	$ 35,852
A/R increases	$ 0	$ 0	$ 0	$ 0	$ 0
Asset purchases	$ 8,351	$ 10,439	$ 11,274	$ 11,691	$ 41,755
Dividends	$ 20,042	$ 25,053	$ 27,057	$ 28,059	$100,211
Total cash outflows	**$ 38,408**	**$ 47,348**	**$ 50,956**	**$ 52,786**	**$189,498**
Net cash flow	**$ 5,021**	**$ 6,938**	**$ 7,673**	**$ 8,015**	**$ 27,647**
Cash balance	**$270,009**	**$276,947**	**$284,620**	**$292,635**	**$292,635**

Auto Detailing

Johnson's Mobile Detail

1550 Wildwood Road
Columbia, MO 65201

Kari Lucke

Johnson's Mobile Detail will provide car washing and detailing services to customers in the Columbia, Missouri, area.

INTRODUCTION

Mission Statement

Johnson's Mobile Detail will provide car washing and detailing services to customers in the Columbia, Missouri, area. As a mobile operation, Johnson's will provide these services at the customers' home, business, or other select location. Johnson's mission is to provide excellent customer service at a reasonable price to individual car owners and car dealerships.

Executive Summary

Owned and operated by Robert and Misty Johnson, Johnson's Mobile Detail provides interior and exterior cleaning of all vehicles, including cars, trucks, SUVs, boats, and airplanes. Individually owned luxury cars and used cars sold by car dealerships are expected to account for the largest percentage of business. Start-up costs are minimal compared to an on-site operation, and customers appreciate the fact that the service comes to them. In today's society, convenience is one of the keys to gaining business in a service industry.

Business Philosophy

Although Johnson's Mobile Detail will obtain some business from local car dealerships, the focus will be on luxury automobiles, such as Lexus, BMW, Mercedes, and so on, owned by individuals. The philosophy at Johnson's is that one's car is a reflection of oneself, and people who drive cars that are clean and neat—both inside and outside—feel better about themselves. A clean car can make a driver feel more in control, less stressed, more professional, and so on. Thus Johnson's is in the business of not only cleaning and detailing cars but also, as a result, making people feel good. Business taken in from used car dealerships, which mainly look for detailers who can make cars presentable for resale, has a different focus and is more reliant on quantity and efficiency.

Luxury car drivers are the main market for the business for the simple reason that they are more likely to be able to afford the types of services offered by Johnson's. Another rationale is that the cost of detailing a luxury automobile represents a small fraction of what the car is worth.

Goals and Objectives

- Realize a profit by the end of the first year of business.

- Establish a reputation as one of the premier auto detailing businesses in the area by the second year of business.

- Establish a list of repeat customers through excellent customer service and quality work.

INDUSTRY AND MARKET

Industry Analysis

According to the International Car Washing Association, the professional car wash industry is a $23 billion dollar industry. The organization made the following statement on its website in 2010:

> The professional car wash industry cleans the world's automobiles in the safest, most convenient, and environmentally responsible manner. With more vehicles on the road and more car washes being purchased by motorists than ever before, this industry's best days are still to come.

There are three types of detailing operations: mobile, express, and site-based. Johnson's will operate as a mobile service for two reasons: (a) start-up costs are minimal and (b) it is easier to generate business if the service comes to where the customers are, rather than vice versa.

Market Analysis

The market for Johnson's Mobile Detail consists of two main groups—individual car owners and car dealerships—in the city of Columbia, Missouri.

Columbia has grown significantly in the past decade and is expected to see continued growth. It is consistently rated one of the best places to live in America by such well-known entities as *Forbes, Money* magazine, and Kiplinger.com due to its excellent educational systems, access to health care, and quality of life. For example, in 2007 *Forbes* ranked Columbia "Third Best Metro for Business and Careers" in its study that factored in the cost of doing business, job growth, and educational attainment. Also, unlike many small towns in Missouri, which are losing population, Columbia's population is growing. Due to these factors of demographics and growth trends as well as others, we see significant potential for an auto detailing service in this location.

Competition

Competition will come from other mobile detailing services in the area that offer the same types of services, including:

- Squeaky Clean Car Wash and Detailing

- Tiger Auto Detailing

- Autos Inc.

Some competition should be expected from the one major on-site service in Columbia, Columbia Car Wash, but operating as a mobile service will give Johnson's the advantage of bringing the service to the customers.

PERSONNEL

Management

Robert and Misty Johnson are the owners and managers of Johnson's Mobile Detail. Misty will act as administrative assistant and will perform such duties as answering the phone, maintaining the website, scheduling appointments, and bookkeeping. Misty has a bachelor of arts degree in accounting from Central Methodist University in Fayette, Missouri. Robert, who will do much of the manual labor as well as supervise other car-wash employees, has a bachelor's degree in business from the University of Missouri and thus has the knowledge and skills needed to run a small business. In addition, Robert worked part-time at a car dealership during high school and college, and his duties included detailing used cars for resale. Robert also has an interest in the business as a result of his participation in the Mid-Missouri Classic Car Club.

Staffing

Johnson's will hire two part-time employees to help wash and detail vehicles. Each employee will work with Robert as the second half of a two-person team and will be trained and closely supervised by Robert. Hours will vary depending on time of year, with the summer months being the busiest, and scheduled appointment times, but each employee is expected to work approximately 20 hours a week. Qualifications include a high school diploma, the ability to perform fairly strenuous manual labor, and the willingness to work a flexible schedule. Employees will be paid $15 an hour, which is slightly higher than average for this type of work in the Columbia area, in order to obtain and retain high-quality staff. Because Columbia is home to three 4-year colleges, most likely these employees will be drawn from this large college student population.

Professional and Advisory Support

Robert is a member of the International Car Wash Association (ICWA), a membership association whose primary mission is to "serve the needs of the car wash and detailing industry's professionals and to represent their interests," according to its website. According to the ICWA, members are 21 percent more successful in their businesses than nonmembers. Some of the benefits of membership in the ICWA include attendance discounts at the annual Car Care World Expo, the opportunity to participate in the organization's Business Improvement Groups, which are peer-networking groups comprised of car wash and detail service providers in noncompeting markets, and access to numerous publications and resources, including a weekly newsletter, a monthly broadcast, and an annual study of U.S. consumer attitudes and habits related to car wash services. Membership fees are $225 per year.

STRATEGIES

Business Strategy

Auto detailing is a service industry; therefore the goal is not to sell products but to provide services to the clients who desire them. Although some industries must advertise to convince customers that they need the service that they provide, auto detailers must advertise to convince customers that their business is the best one to provide those services. For example, many affluent luxury car owners consider car washing and detailing a standard and necessary service. The objective of Johnson's is to convince those people that (a) Johnson's is the best business to provide those services and (b) it will be well worth the money they invest. Once Robert schedules a new client, the goal is to perform the services in a way that keeps that client coming back. This goal is achieved by providing quality service in a timely, professional manner at a competitive rate.

Growth Strategy

The potential for growth in the detailing business is nearly unlimited. Once the business has taken hold in the community and has established a reputation for being a high-quality service provider in the auto detailing industry, expansion can take place in a number of areas. Examples include expanding service to more boat and airplane owners and tapping into markets such as hotels with concierge services, car leasing companies, and other related businesses. In addition, the demand for these services in the used car industry is high and can be expanded on in the future.

PRODUCTS AND SERVICES

Description

Johnson's Mobile Detail will provide the following services:

- Exterior wash, including the engine, exterior of the vehicle, and wheels

- Exterior wax and polish

- Interior cleaning, including removing all trash and dirt; wiping down all surfaces; and vacuuming and shampooing the carpets, seats, and trunk area

- Window cleaning, both inside and outside

- Detailing all interior parts (buttons, switches, vents, crevices, instrument panels, etc.) and exterior parts (chrome and trim moldings, fenders, wheels/tires, etc.).

Unique Features/Niche

Auto detailing can be a messy business. The strength of Johnson's Mobile Detail is that the car is returned looking like new again. In the rare cases that Johnson's cannot clean the vehicle to a high standard, for one reason or another, Robert will discuss the options with the client before the service is performed. However, the main philosophy at Johnson's is "no excuses." Car owners do not want to hear "Well...I might be able to get that spot out, but I can't guarantee it" or "I will do the best I can, and we'll see what we end up with." With the tools and products Robert has learned work best, Johnson's will remove such problems as pet hair and urine, vomit, chewing gum, tar/asphalt, mold, ink stains, and food and beverage spills. In addition, the elimination of bad odors, including cigarette smoke, is guaranteed.

Another unique feature of Johnson's is its professionalism. Robert and all employees will wear uniforms that consist of navy pants and light blue shirts bearing the business's name. Attire such as baseball caps, T-shirts, and worn-out tennis shoes will not be allowed. Employees are expected to be clean-shaven or have neatly trimmed beards or moustaches. These guidelines are put into place in order to provide the impression that Johnson's has a high standard and level of professionalism.

Pricing

The basic full-service car wash and detail package, which includes the following services, will be priced at $125. Robert can adjust cost on a case-by-case basis if the client wants to customize services.

Exterior

- Hand-wash and dry exterior, including windows

- Hand-wax and polish exterior

- Remove (claybar) exterior containments

- Decontaminate paint surface

- Degrease, scrub, and shine tires

- Remove all bugs/tar/soot/salt

- Wash wheel wells

- Polish metal and chrome

- Steam-wash engine

Interior

- Clean all interior surfaces, including windows

- Vacuum and shampoo carpets, floor mats, trunk

- Clean headliner

- Clean and polish door jambs, door panels, consoles, trunk jambs

- Q-tip vents, knobs, buttons, crevices

- Clean and condition all vinyl, rubber, and leather

- Remove odor and add air freshener (if desired)

In addition, Johnson's will offer a maintenance program, which includes the above services once a month in addition to an exterior wash and interior wipe-down and vacuum once a week. The price of this option is $300 a month.

Used car dealerships will be offered a discounted price based on volume (i.e., how many cars the dealership needs washed and how often) and less time spent on detailing. In the future, Johnson's will attempt to obtain monthly contracts with these businesses, which will supply an ongoing source of income.

MARKETING AND SALES

Advertising and Promotion

The main form s of advertising for Johnson's Mobile Detail will consist of (a) a website, (b) brochures placed in select locations, (c) a quarter-page ad in the local monthly magazine *Inside Columbia,* and (d) word-of-mouth. In addition, Robert will attend and provide brochures at local-area car shows. The business name, phone number, and website will also be advertised on the sides of the business' truck and trailer.

Cost

Costs of advertising include $200 a month for the ad in *Inside Columbia.* Misty will create the ad and will change the copy about every three months. Coupons and specials may also be a part of the ad. Misty will also create the brochures, which will be printed on high-quality paper at a local copy shop and will cost approximately $100 a month. Vehicle signs, produced by a local car sign shop, will require a one-time investment of $100.

OPERATIONS

Customers

Customers for Johnson's can be categorized into two main groups: affluent car owners and local car dealerships in the Columbia, Missouri, area. Columbia has a population of about 94,000, and 27 percent of Columbia households have incomes above $75,000. Most of these households are located in the southern part of the city. In addition, there are several large car dealerships in town, including Joe Machens Ford, University Chrysler, and Dodge City, among others. These dealerships sell both new and used cars, and the demand for detailing used cars in order to prepare them for reselling is high. Also, auto detailing customers tend to have a higher level of education. According to the U.S. Census Bureau, more than half of Columbia residents have bachelor's degrees and more than a quarter hold master's degrees, making it the thirteenth most highly educated city in the United States. These demographics also make the city an ideal setting for an auto detailing business.

Equipment

The largest piece of equipment needed for start-up is a mobile detailing trailer. These trailers come with such accessories as water reserves, water reclamation systems, and tanks and hoses and allow Johnson's to wash and detail on-site. Robert will use a 2010 F250 pick-up truck to pull the trailer, and the trailer will be painted to match the truck to ensure a professional image.

Other necessary equipment includes a vacuum and carpet shampooer and a steam cleaner for engines. Cleaning supplies required include sponges/towels, brushes, buckets, exterior soap, interior spray cleaner, degreaser, wax, claybars, air freshener, leather and vinyl conditioner, and window cleaner.

Hours

Customers can schedule service any time between 7 a.m. and 9 p.m. Monday through Saturday. Service will be available on Sunday from noon to 9 p.m.

Facility and Location

Johnson's is a mobile operation, and as such the business address will be the same as the Johnsons' home: 1550 Wildwood Road, Columbia, Missouri.

FINANCIAL ANALYSIS

Start-up expenses	Cost
Detailing trailer	$4,000
Vacuum/carpet shampooer	$ 400
Steam cleaner	$ 600
Uniforms	$ 100
Vehicle signs	$ 100
Association membership dues	$ 225
Cleaning supplies	$ 300
Advertising	$ 300
Business license	$ 100
Office supplies and misc.	$ 100
Total start-up expenses	**$6,225**

Funding for start-up expenses will come from the Johnsons' personal savings account.

Monthly expenses	Cost
Cleaning supplies	$ 100
Gas and oil	$ 500
Insurance	$ 100
Equipment maintenance/repair	$ 100
Part-time employee salaries	$2,400
Advertising	$ 200
Total monthly expenses	**$3,400**

Annual income in the following estimate is averaged across 12 months. Expenses are increased 5 percent annually and 10 percent for each additional 10 clients.

Year	No. individual car washes per month @ $125 each	No. maintenance contracts per month @ $300 each	Total income	Minus expenses	Total gross profit
Year 1	30	5	$ 63,000	$40,800	$22,200
Year 2	40	10	$ 96,000	$48,960	$47,040
Year 3	50	15	$129,000	$58,752	$70,248

Automotive Dealer

Pallisimo Motors

123 Canal St.
New York, NY 10013

BizPlanDB.com

Pallisimo Motors Inc. is a New York based corporation that will provide sales of pre-owned cars to customers in its targeted market.

1.0 EXECUTIVE SUMMARY

The purpose of this business plan is to raise $255,000 for the development of a automotive dealership while showcasing the expected financials and operations over the next three years. Pallisimo Motors Inc. is a New York based corporation that will provide sales of pre-owned cars to customers in its targeted market. The Company was founded in 2010 by Joe Pallisimo.

1.1 The Dealership

The business is actively involved with the sale of quality used cars that have low mileage and are no more than 5 years old. The Company will specialize in offering pre-owned cars that are approximately two to four years in age and have mileage that does not exceed usage of 15,000 miles per year.

The Company will use several online marketing channels to quickly turn over the Company's inventory. Once the business receives its needed capital infusion, the Owner will develop an online eBay Motors account from which to conduct nationwide auto sales.

The third section of the business plan will further describe the vehicles offered by Pallisimo Motors.

1.2 Financing

Mr. Pallisimo is seeking to raise $255,000 from as a bank loan. The interest rate and loan agreement are to be further discussed during negotiation. This business plan assumes that the business will receive a 10 year loan with a 9% fixed interest rate. The financing will be used for the following:

- Development of the location.
- Financing for the first six months of operation.
- Capital to purchase automotive inventory.

Mr. Pallisimo will contribute $10,000 to the venture.

1.3 Mission Statement

The mission of Pallisimo Motors is to become the recognized leader in its targeted market for pre-owned car sales and car services.

1.4 Management Team

The Company was founded by Joe Pallisimo. Mr. Pallisimo has more than 10 years of experience in the auto sales industry. Through his expertise, he will be able to bring the operations of the business to profitability within its first year of operations.

1.5 Sales Forecasts

Mr. Pallisimo expects a strong rate of growth at the start of operations. Below are the expected financials over the next three years.

Proforma profit and loss (yearly)

Year	1	2	3
Sales	$2,473,800	$2,968,560	$3,473,215
Operating costs	$ 579,977	$ 615,947	$ 652,859
EBITDA	$ 344,443	$ 493,357	$ 645,027
Taxes, interest, and depreciation	$ 169,955	$ 217,117	$ 273,703
Net profit	$ 174,488	$ 276,240	$ 371,324

Sales, operating costs, and profit forecast

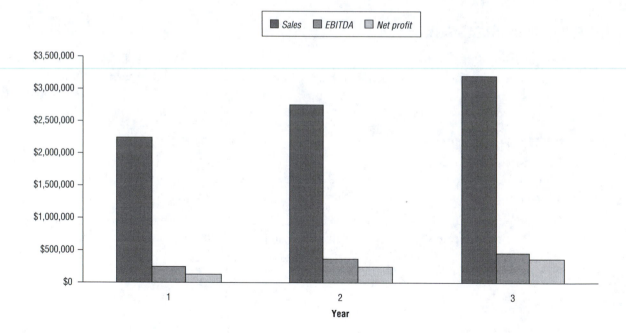

1.6 Expansion Plan

The Founder expects that the business will aggressively expand during the first three years of operation. Mr. Pallisimo intends to implement marketing campaigns that will effectively target individuals within the target market.

2.0 COMPANY AND FINANCING SUMMARY

2.1 Registered Name and Corporate Structure

Pallisimo Motors, Inc. is registered as a corporation in the State of New York.

2.2 Required Funds

At this time, Pallisimo Motors requires $255,000 of debt funds. Below is a breakdown of how these funds will be used:

Projected startup costs

Initial lease payments (3 months)	$ 10,000
Working capital	$ 20,000
FF&E	$ 15,000
Leasehold improvements	$ 5,000
Security deposits	$ 5,000
Insurance	$ 2,500
Automotive inventory	$200,000
Marketing budget	$ 2,500
Miscellaneous and unforeseen costs	$ 5,000
Total startup costs	**$265,000**

Use of funds

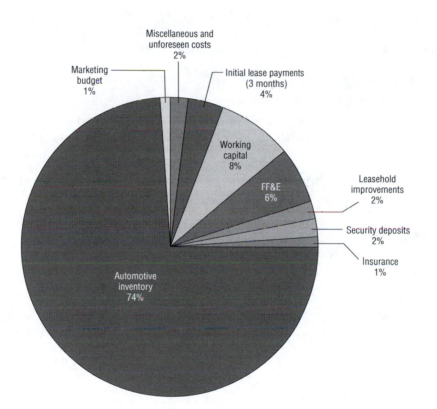

2.3 Investor Equity

Mr. Pallisimo is not seeking an investment from a third party at this time.

2.4 Management Equity

Joe Pallisimo owns 100% of Pallisimo Motors, Inc.

2.5 Exit Strategy

If the business is very successful, Mr. Pallisimo may seek to sell the business to a third party for a significant earnings multiple. Most likely, the Company will hire a qualified business broker to sell the business on behalf of Pallisimo Motors. Based on historical numbers, the business could fetch a sales premium of up to 4 times earnings.

3.0 PRODUCTS AND SERVICES

Below is a description of the car sales and services offered by Pallisimo Motors.

3.1 Sales of Vehicles

After receiving its capital infusion, Mr. Pallisimo anticipates that it will be able to turnover its 10 to 20 (approximate) automobile units from its inventory every month. This will allow the Company to earn a significant profit on the sale of the automobiles it sells in addition to the revenue generated from rentals during this time.

As stated earlier, the business will continue to specialize in purchasing automotive inventories that are relatively new. Management will seek to purchase vehicles that are approximately two to four years of age. The business will also seek cars that have no more than an average annual usage of 15,000 miles per year. In order to promote sales, each car will be certified by a mechanic that will ensure that the car is usable. The business may offer a three month, 3,000 mile bumper to bumper warranty for certain car sales.

3.2 Servicing of Vehicles

The Company will also offer mechanic services to people within the Company's target market. This will ensure a continuous stream of high margin income for the business. Typically, dealerships with associated mechanic shops are able to survive economic downturns because of their servicing revenues.

4.0 STRATEGIC AND MARKET ANALYSIS

4.1 Economic Outlook

This section of the analysis will detail the economic climate, the automotive sales industry, the customer profile, and the competition that the business will face as it progresses through its business operations.

Currently, the economic market condition in the United States is in recession. This slowdown in the economy has also greatly impacted real estate sales, which has halted to historical lows. Many economists expect that this recession will continue until mid-2010, at which point the economy will begin a prolonged recovery period. However, the business will be able to remain profitable and cash flow positive as the vehicle repair services offered by the business will support the underlying operating costs.

4.2 Industry Analysis

In the United States there are over 5,600 established businesses that actively engage in the sale of used automobiles. The industry employs approximately 112,000 people and generates average annual pay-rolls exceeding $3.5 billion dollars. The industry generates approximately $19 billion dollars on an annual basis.

The industry grows at an annual pace of 4.2%. This trend is expected to continue as the availability of the Internet has made it easier for businesses to target individuals seeking to purchase and rent automobiles. Additionally, as the nation's wealth increases, and more people demand luxury services, Management anticipates that the market will begin expand and consolidate.

Overall, the market for all pre-owned cars has had resilient growth in the last decade. The advent of the internet era has created an excellent system that fosters the fast, economically efficient sale of used vehicles. This trend is expected to continue as the overall productivity increases with a corresponding increase in the gross domestic product.

4.3 Customer Profile

Pallisimo Motorss' average client will be a middle- to upper-middle class man or woman living in the Company's target market. Common traits among clients will include:

- Annual household income exceeding $50,000.

- Lives or works no more than 15 miles from the Company's location.

- Will spend approximately $10,000 to $20,000 on a pre-owned vehicle.

4.4 Competition

The Company's targeted market of the New York metropolitan area has approximately 300 automotive dealers that deal in both new and used cars. These automotive dealers consist of both affiliated and non-affiliated manufacturer dealers. The competitive advantage that the business will maintain over others dealers is the low cost infrastructure of the business so that the business can remain very flexible regarding pricing of its vehicle inventories.

5.0 MARKETING PLAN

Pallisimo Motors intends to maintain an extensive marketing campaign that will ensure maximum visibility for the business in its targeted market. Below is an overview of the marketing strategies and objectives of Pallisimo Motors.

5.1 Marketing Objectives

- Develop an online presence by developing a website and placing the Company's name and contact information with online directories.

- Implement a local campaign with the Company's targeted market via the use of flyers, local newspaper advertisements, and word of mouth.

- Establish relationships with other vehicle retailers within the targeted market.

5.2 Marketing Strategies

Mr. Pallisimo intends on using a number of marketing strategies that will allow Pallisimo Motors to easily target men and women within the target market. These strategies include traditional print advertisements and ads placed on search engines on the internet. Below is a description of how the business intends to market its services to the general public.

Pallisimo Motors will also use an internet based strategy. This is very important as many people seeking local services, such as automotive dealers, now the internet to conduct their preliminary searches. Mr. Pallisimo will register Pallisimo Motors with online portals so that potential customers can easily reach the business. The Company will also develop its own online website.

Once the business begins operations, the owner will aggressively develop an eBay account from which the Company will market the cars. Each purchaser of the Company's vehicles will be required to make a deposit on the sold vehicle and arrangements for the delivery of the car. The business will also list its vehicles on several other online used automotive forums including Autotrader.com, cars.com, and several other major online databases of used car inventories. One of the essential elements to developing this sales channel is to quickly develop the Company's online rating within auction sites like eBay. This will give the business credibility among its potential purchasers.

The Company will maintain a sizable amount of print and traditional advertising methods within local markets to promote the vehicles that the Company is selling.

5.3 Pricing

The automobiles sold by the business will carry a sales price of $5,000 to $30,000 depending on the make and model of the car. The business will earn about $75 per hour on labor related to servicing vehicles.

6.0 ORGANIZATIONAL PLAN AND PERSONNEL SUMMARY

6.1 Corporate Organization

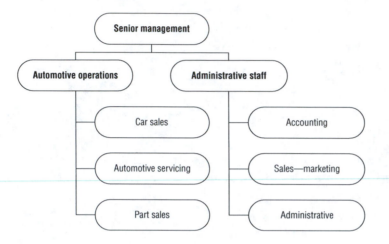

6.2 Organizational Budget

Personnel plan—yearly

Year	1	2	3
Senior management	$ 80,000	$ 82,400	$ 84,872
General manager	$ 35,000	$ 36,050	$ 37,132
Mechanic	$ 97,500	$100,425	$103,438
Sales associate	$ 75,000	$ 77,250	$ 79,568
Administrative	$ 88,000	$ 90,640	$ 93,359
Total	**$375,500**	**$386,765**	**$398,368**

Numbers of personnel

Senior management	2	2	2
General manager	1	1	1
Mechanic	3	3	3
Sales associate	6	6	6
Administrative	4	4	4
Totals	**16**	**16**	**16**

Personnel expense breakdown

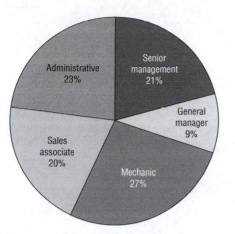

7.0 FINANCIAL PLAN

7.1 Underlying Assumptions

The Company has based its proforma financial statements on the following:

- Pallisimo Motors will have an annual revenue growth rate of 16% per year.

- The Owner will acquire $255,000 of debt funds to develop the business.

- The loan will have a 10 year term with a 9% interest rate.

7.2 Sensitivity Analysis

In the event of an economic downturn, the business may have a decline in its automotive sales revenues. However, mechanic services are demanded during all economic climates and the Company will be able to generate highly predictable streams of revenue from this aspect of the business. As such, the Company will be able to retain profitability despite lagging automotive sales.

7.3 Source of Funds

Financing

Equity contributions	
Management investment	$ 10,000.00
Total equity financing	**$ 10,000.00**
Banks and lenders	
Banks and lenders	$ 255,000.00
Total debt financing	**$ 255,000.00**
Total financing	**$265,000.00**

7.4 General Assumptions

General assumptions

Year	1	2	3
Short term interest rate	9.5%	9.5%	9.5%
Long term interest rate	10.0%	10.0%	10.0%
Federal tax rate	33.0%	33.0%	33.0%
State tax rate	5.0%	5.0%	5.0%
Personnel taxes	15.0%	15.0%	15.0%

7.5 Profit and Loss Statements

Proforma profit and loss (yearly)

Year	1	2	3
Sales	$2,473,800	$2,968,560	$3,473,215
Cost of goods sold	$1,549,380	$1,859,256	$2,175,330
Gross margin	37.37%	37.37%	37.37%
Operating income	$ 924,420	$1,109,304	$1,297,886
Expenses			
Payroll	$ 375,500	$ 386,765	$ 398,368
General and administrative	$ 25,200	$ 26,208	$ 27,256
Marketing expenses	$ 74,214	$ 89,057	$ 104,196
Professional fees and licensure	$ 5,219	$ 5,376	$ 5,537
Insurance costs	$ 1,987	$ 2,086	$ 2,191
Travel and vehicle costs	$ 7,596	$ 8,356	$ 9,191
Rent and utilities	$ 4,250	$ 4,463	$ 4,686
Miscellaneous costs	$ 29,686	$ 35,623	$ 41,679
Payroll taxes	$ 56,325	$ 58,015	$ 59,755
Total operating costs	$ 579,977	$ 615,947	$ 652,859
EBITDA	$ 344,443	$ 493,357	$ 645,027
Federal income tax	$ 113,666	$ 155,965	$ 206,574
State income tax	$ 17,222	$ 23,631	$ 31,299
Interest expense	$ 22,281	$ 20,735	$ 19,044
Depreciation expenses	$ 16,786	$ 16,786	$ 16,786
Net profit	$ 174,488	$ 276,240	$ 371,324
Profit margin	7.05%	9.31%	10.69%

Sales, operating costs, and profit forecast

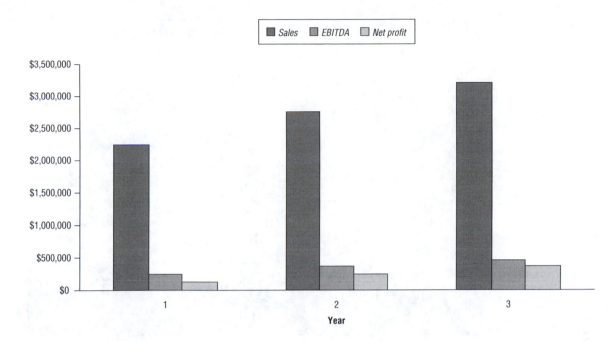

7.6 Cash Flow Analysis

Proforma cash flow analysis—yearly

Year	1	2	3
Cash from operations	$191,274	$293,025	$388,109
Cash from receivables	$ 0	$ 0	$ 0
Operating cash inflow	**$191,274**	**$293,025**	**$388,109**
Other cash inflows			
Equity investment	$ 10,000	$ 0	$ 0
Increased borrowings	$255,000	$ 0	$ 0
Sales of business assets	$ 0	$ 0	$ 0
A/P increases	$ 37,902	$ 43,587	$ 50,125
Total other cash inflows	$302,902	$ 43,587	$ 50,125
Total cash inflow	$494,176	$336,613	$438,235
Cash outflows			
Repayment of principal	$ 16,482	$ 18,028	$ 19,719
A/P decreases	$ 24,897	$ 29,876	$ 35,852
A/R increases	$ 0	$ 0	$ 0
Asset purchases	$235,000	$ 73,256	$ 97,027
Dividends	$133,892	$205,118	$271,677
Total cash outflows	**$410,270**	**$326,278**	**$424,275**
Net cash flow	**$ 83,905**	**$ 10,334**	**$ 13,960**
Cash balance	**$ 83,905**	**$ 94,240**	**$108,200**

Proforma cash flow (yearly)

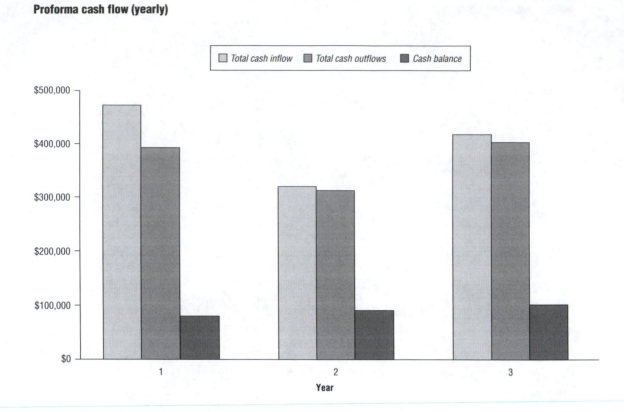

7.7 Balance Sheet

Proforma balance sheet—yearly

Year	1	2	3
Assets			
Cash	$ 83,905	$ 94,240	$108,200
Amortized development and expansion costs	$ 20,000	$ 27,326	$ 37,028
Inventory	$200,000	$254,942	$327,713
FF&E	$ 15,000	$ 25,988	$ 40,543
Accumulated depreciation	($ 16,786)	($ 33,571)	($ 50,357)
Total assets	**$302,120**	**$368,925**	**$463,127**
Liabilities and equity			
Accounts payable	$ 13,005	$ 26,716	$ 40,990
Long term liabilities	$238,518	$220,491	$202,463
Other liabilities	$ 0	$ 0	$ 0
Total liabilities	**$251,523**	**$247,207**	**$243,452**
Net worth	**$ 50,596**	**$121,718**	**$219,674**
Total liabilities and equity	**$302,120**	**$368,925**	**$463,127**

Proforma balance sheet

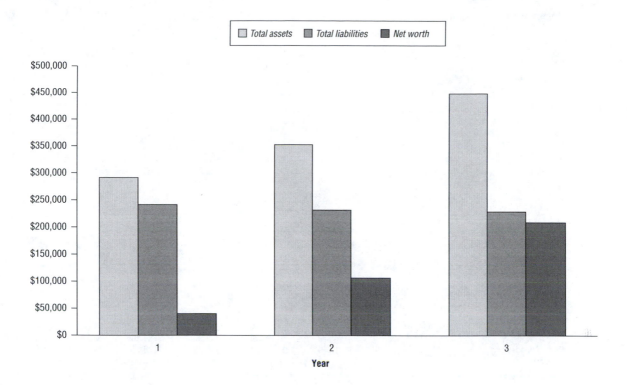

Year

7.8 Breakeven Analysis

Monthly break even analysis

Year	1	2	3
Monthly revenue	$ 129,338	$ 137,359	$ 145,591
Yearly revenue	$1,552,050	$1,648,310	$1,747,087

Break even analysis

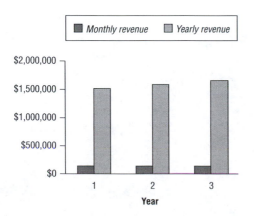

Year

7.9 Business Ratios

Business ratios—yearly

Year	1	2	3
Sales			
Sales growth	0.0%	20.0%	17.0%
Gross margin	37.4%	37.4%	37.4%
Financials			
Profit margin	7.05%	9.31%	10.69%
Assets to liabilities	1.20	1.49	1.90
Equity to liabilities	0.20	0.49	0.90
Assets to equity	5.97	3.03	2.11
Liquidity			
Acid test	0.33	0.38	0.44
Cash to assets	0.28	0.26	0.23

7.10 Three Year Profit and Loss Statement

Profit and loss statement (first year)

Months	1	2	3	4	5	6	7
Sales	$133,000	$146,300	$159,600	$172,900	$186,200	$199,500	$212,800
Cost of goods sold	$ 83,300	$ 91,630	$ 99,960	$108,290	$116,620	$124,950	$133,280
Gross margin	37.4%	37.4%	37.4%	37.4%	37.4%	37.4%	37.4%
Operating income	$ 49,700	$ 54,670	$ 59,640	$ 64,610	$ 69,580	$ 74,550	$ 79,520
Expenses							
Payroll	$ 31,292	$ 31,292	$ 31,292	$ 31,292	$ 31,292	$ 31,292	$ 31,292
General and administrative	$ 2,100	$ 2,100	$ 2,100	$ 2,100	$ 2,100	$ 2,100	$ 2,100
Marketing expenses	$ 6,185	$ 6,185	$ 6,185	$ 6,185	$ 6,185	$ 6,185	$ 6,185
Professional fees and licensure	$ 435	$ 435	$ 435	$ 435	$ 435	$ 435	$ 435
Insurance costs	$ 166	$ 166	$ 166	$ 166	$ 166	$ 166	$ 166
Travel and vehicle costs	$ 633	$ 633	$ 633	$ 633	$ 633	$ 633	$ 633
Rent and utilities	$ 354	$ 354	$ 354	$ 354	$ 354	$ 354	$ 354
Miscellaneous costs	$ 2,474	$ 2,474	$ 2,474	$ 2,474	$ 2,474	$ 2,474	$ 2,474
Payroll taxes	$ 4,694	$ 4,694	$ 4,694	$ 4,694	$ 4,694	$ 4,694	$ 4,694
Total operating costs	$ 48,331	$ 48,331	$ 48,331	$ 48,331	$ 48,331	$ 48,331	$ 48,331
EBITDA	$ 1,369	$ 6,339	$ 11,309	$ 16,279	$ 21,249	$ 26,219	$ 31,189
Federal income tax	$ 6,111	$ 6,722	$ 7,333	$ 7,944	$ 8,556	$ 9,167	$ 9,778
State income tax	$ 926	$ 1,019	$ 1,111	$ 1,204	$ 1,296	$ 1,389	$ 1,481
Interest expense	$ 1,913	$ 1,903	$ 1,893	$ 1,883	$ 1,873	$ 1,862	$ 1,852
Depreciation expense	$ 1,399	$ 1,399	$ 1,399	$ 1,399	$ 1,399	$ 1,399	$ 1,399
Net profit	−$ 8,980	−$ 4,704	−$ 427	$ 3,849	$ 8,125	$ 12,402	$ 16,679

Profit and loss statement (first year cont.)

Month	8	9	10	11	12	1
Sales	$226,100	$239,400	$252,700	$266,000	$279,300	$2,473,800
Cost of goods sold	$141,610	$149,940	$158,270	$166,600	$174,930	$1,549,380
Gross margin	37.4%	37.4%	37.4%	37.4%	37.4%	37.4%
Operating income	$ 84,490	$ 89,460	$ 94,430	$ 99,400	$104,370	$ 924,420
Expenses						
Payroll	$ 31,292	$ 31,292	$ 31,292	$ 31,292	$ 31,292	$ 375,500
General and administrative	$ 2,100	$ 2,100	$ 2,100	$ 2,100	$ 2,100	$ 25,200
Marketing expenses	$ 6,185	$ 6,185	$ 6,185	$ 6,185	$ 6,185	$ 74,214
Professional fees and licensure	$ 435	$ 435	$ 435	$ 435	$ 435	$ 5,219
Insurance costs	$ 166	$ 166	$ 166	$ 166	$ 166	$ 1,987
Travel and vehicle costs	$ 633	$ 633	$ 633	$ 633	$ 633	$ 7,596
Rent and utilities	$ 354	$ 354	$ 354	$ 354	$ 354	$ 4,250
Miscellaneous costs	$ 2,474	$ 2,474	$ 2,474	$ 2,474	$ 2,474	$ 29,686
Payroll taxes	$ 4,694	$ 4,694	$ 4,694	$ 4,694	$ 4,694	$ 56,325
Total operating costs	$ 48,331	$ 48,331	$ 48,331	$ 48,331	$ 48,331	$ 579,977
EBITDA	$ 36,159	$ 41,129	$ 46,099	$ 51,069	$ 56,039	$ 344,443
Federal income tax	$ 10,389	$ 11,000	$ 11,611	$ 12,222	$ 12,833	$ 113,666
State income tax	$ 1,574	$ 1,667	$ 1,759	$ 1,852	$ 1,944	$ 17,222
Interest expense	$ 1,842	$ 1,831	$ 1,821	$ 1,810	$ 1,800	$ 22,281
Depreciation expense	$ 1,399	$ 1,399	$ 1,399	$ 1,399	$ 1,399	$ 16,786
Net profit	$ 20,955	$ 25,232	$ 29,509	$ 33,786	$ 38,062	$ 174,488

Profit and loss statement (second year)

Quarter	Q1	2 Q2	Q3	Q4	2
Sales	$593,712	$742,140	$801,511	$831,197	$2,968,560
Cost of goods sold	$371,851	$464,814	$501,999	$520,592	$1,859,256
Gross margin	37.4%	37.4%	37.4%	37.4%	37.4%
Operating income	$221,861	$277,326	$299,512	$310,605	$1,109,304
Expenses					
Payroll	$ 77,353	$ 96,691	$104,427	$108,294	$ 386,765
General and administrative	$ 5,242	$ 6,552	$ 7,076	$ 7,338	$ 26,208
Marketing expenses	$ 17,811	$ 22,264	$ 24,045	$ 24,936	$ 89,057
Professional fees and licensure	$ 1,075	$ 1,344	$ 1,451	$ 1,505	$ 5,376
Insurance costs	$ 417	$ 522	$ 563	$ 584	$ 2,086
Travel and vehicle costs	$ 1,671	$ 2,089	$ 2,256	$ 2,340	$ 8,356
Rent and utilities	$ 893	$ 1,116	$ 1,205	$ 1,250	$ 4,463
Miscellaneous costs	$ 7,125	$ 8,906	$ 9,618	$ 9,974	$ 35,623
Payroll taxes	$ 11,603	$ 14,504	$ 15,664	$ 16,244	$ 58,015
Total operating costs	$123,189	$153,987	$166,306	$172,465	$ 615,947
EBITDA	$ 98,671	$123,339	$133,206	$138,140	$ 493,357
Federal income tax	$ 31,193	$ 38,991	$ 42,111	$ 43,670	$ 155,965
State income tax	$ 4,726	$ 5,908	$ 6,380	$ 6,617	$ 23,631
Interest expense	$ 5,334	$ 5,235	$ 5,134	$ 5,031	$ 20,735
Depreciation expense	$ 4,196	$ 4,196	$ 4,196	$ 4,196	$ 16,786
Net profit	$ 53,222	$ 69,008	$ 75,385	$ 78,625	$ 276,240

Profit and loss statement (third year)

| | | | | | 3 |
Quarter	Q1	Q2	Q3	Q4	3
Sales	$694,643	$868,304	$937,768	$972,500	$3,473,215
Cost of goods sold	$435,066	$543,832	$587,339	$609,092	$2,175,330
Gross margin	37.4%	37.4%	37.4%	37.4%	37.4%
Operating income	$259,577	$324,471	$350,429	$363,408	$1,297,886
Expenses					
Payroll	$ 79,674	$ 99,592	$107,559	$111,543	$ 398,368
General and administrative	$ 5,451	$ 6,814	$ 7,359	$ 7,632	$ 27,256
Marketing expenses	$ 20,839	$ 26,049	$ 28,133	$ 29,175	$ 104,196
Professional fees and licensure	$ 1,107	$ 1,384	$ 1,495	$ 1,550	$ 5,537
Insurance costs	$ 438	$ 548	$ 591	$ 613	$ 2,191
Travel and vehicle costs	$ 1,838	$ 2,298	$ 2,482	$ 2,574	$ 9,191
Rent and utilities	$ 937	$ 1,171	$ 1,265	$ 1,312	$ 4,686
Miscellaneous costs	$ 8,336	$ 10,420	$ 11,253	$ 11,670	$ 41,679
Payroll taxes	$ 11,951	$ 14,939	$ 16,134	$ 16,731	$ 59,755
Total operating costs	$130,572	$163,215	$176,272	$182,800	$ 652,859
EBITDA	$129,005	$161,257	$174,157	$180,608	$ 645,027
Federal income tax	$ 41,315	$ 51,644	$ 55,775	$ 57,841	$ 206,574
State income tax	$ 6,260	$ 7,825	$ 8,451	$ 8,764	$ 31,299
Interest expense	$ 4,925	$ 4,817	$ 4,707	$ 4,594	$ 19,044
Depreciation expense	$ 4,196	$ 4,196	$ 4,196	$ 4,196	$ 16,786
Net profit	$ 72,309	$ 92,774	$101,028	$105,213	$ 371,324

7.11 Three Year Cash Flow Analysis

Cash flow analysis (first year)

Month	1	2	3	4	5	6	7	8
Cash from operations	−$ 7,581	−$ 3,305	$ 972	$ 5,248	$ 9,524	$13,801	$18,077	$22,354
Cash from receivables	$ 0	$ 0	$ 0	$ 0	$ 0	$ 0	$ 0	$ 0
Operating cash inflow	−$ 7,581	−$ 3,305	$ 972	$ 5,248	$ 9,524	$13,801	$18,077	$22,354
Other cash inflows								
Equity investment	$ 10,000	$ 0	$ 0	$ 0	$ 0	$ 0	$ 0	$ 0
Increased borrowings	$255,000	$ 0	$ 0	$ 0	$ 0	$ 0	$ 0	$ 0
Sales of business assets	$ 0	$ 0	$ 0	$ 0	$ 0	$ 0	$ 0	$ 0
A/P increases	$ 3,159	$ 3,159	$ 3,159	$ 3,159	$ 3,159	$ 3,159	$ 3,159	$ 3,159
Total other cash inflows	$268,159	$ 3,159	$ 3,159	$ 3,159	$ 3,159	$ 3,159	$ 3,159	$ 3,159
Total cash inflow	$260,578	−$ 146	$ 4,130	$ 8,406	$12,683	$16,959	$21,236	$25,512
Cash outflows								
Repayment of principal	$ 1,318	$ 1,328	$ 1,338	$ 1,348	$ 1,358	$ 1,368	$ 1,378	$ 1,388
A/P decreases	$ 2,075	$ 2,075	$ 2,075	$ 2,075	$ 2,075	$ 2,075	$ 2,075	$ 2,075
A/R increases	$ 0	$ 0	$ 0	$ 0	$ 0	$ 0	$ 0	$ 0
Asset purchases	$235,000	$ 0	$ 0	$ 0	$ 0	$ 0	$ 0	$ 0
Dividends	$ 0	$ 0	$ 0	$ 0	$ 0	$ 0	$ 0	$ 0
Total cash outflows	$238,392	$ 3,402	$ 3,412	$ 3,422	$ 3,432	$ 3,443	$ 3,453	$ 3,463
Net cash flow	$ 22,185	−$ 3,549	$ 718	$ 4,984	$ 9,250	$13,517	$17,783	$22,049
Cash balance	$ 22,185	$18,637	$19,354	$24,338	$33,589	$47,105	$64,888	$86,937

Cash flow analysis (first year cont.)

Month	9	10	11	12	1
Cash from operations	$ 26,631	$ 30,907	$ 35,184	$ 39,461	$191,274
Cash from receivables	$ 0	$ 0	$ 0	$ 0	$ 0
Operating cash inflow	**$ 26,631**	**$ 30,907**	**$ 35,184**	**$ 39,461**	**$191,274**
Other cash inflows					
Equity investment	$ 0	$ 0	$ 0	$ 0	$ 10,000
Increased borrowings	$ 0	$ 0	$ 0	$ 0	$255,000
Sales of business assets	$ 0	$ 0	$ 0	$ 0	$ 0
A/P increases	$ 3,159	$ 3,159	$ 3,159	$ 3,159	$ 37,902
Total other cash inflows	**$ 3,159**	**$ 3,159**	**$ 3,159**	**$ 3,159**	**$302,902**
Total cash inflow	**$ 29,789**	**$ 34,066**	**$ 38,343**	**$ 42,620**	**$494,176**
Cash outflows					
Repayment of principal	$ 1,399	$ 1,409	$ 1,420	$ 1,431	$ 16,482
A/P decreases	$ 2,075	$ 2,075	$ 2,075	$ 2,075	$ 24,897
A/R increases	$ 0	$ 0	$ 0	$ 0	$ 0
Asset purchases	$ 0	$ 0	$ 0	$ 0	$235,000
Dividends	$ 0	$ 0	$ 0	$133,892	$133,892
Total cash outflows	**$ 3,474**	**$ 3,484**	**$ 3,495**	**$137,397**	**$410,270**
Net cash flow	**$ 26,316**	**$ 30,582**	**$ 34,848**	**−$ 94,778**	**$ 83,905**
Cash balance	**$113,253**	**$143,835**	**$178,683**	**$ 83,905**	**$ 83,905**

Cash flow analysis (second year)

Quarter	Q1	2 Q2	Q3	Q4	2
Cash from operations	$ 58,605	$ 73,256	$ 79,117	$ 82,047	$293,025
Cash from receivables	$ 0	$ 0	$ 0	$ 0	$ 0
Operating cash inflow	**$ 58,605**	**$ 73,256**	**$ 79,117**	**$ 82,047**	**$293,025**
Other cash inflows					
Equity investment	$ 0	$ 0	$ 0	$ 0	$ 0
Increased borrowings	$ 0	$ 0	$ 0	$ 0	$ 0
Sales of business assets	$ 0	$ 0	$ 0	$ 0	$ 0
A/P increases	$ 8,717	$ 10,897	$ 11,769	$ 12,204	$ 43,587
Total other cash inflows	**$ 8,717**	**$ 10,897**	**$ 11,769**	**$ 12,204**	**$ 43,587**
Total cash inflow	**$ 67,323**	**$ 84,153**	**$ 90,885**	**$ 94,252**	**$336,613**
Cash outflows					
Repayment of principal	$ 4,357	$ 4,455	$ 4,556	$ 4,660	$ 18,028
A/P decreases	$ 5,975	$ 7,469	$ 8,067	$ 8,365	$ 29,876
A/R increases	$ 0	$ 0	$ 0	$ 0	$ 0
Asset purchases	$ 14,651	$ 18,314	$ 19,779	$ 20,512	$ 73,256
Dividends	$ 41,024	$ 51,279	$ 55,382	$ 57,433	$205,118
Total cash outflows	**$ 66,007**	**$ 81,518**	**$ 87,784**	**$ 90,970**	**$326,278**
Net cash flow	**$ 1,316**	**$ 2,635**	**$ 3,101**	**$ 3,282**	**$ 10,334**
Cash balance	**$ 85,221**	**$ 87,857**	**$ 90,958**	**$ 94,240**	**$ 94,240**

Cash flow analysis (third year)

Quarter	Q1	Q2	Q3	Q4	3
Cash from operations	$ 77,622	$ 97,027	$104,790	$108,671	$388,109
Cash from receivables	$ 0	$ 0	$ 0	$ 0	$ 0
Operating cash inflow	**$ 77,622**	**$ 97,027**	**$104,790**	**$108,671**	**$388,109**
Other cash inflows					
Equity investment	$ 0	$ 0	$ 0	$ 0	$ 0
Increased borrowings	$ 0	$ 0	$ 0	$ 0	$ 0
Sales of business assets	$ 0	$ 0	$ 0	$ 0	$ 0
A/P increases	$ 10,025	$ 12,531	$ 13,534	$ 14,035	$ 50,125
Total other cash inflows	**$ 10,025**	**$ 12,531**	**$ 13,534**	**$ 14,035**	**$ 50,125**
Total cash inflow	**$ 87,647**	**$109,559**	**$118,323**	**$122,706**	**$438,235**
Cash outflows					
Repayment of principal	$ 4,765	$ 4,873	$ 4,984	$ 5,097	$ 19,719
A/P decreases	$ 7,170	$ 8,963	$ 9,680	$ 10,038	$ 35,852
A/R increases	$ 0	$ 0	$ 0	$ 0	$ 0
Asset purchases	$ 19,405	$ 24,257	$ 26,197	$ 27,168	$ 97,027
Dividends	$ 54,335	$ 67,919	$ 73,353	$ 76,069	$271,677
Total cash outflows	**$ 85,676**	**$106,012**	**$114,214**	**$118,372**	**$424,275**
Net cash flow	**$ 1,971**	**$ 3,547**	**$ 4,110**	**$ 4,333**	**$ 13,960**
Cash balance	**$ 96,211**	**$ 99,757**	**$103,867**	**$108,200**	**$108,200**

Automotive Repair Service

LR Automotive

6890 Ranch Drive
Traverse City, MI 48963

Paul Greenland

LR Automotive is a full service automotive center with competent and trusting mechanics. This plan originally appeared in Business Plans Handbook, Volume 4, but has been updated for this edition.

EXECUTIVE SUMMARY

The need for a full service automotive center with competent and trusting mechanics is always there. Chuck Liepshur and Rich Rudy have built, and are still accumulating, a clientele that has followed them from location to location through promotions and careers. These clients are loyal and will continue to follow LR Automotive when we move to our new location.

With advertising in local newspapers, online promotions, mailers, and handbills, business should increase by a margin of 10 percent annually. People are always looking for an honest auto repair facility that is committed to customer service, reliability, and promptness. By being fully committed to our clients, our customer base also will increase through word-of-mouth referrals.

Our company will be offering two products: the first being automotive service, which will generate a gross profit margin of 60 percent on average. This will include bumper-to-bumper service on cars and light trucks (i.e., brakes, computer diagnosis, suspension, exhaust, and electrical). The sale of tires will provide a 20 percent profit margin, but will also help us sell service such as front-end parts and front-end alignments as needed. The only time our services will be performed is when and if they are needed or they are recommended on the O.E. manufacturer's maintenance schedule. Service should provide 90 percent of the total sales, with tire sales making up the remaining 10 percent.

The parts and products we will use will also help in our appeal to customers. We will use top of the line, name brand parts such as Auto-X, Reman, and Xilco. Customers always look for a well-known brand name when deciding where to take their vehicle. Counterfeit parts will never be used at LR Automotive. Last but not least, warranties also help when customers are deciding where to get their work done. Our warranties will meet or exceed industry standards.

Our target customers are the owners of automobiles and light trucks. This area of service is always growing, especially during the difficult economic climate of the early 21st century. Instead of purchasing new vehicles, many consumers have chosen to delay new car purchases and keep their existing vehicles, or purchase used vehicles that are more cost effective. As new vehicle prices increase, consumers are inclined to maintain and service their vehicles for longer periods of time. As a result of this trend, the service business will continue to grow.

Our competition will consist of auto dealerships, larger tire and service chains, and gas stations with service departments. These are very successful because they are well-known and offer a wide variety of services. The weakness of these companies will be our advantage. These weaknesses include the need to keep the cars several days to finish work. LR Automotive will make every effort to finish jobs the same day. Also, dealerships tend to distance themselves from their clients, refusing to take the time to educate the customer about their problems. Our employees will take the time to point out our customers' vehicle problems and discuss all the possible solutions, explaining the advantages and disadvantages of each. We are also going to treat our customers as we would like to be treated, spending time with each one so they know they're not just a number to our business. Follow-up calls to ensure satisfaction will also be made after we have completed the work.

Our customers will be made up of our existing clientele, along with a new customer base which we will gain through advertising. Through our satisfied customers, word will spread that LR is the automotive repair shop that customers can trust, which will increase our customer base. These customers will remain satisfied because they will be happy with our service, prices, and the atmosphere we provide.

PARTS & LABOR

We will use only quality parts, which will be readily available in our stock or via our local parts supplier. When we service autos, we will never take short cuts and will never substitute quality in order to obtain a lower price. Our parts warranties will reflect those of the manufacturer.

WARRANTIES

Our labor warranties will be as follows:

- Brakes - Standard brake job - 1 year or 12,000 miles
- Brakes - Brake overhaul - 2 years or 24,000 miles
- Shocks - 1 year or 12,000 miles
- Struts - 3 years or 36,000 miles
- Suspension parts - 1 year or 12,000 miles
- Belts - 1 year or 12,000 miles
- Exhaust - 1 year or 12,000 miles
- Alternator/Starter - 6 months or 6,000 miles
- Alignment - 6 months or 6,000 miles
- Water pump - 1 year or 12,000 miles
- All other warranties - 90 days or 4,000 miles

COMMUNITY ACTIVITY

We plan on being a visible part of the community in which we are based. We will join community groups and participate in local activities in order to understand community needs. As a result of our visibility, we will get to know the local patrons and that will help LR's business to grow within the community.

ORGANIZATION

We plan on working on seven cars per day when LR first opens. Our labor force will include two certified technicians and one salesperson. Every employee in our establishment will be knowledgeable in the auto service area. As our business grows and becomes more profitable, we will add trained personnel to ensure the best service available.

COMPANY PHILOSOPHY

1. To provide an atmosphere where the consumer feels confident about his/her purchase(s) and relationships with LR's service employees.

2. Being honest and sincere with the clientele.

3. Being community oriented.

4. To create a place where customers feel good about recommending LR to friends or relatives for their auto concerns.

5. To provide a comfortable living for ourselves and our employees.

6. To provide a healthy work environment where our employees enjoy coming to work each day.

7. To provide benefits for ourselves, our employees, and families (i.e., 401K, health, and dental plans).

8. Keep our employees long term by treating them as we would wish to be treated ourselves.

JOB DESCRIPTIONS

Co-President

Objective

To ensure survival and growth of LR Automotive Service and control the operation.

Functions

- Act as a team leader, making sure that the LR team stays on track

- Establish and implement company policies, performance standards, and procedures

- Establish and implement employee controls - feedback based on performance standards, indicators, goals, etc.

- Financial planning and controls, including: Paying invoices, Banking, Accounting systems, Sales and expenses, and Assets and liabilities

- Buying and inventory control

- Advertising and promotion

- Reconcile statements

- Planning (long and short range)

- Answer customer complaints

- Maintain the spark to imagine; the daring to innovate; the discipline to plan; the skill to do; the will to achieve; the commitment to be responsible; and the leadership to motivate

- Scheduling, merchandise store, maintain paper flow, housekeeping, and equipment maintenance

- Parts room and warehouse organization

- Business development, fleet accounts, and national accounts

Salesperson

Objective
Take care of customers that come in the door and relieve co-presidents of detail work.

Functions
- Completing work orders and calling customers when job is done.

- All other paper work (i.e., filing work orders daily, inventory management, mailing invoices, filing emissions certificates, getting invoice numbers on parts bills, and clear pending documents.

- Housekeeping - keeping counters clean, displays and vending machines dusted, customer waiting area clean daily, empty waste baskets, rest room detail.

- Supplies - invoices, sales slips, cash receipts, paper towels, keep sufficient change in cash drawer.

- Special assignments as directed by co-presidents.

- Keep all display materials current, window signs, ad boards, manufacturer rebates, and promotions.

Mechanic

Objective
Meet or exceed assigned daily objective. Maximize productivity per hour worked. Get quality work done in the shortest amount of time possible.

Functions
- Get quality work done, fast

- Safety check all cars worked on

- Add-on sales, direct contact with customer (both face to face and on the phone)

- Housekeeping

- Equipment maintenance

- Assist in organizing warehouse and parts room

FINANCIAL ANALYSIS

Start-up Costs

Office equipment

Alarm equipment	$ 1,200
Cash register	$ 750
Coffee machine	$ 75
Deposit for oxygen tank	$ 300
Fax machine	$ 325
Fire extinguishers	$ 300
Incorporation	$ 1,200
Initial supplies	$ 1,200
Office furniture	$ 675
Phone lines (installation)	$ 305
Phone system (4 lines)	$ 1,750
Safe	$ 950
Showroom furniture	$ 1,500
Signage	$ 850
Sub-total	**$11,380**

Shop equipment

2 Post lift	$ 3,500
4 Post lift	$ 8,500
Air compressor	$ 2,000
Alignment machine (wireless)	$11,300
Anti-freeze drum cradle	$ 89
Arbor press	$ 665
Battery charger	$ 700
Bearing packer	$ 350
Catch pan	$ 15
Drain pan	$ 24
Exhaust analyzer	$ 3,900
Exhaust hoses	$ 205
Lab scope	$ 2,155
Lift installation labor	$ 1,000
Mitchel On-Demand (online)	$ 1,908
Oil dispenser	$ 150
Parts washer	$ 450
R134 air-conditioning machine	$ 6,000
Rolling lift	$ 4,500
Strut compressor	$ 760
Tall jack stand	$ 125
Tire changer/wheel balancer	$ 2,400
Tire spreader	$ 75
Tire tank	$ 50
Trans jack	$ 375
Volt amp tester	$ 450
Waste oil tank	$ 150
Welding tank	$ 135
Sub-total	**$51,931**
Total start-up cost	**$63,311**

Operating Expenses

	Weekly	Monthly	Yearly
Miscellaneous service expenses			
Dumpster	$ 13.80	$ 59.80	$ 717.60
Floor dry	$ 1.50	$ 6.50	$ 78.00
Floor soap	$ 4.50	$ 19.50	$ 234.00
Hand soap	$ 11.55	$ 50.05	$ 600.60
Shop towels	$ 18.20	$ 78.87	$ 946.40
Tire removal	$ 13.25	$ 57.42	$ 689.00
Uniforms	$ 20.00	$ 86.67	$ 1,040.00
Waste anti-freeze removal	$ 3.60	$ 15.60	$ 187.20
Waste oil filters removal	$ 7.28	$ 31.55	$ 378.56
Waste oil removal	$ 11.90	$ 51.57	$ 618.80
Welding supplies & services	$ 21.38	$ 92.65	$ 1,111.76
Sub-total	**$ 126.96**	**$ 550.18**	**$ 6,601.92**
Office expenses			
Accountant	$ 38.00	$ 164.67	$ 1,976.00
Advertising	$ 86.50	$ 374.83	$ 4,498.00
Alarm service	$ 6.34	$ 27.47	$ 329.68
Bad debt	$ 25.34	$ 109.81	$ 1,317.68
Bank loan	$ 384.62	$ 1,666.69	$ 20,000.24
Miscellaneous expense (supplies)	$ 300.00	$ 1,300.00	$ 15,600.00
Property rental	$ 425.00	$ 1,841.67	$ 22,100.00
Telephone	$ 65.00	$ 281.67	$ 3,380.00
Utilities (light/heat/water)	$ 77.40	$ 335.40	$ 4,024.80
Sub-total	**$1,408.20**	**$ 6,102.20**	**$ 73,226.40**
Salaries expenses			
Chuck Liepshur	$ 772.00	$ 3,345.33	$ 40,144.00
Rich Rudy	$ 772.00	$ 3,345.33	$ 40,144.00
Abe Sitze	$ 662.00	$ 2,868.67	$ 34,424.00
Sub-total	**$2,206.00**	**$ 9,559.33**	**$114,712.00**
Insurance			
Health	$ 660.69	$ 2,862.99	$ 34,355.88
Liability/comprehensive	$ 111.60	$ 483.60	$ 5,803.20
Sub-total	**$ 772.29**	**$ 3,346.59**	**$ 40,159.08**
Taxes			
FICA (7.65)	$ 169.00	$ 732.33	$ 8,788.00
UIA	$ 33.00	$ 143.00	$ 1,716.00
Sub-total	**$ 202.00**	**$ 875.33**	**$ 10,504.00**
Total	**$4,715.45**	**$20,433.63**	**$245,203.40**

Sales Projection & Cash Flow

First 12 months	Nov.	Dec.	Jan.	Feb.	Mar.	Apr.	May
No. of days	25	25	26	25	26	26	26
Balance	$ 1,000	$ 2,091	$ 3,182	$ 5,134	$ 6,225	$ 8,177	$10,129
Sales	$35,875	$35,875	$37,310	$35,875	$37,310	$37,310	$37,310
Inventory expenses	$14,350	$14,350	$14,924	$14,350	$14,924	$14,924	$14,924
Gross profit	$21,525	$21,525	$22,386	$21,525	$22,386	$22,386	$22,386
Operating expenses	$20,434	$20,434	$20,434	$20,434	$20,434	$20,434	$20,434
Net profit/(loss)	$ 1,091	$ 1,091	$ 1,952	$ 1,091	$ 1,952	$ 1,952	$ 1,952

	June	July	Aug.	Sep.	Oct.	Total
No. of days	25	26	27	24	27	308
Balance	$12,081	$13,172	$15,124	$17,937	$18,167	$ 20,980
Sales	$35,875	$37,310	$38,745	$34,440	$38,745	$441,980
Inventory expenses	$14,350	$14,924	$15,498	$13,776	$15,498	$176,792
Gross profit	$21,525	$22,386	$23,247	$20,664	$23,247	$265,188
Operating expenses	$20,434	$20,434	$20,434	$20,434	$20,434	$245,208
Net profit/(loss)	$ 1,091	$ 1,952	$ 2,813	$ 230	$ 2,813	$ 19,980

Assumptions

Sales

*Average seven vehicles per day @ $205 per vehicle

Inventory Expenses

*40 percent of sales

Operating Expenses

*Average expenses per month

Bowling Alley
Strikers Lanes

9999 60th St.
Brooklyn, NY 11219

BizPlanDB.com

Strikers Lanes is a New York based corporation that will provide usage of its bowling lanes, food/beverage service, shoe rentals, and event management to customers in its targeted market.

1.0 EXECUTIVE SUMMARY

The purpose of this business plan is to raise $900,000 for the development of a bowling alley while showcasing the expected financials and operations over the next three years. Strikers Lanes is a New York based corporation that will provide usage of its bowling lanes, food/beverage service, shoe rentals, and event management to customers in its targeted market. The Company was founded in 2010 by Larry Skozen.

1.1 The Services

The primary revenue stream for the business will come from the ongoing usage of the Company's bowling lanes, which will generate substantial high margin income for the business. The business, much like other bowling alleys, will also provide shoe rentals for its customers.

The Company's secondary stream of revenue will come from the sale of food/beverages and from hosting events. This is an extremely important secondary revenue source for the business as it will substantially increase the average amount of money spent by customer at Strikers Lanes.

The third section of the business plan will further describe the services offered by Strikers Lanes.

1.2 Financing

Mr. Skozen is seeking to raise $900,000 from a bank loan. The interest rate and loan agreement are to be further discussed during negotiation. This business plan assumes that the business will receive a 10 year loan with a 9% fixed interest rate. The financing will be used for the following:

- Development of the bowling alley.

- Financing for the first six months of operation.

- Capital to purchase equipment for the Company's bowling lanes.

Mr. Skozen will contribute $100,000 to the venture.

1.3 Mission Statement

The mission of Strikers Lanes is to become the recognized leader in its targeted market for providing an inviting atmosphere for enjoying bowling.

1.4 Management Team

The Company was founded by Larry Skozen. Mr. Skozen has more than 10 years of experience in the retail management industry. Through his expertise, he will be able to bring the operations of the business to profitability within its first year of operations.

1.5 Sales Forecasts

Mr. Skozen expects a strong rate of growth at the start of operations. Below are the expected financials over the next three years.

Proforma profit and loss (yearly)

Year	1	2	3
Sales	$768,828	$922,594	$1,079,435
Operating costs	$447,709	$467,842	$ 488,690
EBITDA	$244,236	$362,492	$ 482,801
Taxes, interest, and depreciation	$235,306	$246,977	$ 288,994
Net profit	$ 8,930	$115,515	$ 193,807

Sales, operating costs, and profit forecast

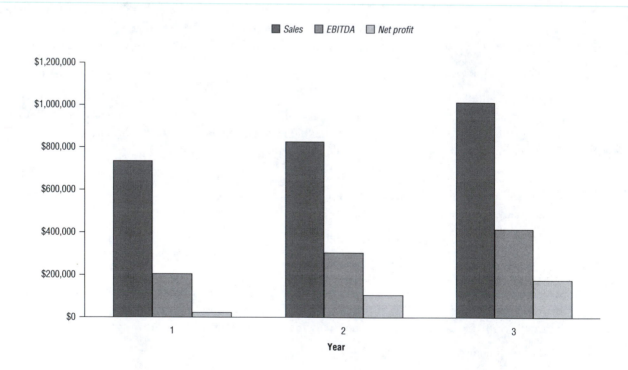

1.6 Expansion Plan

The Founder expects that the business will aggressively expand during the first three years of operation. Mr. Skozen intends to implement marketing campaigns that will effectively target individuals within the target market.

2.0 COMPANY AND FINANCING SUMMARY

2.1 Registered Name and Corporate Structure

Strikers Lanes is registered as a corporation in the State of New York.

2.2 Required Funds

At this time, Strikers Lanes requires $900,000 of debt funds. Below is a breakdown of how these funds will be used:

Projected startup costs

Facility acquisition	$ 350,000
Working capital	$ 100,000
FF&E	$ 150,000
Facility improvements	$ 50,000
Security deposits	$ 25,000
Insurance	$ 12,500
Bowling alley equipment	$ 272,500
Marketing budget	$ 30,000
Miscellaneous and unforeseen costs	$ 10,000
Total startup costs	**$1,000,000**

Use of funds

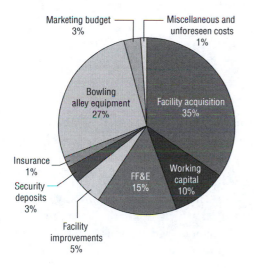

2.3 Investor Equity

Mr. Skozen is not seeking an investment from a third party at this time.

2.4 Management Equity

Larry Skozen owns 100% of Strikers Lanes, Inc.

2.5 Exit Strategy

If the business is very successful, Mr. Skozen may seek to sell the business to a third party for a significant earnings multiple. Most likely, the Company will hire a qualified business broker to sell the business on behalf of Strikers Lanes. Based on historical numbers, the business could fetch a sales premium of up to 6 times earnings.

3.0 PRODUCTS AND SERVICES

Below is a description of the services offered by Strikers Lanes.

3.1 Usage of Bowling Lanes and Rental of Shoes

As stated in the executive summary, the primary revenue stream for the Company will come from the ongoing usage of the Company's bowling lanes coupled with revenues generated from shoe rentals. Management anticipates that the facility will feature 20 to 25 lanes. The Company will also generate revenues from the management of local bowling leagues, which will not only increase revenues, but will further sales of food/beverages.

3.2 Food/Beverage Service

The business will also maintain an area of the retail facility that will provide limited food and beverage service. This revenue center is extremely important for Strikers Lanes because it will provide an additional stream of income for the business.

3.3 Event Management

The final revenue center for the business will be the hosting of birthday parties and other events (primarily for children ages 5 to 12) at Strikers Lanes facility. These parties are anticipated to generate approximately $150 to $200 from each event (with approximately 8 to 10 children).

From an advertising standpoint, this is an important aspect for the business as other children in attendance for a party may want to have their birthday party held at Strikers Lanes. These parties will also increase the visibility of the business among the Company's targeted demographic.

4.0 STRATEGIC AND MARKET ANALYSIS

4.1 Economic Outlook

This section of the analysis will detail the economic climate, the bowling alley industry, the customer profile, and the competition that the business will face as it progresses through its business operations.

Currently, the economic market condition in the United States is in recession. This slowdown in the economy has also greatly impacted real estate sales, which has halted to historical lows. Many economists expect that this recession will continue until mid-2010, at which point the economy will begin a prolonged recovery period. However, bowling allies usually operate with economic stability as the pricing point for the services offered is very low. Only a severe economic recession would impact Strikers Lanes's ability to generate top line income.

4.2 Industry Analysis

The bowling alley industry generates approximately $1.5 billion dollars a year among 2,700 companies that operate retail facilities. These revenue numbers does not include amusement parks, casinos, or resorts that provide bowling alley services as a value added benefit to patrons. The industry employs more than 30,000 people and provides aggregate annual payrolls of $350 million dollars.

As stated earlier, the bowling alley industry is mature. The expected continued growth of these businesses is expected to mirror the general population growth plus the rate of inflation.

4.3 Customer Profile

The average client at Strikers Lanes will be a middle- to upper-middle class man or woman living in the target market. Common traits among clients will include:

- Annual household income exceeding $50,000

- Lives or works no more than 15 miles from Strikers Lanes.

- Will spend $20 per visit.

Within the greater New York metropolitan area, there are more than 1 million people that could become potential customers of Strikers Lanes. Of course, because of the size of this market the business will be able to thrive as a low cost form of entertainment which can serve as an alternative to higher priced forms of entertainment (such as vacations) during deleterious economic conditions.

4.4 Competition

Within the Company's targeted market of the New York metropolitan area, there are 50 businesses that provide bowling alley services to the general public. As such, it is hard to categorize the competition that the business will face as it progresses through its business operations. However, Strikers Lanes intends to maintain a competitive advantage over other firms by pricing its services lower than those of bowling allies within a five mile radius of the business.

5.0 MARKETING PLAN

Strikers Lanes intends to maintain an extensive marketing campaign that will ensure maximum visibility for the business in its targeted market. Below is an overview of the marketing strategies and objectives.

5.1 Marketing Objectives

- Develop an online presence by developing a website and placing the Company's name and contact information with online directories.

- Implement a local campaign with the Company's targeted market via the use of flyers, local newspaper advertisements, and word of mouth.

5.2 Marketing Strategies

Management intends on using a number of advertising and marketing channels to promote traffic to Strikers Lanes. The Company primarily intends to use a broad based advertising campaign that will raise the awareness of the retail location among the targeted demographic.

To that end, Management will place a number of advertisements in locally based newspapers and advertisements from the onset of operations which may include discount coupons or coupons for free. This will create an immediate draw to Strikers Lanes's location.

Management also expects that the business will generate significant word of mouth advertising as the Company hosts events for children's birthday parties. As more and more children are invited to Strikers Lanes for hosted birthday parties, these youngsters may have their parents host their next birthday party at the facility. The Company anticipates that this type of advertising will take three to six months to become effective.

5.3 Pricing

For each round of bowling, the Company anticipates that the business will generate $1.50 of revenue coupled with $2 of revenue for the rental of bowling shoes. As the business will carry a diverse line of beverages and food products, Management anticipates that the business will generate gross margins of approximately 70% on each dollar of income generated through this revenue center.

6.0 ORGANIZATIONAL PLAN AND PERSONNEL SUMMARY

6.1 Corporate Organization

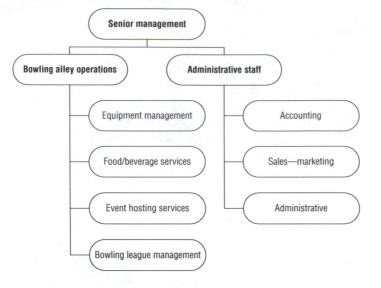

6.2 Organizational Budget

Personnel plan—yearly

Year	1	2	3
Owner	$ 40,000	$ 41,200	$ 42,436
Facility manager	$ 35,000	$ 36,050	$ 37,132
Bowling alley employees	$162,500	$167,375	$172,396
Bookkeeper (P/T)	$ 12,500	$ 12,875	$ 13,261
Administrative	$ 44,000	$ 45,320	$ 46,680
Total	**$294,000**	**$302,820**	**$311,905**

Numbers of personnel

Owner	1	1	1
Facility manager	1	1	1
Bowling alley employees	5	5	5
Bookkeeper (P/T)	1	1	1
Administrative	2	2	2
Total	**10**	**10**	**10**

Personnel expense breakdown

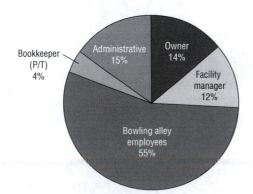

6.3 Management Biographies

Mr. Larry Skozen is a highly experienced entrepreneur with more than 25 years in the entertainment industry. Since beginning his career in the entertainment industry, Mr. Skozen has become well versed in every aspect of the operations of these businesses. Mr. Skozen's skill set includes, but is not limited to:

- The ability to oversee agents and employees.

- A complete understanding of accounting of the complex legal and accounting issues that Strikers Lanes will face on a day to day basis.

7.0 FINANCIAL PLAN

7.1 Underlying Assumptions

The Company has based its proforma financial statements on the following:

- The bowling alley will have an annual revenue growth rate of 16% per year.

- The Owner will acquire $900,000 of debt funds to develop the business.

- The loan will have a 10 year term with a 9% interest rate.

7.2 Sensitivity Analysis

The bowling alley's revenues are somewhat vulnerable to changes in the general economy. The Company is providing bowling lanes for use among customers, which are not a necessity. However, the pricing point for the Company's services is extremely low, and the general economy would need a serious recession before a revenue decline. The high margin revenue generated by the business will allow the Company to operate profitably despite negative economic climates.

7.3 Source of Funds

Financing

Equity contributions	
Management investment	$ 100,000.00
Total equity financing	**$ 100,000.00**
Banks and lenders	
Banks and lenders	$ 900,000.00
Total debt financing	**$ 900,000.00**
Total financing	**$1,000,000.00**

7.4 General Assumptions

General assumptions

Year	1	2	3
Short term interest rate	9.5%	9.5%	9.5%
Long term interest rate	10.0%	10.0%	10.0%
Federal tax rate	33.0%	33.0%	33.0%
State tax rate	5.0%	5.0%	5.0%
Personnel taxes	15.0%	15.0%	15.0%

7.5 Profit and Loss Statements

Proforma profit and loss (yearly)

Year	1	2	3
Sales	$ 768,828	$922,594	$1,079,435
Cost of goods sold	$ 76,883	$ 92,259	$ 107,943
Gross margin	90.00%	90.00%	90.00%
Operating income	**$691,945**	**$830,334**	**$ 971,491**
Expenses			
Payroll	$ 294,000	$302,820	$ 311,905
General and administrative	$ 25,200	$ 26,208	$ 27,256
Marketing expenses	$ 23,065	$ 27,678	$ 32,383
Professional fees and licensure	$ 7,500	$ 7,725	$ 7,957
Insurance costs	$ 12,500	$ 13,125	$ 13,781
Facility maintenance costs	$ 17,500	$ 19,250	$ 21,175
Equipment costs	$ 20,000	$ 21,000	$ 22,050
Miscellaneous costs	$ 3,844	$ 4,613	$ 5,397
Payroll taxes	$ 44,100	$ 45,423	$ 46,786
Total operating costs	**$447,709**	**$467,842**	**$ 488,690**
EBITDA	**$244,236**	**$362,492**	**$ 482,801**
Federal income tax	$ 80,598	$ 95,472	$ 137,144
State income tax	$ 12,212	$ 14,465	$ 20,779
Interest expense	$ 78,639	$ 73,183	$ 67,214
Depreciation expenses	$ 63,857	$ 63,857	$ 63,857
Net profit	**$ 8,930**	**$115,515**	**$ 193,807**
Profit margin	**1.16%**	**12.52%**	**17.95%**

Sales, operating costs, and profit forecast

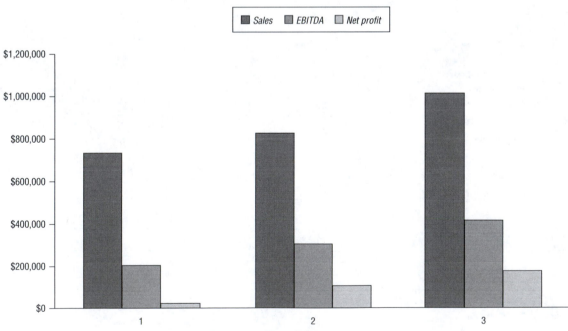

7.6 Cash Flow Analysis

Proforma cash flow analysis—yearly

Year	1	2	3
Cash from operations	$ 72,787	$179,372	$257,664
Cash from receivables	$ 0	$ 0	$ 0
Operating cash inflow	**$ 72,787**	**$179,372**	**$257,664**
Other cash inflows			
Equity investment	$ 100,000	$ 0	$ 0
Increased borrowings	$ 900,000	$ 0	$ 0
Sales of business assets	$ 0	$ 0	$ 0
A/P increases	$ 37,902	$ 43,587	$ 50,125
Total other cash inflows	**$1,037,902**	**$ 43,587**	**$ 50,125**
Total cash inflow	**$1,110,689**	**$222,959**	**$307,790**
Cash outflows			
Repayment of principal	$ 58,171	$ 63,627	$ 69,596
A/P decreases	$ 24,897	$ 29,876	$ 35,852
A/R increases	$ 0	$ 0	$ 0
Asset purchases	$ 870,000	$ 44,843	$ 64,416
Dividends	$ 50,951	$ 71,749	$103,066
Total cash outflows	**$1,004,019**	**$210,096**	**$272,929**
Net cash flow	**$ 106,671**	**$ 12,864**	**$ 34,860**
Cash balance	**$ 106,671**	**$119,534**	**$154,395**

Proforma cash flow (yearly)

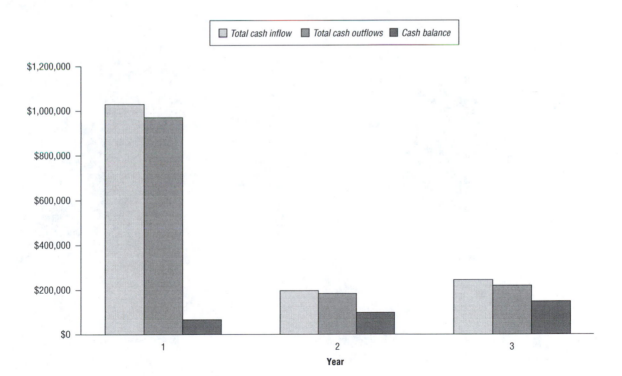

7.7 Balance Sheet

Proforma balance sheet—yearly

Year	1	2	3
Assets			
Cash	$106,671	$119,534	$ 154,395
Amortized development/expansion costs	$ 47,500	$ 51,984	$ 58,426
FF&E	$150,000	$172,422	$ 204,630
Bowling alley equipment	$272,500	$290,437	$ 316,204
Facility	$424,000	$449,440	$ 476,406
Accumulated depreciation	($ 63,857)	($127,714)	($ 191,571)
Total assets	**$936,813**	**$956,103**	**$1,018,489**
Liabilities and equity			
Accounts payable	$ 13,005	$ 26,716	$ 40,990
Long term liabilities	$841,829	$778,202	$ 714,575
Other liabilities	$ 0	$ 0	$ 0
Total liabilities	**$854,834**	**$804,918**	**$ 755,564**
Net worth	**$ 81,979**	**$151,185**	**$ 262,924**
Total liabilities and equity	**$936,813**	**$956,103**	**$1,018,489**

Proforma balance sheet

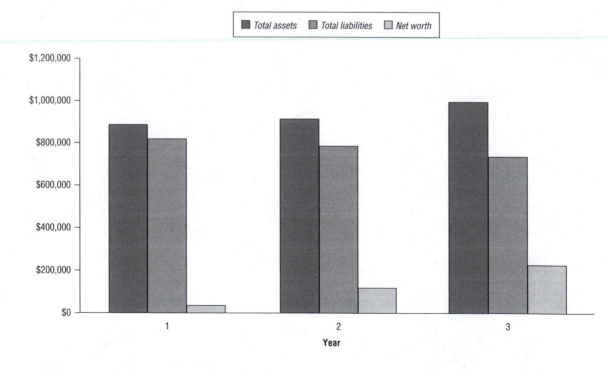

7.8 Breakeven Analysis

Monthly break even analysis

Year	1	2	3
Monthly revenue	$ 41,455	$ 43,319	$ 45,249
Yearly revenue	$497,454	$519,824	$542,989

Break even analysis

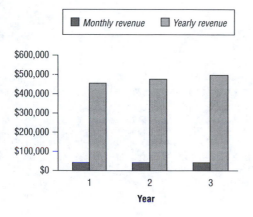

7.9 Business Ratios

Business ratios—yearly

Year	1	2	3
Sales			
Sales growth	0.0%	20.0%	17.0%
Gross margin	90.0%	90.0%	90.0%
Financials			
Profit margin	1.16%	12.52%	17.95%
Assets to liabilities	1.10	1.19	1.35
Equity to liabilities	0.10	0.19	0.35
Assets to equity	11.43	6.32	3.87
Liquidity			
Acid test	0.12	0.15	0.20
Cash to assets	0.11	0.13	0.15

7.10 Three Year Profit and Loss Statement

Profit and loss statement (first year)

Months	1	2	3	4	5	6	7
Sales	$ 63,200	$63,358	$63,516	$63,674	$63,832	$63,990	$64,148
Cost of goods sold	$ 6,320	$ 6,336	$ 6,352	$ 6,367	$ 6,383	$ 6,399	$ 6,415
Gross margin	90.0%	90.0%	90.0%	90.0%	90.0%	90.0%	90.0%
Operating income	$56,880	$57,022	$57,164	$57,307	$57,449	$57,591	$57,733
Expenses							
Payroll	$ 24,500	$24,500	$24,500	$24,500	$24,500	$24,500	$24,500
General and administrative	$ 2,100	$ 2,100	$ 2,100	$ 2,100	$ 2,100	$ 2,100	$ 2,100
Marketing expenses	$ 1,922	$ 1,922	$ 1,922	$ 1,922	$ 1,922	$ 1,922	$ 1,922
Professional fees and licensure	$ 625	$ 625	$ 625	$ 625	$ 625	$ 625	$ 625
Insurance costs	$ 1,042	$ 1,042	$ 1,042	$ 1,042	$ 1,042	$ 1,042	$ 1,042
Facility maintenance costs	$ 1,458	$ 1,458	$ 1,458	$ 1,458	$ 1,458	$ 1,458	$ 1,458
Equipment costs	$ 1,667	$ 1,667	$ 1,667	$ 1,667	$ 1,667	$ 1,667	$ 1,667
Miscellaneous costs	$ 320	$ 320	$ 320	$ 320	$ 320	$ 320	$ 320
Payroll taxes	$ 3,675	$ 3,675	$ 3,675	$ 3,675	$ 3,675	$ 3,675	$ 3,675
Total operating costs	$37,309	$37,309	$37,309	$37,309	$37,309	$37,309	$37,309
EBITDA	$19,571	$19,713	$19,855	$19,998	$20,140	$20,282	$20,424
Federal income tax	$ 6,625	$ 6,642	$ 6,659	$ 6,675	$ 6,692	$ 6,708	$ 6,725
State income tax	$ 1,004	$ 1,006	$ 1,009	$ 1,011	$ 1,014	$ 1,016	$ 1,019
Interest expense	$ 6,750	$ 6,715	$ 6,680	$ 6,645	$ 6,609	$ 6,573	$ 6,537
Depreciation expense	$ 5,321	$ 5,321	$ 5,321	$ 5,321	$ 5,321	$ 5,321	$ 5,321
Net profit	−$ 130	$ 28	$ 187	$ 345	$ 504	$ 663	$ 822

Profit and loss statement (first year cont.)

Month	8	9	10	11	12	1
Sales	$ 64,306	$64,464	$64,622	$64,780	$64,938	$768,828
Cost of goods sold	$ 6,431	$ 6,446	$ 6,462	$ 6,478	$ 6,494	$ 76,883
Gross margin	90.0%	90.0%	90.0%	90.0%	90.0%	90.0%
Operating income	$57,875	$58,018	$58,160	$58,302	$58,444	$691,945
Expenses						
Payroll	$ 24,500	$24,500	$24,500	$24,500	$24,500	$294,000
General and administrative	$ 2,100	$ 2,100	$ 2,100	$ 2,100	$ 2,100	$ 25,200
Marketing expenses	$ 1,922	$ 1,922	$ 1,922	$ 1,922	$ 1,922	$ 23,065
Professional fees and licensure	$ 625	$ 625	$ 625	$ 625	$ 625	$ 7,500
Insurance costs	$ 1,042	$ 1,042	$ 1,042	$ 1,042	$ 1,042	$ 12,500
Facility maintenance costs	$ 1,458	$ 1,458	$ 1,458	$ 1,458	$ 1,458	$ 17,500
Equipment costs	$ 1,667	$ 1,667	$ 1,667	$ 1,667	$ 1,667	$ 20,000
Miscellaneous costs	$ 320	$ 320	$ 320	$ 320	$ 320	$ 3,844
Payroll taxes	$ 3,675	$ 3,675	$ 3,675	$ 3,675	$ 3,675	$ 44,100
Total operating costs	$37,309	$37,309	$37,309	$37,309	$37,309	$447,709
EBITDA	$20,566	$20,709	$20,851	$20,993	$21,135	$244,236
Federal income tax	$ 6,741	$ 6,758	$ 6,774	$ 6,791	$ 6,808	$ 80,598
State income tax	$ 1,021	$ 1,024	$ 1,026	$ 1,029	$ 1,031	$ 12,212
Interest expense	$ 6,500	$ 6,464	$ 6,426	$ 6,389	$ 6,352	$ 78,639
Depreciation expense	$ 5,321	$ 5,321	$ 5,321	$ 5,321	$ 5,321	$ 63,857
Net profit	$ 982	$ 1,142	$ 1,302	$ 1,462	$ 1,623	$ 8,930

Profit and loss statement (second year)

Quarter	Q1	2 Q2	Q3	Q4	2
Sales	$ 184,519	$230,648	$249,100	$258,326	$922,594
Cost of goods sold	$ 18,452	$ 23,065	$ 24,910	$ 25,833	$ 92,259
Gross margin	90.0%	90.0%	90.0%	90.0%	90.0%
Operating income	**$166,067**	**$207,584**	**$224,190**	**$232,494**	**$830,334**
Expenses					
Payroll	$ 60,564	$ 75,705	$ 81,761	$ 84,790	$302,820
General and administrative	$ 5,242	$ 6,552	$ 7,076	$ 7,338	$ 26,208
Marketing expenses	$ 5,536	$ 6,919	$ 7,473	$ 7,750	$ 27,678
Professional fees and licensure	$ 1,545	$ 1,931	$ 2,086	$ 2,163	$ 7,725
Insurance costs	$ 2,625	$ 3,281	$ 3,544	$ 3,675	$ 13,125
Facility maintenance costs	$ 3,850	$ 4,813	$ 5,198	$ 5,390	$ 19,250
Equipment costs	$ 4,200	$ 5,250	$ 5,670	$ 5,880	$ 21,000
Miscellaneous costs	$ 923	$ 1,153	$ 1,246	$ 1,292	$ 4,613
Payroll taxes	$ 9,085	$ 11,356	$ 12,264	$ 12,718	$ 45,423
Total operating costs	**$ 93,568**	**$116,960**	**$126,317**	**$130,996**	**$467,842**
EBITDA	**$ 72,498**	**$ 90,623**	**$ 97,873**	**$101,498**	**$362,492**
Federal income tax	$ 19,094	$ 23,868	$ 25,778	$ 26,732	$ 95,472
State income tax	$ 2,893	$ 3,616	$ 3,906	$ 4,050	$ 14,465
Interest expense	$ 18,826	$ 18,478	$ 18,121	$ 17,757	$ 73,183
Depreciation expense	$ 15,964	$ 15,964	$ 15,964	$ 15,964	$ 63,857
Net profit	**$ 15,720**	**$ 28,697**	**$ 34,104**	**$ 36,994**	**$115,515**

Profit and loss statement (third year)

Quarter	Q1	3 Q2	Q3	Q4	3
Sales	$215,887	$269,859	$291,447	$302,242	$1,079,435
Cost of goods sold	$ 21,589	$ 26,986	$ 29,145	$ 30,224	$ 107,943
Gross margin	90.0%	90.0%	90.0%	90.0%	90.0%
Operating income	**$194,298**	**$242,873**	**$262,303**	**$272,017**	**$ 971,491**
Expenses					
Payroll	$ 62,381	$ 77,976	$ 84,214	$ 87,333	$ 311,905
General and administrative	$ 5,451	$ 6,814	$ 7,359	$ 7,632	$ 27,256
Marketing expenses	$ 6,477	$ 8,096	$ 8,743	$ 9,067	$ 32,383
Professional fees and licensure	$ 1,591	$ 1,989	$ 2,148	$ 2,228	$ 7,957
Insurance costs	$ 2,756	$ 3,445	$ 3,721	$ 3,859	$ 13,781
Facility maintenance costs	$ 4,235	$ 5,294	$ 5,717	$ 5,929	$ 21,175
Equipment costs	$ 4,410	$ 5,513	$ 5,954	$ 6,174	$ 22,050
Miscellaneous costs	$ 1,079	$ 1,349	$ 1,457	$ 1,511	$ 5,397
Payroll taxes	$ 9,357	$ 11,696	$ 12,632	$ 13,100	$ 46,786
Total operating costs	**$ 97,738**	**$122,172**	**$131,946**	**$136,833**	**$ 488,690**
EBITDA	**$ 96,560**	**$120,700**	**$130,356**	**$135,184**	**$ 482,801**
Federal income tax	$ 27,429	$ 34,286	$ 37,029	$ 38,400	$ 137,144
State income tax	$ 4,156	$ 5,195	$ 5,610	$ 5,818	$ 20,779
Interest expense	$ 17,384	$ 17,003	$ 16,613	$ 16,214	$ 67,214
Depreciation expense	$ 15,964	$ 15,964	$ 15,964	$ 15,964	$ 63,857
Net profit	**$ 31,627**	**$ 48,252**	**$ 55,140**	**$ 58,787**	**$ 193,807**

7.11 Three Year Cash Flow Analysis

Cash flow analysis (first year)

Month	1	2	3	4	5	6	7	8
Cash from operations	$ 5,192	$ 5,350	$ 5,508	$ 5,666	$ 5,825	$ 5,984	$ 6,144	$ 6,303
Cash from receivables	$ 0	$ 0	$ 0	$ 0	$ 0	$ 0	$ 0	$ 0
Operating cash inflow	$ 5,192	$ 5,350	$ 5,508	$ 5,666	$ 5,825	$ 5,984	$ 6,144	$ 6,303
Other cash inflows								
Equity investment	$ 100,000	$ 0	$ 0	$ 0	$ 0	$ 0	$ 0	$ 0
Increased borrowings	$ 900,000	$ 0	$ 0	$ 0	$ 0	$ 0	$ 0	$ 0
Sales of business assets	$ 0	$ 0	$ 0	$ 0	$ 0	$ 0	$ 0	$ 0
A/P increases	$ 3,159	$ 3,159	$ 3,159	$ 3,159	$ 3,159	$ 3,159	$ 3,159	$ 3,159
Total other cash inflows	$1,003,159	$ 3,159	$ 3,159	$ 3,159	$ 3,159	$ 3,159	$ 3,159	$ 3,159
Total cash inflow	$1,008,350	$ 8,508	$ 8,666	$ 8,825	$ 8,984	$ 9,143	$ 9,302	$ 9,462
Cash outflows								
Repayment of principal	$ 4,651	$ 4,686	$ 4,721	$ 4,756	$ 4,792	$ 4,828	$ 4,864	$ 4,901
A/P decreases	$ 2,075	$ 2,075	$ 2,075	$ 2,075	$ 2,075	$ 2,075	$ 2,075	$ 2,075
A/R increases	$ 0	$ 0	$ 0	$ 0	$ 0	$ 0	$ 0	$ 0
Asset purchases	$ 870,000	$ 0	$ 0	$ 0	$ 0	$ 0	$ 0	$ 0
Dividends	$ 0	$ 0	$ 0	$ 0	$ 0	$ 0	$ 0	$ 0
Total cash outflows	$ 876,726	$ 6,760	$ 6,796	$ 6,831	$ 6,867	$ 6,903	$ 6,939	$ 6,975
Net cash flow	$ 131,625	$ 1,748	$ 1,871	$ 1,994	$ 2,117	$ 2,240	$ 2,363	$ 2,486
Cash balance	$ 131,625	$133,372	$135,243	$137,237	$139,354	$141,595	$143,958	$146,444

Cash flow analysis (first year cont.)

Month	9	10	11	12	1
Cash from operations	$ 6,463	$ 6,623	$ 6,784	$ 6,944	$ 72,787
Cash from receivables	$ 0	$ 0	$ 0	$ 0	$ 0
Operating cash inflow	$ 6,463	$ 6,623	$ 6,784	$ 6,944	$ 72,787
Other cash inflows					
Equity investment	$ 0	$ 0	$ 0	$ 0	$ 100,000
Increased borrowings	$ 0	$ 0	$ 0	$ 0	$ 900,000
Sales of business assets	$ 0	$ 0	$ 0	$ 0	$ 0
A/P increases	$ 3,159	$ 3,159	$ 3,159	$ 3,159	$ 37,902
Total other cash inflows	$ 3,159	$ 3,159	$ 3,159	$ 3,159	$1,037,902
Total cash inflow	$ 9,622	$ 9,782	$ 9,942	$ 10,103	$1,110,689
Cash outflows					
Repayment of principal	$ 4,937	$ 4,974	$ 5,012	$ 5,049	$ 58,171
A/P decreases	$ 2,075	$ 2,075	$ 2,075	$ 2,075	$ 24,897
A/R increases	$ 0	$ 0	$ 0	$ 0	$ 0
Asset purchases	$ 0	$ 0	$ 0	$ 0	$ 870,000
Dividends	$ 0	$ 0	$ 0	$ 50,951	$ 50,951
Total cash outflows	$ 7,012	$ 7,049	$ 7,086	$ 58,075	$1,004,019
Net cash flow	$ 2,610	$ 2,733	$ 2,856	−$ 47,972	$ 106,671
Cash balance	$149,054	$151,787	$154,643	$106,671	$ 106,671

Cash flow analysis (second year)

Quarter	Q1	2 Q2	Q3	Q4	2
Cash from operations	$ 35,874	$ 44,843	$ 48,430	$ 50,224	$179,372
Cash from receivables	$ 0	$ 0	$ 0	$ 0	$ 0
Operating cash inflow	**$ 35,874**	**$ 44,843**	**$ 48,430**	**$ 50,224**	**$179,372**
Other cash inflows					
Equity investment	$ 0	$ 0	$ 0	$ 0	$ 0
Increased borrowings	$ 0	$ 0	$ 0	$ 0	$ 0
Sales of business assets	$ 0	$ 0	$ 0	$ 0	$ 0
A/P increases	$ 8,717	$ 10,897	$ 11,769	$ 12,204	$ 43,587
Total other cash inflows	**$ 8,717**	**$ 10,897**	**$ 11,769**	**$ 12,204**	**$ 43,587**
Total cash inflow	**$ 44,592**	**$ 55,740**	**$ 60,199**	**$ 62,429**	**$222,959**
Cash outflows					
Repayment of principal	$ 15,376	$ 15,725	$ 16,081	$ 16,446	$ 63,627
A/P decreases	$ 5,975	$ 7,469	$ 8,067	$ 8,365	$ 29,876
A/R increases	$ 0	$ 0	$ 0	$ 0	$ 0
Asset purchases	$ 8,969	$ 11,211	$ 12,108	$ 12,556	$ 44,843
Dividends	$ 14,350	$ 17,937	$ 19,372	$ 20,090	$ 71,749
Total cash outflows	**$ 44,670**	**$ 52,342**	**$ 55,628**	**$ 57,457**	**$210,096**
Net cash flow	**−$ 78**	**$ 3,398**	**$ 4,572**	**$ 4,972**	**$ 12,864**
Cash balance	**$106,593**	**$109,991**	**$114,563**	**$119,534**	**$119,534**

Cash flow analysis (third year)

Quarter	Q1	3 Q2	Q3	Q4	3
Cash from operations	$ 51,533	$ 64,416	$ 69,569	$ 72,146	$257,664
Cash from receivables	$ 0	$ 0	$ 0	$ 0	$ 0
Operating cash inflow	**$ 51,533**	**$ 64,416**	**$ 69,569**	**$ 72,146**	**$257,664**
Other cash inflows					
Equity investment	$ 0	$ 0	$ 0	$ 0	$ 0
Increased borrowings	$ 0	$ 0	$ 0	$ 0	$ 0
Sales of business assets	$ 0	$ 0	$ 0	$ 0	$ 0
A/P increases	$ 10,025	$ 12,531	$ 13,534	$ 14,035	$ 50,125
Total other cash inflows	**$ 10,025**	**$ 12,531**	**$ 13,534**	**$ 14,035**	**$ 50,125**
Total cash inflow	**$ 61,558**	**$ 76,947**	**$ 83,103**	**$ 86,181**	**$307,790**
Cash outflows					
Repayment of principal	$ 16,818	$ 17,200	$ 17,590	$ 17,988	$ 69,596
A/P decreases	$ 7,170	$ 8,963	$ 9,680	$ 10,038	$ 35,852
A/R increases	$ 0	$ 0	$ 0	$ 0	$ 0
Asset purchases	$ 12,883	$ 16,104	$ 17,392	$ 18,036	$ 64,416
Dividends	$ 20,613	$ 25,766	$ 27,828	$ 28,858	$103,066
Total cash outflows	**$ 57,485**	**$ 68,033**	**$ 72,490**	**$ 74,922**	**$272,929**
Net cash flow	**$ 4,073**	**$ 8,914**	**$ 10,614**	**$ 11,259**	**$ 34,860**
Cash balance	**$123,607**	**$132,522**	**$143,135**	**$154,395**	**$154,395**

Commodities Trading Firm

Admirian Commodities

78643 Broadway
New York, NY 10004

BizPlanDB.com

Admirian Commodities is a New York based corporation that will actively trade hard commodities and currencies among the many exchanges within the United States and abroad.

1.0 EXECUTIVE SUMMARY

The purpose of this business plan is to raise $5,000,000 for the development of a commodities trading firm while showcasing the expected financials and operations over the next three years. Admirian Commodities is a New York based corporation that will actively trade hard commodities and currencies among the many exchanges within the United States and abroad. The Company was founded in 2010 by Timm Northup.

1.1 The Services

The primary revenue center for the business will come from the direct trading of commodities including corn, oil, precious metals, and currencies on a day-to-day basis. The Company, through its established relationships with commodities brokers, will be able to amplify its returns through the use of significant leverage for the commodities purchased using the firm's capital. The business expects that it will use 1:5 leverage on all commodities trades executed by the Company.

The Company's secondary stream of income will be derived from interest generated on capital held from short sales that are used in conjunction with the Company's trading operations. Interest income will generate approximately 30% of the Admirian Commodities' aggregate revenue.

The third section of the business plan will further describe the investment management services offered by Admirian Commodities.

1.2 Financing

At this time, the Company is seeking to raise $5,000,000 for the development of operations. Mr. Northup is seeking to sell a 75% ownership interest in the business in exchange for this capital. 90% of the invested capital will be used for direct investments into the firm's commodity trading operations. Briefly, the capital will be used as follows:

- Commodities trading operations.
- Development of the Company's office.
- General working capital.

1.3 Mission Statement

Management's mission is to develop Admirian Commodities into a middle market investment company that specializes in trading specific agricultural, oil, and precious metal commodities with the intent to realize small, but continuous profits on a daily basis.

1.4 Management Team

The Company was founded by Timm Northup. Mr. Northup has more than 10 years of experience in the commodities trading industry. Through his expertise, he will be able to bring the operations of the business to profitability within its first year of operations.

1.5 Income Forecasts

Mr. Northup expects a strong rate of growth at the start of operations. Below are the expected financials over the next three years.

Proforma profit and loss (yearly)

Year	1	2	3
Sales	$2,348,580	$2,935,725	$3,522,870
Operating costs	$ 924,447	$1,162,636	$1,217,863
EBITDA	$1,306,704	$1,626,303	$2,128,863
Taxes, interest, and depreciation	$ 512,929	$ 634,377	$ 825,350
Net profit	$ 793,775	$ 991,926	$1,303,513

Sales, operating costs, and profit forecast

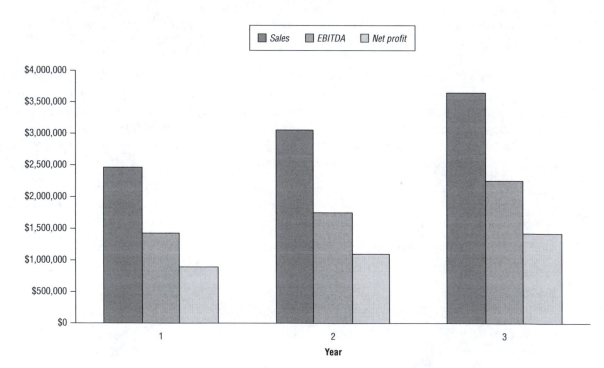

1.6 Expansion Plan

The Company will to undergo an aggressive expansion after the successful completion of the initial capital raising period. As the laws that govern investment pools for commodities trading are different than those for general securities dealers/traders, the business may be able to solicit capital from the general public in a similar capacity to that of a registered investment advisory. Mr. Northup is currently investigating how the business can expand once trading operations commence.

2.0 COMPANY AND FINANCING SUMMARY

2.1 Registered Name and Corporate Structure

Admirian Commodities, Inc. is registered as a corporation in the State of New York.

2.2 Required Funds

At this time, Admirian Commodities requires $5,000,000 of equity funds. Below is a breakdown of how these funds will be used:

Projected startup costs

Initial lease payments and deposits	$ 75,000
Working capital	$ 250,000
FF&E	$ 125,000
Leasehold improvements	$ 125,000
Security deposits	$ 50,000
Insurance	$ 25,000
Commodities trading capital	$ 4,290,000
Marketing budget	$ 50,000
Miscellaneous and unforeseen costs	$ 10,000
Total startup costs	**$5,000,000**

2.3 Investor Equity

At this time, Mr. Northup is seeking to sell a 75% interest in Admirian Commodities in exchange for the capital sought in this business plan.

2.4 Management Equity

Timm Northup currently owns 100% of Admirian Commodities, Inc.

2.5 Exit Strategies

Management has planned for two possible exit strategies that would yield significant capital appreciation for the Company's management team and investors. First, the business could be sold in its entirety to a third party entity. At this point, Management would most likely leave the Company to pursue other ventures.

The second exit strategy would be to engage a secondary capital raising that would allow management and investors to cash out a portion of the equity built into the business while concurrently providing the firm with more capital for trading. This exit strategy would still require that Management operate the firm on a day to day basis, so in actuality it is only a partial exit strategy. However, by raising a secondary or tertiary round of capital, the business could easily expand to become a much larger trading firm after the third year of operations.

2.6 Investor Divesture

This will be discussed during negotiations.

3.0 COMMODITIES TRADING OPERATIONS

As stated in the executive summary, the business intends to actively trade contracts, swaps, and options related to commodities including agricultural commodities, oil, precious metals, and currencies.

The Company, prior to the onset of operations, will develop brokerage relationships with major commodities brokers that will place and manage trades on behalf of the Company. The business will specially select brokers that can offer the firm prime brokerage capabilities which include expanded leverage for the Company's investments. As discussed earlier, the Company intends to use conservative 1:5 leverage for most of its trades. However, most exchanges permit the use of 1:20 leverage for certain commodities. Currency trading can often provide leverage of 1:50 and up to 1:100 leverage depending on the type of trade. Management will only use larger amounts of leverage when the underlying commodities have been properly hedged using counteracting options.

One of the primary strategies that Admirian Commodities intends to engage will be delta neutral trading, which will allow the business to actively purchase options while currently hedging the values of the Company's commodity portfolios. Delta neutral trading allows the firm to generate revenues on commodities (these types of trades are available on all commodities) trading simply through the volatility of the underlying positions. With the pace of inflation increasing significantly in the last year, Management sees a significant opportunity to develop substantial profit streams through volatility style trading rather than attempting to determine the direction of any given market.

4.0 STRATEGIC AND MARKET ANALYSIS

4.1 Economic Outlook

This section of the analysis will detail the economic climate, the commodities trading industry, the customer profile, and the competition that the business will face as it progresses through its business operations.

Currently, the economic market condition in the United States is in recession. This slowdown in the economy has also greatly impacted real estate sales, which has halted to historical lows. Many economists expect that this recession will continue until mid-2010, at which point the economy will begin a prolonged recovery period.

Inflation is somewhat of a concern for the Company. As the inflation rate decreases, the purchasing power parity of the American dollar decreases in relation to other currencies. This may pose a risk to the Company should rampant inflation, much like the inflation experienced in the late 1970s, occur again. This event would significant weaken the Company's ability to borrow funds (should the need arise), but it could also severely impact the gross margins of the business. After the business begins to trade in excess of $20,000,000 per year in revenues, the business may solicit a currency based investment bank to hedge against inflationary risks. This risk has been faced by many companies over the last five years as the value of the Euro/Yuan/Yen has appreciated significantly in its relation to the American dollar.

4.2 Industry Analysis

The financial services sector has become one of the fastest growing business segments in the U.S. economy. Computerized technologies allow financial firms to operate advisory and brokerage services anywhere in the country. In previous decades, most financial firms needed to be within a close proximity to Wall Street in order to provide their clients the highest level of service. This is no longer the case as a firm can access almost every facet of the financial markets through internet connections and specialized trading and investment management software. With these advances, several new firms have been created to address the needs of people in rural and suburban areas.

Within the United States, there are approximately 2,000 companies that independently trade futures and commodities contracts with the intent to generate a profit. Each year, these firms aggregately generate more than $25 billion of revenue while concurrently providing $10 billion of payrolls (including bonuses). More than 60,000 people are employed by the industry.

4.3 Customer Profile

As the Company intends to operate its trading operations via the free trading markets within the U.S. and internationally, the Company will not directly have "customers." In a sense, the customers of this firm are its investors as the Company is trying to develop a wealth and income creating vehicle for them and the Senior Management Team. However, and in the future, the Company may expand its capital base by soliciting additional investments from the general public. In this instance, the Company would need to register itself as a CTA firm with the Commodities and Futures Trading Commission. At this time, it is unclear as to what requirements would be needed in order for an individual to invest with the commodities trading firm as they differ substantially from other private investment vehicles such as hedge funds and private equity groups.

4.4 Competition

Competition among commodities trading firms is next to impossible to discuss as these trades are primarily made on nationwide exchanges that are based in both New York City and Chicago. The prices determined (and locked in through trades by the business) are done so on a free market basis. However, the business will retain a competitive advantage over other firms by having greater access to capital while concurrently operating a low operating cost infrastructure.

5.0 MARKETING PLAN

As Admirian Commodities intends to primarily trade for its own account, the marketing required by the business will be absolutely minimal. Mr. Northup's marketing campaigns will primarily consist of familiarizing the Company's brand name with other commodities traders and brokerages so that future joint ventures and investments can be made in the future. As discussed earlier, there is the possibility that the business may be able to solicit capital from the general public. In that instance, the Company will engage marketing strategies discussed below.

5.1 Marketing Objectives

- Develop ongoing relationships with commodities brokerages within the United States and abroad.

- Develop an informative website if the Company decides to solicit capital from the general public.

5.2 Marketing Strategies

Foremost, the Company will develop ongoing prime brokerage relationships with several commodities brokerages throughout the United States, Europe, and Asia. This will ensure that the Company can amplify its returns through leverage offered by these firms. Mr. Northup will distribute information, via an information packet, to these firms informing them that Admirian Commodities is in business, its capitalization, and what types of trades the company most frequently engages.

In regards to raising capital from the general public, the Company will develop an informative website showcasing the operations of the firm, Mr. Northup's experience as a trader, proper investment disclosures, and relevant contact information. The website may also feature functionality so that investors can log in and track the performance of their account. If this website is built, the Company will hire an internet marketing firm to properly rank the site via search engine optimization and pay per click strategies.

5.3 Pricing

Pricing is not an issue for Admirian Commodities as the business will generate income despite very high commodity prices or low commodity prices. As these exchanges operate on a free market basis, there is always someone standing buy to hold interests in commodities held by the business.

6.0 ORGANIZATIONAL PLAN AND PERSONNEL SUMMARY

6.1 Corporate Organization

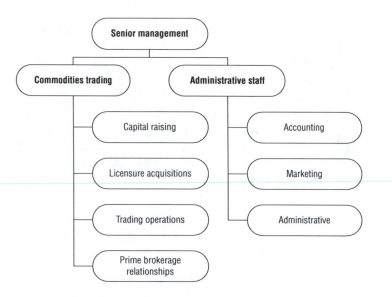

6.2 Organizational Budget

Personnel plan—yearly

Year	1	2	3
Senior management	$200,000	$206,000	$212,180
Economists	$ 85,000	$175,100	$180,353
Accountants	$ 65,000	$ 66,950	$ 68,959
Commodities traders	$150,000	$231,750	$238,703
Administrative	$112,500	$115,875	$119,351
Total	**$612,500**	**$795,675**	**$819,545**

Numbers of personnel

Senior management	2	2	2
Economists	1	2	2
Accountants	1	1	1
Commodities traders	2	3	3
Administrative	3	3	3
Totals	**9**	**11**	**11**

Personnel expense breakdown

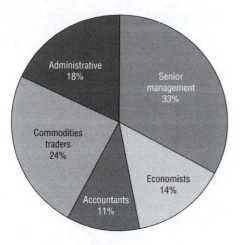

7.0 FINANCIAL PLAN

7.1 Underlying Assumptions

The Company has based its proforma financial statements on the following:

- Admirian Commodities will have an annual revenue growth rate of 19% per year.

- The Founder will acquire $5,000,000 of equity funds to develop the business.

- The Company will earn a compounded annual return of 17% on its commodities portfolio.

7.2 Sensitivity Analysis

The Company's revenues are not sensitive to changes in the general economy. Admirian Commodities will use a number of trading strategies to ensure that the business can generate profits despite increases or decreases in the value of any commodity. As such, the business should have no issues with top line income despite inflationary pressures or downward pricing pressure on specific commodities.

7.3 Source of Funds

Financing

Equity contributions	
Investor(s)	$ 5,000,000.00
Total equity financing	**$5,000,000.00**
Banks and lenders	
Total debt financing	$ 0.00
Total financing	**$5,000,000.00**

7.4 General Assumptions

General assumptions

Year	1	2	3
Short term interest rate	9.5%	9.5%	9.5%
Long term interest rate	10.0%	10.0%	10.0%
Federal tax rate	33.0%	33.0%	33.0%
State tax rate	5.0%	5.0%	5.0%
Personnel taxes	15.0%	15.0%	15.0%

7.5 Profit and Loss Statements

Proforma profit and loss (yearly)

Year	1	2	3
Sales	**$2,348,580**	**$2,935,725**	**$3,522,870**
Cost of goods sold	$ 117,429	$ 146,786	$ 176,144
Gross margin	95.00%	95.00%	95.00%
Operating income	**$2,231,151**	**$2,788,939**	**$3,346,727**
Expenses			
Payroll	$ 612,500	$ 795,675	$ 819,545
General and administrative	$ 48,000	$ 49,920	$ 51,917
Marketing expenses	$ 11,743	$ 14,679	$ 17,614
Professional fees and licensure	$ 30,000	$ 30,900	$ 31,827
Insurance costs	$ 25,000	$ 26,250	$ 27,563
Trading licenses and seat costs	$ 70,457	$ 88,072	$ 105,686
Rent and utilities	$ 29,000	$ 30,450	$ 31,973
Miscellaneous costs	$ 5,871	$ 7,339	$ 8,807
Payroll taxes	$ 91,875	$ 119,351	$ 122,932
Total operating costs	**$ 924,447**	**$1,162,636**	**$1,217,863**
EBITDA	**$1,306,704**	**$1,626,303**	**$2,128,863**
Federal income tax	$ 431,212	$ 536,680	$ 702,525
State income tax	$ 65,335	$ 81,315	$ 106,443
Interest expense	$ 0	$ 0	$ 0
Depreciation expenses	$ 16,382	$ 16,382	$ 16,382
Net profit	**$ 793,775**	**$ 991,926**	**$1,303,513**
Profit margin	**33.80%**	**33.79%**	**37.00%**

Sales, operating costs, and profit forecast

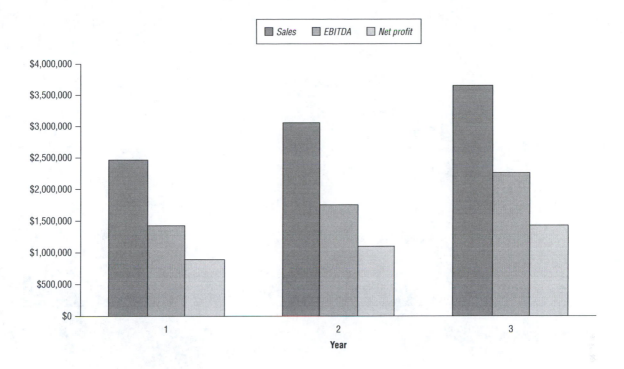

7.6 Cash Flow Analysis

Proforma cash flow analysis—yearly

Year	1	2	3
Cash from operations	$ 810,157	$ 1,008,308	$ 1,319,895
Cash from receivables	$ 0	$ 0	$ 0
Operating cash inflow	**$ 810,157**	**$1,008,308**	**$1,319,895**
Other cash inflows			
Equity investment	$ 5,000,000	$ 0	$ 0
Increased borrowings	$ 0	$ 0	$ 0
Sales of business assets	$ 0	$ 0	$ 0
A/P increases	$ 37,902	$ 43,587	$ 50,125
Total other cash inflows	**$5,037,902**	**$ 43,587**	**$ 50,125**
Total cash inflow	**$5,848,059**	**$1,051,895**	**$1,370,020**
Cash outflows			
Repayment of principal	$ 0	$ 0	$ 0
A/P decreases	$ 24,897	$ 29,876	$ 35,852
A/R increases	$ 0	$ 0	$ 0
Asset purchases	$ 4,700,000	$ 604,985	$ 791,937
Dividends	$ 283,555	$ 352,908	$ 461,963
Total cash outflows	**$5,008,452**	**$ 987,769**	**$1,289,752**
Net cash flow	**$ 839,607**	**$ 64,126**	**$ 80,268**
Cash balance	**$ 839,607**	**$ 903,733**	**$ 984,002**

Proforma cash flow (yearly)

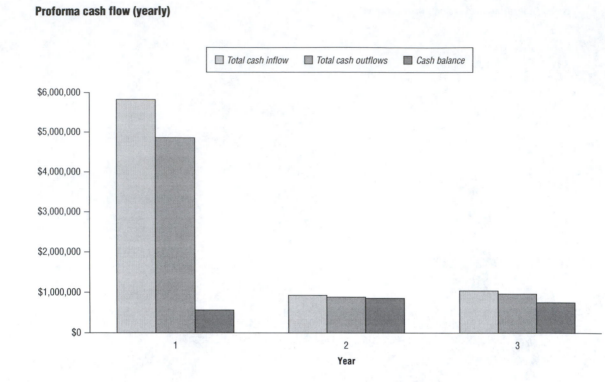

7.7 Balance Sheet

Proforma balance sheet—yearly

Year	1	2	3
Assets			
Cash	$ 839,607	$ 903,733	$ 984,002
Amortized development/expansion costs	$ 285,000	$ 345,498	$ 424,692
Commodities portfolio	$ 4,504,500	$ 5,553,885	$ 6,893,291
FF&E	$ 125,000	$ 185,498	$ 264,692
Accumulated depreciation	($ 16,382)	($ 32,763)	($ 49,145)
Total assets	**$5,737,725**	**$6,955,851**	**$8,517,532**
Liabilities and equity			
Accounts payable	$ 13,005	$ 26,716	$ 40,990
Long term liabilities	$ 0	$ 0	$ 0
Other liabilities	$ 0	$ 0	$ 0
Total liabilities	**$ 13,005**	**$ 26,716**	**$ 40,990**
Net worth	**$5,724,720**	**$6,929,136**	**$8,476,542**
Total liabilities and equity	**$5,737,725**	**$6,955,851**	**$8,517,532**

Proforma balance sheet

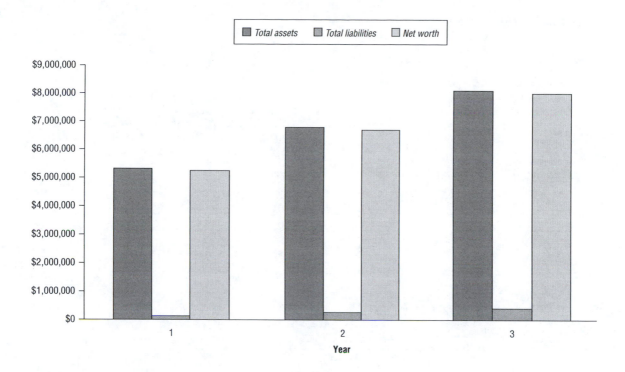

7.8 Breakeven Analysis

Monthly break even analysis

Year	1	2	3
Monthly revenue	$ 81,092	$ 101,986	$ 106,830
Yearly revenue	$973,102	$1,223,827	$1,281,962

Break even analysis

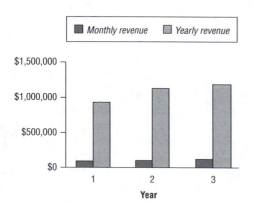

7.9 Business Ratios

Business ratios—yearly

Year	1	2	3
Sales			
Sales growth	0.0%	25.0%	20.0%
Gross margin	95.0%	95.0%	95.0%
Financials			
Profit margin	33.80%	33.79%	37.00%
Assets to liabilities	441.19	260.36	207.80
Equity to liabilities	440.19	259.36	206.80
Assets to equity	1.00	1.00	1.00
Liquidity			
Acid test	64.56	33.83	24.01
Cash to assets	0.15	0.13	0.12

7.10 Three Year Profit and Loss Statement

Profit and loss statement (first year)

Month	1	2	3	4	5	6	7
Sales	$195,000	$195,130	$195,260	$195,390	$195,520	$195,650	$195,780
Cost of goods sold	$ 9,750	$ 9,757	$ 9,763	$ 9,770	$ 9,776	$ 9,783	$ 9,789
Gross margin	95.0%	95.0%	95.0%	95.0%	95.0%	95.0%	95.0%
Operating income	$185,250	$185,374	$185,497	$185,621	$185,744	$185,868	$185,991
Expenses							
Payroll	$ 51,042	$ 51,042	$ 51,042	$ 51,042	$ 51,042	$ 51,042	$ 51,042
General and administrative	$ 4,000	$ 4,000	$ 4,000	$ 4,000	$ 4,000	$ 4,000	$ 4,000
Marketing expenses	$ 979	$ 979	$ 979	$ 979	$ 979	$ 979	$ 979
Professional fees and licensure	$ 2,500	$ 2,500	$ 2,500	$ 2,500	$ 2,500	$ 2,500	$ 2,500
Insurance costs	$ 2,083	$ 2,083	$ 2,083	$ 2,083	$ 2,083	$ 2,083	$ 2,083
Trading licenses and seat costs	$ 5,871	$ 5,871	$ 5,871	$ 5,871	$ 5,871	$ 5,871	$ 5,871
Rent and utilities	$ 2,417	$ 2,417	$ 2,417	$ 2,417	$ 2,417	$ 2,417	$ 2,417
Miscellaneous costs	$ 489	$ 489	$ 489	$ 489	$ 489	$ 489	$ 489
Payroll taxes	$ 7,656	$ 7,656	$ 7,656	$ 7,656	$ 7,656	$ 7,656	$ 7,656
Total operating costs	$ 77,037	$ 77,037	$ 77,037	$ 77,037	$ 77,037	$ 77,037	$ 77,037
EBITDA	$108,213	$108,336	$108,460	$108,583	$108,707	$108,830	$108,954
Federal income tax	$ 35,803	$ 35,827	$ 35,851	$ 35,875	$ 35,899	$ 35,922	$ 35,946
State income tax	$ 5,425	$ 5,428	$ 5,432	$ 5,436	$ 5,439	$ 5,443	$ 5,446
Interest expense	$ 0	$ 0	$ 0	$ 0	$ 0	$ 0	$ 0
Depreciation expense	$ 1,365	$ 1,365	$ 1,365	$ 1,365	$ 1,365	$ 1,365	$ 1,365
Net profit	$ 65,620	$ 65,716	$ 65,812	$ 65,908	$ 66,004	$ 66,100	$ 66,196

Profit and loss statement (first year cont.)

Month	8	9	10	11	12	1
Sales	$195,910	$196,040	$196,170	$196,300	$196,430	$2,348,580
Cost of goods sold	$ 9,796	$ 9,802	$ 9,809	$ 9,815	$ 9,822	$ 117,429
Gross margin	95.0%	95.0%	95.0%	95.0%	95.0%	95.0%
Operating income	$186,115	$186,238	$186,362	$186,485	$186,609	$2,231,151
Expenses						
Payroll	$ 51,042	$ 51,042	$ 51,042	$ 51,042	$ 51,042	$ 612,500
General and administrative	$ 4,000	$ 4,000	$ 4,000	$ 4,000	$ 4,000	$ 48,000
Marketing expenses	$ 979	$ 979	$ 979	$ 979	$ 979	$ 11,743
Professional fees and licensure	$ 2,500	$ 2,500	$ 2,500	$ 2,500	$ 2,500	$ 30,000
Insurance costs	$ 2,083	$ 2,083	$ 2,083	$ 2,083	$ 2,083	$ 25,000
Trading licenses and seat costs	$ 5,871	$ 5,871	$ 5,871	$ 5,871	$ 5,871	$ 70,457
Rent and utilities	$ 2,417	$ 2,417	$ 2,417	$ 2,417	$ 2,417	$ 29,000
Miscellaneous costs	$ 489	$ 489	$ 489	$ 489	$ 489	$ 5,871
Payroll taxes	$ 7,656	$ 7,656	$ 7,656	$ 7,656	$ 7,656	$ 91,875
Total operating costs	$ 77,037	$ 77,037	$ 77,037	$ 77,037	$ 77,037	$ 924,447
EBITDA	$109,077	$109,201	$109,324	$109,448	$109,571	$1,306,704
Federal income tax	$ 35,970	$ 35,994	$ 36,018	$ 36,042	$ 36,066	$ 431,212
State income tax	$ 5,450	$ 5,454	$ 5,457	$ 5,461	$ 5,464	$ 65,335
Interest expense	$ 0	$ 0	$ 0	$ 0	$ 0	$ 0
Depreciation expense	$ 1,365	$ 1,365	$ 1,365	$ 1,365	$ 1,365	$ 16,382
Net profit	$ 66,292	$ 66,388	$ 66,484	$ 66,580	$ 66,676	$ 793,775

Profit and loss statement (second year)

Quarter	Q1	2 Q2	Q3	Q4	2
Sales	$587,145	$733,931	$792,646	$822,003	$2,935,725
Cost of goods sold	$ 29,357	$ 36,697	$ 39,632	$ 41,100	$ 146,786
Gross margin	95.0%	95.0%	95.0%	95.0%	95.0%
Operating income	$557,788	$697,235	$753,013	$780,903	$2,788,939
Expenses					
Payroll	$159,135	$198,919	$214,832	$222,789	$ 795,675
General and administrative	$ 9,984	$ 12,480	$ 13,478	$ 13,978	$ 49,920
Marketing expenses	$ 2,936	$ 3,670	$ 3,963	$ 4,110	$ 14,679
Professional fees and licensure	$ 6,180	$ 7,725	$ 8,343	$ 8,652	$ 30,900
Insurance costs	$ 5,250	$ 6,563	$ 7,088	$ 7,350	$ 26,250
Trading licenses and seat costs	$ 17,614	$ 22,018	$ 23,779	$ 24,660	$ 88,072
Rent and utilities	$ 6,090	$ 7,613	$ 8,222	$ 8,526	$ 30,450
Miscellaneous costs	$ 1,468	$ 1,835	$ 1,982	$ 2,055	$ 7,339
Payroll taxes	$ 23,870	$ 29,838	$ 32,225	$ 33,418	$ 119,351
Total operating costs	$232,527	$290,659	$313,912	$325,538	$1,162,636
EBITDA	$325,261	$406,576	$439,102	$455,365	$1,626,303
Federal income tax	$107,336	$134,170	$144,904	$150,270	$ 536,680
State income tax	$ 16,263	$ 20,329	$ 21,955	$ 22,768	$ 81,315
Interest expense	$ 0	$ 0	$ 0	$ 0	$ 0
Depreciation expense	$ 4,095	$ 4,095	$ 4,095	$ 4,095	$ 16,382
Net profit	$197,566	$247,982	$268,148	$278,231	$ 991,926

Profit and loss statement (third year)

Quarter	Q1	3 Q2	Q3	Q4	3
Sales	$704,574	$880,718	$951,175	$ 986,404	$3,522,870
Cost of goods sold	$ 35,229	$ 44,036	$ 47,559	$ 49,320	$ 176,144
Gross margin	95.0%	95.0%	95.0%	95.0%	95.0%
Operating income	**$669,345**	**$836,682**	**$903,616**	**$ 937,083**	**$3,346,727**
Expenses					
Payroll	$163,909	$204,886	$221,277	$ 229,473	$ 819,545
General and administrative	$ 10,383	$ 12,979	$ 14,018	$ 14,537	$ 51,917
Marketing expenses	$ 3,523	$ 4,404	$ 4,756	$ 4,932	$ 17,614
Professional fees and licensure	$ 6,365	$ 7,957	$ 8,593	$ 8,912	$ 31,827
Insurance costs	$ 5,513	$ 6,891	$ 7,442	$ 7,718	$ 27,563
Trading licenses and seat costs	$ 21,137	$ 26,422	$ 28,535	$ 29,592	$ 105,686
Rent and utilities	$ 6,395	$ 7,993	$ 8,633	$ 8,952	$ 31,973
Miscellaneous costs	$ 1,761	$ 2,202	$ 2,378	$ 2,466	$ 8,807
Payroll taxes	$ 24,586	$ 30,733	$ 33,192	$ 34,421	$ 122,932
Total operating costs	**$243,573**	**$304,466**	**$328,823**	**$341,002**	**$1,217,863**
EBITDA	**$425,773**	**$532,216**	**$574,793**	**$ 596,082**	**$2,128,863**
Federal income tax	$140,505	$175,631	$189,682	$ 196,707	$ 702,525
State income tax	$ 21,289	$ 26,611	$ 28,740	$ 29,804	$ 106,443
Interest expense	$ 0	$ 0	$ 0	$ 0	$ 0
Depreciation expense	$ 4,095	$ 4,095	$ 4,095	$ 4,095	$ 16,382
Net profit	**$259,884**	**$325,878**	**$352,276**	**$ 365,475**	**$1,303,513**

7.11 Three Year Cash Flow Analysis

Cash flow analysis (first year)

Month	1	2	3	4	5	6	7	8
Cash from operations	$ 66,985	$ 67,081	$ 67,177	$ 67,273	$ 67,369	$ 67,465	$ 67,561	$ 67,657
Cash from receivables	$ 0	$ 0	$ 0	$ 0	$ 0	$ 0	$ 0	$ 0
Operating cash inflow	**$ 66,985**	**$ 67,081**	**$ 67,177**	**$ 67,273**	**$ 67,369**	**$ 67,465**	**$ 67,561**	**$ 67,657**
Other cash inflows								
Equity investment	$5,000,000	$ 0	$ 0	$ 0	$ 0	$ 0	$ 0	$ 0
Increased borrowings	$ 0	$ 0	$ 0	$ 0	$ 0	$ 0	$ 0	$ 0
Sales of business assets	$ 0	$ 0	$ 0	$ 0	$ 0	$ 0	$ 0	$ 0
A/P increases	$ 3,159	$ 3,159	$ 3,159	$ 3,159	$ 3,159	$ 3,159	$ 3,159	$ 3,159
Total other cash inflows	**$5,003,159**	**$ 3,159**	**$ 3,159**	**$ 3,159**	**$ 3,159**	**$ 3,159**	**$ 3,159**	**$ 3,159**
Total cash inflow	**$5,070,143**	**$ 70,239**	**$ 70,336**	**$ 70,432**	**$ 70,528**	**$ 70,624**	**$ 70,720**	**$ 70,816**
Cash outflows								
Repayment of principal	$ 0	$ 0	$ 0	$ 0	$ 0	$ 0	$ 0	$ 0
A/P decreases	$ 2,075	$ 2,075	$ 2,075	$ 2,075	$ 2,075	$ 2,075	$ 2,075	$ 2,075
A/R increases	$ 0	$ 0	$ 0	$ 0	$ 0	$ 0	$ 0	$ 0
Asset purchases	$4,700,000	$ 0	$ 0	$ 0	$ 0	$ 0	$ 0	$ 0
Dividends	$ 0	$ 0	$ 0	$ 0	$ 0	$ 0	$ 0	$ 0
Total cash outflows	**$4,702,075**	**$ 2,075**	**$ 2,075**	**$ 2,075**	**$ 2,075**	**$ 2,075**	**$ 2,075**	**$ 2,075**
Net cash flow	**$ 368,069**	**$ 68,165**	**$ 68,261**	**$ 68,357**	**$ 68,453**	**$ 68,549**	**$ 68,645**	**$ 68,741**
Cash balance	**$ 368,069**	**$436,233**	**$504,494**	**$572,851**	**$641,304**	**$709,853**	**$778,497**	**$847,238**

Cash flow analysis (first year cont.)

Month	9	10	11	12	1
Cash from operations	$ 67,753	$ 67,849	$ 67,945	$ 68,041	$ 810,157
Cash from receivables	$ 0	$ 0	$ 0	$ 0	$ 0
Operating cash inflow	**$ 67,753**	**$ 67,849**	**$ 67,945**	**$ 68,041**	**$ 810,157**
Other cash inflows					
Equity investment	$ 0	$ 0	$ 0	$ 0	$5,000,000
Increased borrowings	$ 0	$ 0	$ 0	$ 0	$ 0
Sales of business assets	$ 0	$ 0	$ 0	$ 0	$ 0
A/P increases	$ 3,159	$ 3,159	$ 3,159	$ 3,159	$ 37,902
Total other cash inflows	**$ 3,159**	**$ 3,159**	**$ 3,159**	**$ 3,159**	**$5,037,902**
Total cash inflow	**$ 70,912**	**$ 71,008**	**$ 71,104**	**$ 71,200**	**$5,848,059**
Cash outflows					
Repayment of principal	$ 0	$ 0	$ 0	$ 0	$ 0
A/P decreases	$ 2,075	$ 2,075	$ 2,075	$ 2,075	$ 24,897
A/R increases	$ 0	$ 0	$ 0	$ 0	$ 0
Asset purchases	$ 0	$ 0	$ 0	$ 0	$4,700,000
Dividends	$ 0	$ 0	$ 0	$283,555	$ 283,555
Total cash outflows	**$ 2,075**	**$ 2,075**	**$ 2,075**	**$285,630**	**$5,008,452**
Net cash flow	**$ 68,837**	**$ 68,933**	**$ 69,029**	**−$214,430**	**$ 839,607**
Cash balance	**$916,075**	**$985,008**	**$1,054,037**	**$839,607**	**$ 839,607**

Cash flow analysis (second year)

Quarter	Q1	2 Q2	Q3	Q4	2
Cash from operations	$201,662	$252,077	$272,243	$282,326	$1,008,308
Cash from receivables	$ 0	$ 0	$ 0	$ 0	$ 0
Operating cash inflow	**$201,662**	**$252,077**	**$272,243**	**$282,326**	**$1,008,308**
Other cash inflows					
Equity investment	$ 0	$ 0	$ 0	$ 0	$ 0
Increased borrowings	$ 0	$ 0	$ 0	$ 0	$ 0
Sales of business assets	$ 0	$ 0	$ 0	$ 0	$ 0
A/P increases	$ 8,717	$ 10,897	$ 11,769	$ 12,204	$ 43,587
Total other cash inflows	**$ 8,717**	**$ 10,897**	**$ 11,769**	**$ 12,204**	**$ 43,587**
Total cash inflow	**$210,379**	**$262,974**	**$284,012**	**$294,531**	**$1,051,895**
Cash outflows					
Repayment of principal	$ 0	$ 0	$ 0	$ 0	$ 0
A/P decreases	$ 5,975	$ 7,469	$ 8,067	$ 8,365	$ 29,876
A/R increases	$ 0	$ 0	$ 0	$ 0	$ 0
Asset purchases	$120,997	$151,246	$163,346	$169,396	$ 604,985
Dividends	$ 70,582	$ 88,227	$ 95,285	$ 98,814	$ 352,908
Total cash outflows	**$197,554**	**$246,942**	**$266,698**	**$276,575**	**$ 987,769**
Net cash flow	**$ 12,825**	**$ 16,032**	**$ 17,314**	**$ 17,955**	**$ 64,126**
Cash balance	**$852,432**	**$868,464**	**$885,778**	**$903,733**	**$ 903,733**

Cash flow analysis (third year)

Quarter	Q1	3 Q2	Q3	Q4	3
Cash from operations	$263,979	$329,974	$356,372	$369,571	$1,319,895
Cash from receivables	$ 0	$ 0	$ 0	$ 0	$ 0
Operating cash inflow	**$263,979**	**$329,974**	**$356,372**	**$369,571**	**$1,319,895**
Other cash inflows					
Equity investment	$ 0	$ 0	$ 0	$ 0	$ 0
Increased borrowings	$ 0	$ 0	$ 0	$ 0	$ 0
Sales of business assets	$ 0	$ 0	$ 0	$ 0	$ 0
A/P increases	$ 10,025	$ 12,531	$ 13,534	$ 14,035	$ 50,125
Total other cash inflows	**$ 10,025**	**$ 12,531**	**$ 13,534**	**$ 14,035**	**$ 50,125**
Total cash inflow	**$274,004**	**$342,505**	**$369,906**	**$383,606**	**$1,370,020**
Cash outflows					
Repayment of principal	$ 0	$ 0	$ 0	$ 0	$ 0
A/P decreases	$ 7,170	$ 8,963	$ 9,680	$ 10,038	$ 35,852
A/R increases	$ 0	$ 0	$ 0	$ 0	$ 0
Asset purchases	$158,387	$197,984	$213,823	$221,742	$ 791,937
Dividends	$ 92,393	$115,491	$124,730	$129,350	$ 461,963
Total cash outflows	**$257,950**	**$322,438**	**$348,233**	**$361,131**	**$1,289,752**
Net cash flow	**$ 16,054**	**$ 20,067**	**$ 21,672**	**$ 22,475**	**$ 80,268**
Cash balance	**$919,787**	**$939,854**	**$961,526**	**$984,002**	**$ 984,002**

Diaper Delivery Business

Diapers 'N More

254 Main St.
Bedrock, ME 04403

Paul Greenland

Offering the area's only diaper delivery service, this new business seeks to reach the developing market demanding a more environmentally safe and less expensive option than disposable diapers. This plan offers an example of how to attract a larger customer base by capitalizing on society's changing views. This plan originally appeared in Business Plans Handbook, Volume 1; it has been updated for this volume.

STATEMENT OF PURPOSE

Diapers 'N More is seeking a loan of $36,000 to purchase equipment and inventory, purchase chemicals and softeners, purchase saturation advertising, maintain sufficient cash reserves, and provide adequate working capital to run a diaper delivery and pickup service. This sum, together with the $9,500 equity investment of the principals, will be sufficient to finance transition through the beginning phases of the business and support a profitable enterprise.

DESCRIPTION OF BUSINESS

Diapers 'N More will be a diaper service delivering fresh clean diapers to northeastern Maine. Diapers 'N More plans on offering two sizes of diapers, an infant and a toddler size. The customer will have the added option to buy diaper wraps at an additional cost. Delivery to the various households will occur once a week, at which time any used diapers will be picked up and returned to the Laundromat to be cleaned. A premium service will also be offered for those customers who wish to have the same set of diapers they used returned to them. In essence, they will pay extra for the guarantee that no one else has used their diapers. Deliveries will be made Monday through Saturday, official holidays excluded.

THE MARKET

More than ever before, environmental responsibility has become a high priority for consumers. "Going green" is more than just a passing fad. In fact, for many it has become a way of life. According to *Sustainability: The Rise of Consumer Responsibility*, a 2009 study conducted by the Hartman Group, 88 percent of consumers indicated that they were engaged in sustainable behaviors during the late 2000s.

Our goal is to provide cloth diapers that are cost competitive and more environmentally safe than disposable diapers. Our local market has a total population of 3,200 households with babies under age 2. Currently, 80% of these households use disposable diapers and the remaining 20% use cloth. Of the amount using cloth we conservatively estimate that 20-30% will subscribe to the diaper service. At present birth rates and the above percentages, this will give us a customer base of 130 to 200 households (excerpt on population reports and projections available). However, we feel with the changing viewpoints on waste disposal and the environment that a larger percentage of the people with children under 2 will switch to using cloth diapers.

Customers will be attracted by:

- A local radio advertising campaign

- Fliers placed in care packages to new mothers

- Pamphlets placed with OB/GYNs and Pediatricians' offices

- Promotions done in pre-natal and birthing classes

- A website describing our services and pricing

- Targeted interactive advertising via social media channels such as Facebook to reach new mothers, young parents, and grandparents that may wish to purchase diaper delivery for their grandchildren

- Direct phone solicitation

- Door hangers

- Word-of-mouth advertising

THE COMPETITION

Currently there are no known diaper delivery services in northeastern Maine and the surrounding areas. Clean Babies Inc., part of the General Health Services Corporation, is the only diaper service serving the southeastern area of Maine and has no present plans to deliver in the northeastern Maine area. In fact, Don Taylor, their main diaper salesman, gave us a tour of Clean Babies' operation and offered to answer any questions we might have about beginning our business.

LOCATION

Diapers 'N More will operate from Laundry Inc. located at 254 Main St. The rent for the Laundromat is $1,250 per month, with total square footage of 2,250 feet. The diaper service will occupy approximately 700 square feet, thus contributing to 1/3 of the rent or $417. The water district covering this area is district 9 and has one of the lowest water rates in the region. There will be no charge for sewage as the system is furnished by the building owner. The electric is furnished by Maine Electric Cooperative. The facility is approximately 1/4 a mile from the Interstate.

MANAGEMENT AND MAINTENANCE

Barney Smith was born July 10, 1969. He was a journeyman electrician in Bangor for two years. He has 140 hours of college education in the areas of electrical and mechanical engineering. He currently owns and operates a company specializing in commercial refrigeration, heating, and air conditioning repair.

He is also a member of the Maine Army National Guard. After four years of service he has obtained the rank of Sergeant (E-5). He presently is a subcontractor.

He has extensive long-term knowledge in pickup and delivery service in the surrounding areas. His mechanical expertise is the real cost savings to this project. Mechanical repairs tend to be one of the most variable and highly unpredictable costs to a business of this sort. Barney has enough knowledge and experience to handle just about any breakdown that may occur, whether it be with the machinery or with the trucks.

Betty Smith was born on February 14, 1972. She graduated with honors from UMC in 1994 with a Bachelor of Arts degree in Economics. She then earned a Masters degree in Economics and is currently working on her Ph.D. in the same field. She is an instructor for University of Maine in the evening program. Classes taught include basic Micro and Macro Economics, Theory of the Firm, Money and Banking, Real Estate, Corporate Finance, and Investment Management. Betty handles the books of a local company named MGL Service and Maintenance. She is the mother of two children: Abbey, age three, and Jack, age one. Both children were raised in cloth diapers from birth and Jack is still using them.

Barney will be responsible primarily for set up of the routes, delivery, and maintenance of equipment. Betty will be responsible for the cleaning and packaging of the diapers, customer consultations, inventory control, and the basic accounting. In order to augment their skills, they have enlisted the help of a CPA who currently handles the tax accounting for MGL Service and Maintenance and the Smiths' personal finances.

SALARIES

Betty will be earning a salary from MGL Service and the University of Maine, and Barney will be earning a salary from the Maine National Guard, his present employer, and profit from his existing business. This money, coupled with the earnings from their real estate and the Laundromat, will enable them to support their family with very little help from the diaper service. At the end of the first fiscal year any net profit will be retained and reinvested in the diaper service to further enhance future earnings. In future years approximately 50% of the net profits will be drawn to pay the salaries of Mr. and Mrs. Smith. The remaining half will be retained to either continue expansion or accelerate payoff of the SBA note in an effort to improve the company's financial position.

APPLICATION AND EXPECTED EFFECT OF LOAN

The $36,000 will be used as follows:

Purchases:

Diapers, infant and toddler size (Diapers last approximately 3 years w/150+ washes)—$10,995

Hampers—$733

Diaper wraps—$1,230

Plastic Bags—$615

Diaper wraps (to replenish inventory in month 9)—$615

Supplies:

3 months supply of salt—$175

Chemicals, approximately 1 year's supply—$950

Advertising:

Door hangers—$290

Radio for first week—$750

Equipment:

Washer/dryer—$13,000

Setup charges—$586

Shelving—$586

Water softener (used, four years old)—$2,200

Reserve (not disbursed)—$3,275

Total—$36,000

The reserve will be held in an interest bearing account at the bank, to take advantage of special opportunities or to meet any unforeseen expenses not mentioned above. The setup charge will be for parts and material used in installing the washing machine and dryer, as Mr. Smith will furnish the labor involved. Chemicals needed included 400lb. drums of detergent and bleach, 100 lb. drums of fabric softener/bactericide, and sours. Washing machine will be a Unimac UHM027D Barrier Washer (60 lb.). Dryer will be a 75lb. Unimac UTO75N.

Small Business Development Program

We wish to thank the University of Maine Small Business Development Program for all of their help in preparing this proposal and for their general overall good advice. Special thanks are extended to Lydia Ferris for her time, dedication, and hard work.

SUMMARY

Diapers 'N More will be a diaper delivery service covering the northeastern Maine area. We offer an alternative to popular, but often environmentally harmful, disposable diapers, and convenience for those households currently handling their own cloth diapers. The owners are seeking a $36,000 loan to help begin and maintain this potentially profitable venture. Careful analysis of the potential market shows an unfilled and growing demand for cloth diapers. We feel that the time is right for entry into this type of business. The city landfill has approximately 2-3 years of life left and the landfill problem has reached such proportions that they have resorted to charging "by the bag" for trash in an effort to encourage recycling. Possible further markets include entrance into the geriatric field of cloth diapers to handle the urinary incontinence that affects millions of the elderly in America. This type of service is a major part of the Rockport General Diaper's business. Several of the nursing care facilities and hospitals (including Tri-County and Maine Regional) have expressed an interest in this type of service and would entertain a bid at some later date.

CASH FLOW PROJECTION

A monthly cash flow projection worksheet has been prepared.

Monthly Cash Flow Projections—Notes and Explanations

- Cash sales: Estimate 50 customers x $20/week = $80 per month, which comes out to a total of $4,000 for month 1; month 2, 55 customers; month 3, 60 customers; month 4, 65 customers, etc.

- Supplies include $58 in salt per month for water softener and a $500 expenditure to replenish chemical supplies in month 12.

- Advertising includes $290 for door hangers and fliers each month.

- Maintenance is only $29 per month because the business is renting the facilities and part is for laundry.

- Car & Travel is $850 per month and will stay about the same even when more customers are added because of the route layout.

- Accounting & Legal: The accounting is based on a quarterly retainer.

- Telephone & Utilities: Based upon the knowledge of laundry business.

- Insurance: Insurance quote from Morgan Mutual.

- Loan Payment: Based upon a $36,000 loan, 8% interest for 5 years.

INCOME PROJECTION: THREE-YEAR SUMMARY

Pro Forma Profit & Loss

	Year 1	Year 2	Year 3
Service revenues	$74,400	$144,000	$192,000
Purchases	$ 617	$ 1,200	$ 1,600
Gross sales	$75,017	$145,200	$193,600
Operating expenses			
Supplies	$ 1,441	$ 2,804	$ 3,739
Maintenance	$ 350	$ 350	$ 350
Advertising	$ 3,500	$ 3,500	$ 3,500
Car	$10,200	$ 10,500	$ 10,500
Accounting & legal	$ 800	$ 800	$ 800
Rent	$ 5,004	$ 5,004	$ 5,004
Telephone	$ 1,000	$ 1,000	$ 1,000
Utilities	$ 3,600	$ 4,000	$ 4,556
Insurance	$ 2,600	$ 2,600	$ 2,600
Loan payment	$ 8,760	$ 8,760	$ 8,760
Total	**$37,255**	**$ 39,318**	**$ 40,809**
Net profit pre-tax	$37,762	$105,882	$152,791
Salaries	$ 0	$ 52,941	$ 76,396

Notes and Explanations

- Sales: year 2 based upon a constant 150 customers per month; year 3 based upon a constant 200 customers per month.

- Purchases: based upon the percentage change of customer sales.

- Supplies: based upon the percentage change of customer sales.

- Maintenance should remain relatively constant.

- Car & Travel is $875 per month and will stay about the same even when more customers are added because of the route layout.

- Rent will stay constant since the building is leased for five years.

- Utilities are increased based upon percentage of additional customers.

- Insurance should remain constant since the quote is based on a gross of $200,000 a year.

SUPPORTING DOCUMENTS

Population Projections

A table of actual and projected births through 2015 for the northeastern Maine region has been prepared and is available upon request.

Floor Plan

A floor plan of the Laundromat from which we propose to do business is available upon request.

Digital Presentations

Martin Productions

8975 Strawberry Lane
Royal Oak, MI 48067

Heidi Denler

Martin Productions will begin as a home–based sole proprietorship with a goal of growing to include support staff and, within three years, at least one partner. As an art director for a one of the U.S. automotive companies, Douglas Martin gained 25 years of experience creating presentations for the company, its advertising agencies, and investors, among others. Following an early retirement brought about by the slump in the economy and the automotive industry, Martin decided to put his expertise to use by forming a company that would create presentations.

COMPANY SUMMARY

Martin Productions will begin as a home–based sole proprietorship with a goal of growing to include support staff and, within three years, at least one partner. As an art director for a one of the U.S. automotive companies, Douglas Martin gained 25 years of experience creating presentations for the company, its advertising agencies, and investors, among others. Following an early retirement brought about by the slump in the economy and the automotive industry, Martin decided to put his expertise to use by forming a company that would create presentations. He expects that his work will be outsourced by not only the automakers, but also by businesses of all sizes and non–profit organizations that can no longer afford to maintain such a department or position within their own enterprises. Martin expects that this market will continue to grow regardless of the economic climate.

MANAGEMENT SUMMARY

Douglas Martin has an extensive background in the field of digital presentations. He holds an MBA from Wayne State University in Detroit as well as a BFA and a BS in computer science and logistics. He has continued his technology education through online classes and classes at the local community college. Martin recognizes that technology is a fast–paced, ever–changing field, and has worked to keep up with all of the changes.

MISSION STATEMENT

Martin Productions will offer affordable, quality digital presentations to businesses and non–profit organizations for use at banquets, stockholder meetings, etc. Quality digital presentations that include exactly what the client seeks, using client–provided information, with graphics provided either by the client or by Martin Productions.

BUSINESS PHILOSOPHY

Customer satisfaction will be central to Martin Productions' success through friendly, timely, quality service for all clients.

VALUES STATEMENT

Douglas Martin will provide clients with quality presentations that even a novice will be able to use in any business setting.

GOALS AND OBJECTIVES

Doug Martin has determined to build a customer base through networking of former co–workers, former contacts who have requested that he do freelance work for them, and by providing friendly, high–quality, timely, and reliable service. Promotion and advertising will start strong and build, as Martin makes use of a wide network of friends and former colleagues.

Within three years, Martin expects to have added at least one partner to handle what he expects to be an ever–expanding business. He plans an extensive Internet presence, local clients, and, after some time, international clients.

Advertising will play a key role in growth, as will referrals made by satisfied clients. Repeat business will also come into play, specifically for such business events as shareholder meetings.

ORGANIZATION STRUCTURE

As sole proprietor, Martin will assume all responsibility and expense for Martin Productions. However, should he find himself in a position where he has overlapping assignments, he will refer to a list of available contacts he has made over the years to identify someone to help him with minor work.

Within three years, Martin expects to have enough business locally and worldwide, thanks to an Internet presence, to hire at least one assistant. That assistant could potentially become Martin's partner in Martin Productions. At that time, the sole proprietorship would become a partnership, and possibly a corporation or LLC.

Martin projects immediate profitability for Martin Productions, given that there is minimal overhead and under $25,000 in the way of start–up expense.

ADVERTISING AND PROMOTION

Advertising and promotion will begin immediately and will remain strong. Announcements of the "grand opening" of Martin Productions will be sent to contacts, former employers, local businesses, and local nonprofit organizations from PTOs and churches to symphony orchestras and such health–based non-profits as local chapters of the American Lung Association and the Muscular Dystrophy Association.

Local media, including television, newspapers, and magazines, will be sent press releases outlining company offerings and giving discounts for presentations to be created by Martin for those media.

Martin will launch a Web site where prospective and current clients will be able to contact him with questions and/or changes to their presentations. Sample presentations will be available for viewing as well. These will be copyrighted to protect Martin's intellectual property.

CUSTOMER BASE

The primary customer base for Martin Productions will comprise individuals, small community groups; home–based business owners; small, medium, and large businesses; schools and school–sponsored organizations; all sizes of community service organizations; and political groups. No one in the community will be exempt from being a potential client. With a vast and diverse customer base, Martin projects immediate and long–term success, growth, and profitability for the company.

PRODUCTS AND SERVICES

Martin will offer his clients a range of presentation options from PowerPoint to interactive meetings for companies with multiple office locations. Clients may provide graphics and photos or ask Martin to create them.

Martin Productions will work with clients to prepare an outline of major concepts and principal points, as well as to consult on visual needs for the presentation. Martin will provide a draft with sketches of the visuals, which will include clip art, graphs, tables, photographs. The draft will incorporate proposed title slides that will identify topics that Martin and the client agree should be retained by the audience.

Martin has determined that presentations should be big, clear, and consistent, while adopting the KISS (Keep It Short and Simple) theory for his clients. When he first contracts with the client, ample time for changes will be in the proposed delivery timeline, as will time for the client to practice the actual presentation, with Martin's assistance, should the client request or require it. Back–up copies of the final product will be provided for each client.

The company will offer a diverse range of presentations from informal interactive "chats" to seminars to formal presentations that end with a question and answer session. Martin recognizes that the audience will be an integral part of decision making for all presentations. Specialists will require a different approach than a general audience; seminars will require timing for interaction. Length of the presentation will determine the exploration of the subject matter.

Expectations will be discussed with the client prior to Martin beginning production of all presentations. Martin will determine the purpose of the presentation and build an understanding of the topic to ensure audience attention.

Martin will attempt to work within the 10–20–30 rule of PowerPoint decreed by Guy Kawasaki: fewer than 10 slides, no more than 20 minutes, and font size of 30. It is important to get the the point across quickly and clearly. He will make good use of visual aids to reinforce the message, clarify points, and keep the audience's interest.

Presentations will also be developed to move smoothly from one topic to the next, using PowerPoint animations and transitions. Martin will provide clients with a web–style graphic organizer and story-board that will be approved before actual work on the presentation begins.

Martin will offer consulting services to aid his clients' preparations for the actual presentation. He will work with them on pacing their presentation, helping them make smooth, logical transitions that will work with the visual presentation. He will also ensure that his software and programs are compatible with those where the presentation will be made.

Handouts based on each presentation will be prepared for clients to distribute, the format of which will be dependent on the audience and the presentation itself. These handouts will offer a summary of each concept presented and include the graphics used, especially graphs and tables with detailed data pertinent to the presentation. The handouts will reinforce the information presented digitally.

In addition to such digital presentations created in PowerPoint, Martin Productions will also create presentations for overhead projectors, Elmo document cameras, and posters for single message pre-sentations. These presentations will include all of the services available to digital presentation clients.

Other services will be presentation makeovers (for the dynamite presentation that requires updating), and workshops on presentations. In addition, Martin Productions will offer rental of equipment, including projectors, Elmo document cameras, plasma TVs, video cameras, projector screens, cables and accessories, microphones and PA systems, speakers, computers (laptop, Mac & PC), printers, podiums, and conference phones. Audio–visual consulting will offer on–site technical service, editing, and conversion to digital.

EQUIPMENT

Martin Productions will maintain an inventory of projectors, Elmo document cameras, plasma TVs, video cameras, projector screens, cables and accessories, microphones and PA systems, speakers, computers (laptop, Mac & PC), printers, podiums, and conference phones for their own use as well as for renting to clients locally.

As equipment in their inventory becomes technologically obsolete, they will replace and update it. Martin recognizes the need to stay technologically up–to–date and use state–of–the–art equipment on all levels of the enterprise. Old equipment will be donated to local schools and non–profit organizations.

LOCATION

With products and services that can easily be e–mailed or sent on CDs, Martin Productions' home–based location in Royal Oak, Michigan, is not detrimental to the success of the company. While it is not necessary for Martin to meet face–to–face with clients or prospective clients, he has planned to make himself available for such meetings should they be requested.

FINANCIAL

Start–up costs will include purchase of new, state–of–the art computers (one laptop and one desktop), color laser printer, fax machine, and supplies for each (toner, blank CDs and jewel cases, paper, etc.). In addition, two projectors and screens will be purchased. Martin will be able to continue to use his current office furniture in his home office, although he will add a filing cabinet and shelving/cabinets to hold office supplies.

Other costs will be fees and registration for the company name, home–based business insurance coverage, additional life insurance for Martin, and any fees required by local, state, and federal government agencies. Martin will also incur legal and CPA fees not only for the start up of the business, but also for ongoing small business and tax coverage.

Overhead will include a portion of the current mortgage payments and telephone and utilities, business taxes an alarm system, advertising, and wi–fi Internet access from AT&T.

PROFESSIONAL AND ADVISORY SUPPORT

Martin will use his personal attorney to get things started, but will act on that attorney's advice to locate an attorney well–versed in small business and intellectual property law.

The company will work with J. Franklin of Prudential to provide optimal coverage for life, health, and dental insurance and retirement savings. Mr. Franklin will work with the property–casualty arm of the agency to secure home–business owners insurance coverage.

Martin will bank with Chase, where he has established a personal relationship and secured a line of credit to cover start–up expenses.

BUSINESS AND GROWTH STRATEGY

Martin plans to build his business by networking with former co–workers and other contacts who have requested that he do freelance work for them. He will begin with an aggressive advertising and promotion campaign, working with a friend who is a graphic artist for a local advertising agency. They will create ads for local media, as well as a press kit for announcing the grand opening of the business and the launch of the company web site. Martin's business acumen is centered around presentations and computer technology, so he had determined that it will be to his advantage to hire someone else to handle advertising. This will also allow him to concentrate on creating memorable presentations that will provide opportunities for repeat business from clients, along with referrals from those clients.

COMPETITION

In early 2010 there was little competition for a company preparing digital presentations. Many companies do this type of work in–house, but with a faltering economy, these companies are expected to begin outsourcing the work rather than paying to have a staff on hand. This will provide Doug Martin with a multitude of opportunities to use his networking skills to increase his customer base.

WEB SITE

Martin Productions plans an immediate online presence with the launch of a colorful, informative website that will offer examples of presentations, contact information, a contact form, and a listing of equipment that can be rented.

Once a client has signed a contract to work with Martin Productions, he or she will be able to check on the progress of the presentation online and even view it while it is being prepared.

CONCLUSION

Doug Martin projects that Martin Productions will be profitable within six months. He has solid backing from his bank and a solid network for his initial stable of clients. With his background and experience, along with statistics provided by Jeff Radel of the KU Medical Center that show that combined oral and visual presentations, such as those available from Martin Productions, have a 65 percent retention by the audience (oral presentations have 10 percent retention and visual presentations have 35 percent retention), Martin is assured a good measure of success in what promises to be a growing field.

Farm

Gilmore Farms

123 Old Mill Rd.
Binghamton, NY 13905

BizPlanDB.com

Gilmore Farms is a New York based corporation that will produce and sell a variety of crops to farmer's markets and produce distributors.

1.0 EXECUTIVE SUMMARY

The purpose of this business plan is to raise $400,000 for the development of a farm while showcasing the expected financials and operations over the next three years. Gilmore Farms ("the Company") is a New York based corporation that will produce and sell a variety of crops to farmer's markets and produce distributors. The Company was founded in 2010 by John Gilmore.

1.1 The Services

Gilmore Farms will produce a number of crops on a yearly basis depending on the demand for produce products. Mr. Gilmore anticipates that Gilmore Farms will encompass 15 to 20 acres of arable land that can be used to plant and grow a host of different produce goods.

At the onset of operations, Gilmore Farms will have approximately 4 farmhands to assist with the day to day operations of the farm.

The third section of the business plan will further describe the services offered by Gilmore Farms.

1.2 Financing

Mr. Gilmore is seeking to raise $400,000 from as a bank loan. The interest rate and loan agreement are to be further discussed during negotiation. This business plan assumes that the business will receive a 10 year loan with a 9% fixed interest rate. The financing will be used for the following:

- Development of the Company's Farm location.

- Financing for the first six months of operation.

- Capital to purchase FF&E and equipment associated with the Company's operations.

Mr. Gilmore will contribute $100,000 to the venture.

1.3 Mission Statement

Gilmore Farms' mission is to provide its buyers with the freshest quality produce available while concurrently using economically viable and ecologically sustainable practices.

1.4 Management Team

The Company was founded by John Gilmore. Mr. Gilmore has more than 10 years of experience in the farming industry. Through his expertise, he will be able to bring the operations of the business to profitability within its first year of operations.

1.5 Sales Forecasts

Mr. Gilmore expects a strong rate of growth at the start of operations. Below are the expected financials over the next three years.

Proforma profit and loss (yearly)

Year	1	2	3
Sales	$753,000	$828,300	$911,130
Operating costs	$331,787	$346,822	$362,770
EBITDA	$120,013	$150,158	$183,908
Taxes, interest, and depreciation	$110,841	$107,512	$118,692
Net profit	$ 9,172	$ 42,646	$ 65,216

Sales, operating costs, and profit forecast

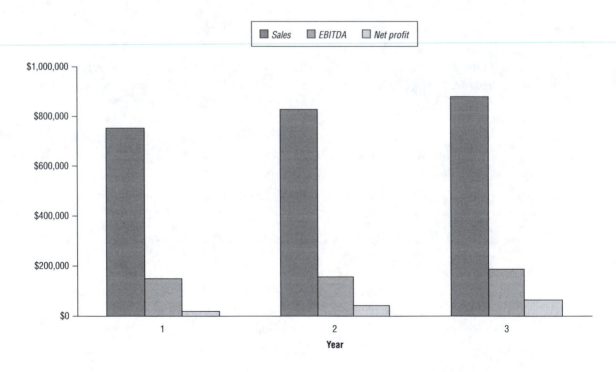

1.6 Expansion Plan

Mr. Gilmore expects that the business will aggressively expand during the first three years of operation. To this end, he intends to implement marketing campaigns that will effectively target farmer's markets and produce buyers within the target market.

2.0 COMPANY AND FINANCING SUMMARY

2.1 Registered Name and Corporate Structure

The Company is registered as a corporation in the State of New York.

2.2 Required Funds

At this time, Gilmore Farms requires $400,000 of debt funds. Below is a breakdown of how these funds will be used:

Projected startup costs

Land	$150,000
Working capital	$ 40,000
FF&E	$ 50,000
Improvements	$ 15,000
Security deposits	$ 10,000
Insurance	$ 5,000
Farming equipment	$200,000
Marketing budget	$ 20,000
Miscellaneous and unforeseen costs	$ 10,000
Total startup costs	**$500,000**

Use of funds

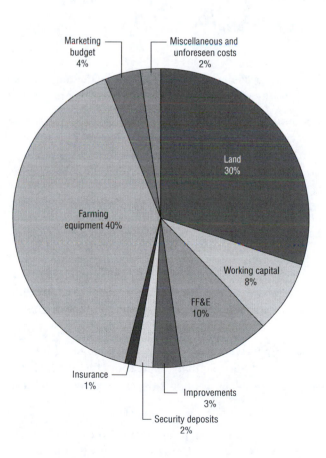

2.3 Investor Equity

Mr. Gilmore is not seeking an investment from a third party at this time.

2.4 Management Equity

John Gilmore owns 100% of Gilmore Farms.

2.5 Exit Strategy

If the business is very successful, Mr. Gilmore may seek to sell the business to a third party for a significant earnings multiple. Most likely, the Company will hire a qualified business broker to sell the business on behalf of Gilmore Farms. Based on historical numbers, the business could fetch a sales premium of up to 3 to 5 times the previous year's net earnings.

3.0 FARMING OPERATIONS

As stated in the executive summary, Mr. Gilmore intends to develop Gilmore Farms as a multi-produce property that will plant, grow, and distribute its products to farmer's markets and produce wholesalers throughout the target market.

Mr. Gilmore has already sourced the potential land and the equipment that will be used for Gilmore Farms' operations. Additionally, it should be noted that Mr. Gilmore may join a produce co-op that will assist with the distribution and sale of Gilmore Farms' produce.

4.0 STRATEGIC AND MARKET ANALYSIS

4.1 Economic Outlook

This section of the analysis will detail the economic climate, the farm/agriculture industry, the customer profile, and the competition that the business will face as it progresses through its business operations.

Currently, the economic market condition in the United States is in recession. This slowdown in the economy has also greatly impacted real estate sales, which has halted to historical lows. Many economists expect that this recession will continue until mid-2010, at which point the economy will begin a prolonged recovery period. However, this should have a minimal impact on Gilmore Farms' ability to generate revenues as much of its crops will be geared towards staple foods that are constantly in demand regardless of the general economic climate.

4.2 Industry Analysis

Within the United States, agriculture producers (of produce) generate more than $130 billion per year of revenue and provide jobs to more than 1.5 million people. Aggregate payrolls in each of the last five years have exceeded $20 billion. This is a mature industry (and one of America's oldest industries), and the expected future growth rate is expected to mirror that of the general economy and population growth.

One of the most common trends in the farming and agriculture industry is that newer technologies and genetically engineered seeds are actually increasing the net profit margins of the business while concurrently lessening the ecological impact of farming on the environment.

4.3 Customer Profile

It is extremely difficult to determine the customer profile of people that will acquire the produce produced by Gilmore Farms, Inc. The Company intends to do business with farmer's markets, co-ops, and produce wholesalers that will acquire the Company's inventories of produce. However, Management has outlined the following buying groups that are expected to visit Gilmore Farms on a regular basis:

- Local grocery stores that want to purchase from local suppliers.

- Individuals seeking to purchase organic produce.

- Major national brokers of food commodities.

Within the Company's target market radius, there are approximately 2,000 people that could potentially become regular buyers of Gilmore Farms' organic produce via the distribution of farm shares on an annual basis. This would assist greatly with predicting the revenues of Gilmore Farms on a per annum basis.

4.4 Competition

As will be discussed further in the next section of the business plan, competition within the farming industry is hard to gauge given the fact the business' revenues are heavily dependent on the fluctuations of the value of food stuff commodities that are traded among major exchanges on a worldwide basis. However, the business—in its local market—intends to maintain a strong competitive advantage by providing only fresh organic produce to its customers.

5.0 MARKETING PLAN

Gilmore Farms intends to maintain an extensive marketing campaign that will ensure maximum visibility for the business in its targeted market. Below is an overview of the marketing strategies and objectives of Gilmore Farms.

5.1 Marketing Objectives
- Develop ongoing purchase order relationships with co-ops throughout the target market.

- Develop relationships with major groceries and produce wholesalers that will acquire bulk inventories from Gilmore Farms.

5.2 Marketing Strategies

Gilmore Farms' marketing operations will be minimal as once the Company solidifies ongoing relationships with produce co-ops and wholesalers, very little marketing will be required to maintain these relationships. At the onset of operations, Mr. Gilmore intends to aggressively develop relationships with local and regional farming co-ops that will assist the farm in maintaining stringent pricing (through forward and futures contracts) so that Gilmore Farms always has a predictable stream of income.

However, in the future, Mr. Gilmore may seek to brand certain produce items that are produced on Gilmore Farms. In this instance, the Company will hire a marketing/advertising firm to properly position the Company's image and brand so that it can directly sell packaged produce to major grocers, supermarkets, farmer's markets, and select retailers.

5.3 Pricing

Pricing is the most difficult aspect in regards to Gilmore Farms' operations as the business will rely heavily on free market pricing models and commodities markets that trade the farm produced goods distributed by the business. As such, the pricing structures used by the business will vary on a year to year basis. Management intends to ameliorate these risks by working with farm co-ops that can effectively assist the business with locking in pricing for its produce prior to the onset of the harvesting season for each of the crops produced by Gilmore Farms.

6.0 ORGANIZATIONAL PLAN AND PERSONNEL SUMMARY

6.1 Corporate Organization

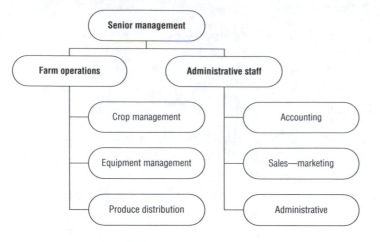

6.2 Organizational Budget

Personnel plan—yearly

Year	1	2	3
Owner	$ 50,000	$ 51,500	$ 53,045
Site and facility manager	$ 35,000	$ 36,050	$ 37,132
Farm hands	$ 70,000	$ 72,100	$ 74,263
Bookkeeper (P/T)	$ 10,000	$ 10,300	$ 10,609
Administrative	$ 22,500	$ 23,175	$ 23,870
Total	**$187,500**	**$193,125**	**$198,919**

Numbers of personnel

Owner	1	1	1
Site and facility manager	1	1	1
Farm hands	4	4	4
Bookkeeper (P/T)	1	1	1
Administrative	1	1	1
Totals	**8**	**8**	**8**

Personnel expense breakdown

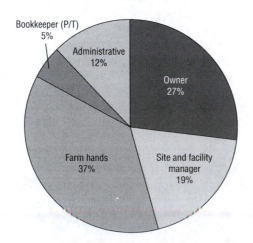

7.0 FINANCIAL PLAN

7.1 Underlying Assumptions

The Company has based its proforma financial statements on the following:

• Gilmore Farms will have an annual revenue growth rate of 10% per year.

• The Owner will acquire $400,000 of debt funds to develop the business.

• The loan will have a 10 year term with a 9% interest rate.

7.2 Sensitivity Analysis

In the event of an economic downturn, the business should not have a major decline in its revenues. Gilmore Farms intends to grow in demand produce that will be readily purchased by wholesalers, grocers, co-ops, and other organizations that deal in produce. As such, the Company will be able to remain profitable and cash flow positive in any economic climate.

7.3 Source of Funds

Financing

Equity contributions	
Management investment	$ 100,000.00
Total equity financing	**$100,000.00**
Banks and lenders	
Banks and lenders	$ 400,000.00
Total debt financing	$ 400,000.00
Total financing	**$500,000.00**

7.4 General Assumptions

General assumptions

Year	1	2	3
Short term interest rate	9.5%	9.5%	9.5%
Long term interest rate	10.0%	10.0%	10.0%
Federal tax rate	33.0%	33.0%	33.0%
State tax rate	5.0%	5.0%	5.0%
Personnel taxes	15.0%	15.0%	15.0%

7.5 Profit and Loss Statements

Proforma profit and loss (yearly)

Year	1	2	3
Sales	**$753,000**	**$828,300**	**$911,130**
Cost of goods sold	$301,200	$331,320	$364,452
Gross margin	60.00%	60.00%	60.00%
Operating income	**$451,800**	**$496,980**	**$546,678**
Expenses			
Payroll	$187,500	$193,125	$198,919
General and administrative	$ 12,500	$ 13,000	$ 13,520
Product distribution expenses	$ 37,650	$ 41,415	$ 45,557
Professional fees and licensure	$ 5,000	$ 5,150	$ 5,305
Insurance costs	$ 14,000	$ 14,700	$ 15,435
Travel and vehicle costs	$ 19,000	$ 20,900	$ 22,990
Utility costs	$ 25,000	$ 26,250	$ 27,563
Miscellaneous costs	$ 3,012	$ 3,313	$ 3,645
Payroll taxes	$ 28,125	$ 28,969	$ 29,838
Total operating costs	**$331,787**	**$346,822**	**$362,770**
EBITDA	**$120,013**	**$150,158**	**$183,908**
Federal income tax	$ 39,604	$ 38,819	$ 50,832
State income tax	$ 6,001	$ 5,882	$ 7,702
Interest expense	$ 34,951	$ 32,526	$ 29,873
Depreciation expenses	$ 30,286	$ 30,286	$ 30,286
Net profit	**$ 9,172**	**$ 42,646**	**$ 65,216**
Profit margin	**1.22%**	**5.15%**	**7.16%**

Sales, operating costs, and profit forecast

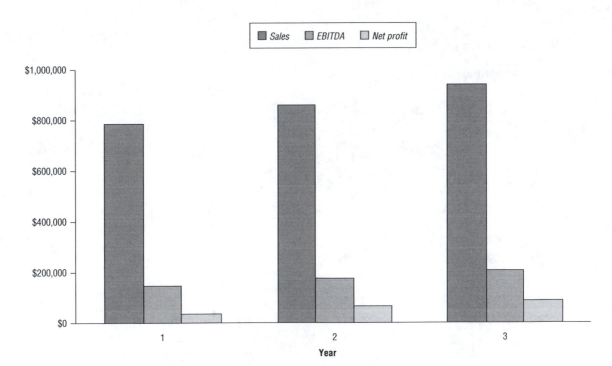

7.6 Cash Flow Analysis

Proforma cash flow analysis—yearly

Year	1	2	3
Cash from operations	$ 39,457	$72,932	$ 95,502
Cash from receivables	$ 0	$ 0	$ 0
Operating cash inflow	**$ 39,457**	**$72,932**	**$ 95,502**
Other cash inflows			
Equity investment	$100,000	$ 0	$ 0
Increased borrowings	$400,000	$ 0	$ 0
Sales of business assets	$ 0	$ 0	$ 0
A/P increases	$ 10,000	$11,500	$ 13,225
Total other cash inflows	**$510,000**	**$11,500**	**$ 13,225**
Total cash inflow	**$549,457**	**$84,432**	**$108,727**
Cash outflows			
Repayment of principal	$ 25,854	$28,279	$ 30,932
A/P decreases	$ 9,000	$10,800	$ 12,960
A/R increases	$ 0	$ 0	$ 0
Asset purchases	$471,500	$ 7,293	$ 9,550
Dividends	$ 31,566	$36,466	$ 47,751
Total cash outflows	**$537,919**	**$82,838**	**$101,193**
Net cash flow	**$ 11,538**	**$ 1,594**	**$ 7,534**
Cash balance	**$ 11,538**	**$13,132**	**$ 20,666**

Proforma cash flow (yearly)

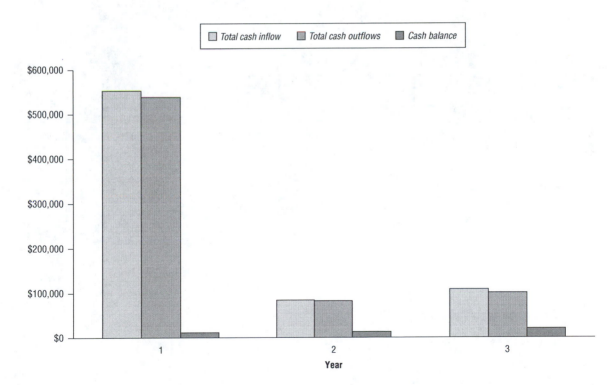

7.7 Balance Sheet

Proforma balance sheet—yearly

Year	1	2	3
Assets			
Cash	$ 11,538	$ 13,132	$ 20,666
Amortized development/expansion costs	$ 40,000	$ 40,729	$ 41,684
Farm equipment	$175,000	$178,647	$183,422
FF&E	$ 50,000	$ 52,917	$ 56,737
Property	$159,000	$168,540	$178,652
Accumulated depreciation	($ 30,286)	($ 60,571)	($ 90,857)
Total assets	**$405,252**	**$393,394**	**$390,305**
Liabilities and equity			
Accounts payable	$ 1,000	$ 1,700	$ 1,965
Long term liabilities	$374,146	$345,868	$317,589
Other liabilities	$ 0	$ 0	$ 0
Total liabilities	**$375,146**	**$347,568**	**$319,554**
Net worth	**$ 30,106**	**$ 45,826**	**$ 70,751**
Total liabilities and equity	**$405,252**	**$393,394**	**$390,305**

Proforma balance sheet

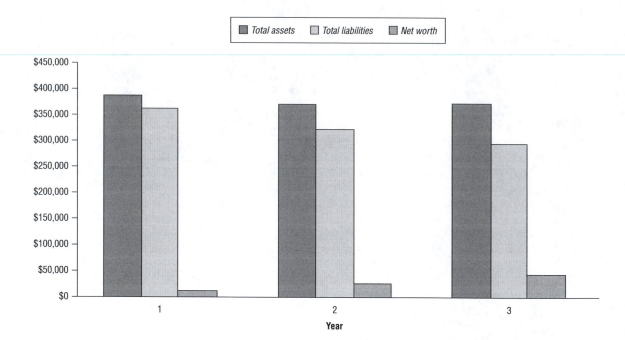

7.8 Breakeven Analysis

Monthly break even analysis

Year	1	2	3
Monthly revenue	$ 46,082	$ 48,170	$ 50,385
Yearly revenue	$552,978	$578,037	$604,616

Break even analysis

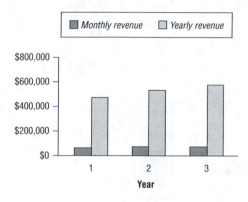

7.9 Business Ratios

Business ratios—yearly

Year	1	2	3
Sales			
Sales growth	0.0%	10.0%	10.0%
Gross margin	60.0%	60.0%	60.0%
Financials			
Profit margin	1.22%	5.15%	7.16%
Assets to liabilities	1.08	1.13	1.22
Equity to liabilities	0.08	0.13	0.22
Assets to equity	13.46	8.58	5.52
Liquidity			
Acid test	0.03	0.04	0.06
Cash to assets	0.03	0.03	0.05

7.10 Three Year Profit and Loss Statement

Profit and loss statement (first year)

Months	1	2	3	4	5	6	7
Sales	$60,000	$60,500	$61,000	$61,500	$62,000	$62,500	$63,000
Cost of goods sold	$24,000	$24,200	$24,400	$24,600	$24,800	$25,000	$25,200
Gross margin	60.0%	60.0%	60.0%	60.0%	60.0%	60.0%	60.0%
Operating income	$36,000	$36,300	$36,600	$36,900	$37,200	$37,500	$37,800
Expenses							
Payroll	$15,625	$15,625	$15,625	$15,625	$15,625	$15,625	$15,625
General and administrative	$ 1,042	$ 1,042	$ 1,042	$ 1,042	$ 1,042	$ 1,042	$ 1,042
Product distribution expenses	$ 3,138	$ 3,138	$ 3,138	$ 3,138	$ 3,138	$ 3,138	$ 3,138
Professional fees and licensure	$ 417	$ 417	$ 417	$ 417	$ 417	$ 417	$ 417
Insurance costs	$ 1,167	$ 1,167	$ 1,167	$ 1,167	$ 1,167	$ 1,167	$ 1,167
Travel and vehicle costs	$ 1,583	$ 1,583	$ 1,583	$ 1,583	$ 1,583	$ 1,583	$ 1,583
Utility costs	$ 2,083	$ 2,083	$ 2,083	$ 2,083	$ 2,083	$ 2,083	$ 2,083
Miscellaneous costs	$ 251	$ 251	$ 251	$ 251	$ 251	$ 251	$ 251
Payroll taxes	$ 2,344	$ 2,344	$ 2,344	$ 2,344	$ 2,344	$ 2,344	$ 2,344
Total operating costs	$27,649	$27,649	$27,649	$27,649	$27,649	$27,649	$27,649
EBITDA	$ 8,351	$ 8,651	$ 8,951	$ 9,251	$ 9,551	$ 9,851	$10,151
Federal income tax	$ 3,156	$ 3,182	$ 3,208	$ 3,235	$ 3,261	$ 3,287	$ 3,314
State income tax	$ 478	$ 482	$ 486	$ 490	$ 494	$ 498	$ 502
Interest expense	$ 3,000	$ 2,984	$ 2,969	$ 2,953	$ 2,937	$ 2,921	$ 2,905
Depreciation expense	$ 2,524	$ 2,524	$ 2,524	$ 2,524	$ 2,524	$ 2,524	$ 2,524
Net profit	−$ 807	−$ 521	−$ 236	$ 49	$ 335	$ 621	$ 906

Profit and loss statement (first year cont.)

Month	8	9	10	11	12	1
Sales	**$63,500**	**$64,000**	**$64,500**	**$65,000**	**$65,500**	**$753,000**
Cost of goods sold	$25,400	$25,600	$25,800	$26,000	$26,200	$301,200
Gross margin	60.0%	60.0%	60.0%	60.0%	60.0%	60.0%
Operating income	**$38,100**	**$38,400**	**$38,700**	**$39,000**	**$39,300**	**$451,800**
Expenses						
Payroll	$15,625	$15,625	$15,625	$15,625	$15,625	$187,500
General and administrative	$ 1,042	$ 1,042	$ 1,042	$ 1,042	$ 1,042	$ 12,500
Product distribution expenses	$ 3,138	$ 3,138	$ 3,138	$ 3,138	$ 3,138	$ 37,650
Professional fees and licensure	$ 417	$ 417	$ 417	$ 417	$ 417	$ 5,000
Insurance costs	$ 1,167	$ 1,167	$ 1,167	$ 1,167	$ 1,167	$ 14,000
Travel and vehicle costs	$ 1,583	$ 1,583	$ 1,583	$ 1,583	$ 1,583	$ 19,000
Utility costs	$ 2,083	$ 2,083	$ 2,083	$ 2,083	$ 2,083	$ 25,000
Miscellaneous costs	$ 251	$ 251	$ 251	$ 251	$ 251	$ 3,012
Payroll taxes	$ 2,344	$ 2,344	$ 2,344	$ 2,344	$ 2,344	$ 28,125
Total operating costs	**$27,649**	**$27,649**	**$27,649**	**$27,649**	**$27,649**	**$331,787**
EBITDA	**$10,451**	**$10,751**	**$11,051**	**$11,351**	**$11,651**	**$120,013**
Federal income tax	$ 3,340	$ 3,366	$ 3,392	$ 3,419	$ 3,445	$ 39,604
State income tax	$ 506	$ 510	$ 514	$ 518	$ 522	$ 6,001
Interest expense	$ 2,889	$ 2,873	$ 2,856	$ 2,840	$ 2,823	$ 34,951
Depreciation expense	$ 2,524	$ 2,524	$ 2,524	$ 2,524	$ 2,524	$ 30,286
Net profit	**$ 1,192**	**$ 1,478**	**$ 1,765**	**$ 2,051**	**$ 2,337**	**$ 9,172**

Profit and loss statement (second year)

Quarter	Q1	2 Q2	Q3	Q4	2
Sales	**$165,660**	**$207,075**	**$223,641**	**$231,924**	**$828,300**
Cost of goods sold	$ 66,264	$ 82,830	$ 89,456	$ 92,770	$ 331,320
Gross margin	60.0%	60.0%	60.0%	60.0%	60.0%
Operating income	**$ 99,396**	**$124,245**	**$134,185**	**$139,154**	**$496,980**
Expenses					
Payroll	$ 38,625	$ 48,281	$ 52,144	$ 54,075	$193,125
General and administrative	$ 2,600	$ 3,250	$ 3,510	$ 3,640	$ 13,000
Product distribution expenses	$ 8,283	$ 10,354	$ 11,182	$ 11,596	$ 41,415
Professional fees and licensure	$ 1,030	$ 1,288	$ 1,391	$ 1,442	$ 5,150
Insurance costs	$ 2,940	$ 3,675	$ 3,969	$ 4,116	$ 14,700
Travel and vehicle costs	$ 4,180	$ 5,225	$ 5,643	$ 5,852	$ 20,900
Utility costs	$ 5,250	$ 6,563	$ 7,088	$ 7,350	$ 26,250
Miscellaneous costs	$ 663	$ 828	$ 895	$ 928	$ 3,313
Payroll taxes	$ 5,794	$ 7,242	$ 7,822	$ 8,111	$ 28,969
Total operating costs	**$ 69,364**	**$ 86,705**	**$ 93,642**	**$ 97,110**	**$346,822**
EBITDA	**$ 30,032**	**$ 37,540**	**$ 40,543**	**$ 42,044**	**$150,158**
Federal income tax	$ 7,764	$ 9,705	$ 10,481	$ 10,869	$ 38,819
State income tax	$ 1,176	$ 1,470	$ 1,588	$ 1,647	$ 5,882
Interest expense	$ 8,367	$ 8,212	$ 8,054	$ 7,892	$ 32,526
Depreciation expense	$ 7,571	$ 7,571	$ 7,571	$ 7,571	$ 30,286
Net profit	**$ 5,153**	**$ 10,581**	**$ 12,848**	**$ 14,065**	**$ 42,646**

Profit and loss statement (third year)

Quarter	Q1	Q2	Q3	Q4	3
Sales	$182,226	$227,783	$246,005	$255,116	$911,130
Cost of goods sold	$ 72,890	$ 91,113	$ 98,402	$102,047	$364,452
Gross margin	60.0%	60.0%	60.0%	60.0%	60.0%
Operating income	$109,336	$136,670	$147,603	$153,070	$546,678
Expenses					
Payroll	$ 39,784	$ 49,730	$ 53,708	$ 55,697	$198,919
General and administrative	$ 2,704	$ 3,380	$ 3,650	$ 3,786	$ 13,520
Product distribution expenses	$ 9,111	$ 11,389	$ 12,300	$ 12,756	$ 45,557
Professional fees and licensure	$ 1,061	$ 1,326	$ 1,432	$ 1,485	$ 5,305
Insurance costs	$ 3,087	$ 3,859	$ 4,167	$ 4,322	$ 15,435
Travel and vehicle costs	$ 4,598	$ 5,748	$ 6,207	$ 6,437	$ 22,990
Utility costs	$ 5,513	$ 6,891	$ 7,442	$ 7,718	$ 27,563
Miscellaneous costs	$ 729	$ 911	$ 984	$ 1,020	$ 3,645
Payroll taxes	$ 5,968	$ 7,459	$ 8,056	$ 8,355	$ 29,838
Total operating costs	$ 72,554	$ 90,692	$ 97,948	$101,575	$362,770
EBITDA	$ 36,782	$ 45,977	$ 49,655	$ 51,494	$183,908
Federal income tax	$ 10,166	$ 12,708	$ 13,725	$ 14,233	$ 50,832
State income tax	$ 1,540	$ 1,925	$ 2,079	$ 2,156	$ 7,702
Interest expense	$ 7,726	$ 7,557	$ 7,384	$ 7,206	$ 29,873
Depreciation expense	$ 7,571	$ 7,571	$ 7,571	$ 7,571	$ 30,286
Net profit	$ 9,777	$ 16,216	$ 18,896	$ 20,327	$ 65,216

7.11 Three Year Cash Flow Analysis

Cash flow analysis (first year)

Month	1	2	3	4	5	6	7	8
Cash from operations	$ 1,717	$ 2,002	$ 2,288	$ 2,573	$ 2,859	$ 3,144	$ 3,430	$ 3,716
Cash from receivables	$ 0	$ 0	$ 0	$ 0	$ 0	$ 0	$ 0	$ 0
Operating cash inflow	$ 1,717	$ 2,002	$ 2,288	$ 2,573	$ 2,859	$ 3,144	$ 3,430	$ 3,716
Other cash inflows								
Equity investment	$100,000	$ 0	$ 0	$ 0	$ 0	$ 0	$ 0	$ 0
Increased borrowings	$400,000	$ 0	$ 0	$ 0	$ 0	$ 0	$ 0	$ 0
Sales of business assets	$ 0	$ 0	$ 0	$ 0	$ 0	$ 0	$ 0	$ 0
A/P increases	$ 833	$ 833	$ 833	$ 833	$ 833	$ 833	$ 833	$ 833
Total other cash inflows	$500,833	$ 833	$ 833	$ 833	$ 833	$ 833	$ 833	$ 833
Total cash inflow	$502,551	$ 2,836	$ 3,121	$ 3,407	$ 3,692	$ 3,978	$ 4,264	$ 4,550
Cash outflows								
Repayment of principal	$ 2,067	$ 2,083	$ 2,098	$ 2,114	$ 2,130	$ 2,146	$ 2,162	$ 2,178
A/P decreases	$ 750	$ 750	$ 750	$ 750	$ 750	$ 750	$ 750	$ 750
A/R increases	$ 0	$ 0	$ 0	$ 0	$ 0	$ 0	$ 0	$ 0
Asset purchases	$471,500	$ 0	$ 0	$ 0	$ 0	$ 0	$ 0	$ 0
Dividends	$ 0	$ 0	$ 0	$ 0	$ 0	$ 0	$ 0	$ 0
Total cash outflows	$474,317	$ 2,833	$ 2,848	$ 2,864	$ 2,880	$ 2,896	$ 2,912	$ 2,928
Net cash flow	$ 28,234	$ 3	$ 273	$ 543	$ 812	$ 1,082	$ 1,352	$ 1,622
Cash balance	$ 28,234	$28,237	$28,510	$29,052	$29,865	$30,947	$32,299	$33,920

Cash flow analysis (first year cont.)

Month	9	10	11	12	1
Cash from operations	$ 4,002	$ 4,288	$ 4,575	$ 4,861	$ 39,457
Cash from receivables	$ 0	$ 0	$ 0	$ 0	$ 0
Operating cash inflow	**$ 4,002**	**$ 4,288**	**$ 4,575**	**$ 4,861**	**$ 39,457**
Other cash inflows					
Equity investment	$ 0	$ 0	$ 0	$ 0	$100,000
Increased borrowings	$ 0	$ 0	$ 0	$ 0	$400,000
Sales of business assets	$ 0	$ 0	$ 0	$ 0	$ 0
A/P increases	$ 833	$ 833	$ 833	$ 833	$ 10,000
Total other cash inflows	**$ 833**	**$ 833**	**$ 833**	**$ 833**	**$510,000**
Total cash inflow	**$ 4,836**	**$ 5,122**	**$ 5,408**	**$ 5,695**	**$549,457**
Cash outflows					
Repayment of principal	$ 2,194	$ 2,211	$ 2,227	$ 2,244	$ 25,854
A/P decreases	$ 750	$ 750	$ 750	$ 750	$ 9,000
A/R increases	$ 0	$ 0	$ 0	$ 0	$ 0
Asset purchases	$ 0	$ 0	$ 0	$ 0	$471,500
Dividends	$ 0	$ 0	$ 0	$31,566	$ 31,566
Total cash outflows	**$ 2,944**	**$ 2,961**	**$ 2,977**	**$34,560**	**$537,919**
Net cash flow	**$ 1,891**	**$ 2,161**	**$ 2,431**	**−$28,866**	**$ 11,538**
Cash balance	**$35,812**	**$37,973**	**$40,403**	**$11,538**	**$ 11,538**

Cash flow analysis (second year)

Quarter	Q1	2 Q2	Q3	Q4	2
Cash from operations	$14,586	$18,233	$19,692	$20,421	$72,932
Cash from receivables	$ 0	$ 0	$ 0	$ 0	$ 0
Operating cash inflow	**$14,586**	**$18,233**	**$19,692**	**$20,421**	**$72,932**
Other cash inflows					
Equity investment	$ 0	$ 0	$ 0	$ 0	$ 0
Increased borrowings	$ 0	$ 0	$ 0	$ 0	$ 0
Sales of business assets	$ 0	$ 0	$ 0	$ 0	$ 0
A/P increases	$ 2,300	$ 2,875	$ 3,105	$ 3,220	$11,500
Total other cash inflows	**$ 2,300**	**$ 2,875**	**$ 3,105**	**$ 3,220**	**$11,500**
Total cash inflow	**$16,886**	**$21,108**	**$22,797**	**$23,641**	**$84,432**
Cash outflows					
Repayment of principal	$ 6,834	$ 6,989	$ 7,147	$ 7,309	$28,279
A/P decreases	$ 2,160	$ 2,700	$ 2,916	$ 3,024	$10,800
A/R increases	$ 0	$ 0	$ 0	$ 0	$ 0
Asset purchases	$ 1,459	$ 1,823	$ 1,969	$ 2,042	$ 7,293
Dividends	$ 7,293	$ 9,117	$ 9,846	$10,211	$36,466
Total cash outflows	**$17,746**	**$20,629**	**$21,878**	**$22,586**	**$82,838**
Net cash flow	**−$ 859**	**$ 480**	**$ 919**	**$ 1,055**	**$ 1,594**
Cash balance	**$10,679**	**$11,158**	**$12,077**	**$13,132**	**$13,132**

Cash flow analysis (third year)

Quarter	Q1	3 Q2	Q3	Q4	3
Cash from operations	$19,100	$23,876	$25,786	$26,741	$ 95,502
Cash from receivables	$ 0	$ 0	$ 0	$ 0	$ 0
Operating cash inflow	**$19,100**	**$23,876**	**$25,786**	**$26,741**	**$ 95,502**
Other cash inflows					
Equity investment	$ 0	$ 0	$ 0	$ 0	$ 0
Increased borrowings	$ 0	$ 0	$ 0	$ 0	$ 0
Sales of business assets	$ 0	$ 0	$ 0	$ 0	$ 0
A/P increases	$ 2,645	$ 3,306	$ 3,571	$ 3,703	$ 13,225
Total other cash inflows	**$ 2,645**	**$ 3,306**	**$ 3,571**	**$ 3,703**	**$ 13,225**
Total cash inflow	**$21,745**	**$27,182**	**$29,356**	**$30,444**	**$108,727**
Cash outflows					
Repayment of principal	$ 7,475	$ 7,644	$ 7,818	$ 7,995	$ 30,932
A/P decreases	$ 2,592	$ 3,240	$ 3,499	$ 3,629	$ 12,960
A/R increases	$ 0	$ 0	$ 0	$ 0	$ 0
Asset purchases	$ 1,910	$ 2,388	$ 2,579	$ 2,674	$ 9,550
Dividends	$ 9,550	$11,938	$12,893	$13,370	$ 47,751
Total cash outflows	**$21,527**	**$25,210**	**$26,788**	**$27,668**	**$101,193**
Net cash flow	**$ 218**	**$ 1,972**	**$ 2,568**	**$ 2,776**	**$ 7,534**
Cash balance	**$13,350**	**$15,322**	**$17,891**	**$20,666**	**$ 20,666**

Furniture Store
Collins Furniture

78901 High Ave.
Rochester, NY 14620

BizPlanDB.com

Collins Furniture is a New York based corporation that will provide extensive inventories of mid-range to high end furniture pieces to customers in its targeted market.

1.0 EXECUTIVE SUMMARY

The purpose of this business plan is to raise $300,000 for the development of a furniture store while showcasing the expected financials and operations over the next three years. Collins Furniture is a New York based corporation that will provide extensive inventories of mid-range to high end furniture pieces to customers in its targeted market. The Company was founded by Martin Collins.

1.1 The Products and Services

As stated above, Collins Furniture will carry extensive brand name lines of mid-range and high end furniture pieces for sale to the general public from its retail showroom location. Mr. Collins is currently sourcing a number of furniture manufacturers, distributors, and wholesalers that will provide the Company with its inventories via direct purchases and on credit until sales are made.

Mr. Collins will also develop relationships with interior decorators and design firms so that these businesses can source furniture for their clients through Collins Furniture.

The third section of the business plan will further describe the services offered by Collins Furniture.

1.2 Financing

Mr. Collins is seeking to raise $300,000 from as a bank loan. The interest rate and loan agreement are to be further discussed during negotiation. This business plan assumes that the business will receive a 10 year loan with a 9% fixed interest rate. The financing will be used for the following:

- Development of the storefront location.

- Financing for the first six months of operation.

- Capital to purchase the Company's initial inventory of furniture.

Mr. Collins will contribute $50,000 to the venture.

1.3 Mission Statement

Collins Furniture's mission is to provide the general public and interior decorators with an expansive inventory of mid-range and high end furniture pieces at affordable prices.

1.4 Management Team

The Company was founded by Martin Collins. Mr. Collins has more than 10 years of experience in the retail management industry. Through his expertise, he will be able to bring the operations of the business to profitability within its first year of operations.

1.5 Sales Forecasts

Mr. Collins expects a strong rate of growth at the start of operations. Below are the expected financials over the next three years.

Proforma profit and loss (yearly)

Year	1	2	3
Sales	$1,324,680	$1,589,616	$1,859,851
Operating costs	$ 432,788	$ 485,471	$ 510,798
EBITDA	$ 130,948	$ 191,012	$ 280,687
Taxes, interest, and depreciation	$ 96,866	$ 108,602	$ 141,445
Net profit	$ 34,082	$ 82,410	$ 139,242

Sales, operating costs, and profit forecast

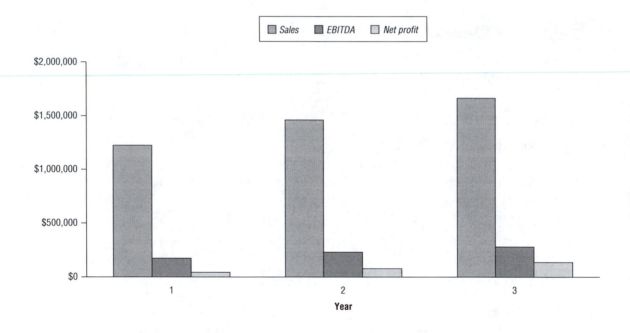

1.6 Expansion Plan

The Founder expects that the business will aggressively expand during the first three years of operation. Mr. Collins intends to implement marketing campaigns that will effectively target individuals and interior design firms within the target market.

2.0 COMPANY AND FINANCING SUMMARY

2.1 Registered Name and Corporate Structure

The Company is registered as a corporation in the State of New York.

2.2 Required Funds

At this time, Collins Furniture requires $300,000 of debt funds. Below is a breakdown of how these funds will be used:

Projected startup costs

Initial lease payments and deposits	$ 17,500
Working capital	$ 40,000
FF&E	$ 65,000
Leasehold improvements	$ 25,000
Security deposits	$ 10,000
Insurance	$ 5,000
Furniture inventory	$165,000
Marketing budget	$ 17,500
Miscellaneous and unforeseen costs	$ 5,000
Total startup costs	**$350,000**

Use of funds

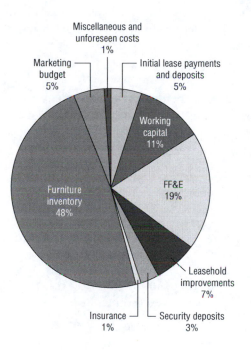

2.3 Investor Equity

Mr. Collins is not seeking an investment from a third party at this time.

2.4 Management Equity

Martin Collins owns 100% of Collins Furniture.

2.5 Exit Strategy

If the business is very successful, Mr. Collins may seek to sell the business to a third party for a significant earnings multiple. Most likely, the Company will hire a qualified business broker to sell the business on behalf of Collins Furniture. Based on historical numbers, the business could fetch a sales premium of up to 6 times earnings.

3.0 PRODUCTS AND SERVICES

Below is a description of the products services offered by Collins Furniture.

3.1 Sales of Furniture

The primary source of revenue for the business will come from the direct retail sale of mid-range and high end furniture pieces that are sold throughout the Company's showroom. As stated in the executive summary, Mr. Collins is currently sourcing a number of manufacturers, distributors, and wholesalers that will provide the business with its inventories via direct sales and on credit until sales are made. All of the furniture sold by the business will be of the highest retail quality. Mr. Collins will also seek to gain distributor status among popular furniture manufacturers so that the business can increase its gross margins.

The business will also develop an online sales platform which will include a proprietary website as well as online stores developed in conjunction with major online sales platforms such as Yahoo, Google, Amazon.com, and eBay. This will allow the Company to more rapidly turnover its inventory at the onset of operation.

Finally, the Company will work closely with a sourced financing provider so that customers can apply for credit in regards to their big ticket furniture purchases. Customers will be able to receive immediate financing decisions through an online platform that will be integrated into the Company's point of sale terminals. This is common practice among furniture stores.

3.2 Delivery Services

The Company's secondary source of revenue will come from the delivery services that are offered in conjunction with the furniture sales discussed above. While this will be a smaller segment of the Company's operations, the business will be able to markup its direct delivery costs by 25% to the customer. Management anticipates that approximately 20% of Collins Furniture's aggregate revenues will come from this operating segment.

4.0 STRATEGIC AND MARKET ANALYSIS

4.1 Economic Outlook

This section of the analysis will detail the economic climate, the furniture industry, the customer profile, and the competition that the business will face as it progresses through its business operations.

Currently, the economic market condition in the United States is in recession. This slowdown in the economy has also greatly impacted real estate sales, which has halted to historical lows. Many economists expect that this recession will continue until mid-2010, at which point the economy will begin a prolonged recovery period. As such, the business may have issues with top line income as customers scale back on major purchases like furniture.

4.2 Industry Analysis

Within the United States, there are more than 28,000 companies that operate in a furniture retailing capacity. Each year, these businesses aggregately generate more than $53 billion of revenue while providing jobs for more than 250,000 people. Aggregate payrolls in each of the last five years have exceeded $12.9 billion.

This is a mature industry, and the expected future growth rate of this market is expected to mirror that of the general economy. One of the most common trends among furniture retailers is to develop e-commerce platforms that operate concurrently with their traditional brick and mortar retail locations.

4.3 Customer Profile

Collins Furniture's average client will be a middle- to upper-middle class man or woman living in the Company's target market. Common traits among clients will include:

- Annual household income exceeding $50,000

- Lives or works no more than 15 miles from the Company's location.

- Will spend $250 to $2,000 per visit to Collins Furniture.

- May require financing for their furniture purchases.

Based on demographic information regarding the Rochester, New York metropolitan area, there are more than12 million people located within the Company's targeted market. Among these residents, the annual household income within this area is $45,000 while median family income has remained stable around $55,000. However, incomes over the past three years within this area have declined slightly given the current economic climate.

4.4 Competition

There are several major retailers that specialize in the distribution and sale of furniture that are identical to Collins Furniture. This has become a highly commoditized industry and businesses within this industry retain competitive advantages based on their pricing and their ability to extend credit to their customers. Mr. Collins intends to further the Company's pricing advantage by maintaining lines of credit with furniture manufacturers that ensure that customers can receive 0% or low APR interest rates on the furniture that they intend to finance.

5.0 MARKETING PLAN

Collins Furniture intends to maintain an extensive marketing campaign that will ensure maximum visibility for the business in its targeted market. Below is an overview of the marketing strategies and objectives of the Company.

5.1 Marketing Objectives
- Develop an online presence by developing a website and placing the Company's name and contact information with online directories.

- Implement a local campaign with the Company's targeted market via the use of flyers, local newspaper advertisements, and word of mouth advertising.

- Establish relationships with interior decorators and design firms in the target market.

5.2 Marketing Strategies

Mr. Collins intends on using a number of marketing strategies that will allow Collins Furniture to easily target men and women within the target market. These strategies include traditional print advertisements and ads placed on search engines on the Internet. Below is a description of how the business intends to market its services to the general public.

Collins Furniture will also use an internet based strategy. This is very important as many people seeking local retailers, such as furniture stores, now the Internet to conduct their preliminary searches. Mr. Collins will register Collins Furniture with online portals so that potential customers can easily reach the business. The Company will also develop its own online website which will feature e-commerce functionality while concurrently developing relationships with third party e-commerce store hosts such as Yahoo, Google, eBay, and Amazon.com.

Finally, Mr. Collins will develop ongoing purchase order relationships with local interior decorators and design firms that will use Collins Furniture as their source for the client's furniture purchasing needs.

5.3 Pricing

As the business will carry a diverse line of furniture, it is difficult to determine the pricing of each product sold by Collins Furniture. A full pricing matrix of the Company's products are available upon request. On each dollar of revenue generated, the business anticipates that the business will generate approximately 43 cents of contribution margins.

6.0 ORGANIZATIONAL PLAN AND PERSONNEL SUMMARY

6.1 Corporate Organization

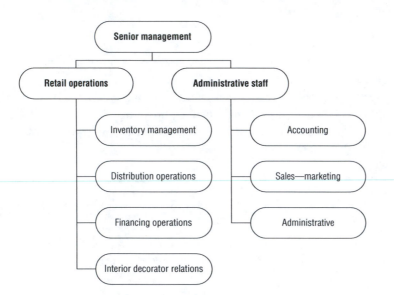

6.2 Organizational Budget

Personnel plan—yearly

Year	1	2	3
Owner	$ 50,000	$ 51,500	$ 53,045
Store manager	$ 45,000	$ 46,350	$ 47,741
Store employees	$ 98,000	$126,175	$129,960
Bookkeeper (P/T)	$ 12,500	$ 12,875	$ 13,261
Administrative	$ 50,000	$ 51,500	$ 53,045
Total	**$255,500**	**$288,400**	**$297,052**

Numbers of personnel

Owner	1	1	1
Store manager	1	1	1
Store employees	4	5	5
Bookkeeper (P/T)	1	1	1
Administrative	2	2	2
Totals	**9**	**10**	**10**

Personnel expense breakdown

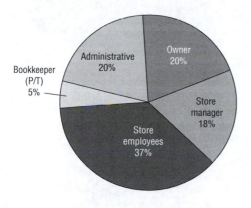

7.0 FINANCIAL PLAN

7.1 Underlying Assumptions

The Company has based its proforma financial statements on the following:

*   Collins Furniture will have an annual revenue growth rate of 16% per year.

*   The Owner will acquire $300,000 of debt funds to develop the business.

*   The loan will have a 10 year term with a 9% interest rate.

7.2 Sensitivity Analysis

In the event of an economic downturn, the business may have a decline in its revenues. Furniture purchases are considered big ticket items, and during an economic downturn, the business will most likely see a drop in its top line income. However, the Company will earn significant margins on each piece of furniture sold and Mr. Collins intends to operate a very lean operating and overhead infrastructure. As such, the business will be able to remain profitable and cash flow positive despite moderate declines in revenue.

7.3 Source of Funds

Financing

Equity contributions	
Management investment	$ 50,000.00
Total equity financing	**$ 50,000.00**
Banks and lenders	
Banks and lenders	$ 300,000.00
Total debt financing	**$ 300,000.00**
Total financing	**$350,000.00**

7.4 General Assumptions

General assumptions

Year	1	2	3
Short term interest rate	9.5%	9.5%	9.5%
Long term interest rate	10.0%	10.0%	10.0%
Federal tax rate	33.0%	33.0%	33.0%
State tax rate	5.0%	5.0%	5.0%
Personnel taxes	15.0%	15.0%	15.0%

7.5 Profit and Loss Statements

Proforma profit and loss (yearly)

Year	1	2	3
Sales	$1,324,680	$1,589,616	$1,859,851
Cost of goods sold	$ 760,944	$ 913,133	$1,068,365
Gross margin	42.56%	42.56%	42.56%
Operating income	$ 563,736	$ 676,483	$ 791,485
Expenses			
Payroll	$ 255,500	$ 288,400	$ 297,052
General and administrative	$ 25,200	$ 26,208	$ 27,256
Marketing expenses	$ 42,390	$ 50,868	$ 59,515
Professional fees and licensure	$ 7,500	$ 7,725	$ 7,957
Insurance costs	$ 14,000	$ 14,700	$ 15,435
Travel and vehicle costs	$ 19,000	$ 20,900	$ 22,990
Rent and utilities	$ 24,250	$ 25,463	$ 26,736
Miscellaneous costs	$ 6,623	$ 7,948	$ 9,299
Payroll taxes	$ 38,325	$ 43,260	$ 44,558
Total operating costs	$ 432,788	$ 485,471	$ 510,798
EBITDA	$ 130,948	$ 191,012	$ 280,687
Federal income tax	$ 43,213	$ 54,984	$ 85,233
State income tax	$ 6,547	$ 8,331	$ 12,914
Interest expense	$ 26,213	$ 24,394	$ 22,405
Depreciation expenses	$ 20,893	$ 20,893	$ 20,893
Net profit	$ 34,082	$ 82,410	$ 139,242
Profit margin	2.57%	5.18%	7.49%

Sales, operating costs, and profit forecast

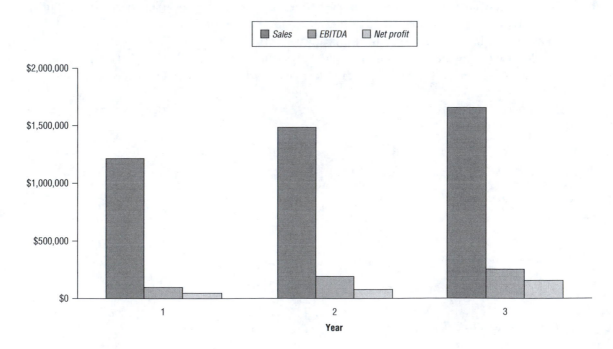

7.6 Cash Flow Analysis

Proforma cash flow analysis—yearly

Year	1	2	3
Cash from operations	$ 54,975	$103,303	$160,135
Cash from receivables	$ 0	$ 0	$ 0
Operating cash inflow	**$ 54,975**	**$103,303**	**$160,135**
Other cash inflows			
Equity investment	$ 50,000	$ 0	$ 0
Increased borrowings	$300,000	$ 0	$ 0
Sales of business assets	$ 0	$ 0	$ 0
A/P increases	$ 37,902	$ 43,587	$ 50,125
Total other cash inflows	**$387,902**	**$ 43,587**	**$ 50,125**
Total cash inflow	**$442,877**	**$146,890**	**$210,261**
Cash outflows			
Repayment of principal	$ 19,390	$ 21,209	$ 23,199
A/P decreases	$ 24,897	$ 29,876	$ 35,852
A/R increases	$ 0	$ 0	$ 0
Asset purchases	$292,500	$ 25,826	$ 40,034
Dividends	$ 38,482	$ 61,982	$ 96,081
Total cash outflows	**$375,269**	**$138,893**	**$195,165**
Net cash flow	**$ 67,607**	**$ 7,997**	**$ 15,095**
Cash balance	**$ 67,607**	**$ 75,604**	**$ 90,700**

Proforma cash flow (yearly)

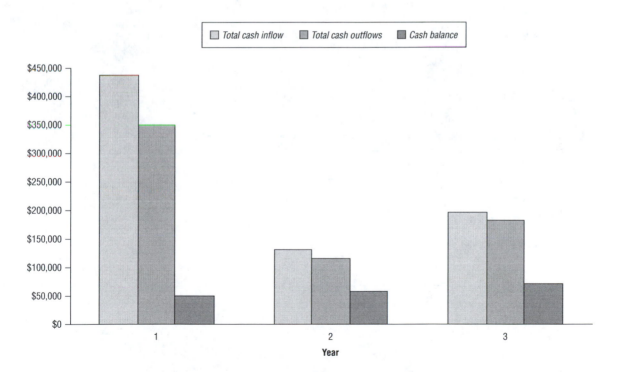

7.7 Balance Sheet

Proforma balance sheet—yearly

Year	1	2	3
Assets			
Cash	$ 67,607	$ 75,604	$ 90,700
Amortized development/expansion costs	$ 62,500	$ 65,083	$ 69,086
Furniture inventory	$165,000	$177,913	$197,930
FF&E	$ 65,000	$ 75,330	$ 91,344
Accumulated depreciation	($ 20,893)	($ 41,786)	($ 62,679)
Total assets	**$339,214**	**$352,144**	**$386,381**
Liabilities and equity			
Accounts payable	$ 13,005	$ 26,716	$ 40,990
Long term liabilities	$280,610	$259,401	$238,192
Other liabilities	$ 0	$ 0	$ 0
Total liabilities	**$293,615**	**$286,117**	**$279,181**
Net worth	**$ 45,600**	**$ 66,028**	**$107,200**
Total liabilities and equity	**$339,214**	**$352,144**	**$386,381**

Proforma balance sheet

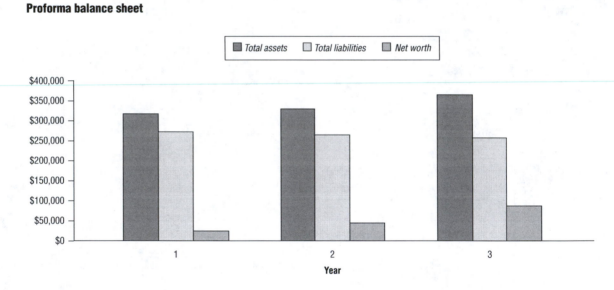

7.8 Breakeven Analysis

Monthly break even analysis

Year	1	2	3
Monthly revenue	$ 84,748	$ 95,064	$ 100,024
Yearly revenue	$1,016,976	$1,140,772	$1,200,285

Break even analysis

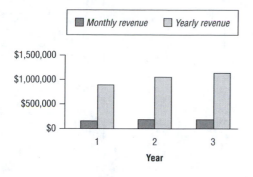

7.9 Business Ratios

Business ratios—yearly

Year	1	2	3
Sales			
Sales growth	0.0%	20.0%	17.0%
Gross margin	42.6%	42.6%	42.6%
Financials			
Profit margin	2.57%	5.18%	7.49%
Assets to liabilities	1.16	1.23	1.38
Equity to liabilities	0.16	0.23	0.38
Assets to equity	7.44	5.33	3.60
Liquidity			
Acid test	0.23	0.26	0.32
Cash to assets	0.20	0.21	0.23

7.10 Three Year Profit and Loss Statement

Profit and loss statement (first year)

Month	1	2	3	4	5	6	7
Sales	**$103,075**	**$104,405**	**$105,735**	**$107,065**	**$108,395**	**$109,725**	**$111,055**
Cost of goods sold	$ 59,210	$ 59,974	$ 60,738	$ 61,502	$ 62,266	$ 63,030	$ 63,794
Gross margin	42.6%	42.6%	42.6%	42.6%	42.6%	42.6%	42.6%
Operating income	**$ 43,865**	**$ 44,431**	**$ 44,997**	**$ 45,563**	**$ 46,129**	**$ 46,695**	**$ 47,261**
Expenses							
Payroll	$ 21,292	$ 21,292	$ 21,292	$ 21,292	$ 21,292	$ 21,292	$ 21,292
General and administrative	$ 2,100	$ 2,100	$ 2,100	$ 2,100	$ 2,100	$ 2,100	$ 2,100
Marketing expenses	$ 3,532	$ 3,532	$ 3,532	$ 3,532	$ 3,532	$ 3,532	$ 3,532
Professional fees and licensure	$ 625	$ 625	$ 625	$ 625	$ 625	$ 625	$ 625
Insurance costs	$ 1,167	$ 1,167	$ 1,167	$ 1,167	$ 1,167	$ 1,167	$ 1,167
Travel and vehicle costs	$ 1,583	$ 1,583	$ 1,583	$ 1,583	$ 1,583	$ 1,583	$ 1,583
Rent and utilities	$ 2,021	$ 2,021	$ 2,021	$ 2,021	$ 2,021	$ 2,021	$ 2,021
Miscellaneous costs	$ 552	$ 552	$ 552	$ 552	$ 552	$ 552	$ 552
Payroll taxes	$ 3,194	$ 3,194	$ 3,194	$ 3,194	$ 3,194	$ 3,194	$ 3,194
Total operating costs	**$ 36,066**	**$ 36,066**	**$ 36,066**	**$ 36,066**	**$ 36,066**	**$ 36,066**	**$ 36,066**
EBITDA	**$ 7,799**	**$ 8,365**	**$ 8,931**	**$ 9,497**	**$ 10,063**	**$ 10,629**	**$ 11,195**
Federal income tax	$ 3,362	$ 3,406	$ 3,449	$ 3,493	$ 3,536	$ 3,579	$ 3,623
State income tax	$ 509	$ 516	$ 523	$ 529	$ 536	$ 542	$ 549
Interest expense	$ 2,250	$ 2,238	$ 2,227	$ 2,215	$ 2,203	$ 2,191	$ 2,179
Depreciation expense	$ 1,741	$ 1,741	$ 1,741	$ 1,741	$ 1,741	$ 1,741	$ 1,741
Net profit	**−$ 64**	**$ 464**	**$ 992**	**$ 1,520**	**$ 2,048**	**$ 2,576**	**$ 3,104**

Profit and loss statement (first year cont.)

Month	8	9	10	11	12	1
Sales	$112,385	$113,715	$115,045	$116,375	$117,705	$1,324,680
Cost of goods sold	$ 64,558	$ 65,322	$ 66,086	$ 66,850	$ 67,614	$ 760,944
Gross margin	42.6%	42.6%	42.6%	42.6%	42.6%	42.6%
Operating income	**$ 47,827**	**$ 48,393**	**$ 48,959**	**$ 49,525**	**$ 50,091**	**$ 563,736**
Expenses						
Payroll	$ 21,292	$ 21,292	$ 21,292	$ 21,292	$ 21,292	$ 255,500
General and administrative	$ 2,100	$ 2,100	$ 2,100	$ 2,100	$ 2,100	$ 25,200
Marketing expenses	$ 3,532	$ 3,532	$ 3,532	$ 3,532	$ 3,532	$ 42,390
Professional fees and licensure	$ 625	$ 625	$ 625	$ 625	$ 625	$ 7,500
Insurance costs	$ 1,167	$ 1,167	$ 1,167	$ 1,167	$ 1,167	$ 14,000
Travel and vehicle costs	$ 1,583	$ 1,583	$ 1,583	$ 1,583	$ 1,583	$ 19,000
Rent and utilities	$ 2,021	$ 2,021	$ 2,021	$ 2,021	$ 2,021	$ 24,250
Miscellaneous costs	$ 552	$ 552	$ 552	$ 552	$ 552	$ 6,623
Payroll taxes	$ 3,194	$ 3,194	$ 3,194	$ 3,194	$ 3,194	$ 38,325
Total operating costs	**$ 36,066**	**$ 36,066**	**$ 36,066**	**$ 36,066**	**$ 36,066**	**$ 432,788**
EBITDA	**$ 11,761**	**$ 12,327**	**$ 12,893**	**$ 13,459**	**$ 14,025**	**$ 130,948**
Federal income tax	$ 3,666	$ 3,710	$ 3,753	$ 3,796	$ 3,840	$ 43,213
State income tax	$ 555	$ 562	$ 569	$ 575	$ 582	$ 6,547
Interest expense	$ 2,167	$ 2,155	$ 2,142	$ 2,130	$ 2,117	$ 26,213
Depreciation expense	$ 1,741	$ 1,741	$ 1,741	$ 1,741	$ 1,741	$ 20,893
Net profit	**$ 3,632**	**$ 4,160**	**$ 4,689**	**$ 5,217**	**$ 5,746**	**$ 34,082**

Profit and loss statement (second year)

Quarter	Q1	2 Q2	Q3	Q4	2
Sales	$317,923	$397,404	$429,196	$445,092	$1,589,616
Cost of goods sold	$182,627	$228,283	$246,546	$255,677	$ 913,133
Gross margin	42.6%	42.6%	42.6%	42.6%	42.6%
Operating income	**$135,297**	**$169,121**	**$182,650**	**$189,415**	**$ 676,483**
Expenses					
Payroll	$ 57,680	$ 72,100	$ 77,868	$ 80,752	$ 288,400
General and administrative	$ 5,242	$ 6,552	$ 7,076	$ 7,338	$ 26,208
Marketing expenses	$ 10,174	$ 12,717	$ 13,734	$ 14,243	$ 50,868
Professional fees and licensure	$ 1,545	$ 1,931	$ 2,086	$ 2,163	$ 7,725
Insurance costs	$ 2,940	$ 3,675	$ 3,969	$ 4,116	$ 14,700
Travel and vehicle costs	$ 4,180	$ 5,225	$ 5,643	$ 5,852	$ 20,900
Rent and utility	$ 5,093	$ 6,366	$ 6,875	$ 7,130	$ 25,463
Miscellaneous costs	$ 1,590	$ 1,987	$ 2,146	$ 2,225	$ 7,948
Payroll taxes	$ 8,652	$ 10,815	$ 11,680	$ 12,113	$ 43,260
Total operating costs	**$ 97,094**	**$121,368**	**$131,077**	**$135,932**	**$ 485,471**
EBITDA	**$ 38,202**	**$ 47,753**	**$ 51,573**	**$ 53,483**	**$ 191,012**
Federal income tax	$ 10,997	$ 13,746	$ 14,846	$ 15,395	$ 54,984
State income tax	$ 1,666	$ 2,083	$ 2,249	$ 2,333	$ 8,331
Interest expense	$ 6,275	$ 6,159	$ 6,040	$ 5,919	$ 24,394
Depreciation expense	$ 5,223	$ 5,223	$ 5,223	$ 5,223	$ 20,893
Net profit	**$ 14,041**	**$ 20,542**	**$ 23,215**	**$ 24,613**	**$ 82,410**

Profit and loss statement (third year)

Quarter	Q1	Q2	Q3	Q4	3
Sales	$371,970	$464,963	$502,160	$520,758	$1,859,851
Cost of goods sold	$213,673	$267,091	$288,459	$299,142	$1,068,365
Gross margin	42.6%	42.6%	42.6%	42.6%	42.6%
Operating income	$158,297	$197,871	$213,701	$221,616	$ 791,485
Expenses					
Payroll	$ 59,410	$ 74,263	$ 80,204	$ 83,175	$ 297,052
General and administrative	$ 5,451	$ 6,814	$ 7,359	$ 7,632	$ 27,256
Marketing expenses	$ 11,903	$ 14,879	$ 16,069	$ 16,664	$ 59,515
Professional fees and licensure	$ 1,591	$ 1,989	$ 2,148	$ 2,228	$ 7,957
Insurance costs	$ 3,087	$ 3,859	$ 4,167	$ 4,322	$ 15,435
Travel and vehicle costs	$ 4,598	$ 5,748	$ 6,207	$ 6,437	$ 22,990
Rent and utilities	$ 5,347	$ 6,684	$ 7,219	$ 7,486	$ 26,736
Miscellaneous costs	$ 1,860	$ 2,325	$ 2,511	$ 2,604	$ 9,299
Payroll taxes	$ 8,912	$ 11,139	$ 12,031	$ 12,476	$ 44,558
Total operating costs	$102,160	$127,699	$137,915	$143,023	$ 510,798
EBITDA	$ 56,137	$ 70,172	$ 75,786	$ 78,592	$ 280,687
Federal income tax	$ 17,047	$ 21,308	$ 23,013	$ 23,865	$ 85,233
State income tax	$ 2,583	$ 3,229	$ 3,487	$ 3,616	$ 12,914
Interest expense	$ 5,795	$ 5,668	$ 5,538	$ 5,405	$ 22,405
Depreciation expense	$ 5,223	$ 5,223	$ 5,223	$ 5,223	$ 20,893
Net profit	$ 25,490	$ 34,744	$ 38,525	$ 40,483	$ 139,242

7.11 Three Year Cash Flow Analysis

Cash flow analysis (first year)

Month	1	2	3	4	5	6	7	8
Cash from operations	$ 1,677	$ 2,205	$ 2,733	$ 3,261	$ 3,789	$ 4,317	$ 4,845	$ 5,373
Cash from receivables	$ 0	$ 0	$ 0	$ 0	$ 0	$ 0	$ 0	$ 0
Operating cash inflow	$ 1,677	$ 2,205	$ 2,733	$ 3,261	$ 3,789	$ 4,317	$ 4,845	$ 5,373
Other cash inflows								
Equity investment	$ 50,000	$ 0	$ 0	$ 0	$ 0	$ 0	$ 0	$ 0
Increased borrowings	$300,000	$ 0	$ 0	$ 0	$ 0	$ 0	$ 0	$ 0
Sales of business assets	$ 0	$ 0	$ 0	$ 0	$ 0	$ 0	$ 0	$ 0
A/P increases	$ 3,159	$ 3,159	$ 3,159	$ 3,159	$ 3,159	$ 3,159	$ 3,159	$ 3,159
Total other cash inflows	$353,159	$ 3,159	$ 3,159	$ 3,159	$ 3,159	$ 3,159	$ 3,159	$ 3,159
Total cash inflow	$354,836	$ 5,364	$ 5,891	$ 6,419	$ 6,947	$ 7,475	$ 8,003	$ 8,531
Cash outflows								
Repayment of principal	$ 1,550	$ 1,562	$ 1,574	$ 1,585	$ 1,597	$ 1,609	$ 1,621	$ 1,634
A/P decreases	$ 2,075	$ 2,075	$ 2,075	$ 2,075	$ 2,075	$ 2,075	$ 2,075	$ 2,075
A/R increases	$ 0	$ 0	$ 0	$ 0	$ 0	$ 0	$ 0	$ 0
Asset purchases	$292,500	$ 0	$ 0	$ 0	$ 0	$ 0	$ 0	$ 0
Dividends	$ 0	$ 0	$ 0	$ 0	$ 0	$ 0	$ 0	$ 0
Total cash outflows	$296,125	$ 3,637	$ 3,648	$ 3,660	$ 3,672	$ 3,684	$ 3,696	$ 3,708
Net cash flow	$ 58,711	$ 1,727	$ 2,243	$ 2,759	$ 3,275	$ 3,791	$ 4,307	$ 4,823
Cash balance	$ 58,711	$60,438	$62,681	$65,440	$68,715	$72,506	$76,813	$81,636

Cash flow analysis (first year cont.)

Month	9	10	11	12	1
Cash from operations	$ 5,901	$ 6,430	$ 6,958	$ 7,487	$ 54,975
Cash from receivables	$ 0	$ 0	$ 0	$ 0	$ 0
Operating cash inflow	**$ 5,901**	**$ 6,430**	**$ 6,958**	**$ 7,487**	**$ 54,975**
Other cash inflows					
Equity investment	$ 0	$ 0	$ 0	$ 0	$ 50,000
Increased borrowings	$ 0	$ 0	$ 0	$ 0	$300,000
Sales of business assets	$ 0	$ 0	$ 0	$ 0	$ 0
A/P increases	$ 3,159	$ 3,159	$ 3,159	$ 3,159	$ 37,902
Total other cash inflows	**$ 3,159**	**$ 3,159**	**$ 3,159**	**$ 3,159**	**$387,902**
Total cash inflow	**$ 9,060**	**$ 9,588**	**$10,117**	**$10,645**	**$442,877**
Cash outflows					
Repayment of principal	$ 1,646	$ 1,658	$ 1,671	$ 1,683	$ 19,390
A/P decreases	$ 2,075	$ 2,075	$ 2,075	$ 2,075	$ 24,897
A/R increases	$ 0	$ 0	$ 0	$ 0	$ 0
Asset purchases	$ 0	$ 0	$ 0	$ 0	$292,500
Dividends	$ 0	$ 0	$ 0	$38,482	$ 38,482
Total cash outflows	**$ 3,721**	**$ 3,733**	**$ 3,745**	**$42,240**	**$375,269**
Net cash flow	**$ 5,339**	**$ 5,855**	**$ 6,371**	**−$31,595**	**$ 67,607**
Cash balance	**$86,975**	**$92,831**	**$99,202**	**$67,607**	**$ 67,607**

Cash flow analysis (second year)

Quarter	Q1	Q2	Q3	Q4	2
Cash from operations	$20,661	$25,826	$27,892	$28,925	$103,303
Cash from receivables	$ 0	$ 0	$ 0	$ 0	$ 0
Operating cash inflow	**$20,661**	**$25,826**	**$27,892**	**$28,925**	**$103,303**
Other cash inflows					
Equity investment	$ 0	$ 0	$ 0	$ 0	$ 0
Increased borrowings	$ 0	$ 0	$ 0	$ 0	$ 0
Sales of business assets	$ 0	$ 0	$ 0	$ 0	$ 0
A/P increases	$ 8,717	$10,897	$11,769	$12,204	$ 43,587
Total other cash inflows	**$ 8,717**	**$10,897**	**$11,769**	**$12,204**	**$ 43,587**
Total cash inflow	**$29,378**	**$36,723**	**$39,660**	**$41,129**	**$146,890**
Cash outflows					
Repayment of principal	$ 5,125	$ 5,242	$ 5,360	$ 5,482	$ 21,209
A/P decreases	$ 5,975	$ 7,469	$ 8,067	$ 8,365	$ 29,876
A/R increases	$ 0	$ 0	$ 0	$ 0	$ 0
Asset purchases	$ 5,165	$ 6,456	$ 6,973	$ 7,231	$ 25,826
Dividends	$12,396	$15,495	$16,735	$17,355	$ 61,982
Total cash outflows	**$28,662**	**$34,663**	**$37,135**	**$38,433**	**$138,893**
Net cash flow	**$ 716**	**$ 2,060**	**$ 2,525**	**$ 2,696**	**$ 7,997**
Cash balance	**$68,323**	**$70,383**	**$72,909**	**$75,604**	**$ 75,604**

Cash flow analysis (third year)

Quarter	Q1	3 Q2	Q3	Q4	3
Cash from operations	$32,027	$40,034	$43,237	$44,838	$160,135
Cash from receivables	$ 0	$ 0	$ 0	$ 0	$ 0
Operating cash inflow	**$32,027**	**$40,034**	**$43,237**	**$44,838**	**$160,135**
Other cash inflows					
Equity investment	$ 0	$ 0	$ 0	$ 0	$ 0
Increased borrowings	$ 0	$ 0	$ 0	$ 0	$ 0
Sales of business assets	$ 0	$ 0	$ 0	$ 0	$ 0
A/P increases	$10,025	$12,531	$13,534	$14,035	$ 50,125
Total other cash inflows	**$10,025**	**$12,531**	**$13,534**	**$14,035**	**$ 50,125**
Total cash inflow	**$42,052**	**$52,565**	**$56,770**	**$58,873**	**$210,261**
Cash outflows					
Repayment of principal	$ 5,606	$ 5,733	$ 5,863	$ 5,996	$ 23,199
A/P decreases	$ 7,170	$ 8,963	$ 9,680	$10,038	$ 35,852
A/R increases	$ 0	$ 0	$ 0	$ 0	$ 0
Asset purchases	$ 8,007	$10,008	$10,809	$11,209	$ 40,034
Dividends	$19,216	$24,020	$25,942	$26,903	$ 96,081
Total cash outflows	**$39,999**	**$48,725**	**$52,294**	**$54,147**	**$195,165**
Net cash flow	**$ 2,053**	**$ 3,840**	**$ 4,476**	**$ 4,726**	**$ 15,095**
Cash balance	**$77,657**	**$81,497**	**$85,974**	**$90,700**	**$ 90,700**

Gas Station

Rapid Roger's Gas Station

9999 Plainfield Ave.
Edison, NJ 08820

BizPlanDB.com

Rapid Roger's Gas Station is a New Jersey based corporation that will provide dispensing of gasoline/diesel fuel as well as convenience store items to customers in its targeted market.

1.0 EXECUTIVE SUMMARY

The purpose of this business plan is to raise $750,000 for the development of a gas station and convenience store while showcasing the expected financials and operations over the next three years. Rapid Roger's Gas Station is a New Jersey based corporation that will provide dispensing of gasoline/diesel fuel as well as convenience store items to customers in its targeted market. The Company was founded in 2010 by Roger Dunn.

1.1 The Services

Through Rapid Roger's Gas Station's retail location (where most profits are realized), the store will provide an expansive variety of food, beverage products, packaged food goods, bottled beverages, and ancillary merchandise such as toiletries, automotive products, and other small life essentials.

A vast majority of the revenues (not the profits) will from the sale of gasoline products and diesel fuel.

The third section of the business plan will further describe the services offered by Rapid Roger's Gas Station.

1.2 Financing

Mr. Dunn is seeking to raise $750,000 from as a bank loan. The interest rate and loan agreement are to be further discussed during negotiation. This business plan assumes that the business will receive a 10 year loan with a 9% fixed interest rate. The financing will be used for the following:

*   Development of the location.

*   Financing for the first six months of operation.

*   Capital to purchase the Company's inventory of gasoline and convenience store items.

Mr. Dunn will contribute $100,000 to the venture.

1.3 Mission Statement

The mission of Rapid Roger's Gas Station is to become the recognized local leader in its targeted market for convenience store products and gasoline dispensing services.

1.4 Management Team

The Company was founded by Roger Dunn. Mr. Dunn has more than 10 years of experience in the retail management industry. Through his expertise, he will be able to bring the operations of the business to profitability within its first year of operations.

1.5 Sales Forecasts

Mr. Dunn expects a strong rate of growth at the start of operations. Below are the expected financials over the next three years.

Proforma profit and loss (yearly)

Year	1	2	3
Sales	$5,635,739	$6,762,886	$7,912,577
Operating costs	$ 520,585	$ 554,903	$ 590,239
EBITDA	$ 184,784	$ 291,539	$ 400,099
Taxes, interest, and depreciation	$ 162,879	$ 176,736	$ 216,412
Net profit	$ 21,905	$ 114,803	$ 183,687

Sales, operating costs, and profit forecast

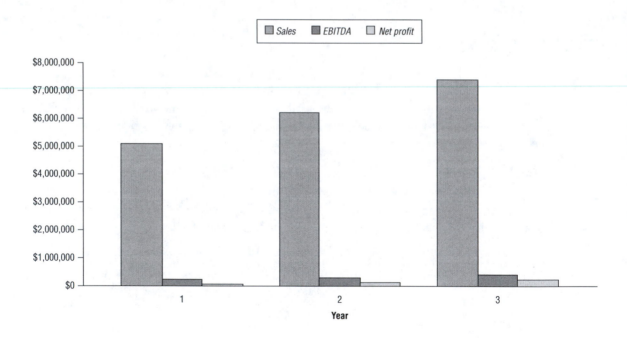

1.6 Expansion Plan

Mr. Dunn expects that the business will aggressively expand during the first three years of operation. He intends to implement marketing campaigns that will effectively target individuals within the target market.

2.0 COMPANY AND FINANCING SUMMARY

2.1 Registered Name and Corporate Structure

Rapid Roger's Gas Station is registered as a corporation in the State of New Jersey.

2.2 Required Funds

At this time, Rapid Roger's Gas Station requires $750,000 of debt funds. Below is a breakdown of how these funds will be used:

Projected startup costs

Initial lease payments and deposits	$150,000
Working capital	$ 52,500
FF&E	$150,000
Leasehold improvements	$200,000
Security deposits	$ 25,000
Store inventory	$ 12,500
Fuel pumps and related equipment	$175,000
Gasoline inventory	$ 75,000
Miscellaneous and unforeseen costs	$ 10,000
Total startup costs	**$850,000**

Use of funds

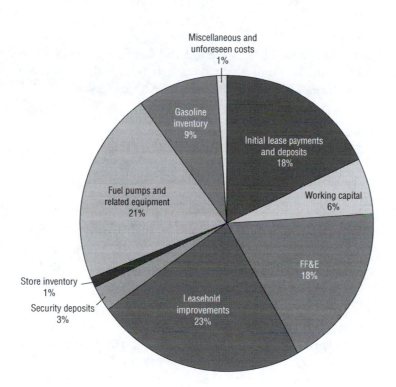

2.3 Investor Equity

Mr. Dunn is not seeking an investment from a third party at this time.

2.4 Management Equity

Roger Dunn owns 100% of Rapid Roger's Gas Station.

2.5 Exit Strategy

If the business is very successful, Mr. Dunn may seek to sell the business to a third party for a significant earnings multiple. Most likely, the Company will hire a qualified business broker to sell the business on behalf of Mr. Dunn. Based on historical numbers, the business could fetch a sales premium of up to 4 times earnings.

3.0 PRODUCTS AND SERVICES

Below is a description of the products offered by Rapid Roger's Gas Station.

3.1 Gasoline Sales

Management expects to sell more than 320,000 gallons of fuel per month to motorists within the target market area. This is by far the largest revenue center for the business, but it does not generate an overwhelming amount of profit. The Company will use the gas sales as a primary vehicle for bringing people into the convenience store.

3.2 Food, Beverage, Merchandise Sales

The primary profit center of Rapid Roger's Gas Station will be the retail sale of packaged food items, prepared food items, beverages (sodas, coffees, and bottled beverages), as well as other merchandise such as small toiletries, ancillary automotive merchandise (oil, fluids, ice scrapers, air fresheners, etc). The Company will offer an expansive number of these items throughout the location. On each item sold, the business generates approximately 40 cents of operating income.

3.3 Lottery Ticket Sales

In addition to the aforementioned food, beverage, and merchandise sales, the business will also provide sales of lottery tickets. This is an important revenue center for the franchise as this provides a highly predictable stream of revenue for the business on a day to day basis.

4.0 STRATEGIC AND MARKET ANALYSIS

4.1 Economic Outlook

This section of the analysis will detail the economic climate, the gas station industry, the customer profile, and the competition that the business will face as it progresses through its business operations.

Currently, the economic market condition in the United States is in recession. This slowdown in the economy has also greatly impacted real estate sales, which has halted to historical lows. Many economists expect that this recession will continue until mid-2010, at which point the economy will begin a prolonged recovery period.

A primary concern for the Company is its ability to price its services affordably during times of economic recession or spikes of oil prices. As of 2010, the price of oil and its associated refined energy products have reached multiyear highs with a moderate retraction in price. This increase in oil prices has caused costs increases among all industries. The reason Management is concerned about this increase in gas prices is that the discretionary income of customer's may decrease, and thus they will have less money to spend on convenience store items. However, the items sold within Rapid Roger's Gas Station are very affordable, and during times of higher living costs, Management does not expect that slight decreases in customer's discretionary income will have an impact on the business's ability to generate revenue.

4.2 Industry Analysis

Gas Stations

Within the United States, fueling stations within convenience stores generate more than $490 billion dollars a year of aggregate revenues and provide jobs for almost 1 million Americans. These locations are the heart of America's power infrastructure for individuals and commercial enterprises. The growth of this industry is expected to remain on pace with that of the general economy. There are approximately 100,000 companies that own and operate one or more fuel stations within the country.

However, there are substantial changes expected to occur within the industry over the next ten to twenty years as alternative fuels and energy sources become prevalent within the US economy. There are now several stations that beginning to offer alternative fuels such as ethanol, Biodiesel mixes, and electricity for hybrid vehicles.

Convenience Stores

Within the Untied States, there are more than 30,000 companies that operate one or more convenience store locations. Among these market providers, the aggregate revenue generated by these businesses on a yearly basis exceeds $20.3 billion dollars. The industry employs more than 138,000 and provides annual payrolls of $1.8 billion per year. This is a mature industry and Management expects that the future growth of the industry will remain on par with the US economy.

4.3 Customer Profile

Rapid Roger's Gas Station's average client will be a middle to upper middle class man or woman living in the Company's target market. Common traits among clients will include:

- Annual household income exceeding $30,000

- Lives or works no more than 15 miles from Rapid Roger's Gas Station

- Will spend $50 to $75 per visit

4.4 Competition

Competition within the gas station industry is difficult to gauge as gasoline is a commodity. The gasoline sold by one retailer is identical (or nearly identical) to the gasoline sold by any other retailer. However, the business will be able to retain a competitive advantage by maintaining stringent protocols for gasoline purchasing so that the business can remain modestly price flexible against other retailers within the area while providing convenience store products at reasonable prices.

5.0 MARKETING PLAN

Rapid Roger's Gas Station intends to maintain an extensive marketing campaign that will ensure maximum visibility for the business in its targeted market. Below is an overview of the marketing strategies and objectives of Rapid Roger's Gas Station.

5.1 Marketing Objectives

- Acquire a highly visible location from which Rapid Roger's Gas Station can conduct business operations.

- Regularly offer discounts on convenience store items to further drive sales.

5.2 Marketing Strategies

Mr. Dunn intends on using a number of marketing strategies that will allow Rapid Roger's Gas Station to easily target men and women within the target market. These strategies include traditional print advertisements, acquiring a highly visible retail location, and offering regular discounts on products sold throughout Rapid Roger's Gas Station's convenience store.

Foremost, the Company intends to acquire a highly visible retail location from which is can sell its gasoline and convenience store products. As gas stations typically maintain only minimal marketing campaigns, it is imperative that Mr. Dunn choose a location that will be easily seen by passers-by and motorists. Mr. Dunn is currently working with a number of real estate agents to find a prime location for Rapid Roger's Gas Station.

The Company will maintain a sizable amount of print and traditional advertising methods within local markets to promote the gasoline and convenience store products that the Company is selling.

5.3 Pricing

The Company's revenues are heavily dependent on the prevailing cost of gasoline inventories (and the underlying value of crude oil within the United States). As such, it is difficult to determine the income that the business will receive from gasoline sales as these prices are updated on a per diem basis. However, in regards to products sold through Rapid Roger's Gas Station's store, Management anticipates that the business will receive gross margins of 40% to 50% on each item sold.

6.0 ORGANIZATIONAL PLAN AND PERSONNEL SUMMARY

6.1 Corporate Organization

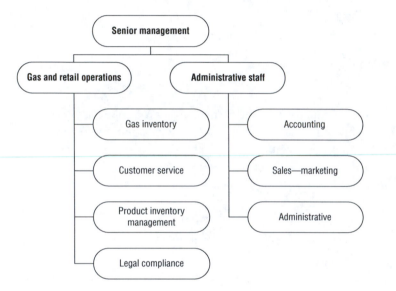

6.2 Organizational Budget

Personnel plan—yearly

Year	1	2	3
Owner	$ 40,000	$ 41,200	$ 42,436
Managers	$ 35,000	$ 36,050	$ 37,132
Store employees	$162,500	$167,375	$172,396
Bookkeeper	$ 19,000	$ 19,570	$ 20,157
Administrative	$ 22,000	$ 22,660	$ 23,340
Total	**$278,500**	**$286,855**	**$295,461**

Numbers of personnel

Owner	1	1	1
Managers	1	1	1
Store employees	5	5	5
Bookkeeper	1	1	1
Administrative	1	1	1
Totals	**9**	**9**	**9**

Personnel expense breakdown

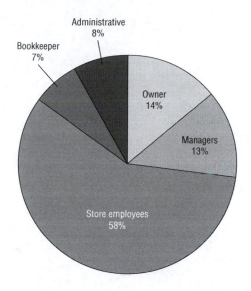

7.0 FINANCIAL PLAN

7.1 Underlying Assumptions

The Company has based its proforma financial statements on the following:

- Rapid Roger's Gas Station will have an annual revenue growth rate of 16% per year.

- The Owner will acquire $750,000 of debt funds to develop the business.

- The loan will have a 15 year term with a 9% interest rate.

7.2 Sensitivity Analysis

The Company's revenues are moderately sensitive to changes in the general economy. The price of oil and its associated refined energy products has hit all time highs, and as such, drivers have reduced their driving to offset these high energy prices. As such, this may translate into less traffic into Rapid Roger's Gas Station's convenience store. However, gasoline is a necessity, and only a severe economic recession would result in a decline in the Company's ability to maintain profitability.

7.3 Source of Funds

Financing

Equity contributions	
Management investment	$ 100,000.00
Total equity financing	**$100,000.00**
Banks and lenders	
Banks and lenders	$ 750,000.00
Total debt financing	$ 750,000.00
Total financing	**$850,000.00**

7.4 General Assumptions

General assumptions

Year	1	2	3
Short term interest rate	9.5%	9.5%	9.5%
Long term interest rate	10.0%	10.0%	10.0%
Federal tax rate	33.0%	33.0%	33.0%
State tax rate	5.0%	5.0%	5.0%
Personnel taxes	15.0%	15.0%	15.0%

7.5 Profit and Loss Statements

Proforma profit and loss (yearly)

Year	1	2	3
Sales	**$5,635,739**	**$6,762,886**	**$7,912,577**
Cost of goods sold	$4,930,370	$5,916,444	$6,922,239
Gross margin	12.52%	12.52%	12.52%
Operating income	**$ 705,369**	**$ 846,442**	**$ 990,337**
Expenses			
Payroll	$ 278,500	$ 286,855	$ 295,461
General and administrative	$ 25,200	$ 26,208	$ 27,256
Marketing expenses	$ 28,179	$ 33,814	$ 39,563
Professional fees and licensure	$ 15,219	$ 15,676	$ 16,146
Insurance costs	$ 21,987	$ 23,086	$ 24,241
Travel and vehicle costs	$ 17,596	$ 19,356	$ 21,291
Rent and utilities	$ 24,500	$ 25,725	$ 27,011
Miscellaneous costs	$ 67,629	$ 81,155	$ 94,951
Payroll taxes	$ 41,775	$ 43,028	$ 44,319
Total operating costs	**$ 520,585**	**$ 554,903**	**$ 590,239**
EBITDA	**$ 184,784**	**$ 291,539**	**$ 400,099**
Federal income tax	$ 60,979	$ 75,032	$ 111,696
State income tax	$ 9,239	$ 11,369	$ 16,924
Interest expense	$ 66,494	$ 64,168	$ 61,625
Depreciation expenses	$ 26,167	$ 26,167	$ 26,167
Net profit	**$ 21,905**	**$ 114,803**	**$ 183,687**
Profit margin	**0.39%**	**1.70%**	**2.32%**

Sales, operating costs, and profit forecast

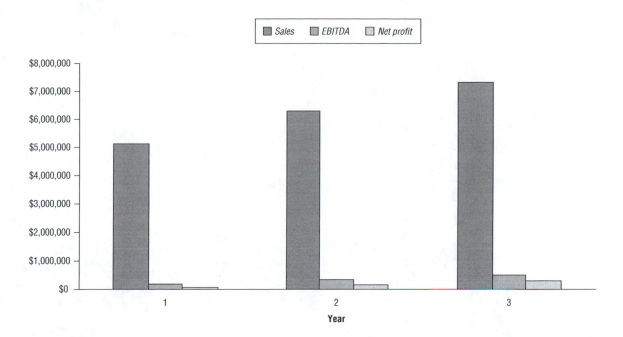

7.6 Cash Flow Analysis

Proforma cash flow analysis—yearly

Year	1	2	3
Cash from operations	$ 48,072	$140,970	$209,854
Cash from receivables	$ 0	$ 0	$ 0
Operating cash inflow	**$ 48,072**	**$140,970**	**$209,854**
Other cash inflows			
Equity investment	$100,000	$ 0	$ 0
Increased borrowings	$750,000	$ 0	$ 0
Sales of business assets	$ 0	$ 0	$ 0
A/P increases	$ 37,902	$ 43,587	$ 50,125
Total other cash inflows	**$887,902**	**$ 43,587**	**$ 50,125**
Total cash inflow	**$935,974**	**$184,557**	**$259,979**
Cash outflows			
Repayment of principal	$ 24,790	$ 27,116	$ 29,659
A/P decreases	$ 24,897	$ 29,876	$ 35,852
A/R increases	$ 0	$ 0	$ 0
Asset purchases	$797,500	$ 11,385	$ 18,019
Dividends	$ 18,626	$ 91,084	$144,156
Total cash outflows	**$865,813**	**$159,461**	**$227,686**
Net cash flow	**$ 70,161**	**$ 25,096**	**$ 32,293**
Cash balance	**$ 70,161**	**$ 95,258**	**$127,551**

Proforma cash flow (yearly)

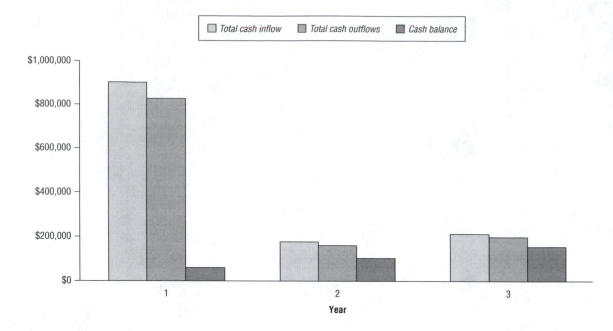

7.7 Balance Sheet

Proforma balance sheet—yearly

Year	1	2	3
Assets			
Cash	$ 70,161	$ 95,258	$127,551
Amortized development/expansion costs	$385,000	$386,139	$387,940
Fueling equipment	$175,000	$176,708	$179,411
FF&E	$150,000	$152,846	$157,351
Fuel inventories	$ 75,000	$ 78,985	$ 85,292
Store inventory	$ 12,500	$ 14,208	$ 16,911
Accumulated depreciation	($ 26,167)	($ 52,333)	($ 78,500)
Total assets	**$841,495**	**$851,810**	**$875,956**
Liabilities and equity			
Accounts payable	$ 13,005	$ 26,716	$ 40,990
Long term liabilities	$725,210	$698,094	$670,979
Other liabilities	$ 0	$ 0	$ 0
Total liabilities	**$738,215**	**$724,810**	**$711,969**
Net worth	**$103,280**	**$127,000**	**$163,987**
Total liabilities and equity	**$841,495**	**$851,810**	**$875,956**

Proforma balance sheet

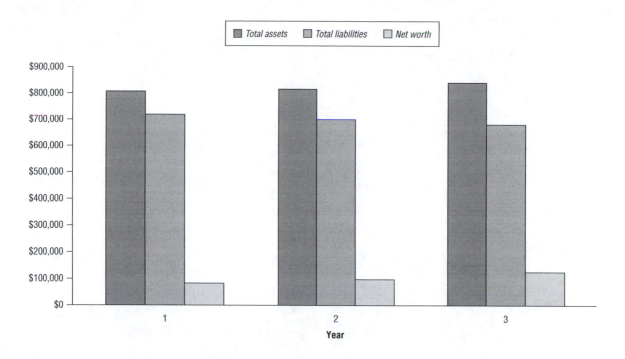

7.8 Breakeven Analysis

Monthly break even analysis

Year	1	2	3
Monthly revenue	$ 346,613	$ 369,463	$ 392,990
Yearly revenue	$4,159,355	$4,433,551	$4,715,877

Break even analysis

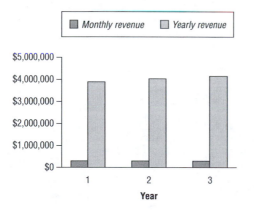

7.9 Business Ratios

Business ratios—yearly

Year	1	2	3
Sales			
Sales growth	0.0%	20.0%	17.0%
Gross margin	12.5%	12.5%	12.5%
Financials			
Profit margin	0.39%	1.70%	2.32%
Assets to liabilities	1.14	1.18	1.23
Equity to liabilities	0.14	0.18	0.23
Assets to equity	8.15	6.71	5.34
Liquidity			
Acid test	0.10	0.13	0.18
Cash to assets	0.08	0.11	0.15

7.10 Three Year Profit and Loss Statement

Profit and loss statement (first year)

Month	1	2	3	4	5	6	7
Sales	$469,000	$469,117	$469,235	$469,352	$469,469	$469,586	$469,704
Cost of goods sold	$410,300	$410,403	$410,505	$410,608	$410,710	$410,813	$410,915
Gross margin	12.5%	12.5%	12.5%	12.5%	12.5%	12.5%	12.5%
Operating income	$ 58,700	$ 58,715	$ 58,729	$ 58,744	$ 58,759	$ 58,773	$ 58,788
Expenses							
Payroll	$ 23,208	$ 23,208	$ 23,208	$ 23,208	$ 23,208	$ 23,208	$ 23,208
General and administrative	$ 2,100	$ 2,100	$ 2,100	$ 2,100	$ 2,100	$ 2,100	$ 2,100
Marketing expenses	$ 2,348	$ 2,348	$ 2,348	$ 2,348	$ 2,348	$ 2,348	$ 2,348
Professional fees and licensure	$ 1,268	$ 1,268	$ 1,268	$ 1,268	$ 1,268	$ 1,268	$ 1,268
Insurance costs	$ 1,832	$ 1,832	$ 1,832	$ 1,832	$ 1,832	$ 1,832	$ 1,832
Travel and vehicle costs	$ 1,466	$ 1,466	$ 1,466	$ 1,466	$ 1,466	$ 1,466	$ 1,466
Rent and utilities	$ 2,042	$ 2,042	$ 2,042	$ 2,042	$ 2,042	$ 2,042	$ 2,042
Miscellaneous costs	$ 5,636	$ 5,636	$ 5,636	$ 5,636	$ 5,636	$ 5,636	$ 5,636
Payroll taxes	$ 3,481	$ 3,481	$ 3,481	$ 3,481	$ 3,481	$ 3,481	$ 3,481
Total operating costs	$ 43,382	$ 43,382	$ 43,382	$ 43,382	$ 43,382	$ 43,382	$ 43,382
EBITDA	$ 15,318	$ 15,333	$ 15,347	$ 15,362	$ 15,377	$ 15,391	$ 15,406
Federal income tax	$ 5,075	$ 5,076	$ 5,077	$ 5,078	$ 5,080	$ 5,081	$ 5,082
State income tax	$ 769	$ 769	$ 769	$ 769	$ 770	$ 770	$ 770
Interest expense	$ 5,625	$ 5,610	$ 5,595	$ 5,580	$ 5,565	$ 5,550	$ 5,534
Depreciation expense	$ 2,181	$ 2,181	$ 2,181	$ 2,181	$ 2,181	$ 2,181	$ 2,181
Net profit	$ 1,669	$ 1,697	$ 1,725	$ 1,754	$ 1,782	$ 1,810	$ 1,839

Profit and loss statement (first year cont.)

Month	8	9	10	11	12	1
Sales	$469,821	$469,938	$470,055	$470,173	$470,290	$5,635,739
Cost of goods sold	$411,018	$411,121	$411,223	$411,326	$411,428	$4,930,370
Gross margin	12.5%	12.5%	12.5%	12.5%	12.5%	12.5%
Operating income	**$ 58,803**	**$ 58,817**	**$ 58,832**	**$ 58,847**	**$ 58,861**	**$ 705,369**
Expenses						
Payroll	$ 23,208	$ 23,208	$ 23,208	$ 23,208	$ 23,208	$ 278,500
General and administrative	$ 2,100	$ 2,100	$ 2,100	$ 2,100	$ 2,100	$ 25,200
Marketing expenses	$ 2,348	$ 2,348	$ 2,348	$ 2,348	$ 2,348	$ 28,179
Professional fees and licensure	$ 1,268	$ 1,268	$ 1,268	$ 1,268	$ 1,268	$ 15,219
Insurance costs	$ 1,832	$ 1,832	$ 1,832	$ 1,832	$ 1,832	$ 21,987
Travel and vehicle costs	$ 1,466	$ 1,466	$ 1,466	$ 1,466	$ 1,466	$ 17,596
Rent and utilities	$ 2,042	$ 2,042	$ 2,042	$ 2,042	$ 2,042	$ 24,500
Miscellaneous costs	$ 5,636	$ 5,636	$ 5,636	$ 5,636	$ 5,636	$ 67,629
Payroll taxes	$ 3,481	$ 3,481	$ 3,481	$ 3,481	$ 3,481	$ 41,775
Total operating costs	**$ 43,382**	**$ 43,382**	**$ 43,382**	**$ 43,382**	**$ 43,382**	**$ 520,585**
EBITDA	**$ 15,421**	**$ 15,435**	**$ 15,450**	**$ 15,465**	**$ 15,479**	**$ 184,784**
Federal income tax	$ 5,083	$ 5,085	$ 5,086	$ 5,087	$ 5,089	$ 60,979
State income tax	$ 770	$ 770	$ 771	$ 771	$ 771	$ 9,239
Interest expense	$ 5,519	$ 5,503	$ 5,487	$ 5,471	$ 5,455	$ 66,494
Depreciation expense	$ 2,181	$ 2,181	$ 2,181	$ 2,181	$ 2,181	$ 26,167
Net profit	**$ 1,868**	**$ 1,897**	**$ 1,926**	**$ 1,955**	**$ 1,984**	**$ 21,905**

Profit and loss statement (second year)

Quarter	Q1	2 Q2	Q3	Q4	2
Sales	$1,352,577	$1,690,722	$1,825,979	$1,893,608	$6,762,886
Cost of goods sold	$1,183,289	$1,479,111	$1,597,440	$1,656,604	$5,916,444
Gross margin	12.5%	12.5%	12.5%	12.5%	12.5%
Operating income	**$ 169,288**	**$ 211,611**	**$ 228,539**	**$ 237,004**	**$ 846,442**
Expenses					
Payroll	$ 57,371	$ 71,714	$ 77,451	$ 80,319	$ 286,855
General and administrative	$ 5,242	$ 6,552	$ 7,076	$ 7,338	$ 26,208
Marketing expenses	$ 6,763	$ 8,454	$ 9,130	$ 9,468	$ 33,814
Professional fees and licensure	$ 3,135	$ 3,919	$ 4,232	$ 4,389	$ 15,676
Insurance costs	$ 4,617	$ 5,772	$ 6,233	$ 6,464	$ 23,086
Travel and vehicle costs	$ 3,871	$ 4,839	$ 5,226	$ 5,420	$ 19,356
Rent and utilities	$ 5,145	$ 6,431	$ 6,946	$ 7,203	$ 25,725
Miscellaneous costs	$ 16,231	$ 20,289	$ 21,912	$ 22,723	$ 81,155
Payroll taxes	$ 8,606	$ 10,757	$ 11,618	$ 12,048	$ 43,028
Total operating costs	**$ 110,981**	**$ 138,726**	**$ 149,824**	**$ 155,373**	**$ 554,903**
EBITDA	**$ 58,308**	**$ 72,885**	**$ 78,716**	**$ 81,631**	**$ 291,539**
Federal income tax	$ 15,006	$ 18,758	$ 20,259	$ 21,009	$ 75,032
State income tax	$ 2,274	$ 2,842	$ 3,070	$ 3,183	$ 11,369
Interest expense	$ 16,268	$ 16,120	$ 15,968	$ 15,813	$ 64,168
Depreciation expense	$ 6,542	$ 6,542	$ 6,542	$ 6,542	$ 26,167
Net profit	**$ 18,218**	**$ 28,623**	**$ 32,878**	**$ 35,085**	**$ 114,803**

Profit and loss statement (third year)

Quarter	Q1	3 Q2	Q3	Q4	3
Sales	$1,582,515	$1,978,144	$2,136,396	$2,215,522	$7,912,577
Cost of goods sold	$1,384,448	$1,730,560	$1,869,005	$1,938,227	$6,922,239
Gross margin	12.5%	12.5%	12.5%	12.5%	12.5%
Operating income	$ 198,067	$ 247,584	$ 267,391	$ 277,294	$ 990,337
Expenses					
Payroll	$ 59,092	$ 73,865	$ 79,774	$ 82,729	$ 295,461
General and administrative	$ 5,451	$ 6,814	$ 7,359	$ 7,632	$ 27,256
Marketing expenses	$ 7,913	$ 9,891	$ 10,682	$ 11,078	$ 39,563
Professional fees and licensure	$ 3,229	$ 4,036	$ 4,359	$ 4,521	$ 16,146
Insurance costs	$ 4,848	$ 6,060	$ 6,545	$ 6,787	$ 24,241
Travel and vehicle costs	$ 4,258	$ 5,323	$ 5,749	$ 5,962	$ 21,291
Rent and utilities	$ 5,402	$ 6,753	$ 7,293	$ 7,563	$ 27,011
Miscellaneous costs	$ 18,990	$ 23,738	$ 25,637	$ 26,586	$ 94,951
Payroll taxes	$ 8,864	$ 11,080	$ 11,966	$ 12,409	$ 44,319
Total operating costs	$ 118,048	$ 147,560	$ 159,364	$ 165,267	$ 590,239
EBITDA	$ 80,020	$ 100,025	$ 108,027	$ 112,028	$ 400,099
Federal income tax	$ 22,339	$ 27,924	$ 30,158	$ 31,275	$ 111,696
State income tax	$ 3,385	$ 4,231	$ 4,569	$ 4,739	$ 16,924
Interest expense	$ 15,654	$ 15,491	$ 15,325	$ 15,155	$ 61,625
Depreciation expense	$ 6,542	$ 6,542	$ 6,542	$ 6,542	$ 26,167
Net profit	$ 32,100	$ 45,837	$ 51,433	$ 54,317	$ 183,687

7.11 Three Year Cash Flow Analysis

Cash flow analysis (first year)

Month	1	2	3	4	5	6	7	8
Cash from operations	$ 3,849	$ 3,878	$ 3,906	$ 3,934	$ 3,962	$ 3,991	$ 4,020	$ 4,048
Cash from receivables	$ 0	$ 0	$ 0	$ 0	$ 0	$ 0	$ 0	$ 0
Operating cash inflow	$ 3,849	$ 3,878	$ 3,906	$ 3,934	$ 3,962	$ 3,991	$ 4,020	$ 4,048
Other cash inflows								
Equity investment	$100,000	$ 0	$ 0	$ 0	$ 0	$ 0	$ 0	$ 0
Increased borrowings	$750,000	$ 0	$ 0	$ 0	$ 0	$ 0	$ 0	$ 0
Sales of business assets	$ 0	$ 0	$ 0	$ 0	$ 0	$ 0	$ 0	$ 0
A/P increases	$ 3,159	$ 3,159	$ 3,159	$ 3,159	$ 3,159	$ 3,159	$ 3,159	$ 3,159
Total other cash inflows	$853,159	$ 3,159	$ 3,159	$ 3,159	$ 3,159	$ 3,159	$ 3,159	$ 3,159
Total cash inflow	$857,008	$ 7,036	$ 7,064	$ 7,093	$ 7,121	$ 7,150	$ 7,178	$ 7,207
Cash outflows								
Repayment of principal	$ 1,982	$ 1,997	$ 2,012	$ 2,027	$ 2,042	$ 2,057	$ 2,073	$ 2,088
A/P decreases	$ 2,075	$ 2,075	$ 2,075	$ 2,075	$ 2,075	$ 2,075	$ 2,075	$ 2,075
A/R increases	$ 0	$ 0	$ 0	$ 0	$ 0	$ 0	$ 0	$ 0
Asset purchases	$797,500	$ 0	$ 0	$ 0	$ 0	$ 0	$ 0	$ 0
Dividends	$ 0	$ 0	$ 0	$ 0	$ 0	$ 0	$ 0	$ 0
Total cash outflows	$801,557	$ 4,072	$ 4,087	$ 4,102	$ 4,117	$ 4,132	$ 4,148	$ 4,163
Net cash flow	$ 55,451	$ 2,964	$ 2,978	$ 2,991	$ 3,004	$ 3,017	$ 3,031	$ 3,044
Cash balance	$ 55,451	$58,416	$61,393	$64,384	$67,388	$70,406	$73,436	$76,480

Cash flow analysis (first year cont.)

Month	9	10	11	12	1
Cash from operations	$ 4,077	$ 4,106	$ 4,135	$ 4,165	$ 48,072
Cash from receivables	$ 0	$ 0	$ 0	$ 0	$ 0
Operating cash inflow	**$ 4,077**	**$ 4,106**	**$ 4,135**	**$ 4,165**	**$ 48,072**
Other cash inflows					
Equity investment	$ 0	$ 0	$ 0	$ 0	$100,000
Increased borrowings	$ 0	$ 0	$ 0	$ 0	$750,000
Sales of business assets	$ 0	$ 0	$ 0	$ 0	$ 0
A/P increases	$ 3,159	$ 3,159	$ 3,159	$ 3,159	$ 37,902
Total other cash inflows	**$ 3,159**	**$ 3,159**	**$ 3,159**	**$ 3,159**	**$887,902**
Total cash inflow	**$ 7,236**	**$ 7,265**	**$ 7,294**	**$ 7,323**	**$935,974**
Cash outflows					
Repayment of principal	$ 2,104	$ 2,120	$ 2,136	$ 2,152	$ 24,790
A/P decreases	$ 2,075	$ 2,075	$ 2,075	$ 2,075	$ 24,897
A/R increases	$ 0	$ 0	$ 0	$ 0	$ 0
Asset purchases	$ 0	$ 0	$ 0	$ 0	$797,500
Dividends	$ 0	$ 0	$ 0	$18,626	$ 18,626
Total cash outflows	**$ 4,179**	**$ 4,195**	**$ 4,211**	**$22,853**	**$865,813**
Net cash flow	**$ 3,057**	**$ 3,070**	**$ 3,083**	**−$15,529**	**$ 70,161**
Cash balance	**$79,537**	**$82,607**	**$ 85,690**	**$70,161**	**$ 70,161**

Cash flow analysis (second year)

Quarter	Q1	2 Q2	Q3	Q4	2
Cash from operations	$28,194	$35,242	$38,062	$39,472	$140,970
Cash from receivables	$ 0	$ 0	$ 0	$ 0	$ 0
Operating cash inflow	**$28,194**	**$35,242**	**$38,062**	**$39,472**	**$140,970**
Other cash inflows					
Equity investment	$ 0	$ 0	$ 0	$ 0	$ 0
Increased borrowings	$ 0	$ 0	$ 0	$ 0	$ 0
Sales of business assets	$ 0	$ 0	$ 0	$ 0	$ 0
A/P increases	$ 8,717	$10,897	$11,769	$12,204	$ 43,587
Total other cash inflows	**$ 8,717**	**$10,897**	**$11,769**	**$12,204**	**$ 43,587**
Total cash inflow	**$36,911**	**$46,139**	**$49,830**	**$51,676**	**$184,557**
Cash outflows					
Repayment of principal	$ 6,553	$ 6,701	$ 6,853	$ 7,008	$ 27,116
A/P decreases	$ 5,975	$ 7,469	$ 8,067	$ 8,365	$ 29,876
A/R increases	$ 0	$ 0	$ 0	$ 0	$ 0
Asset purchases	$ 2,277	$ 2,846	$ 3,074	$ 3,188	$ 11,385
Dividends	$18,217	$22,771	$24,593	$25,503	$ 91,084
Total cash outflows	**$33,022**	**$39,788**	**$42,586**	**$44,065**	**$159,461**
Net cash flow	**$ 3,890**	**$ 6,352**	**$ 7,244**	**$ 7,611**	**$ 25,096**
Cash balance	**$74,051**	**$80,403**	**$87,647**	**$95,258**	**$ 95,258**

Cash flow analysis (third year)

Quarter	Q1	3 Q2	Q3	Q4	3
Cash from operations	$ 41,971	$ 52,463	$ 56,661	$ 58,759	$ 209,854
Cash from receivables	$ 0	$ 0	$ 0	$ 0	$ 0
Operating cash inflow	**$ 41,971**	**$ 52,463**	**$ 56,661**	**$ 58,759**	**$ 209,854**
Other cash inflows					
Equity investment	$ 0	$ 0	$ 0	$ 0	$ 0
Increased borrowings	$ 0	$ 0	$ 0	$ 0	$ 0
Sales of business assets	$ 0	$ 0	$ 0	$ 0	$ 0
A/P increases	$ 10,025	$ 12,531	$ 13,534	$ 14,035	$ 50,125
Total other cash inflows	**$ 10,025**	**$ 12,531**	**$ 13,534**	**$ 14,035**	**$ 50,125**
Total cash inflow	**$ 51,996**	**$ 64,995**	**$ 70,194**	**$ 72,794**	**$ 259,979**
Cash outflows					
Repayment of principal	$ 7,167	$ 7,330	$ 7,496	$ 7,666	$ 29,659
A/P decreases	$ 7,170	$ 8,963	$ 9,680	$ 10,038	$ 35,852
A/R increases	$ 0	$ 0	$ 0	$ 0	$ 0
Asset purchases	$ 3,604	$ 4,505	$ 4,865	$ 5,045	$ 18,019
Dividends	$ 28,831	$ 36,039	$ 38,922	$ 40,364	$ 144,156
Total cash outflows	**$ 46,773**	**$ 56,837**	**$ 60,963**	**$ 63,113**	**$ 227,686**
Net cash flow	**$ 5,223**	**$ 8,158**	**$ 9,231**	**$ 9,681**	**$ 32,293**
Cash balance	**$100,481**	**$108,639**	**$117,870**	**$127,551**	**$ 127,551**

Ice Cream Shop

Fran's Ice

Davis Plaza Regional Mall
19 Orchard Avenue
Davis, CA 95616

Paul Greenland

This plan originally appeared in Business Plans Handbook, Volume 3. It has been updated for this edition.

INTRODUCTION

The purpose of this business plan is to outline the parameters under which the principals will pursue the construction, development, and operation of a franchised Fran's Ice Cream Shoppe in a key location at the mall entrance to the food court of Davis Plaza, a successful, dominant, super regional shopping center in metropolitan Woodland - Sacramento.

Davis Plaza's management company, Martin Richardson, and the franchisor, the Fran's Ice Shoppe Company, Inc., are optimistic and enthusiastic about locating a high-volume shop within Davis Plaza.

Martin Richardson, The Fran's Ice Shoppe Company, Inc., and the franchisees, Augustus and Cheryl Dwyer, are all confident that this Fran's shop will be successful among the other national stores already committed to doing business in Davis Plaza.

EXECUTIVE SUMMARY

The Fran's Ice Shoppe of Davis (franchisee) will construct, develop, and operate a licensed franchised ice cream dipping shop of The Fran's Ice Shoppe Company, Inc. (franchisor). This single retail dipping shop will sell Fran's ice cream and related products, all manufactured by the franchisor under its name.

Revenue will be primarily from the sale of hand-dipped ice cream and related products consumed within Davis Plaza. Franchisees will also sell ice cream cakes, traditional gourmet cakes, birthday cakes, and assorted beverages. Sales are anticipated to be $497,400 in the first year and to increase at an average annual rate of 4 percent per year in the first five years of operation.

The franchise will be located in Davis Plaza in Davis, California. Because of its location in the center of the Woodland - Sacramento areas, Davis Plaza serves many communities and is commonly considered the Tri-Cities' premier retail facility. Davis Plaza, which opened in 1968, is a two-level, enclosed regional shopping center containing a total of 1.2 million square feet and 200 stores, shops, and food service establishments. The Plaza is anchored by Hank's, B.P.'s, and Westbury's. Fran's Ice Shoppe of Davis will be located in "The Outdoorum," Davis Plaza's 40,000-square-foot food court, which contains 17 food service establishments, including Cheese Pleese, Beefeaters, and Sweet Dreams.

Franchisee's primary customers will be drawn from Davis Plaza's 2009 trade area population of over 853,000 people, which is projected to reach 940,000 people by 2019. Customers shopping The Plaza will purchase Fran's hand-dipped ice cream and other products on an impulse basis during their shopping trip, or as a dessert treat upon completing a meal at The Outdoorum. Franchisee also anticipates that many patrons will make the shop their primary destination due to name recognition and product quality. Except for a small Earl's Ice Cream Shop and a Frozen Treat selling soft serve vanilla only, there is no other competition within Davis Plaza, and no outside competition within 2 miles of The Plaza.

The principals will be managing their own shop. Augustus Dwyer will be the hands-on manager for daily operations. Cheryl Dwyer will retain her present position as a nurse clinician for J. Landers, but will assist with her employee management and accounting skills. In addition, approximately six to ten high school and/or college students will be hired to work shifts during peak sales periods. Other part-time employees may be hired on an "as needed" basis for special projects such as cake decorating, preparing large orders for caterers, and the servicing of other special functions.

Project costs are projected to be $300,000 which includes leasehold improvements (build-out of the shop), equipment purchases, opening inventory, and working capital needs. This amount does not include the $35,000 franchise fee, Fran's $3,500 grand opening contribution, or the $7,870 cost of architect's plans for the store which Gus and Cheryl Dwyer have already invested in this business from their own funds. The principals are seeking to finance the remainder of this project through a local lending institution using the assistance of a Small Business Administration (SBA) guarantee, with an agreement that allows for loan repayment over 10 years.

Based on a preliminary timetable it is anticipated that the shop will be operational for business no later than April, 1, 2010.

FACT SHEET

Requested Loan: $300,000

Cash Invested: $50,000

Business Type: Fran's Ice Franchise Ice Cream Shop

Location: In the food court of Davis Plaza Regional Mall in Davis, California

Size: 556 Sq. Ft.

Rent: $5,000 gross (includes all CAM charges) or $8.99/sq. ft.

Projected Sales - Year 1: $497,400

Sales Break-even: $408,490

Loan Collateral Available: $125,000 Equipment Value, $50,000 Equity in home, and $16,000 Opening Inventory

Principals: Augustus and Cheryl Dwyer

Home Address: 37 Huckleberry Lane, Fair Oaks CA 95628

Other Noteworthy Facts:

- A 2.5 gallon tub of ice cream from Fran's costs $40

- From a 2.5 gallon tub come 72 4 oz. scoops which sell for $2.00 to $2.75 a scoop. Therefore, a tub will sell for $144 to $198.

- Average ticket for a Fran's shop runs around $3.20.

DESCRIPTION OF BUSINESS OBJECTIVES

The Fran's Ice Shoppe of Davis (Shoppe), will be a franchised operation of The Fran's Ice Shoppe Company, Inc. licensed to sell Fran's ice cream and related products. The Fran's name has been associated with the ice cream business since 1961. The company manufactures a large and growing volume of Fran's products, which it distributes through a variety of channels. The ice cream ordinarily is not sold for retail dipping except to franchised dipping shops.

The Franchisor is a Connecticut corporation, with principal offices in New Haven, Connecticut. The ultimate parent of the company is Drake PLC, a public corporation listed on the London Stock Exchange, via ownership of The Harley Company.

Franchisees have been granted a license to sell certain ice cream products under the Fran's name since 1977, although the franchisor has been conducting a business of the type operated by the franchisee since 1983. Affiliates of the franchisor are actively engaged in various other sectors of the food service industry, including fast service restaurants, theme restaurants, food service supply, institutional and retail food production, distribution and sales, and food commodity transactions.

The main items for sale will be hand dipped ice cream and yogurt cups/cones; sundaes finished with a variety of toppings such as hot fudge, caramel, butterscotch, or fruit; banana splits; shakes; malts; and ice cream sodas and floats. Most of these items will be consumed immediately on the premises. Davis Plaza provides extensive indoor seating for the food court customers.

In addition to hand-dipped ice cream sales, the Shoppe anticipates doing a material business in the sale of both ice cream cakes and gourmet traditional cakes and birthday cakes. These cakes will be displayed for immediate sale at all times during business hours and can also be produced in quantity on a special order basis for caterers and parties. Phenomenal foot traffic in the plaza and employees from the 200 shops in the mall can support a lucrative cake business for the Shoppe.

The goals and objectives of The Fran's Ice Shoppe of Davis are as follows:

> To deliver a quality product in a consistent, courteous and timely manner in order to have the customer return again for another satisfying, flavorsome treat, while at the same time earning a reasonable return on the initial investment.

The principals believe that for an organization to be successful, the organization must ensure that the customer continues to return to purchase the product, again and again. One way to ensure repeat business is to provide consistency in both the product and service. Fran's product speaks for itself; the service our Shoppe provides will be a function of training, evaluation, and retraining in order to deliver it courteously and in a timely manner.

In order to earn a reasonable return on the investment, along with the ability to repay debt, strict cost-control measures will be implemented. These measures will include, among others, proper and prudent purchasing practices, maximization of product distribution through strict adherence to weights, amounts and recipes (portion control), effective utilization of personnel, and the constant search for ways to reduce the cost of sales of our products without sacrificing quality and service.

In summary, the principals are committed to ensuring that this operation is successful.

THE MARKET

The purchase of hand-dipped ice cream and related products is basically an impulse-type purchase by a consumer relating to one of the following stimuli:

- Passing by the Shoppe on the way to another destination

- Visual contact with the Shoppe's signs

- Observing someone else consuming one of the Shoppe's products

- The final course (dessert) after a meal has been consumed elsewhere

Locating the Shoppe in Davis Plaza gives the business the opportunity to take advantage of all of them and the above mentioned ways that motivate the consumer to purchase the products offered.

Passing by on the Way to Another Destination

Davis Plaza is comprised of the best known, nationally recognized retail stores and outlets. The unique blend of these operations draws a large cross section of the population to the Plaza to shop for a variety of goods and services. The Fran's Ice Shoppe of Davis will be a 556-square-foot store located at the entrance to the mall's food court. It is on the second level, right across from the main escalators carrying shoppers from the lower to the second level. It is between the main parking structure and B.P.'s, requiring all B.P.'s patrons entering from the main parking structure to pass directly in front of the Shoppe on their way to B.P.'s. The Shoppe is well within walking distance from anywhere in Davis Plaza in five minutes or less. Because of its location, many patrons of the Plaza will pass by the Shoppe on the way to and from another store, making it convenient for an impulse purchase.

Visual Contact from the Shoppe's Sign

Signage is planned for the Shoppe in two locations. Large, colorful neon signs will be located over the dipping cabinets, making them visible from both the food court and from down the mall. Since the Shoppe will be in a corner location, the Shoppe will be visible from several directions in the "I" shaped mall. There is also an opening to below directly in front of the Shoppe, allowing visibility to patrons on the lower level. The location for the Shoppe has the greatest amount of foot traffic in front of it than any other food service in Davis Plaza.

Observing Someone Else Consuming One of the Products

As previously mentioned, the Shoppe's products more than likely will be consumed on or nearby the premises. The fact that Davis Plaza is enclosed and self-contained will make Fran's products very visible to many shoppers, particularly since all products will be served in containers that display the Fran's logo.

The Final Course (Dessert) After a Meal has been Consumed Elsewhere

In addition to the tremendous foot traffic generated by the major department stores and numerous nationally renowned shops surrounding The Fran's Ice Shoppe of Davis, the Shoppe is to be located at the entrance to The Outdoorum, the Plaza's food court. The food court houses 17 places to eat. The Shoppe can be seen from anywhere in the food court, making it a likely destination for a dessert treat following a meal for the entire family. The Shoppe will have two 3-foot-wide, 4-shelf display cases for cakes. One 3-foot display will be for frozen ice cream cakes, and the other will be refrigerated for display of traditional gourmet cakes and gourmet birthday cakes. The principals believe that tremendous potential exists for the sale of birthday cakes in the Plaza since many gifts are purchased there and no competition exists for these items in the Plaza.

An additional marketing strategy of the Shoppe will be sales generated from freezer carts bearing the Fran's logo and colors off site from Davis Plaza. There are many fairs, festivals, and parties within the Shoppe's geographic service area (including the Sacramento County Fair and Renaissance Days) where significant additional sales may be generated on ice cream bars and other novelties. Most importantly, these outside sales will give the Shoppe name recognition, which will help make it a primary destination for an expanded segment of the market.

Additional methods of enhancing the Shoppe's name recognition will include Web marketing (a Fran's Web site is included as part of the franchise agreement), the use of social media channels like Twitter to communicate specials, local newspaper advertising with coupons, special promotions and discounts to employees of Davis Plaza, companion promotions and discounts with other merchants in the Plaza, and offers to local schools for discounts to students with good grades.

Lastly, additional sales revenue and name recognition for the Shoppe will be generated by sponsoring sports, social, educational, and fund-raising activities within the communities served by Davis Plaza. The principals have numerous fund-raising ideas and plans for community involvement that will help make the Shoppe a money-maker.

COMPETITIVE ANALYSIS

The primary competitors of The Fran's Ice Shoppe of Davis are within the Davis Plaza itself. The principals have done a detailed analysis of the existing ice cream and yogurt shops outside Davis Plaza, and this study is available upon request. The principals believe that the two ice cream and yogurt related businesses inside Davis Plaza are the Shoppe's main competition. They are:

Frozen Treat

Frozen Treat (located across The Outdoorum from the Shoppe) does not serve real ice cream at all. They serve only one flavor of soft serve—vanilla. They make cones, cups, sundaes, and shakes and, according to Davis Plaza management, enjoyed $$650,000 in sales volume in 2008 and approximately the same sales volume in 2009.

Earl's Ice Cream and Yogurt

Earl's Ice Cream and Yogurt is located in the Westbury wing of Davis Plaza. This is a small shop with extremely limited visibility. It is not located in The Outdoorum but is on the outskirts of the heavy traffic area of the Plaza.

Earl's serves 24 flavors of real ice cream and two flavors of frozen yogurt. No cakes are offered for sale. According to Davis Plaza management, Earl's enjoyed $420,000 in sales volume in 2008 and approximately the same sales volume in 2009.

The principals believe that there is outstanding potential for the sale of Fran's super premium quality ice cream, yogurt, and related products in Davis Plaza. As just noted, in 2008 and 2009 the sales volume generated for ice cream, frozen yogurt, and soft serve in Davis Plaza was nearly $1.1 million. The Fran's Ice Shoppe of Davis will be located in the most visible food service location in Davis Plaza. The principals feel that Frozen Treat will not hinder the Shoppe's sales because Frozen Treat serves only average quality soft serve vanilla products. The Shoppe will have 32 flavors of the finest quality ice cream and six flavors of frozen yogurt and sorbet ready for sale at all times, as well as ice cream cakes, birthday cakes, gourmet traditional cakes by the slice or whole, and shakes, malts, sundaes, ice cream bars, frozen yogurt and sorbet bars, and sodas.

Other ice cream and frozen yogurt stores exist within a 3-mile radius of Davis Plaza. There are four small independent stores and three Scoops stores in this 3-mile circle. The closest independent to the Plaza is approximately 2 miles away. As stated previously, the principals strongly believe that the Shoppe's main and most important competitors are inside Davis Plaza. The principals also firmly believe that the quality and selection of Fran's products, coupled with a superior location within the Davis Plaza, will help them achieve the success. The principals are also actively engaged in negotiations with the landlord to exclude any new competition from the Plaza during the term of their lease.

MANAGEMENT

The principals will personally manage this business. Augustus Dwyer will be the hands-on manager for the daily operation of the Shoppe, assisted by Cheryl Dwyer. Gus Dwyer shall have the following responsibilities and perform the following duties:

- Oversee the design, development, and construction of the Shoppe

- Collect competitive bids for the build-out of the Shoppe and for the equipment needed for the Shoppe.

- Select contractors and equipment suppliers to complete the Shoppe.

- Seek and obtain the necessary financing for this project.

- Attend and successfully complete Fran's Ice Basic Management Training Course # 318 at The Fran's Ice Shoppe Company, Inc. corporate offices in New Haven Connecticut. This is an 11-day training course that will prepare Gus to successfully operate a Fran's ice cream shop.

- Plan, coordinate, and execute merchandising and promotion of the Shoppe, including grand opening activities, and a year-round calendar of holidays, special events, and numerous other promotional activities.

- Prepare all products to be sold, sourcing the most cost effective suppliers on goods not purchased from Fran's directly. Maintain adequate levels of inventory, while maximizing inventory turns and losing no sales due to out-of-stocks.

- Ensure that standards of product quality control and shop cleanliness required by the franchisor are maintained on a daily basis.

- Recruit, select, interview, and hire all Shoppe personnel.

- Perform orientation, training, and re-training of all Shoppe personnel.

- Perform all required accounting functions for the Shoppe.

- Personally make a commitment to give 100 percent best effort and a personal full-time commitment to operating the Shoppe to its greatest potential. Gus will demonstrate the leadership necessary to operate the Shoppe successfully on a daily basis, and to ensure an acceptable return on the initial investment and repayment of debt.

The principals will designate certain properly trained personnel who will coordinate the activities of the other employees during periods when Augustus Dwyer is not on the premises. Those employees will be trained to make prudent decisions in the absence of Gus Dwyer and to carry out the duties of the manager on an as-needed basis. In the event of an emergency, the principals can be contacted by cell phone and be on-site within 15 minutes.

PERSONNEL

Six to eight high school and/or college students will be hired to work at the Shoppe on a part-time basis. There will be no full-time employees of the Shoppe other than management.

The principals are developing a program of orientation and training which all Shoppe employees must complete prior to starting work. A written policies and procedures manual will be the foundation for that that training. All Shoppe employees will be trained to perform all customer service, quality control, and cleanliness and sanitation procedures utilized by the Shoppe, and will know exactly what is expected of them as a Fran's Ice Shoppe employee.

The principals have worked for many different supervisors in their 37 years of combined work experience, and have seen many different management techniques and styles. Augustus Dwyer has extensive management experience in both retail and wholesale sales and customer service. Cheryl Dwyer brings to Fran's a wealth of experience as house supervisor at the 205-bed J. Landers Hospital, supervising 60 or more nurses at a time. The combined management experience that the principals have will be an asset to them in training and managing a productive team of Shoppe employees.

DEVELOPMENT TIMETABLE

The proposed timetable for the project is as follows:

Activity Target Timetable

- Site selection approved by Fran's—May 11, 2009

- Franchise Agreement signed and franchise fee/grand opening contribution paid to Fran's by principals—Nov. 26, 2009

- Submitted lease proposal to Martin Richardson (Davis Plaza management firm)—Nov. 28, 2009

- Received draft lease from attorneys for Martin Richardson and forwarded lease to principals' lease attorney, Chip Barker of Burns, Webster, Paquette, Walton, and Weigand—Dec. 20, 2009

- Submit business plan and loan application to financing institution for review and approval of loan request—Jan. 8, 2010

- Receive loan approval from lender and SBA—Jan. 15, 2010

- Receive complete blueprints and drawings of leasehold improvements for the Shoppe from Lee Freemont Architecture & Design, Detroit, Mich.—Jan 15, 2010

- Attend and successfully complete all courses offered at Fran's Ice Basic Management Training Course 318 in New Haven, Conn.—Jan. 16-26, 2010

- Perform competitive bid process for leasehold improvements (buildout of Shoppe), purchase all Shoppe equipment—Jan. 27, 2010

- Award contracts and commence buildout of Shoppe—Feb. 1, 2010

- Grand Opening—April 1, 2010

PRINCIPALS' PROFILES

Augustus Herman Dwyer

A strong, responsible businessman and manager, Augustus Dwyer has over 21 years experience in retailing, wholesaling, and customer service. Gus' roots are in the grocery industry, where he was employed for 14 years. The first five years Gus spent working at store level as a boxboy, grocery clerk, produce clerk, and produce department manager. He was elevated by division corporate personnel who felt that his talents would be best utilized at the division level and promoted to division produce and floral buyer.

During this nine-year period, Gus' hands-on approach to his work greatly benefited his company. Gus planned, researched, and implemented a program of fresh fruit, soup, and salad bars for the company and personally assisted in the set-up of 41 new salad bars division-wide. Gus was also responsible for planning the division's floral program and purchased cut flowers and plants for 110 stores for four years.

Utilizing his knowledge and experience in the floral trade, Gus now works as national sales manager for a flower wholesaling company in San Francisco. He has an outstanding record in high volume sales and increasing sales revenues. He has expanded the customer base, sourced new suppliers, and increased the variety of product his company sells, resulting in a 30 percent increase in sales since coming on board with the company.

Gus' strengths include the ability to plan, organize, achieve results quickly, and evaluate and implement winning marketing strategies. He has significant influence with other employees and positively motivates his subordinates and peers. He is an experienced buyer, merchandiser, salesman, and customer satisfaction specialist.

Cheryl Lynn Dwyer

An experienced nurse manager, Cheryl's nursing background involves a total of 10 years as a Registered Nurse, all employed with J. Landers. Seven of these years have been dedicated to the management of medical-surgical and maternal child health nursing services. Accountabilities include yearly performance evaluations of approximately 45 employees and the general supervision of J. Landers Florin on the evening shift of the entire hospital, which averages 120 employees. All problems unresolved are directed to her for her successful resolution and follow-up.

Cheryl is responsible for the successful planning and implementation of the Medical-Surgical Department Quality Management Program, which encompasses directing nurses in data collection, action plans, and evaluation on a monthly basis. She has completed a 12-week, total quality management (TQM) course and participated in two task forces utilizing TQM.

Cheryl's strengths include effective organization and leadership abilities and extensive interpersonal skills. Cheryl has seven years of experience hiring successful employees and coaching, counseling, and motivating them to deliver the best nursing care to J. Landers members.

FINANCIAL INFORMATION

Equipment schedule

Item description	Lowest bid
16 can illuminated dipping cabinet	$ 4,459
8 can illuminated dipping cabinet—2 units	$ 5,490
Dipper well—4 units	$ 612
Upright pie & freezer display case	$ 8,086
Refrigerated pastry display case	$ 6,482
27" Fountainette cabinet	$ 2,406
Drop-in ice cream bar freezer	$ 1,721
Single door reach-in freezer	$ 2,645
Single door reach-in flash freezer	$ 4,474
Single door reach-in refrigerator	$ 2,214
6 x 8 ft - 15 degree walk-in freezer	$ 5,990
Medium capacity (1 phase-air cooled) ice machine	$ 3,280
Soft-serve (3 phase-AC) machine w/ faucet—2 units	$ 24,130

Dispensing & topping units

Dip-coat warmer—2 units	$ 336
Butterscotch & fudge warmer with pump—3 units	$ 816
Milk shake machine	$ 730
5-quart mixer	$ 534
Spoon dispenser—4 units	$ 46

Sink units

2-compartment sink	$ 2,046
Counter MTD 2-comp hand sink	$ 410
Wall mounted hand sink	$ 350

Beverage dispensing equipment

Soft drink dispenser with ice bin (supplied by Coca-Cola at no charge)	$ 0
Carbonator with double check valve (supplied by Coca-Cola at no charge)	$ 0
Wall mounted syrup pumps (supplied by Coca-Cola at no charge)	$ 0
CO-2 tanks (supplied by Coca-Cola at no charge)	$ 0
Automatic coffee maker	$ 656
Coffee grinder	$ 742
Cup dispensers—10 units required	$ 539
Lid organizer	$ 79

Storage equipment units

6 x 8 Freezer storage shelving set	$ 873
18" x 36" Storage shelf unit—4 units required	$ 952
18" x 38" Storage shelf unit—4 units required	$ 1,076
42" Overshelves—2 units required	$ 406
Electric can opener	$ 65

Sales & display equipment

Cash register—2 units required	$ 7,645
Menu board—1 8-panel unit and 1 4-panel unit required	$ 6,950
Quality statement panel	$ 125
36" x 33" Topping unit (Cabinet work by gen. contr.—includ. in quote)	$ 0
Dry topping bowls with covers—8 units required	$ 97
1/9th S/S insert pan—4 units required	$ 26
36" Sneeze guard assembly	$ 1,960

Miscellaneous equipment

Work table	$ 1,108
File cabinet	$ 348
7-Person locker	$ 242
Safe	$ 1,390
Tackboard	$ 209
Mop & broom holder	$ 22
Acrylic cone/bowl holders—18 units required various sizes	$ 695
Personal computer, printer and software	$ 4,170
2 Haagen-Dazs logo neon signs (Incl. freight)	$ 1,738
Translites (pictures/ads) for menu boards—12 units incl. freight	$ 1,043
Freight and sales tax for major equipment purchased	$ 9,271
Total	**$119,684**

Projected income & expense (year one)

	Apr 1	May 2	Jun 3	Jul 4	Aug 5	Sep 6	Oct 7
Income							
Total sales	$35,046	$36,831	$41,351	$48,204	$44,007	$44,480	$36,140
Cost of goods sold	$11,215	$11,786	$13,232	$15,425	$15,043	$14,234	$11,565
Labor cost	$ 6,405	$ 6,730	$ 7,557	$ 8,808	$ 8,590	$ 8,128	$ 6,604
Total cost of goods sold	$17,620	$18,516	$20,789	$24,233	$23,633	$22,362	$18,169
Gross profit	$17,426	$18,315	$20,562	$23,971	$20,374	$22,118	$17,971
Expenses							
Advertising & marketing fee	$ 353	$ 353	$ 353	$ 353	$ 353	$ 353	$ 353
Accounting & legal	$ 584	$ 584	$ 584	$ 584	$ 584	$ 584	$ 584
Insurance	$ 813	$ 813	$ 813	$ 813	$ 813	$ 813	$ 813
Interest expense	$ 2,250	$ 2,250	$ 2,250	$ 2,250	$ 2,250	$ 2,250	$ 2,250
Rent	$ 5,000	$ 5,000	$ 5,000	$ 5,000	$ 5,000	$ 5,000	$ 5,000
Sales tax	$ 285	$ 285	$ 285	$ 285	$ 285	$ 285	$ 285
Telephone	$ 150	$ 150	$ 150	$ 150	$ 150	$ 150	$ 150
Utilities	$ 1,100	$ 1,100	$ 1,100	$ 1,100	$ 1,100	$ 1,100	$ 1,100
Owner draw	$ 3,000	$ 3,000	$ 3,000	$ 3,000	$ 3,000	$ 3,000	$ 3,000
Total expenses	$13,535	$13,535	$13,535	$13,535	$13,535	$13,535	$13,535
Net income before taxes	$ 3,891	$ 4,780	$ 7,027	$10,436	$ 6,839	$ 8,583	$ 4,436

	Nov 8	Dec 9	Jan 10	Feb 11	Mar 12	Total
Income						
Total sales	$37,530	$61,160	$37,591	$36,140	$38,920	$497,400
Cost of goods sold	$12,010	$19,571	$12,029	$11,982	$12,454	$160,546
Labor cost	$ 6,858	$11,176	$ 6,869	$ 6,604	$ 7,112	$ 91,441
Total cost of goods sold	$18,868	$30,747	$18,898	$18,586	$19,566	$251,987
Gross profit	$18,662	$30,413	$18,693	$17,554	$19,354	$245,413
Expenses						
Advertising & marketing fee	$ 353	$ 353	$ 353	$ 353	$ 353	$ 4,236
Accounting & legal	$ 584	$ 584	$ 584	$ 584	$ 584	$ 7,008
Insurance	$ 813	$ 813	$ 813	$ 813	$ 813	$ 9,756
Interest expense	$ 2,250	$ 2,250	$ 2,250	$ 2,250	$ 2,250	$ 27,000
Rent	$ 5,000	$ 5,000	$ 5,000	$ 5,000	$ 5,000	$ 60,000
Sales tax	$ 285	$ 285	$ 285	$ 285	$ 285	$ 3,420
Telephone	$ 150	$ 150	$ 150	$ 150	$ 150	$ 1,800
Utilities	$ 1,100	$ 1,100	$ 1,100	$ 1,100	$ 1,100	$ 13,200
Owner draw	$ 3,000	$ 3,000	$ 3,000	$ 3,000	$ 3,000	$ 36,000
Total expenses	$13,535	$13,535	$13,535	$13,535	$13,535	$162,420
Net income before taxes	$ 5,127	$16,878	$ 5,158	$ 4,019	$ 5,819	$ 82,993

Notes

Principal reduction on the business loan is not shown as an expense on the Income and Expense Statement.

Financial projections (years 1–5)

	Year 1	Year 2	Year 3	Year 4	Year 5
Gross sales	$497,400	$517,296	$537,988	$559,507	$581,887
Net income (before taxes)	$ 82,993	$ 86,313	$ 89,765	$ 93,356	$ 97,090

Interior Decorator

Lindsay Smith Interiors LLC

125 Knotty Pine Lane
Chadwood, MA 01012

Paul Greenland

Lindsay Smith is an interior decorator who helps clients discover the potential of residential spaces and transform creative visions into reality.

EXECUTIVE SUMMARY

Business Overview

Lindsay Smith is an interior decorator who helps clients discover the potential of residential spaces and transform creative visions into reality. After working for several years as a Registered Nurse, Lindsay realized that interior decorating was her true calling. After earning a diploma in residential planning from the Carlsberg Institute of Design, a nearby technical college, Lindsay has formally established Lindsay Smith Interiors LLC, which she will initially operate on a part-time basis. Her goal is to leave the nursing profession and operate her interior decorating business full-time during the third year of operations.

Business Philosophy

Lindsay Smith is committed to helping others create environments that complement their individual attributes and personalities.

MARKET ANALYSIS

According to data from Central Point Research Associates, Chadwood was home to an estimated 91,549 people in 2009. That year, the community consisted of 43,000 housing units. Of these, 43.7 percent were owner-occupied, 47.7 percent were renter occupied, and 8.5 percent were vacant. Central Point Research projects that, by 2014, the number of owner-occupied housing units will increase by 9 percent.

In 2009 the average household income in Chadwood was $60,005. This number is projected to increase 4.7 percent by 2014, reaching $71,213. The largest household income category consists of those earning between $50,000 and $74,999 (19.9%). The second-largest category includes those earning between $35,000 and $49,999 (15.8%).

INDUSTRY ANALYSIS

The interior decorating field is highly fragmented and includes many independent contractors. Indications of the industry's growth potential are evident in reports from the U.S. Bureau of Labor Statistics regarding the separate (but closely related) field of interior design. Although interior designers also focus on decorating, these professionals (who must be licensed in many states) are involved in planning the layout of commercial buildings, such as airports and hospitals, in collaboration with architects, building contractors, electricians, etc.

The Bureau of Labor Statistics projects that the employment of interior designers will increase 19 percent between 2008 and 2018. Part of this increase is due to the fact that homeowners are relying upon the services of professionals when performing remodeling projects, planning additions to their homes, developing home theaters, or simply choosing the appropriate decor.

Some educational programs within the interior decorating industry are either approved or accredited by Certified Interior Decorators International (C.I.D.). In addition, this organization provides the professional designation of Certified Interior Decorator to individuals who meet specific requirements, including the successful completion of an approved study course and entrance exam.

PERSONNEL

Lindsay Smith

Lindsay Smith's creative abilities were evident at an early age. In high school she used her talents to decorate a bedroom that was the envy of all her friends. In college, the same was true of her studio apartment. All the while, she never considered pursuing interior decorating as a career. After graduating from nursing school and working as a hospital nurse for three years, Lindsay purchased her first home which, like every residential space she had ever occupied, became an exhibit of her creative flair. Her spare time was occupied by watching popular design-related television programs, reading books about decorating, and sketching out ideas for her house.

After being called upon to provide decorating advice for friends and family, Lindsay soon realized that interior decorating was her true calling. She began attending Carlsberg Institute of Design, a nearby technical college, which offered formal training in residential planning. The school's program offered a combination of online, evening, and weekend courses, which was compatible with her nursing work schedule. After graduating with a diploma in residential planning, Lindsay now had the formal training to complement her natural creative talents and abilities and establish Lindsay Smith Interiors LLC.

Professional & Advisory Support

Lindsay Smith Interiors has established a business banking account with Chadwood Community Bank. In addition, the bank has provided her with a merchant account for accepting credit card payments. Legal services are provided by the law offices of Barnes, Field & O'Neill, and tax advisory services are provided by Chadwood Financial Services Inc.

BUSINESS STRATEGY

During its first year of operations, Lindsay Smith Interiors will operate as a part-time business while the owner continues to work full-time in the nursing field. At this time the focus will be on establishing a solid client base and generating awareness about the business among referral sources, including realtors and contractors. In addition, Lindsay Smith will work on honing her negotiation, estimation, and business management skills. At the beginning of year two Lindsay Smith plans to scale back her nursing career to part-time and increase her interior decorating workload. Finally, in year three the owner plans to leave the nursing profession and operate Lindsey Smith Interiors on a full-time basis.

SERVICES

When meeting with new clients, Lindsay Smith Interiors will follow a pre-defined process. This begins with a brief conversation (usually by telephone) to discuss client's needs and desires. At this stage it is determined whether or not the project is something Lindsay Smith is able to take on. If the project goes beyond the scope of services offered, a referral will be made to an interior designer, architect, or contractor who can meet the customer's needs.

If the project appears to be a good fit for Lindsay Smith Interiors, a meeting will be scheduled with the prospective client. At this stage of the process, Lindsay will discuss the client's goals and objectives in greater detail, gathering enough information to produce a written estimate. If the client wishes to move forward, a formal budget and completion timeline will be developed. This information will be included in a written service agreement to be signed by the customer and Lindsay Smith.

Specific services offered by Lindsay Smith Interiors include:

- Space Planning
- Design Concepting
- Color Consulting
- Fabric Selection
- Furniture Selection
- Fixture Selection
- Decorations/Accessories
- Flooring
- Tiling
- Soft Furnishings
- Window Treatments
- Storage Solutions
- Kid-Friendly Decor
- Painting
- Wallpapering
- Trim

Services typically are focused on one or more specific residential living spaces:

- Adult Bedrooms
- Children's Bedrooms
- Bathrooms
- Basements
- Kitchens

- Dining Rooms
- Family Rooms
- Living Rooms
- Home Theaters
- Home Offices

MARKETING & SALES

Lindsay Smith Interiors has developed a formal marketing plan includes the following tactics:

1. Business cards with Lindsay's contact information.

2. A website describing Lindsay's design philosophy, approach to projects, services provided, as well as a contact form.

3. Exhibition at home improvement shows. To give potential customers a feel for her creative skills, Lindsay has created (from basic building materials) a unique trade show exhibit. In addition, she bartered with a local freelance videographer to create a video about her business that showcases some of her most impressive interior design projects. This video is displayed on a large LCD monitor at all of the trade shows that Lindsay attends.

4. Targeted direct-mail campaigns. Lindsay will work with a list broker to obtain mailing lists of new homeowners, as well as newly divorced individuals who may need to freshen up the appearance of an existing home (to maximize its selling power) or decorate a new home. Lindsay also will send a periodic postcard mailer to realtors, home builders, and art dealers to raise awareness about her services. Finally, she will send mailings to individuals who have applied for permits to improve their homes (e.g., those making additions to their homes, renovating rooms, or finishing basements).

5. Because word-of-mouth is very powerful in the interior decorating business, Lindsay will encourage all of her customers to tell their friends and family about her business. In addition, she will offer a special discount on future services to customers who make referrals.

OPERATIONS

Location

To keep overhead low, Lindsay Smith Interiors will operate from a home office. This arrangement should prove to be sufficient for the foreseeable future, since Lindsay will typically meet with clients in their homes, and with contractors and suppliers at their places of business. Her home office is equipped with a computer, multi-functional peripheral device (e.g., a combination copier-fax-scanner), and file storage area. Lindsay also has purchased a mobile phone, which will allow her to be accessible via voice, text message, and e-mail at all times.

Hour

Because Lindsay Smith Interiors is a part-time operation and the owner initially will continue to work her regular full-time job, hours of operation will be variable. Lindsay typically works three 12-hour shifts per week (three days on, four days off) at her nursing job, which gives her ample time to meet with potential customers and oversee interior decorating projects.

Suppliers

The number of suppliers for interior decorating projects is virtually unlimited. Lindsay Smith has identified many reputable manufacturers from whom she can obtain materials for her customers. These include:

- A. Smith Furniture Company Ltd.
- A.B. Fabrics
- Ace Decor
- ADO International
- Anna French
- Anya Larkin, Ltd.
- Archive Fabrics
- Arizio Mirror Decor
- Austin Horn Bedding
- Beacon Hill Fabrics
- Brandenburg Furniture
- Brown Jordan International
- Broyhill Furniture
- Butler Specialty Company
- Callahan Company
- Carlton V, Ltd.
- Century Furniture
- Coraggio Fabrics
- Cowtan & Tout
- Creation Baumann
- Cutler-McDonald
- Decorative Crafts
- Donghia
- Dresden Furniture Elements
- Duralee Fabrics
- Durkan Carpet
- E.J. Victor
- F. Schumacher & Co.
- Fine Art Lamps
- Frederick Cooper Lamp Co., Inc.
- Gentano Floor Coverings Inc.
- Gramercy Fabrics
- Greff Fabrics
- Gretzky Carpets

- Harden Furniture Company
- Harrison & Gil Mirrors
- Heady Karcher
- Hekman Furniture
- Hinson & Company
- Hokanson Carpets
- Hooker Furniture
- Houles Trims
- Hubley Worldwide
- Hunter Douglas
- Innovative Wallcoverings
- Jennifer Westen
- Jumeranian
- Karastan
- Kensington Trims
- Kravet Furniture
- LaBarge
- Landsman
- Lane Furniture
- Laneventure
- Lapier Furniture
- Lazar Industries
- Lee Jofa
- Lexicon
- Lexington Furniture Industries
- Libas Limited
- Maitland-Smith
- Marge Carson Furniture
- Mariner Pacific Trims
- McGuire Furniture
- Neo
- Nina Campbell
- Nobilis
- NOMI Fabrics
- Old World Weavers
- Osborne & Little

- Pago Lamp Co.
- Patina
- Perry Creek Furniture
- Pierre Deux
- Pierre Frey
- Pindler & Pindler
- Prismatek Fabrics
- Pulaski Furniture
- Quadrille
- Ralph Lauren
- Raymond Waites
- Richardson Temple Designs
- Robert Allen Fabrics
- Robinson Wallcoverings
- Ronald Redding Designs
- Rubric Fabric Co.
- S. Harris & Co.
- Sam Moore Upholstery
- Scalamandre' Fabrics
- Stenberg Furnishings
- Stickley Furniture
- Stout Brothers Company
- Stroheim & Romann
- Swaim
- Taylor King
- The John Richard Company
- Thibaut, Inc.
- Thybony Wallcoverings
- Travers & Company
- Tyndale Lamps
- Universal Furniture
- Van Luit
- Wesley Allen
- Westgate Fabrics
- William Ashby, Inc.
- William Switzer

- Winton Fabrics
- Zoffany, Ltd.
- Zuber

Pricing

Lindsay Smith Interiors typically charges a flat fee for projects. Estimates are based on an hourly rate of $75. One-third of the project fee must be received prior to the beginning of the project. One-third is due at an agreeable milestone (typically when the project is half done). Finally, the remaining balance is due upon completion. Customers who simply want an hour or two of Lindsay's time (e.g., for consultations, etc.) pay a flat hourly rate of $75. Depending on the project, Lindsay Smith Interiors typically will mark up the price of furniture, fixtures, and other items purchased for clients at wholesale.

LEGAL

Lindsay Smith Interiors is structured as a limited liability corporation. Massachusetts does not require a unique license to operate an interior decorating business. However, we have secured a local business license from the city of Chadwood. In addition, Lindsay Smith Interiors has conducted a thorough risk assessment to determine the appropriate level of business insurance coverage, and a specialized policy has been obtained from Stronghold Insurance Inc.

FINANCIAL ANALYSIS

Following are three-year financial projections for Lindsay Smith Interiors. Projected revenues are based on a 48-week work year, with 10 hours of weekly billable time during year one, 20 hours in year two, and 40 hours in year three. These figures will likely be higher when product markups (e.g., furniture and fixtures purchased for clients at wholesale) are factored in. Estimating markups is difficult, due to the great variability in purchases from project to project, and client to client.

Lindsay Smith will fund initial start-up costs (e.g., accounting and legal expenses, office supplies, etc.) from personal savings. To reduce her tax liability, Lindsay Smith plans to meet with an investment advisor and discuss the establishment of an individual retirement account. This business plan will be revised annually, based on the actual performance of the business.

	2011	2012	2013
Revenue	$36,000	$72,000	$144,000
Expenses			
Advertising & marketing	$ 500	$ 500	$ 500
Miscellaneous items	$ 750	$ 500	$ 500
Accounting & legal	$ 600	$ 350	$ 350
Office supplies	$ 250	$ 250	$ 250
Computers/peripherals	$ 1,500	$ 0	$ 0
Business insurance	$ 750	$ 750	$ 750
Health insurance	$ 0	$ 0	$ 10,000
Salaries	$18,000	$40,000	$ 80,000
Taxes	$10,800	$21,600	$ 43,200
Postage	$ 350	$ 350	$ 350
Telecommunications	$ 500	$ 500	$ 500
Travel	$ 650	$ 750	$ 1,000
Subscriptions	$ 350	$ 350	$ 350
Total expenses	**$35,000**	**$65,900**	**$137,750**
Net income	**$ 1,000**	**$ 6,100**	**$ 6,250**

Interior Design Firm

Gable & Nash LLC

43 N. State Street
Belvidere, IL 61008

Paul Greenland

Gable & Nash LLC is an interior design firm focusing on the commercial market, with specialized expertise in the areas of ergonomics and green design.

EXECUTIVE SUMMARY

Business Overview

Gable & Nash LLC is a new interior design firm that focuses on the commercial market. We have specialized expertise in several areas, including ergonomics, which allows us to design furniture and workspaces that minimize muscle strain and repetitive stress injuries. In addition, our experience with green design makes us the perfect choice for clients who wish to use construction materials, carpets, and furnishings that are made from renewable materials, hypoallergenic, chemical-free, and/or energy-efficient.

Our firm is owned by Josh Gable and Mary Nash. Former classmates from Hirschfield Design College, Gable and Nash each began their careers working for different employers. In addition to general training as interior designers, each partner brings specialized expertise to the firm. Gable became versed in the field of green design while working for William Smith Architecture, a firm in Providence, Rhode Island. Nash developed specialized knowledge and experience related to ergonomics while working for Cogerlomo Worldwide, a large corporation.

Business Philosophy

Gable & Nash is committed to designing commercial spaces that are friendly to humans and the environment.

MARKET ANALYSIS

Our firm is located in the city of Belvidere, in Illinois' Boone County. Our location gives us easy access to the city of Rockford, which is one of the state's larger cities. In addition, our position near Interstate 90 provides quick access to McHenry County and the far western suburbs of Chicago. We also serve some smaller communities to the south, including Rochelle, located in Ogle County. Compared to the Chicago market, where competition is fierce, our primary service area (Winnebago, Boone, McHenry, and Ogle counties) is somewhat underserved by interior design firms.

According to DemographicsNow, our primary service area included 25,491 establishments in 2009 (338,891 employees). Nearly 60 percent of our market is comprised of white collar workers. Specifically, services comprise the largest industry sector, with 130,240 employees (38.4%). Other important industry sectors for us include retail trade, with 69,942 employees (20.6%); finance, insurance, and real estate, with 18,124 employees (5.3%); and public administration, with 13,036 employees (3.8%).

Within the services sector, we will concentrate on several key segments, including:

- Hospitals (the largest segment, accounting for 19.5% of service employees)

- Primary & Secondary Education (16%)

- Health & Medical Services (14.9%)

- Social Services (8.1%)

- Membership Organizations (3.9%)

- Legal Services (1.8%)

- Hotels & Lodging (1.4%)

- Computer Services (1%)

- Colleges & Universities (0.9%)

- Advertising (0.9%)

INDUSTRY ANALYSIS

The interior design field is different from, but closely related to, the field of interior decorating. While interior decorators concentrate mainly on the decorative elements of interior furnishing and design, interior designers (who must be licensed in many states) are involved in planning the overall layout and design of an interior space. Many interior designers, such as our firm, concentrate on commercial buildings, such as airports and hospitals, in collaboration with architects, building contractors, electricians, etc.

The interior design field is highly fragmented and includes many independent contractors. Indications of the industry's growth potential are evident in reports from the U.S. Bureau of Labor Statistics, which reported that interior designers held some 71,700 jobs in 2008. Of this total, an estimated 30 percent of designers worked in specialized areas and 14 percent worked for architectural or landscape architecture services. Finally, home furnishings and furniture stores employed 9 percent of designers. In addition to the many designers who work as independent contractors, many of those holding regular positions also perform freelance work.

The Bureau of Labor Statistics projects that the employment of interior designers will increase 19 percent between 2008 and 2018, when employment will total 85,600 people. Within the commercial sector, growth will be driven by the healthcare industry as it addresses the needs of an aging population. In addition, restaurants, resorts, and hotels also will have a strong need for interior designers. Specialized services such as ergonomics and green design, which we offer, will be in great demand.

The largest and oldest professional organization within our industry is the American Society of Interior Designers (ASID). Established in 1975, the society had approximately 36,000 members in 48 chapters across the United States and Canada. As part of its effort to advance the interior design industry, the society engages in education, advocacy, outreach, community building, and knowledge sharing. Professional ASID members are required to pass a two-day accreditation exam administered by the National Council for Interior Design Qualification and meet minimum full-time work experience/accredited design education standards. In addition to professional members, ASID's membership base includes students and industry partners.

PERSONNEL

Gable & Nash is owned by business partners Josh Gable and Mary Nash.

Josh Gabel, ASID

A native of San Jose, California, Josh Gable earned an undergraduate degree (BFA) in interior design from Hirschfield Design College in Denver, Colorado. Gabel began his career with William Smith Architecture, a firm in Providence, Rhode Island. After working as an apprentice for three years, Gable was promoted to a regular interior designer position, which he held for four years. While working for William Smith, Gable became versed in the field of green design while helping to create new facilities for leading corporations such as Parkinson Manufacturing Inc. and Rocket Corp., as well as hotel projects for the likes of Sherrington Hospitality. Josh has successfully passed a competency examination offered by the National Council for Interior Design Qualification (NCIDQ) and is licensed as an interior designer in the state of Illinois.

Mary Nash, ASID

A native of Dallas, Texas, Mary Nash also earned a BFA in interior design from Hirschfield Design College, where she was a classmate of Josh Gabel's. Like Josh, she began her career as an apprentice with an architecture firm. However, after three years she was hired by Cogerlomo Worldwide, a large corporation, which needed an interior designer in its property & construction department. In that role, she spent four years developing specialized expertise in ergonomics and was involved in the design of a telesales facility for 750 employees that included cubical areas, as well as private offices and meeting rooms. Mary also has successfully passed the NCIDQ examination and is licensed as an interior designer in the state of Illinois.

Professional & Advisory Support

Gable & Nash has established a business banking account with the Community Bank of Illinois. In addition, the bank has provided their firm with a merchant account for accepting credit card payments. Legal services are provided by the law offices of Royce & Holloway, and tax advisory services are provided by Belvidere Tax Advisors Inc.

BUSINESS STRATEGY

Gable & Nash will devote its first year of operations to becoming established within its primary service area. We are fortunate to begin our new company with several large projects, thanks to relationships developed while working for our previous employers. Along with start-up funding provided by the partners, these early projects will allow us to commence operations with positive cash flow. We realize that our first year will be difficult, in terms of balancing the amount of time spent on marketing/customer acquisition and actual project work. We are preparing to hire an administrative assistant to help with administrative tasks and project coordination. During our second year we will focus on increasing our market share. Finally, during our third year we will consider the addition of a third interior designer, as well as a full-time marketing professional to assist us in growing the business.

SERVICES

When meeting with clients, Gable & Nash takes the following approach to service delivery:

1. Programming—We begin all projects by meeting with clients to understand their objectives and vision, and to discuss budget guidelines.

2. Plan Development—After we have a clear understanding of the client's needs, we then develop an interior design plan utilizing computer-aided design (CAD) software and present the plan to the client.

3. Specification—At this stage, specifications regarding furnishings, finishes, and materials are identified. Examples include wallcoverings, furniture, flooring, and lighting. If needed, drawings are produced for review and approval by construction inspectors, in order to ensure compliance with building codes. Engineers or architects are consulted for projects involving structural work.

4. Contractor Selection—Contractors are hired to perform painting, flooring, electrical, and plumbing work if necessary.

5. Timeline Development—A project timeline is established at this phase, taking into consideration the client's needs, as well as the work schedules of contractors.

6. Material Selection—Based upon established specifications, materials such as light fixtures, artwork, etc., are selected and procured.

7. Installation/Construction—Our firm supervises and coordinates the entire design project through completion, ensuring the total satisfaction of our clients.

Beyond general interior design services, our firm offers specialized expertise. For example, our experience in the field of ergonomics allows us to design furniture and workspaces that minimize muscle strain and repetitive stress injuries. In addition, we are very knowledgeable about construction materials, carpets, and furnishings that are made from renewable materials, hypoallergenic, chemical-free, and/or energy-efficient.

MARKETING & SALES

Gable & Nash has developed a formal marketing plan includes the following tactics:

- Business cards with contact information for our partners.

- A website describing our firm's design philosophy, approach to projects, services provided, as well as a contact form.

- Four-color, high-quality sales literature for presentation to potential clients. In addition to a general capabilities brochure, we also have developed panel cards describing our expertise in special areas, including ergonomics and green design. A less expensive tri-fold brochure also has been developed, for distribution via direct mail and at professional trade shows.

- Targeted direct-mail campaigns. Our firm will work with a list broker to secure mailing lists for commercial prospects in our primary service area. During our first year of operations, direct marketing efforts will focus on hospitals, primary & secondary education, and health & medical services. In addition, we also will target campaigns toward finance, insurance, and real estate firms.

- Gable & Nash will secure Chamber of Commerce memberships within our primary service area, in order to network with government officials, decision-makers, and business leaders.

OPERATIONS

Location

Gable & Nash has rented affordable office space in a former storefront. Although we mainly meet with customers at their places of business, our location includes a conference room for meetings; a storage area for files, material samples, and catalogs; and office areas for the partners. In the near future, it will accommodate working space for one additional partner and an assistant, after which time we will likely need to find new office space.

Hours

Generally speaking, Gable & Nash maintains office hours from 8 AM to 5 PM, Monday through Friday. However, we will work around customers' schedules as needed. We have secured an answering service that will take calls after hours and forward them to the appropriate partner.

Suppliers

The number of suppliers for interior design projects is virtually unlimited. Gable & Nash has identified many reputable manufacturers from whom they can obtain materials for their clients. Examples include:

Furniture

- Steelcase Inc.
- Ashley Furniture Industries Inc.
- PinskDrev Industrial Woodworking Co.
- Kohler Co.
- Aaron's Inc.
- Haworth Inc.
- HNI Corp.
- Herman Miller Inc.
- Grammer AG
- La-Z-Boy Inc.
- Kimball International Inc.
- Knoll Inc.

Carpet & Flooring

- Mohawk Carpet Corp.
- Shaw Industries Group Inc.
- Leggett and Platt Inc.
- Modern Carpet
- Shaw Contract Flooring
- ABC Carpet Company Inc.

Lighting

- Seattle Lighting Fixtures Co.
- ACME Lighting Supply
- Frederick Cooper L.L.C.
- Weinstock Lamp Company Inc.
- Accent Lamp Company Inc.
- Arkansas Lamp Manufacturing Co.
- Deran International Inc.
- B and P Lamp Supply Company Inc.
- Pacific Lamp and Supply Co.

Pricing

Gable & Nash typically charges a flat fee for projects. Estimates are based on an hourly rate of $100. One-third of the project fee must be received prior to the beginning of the project. One-third is due at an agreeable milestone (typically when the project is half done). Finally, the remaining balance is due upon completion. If contractors are hired as part of a project, we typically receive a percentage of their earnings as well.

LEGAL

Gable & Nash is structured as a limited liability corporation. The partners are both registered as interior designers in the state of Illinois. Our state registrations, which cost $100 each, expire on August 31 of every odd-numbered year. Gable & Nash has conducted a thorough risk assessment to determine the appropriate level of business insurance coverage, and a specialized policy has been obtained from Fortress Insurance Inc.

FINANCIAL ANALYSIS

Following are three-year financial projections for Gable & Nash. Projected revenues are based on a 48-week work year, with 30 hours of weekly billable time during year one (15 hours per partner), 50 hours in year two, and 60 hours in year three. These estimates are conservative; actual figures will likely be higher when percentages of contractor fees are included. Estimating contractor fee markups is difficult, due to the great variability in purchases from project to project, and client to client. This plan will be revised annually, based on the actual performance of the business.

	2011	2012	2013
Revenue	$192,000	$240,000	$288,000
Expenses			
Advertising & marketing	$ 10,000	$ 8,500	$ 8,500
Office lease	$ 5,400	$ 5,400	$ 5,400
Utilities	$ 3,000	$ 3,500	$ 4,000
Miscellaneous items	$ 1,000	$ 1,000	$ 1,000
Accounting & legal	$ 1,500	$ 1,000	$ 1,000
Office supplies	$ 850	$ 850	$ 850
Computers/peripherals	$ 7,500	$ 2,500	$ 2,500
Business insurance	$ 850	$ 850	$ 850
Health insurance	$ 15,000	$ 15,000	$ 15,000
Salaries	$120,000	$150,000	$165,000
Taxes	$ 16,500	$ 17,325	$ 18,191
Postage	$ 3,500	$ 2,000	$ 2,000
Telecommunications	$ 1,200	$ 1,200	$ 1,200
Travel	$ 1,500	$ 1,750	$ 2,000
Subscriptions	$ 750	$ 750	$ 750
Total expenses	**$188,550**	**$211,625**	**$228,241**
Net income	**$ 3,450**	**$ 28,375**	**$ 59,759**

Josh Gable and Mary Nash will each contribute $30,000 from personal savings to fund certain start-up costs (e.g., marketing materials, computer hardware and software, accounting and legal expenses, office supplies, etc.). As previously mentioned, our firm is fortunate to begin operations with several large projects, providing us with positive cash flow.

Laundry Mat

Duds and Suds Laundry Mat

99876 Canton Ave.
Brooklyn, NY 11215

BizPlanDB.com

Duds and Suds Laundry Mat is a New York based corporation that will provide usage of coin operated washers/ dryers, outsourced dry cleaning services, and drop off washing/drying/folding services to customers in its targeted market. It was founded in 2010 by Jacob Lewis.

1.0 EXECUTIVE SUMMARY

The purpose of this business plan is to raise $125,000 for the development of a coin operated laundry mat while showcasing the expected financials and operations over the next three years. Duds and Suds Laundry Mat is a New York based corporation that will provide usage of coin operated washers/dryers, outsourced dry cleaning services, and drop off washing/drying/folding services to customers in its targeted market. It was founded in 2010 by Jacob Lewis.

1.1 The Services

As stated above, the primary revenue stream for Duds and Suds Laundry Mat is the usage of the Company's coin operated washing and drying machines. At the onset of operations, Management expects that the business will have approximately 20 machines (10 washers/10 dryers) that will be available for customer use.

Duds and Suds will also offer drop off services where the company will provide the washing, drying, and folding of clothes. This is an important secondary stream of revenue for the business as the margins from this service are very high. The business will also contract with a local dry cleaner so that certain garments can be sent for dry cleaning offsite, while again providing the business with a strong source of secondary income.

The third section of the business plan will further describe the services offered by Duds and Suds Laundry Mat.

1.2 Financing

Mr. Lewis is seeking to raise $125,000 from as a bank loan. The interest rate and loan agreement are to be further discussed during negotiation. This business plan assumes that the business will receive a 10 year loan with a 9% fixed interest rate. The financing will be used for the following:

- Development of the Company's Duds and Suds Laundry Mat location.

- Financing for the first six months of operation.

- Capital to purchase coin operated washing machines and dryers.

Mr. Lewis will contribute $25,000 to the venture.

1.3 Mission Statement

Management's mission is to provide customers with a convenient and affordable way of having their clothes washed and cleaned.

1.4 Management Team

The Company was founded by Jacob Lewis. Mr. Lewis has more than 10 years of experience in the retail management industry. Through his expertise, he will be able to bring the operations of the business to profitability within its first year of operations.

1.5 Sales Forecasts

Mr. Lewis expects a strong rate of growth at the start of operations. Below are the expected financials over the next three years.

Proforma profit and loss (yearly)

Year	1	2	3
Sales	$381,708	$408,428	$437,017
Operating costs	$209,146	$216,822	$224,831
EBITDA	$ 93,731	$107,256	$121,933
Taxes, interest, and depreciation	$ 54,219	$ 54,738	$ 59,801
Net profit	$ 39,513	$ 52,519	$ 62,132

Sales, operating costs, and profit forecast

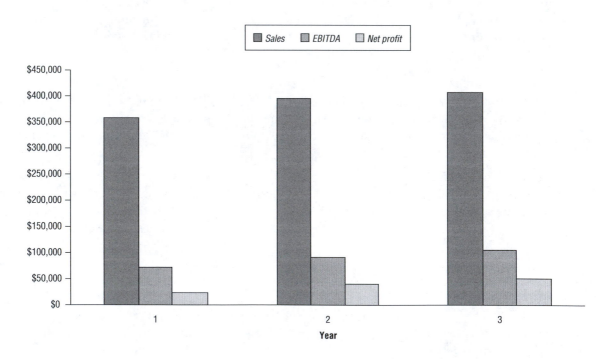

1.6 Expansion Plan

The business will aggressively expand during the first three years of operation. Mr. Lewis intends to implement marketing campaigns that will effectively target individuals within the target market.

2.0 COMPANY AND FINANCING SUMMARY

2.1 Registered Name and Corporate Structure

Duds and Suds Laundry Mat is registered as a corporation in the State of New York.

2.2 Required Funds

At this time, Duds and Suds Laundry Mat requires $125,000 of debt funds. Below is a breakdown of how these funds will be used:

Projected startup costs

Initial lease payments and deposits	$ 10,000
Working capital	$ 35,000
FF&E	$ 25,000
Leasehold improvements	$ 5,000
Security deposits	$ 5,000
Insurance	$ 2,500
Washing machines and dryers	$ 55,000
Marketing budget	$ 7,500
Miscellaneous and unforeseen costs	$ 5,000
Total startup costs	**$150,000**

Use of funds

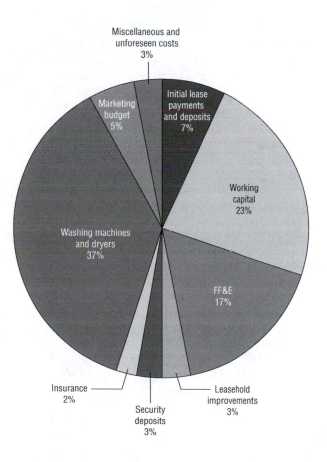

2.3 Investor Equity

Mr. Lewis is not seeking an investment from a third party at this time.

2.4 Management Equity

Jacob Lewis owns 100% of Duds and Suds Laundry Mat, Inc.

2.5 Exit Strategy

If the business is very successful, Mr. Lewis may seek to sell the business to a third party for a significant earnings multiple. Most likely, the Company will hire a qualified business broker to sell the business on behalf of Duds and Suds Laundry Mat. Based on historical numbers, the business could fetch a sales premium of up to 4 times earnings.

3.0 PRODUCTS AND SERVICES

Below is a description of the laundering services offered by Duds and Suds Laundry Mat.

3.1 Usage of Washers and Dryers

The primary business of Duds and Suds Laundry Mat will be to provide coin operated laundry machines that customers can come in and use to wash and dry their clothes. Management intends to maintain approximately 20 machines that will provide customers with a low cost method of doing their laundry. At this time, Mr. Lewis is sourcing several manufacturers from which he will purchase these machines.

3.2 Outsourced Dry Cleaning and Drop Off Washing Services

The Company will also offer wash/dry services where customers can simply drop off their laundry, which will be completed by the Company's staff. The Company will also develop an ongoing relationship with a local dry cleaner so that the Company can offer this service, on an outsourced basis, to its customers. Mr. Lewis anticipates that approximately 25% of the Company's revenues will come from these services.

3.3 Sales of Soap/Detergent

The Company's final revenue stream will come from the sale of soap and detergent from small vending machines for customer use. This aspect of the Company's operations will account for 2% to 4% of the business's top line income.

4.0 STRATEGIC AND MARKET ANALYSIS

4.1 Economic Outlook

This section of the analysis will detail the economic climate, the laundry mat industry, the customer profile, and the competition that the business will face as it progresses through its business operations.

Currently, the economic market condition in the United States is in recession. This slowdown in the economy has also greatly impacted real estate sales, which has halted to historical lows. Many economists expect that this recession will continue until mid-2010, at which point the economy will begin a prolonged recovery period.

4.2 Industry Analysis

Within the United States, there are approximately 13,000 businesses that operate one of more coin operated laundry locations. Each year, these companies aggregately generate more than $3.5 billion dollars per while providing jobs to 50,000 people. Payrolls in each of the last five years have exceeded $625 million dollars.

This is a mature industry that enjoys insulation from changes in the general economy. Regardless of the general economic environment, people will continue to need to have their clothes cleaned. Additionally, revenues during economic recessions may actually increase as consumers forego purchases of their own washers and dryers. This is a very stable type of business to operate, and Mr. Lewis intends to capitalize on the stability of this industry.

4.3 Customer Profile

Management has developed the following demographic profile of people that the business will have as its average customer:

- Between the ages of 21 and 60

- Annual household income of $25,000 to $35,000 per year

- Lives within 5 miles of Duds and Suds Laundry Mat location

Management intends to place Duds and Suds Laundry Mat within a lower middle class to working class area within the New York metropolitan area. People that have higher incomes tend to own their own washer and dryer once they hit an income level that exceeds $50,000 per year. At this time, Mr. Lewis is scouting locations within the Bronx, Brooklyn, and Queens. Management has also looked at places within Northern Manhattan. Mr. Lewis wants to ensure the effective market radius of the business has at least 20,000 people within walking distance of the business.

4.4 Competition

The business of providing laundry services is a commoditized industry. The washing and drying services provided by one Duds and Suds Laundry Mat is identical to that of another location. As such, it is imperative that the business find a location that is in need of a coin operated laundry mat. The business will remain price competitive within any other laundry mat within the other.

5.0 MARKETING PLAN

Duds and Suds Laundry Mat intends to maintain an extensive marketing campaign that will ensure maximum visibility for the business in its targeted market. Below is an overview of the marketing strategies and objectives.

5.1 Marketing Objectives

- Implement a local campaign with the Company's targeted market via the use of flyers, local newspaper advertisements, and word of mouth advertising.

- Establish relationships with dry cleaners within the targeted market.

5.2 Marketing Strategies

The Company intends to use a localized marketing campaign to develop the customer base for the business. To that end, Mr. Lewis has developed the following marketing campaigns that he will use at the onset of operations. Foremost, Mr. Lewis intends to acquire a highly visible retail location that will attract a significant amount of foot traffic. This will ensure that the marketing campaign budgets can be kept to a minimum, and that the signage of the facility will provide a significant amount of visibility.

The Company will also maintain a strong level of print and media advertising among local newspapers, The business will also maintain listings in the local Yellow Books.

At the onset of operations, Mr. Lewis will distribute discount coupons and flyers to local residents, which will create instant visibility of the Duds and Suds Laundry Mat's brand name. This discount coupon campaign will run for the first two months of operation. Primarily these discounts will be geared towards the Company's in-house wash/fold and dry cleaning services.

5.3 Pricing

Each run of a standard sized wash will be $1.50. Each 12 minutes of usage of a dryer (which is the standard timing for a commercial dryer) will run $.50. The average drying of clothes will generate $2.00 per customer on a per visit basis.

6.0 ORGANIZATIONAL PLAN AND PERSONNEL SUMMARY

6.1 Corporate Organization

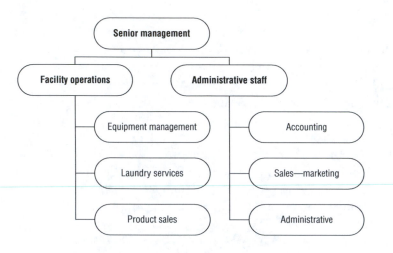

6.2 Organizational Budget

Personnel plan—yearly

Year	1	2	3
Owner	$ 30,000	$ 30,900	$ 31,827
Laundry mat manager	$ 24,500	$ 25,235	$ 25,992
Laundry mat employees	$ 46,500	$ 47,895	$ 49,332
Bookkeeper (P/T)	$ 12,500	$ 12,875	$ 13,261
Administrative	$ 22,000	$ 22,660	$ 23,340
Total	**$135,500**	**$139,565**	**$143,752**

Numbers of personnel

Owner	1	1	1
Laundry mat manager	1	1	1
Laundry mat employees	3	3	3
Bookkeeper (P/T)	1	1	1
Administrative	1	1	1
Totals	**7**	**7**	**7**

Personnel expense breakdown

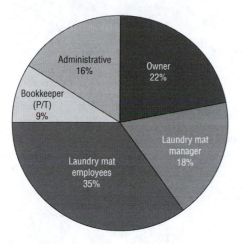

7.0 FINANCIAL PLAN

7.1 Underlying Assumptions

The Company has based its proforma financial statements on the following:

* Duds and Suds Laundry Mat will have an annual revenue growth rate of 7% per year.

* The Owner will acquire $125,000 of debt funds to develop the business.

* The loan will have a 10 year term with a 9% interest rate.

7.2 Sensitivity Analysis

The Company's revenues are not sensitive to changes in the general economy. People will be required to wash their clothing in any economic climate. As such, Management does not expect that any change in the economy will impact the business's top line income. Additionally, revenues may actually increase during economic recession as people will not be able to afford their own washers/dryers for their homes.

7.3 Source of Funds

Financing

Equity contributions	
Management investment	$ 25,000.00
Total equity financing	**$ 25,000.00**
Banks and lenders	
Banks and lenders	$ 125,000.00
Total debt financing	**$125,000.00**
Total financing	**$150,000.00**

7.4 General Assumptions

General assumptions

Year	1	2	3
Short term interest rate	9.5%	9.5%	9.5%
Long term interest rate	10.0%	10.0%	10.0%
Federal tax rate	33.0%	33.0%	33.0%
State tax rate	5.0%	5.0%	5.0%
Personnel taxes	15.0%	15.0%	15.0%

7.5 Profit and Loss Statements

Proforma profit and loss (yearly)

Year	1	2	3
Sales	**$381,708**	**$408,428**	**$437,017**
Cost of goods sold	$ 78,831	$ 84,349	$ 90,254
Gross margin	79.35%	79.35%	79.35%
Operating income	**$302,877**	**$324,078**	**$346,764**
Expenses			
Payroll	$135,500	$139,565	$143,752
General and administrative	$ 13,200	$ 13,728	$ 14,277
Marketing expenses	$ 5,726	$ 6,126	$ 6,555
Professional fees and licensure	$ 3,500	$ 3,605	$ 3,713
Insurance costs	$ 2,500	$ 2,625	$ 2,756
Equipment maintenance costs	$ 8,000	$ 8,800	$ 9,680
Rent and utilities	$ 19,250	$ 20,213	$ 21,223
Miscellaneous costs	$ 1,145	$ 1,225	$ 1,311
Payroll taxes	$ 20,325	$ 20,935	$ 21,563
Total operating costs	**$209,146**	**$216,822**	**$224,831**
EBITDA	**$ 93,731**	**$107,256**	**$121,933**
Federal income tax	$ 30,931	$ 32,040	$ 37,157
State income tax	$ 4,687	$ 4,855	$ 5,630
Interest expense	$ 10,922	$ 10,164	$ 9,335
Depreciation expenses	$ 7,679	$ 7,679	$ 7,679
Net profit	**$ 39,513**	**$ 52,519**	**$ 62,132**
Profit margin	**10.35%**	**12.86%**	**14.22%**

Sales, operating costs, and profit forecast

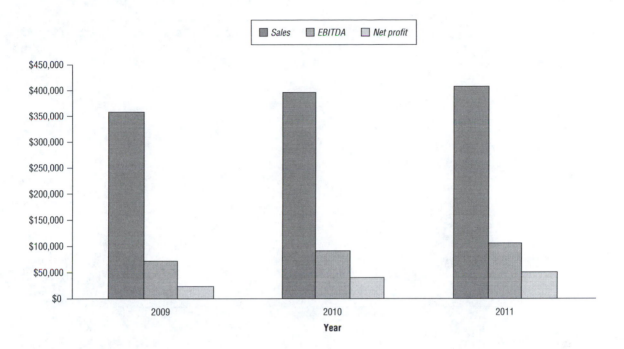

7.6 Cash Flow Analysis

Proforma cash flow analysis—yearly

Year	1	2	3
Cash from operations	$ 47,191	$60,197	$69,811
Cash from receivables	$ 0	$ 0	$ 0
Operating cash inflow	**$ 47,191**	**$60,197**	**$69,811**
Other cash inflows			
Equity investment	$ 25,000	$ 0	$ 0
Increased borrowings	$125,000	$ 0	$ 0
Sales of business assets	$ 0	$ 0	$ 0
A/P increases	$ 3,790	$ 4,359	$ 5,012
Total other cash inflows	**$153,790**	**$ 4,359**	**$ 5,012**
Total cash inflow	**$200,981**	**$64,556**	**$74,823**
Cash outflows			
Repayment of principal	$ 8,079	$ 8,837	$ 9,666
A/P decreases	$ 2,489	$ 2,987	$ 3,584
A/R increases	$ 0	$ 0	$ 0
Asset purchases	$107,500	$ 6,020	$ 6,981
Dividends	$ 33,034	$42,138	$48,867
Total cash outflows	**$151,102**	**$59,982**	**$69,099**
Net cash flow	**$ 49,879**	**$ 4,574**	**$ 5,724**
Cash balance	**$ 49,879**	**$54,453**	**$60,177**

Proforma cash flow (yearly)

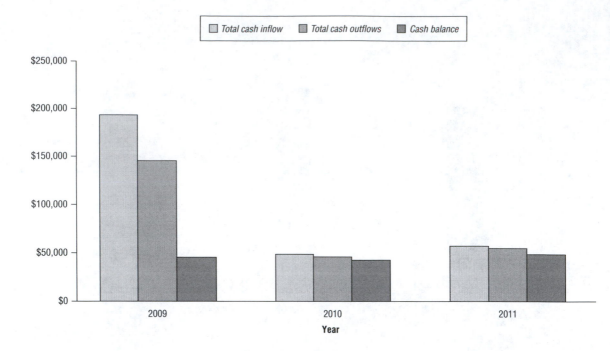

7.7 Balance Sheet

Proforma balance sheet—yearly

Year	1	2	3
Assets			
Cash	$ 49,879	$ 54,453	$ 60,177
Amortized development/expansion costs	$ 27,500	$ 28,102	$ 28,800
Washing machines and dryers	$ 55,000	$ 58,010	$ 61,500
FF&E	$ 25,000	$ 27,408	$ 30,200
Accumulated depreciation	($ 7,679)	($ 15,357)	($ 23,036)
Total assets	**$149,701**	**$152,616**	**$157,642**
Liabilities and equity			
Accounts payable	$ 1,301	$ 2,673	$ 4,101
Long term liabilities	$116,921	$108,084	$ 99,247
Other liabilities	$ 0	$ 0	$ 0
Total liabilities	**$118,222**	**$110,756**	**$103,347**
Net worth	**$ 31,479**	**$ 41,859**	**$ 54,295**
Total liabilities and equity	**$149,701**	**$152,616**	**$157,642**

Proforma balance sheet

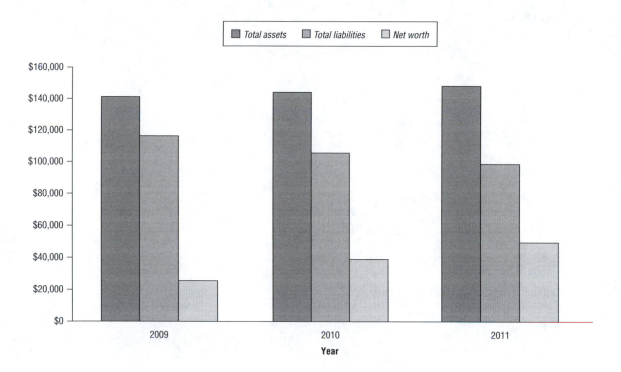

7.8 Breakeven Analysis

Monthly break even analysis

Year	1	2	3
Monthly revenue	$ 21,965	$ 22,771	$ 23,612
Yearly revenue	$263,581	$273,255	$283,348

Break even analysis

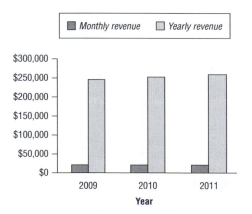

7.9 Business Ratios

Business ratios—yearly

Year	1	2	3
Sales			
Sales growth	0.0%	7.0%	7.0%
Gross margin	79.3%	79.3%	79.3%
Financials			
Profit margin	10.35%	12.86%	14.22%
Assets to liabilities	1.27	1.38	1.53
Equity to liabilities	0.27	0.38	0.53
Assets to equity	4.76	3.65	2.90
Liquidity			
Acid test	0.42	0.49	0.58
Cash to assets	0.33	0.36	0.38

7.10 Three Year Profit and Loss Statement

Profit and loss statement (first year)

Month	1	2	3	4	5	6	7
Sales	$31,050	$31,188	$31,326	$31,464	$31,602	$31,740	$31,878
Cost of goods sold	$ 6,413	$ 6,441	$ 6,470	$ 6,498	$ 6,527	$ 6,555	$ 6,584
Gross margin	79.3%	79.3%	79.3%	79.3%	79.3%	79.3%	79.3%
Operating income	$24,638	$24,747	$24,857	$24,966	$25,076	$25,185	$25,295
Expenses							
Payroll	$11,292	$11,292	$11,292	$11,292	$11,292	$11,292	$11,292
General and administrative	$ 1,100	$ 1,100	$ 1,100	$ 1,100	$ 1,100	$ 1,100	$ 1,100
Marketing expenses	$ 477	$ 477	$ 477	$ 477	$ 477	$ 477	$ 477
Professional fees and licensure	$ 292	$ 292	$ 292	$ 292	$ 292	$ 292	$ 292
Insurance costs	$ 208	$ 208	$ 208	$ 208	$ 208	$ 208	$ 208
Equipment maintenance costs	$ 667	$ 667	$ 667	$ 667	$ 667	$ 667	$ 667
Rent and utilities	$ 1,604	$ 1,604	$ 1,604	$ 1,604	$ 1,604	$ 1,604	$ 1,604
Miscellaneous costs	$ 95	$ 95	$ 95	$ 95	$ 95	$ 95	$ 95
Payroll taxes	$ 1,694	$ 1,694	$ 1,694	$ 1,694	$ 1,694	$ 1,694	$ 1,694
Total operating costs	$17,429	$17,429	$17,429	$17,429	$17,429	$17,429	$17,429
EBITDA	$ 7,209	$ 7,318	$ 7,428	$ 7,537	$ 7,647	$ 7,756	$ 7,866
Federal income tax	$ 2,516	$ 2,527	$ 2,538	$ 2,550	$ 2,561	$ 2,572	$ 2,583
State income tax	$ 381	$ 383	$ 385	$ 386	$ 388	$ 390	$ 391
Interest expense	$ 938	$ 933	$ 928	$ 923	$ 918	$ 913	$ 908
Depreciation expense	$ 640	$ 640	$ 640	$ 640	$ 640	$ 640	$ 640
Net profit	$ 2,734	$ 2,835	$ 2,937	$ 3,038	$ 3,140	$ 3,242	$ 3,343

Profit and loss statement (first year cont.)

Month	8	9	10	11	12	1
Sales	$32,016	$32,154	$32,292	$32,430	$32,568	$381,708
Cost of goods sold	$ 6,612	$ 6,641	$ 6,669	$ 6,698	$ 6,726	$ 78,831
Gross margin	79.3%	79.3%	79.3%	79.3%	79.3%	79.3%
Operating income	$25,404	$25,514	$25,623	$25,733	$25,842	$302,877
Expenses						
Payroll	$11,292	$11,292	$11,292	$11,292	$11,292	$135,500
General and administrative	$ 1,100	$ 1,100	$ 1,100	$ 1,100	$ 1,100	$ 13,200
Marketing expenses	$ 477	$ 477	$ 477	$ 477	$ 477	$ 5,726
Professional fees and licensure	$ 292	$ 292	$ 292	$ 292	$ 292	$ 3,500
Insurance costs	$ 208	$ 208	$ 208	$ 208	$ 208	$ 2,500
Equipment maintenance costs	$ 667	$ 667	$ 667	$ 667	$ 667	$ 8,000
Rent and utilities	$ 1,604	$ 1,604	$ 1,604	$ 1,604	$ 1,604	$ 19,250
Miscellaneous costs	$ 95	$ 95	$ 95	$ 95	$ 95	$ 1,145
Payroll taxes	$ 1,694	$ 1,694	$ 1,694	$ 1,694	$ 1,694	$ 20,325
Total operating costs	$17,429	$17,429	$17,429	$17,429	$17,429	$209,146
EBITDA	$ 7,975	$ 8,085	$ 8,194	$ 8,304	$ 8,413	$ 93,731
Federal income tax	$ 2,594	$ 2,606	$ 2,617	$ 2,628	$ 2,639	$ 30,931
State income tax	$ 393	$ 395	$ 396	$ 398	$ 400	$ 4,687
Interest expense	$ 903	$ 898	$ 893	$ 887	$ 882	$ 10,922
Depreciation expense	$ 640	$ 640	$ 640	$ 640	$ 640	$ 7,679
Net profit	$ 3,445	$ 3,547	$ 3,649	$ 3,750	$ 3,852	$ 39,513

Profit and loss statement (second year)

Quarter	Q1	2 Q2	Q3	Q4	2
Sales	$81,686	$102,107	$110,275	$114,360	$408,428
Cost of goods sold	$16,870	$ 21,087	$ 22,774	$ 23,618	$ 84,349
Gross margin	79.3%	79.3%	79.3%	79.3%	79.3%
Operating income	$64,816	$ 81,020	$ 87,501	$ 90,742	$324,078
Expenses					
Payroll	$27,913	$ 34,891	$ 37,683	$ 39,078	$139,565
General and administrative	$ 2,746	$ 3,432	$ 3,707	$ 3,844	$ 13,728
Marketing expenses	$ 1,225	$ 1,532	$ 1,654	$ 1,715	$ 6,126
Professional fees and licensure	$ 721	$ 901	$ 973	$ 1,009	$ 3,605
Insurance costs	$ 525	$ 656	$ 709	$ 735	$ 2,625
Equipment maintenance costs	$ 1,760	$ 2,200	$ 2,376	$ 2,464	$ 8,800
Rent and utilities	$ 4,043	$ 5,053	$ 5,457	$ 5,660	$ 20,213
Miscellaneous costs	$ 245	$ 306	$ 331	$ 343	$ 1,225
Payroll taxes	$ 4,187	$ 5,234	$ 5,652	$ 5,862	$ 20,935
Total operating costs	$43,364	$ 54,205	$ 58,542	$ 60,710	$216,822
EBITDA	$21,451	$ 26,814	$ 28,959	$ 30,032	$107,256
Federal income tax	$ 6,408	$ 8,010	$ 8,651	$ 8,971	$ 32,040
State income tax	$ 971	$ 1,214	$ 1,311	$ 1,359	$ 4,855
Interest expense	$ 2,615	$ 2,566	$ 2,517	$ 2,466	$ 10,164
Depreciation expense	$ 1,920	$ 1,920	$ 1,920	$ 1,920	$ 7,679
Net profit	$ 9,538	$ 13,104	$ 14,561	$ 15,315	$ 52,519

Profit and loss statement (third year)

Quarter	Q1	Q2	Q3	Q4	3
Sales	$87,403	$109,254	$117,995	$122,365	$437,017
Cost of goods sold	$18,051	$ 22,563	$ 24,368	$ 25,271	$ 90,254
Gross margin	79.3%	79.3%	79.3%	79.3%	79.3%
Operating income	**$69,353**	**$ 86,691**	**$ 93,626**	**$ 97,094**	**$346,764**
Expenses					
Payroll	$28,750	$ 35,938	$ 38,813	$ 40,251	$143,752
General and administrative	$ 2,855	$ 3,569	$ 3,855	$ 3,998	$ 14,277
Marketing expenses	$ 1,311	$ 1,639	$ 1,770	$ 1,835	$ 6,555
Professional fees and licensure	$ 743	$ 928	$ 1,003	$ 1,040	$ 3,713
Insurance costs	$ 551	$ 689	$ 744	$ 772	$ 2,756
Equipment maintenance costs	$ 1,936	$ 2,420	$ 2,614	$ 2,710	$ 9,680
Rent and utilities	$ 4,245	$ 5,306	$ 5,730	$ 5,942	$ 21,223
Miscellaneous costs	$ 262	$ 328	$ 354	$ 367	$ 1,311
Payroll taxes	$ 4,313	$ 5,391	$ 5,822	$ 6,038	$ 21,563
Total operating costs	**$44,966**	**$ 56,208**	**$ 60,704**	**$ 62,953**	**$224,831**
EBITDA	**$24,387**	**$ 30,483**	**$ 32,922**	**$ 34,141**	**$121,933**
Federal income tax	$ 7,431	$ 9,289	$ 10,032	$ 10,404	$ 37,157
State income tax	$ 1,126	$ 1,407	$ 1,520	$ 1,576	$ 5,630
Interest expense	$ 2,414	$ 2,361	$ 2,307	$ 2,252	$ 9,335
Depreciation expense	$ 1,920	$ 1,920	$ 1,920	$ 1,920	$ 7,679
Net profit	**$11,495**	**$ 15,505**	**$ 17,142**	**$ 17,989**	**$ 62,132**

7.11 Three Year Cash Flow Analysis

Cash flow analysis (first year)

Month	1	2	3	4	5	6	7	8
Cash from operations	$ 3,374	$ 3,475	$ 3,577	$ 3,678	$ 3,780	$ 3,882	$ 3,983	$ 4,085
Cash from receivables	$ 0	$ 0	$ 0	$ 0	$ 0	$ 0	$ 0	$ 0
Operating cash inflow	**$ 3,374**	**$ 3,475**	**$ 3,577**	**$ 3,678**	**$ 3,780**	**$ 3,882**	**$ 3,983**	**$ 4,085**
Other cash inflows								
Equity investment	$ 25,000	$ 0	$ 0	$ 0	$ 0	$ 0	$ 0	$ 0
Increased borrowings	$125,000	$ 0	$ 0	$ 0	$ 0	$ 0	$ 0	$ 0
Sales of business assets	$ 0	$ 0	$ 0	$ 0	$ 0	$ 0	$ 0	$ 0
A/P increases	$ 316	$ 316	$ 316	$ 316	$ 316	$ 316	$ 316	$ 316
Total other cash inflows	**$150,316**	**$ 316**	**$ 316**	**$ 316**	**$ 316**	**$ 316**	**$ 316**	**$ 316**
Total cash inflow	**$153,690**	**$ 3,791**	**$ 3,893**	**$ 3,994**	**$ 4,096**	**$ 4,197**	**$ 4,299**	**$ 4,401**
Cash outflows								
Repayment of principal	$ 646	$ 651	$ 656	$ 661	$ 666	$ 671	$ 676	$ 681
A/P decreases	$ 207	$ 207	$ 207	$ 207	$ 207	$ 207	$ 207	$ 207
A/R increases	$ 0	$ 0	$ 0	$ 0	$ 0	$ 0	$ 0	$ 0
Asset purchases	$107,500	$ 0	$ 0	$ 0	$ 0	$ 0	$ 0	$ 0
Dividends	$ 0	$ 0	$ 0	$ 0	$ 0	$ 0	$ 0	$ 0
Total cash outflows	**$108,353**	**$ 858**	**$ 863**	**$ 868**	**$ 873**	**$ 878**	**$ 883**	**$ 888**
Net cash flow	**$ 45,336**	**$ 2,933**	**$ 3,030**	**$ 3,126**	**$ 3,223**	**$ 3,319**	**$ 3,416**	**$ 3,513**
Cash balance	**$ 45,336**	**$48,269**	**$51,299**	**$54,425**	**$57,648**	**$60,967**	**$64,383**	**$67,896**

Cash flow analysis (first year cont.)

Month	9	10	11	12	1
Cash from operations	$ 4,187	$ 4,288	$ 4,390	$ 4,492	$ 47,191
Cash from receivables	$ 0	$ 0	$ 0	$ 0	$ 0
Operating cash inflow	**$ 4,187**	**$ 4,288**	**$ 4,390**	**$ 4,492**	**$ 47,191**
Other cash inflows					
Equity investment	$ 0	$ 0	$ 0	$ 0	$ 25,000
Increased borrowings	$ 0	$ 0	$ 0	$ 0	$125,000
Sales of business assets	$ 0	$ 0	$ 0	$ 0	$ 0
A/P increases	$ 316	$ 316	$ 316	$ 316	$ 3,790
Total other cash inflows	**$ 316**	**$ 316**	**$ 316**	**$ 316**	**$153,790**
Total cash inflow	**$ 4,502**	**$ 4,604**	**$ 4,706**	**$ 4,808**	**$200,981**
Cash outflows					
Repayment of principal	$ 686	$ 691	$ 696	$ 701	$ 8,079
A/P decreases	$ 207	$ 207	$ 207	$ 207	$ 2,489
A/R increases	$ 0	$ 0	$ 0	$ 0	$ 0
Asset purchases	$ 0	$ 0	$ 0	$ 0	$107,500
Dividends	$ 0	$ 0	$ 0	$33,034	$ 33,034
Total cash outflows	**$ 893**	**$ 898**	**$ 903**	**$33,943**	**$151,102**
Net cash flow	**$ 3,609**	**$ 3,706**	**$ 3,803**	**−$29,135**	**$ 49,879**
Cash balance	**$71,505**	**$75,211**	**$79,014**	**$49,879**	**$ 49,879**

Cash flow analysis (second year)

Quarter	Q1	2 Q2	Q3	Q4	2
Cash from operations	$12,039	$15,049	$16,253	$16,855	$60,197
Cash from receivables	$ 0	$ 0	$ 0	$ 0	$ 0
Operating cash inflow	**$12,039**	**$15,049**	**$16,253**	**$16,855**	**$60,197**
Other cash inflows					
Equity investment	$ 0	$ 0	$ 0	$ 0	$ 0
Increased borrowings	$ 0	$ 0	$ 0	$ 0	$ 0
Sales of business assets	$ 0	$ 0	$ 0	$ 0	$ 0
A/P increases	$ 872	$ 1,090	$ 1,177	$ 1,220	$ 4,359
Total other cash inflows	**$ 872**	**$ 1,090**	**$ 1,177**	**$ 1,220**	**$ 4,359**
Total cash inflow	**$12,911**	**$16,139**	**$17,430**	**$18,076**	**$64,556**
Cash outflows					
Repayment of principal	$ 2,136	$ 2,184	$ 2,233	$ 2,284	$ 8,837
A/P decreases	$ 597	$ 747	$ 806	$ 836	$ 2,987
A/R increases	$ 0	$ 0	$ 0	$ 0	$ 0
Asset purchases	$ 1,204	$ 1,505	$ 1,625	$ 1,686	$ 6,020
Dividends	$ 8,428	$10,535	$11,377	$11,799	$42,138
Total cash outflows	**$12,364**	**$14,970**	**$16,043**	**$16,605**	**$59,982**
Net cash flow	**$ 547**	**$ 1,169**	**$ 1,388**	**$ 1,471**	**$ 4,574**
Cash balance	**$50,426**	**$51,595**	**$52,982**	**$54,453**	**$54,453**

Cash flow analysis (third year)

Quarter	Q1	Q2	Q3	Q4	3
Cash from operations	$13,962	$17,453	$18,849	$19,547	$69,811
Cash from receivables	$ 0	$ 0	$ 0	$ 0	$ 0
Operating cash inflow	**$13,962**	**$17,453**	**$18,849**	**$19,547**	**$69,811**
Other cash inflows					
Equity investment	$ 0	$ 0	$ 0	$ 0	$ 0
Increased borrowings	$ 0	$ 0	$ 0	$ 0	$ 0
Sales of business assets	$ 0	$ 0	$ 0	$ 0	$ 0
A/P increases	$ 1,002	$ 1,253	$ 1,353	$ 1,403	$ 5,012
Total other cash inflows	**$ 1,002**	**$ 1,253**	**$ 1,353**	**$ 1,403**	**$ 5,012**
Total cash inflow	**$14,965**	**$18,706**	**$20,202**	**$20,950**	**$74,823**
Cash outflows					
Repayment of principal	$ 2,336	$ 2,389	$ 2,443	$ 2,498	$ 9,666
A/P decreases	$ 717	$ 896	$ 968	$ 1,004	$ 3,584
A/R increases	$ 0	$ 0	$ 0	$ 0	$ 0
Asset purchases	$ 1,396	$ 1,745	$ 1,885	$ 1,955	$ 6,981
Dividends	$ 9,773	$12,217	$13,194	$13,683	$48,867
Total cash outflows	**$14,222**	**$17,247**	**$18,490**	**$19,140**	**$69,099**
Net cash flow	**$ 742**	**$ 1,459**	**$ 1,712**	**$ 1,811**	**$ 5,724**
Cash balance	**$55,195**	**$56,654**	**$58,366**	**$60,177**	**$60,177**

Marina

The Bayshore Marina

3456 Bayshore Dr.
St. Petersburg, FL 33712

BizPlanDB.com

The Bayshore Marina is a Florida based corporation that will provide rental spaces for customers with boats and yachts as well as boat/yacht maintenance services to customers in its targeted market.

1.0 EXECUTIVE SUMMARY

The purpose of this business plan is to raise $5,000,000 for the development of a marina while showcasing the expected financials and operations over the next three years. The Bayshore Marina is a Florida based corporation that will provide rental spaces for customers with boats and yachts as well as boat/yacht maintenance services to customers in its targeted market. The Company was founded in 2010 by Edward Dorrington.

1.1 The Services

The primary source of revenue for The Bayshore Marina will come from the rental of boat slips and spaces for yachts within its facility. Approximately 60% of the aggregate revenues of the business will come from this service. Management is currently sourcing the location of the planned marina site. Mr. Dorrington expects that The Bayshore Marina will feature 100 slips and yacht spaces that will generate an approximate monthly income of $50,000.

The Bayshore Marina will also provide boat/yacht maintenance services, which will greatly enhance the profitability of the business. Mr. Dorrington expects that 35% of the Company's income will be derived from these services.

The third section of the business plan will further describe the services offered by The Bayshore Marina.

1.2 Financing

At this time, Mr. Dorrington is seeking to raise $5,000,000 for the development of The Bayshore Marina. Tentatively, he is seeking to sell a 49% equity interest in the business in exchange for the requisite capital. The financing will be used for the following:

- Development of the marina location.
- Financing for the first six months of operation.
- Capital to purchase equipment related to the maintenance of boats/yachts.

The second section of the business plan will further document the usage of funds and the potential returns for an investor.

1.3 Mission Statement

The Bayshore Marina's mission is to become the recognized local leader in its targeted market for slip rental and boat/yacht maintenance services.

1.4 Management Team

The Company was founded by Edward Dorrington. Mr. Dorrington has more than 10 years of experience in the marine industry. Through his expertise, he will be able to bring the operations of the business to profitability within its first year of operations.

1.5 Sales Forecasts

Mr. Dorrington expects a strong rate of growth at the start of operations. Below are the expected financials over the next three years.

Proforma profit and loss (yearly)

Year	1	2	3
Sales	$1,091,880	$1,201,068	$1,321,175
Operating costs	$ 566,423	$ 620,080	$ 643,120
EBITDA	$ 419,302	$ 464,218	$ 549,607
Taxes, interest, and depreciation	$ 257,225	$ 274,293	$ 306,741
Net profit	$ 162,077	$ 189,925	$ 242,867

Sales, operating costs, and profit forecast

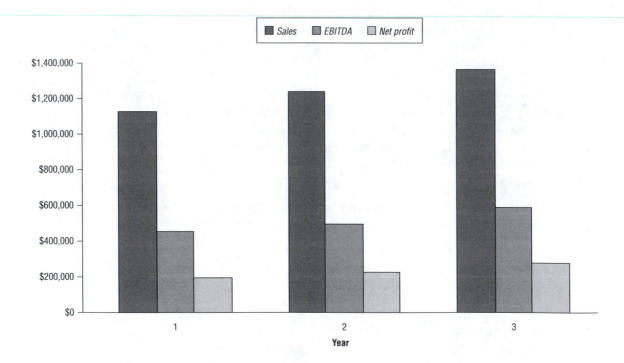

1.6 Expansion Plan

The business will aggressively expand during the first three years of operation. Mr. Dorrington intends to implement marketing campaigns that will effectively target wealthy individuals within the target market. Mr. Dorrington will also target boat/yacht dealers that will refer their clients to The Bayshore Marina.

2.0 COMPANY AND FINANCING SUMMARY

2.1 Registered Name and Corporate Structure

The Company is registered as a corporation in the State of Florida.

2.2 Required Funds

At this time, The Bayshore Marina requires $5,000,000 of investor funds. Below is a breakdown of how these funds will be used:

Projected startup costs

Marina development	$3,775,000
Working capital	$ 350,000
FF&E	$ 250,000
Property improvements	$ 300,000
Security deposits	$ 50,000
Insurance	$ 25,000
Boat/Yacht equipment	$ 175,000
Marketing budget	$ 50,000
Miscellaneous and unforeseen costs	$ 25,000
Total startup costs	**$5,000,000**

2.3 Investor Equity

Mr. Dorrington is seeking to sell a 49% ownership interest in The Bayshore Marina in exchange for the capital sought in this business plan. The investor will also receive a seat on the board of directors and a regular stream of dividends starting in the first year of operations. Please reference the Company's private placement memorandum for more information regarding this investment.

2.4 Management Equity

Edward Dorrington will retain a 51% ownership stake in the business once the requisite capital is raised.

2.5 Exit Strategy

In the event that Management wishes to sell The Bayshore Marina, the business will contract a real estate or business brokerage to market the property for sale to a third party. Based on historical sales figures, marinas typically sell for 9 to 15 times earnings as a substantial portion of the equity of the business is real estate based. Mr. Dorrington expects that the completed marina property will have a fair market value of nearly $6.1 million by the third year of operation.

3.0 MARINA SERVICES

Below is a description of the services offered by The Bayshore Marina.

3.1 Marina Rental Services

The Bayshore Marina will have approximately 100 total slips with 85 reserved for small and medium sized boats and 15 for large scale yachts. Each month, the Company expects to generate approximately $50,000 of rental income from its client base. One of the most positive aspects of operating a marina is that the clientele tend to be wealthy people that will be able to continually afford the services and rental fees associated with The Bayshore Marina. Smaller slips will rent for approximately $300 to $450 per month while yacht docking fees will range from $1,000 to $1,500 depending on the size of the boat.

3.2 Maintenance of Boats/Yachts

The Company's second revenue center will be the ongoing maintenance of boats and yachts on behalf of customers. At the onset of operations, Management will have two to three employees on staff that will wash and care for all boats docked at The Bayshore Marina. The business may also contract (or hire in-house) a boat/yacht mechanic that can perform simple to moderately complex mechanical repairs on site on behalf of clients. As stated in the executive summary, Mr. Dorrington expects that approximately 35% of the gross income will come from this revenue center.

It should be noted that this is an extremely important revenue center for the business as it will provide the business with a continuous stream of income despite deleterious changes in the economy.

3.3 Ancillary Income

The business will also generate a modest amount of ancillary income from miscellaneous service charges, marine gasoline filling fees, and late rental fees applied to customer's accounts. This revenue center will generate approximately 5% of the Company's gross revenues.

4.0 STRATEGIC AND MARKET ANALYSIS

4.1 Economic Outlook

This section of the analysis will detail the economic climate, the marina industry, the customer profile, and the competition that the business will face as it progresses through its business operations.

Currently, the economic market condition in the United States is in recession. This slowdown in the economy has also greatly impacted real estate sales, which has halted to historical lows. Many economists expect that this recession will continue until mid-2010, at which point the economy will begin a prolonged recovery period.

4.2 Industry Analysis

Within the United States, there are more than 4,300 marinas that aggregately generate more than $3.3 billion per year and provide jobs for more than 30,000 people. In each of the last five years, aggregate income paid to employees has exceeded $750,000,000.

This is a mature industry, and the future expected growth rate will be on par with that of the general economy. As stated earlier, marinas tend to operate with strong economic stability as the clients of these businesses tend to be wealthier people that can continue to afford marina fees and boat maintenance despite negative economic climates.

4.3 Customer Profile

The Bayshore Marina's average client will be an upper middle class to upper class man or woman living in the Company's target market. Common traits among clients will include:

- Annual household income exceeding $150,000

- Lives or works no more than 15 miles from the Company's location.

- Will spend $300 to $1,500 on slip rentals and boat maintenance fees.

- Has a boat with a value in excess of $30,000.

Within the Company's targeted market within the Tampa Bay-St. Petersburg Metropolitan Area, there are approximately 10,000 people that own registered boats and yachts that would require the services of a marina on an ongoing basis. Additionally, it should be noted that among the people that will enroll in the Company's marina and boat care service, the incomes generated by these customers are typically very high and immune from deleterious changes in the economy. As such, the business will be able to remain profitable and cash flow positive at all times.

4.4 Competition

The Tampa Bay-St. Petersburg Metropolitan Area currently has seven operating marinas that provide both a location to dock a vessel as well as boat/yacht maintenance services. At this time, the demand for marina services is extremely strong as all other marinas are operating at near or full capacity. In fact, marinas that are located within the Tampa Bay-St. Petersburg Metropolitan Area have extensive waiting lists among people that are looking to obtain a boat to dock. As such, the business will be able to immediately generate revenues once the completion of the marina is complete.

5.0 MARKETING PLAN

The Bayshore Marina intends to maintain an extensive marketing campaign that will ensure maximum visibility for the business in its targeted market. Below is an overview of the marketing strategies and objectives of the business.

5.1 Marketing Objectives

- Develop an online presence by developing a website and placing the Company's name and contact information with online directories.

- Implement a local campaign with the Company's targeted market via the use of local newspaper advertisements, and word of mouth advertising.

- Establish relationships with boat/yacht dealers that will refer business to The Bayshore Marina.

5.2 Marketing Strategies

Mr. Dorrington intends on using a number of marketing strategies to generate immediate rental of slips within The Bayshore Marina. Foremost, the Company will develop relationships with nearby boat and yacht dealers that will provide The Bayshore Marina with an influx of referrals among people that have recently purchased boats of yachts. This will ensure that the business reaches maximum occupancy by the end of the first year of operations.

The Bayshore Marina will also use an internet based strategy. This is very important as many people seeking local services, such as marinas, now the Internet to conduct their preliminary searches. Mr. Dorrington will register The Bayshore Marina with online portals so that potential customers can easily reach the business. The Company will also develop its own online website showcasing the marina, its facilities, its Management, preliminary pricing information, and relevant contact information along with directions to the facility.

The Company will maintain a sizable amount of print and traditional advertising methods within local markets to promote the marina rental and boat/yacht maintenance services that the Company is selling.

5.3 Pricing

Due to the strong demand among wealthy Floridians for marina services, Management anticipates that it can charge $300 to $450 per month for each slip rented to an individual that has a small or medium sized boat; large Yacht docking fees will range from $1,000 to $1,500. Revenues generated from boat care services will vary depending on the vessel and its ongoing needs.

6.0 ORGANIZATIONAL PLAN AND PERSONNEL SUMMARY

6.1 Corporate Organization

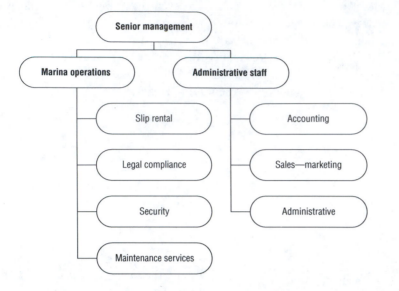

6.2 Organizational Budget

Personnel plan—yearly

Year	1	2	3
Owner	$ 75,000	$ 77,250	$ 79,568
Marina manager	$ 65,000	$ 66,950	$ 68,959
Marina employees	$137,500	$169,950	$175,049
Accountant	$ 37,500	$ 38,625	$ 39,784
Administrative	$ 66,000	$ 67,980	$ 70,019
Total	**$381,000**	**$420,755**	**$433,378**

Numbers of personnel

Owner	1	1	1
Marina manager	1	1	1
Marina employees	5	6	6
Accountant	1	1	1
Administrative	3	3	3
Totals	**11**	**12**	**12**

Personnel expense breakdown

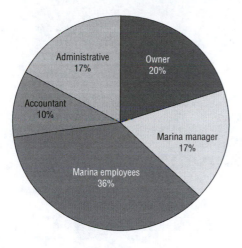

7.0 FINANCIAL PLAN

7.1 Underlying Assumptions

The Company has based its proforma financial statements on the following:

- The marina will have an annual revenue growth rate of 10% per year.

- Mr. Dorrington will acquire $5,000,000 of equity funds to develop the marina.

- The marina property will appreciate at an annual rate of 6% per year.

7.2 Sensitivity Analysis

In the event of an economic downturn, the business may have a decline in its revenues. Boats and yachts are a luxury, and during an economic slowdown the business may see a drop in its top line revenues as people sell their boats. However, and as stated earlier, The Bayshore Marina's primary clientele will consist of wealthy people who can continue to afford slip rentals and boat maintenance services despite deleterious changes in the economy.

7.3 Source of Funds

Financing

Equity contributions	
Investor(s)	$ 5,000,000.00
Total equity financing	**$5,000,000.00**
Banks and lenders	
Total debt financing	$ 0.00
Total financing	**$5,000,000.00**

7.4 General Assumptions

General assumptions

Year	1	2	3
Short term interest rate	9.5%	9.5%	9.5%
Long term interest rate	10.0%	10.0%	10.0%
Federal tax rate	33.0%	33.0%	33.0%
State tax rate	5.0%	5.0%	5.0%
Personnel taxes	15.0%	15.0%	15.0%

7.5 Profit and Loss Statements

Proforma profit and loss (yearly)

Year	1	2	3
Sales	$1,091,880	$1,201,068	$1,321,175
Cost of goods sold	$ 106,155	$ 116,771	$ 128,448
Gross margin	90.28%	90.28%	90.28%
Operating income	$ 985,725	$1,084,298	$1,192,727
Expenses			
Payroll	$ 381,000	$ 420,755	$ 433,378
General and administrative	$ 25,200	$ 26,208	$ 27,256
Marketing expenses	$ 10,919	$ 12,011	$ 13,212
Professional fees and licensure	$ 15,219	$ 15,676	$ 16,146
Insurance costs	$ 21,987	$ 23,086	$ 24,241
Travel and vehicle costs	$ 17,596	$ 19,356	$ 21,291
Marina maintenance	$ 24,250	$ 25,463	$ 26,736
Miscellaneous costs	$ 13,103	$ 14,413	$ 15,854
Payroll taxes	$ 57,150	$ 63,113	$ 65,007
Total operating costs	$ 566,423	$ 620,080	$ 643,120
EBITDA	$ 419,302	$ 464,218	$ 549,607
Federal income tax	$ 138,370	$ 153,192	$ 181,370
State income tax	$ 20,965	$ 23,211	$ 27,480
Interest expense	$ 0	$ 0	$ 0
Depreciation expenses	$ 97,890	$ 97,890	$ 97,890
Net profit	$ 162,077	$ 189,925	$ 242,867
Profit margin	14.84%	15.81%	18.38%

Sales, operating costs, and profit forecast

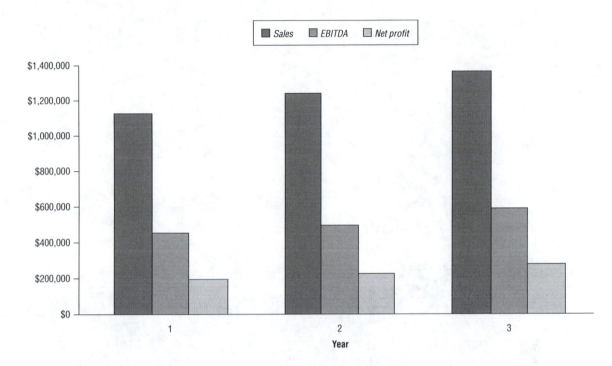

7.6 Cash Flow Analysis

Proforma cash flow analysis—yearly

Year	1	2	3
Cash from operations	$ 259,967	$287,815	$340,757
Cash from receivables	$ 0	$ 0	$ 0
Operating cash inflow	**$ 259,967**	**$287,815**	**$340,757**
Other cash inflows			
Equity investment	$5,000,000	$ 0	$ 0
Increased borrowings	$ 0	$ 0	$ 0
Sales of business assets	$ 0	$ 0	$ 0
A/P increases	$ 37,902	$ 43,587	$ 50,125
Total other cash inflows	**$5,037,902**	**$ 43,587**	**$ 50,125**
Total cash inflow	**$5,297,869**	**$331,402**	**$390,882**
Cash outflows			
Repayment of principal	$ 0	$ 0	$ 0
A/P decreases	$ 24,897	$ 29,876	$ 35,852
A/R increases	$ 0	$ 0	$ 0
Asset purchases	$4,600,000	$ 71,954	$ 85,189
Dividends	$ 181,977	$201,470	$238,530
Total cash outflows	**$4,806,874**	**$303,301**	**$359,570**
Net cash flow	**$ 490,995**	**$ 28,102**	**$ 31,312**
Cash balance	**$ 490,995**	**$519,097**	**$550,408**

Proforma cash flow (yearly)

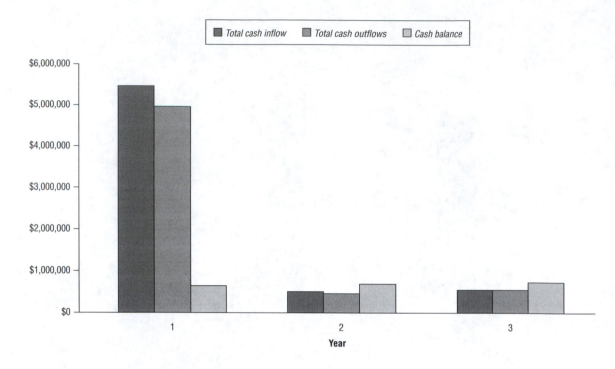

7.7 Balance Sheet

Proforma balance sheet—yearly

Year	1	2	3
Assets			
Cash	$ 490,995	$ 519,097	$ 550,408
Amortized development/expansion costs	$ 150,000	$ 157,195	$ 165,714
Marina property	$ 4,319,500	$ 4,578,670	$ 4,853,390
FF&E	$ 250,000	$ 278,781	$ 312,857
Boat/Yacht equipment	$ 175,000	$ 210,977	$ 253,571
Accumulated depreciation	($ 97,890)	($ 195,780)	($ 293,670)
Total assets	**$5,287,605**	**$5,548,941**	**$5,842,271**
Liabilities and equity			
Accounts payable	$ 13,005	$ 26,716	$ 40,990
Long term liabilities	$ 0	$ 0	$ 0
Other liabilities	$ 0	$ 0	$ 0
Total liabilities	**$ 13,005**	**$ 26,716**	**$ 40,990**
Net worth	**$5,274,600**	**$5,522,225**	**$5,801,282**
Total liabilities and equity	**$5,287,605**	**$5,548,941**	**$5,842,271**

Proforma balance sheet

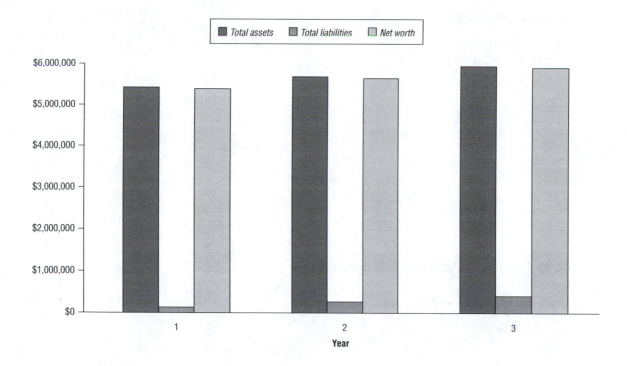

7.8 Breakeven Analysis

Monthly break even analysis

Year	1	2	3
Monthly revenue	$ 52,285	$ 57,238	$ 59,365
Yearly revenue	$627,423	$686,858	$712,379

Break even analysis

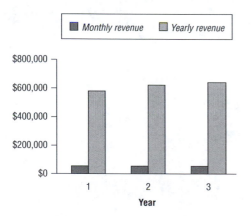

7.9 Business Ratios

Business ratios—yearly

Year	1	2	3
Sales			
Sales growth	0.0%	10.0%	10.0%
Gross margin	90.3%	90.3%	90.3%
Financials			
Profit margin	14.84%	15.81%	18.38%
Assets to liabilities	406.58	207.70	142.53
Equity to liabilities	405.58	206.70	141.53
Assets to equity	1.00	1.00	1.01
Liquidity			
Acid test	37.75	19.43	13.43
Cash to assets	0.09	0.09	0.09

7.10 Three Year Profit and Loss Statement

Profit and loss statement (first year)

Month	1	2	3	4	5	6	7
Sales	**$90,000**	**$90,180**	**$90,360**	**$90,540**	**$90,720**	**$90,900**	**$91,080**
Cost of goods sold	$ 8,750	$ 8,768	$ 8,785	$ 8,803	$ 8,820	$ 8,838	$ 8,855
Gross margin	90.3%	90.3%	90.3%	90.3%	90.3%	90.3%	90.3%
Operating income	**$81,250**	**$81,413**	**$81,575**	**$81,738**	**$81,900**	**$82,063**	**$82,225**
Expenses							
Payroll	$31,750	$31,750	$31,750	$31,750	$31,750	$31,750	$31,750
General and administrative	$ 2,100	$ 2,100	$ 2,100	$ 2,100	$ 2,100	$ 2,100	$ 2,100
Marketing expenses	$ 910	$ 910	$ 910	$ 910	$ 910	$ 910	$ 910
Professional fees and licensure	$ 1,268	$ 1,268	$ 1,268	$ 1,268	$ 1,268	$ 1,268	$ 1,268
Insurance costs	$ 1,832	$ 1,832	$ 1,832	$ 1,832	$ 1,832	$ 1,832	$ 1,832
Travel and vehicle costs	$ 1,466	$ 1,466	$ 1,466	$ 1,466	$ 1,466	$ 1,466	$ 1,466
Marina maintenance	$ 2,021	$ 2,021	$ 2,021	$ 2,021	$ 2,021	$ 2,021	$ 2,021
Miscellaneous costs	$ 1,092	$ 1,092	$ 1,092	$ 1,092	$ 1,092	$ 1,092	$ 1,092
Payroll taxes	$ 4,763	$ 4,763	$ 4,763	$ 4,763	$ 4,763	$ 4,763	$ 4,763
Total operating costs	**$47,202**	**$47,202**	**$47,202**	**$47,202**	**$47,202**	**$47,202**	**$47,202**
EBITDA	**$34,048**	**$34,211**	**$34,373**	**$34,536**	**$34,698**	**$34,861**	**$35,023**
Federal income tax	$11,405	$11,428	$11,451	$11,474	$11,497	$11,519	$11,542
State income tax	$ 1,728	$ 1,732	$ 1,735	$ 1,738	$ 1,742	$ 1,745	$ 1,749
Interest expense	$ 0	$ 0	$ 0	$ 0	$ 0	$ 0	$ 0
Depreciation expense	$ 8,158	$ 8,158	$ 8,158	$ 8,158	$ 8,158	$ 8,158	$ 8,158
Net profit	**$12,757**	**$12,893**	**$13,030**	**$13,166**	**$13,302**	**$13,438**	**$13,575**

Profit and loss statement (first year cont.)

Month	8	9	10	11	12	1
Sales	$91,260	$91,440	$91,620	$91,800	$91,980	$1,091,880
Cost of goods sold	$ 8,873	$ 8,890	$ 8,908	$ 8,925	$ 8,943	$ 106,155
Gross margin	90.3%	90.3%	90.3%	90.3%	90.3%	90.3%
Operating income	$82,388	$82,550	$82,713	$82,875	$83,038	$ 985,725
Expenses						
Payroll	$31,750	$31,750	$31,750	$31,750	$31,750	$ 381,000
General and administrative	$ 2,100	$ 2,100	$ 2,100	$ 2,100	$ 2,100	$ 25,200
Marketing expenses	$ 910	$ 910	$ 910	$ 910	$ 910	$ 10,919
Professional fees and licensure	$ 1,268	$ 1,268	$ 1,268	$ 1,268	$ 1,268	$ 15,219
Insurance costs	$ 1,832	$ 1,832	$ 1,832	$ 1,832	$ 1,832	$ 21,987
Travel and vehicle costs	$ 1,466	$ 1,466	$ 1,466	$ 1,466	$ 1,466	$ 17,596
Marina maintenance	$ 2,021	$ 2,021	$ 2,021	$ 2,021	$ 2,021	$ 24,250
Miscellaneous costs	$ 1,092	$ 1,092	$ 1,092	$ 1,092	$ 1,092	$ 13,103
Payroll taxes	$ 4,763	$ 4,763	$ 4,763	$ 4,763	$ 4,763	$ 57,150
Total operating costs	$47,202	$47,202	$47,202	$47,202	$47,202	$ 566,423
EBITDA	$35,186	$35,348	$35,511	$35,673	$35,836	$ 419,302
Federal income tax	$11,565	$11,588	$11,611	$11,633	$11,656	$ 138,370
State income tax	$ 1,752	$ 1,756	$ 1,759	$ 1,763	$ 1,766	$ 20,965
Interest expense	$ 0	$ 0	$ 0	$ 0	$ 0	$ 0
Depreciation expense	$ 8,158	$ 8,158	$ 8,158	$ 8,158	$ 8,158	$ 97,890
Net profit	$13,711	$13,847	$13,983	$14,119	$14,256	$ 162,077

Profit and loss statement (second year)

Quarter	Q1	Q2	Q3	Q4	2
Sales	$240,214	$300,267	$324,288	$336,299	$1,201,068
Cost of goods sold	$ 23,354	$ 29,193	$ 31,528	$ 32,696	$ 116,771
Gross margin	90.3%	90.3%	90.3%	90.3%	90.3%
Operating income	$216,860	$271,074	$292,760	$303,603	$1,084,298
Expenses					
Payroll	$ 84,151	$105,189	$113,604	$117,811	$ 420,755
General and administrative	$ 5,242	$ 6,552	$ 7,076	$ 7,338	$ 26,208
Marketing expenses	$ 2,402	$ 3,003	$ 3,243	$ 3,363	$ 12,011
Professional fees and licensure	$ 3,135	$ 3,919	$ 4,232	$ 4,389	$ 15,676
Insurance costs	$ 4,617	$ 5,772	$ 6,233	$ 6,464	$ 23,086
Travel and vehicle costs	$ 3,871	$ 4,839	$ 5,226	$ 5,420	$ 19,356
Marina maintenance	$ 5,093	$ 6,366	$ 6,875	$ 7,130	$ 25,463
Miscellaneous costs	$ 2,883	$ 3,603	$ 3,891	$ 4,036	$ 14,413
Payroll taxes	$ 12,623	$ 15,778	$ 17,041	$ 17,672	$ 63,113
Total operating costs	$124,016	$155,020	$167,422	$173,622	$ 620,080
EBITDA	$ 92,844	$116,054	$125,339	$129,981	$ 464,218
Federal income tax	$ 30,638	$ 38,298	$ 41,362	$ 42,894	$ 153,192
State income tax	$ 4,642	$ 5,803	$ 6,267	$ 6,499	$ 23,211
Interest expense	$ 0	$ 0	$ 0	$ 0	$ 0
Depreciation expense	$ 24,473	$ 24,473	$ 24,473	$ 24,473	$ 97,890
Net profit	$ 33,090	$ 47,481	$ 53,238	$ 56,116	$ 189,925

Profit and loss statement (third year)

Quarter	Q1	3 Q2	Q3	Q4	3
Sales	$264,235	$330,294	$356,717	$369,929	$1,321,175
Cost of goods sold	$ 25,690	$ 32,112	$ 34,681	$ 35,965	$ 128,448
Gross margin	90.3%	90.3%	90.3%	90.3%	90.3%
Operating income	**$238,545**	**$298,182**	**$322,036**	**$333,964**	**$1,192,727**
Expenses					
Payroll	$ 86,676	$108,344	$117,012	$121,346	$ 433,378
General and administrative	$ 5,451	$ 6,814	$ 7,359	$ 7,632	$ 27,256
Marketing expenses	$ 2,642	$ 3,303	$ 3,567	$ 3,699	$ 13,212
Professional fees and licensure	$ 3,229	$ 4,036	$ 4,359	$ 4,521	$ 16,146
Insurance costs	$ 4,848	$ 6,060	$ 6,545	$ 6,787	$ 24,241
Travel and vehicle costs	$ 4,258	$ 5,323	$ 5,749	$ 5,962	$ 21,291
Marina maintenance	$ 5,347	$ 6,684	$ 7,219	$ 7,486	$ 26,736
Miscellaneous costs	$ 3,171	$ 3,964	$ 4,281	$ 4,439	$ 15,854
Payroll taxes	$ 13,001	$ 16,252	$ 17,552	$ 18,202	$ 65,007
Total operating costs	**$128,624**	**$160,780**	**$173,642**	**$180,074**	**$ 643,120**
EBITDA	**$109,921**	**$137,402**	**$148,394**	**$153,890**	**$ 549,607**
Federal income tax	$ 36,274	$ 45,343	$ 48,970	$ 50,784	$ 181,370
State income tax	$ 5,496	$ 6,870	$ 7,420	$ 7,695	$ 27,480
Interest expense	$ 0	$ 0	$ 0	$ 0	$ 0
Depreciation expense	$ 24,473	$ 24,473	$ 24,473	$ 24,473	$ 97,890
Net profit	**$ 43,679**	**$ 60,717**	**$ 67,532**	**$ 70,939**	**$ 242,867**

7.11 Three Year Cash Flow Analysis

Cash flow analysis (first year)

Month	1	2	3	4	5	6	7	8
Cash from operations	$ 20,915	$ 21,051	$ 21,187	$ 21,323	$ 21,460	$ 21,596	$ 21,732	$ 21,868
Cash from receivables	$ 0	$ 0	$ 0	$ 0	$ 0	$ 0	$ 0	$ 0
Operating cash inflow	**$ 20,915**	**$ 21,051**	**$ 21,187**	**$ 21,323**	**$ 21,460**	**$ 21,596**	**$ 21,732**	**$ 21,868**
Other cash inflows								
Equity investment	$5,000,000	$ 0	$ 0	$ 0	$ 0	$ 0	$ 0	$ 0
Increased borrowings	$ 0	$ 0	$ 0	$ 0	$ 0	$ 0	$ 0	$ 0
Sales of business assets	$ 0	$ 0	$ 0	$ 0	$ 0	$ 0	$ 0	$ 0
A/P increases	$ 3,159	$ 3,159	$ 3,159	$ 3,159	$ 3,159	$ 3,159	$ 3,159	$ 3,159
Total other cash inflows	**$5,003,159**	**$ 3,159**	**$ 3,159**	**$ 3,159**	**$ 3,159**	**$ 3,159**	**$ 3,159**	**$ 3,159**
Total cash inflow	**$5,024,073**	**$ 24,209**	**$ 24,346**	**$ 24,482**	**$ 24,618**	**$ 24,754**	**$ 24,891**	**$ 25,027**
Cash outflows								
Repayment of principal	$ 0	$ 0	$ 0	$ 0	$ 0	$ 0	$ 0	$ 0
A/P decreases	$ 2,075	$ 2,075	$ 2,075	$ 2,075	$ 2,075	$ 2,075	$ 2,075	$ 2,075
A/R increases	$ 0	$ 0	$ 0	$ 0	$ 0	$ 0	$ 0	$ 0
Asset purchases	$4,600,000	$ 0	$ 0	$ 0	$ 0	$ 0	$ 0	$ 0
Dividends	$ 0	$ 0	$ 0	$ 0	$ 0	$ 0	$ 0	$ 0
Total cash outflows	**$4,602,075**	**$ 2,075**	**$ 2,075**	**$ 2,075**	**$ 2,075**	**$ 2,075**	**$ 2,075**	**$ 2,075**
Net cash flow	**$ 421,998**	**$ 22,135**	**$ 22,271**	**$ 22,407**	**$ 22,543**	**$ 22,680**	**$ 22,816**	**$ 22,952**
Cash balance	**$ 421,998**	**$444,133**	**$466,404**	**$488,811**	**$511,354**	**$534,034**	**$556,850**	**$579,802**

Cash flow analysis (first year cont.)

Month	9	10	11	12	1
Cash from operations	$ 22,005	$ 22,141	$ 22,277	$ 22,413	$ 259,967
Cash from receivables	$ 0	$ 0	$ 0	$ 0	$ 0
Operating cash inflow	**$ 22,005**	**$ 22,141**	**$ 22,277**	**$ 22,413**	**$ 259,967**
Other cash inflows					
Equity investment	$ 0	$ 0	$ 0	$ 0	$5,000,000
Increased borrowings	$ 0	$ 0	$ 0	$ 0	$ 0
Sales of business assets	$ 0	$ 0	$ 0	$ 0	$ 0
A/P increases	$ 3,159	$ 3,159	$ 3,159	$ 3,159	$ 37,902
Total other cash inflows	$ 3,159	$ 3,159	$ 3,159	$ 3,159	$5,037,902
Total cash inflow	$ 25,163	$ 25,299	$ 25,435	$ 25,572	$5,297,869
Cash outflows					
Repayment of principal	$ 0	$ 0	$ 0	$ 0	$ 0
A/P decreases	$ 2,075	$ 2,075	$ 2,075	$ 2,075	$ 24,897
A/R increases	$ 0	$ 0	$ 0	$ 0	$ 0
Asset purchases	$ 0	$ 0	$ 0	$ 0	$4,600,000
Dividends	$ 0	$ 0	$ 0	$181,977	$ 181,977
Total cash outflows	$ 2,075	$ 2,075	$ 2,075	$184,052	$4,806,874
Net cash flow	**$ 23,088**	**$ 23,224**	**$ 23,361**	**−$158,480**	**$ 490,995**
Cash balance	**$602,890**	**$626,114**	**$649,475**	**$490,995**	**$ 490,995**

Cash flow analysis (second year)

Quarter	Q1	2 Q2	Q3	Q4	2
Cash from operations	$ 57,563	$ 71,954	$ 77,710	$ 80,588	$287,815
Cash from receivables	$ 0	$ 0	$ 0	$ 0	$ 0
Operating cash inflow	**$ 57,563**	**$ 71,954**	**$ 77,710**	**$ 80,588**	**$287,815**
Other cash inflows					
Equity investment	$ 0	$ 0	$ 0	$ 0	$ 0
Increased borrowings	$ 0	$ 0	$ 0	$ 0	$ 0
Sales of business assets	$ 0	$ 0	$ 0	$ 0	$ 0
A/P increases	$ 8,717	$ 10,897	$ 11,769	$ 12,204	$ 43,587
Total other cash inflows	$ 8,717	$ 10,897	$ 11,769	$ 12,204	$ 43,587
Total cash inflow	$ 66,280	$ 82,851	$ 89,479	$ 92,793	$331,402
Cash outflows					
Repayment of principal	$ 0	$ 0	$ 0	$ 0	$ 0
A/P decreases	$ 5,975	$ 7,469	$ 8,067	$ 8,365	$ 29,876
A/R increases	$ 0	$ 0	$ 0	$ 0	$ 0
Asset purchases	$ 14,391	$ 17,988	$ 19,428	$ 20,147	$ 71,954
Dividends	$ 40,294	$ 50,368	$ 54,397	$ 56,412	$201,470
Total cash outflows	$ 60,660	$ 75,825	$ 81,891	$ 84,924	$303,301
Net cash flow	**$ 5,620**	**$ 7,025**	**$ 7,587**	**$ 7,868**	**$ 28,102**
Cash balance	**$496,615**	**$503,641**	**$511,228**	**$519,097**	**$519,097**

Cash flow analysis (third year)

| Quarter | Q1 | 3 | | | |
		Q2	Q3	Q4	3
Cash from operations	$ 68,151	$ 85,189	$ 92,004	$ 95,412	$340,757
Cash from receivables	$ 0	$ 0	$ 0	$ 0	$ 0
Operating cash inflow	**$ 68,151**	**$ 85,189**	**$ 92,004**	**$ 95,412**	**$340,757**
Other cash inflows					
Equity investment	$ 0	$ 0	$ 0	$ 0	$ 0
Increased borrowings	$ 0	$ 0	$ 0	$ 0	$ 0
Sales of business assets	$ 0	$ 0	$ 0	$ 0	$ 0
A/P increases	$ 10,025	$ 12,531	$ 13,534	$ 14,035	$ 50,125
Total other cash inflows	**$ 10,025**	**$ 12,531**	**$ 13,534**	**$ 14,035**	**$ 50,125**
Total cash inflow	**$ 78,176**	**$ 97,721**	**$105,538**	**$109,447**	**$390,882**
Cash outflows					
Repayment of principal	$ 0	$ 0	$ 0	$ 0	$ 0
A/P decreases	$ 7,170	$ 8,963	$ 9,680	$ 10,038	$ 35,852
A/R increases	$ 0	$ 0	$ 0	$ 0	$ 0
Asset purchases	$ 17,038	$ 21,297	$ 23,001	$ 23,853	$ 85,189
Dividends	$ 47,706	$ 59,632	$ 64,403	$ 66,788	$238,530
Total cash outflows	**$ 71,914**	**$ 89,893**	**$ 97,084**	**$100,680**	**$359,570**
Net cash flow	**$ 6,262**	**$ 7,828**	**$ 8,454**	**$ 8,767**	**$ 31,312**
Cash balance	**$525,359**	**$533,187**	**$541,641**	**$550,408**	**$550,408**

Mobile Pizza Kitchen Business

Pizza2go–go Inc.

2381 Laramie Lane
College Park, Iowa 50017

Paul Greenland

Pizza2go–go Inc. is a mobile pizza kitchen business. Beyond the flexibility of being able to bring a great product directly to the target market, our mobile business model offers a number of other distinct advantages over a brick–and–mortar model. Specifically, we avoid the need to lease/purchase or maintain a physical facility, or pay property taxes. We also save on energy costs.

EXECUTIVE SUMMARY

Business Overview

In the ultracompetitive restaurant business, several factors are essential for success. Beyond delicious food and excellent customer service are the differentials that set one eatery apart from another. As a mobile pizza kitchen, we will bring good pizza to the hungry masses—wherever they are. By day, we will serve lunch and dinner to working people, usually in the Central City business district or directly on the premises of large organizations. By night, we will cater to college students who frequent the city's popular bars and night clubs.

Our promotional strategy will focus heavily on the use of social media (especially Twitter) to promote our whereabouts and specials, and build relationships with loyal followers. We also plan to forge alliances with some of the College Park's most popular bars and clubs, whereby we will promote planned appearances outside of their establishments via handbills and other tactics.

Beyond the flexibility of being able to bring a great product directly to the target market, our mobile business model offers a number of other distinct advantages over a brick–and–mortar model. Specifically, we avoid the need to lease/purchase or maintain a physical facility, or pay property taxes. We also save on energy costs.

MARKET ANALYSIS

According to data from the research firm TargetFind LLC, College Park, Iowa, was home to 58,600 residents in 2009 (20,500 households). By 2014 the population is projected to increase approximately 21 percent, reaching 71,300 (22,200 households).

As a "college town," which includes Smithfield Community College, Jonathan Roberts Technical College, and College Park University, the community of College Park is home to a disproportionately high concentration of younger people. Those aged 25 to 34 represent the largest population group (32%), followed by those aged 20 to 24 (21%). The next largest categories are those aged 45 to 54 (9%) and 35 to 44 (8%).

Additional research from TargetFind reveals that the College Park community was home to 1,576 business establishments in 2009. Among the total estimated employee population of 27,663, roughly half worked in the services field (13,323). Within this category, about 46 percent of all service employees worked for colleges and universities. Retail trade is the next–largest employer category, with 7,458 establishments.

Competition

As a pizzeria, Pizza2go–go competes with traditional brick–and–mortar restaurants. Within retail trade, restaurants are the largest employers in College Park, accounting for 78 establishments and 2,055 employees, or 27.6 percent of the category total. There currently are 18 pizzerias in College Park. Hands down, Frankie's on Main is the most popular pizzeria in town. Established during the 1940s, the restaurant has a loyal following that spans several generations. Papa Pietro's is the second–most–popular pizzeria. Together, these two locations probably corner 20 percent of the local pizza market, with smaller pizzerias accounting for the remainder.

Fortunately, Pizza2go–go is among the first mobile food operations in College Park. Currently, the only other mobile food operation is TacoTyme, a mobile taco unit. There clearly is plenty of capacity in the market for additional competitors.

INDUSTRY ANALYSIS

There is no questioning the popularity of pizza. According to Blumenfeld and Associates, the U.S. pizza industry is comprised of approximately 69,000 pizzerias, which generate more than $30 billion annually. Bolla Wines estimates that 93 percent of Americans consume at least one pizza every month. In addition, Packaged Facts estimates that the average American consumes about 23 pounds (46 slices) of pizza annually.

During the late 2000s pizzerias faced rising costs in a number of areas. Specifically, business operators contended with record high cheese prices and skyrocketing wheat costs, attributed to factors ranging from government ethanol subsidies to rising overseas demand. Collectively, these conditions made operating a pizza business more expensive. Coupled with weak economic conditions, cost–cutting became more important than ever before.

The mobile pizza kitchen model, which is considerably less expensive than operating a brick–and–mortar restaurant, is already well established in Europe. In recent years, the model has been catching on in the United States as well. Mobile pizza kitchens currently operate in Houston, Texas; New York City; Long Island, New York; Milwaukee, Wisconsin; Los Angeles; and Connecticut.

Although they don't currently operate in our market, one of Domino's Pizza's largest franchises operates a fleet of mobile pizza vehicles for events in a number of markets nationwide. In addition, Unique Pizza and Subs Corp. announced plans to produce 30 mobile pizza kitchens in mid–2008. Beyond pizza, the mobile model has been applied to other food types, including frozen yogurt, Swedish meatballs, barbecue, hot dogs, waffles, schnitzel, pastries, and even African and Bosnian cuisine.

In 2010 the National Restaurant Association (NRA) began featuring mobile food trucks at its annual trade show for the first time. In a May 2010 Associated Press article, NRA Senior Vice President of Research Hudson Riehle commented on the mobile food model, explaining: "This is definitely not a fad, it is the evolving of the restaurant industry."

According to NRA data, the restaurant industry had sales of $580 billion in 2010. According to the association's *2010 Restaurant Industry Overview,* the industry is a leading private–sector employer, providing jobs for approximately 12.7 million people who work at about 945,000 locations. Our establishment is part of the Eating Places segment of the industry, which generated sales of $388.5 billion in 2010.

PERSONNEL

Pizza2go–go is owned by Ed Cascio, a self–described industry veteran who made his first pizza pie in 1983. After working in the kitchen of a Chicago–area pizzeria throughout his high school years, Ed moved to Des Moines, Iowa, where he became manager of Tony's Pizza. In that role, he spent five years managing a family–owned restaurant that was frequently recognized as one of the city's best.

When Tony's decided to open two new locations, Ed was a natural choice to oversee the expansion effort. Once open, management of all three locations was entrusted to him. Under Ed's guidance, Tony's grew from a successful one–location operation to a thriving family–owned chain. A unique opportunity presented itself in 2002 when Ed became regional manager of PizzaTime Playhouse, a national pizzeria/arcade chain. There, he honed his management skills and received valuable training—especially in the areas of sales and marketing.

Throughout his 27–year career, Cascio has become intimately familiar with all aspects of pizza restaurant management and operations. Combined with his sales and marketing knowledge, and an entrepreneurial spirit, Ed has what it takes to make Pizza2go–go a success.

Ed Cascio will be responsible for the day–to–day management and operation of Pizza2go–go. Initially, he will employ four part–time staff members. Following a period of formal training (provided by Ed), his cross–trained staff will be able to operate the cash register and manage mobile unit receipts, and also make pizzas in accordance with pre–established standards. Temporary staff will be utilized when needed for large events.

Professional & Advisory Support

Pizza2go–go has established a business banking account with College Park Bank, including a merchant account for credit card payments. Tax advisement is provided by A–1 Financial Services LLC. In addition, legal services are provided by the law offices of Shelly Roberts & Associates.

GROWTH STRATEGY

Based upon our observation of the aforementioned mobile taco business, TacoTyme, as well as discussions with operators of other mobile pizza businesses nationwide, we are convinced that a mobile food service model will be tremendously successful in College Park. Even so, Ed Cascio realizes that there will be much to learn during the initial period of operation. To ensure excellent customer service and quality, the first year of our operations will be devoted to developing relationships with area customers and gaining a firm understanding of their tastes. The addition of a second mobile unit (or perhaps a completely different type of mobile food operation) is tentatively planned for our third year of operation, once our brand and reputation is firmly established in College Park.

SERVICES

Pizza2go–go will generate sales via two main channels: traditional street vending and on–site sales (e.g., events, company–sponsored lunches, etc.).

Menu

Pizza2go–go will offer the following types of pizza for $3.00 per slice, or $18 for an entire pie:

- Cheese
- Pepperoni

- Sausage
- Veggie
- Barbecue Chicken Pizza
- Meatball Pizza
- Slice of the Day

Our Slice of the Day selection could be named Surprise of the Day, because it is a special creation (not a choice from our regular menu). Drawing upon his many years in the pizza business, Ed Cascio has a relatively long list of specialty pizza recipes. These are customer favorites from popular restaurants throughout the country. Every day, Pizza2go–go customers will be to experience one of these delicious pies.

We will offer beverage products from the Coca–Cola Company, including:

- Coca–Cola Classic
- Caffeine–Free Coke
- Diet Coke
- Coke Zero
- Sprite
- Canada Dry Ginger Ale
- Caffeine–Free Diet Coke
- Cherry Coke
- Barq's Rootbeer
- Sunkist Orange
- Bottled water

MARKETING & SALES

Pizza2go–go's primary target markets are large companies who will sponsor our mobile pizza operation for employee lunch days and corporate events; the Central City business district lunch crowd; as well as college students who frequent one of the city's 27 bars and nightclubs.

In addition, other significant marketing opportunities include:

- College sporting events
- High school sporting events
- Special events
- Tailgating parties
- Fundraisers
- Festivals
- Concerts
- Carnivals and fairs
- Church functions
- PTA events

Our marketing plan focuses heavily on online promotion, and includes the following four tactics:

1. *Coupons and Specials:* We will promote special discounts (on single slices, entire pizzas, and beverages) via Facebook, Twitter, and handbills distributed at select bars and nightclubs.

2. *Loyalty Program:* We will develop a database of loyal customers, to whom we will e–mail special member–only coupons. In addition, for our loyalty club members, every 10th slice of pizza is free (something we can track via our electronic POS system), and a free Pizza2go–go T–shirt is received after they purchase their 100th slice.

3. *Online Advertising:* Pizza2go–go will advertise regularly on popular social media sites, such as Facebook. Compared to traditional print advertising, this is a cost effective tactic that will allow us to reach prospects in a highly targeted way (e.g., based on criteria such as age, gender, geography, etc.).

4. *Web Site:* Pizza2go–go will develop a Web site where customers can find details about our menu, submit ideas for new Slice of the Day pizza selections, link to our social media channels, view items in our online photo gallery, read special announcements, buy items from the Pizza2go–go mer- chandise store (e.g., hats, T–shirts, keychains, etc.), sign up for our loyalty club, and more.

OPERATIONS

Hours

As a mobile operation, Pizza2go–go's hours will be variable. However, we typically will serve lunch in the Central City business district Monday through Friday, from 11:00 AM to 2:00 PM. We will serve pizza from 9:00 PM to 2:30 AM on Wednesday, Friday, and Saturday, when area bars and nightclubs are the busiest.

Suppliers

Pizza2go–go has negotiated supplier agreements with food–service distributors and wholesalers in the College Park area that have a reputation for quality and reliability, including:

- Cacciatore's Meat Market

- Paul's Organic Produce

- Falstaff Dairy Distribution

Additionally, we also have made arrangements with several regional and national suppliers that can meet our needs for cheeses, meats, dough, and general cooking/restaurant supplies:

- Brookfield Foods LLC

- Vettore Italian Foods Co.

- Reynolds Supply Inc.

- Elton Beverage Distributors Co.

Mobile Pizza Kitchen (Facility)

Our 26–foot mobile pizza kitchen, which costs $45,000, is fully equipped for operation and includes:

- Automatic transmission

- Air conditioning

- Tow package

- Refrigeration units
- Double-deck pizza ovens
- 7,000–watt generator
- 10–gallon propane tank
- 3–basin sink
- Hot water
- Microwave
- Warming cabinets
- Storage area
- Refrigerator
- Fold–up awning
- Removable windows

Supplies

We will need a variety of routine supplies for daily operations, including:

- Disposable plates
- Disposable silverware
- Disposable cups
- Kitchen utensils
- Plastic wrap
- Tinfoil
- Hand sanitizer
- Garbage bags
- Cleaning rags
- Paper towels

LEGAL

Pizza2go–go adheres to all local, state, and federal regulations pertaining to food handling and safety. Specifically, we adhere to regulations enforced by the Iowa Department of Inspections and Appeals, Administration Division, Food and Consumer Safety Bureau. In particular, we comply with the Iowa Food Code, which is based on food safety recommendations developed by the Food and Drug Administration. In addition to the Iowa Food Code, our business is required to comply with specific state regulations pertaining to mobile food units. Our operations must be inspected and licensed by the Department of Inspections and Appeals.

Even when following recommended practices, food poisoning is always a potential risk for businesses in the food industry (e.g., due to negligence on the part of a food distributor, wholesaler, equipment manufacturer, or supplier). In order to mitigate our risk, Pizza2go–go has obtained appropriate business, liability, and vehicle insurance.

FINANCIAL ANALYSIS

Following is Pizza2go–go's projected balance sheet for its first three years of operations (fiscal year beginning June 1). Ed Cascio is seeking a five–year, $50,000 business loan from College Park Bank to cover the purchase of the mobile pizza kitchen and an electronic point–of–sale system. He will contribute $25,000 of his own money from personal savings to cover daily operations and initial startup costs (e.g., supplies and food). Ed has established accounts and lines of credit with most of the suppliers named in this plan, based on his existing relationships with them.

	2011	2012	2013
Sales			
Total sales	$235,680	$247,464	$259,837
Cost of goods sold	$ 75,265	$ 79,188	$ 83,148
Labor cost	$ 86,000	$ 89,500	$ 93,000
Total cost of goods sold	$161,265	$168,688	$176,148
Gross profit	$ 74,415	$ 78,776	$ 83,689
Expenses			
Marketing & advertising	$ 3,000	$ 3,000	$ 3,000
General/administrative	$ 1,500	$ 1,500	$ 1,500
Accounting/legal	$ 1,500	$ 1,500	$ 1,500
Office supplies	$ 450	$ 450	$ 450
Business loan	$ 12,024	$ 12,024	$ 12,024
Insurance	$ 4,500	$ 4,750	$ 5,000
Payroll taxes	$ 10,320	$ 10,740	$ 11,160
Vendor permits & licenses	$ 2,500	$ 3,000	$ 3,500
Postage	$ 350	$ 350	$ 350
Propane	$ 2,500	$ 3,000	$ 3,500
Gasoline	$ 15,000	$ 16,000	$ 17,000
Maintenance & repairs	$ 2,500	$ 2,500	$ 2,500
Wireless telecommunications	$ 2,000	$ 2,000	$ 2,000
Total expenses	**$ 58,144**	**$ 60,814**	**$ 63,484**
Net income	**$ 16,271**	**$ 17,962**	**$ 20,205**

Roller Skating Rink

Dancing Wheels Roller Rink

199 Hillside St.
Hempstead, NY 11550

BizPlanDB.com

Dancing Wheels Roller Rink is a New York–based corporation that will provide roller skating rink facilities, hockey tournament hosting, food concessions, and event hosting to customers.

1.0 EXECUTIVE SUMMARY

The purpose of this business plan is to raise $1,000,000 for the development of a roller skating rink while showcasing the expected financials and operations over the next three years. Dancing Wheels Roller Rink ("the Company") is a New York–based corporation that will provide roller skating rink facilities, hockey tournament hosting, food concessions, and event hosting to customers in its targeted market. The Company was founded in 2010 by Henry Mullins.

1.1 The Services

The primary service offered by the Dancing Wheels Roller Rink is the use of its roller rink facility. Within the rink, the Company will provide skate rentals, public skate sessions, group/individual lessons, birthday/event hosting, and hockey management.

Additionally, the business will offer a limited food and beverage service which will include candy, hot dogs, hamburgers, hot wings, small sandwiches, coffee, and fountain drinks. This aspect of the business is very important because it will provide an additional stream of revenue for the business while concurrently allowing parents of children to stay at the facility longer. Finally, the business will generate revenue streams from hosting birthday parties and other events within the facility.

The third section of the business plan will further describe the services offered by the Dancing Wheels Roller Rink.

1.2 Financing

Mr. Mullins is seeking to raise $100,000 from a bank loan. The interest rate and loan agreement are to be further discussed during negotiation. This business plan assumes that the business will receive a 15 year loan with a 7% fixed interest rate. The financing will be used for the following:

- Development of the Company's roller skating rink location.

- Financing for the first six months of operation.

- Capital to purchase FF&E-related to the food concession and facility maintenance operations of the business.

Mr. Mullins will contribute $50,000 to the venture.

1.3 Mission Statement

Management's mission is to provide customers (adults and children) with an expansive roller rink that they can use for public skating, lessons, hockey, and birthday parties. The Owner is committed to responsible fiscal and business management practices.

1.4 Management Team

The Company was founded by Henry Mullins. Mr. Mullins has more than 10 years of experience in the retail management industry. Through his expertise, he will be able to bring the operations of the business to profitability within its first year of operations.

1.5 Sales Forecasts

Mr. Mullins expects a strong rate of growth at the start of operations. Below are the expected financials over the next three years.

Proforma profit and loss (yearly)

Year	1	2	3
Sales	$780,678	$936,814	$1,096,072
Operating costs	$346,724	$361,290	$ 376,386
EBITDA	$306,401	$422,460	$ 540,601
Taxes, interest, and depreciation	$216,060	$232,281	$ 275,296
Net profit	$ 90,341	$190,179	$ 265,305

Sales, operating costs, and profit forecast

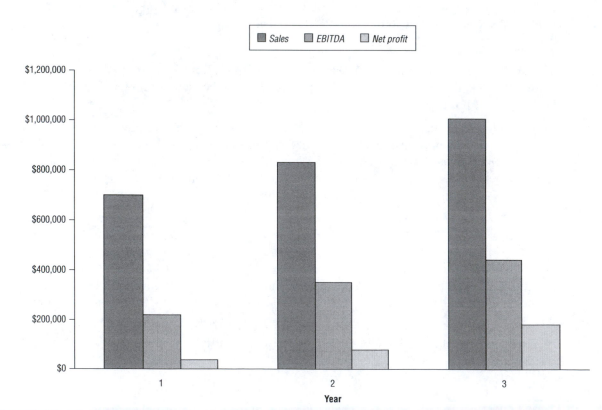

1.6 Expansion Plan

Mr. Mullins expects that the business will aggressively expand during the first three years of operation. He intends to implement marketing campaigns that will effectively target individuals within the target market.

2.0 COMPANY AND FINANCING SUMMARY

2.1 Registered Name and Corporate Structure

The Company is registered as a corporation in the State of New York.

2.2 Required Funds

At this time, Dancing Wheels Roller Rink requires $1,000,000 of debt funds. Below is a breakdown of how these funds will be used:

Projected startup costs

Facility acquisition	$ 600,000
Working capital	$ 125,000
FF&E	$ 72,500
Facility improvements	$ 100,000
Security deposits	$ 15,000
Insurance	$ 12,500
Facility maintenance equipment	$ 75,000
Marketing budget	$ 35,000
Miscellaneous and unforeseen costs	$ 15,000
Total startup costs	**$1,050,000**

Use of funds

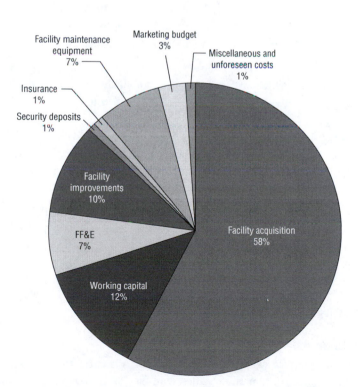

2.3 Investor Equity

Mr. Mullins is not seeking an investment from a third party at this time.

2.4 Management Equity

Henry Mullins owns 100% of the Dancing Wheels Roller Rink.

2.5 Exit Strategy

If the business is very successful, Mr. Mullins may seek to sell the business to a third party for a significant earnings multiple. Most likely, the Company will hire a qualified business broker to sell the business on behalf of Mr. Mullins. Based on historical numbers, the business could fetch a sales premium of up to 4 times earnings.

3.0 PRODUCTS AND SERVICES

Below is a description of the services offered by the Dancing Wheels Roller Rink.

3.1 Roller Rink Usage

The primary revenue center for the business is the direct usage of the facility's roller rink. Through this area of the facility, the Company provides public skating, skating lessons, and hockey league programs, as well as birthday party/event hosting. The business generates substantial gross margins from the usage of the facility. Within the facility, people of all ages are free to enjoy public skating times, which are held regularly on a daily basis. The Company will also provide rental of hockey and skating equipment. Of course, people are free to use their own skates or hockey equipment at the facility.

3.2 Food and Beverage Service

The business will also maintain an area of the retail facility that will provide limited food and beverage service. This revenue center is extremely important for the business because it will provide an additional stream of income for the business and by providing parents of children using the arcade an incentive to stay at the facility longer. This business model is akin to Barnes and Noble's installation of cafes in most of their bookstores.

This part of the business will serve hot dogs, small sandwiches, coffee/tea, and fountain drinks. The preliminary pricing schedule for these products can be found in the fifth section of the business plan.

3.3 Event Hosting

The final revenue center for the business will be the hosting of birthday parties and other events (primarily for children ages 3 to 10) at the facility. These parties are anticipated to generate approximately $150 to $225 from each event.

From an advertising standpoint, this is an important aspect for the business as other children in attendance for a party may want to have their birthday party held at facility. These parties will also increase the visibility of the business among the Company's targeted demographic.

4.0 STRATEGIC AND MARKET ANALYSIS

4.1 Economic Outlook

This section of the analysis will detail the economic climate, the roller rink industry, the customer profile, and the competition that the business will face as it progresses through its business operations.

Currently, the economic market condition in the United States is in recession. This slowdown in the economy has also greatly impacted real estate sales, which has halted to historical lows. Many economists expect that this recession will continue until mid–2010, at which point the economy will begin a prolonged recovery period. However, the low pricing point of the Company's services will allow the business to remain profitable and cash flow positive at all times.

4.2 Industry Analysis

In the United States, there are 443 roller rinks currently in operation. Each year, these businesses aggregate generate more than $419 million dollars of revenue and provide $114 million dollars of payrolls for 11,500 Americans. The roller rink industry is mature. The expected continued growth of these businesses is expected to mirror the general population growth plus the rate of inflation.

One of the common trends within the industry is for facilities to integrate secondary forms of entertainment into their businesses. These additional revenue streams income arcade machines, fuse ball tables, pool tables, and other forms of secondary entertainment. After Management completes the development of the facility, the Company may introduce other entertainment items such as arcade games to compliment the entertainment nature of Dancing Wheels Roller Rink.

4.3 Customer Profile

Dancing Wheels Roller Rink's average client will be a middle– to upper–middle class man or woman living in the Company's target market. Common traits among clients will include:

- Annual household income exceeding $30,000

- Lives or works no more than 15 miles from the Company's location.

- Will spend $35 per visit to Dancing Wheels Roller Rink

- Has two or more children

Based on the demographic profile outlined above, there are approximately 500,000 people that could become potential customers of the business on a yearly basis. Within the Company's targeted market, the annual median household income is $50,000 while median family is $60,000.

4.4 Competition

There are only seven roller skating rinks within the New York metropolitan area that provide services that are substantially to that of the Company. The business intends to maintain a modest competitive advantage by operating slightly outside of the five boroughs which will provide the business with a pricing competitive advantage over companies that operate directly within New York City.

5.0 MARKETING PLAN

Dancing Wheels Roller Rink intends to maintain an extensive marketing campaign that will ensure maximum visibility for the business in its targeted market. Below is an overview of the marketing strategies and objectives of Dancing Wheels Roller Rink.

5.1 Marketing Objectives

- Develop an online presence by developing a website and placing the Company's name and contact information with online directories.

- Implement a local campaign with the Company's targeted market via the use of flyers, local newspaper advertisements, and word of mouth advertising.

5.2 Marketing Strategies

Management intends to use a broad based advertising campaign that will raise the awareness of the retail location among the targeted young child and adolescent demographic. To that end, Management will place a number of advertisements in locally based newspapers and advertisements from the onset of operations which may include discount coupons or coupons for free admission. This will create an immediate draw to the Dancing Wheels Roller Rink location.

Management also expects that the business will generate significant word of mouth advertising as the Company hosts events for children's birthday parties. As more and more children are invited to Dancing Wheels Roller Rink hosted birthday parties, these youngsters may have their parents host their next birthday party at the roller rink facility. The Company anticipates that this type of advertising will take three to six months to become effective.

Dancing Wheels Roller Rink will also use an internet based strategy. This is very important as many people seeking local services, such as local entertainment, now the Internet to conduct their preliminary searches. Mr. Mullins will register the Roller Skating with online portals so that potential customers can easily reach the business. The Company will also develop its own online website.

5.3 Pricing

For each session of a roller skating, the Company anticipates that the business will receive $10 of revenue. Concessions pricing will range from $2 to $6 depending on the food or beverage served to the customer.

6.0 ORGANIZATIONAL PLAN AND PERSONNEL SUMMARY

6.1 Corporate Organization

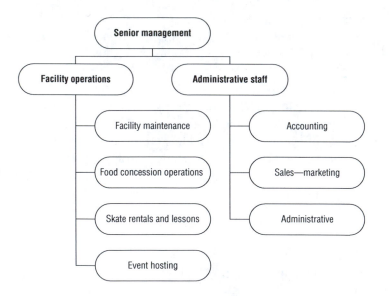

6.2 Organizational Budget

Personnel plan—yearly

Year	1	2	3
Owner	$ 40,000	$ 41,200	$ 42,436
Assistant manager	$ 29,000	$ 29,870	$ 30,766
Rink employees	$ 96,000	$ 98,880	$101,846
Bookkeeper (P/T)	$ 9,000	$ 9,270	$ 9,548
Administrative (P/T)	$ 34,000	$ 35,020	$ 36,071
Total	**$208,000**	**$214,240**	**$220,667**

Numbers of personnel

Owner	1	1	1
Assistant manager	1	1	1
Rink employees	6	6	6
Bookkeeper (P/T)	1	1	1
Administrative (P/T)	2	2	2
Totals	**11**	**11**	**11**

Personnel expense breakdown

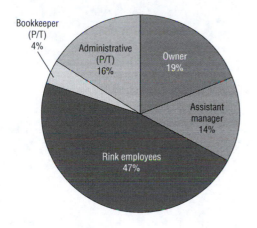

7.0 FINANCIAL PLAN

7.1 Underlying Assumptions

The Company has based its proforma financial statements on the following:

- Dancing Wheels Roller Rink will have an annual revenue growth rate of 16% per year.

- The Owner will acquire $1,000,000 of debt funds to develop the business.

- The loan will have a 15 year term with a 7% interest rate.

7.2 Sensitivity Analysis

The Company's revenues are moderately sensitive to changes in the general economy. Roller skating is not an essential life activity, and as such, severe economic pullbacks may hamper the Company's ability to continually increase top line income. However, the pricing structure that Management will use for its roller rink services will allow almost all residents to afford the skating, hockey, public session, and snack bar products offered by the business on a year round basis.

7.3 Source of Funds

Financing

Equity contributions

Management investment	$ 50,000.00
Total equity financing	**$ 50,000.00**

Banks and lenders

Banks and lenders	$ 1,000,000.00
Total debt financing	**$1,000,000.00**
Total financing	**$1,050,000.00**

7.4 General Assumptions

General assumptions

Year	1	2	3
Short term interest rate	9.5%	9.5%	9.5%
Long term interest rate	10.0%	10.0%	10.0%
Federal tax rate	33.0%	33.0%	33.0%
State tax rate	5.0%	5.0%	5.0%
Personnel taxes	15.0%	15.0%	15.0%

7.5 Profit and Loss Statements

Proforma profit and loss (yearly)

Year	1	2	3
Sales	**$780,678**	**$936,814**	**$1,096,072**
Cost of goods sold	$127,553	$153,064	$ 179,085
Gross margin	83.66%	83.66%	83.66%
Operating income	**$653,125**	**$783,750**	**$ 916,987**
Expenses			
Payroll	$208,000	$214,240	$ 220,667
General and administrative	$ 25,200	$ 26,208	$ 27,256
Marketing expenses	$ 3,903	$ 4,684	$ 5,480
Professional fees and licensure	$ 5,219	$ 5,376	$ 5,537
Insurance costs	$ 21,987	$ 23,086	$ 24,241
Facility maintenance costs	$ 7,596	$ 8,356	$ 9,191
Rent and utilities	$ 34,250	$ 35,963	$ 37,761
Miscellaneous costs	$ 9,368	$ 11,242	$ 13,153
Payroll taxes	$ 31,200	$ 32,136	$ 33,100
Total operating costs	**$346,724**	**$361,290**	**$ 376,386**
EBITDA	**$306,401**	**$422,460**	**$ 540,601**
Federal income tax	$101,112	$117,653	$ 157,640
State income tax	$ 15,320	$ 17,826	$ 23,885
Interest expense	$ 68,761	$ 65,935	$ 62,904
Depreciation expenses	$ 30,867	$ 30,867	$ 30,867
Net profit	**$ 90,341**	**$190,179**	**$ 265,305**
Profit margin	**11.57%**	**20.30%**	**24.21%**

Sales, operating costs, and profit forecast

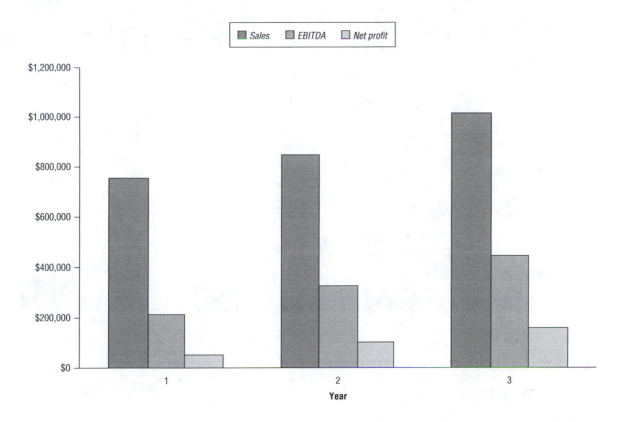

7.6 Cash Flow Analysis

Proforma cash flow analysis—yearly

Year	1	2	3
Cash from operations	$ 121,207	$221,045	$296,172
Cash from receivables	$ 0	$ 0	$ 0
Operating cash inflow	**$ 121,207**	**$221,045**	**$296,172**
Other cash inflows			
Equity investment	$ 50,000	$ 0	$ 0
Increased borrowings	$ 1,000,000	$ 0	$ 0
Sales of business assets	$ 0	$ 0	$ 0
A/P increases	$ 37,902	$ 43,587	$ 50,125
Total other cash inflows	**$1,087,902**	**$ 43,587**	**$ 50,125**
Total cash inflow	**$1,209,109**	**$264,633**	**$346,297**
Cash outflows			
Repayment of principal	$ 39,098	$ 41,924	$ 44,955
A/P decreases	$ 24,897	$ 29,876	$ 35,852
A/R increases	$ 0	$ 0	$ 0
Asset purchases	$ 890,000	$ 22,105	$ 29,617
Dividends	$ 84,845	$154,732	$207,320
Total cash outflows	**$1,038,840**	**$248,637**	**$317,744**
Net cash flow	**$ 170,269**	**$ 15,996**	**$ 28,553**
Cash balance	**$ 170,269**	**$186,265**	**$214,818**

Proforma cash flow (yearly)

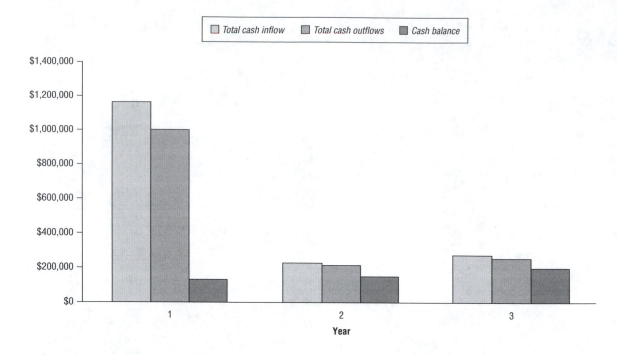

Legend	
☐ Total cash inflow	☐ Total cash outflows	☐ Cash balance

7.7 Balance Sheet

Proforma balance sheet—yearly

Year	1	2	3
Assets			
Cash	$ 170,269	$ 186,265	$ 214,818
Amortized development/expansion costs	$ 142,500	$ 144,710	$ 147,672
Facility maintenance equipment	$ 75,000	$ 91,578	$ 113,791
FF&E	$ 72,500	$ 75,816	$ 80,258
Facility	$ 636,000	$ 674,160	$ 714,610
Accumulated depreciation	($ 30,867)	($ 61,733)	($ 92,600)
Total assets	**$1,065,403**	**$1,110,796**	**$1,178,549**
Liabilities and equity			
Accounts payable	$ 13,005	$ 26,716	$ 40,990
Long term liabilities	$ 960,902	$ 918,978	$ 877,053
Other liabilities	$ 0	$ 0	$ 0
Total liabilities	**$ 973,907**	**$ 945,694**	**$ 918,043**
Net worth	**$ 91,496**	**$ 165,102**	**$ 260,506**
Total liabilities and equity	**$1,065,403**	**$1,110,796**	**$1,178,549**

Proforma balance sheet

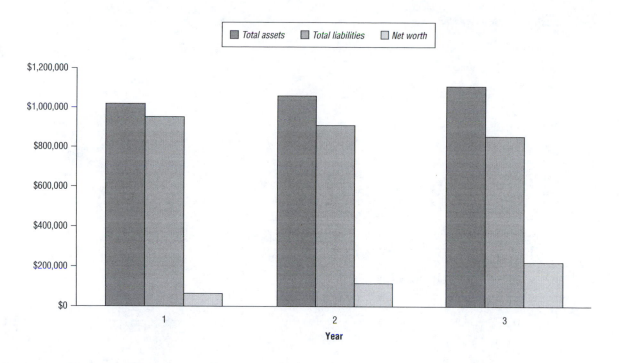

7.8 Breakeven Analysis

Monthly break even analysis

Year	1	2	3
Monthly revenue	$ 34,536	$ 35,987	$ 37,491
Yearly revenue	$414,438	$431,849	$449,893

Break even analysis

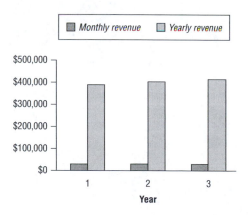

7.9 Business Ratios

Business ratios—yearly

Year	1	2	3
Sales			
Sales growth	0.0%	20.0%	17.0%
Gross margin	83.7%	83.7%	83.7%
Financials			
Profit margin	11.57%	20.30%	24.21%
Assets to liabilities	1.09	1.17	1.28
Equity to liabilities	0.09	0.17	0.28
Assets to equity	11.64	6.73	4.52
Liquidity			
Acid test	0.17	0.20	0.23
Cash to assets	0.16	0.17	0.18

7.10 Three Year Profit and Loss Statement

Profit and loss statement (first year)

Month	1	2	3	4	5	6	7
Sales	$64,050	$64,233	$64,416	$64,599	$64,782	$64,965	$65,148
Cost of goods sold	$10,465	$10,495	$10,525	$10,555	$10,585	$10,615	$10,644
Gross margin	83.7%	83.7%	83.7%	83.7%	83.7%	83.7%	83.7%
Operating income	**$53,585**	**$53,738**	**$53,891**	**$54,044**	**$54,197**	**$54,351**	**$54,504**
Expenses							
Payroll	$17,333	$17,333	$17,333	$17,333	$17,333	$17,333	$17,333
General and administrative	$ 2,100	$ 2,100	$ 2,100	$ 2,100	$ 2,100	$ 2,100	$ 2,100
Marketing expenses	$ 325	$ 325	$ 325	$ 325	$ 325	$ 325	$ 325
Professional fees and licensure	$ 435	$ 435	$ 435	$ 435	$ 435	$ 435	$ 435
Insurance costs	$ 1,832	$ 1,832	$ 1,832	$ 1,832	$ 1,832	$ 1,832	$ 1,832
Facility maintenance costs	$ 633	$ 633	$ 633	$ 633	$ 633	$ 633	$ 633
Rent and utilities	$ 2,854	$ 2,854	$ 2,854	$ 2,854	$ 2,854	$ 2,854	$ 2,854
Miscellaneous costs	$ 781	$ 781	$ 781	$ 781	$ 781	$ 781	$ 781
Payroll taxes	$ 2,600	$ 2,600	$ 2,600	$ 2,600	$ 2,600	$ 2,600	$ 2,600
Total operating costs	**$28,894**	**$28,894**	**$28,894**	**$28,894**	**$28,894**	**$28,894**	**$28,894**
EBITDA	**$24,691**	**$24,844**	**$24,998**	**$25,151**	**$25,304**	**$25,457**	**$25,610**
Federal income tax	$ 8,296	$ 8,319	$ 8,343	$ 8,367	$ 8,390	$ 8,414	$ 8,438
State income tax	$ 1,257	$ 1,261	$ 1,264	$ 1,268	$ 1,271	$ 1,275	$ 1,278
Interest expense	$ 5,833	$ 5,815	$ 5,796	$ 5,778	$ 5,759	$ 5,740	$ 5,721
Depreciation expense	$ 2,572	$ 2,572	$ 2,572	$ 2,572	$ 2,572	$ 2,572	$ 2,572
Net profit	**$ 6,733**	**$ 6,877**	**$ 7,022**	**$ 7,166**	**$ 7,311**	**$ 7,455**	**$ 7,600**

Profit and loss statement (first year cont.)

Month	8	9	10	11	12	1
Sales	$65,331	$65,514	$65,697	$65,880	$66,063	$780,678
Cost of goods sold	$10,674	$10,704	$10,734	$10,764	$10,794	$127,553
Gross margin	83.7%	83.7%	83.7%	83.7%	83.7%	83.7%
Operating income	$54,657	$54,810	$54,963	$55,116	$55,269	$653,125
Expenses						
Payroll	$17,333	$17,333	$17,333	$17,333	$17,333	$208,000
General and administrative	$ 2,100	$ 2,100	$ 2,100	$ 2,100	$ 2,100	$ 25,200
Marketing expenses	$ 325	$ 325	$ 325	$ 325	$ 325	$ 3,903
Professional fees and licensure	$ 435	$ 435	$ 435	$ 435	$ 435	$ 5,219
Insurance costs	$ 1,832	$ 1,832	$ 1,832	$ 1,832	$ 1,832	$ 21,987
Facility maintenance costs	$ 633	$ 633	$ 633	$ 633	$ 633	$ 7,596
Rent and utilities	$ 2,854	$ 2,854	$ 2,854	$ 2,854	$ 2,854	$ 34,250
Miscellaneous costs	$ 781	$ 781	$ 781	$ 781	$ 781	$ 9,368
Payroll taxes	$ 2,600	$ 2,600	$ 2,600	$ 2,600	$ 2,600	$ 31,200
Total operating costs	$28,894	$28,894	$28,894	$28,894	$28,894	$346,724
EBITDA	$25,763	$25,916	$26,069	$26,222	$26,375	$306,401
Federal income tax	$ 8,462	$ 8,485	$ 8,509	$ 8,533	$ 8,556	$101,112
State income tax	$ 1,282	$ 1,286	$ 1,289	$ 1,293	$ 1,296	$ 15,320
Interest expense	$ 5,702	$ 5,683	$ 5,664	$ 5,644	$ 5,625	$ 68,761
Depreciation expense	$ 2,572	$ 2,572	$ 2,572	$ 2,572	$ 2,572	$ 30,867
Net profit	$ 7,745	$ 7,890	$ 8,035	$ 8,180	$ 8,326	$ 90,341

Profit and loss statement (second year)

Quarter	Q1	2 Q2	Q3	Q4	2
Sales	$187,363	$234,203	$252,940	$ 262,308	$936,814
Cost of goods sold	$ 30,613	$ 38,266	$ 41,327	$ 42,858	$153,064
Gross margin	83.7%	83.7%	83.7%	83.7%	83.7%
Operating income	$156,750	$195,937	$211,612	$ 219,450	$783,750
Expenses					
Payroll	$ 42,848	$ 53,560	$ 57,845	$ 59,987	$214,240
General and administrative	$ 5,242	$ 6,552	$ 7,076	$ 7,338	$ 26,208
Marketing expenses	$ 937	$ 1,171	$ 1,265	$ 1,312	$ 4,684
Professional fees and licensure	$ 1,075	$ 1,344	$ 1,451	$ 1,505	$ 5,376
Insurance costs	$ 4,617	$ 5,772	$ 6,233	$ 6,464	$ 23,086
Facility maintenance costs	$ 1,671	$ 2,089	$ 2,256	$ 2,340	$ 8,356
Rent and utilities	$ 7,193	$ 8,991	$ 9,710	$ 10,070	$ 35,963
Miscellaneous costs	$ 2,248	$ 2,810	$ 3,035	$ 3,148	$ 11,242
Payroll taxes	$ 6,427	$ 8,034	$ 8,677	$ 8,998	$ 32,136
Total operating costs	$ 72,258	$ 90,322	$ 97,548	$ 101,161	$361,290
EBITDA	$ 84,492	$105,615	$114,064	$ 118,289	$422,460
Federal income tax	$ 23,531	$ 29,413	$ 31,766	$ 32,943	$117,653
State income tax	$ 3,565	$ 4,457	$ 4,813	$ 4,991	$ 17,826
Interest expense	$ 16,756	$ 16,577	$ 16,394	$ 16,208	$ 65,935
Depreciation expense	$ 7,717	$ 7,717	$ 7,717	$ 7,717	$ 30,867
Net profit	$ 32,923	$ 47,452	$ 53,374	$ 56,430	$190,179

Profit and loss statement (third year)

Quarter	Q1	3 Q2	Q3	Q4	3
Sales	$219,214	$274,018	$295,939	$ 306,900	$1,096,072
Cost of goods sold	$ 35,817	$ 44,771	$ 48,353	$ 50,144	$ 179,085
Gross margin	83.7%	83.7%	83.7%	83.7%	83.7%
Operating income	**$183,397**	**$229,247**	**$247,586**	**$ 256,756**	**$ 916,987**
Expenses					
Payroll	$ 44,133	$ 55,167	$ 59,580	$ 61,787	$ 220,667
General and administrative	$ 5,451	$ 6,814	$ 7,359	$ 7,632	$ 27,256
Marketing expenses	$ 1,096	$ 1,370	$ 1,480	$ 1,535	$ 5,480
Professional fees and licensure	$ 1,107	$ 1,384	$ 1,495	$ 1,550	$ 5,537
Insurance costs	$ 4,848	$ 6,060	$ 6,545	$ 6,787	$ 24,241
Facility maintenance costs	$ 1,838	$ 2,298	$ 2,482	$ 2,574	$ 9,191
Rent and utilities	$ 7,552	$ 9,440	$ 10,195	$ 10,573	$ 37,761
Miscellaneous costs	$ 2,631	$ 3,288	$ 3,551	$ 3,683	$ 13,153
Payroll taxes	$ 6,620	$ 8,275	$ 8,937	$ 9,268	$ 33,100
Total operating costs	**$ 75,277**	**$ 94,097**	**$101,624**	**$ 105,388**	**$ 376,386**
EBITDA	**$108,120**	**$135,150**	**$145,962**	**$ 151,368**	**$ 540,601**
Federal income tax	$ 31,528	$ 39,410	$ 42,563	$ 44,139	$ 157,640
State income tax	$ 4,777	$ 5,971	$ 6,449	$ 6,688	$ 23,885
Interest expense	$ 16,019	$ 15,826	$ 15,630	$ 15,430	$ 62,904
Depreciation expense	$ 7,717	$ 7,717	$ 7,717	$ 7,717	$ 30,867
Net profit	**$ 48,080**	**$ 66,227**	**$ 73,604**	**$ 77,394**	**$ 265,305**

7.11 Three Year Cash Flow Analysis

Cash flow analysis (first year)

Month	1	2	3	4	5	6	7	8
Cash from operations	$ 9,305	$ 9,450	$ 9,594	$ 9,738	$ 9,883	$ 10,028	$ 10,172	$ 10,317
Cash from receivables	$ 0	$ 0	$ 0	$ 0	$ 0	$ 0	$ 0	$ 0
Operating cash inflow	**$ 9,305**	**$ 9,450**	**$ 9,594**	**$ 9,738**	**$ 9,883**	**$ 10,028**	**$ 10,172**	**$ 10,317**
Other cash inflows								
Equity investment	$ 50,000	$ 0	$ 0	$ 0	$ 0	$ 0	$ 0	$ 0
Increased borrowings	$1,000,000	$ 0	$ 0	$ 0	$ 0	$ 0	$ 0	$ 0
Sales of business assets	$ 0	$ 0	$ 0	$ 0	$ 0	$ 0	$ 0	$ 0
A/P increases	$ 3,159	$ 3,159	$ 3,159	$ 3,159	$ 3,159	$ 3,159	$ 3,159	$ 3,159
Total other cash inflows	**$1,053,159**	**$ 3,159**	**$ 3,159**	**$ 3,159**	**$ 3,159**	**$ 3,159**	**$ 3,159**	**$ 3,159**
Total cash inflow	**$1,062,464**	**$ 12,608**	**$ 12,752**	**$ 12,897**	**$ 13,041**	**$ 13,186**	**$ 13,331**	**$ 13,476**
Cash outflows								
Repayment of principal	$ 3,155	$ 3,173	$ 3,192	$ 3,210	$ 3,229	$ 3,248	$ 3,267	$ 3,286
A/P decreases	$ 2,075	$ 2,075	$ 2,075	$ 2,075	$ 2,075	$ 2,075	$ 2,075	$ 2,075
A/R increases	$ 0	$ 0	$ 0	$ 0	$ 0	$ 0	$ 0	$ 0
Asset purchases	$ 890,000	$ 0	$ 0	$ 0	$ 0	$ 0	$ 0	$ 0
Dividends	$ 0	$ 0	$ 0	$ 0	$ 0	$ 0	$ 0	$ 0
Total cash outflows	**$ 895,230**	**$ 5,248**	**$ 5,267**	**$ 5,285**	**$ 5,304**	**$ 5,323**	**$ 5,342**	**$ 5,361**
Net cash flow	**$ 167,234**	**$ 7,360**	**$ 7,486**	**$ 7,612**	**$ 7,737**	**$ 7,863**	**$ 7,989**	**$ 8,115**
Cash balance	**$ 167,234**	**$174,594**	**$182,080**	**$189,692**	**$197,429**	**$205,293**	**$213,282**	**$221,397**

Cash flow analysis (first year cont.)

Month	9	10	11	12	1
Cash from operations	$ 10,462	$ 10,607	$ 10,752	$ 10,898	$ 121,207
Cash from receivables	$ 0	$ 0	$ 0	$ 0	$ 0
Operating cash inflow	**$ 10,462**	**$ 10,607**	**$ 10,752**	**$ 10,898**	**$ 121,207**
Other cash inflows					
Equity investment	$ 0	$ 0	$ 0	$ 0	$ 50,000
Increased borrowings	$ 0	$ 0	$ 0	$ 0	$1,000,000
Sales of business assets	$ 0	$ 0	$ 0	$ 0	$ 0
A/P increases	$ 3,159	$ 3,159	$ 3,159	$ 3,159	$ 37,902
Total other cash inflows	**$ 3,159**	**$ 3,159**	**$ 3,159**	**$ 3,159**	**$1,087,902**
Total cash inflow	**$ 13,621**	**$ 13,766**	**$ 13,911**	**$ 14,056**	**$1,209,109**
Cash outflows					
Repayment of principal	$ 3,305	$ 3,325	$ 3,344	$ 3,363	$ 39,098
A/P decreases	$ 2,075	$ 2,075	$ 2,075	$ 2,075	$ 24,897
A/R increases	$ 0	$ 0	$ 0	$ 0	$ 0
Asset purchases	$ 0	$ 0	$ 0	$ 0	$ 890,000
Dividends	$ 0	$ 0	$ 0	$ 84,845	$ 84,845
Total cash outflows	**$ 5,380**	**$ 5,399**	**$ 5,419**	**$ 90,283**	**$1,038,840**
Net cash flow	**$ 8,241**	**$ 8,367**	**$ 8,492**	**−$ 76,227**	**$ 170,269**
Cash balance	**$229,637**	**$238,004**	**$246,496**	**$170,269**	**$ 170,269**

Cash flow analysis (second year)

Quarter	Q1	2 Q2	Q3	Q4	2
Cash from operations	$ 44,209	$ 55,261	$ 59,682	$ 61,893	$221,045
Cash from receivables	$ 0	$ 0	$ 0	$ 0	$ 0
Operating cash inflow	**$ 44,209**	**$ 55,261**	**$ 59,682**	**$ 61,893**	**$221,045**
Other cash inflows					
Equity investment	$ 0	$ 0	$ 0	$ 0	$ 0
Increased borrowings	$ 0	$ 0	$ 0	$ 0	$ 0
Sales of business assets	$ 0	$ 0	$ 0	$ 0	$ 0
A/P increases	$ 8,717	$ 10,897	$ 11,769	$ 12,204	$ 43,587
Total other cash inflows	**$ 8,717**	**$ 10,897**	**$ 11,769**	**$ 12,204**	**$ 43,587**
Total cash inflow	**$ 52,927**	**$ 66,158**	**$ 71,451**	**$ 74,097**	**$264,633**
Cash outflows					
Repayment of principal	$ 10,208	$ 10,388	$ 10,571	$ 10,757	$ 41,924
A/P decreases	$ 5,975	$ 7,469	$ 8,067	$ 8,365	$ 29,876
A/R increases	$ 0	$ 0	$ 0	$ 0	$ 0
Asset purchases	$ 4,421	$ 5,526	$ 5,968	$ 6,189	$ 22,105
Dividends	$ 30,946	$ 38,683	$ 41,778	$ 43,325	$154,732
Total cash outflows	**$ 51,551**	**$ 62,066**	**$ 66,383**	**$ 68,637**	**$248,637**
Net cash flow	**$ 1,376**	**$ 4,092**	**$ 5,067**	**$ 5,461**	**$ 15,996**
Cash balance	**$171,645**	**$175,737**	**$180,804**	**$186,265**	**$186,265**

Cash flow analysis (third year)

Quarter	Q1	Q2	Q3	Q4	3
Cash from operations	$ 59,234	$ 74,043	$ 79,966	$ 82,928	$296,172
Cash from receivables	$ 0	$ 0	$ 0	$ 0	$ 0
Operating cash inflow	**$ 59,234**	**$ 74,043**	**$ 79,966**	**$ 82,928**	**$296,172**
Other cash inflows					
Equity investment	$ 0	$ 0	$ 0	$ 0	$ 0
Increased borrowings	$ 0	$ 0	$ 0	$ 0	$ 0
Sales of business assets	$ 0	$ 0	$ 0	$ 0	$ 0
A/P increases	$ 10,025	$ 12,531	$ 13,534	$ 14,035	$ 50,125
Total other cash inflows	**$ 10,025**	**$ 12,531**	**$ 13,534**	**$ 14,035**	**$ 50,125**
Total cash inflow	**$ 69,259**	**$ 86,574**	**$ 93,500**	**$ 96,963**	**$346,297**
Cash outflows					
Repayment of principal	$ 10,946	$ 11,139	$ 11,335	$ 11,535	$ 44,955
A/P decreases	$ 7,170	$ 8,963	$ 9,680	$ 10,038	$ 35,852
A/R increases	$ 0	$ 0	$ 0	$ 0	$ 0
Asset purchases	$ 5,923	$ 7,404	$ 7,997	$ 8,293	$ 29,617
Dividends	$ 41,464	$ 51,830	$ 55,976	$ 58,050	$207,320
Total cash outflows	**$ 65,504**	**$ 79,336**	**$ 84,988**	**$ 87,916**	**$317,744**
Net cash flow	**$ 3,755**	**$ 7,238**	**$ 8,512**	**$ 9,048**	**$ 28,553**
Cash balance	**$190,020**	**$197,258**	**$205,770**	**$214,818**	**$214,818**

Stained Glass Business

Rose's Colored Glass

18765 Luther Way
Lansing Hills, WI 53575

Paul Greenland

Rose's Colored Glass is a stained glass business that makes custom stained glass lamps, windows, sun catchers, ornaments, votives, nightlights, and more.

EXECUTIVE SUMMARY

Business Overview

Rose's Colored Glass is a new stained glass business that makes custom stained glass lamps, windows, sun catchers, ornaments, votives, nightlights, and more. We are located in the popular tourist town of Lansing Hills, Wisconsin, where we plan to make the bulk of our sales. In addition, we also will offer workshops and educational seminars for amateur crafters, and provide contract services to home-owners, builders, and churches in need of custom stained glass windows.

Incorporated in the state of Wisconsin, our business is owned by Rose and Stanley Maxwell. For more than 15 years, the Maxwells have been making and selling stained glass items on a part–time basis, selling their wares at craft fairs, bazaars, and festivals. During that time Stanley has worked as a carpenter for Golden Hammer Construction Co., while Rose has worked as the office manager/book-keeper for Gustafson Fastener Manufacturing Co.

MARKET ANALYSIS

Lansing Hills is home to many small shops that sell artwork and gift items, as well as specialty food and beverage selections such as wine, cheese, sausage, and preserves. Although we are the only stained glass merchant in Lansing Hills, we compete against other gift and specialty stores for consumers' discretionary spending. According to Nelson Marketing Research, the town of Lansing Hills (our primary service area) was home to 29 specialty stores in 2009.

Our secondary service area extends beyond Lansing Hills in a 50–mile radius. There presently are 85 specialty stores within a 15–mile radius of our location, 117 specialty stores within a 25–mile radius, and 372 specialty stores within a 50–mile radius. Most of these specialty stores sell antiques, collectibles, and custom home decor, but are not focused exclusively on the production and sale of stained glass items.

Benefiting our business is the economic health of consumers in our primary and secondary market areas. Within a 10–mile radius of our business, there are 5,351 households with an average household income of $70,431. Within a 15–mile radius there are 21,443 households with an average household income of $75,399. Expanding the radius to 25 miles, there are 149,831 households with an average household income of $74,315. Finally, at 50 miles there are 474,535 households with an average household income of $67,205. Our entire market area includes a grand total of 651,160 households with an average household income of $69,137.

In addition to our relatively unique focus on stained glass, our educational programs also will set us apart from other merchants in Lansing Hills and the surrounding area. Over the last 15 years Rose and Stanley Maxwell have offered a number of stained glass workshops at the Lansing Hills Community Center. These have been well received by amateur crafters in our local and regional markets, as well as tourists who have driven as far as 120 miles in order to attend.

Finally, contract services will be another key differential for Rose's Colored Glass. Presently, homeowners, builders, and churches in need of custom stained glass windows rely upon the services of stained glass professionals in and around Milwaukee, Wisconsin, which is several hours away. As long–time local residents with a reputation for quality workmanship (we have performed several contract jobs independently over the years), we are confident that Rose's Colored Glass will be able to secure most of the market in the 50–mile radius surrounding Lansing Hills. As a carpenter, Stanley's status as a licensed contractor and relationships with area builders and developers will be very beneficial to us.

PRODUCTS & SERVICES

Lamps

A large percentage of the products we sell will be different types of stained–glass lamps, including:

- Fan lamps
- Sconces
- Nightlights
- Table lamps
- Bankers lamps
- Piano lamps
- Tiffany style lamps
- Lamp shades
- Lanterns

Our lamps will be available in a number of different styles and patterns, including:

- Prairie style
- Falling leaves
- South beach
- Floral
- Diamond
- Art nouveau
- Waterlily
- Tulip

- Dogwood

- Black–Eyed susan

- Hollyhock

- Patriotic

- Celtic

- Insect

Other Stained–Glass Goods

We also will produce and sell a variety other items, such as:

- Sun catchers

- Paperweights

- Votives

- Garden stakes

- Steppingstones

- Crosses

- Snowflakes

- Seasonal items

- Holiday items

- Garden tables

- Jewelry boxes

- Watch boxes

- Windows

Educational Workshops

Our educational workshops will provide amateur hobbyists with the knowledge needed to complete simple stained glass projects, including lanterns and lamps. We will offer 10 half–day classes per year (on Saturdays) at our store (limited to 15 participants per session). In addition to paying a fee for the workshop, we will sell attendees the supply kits, at a mark–up, needed to complete the featured projects that we choose in advance.

Contract Services

Rose's Colored Glass will provide installation and repair services on a contract basis to homeowners, builders, and churches in need of custom stained glass windows and sidelights. Over the years we have provided this service on an occasional basis as independent contractors. Our experience, coupled with Stanley's contractors license and carpentry knowledge, positions us for success in this niche area.

Projects will always begin with a discovery session, where we meet with clients to gain a clear understanding of their needs. Whether we are re–creating something from an existing design (e.g., in the case of a damaged window) or developing something new, we will provide a sketch to the client, which they will approve before we provide a formal time and cost estimate for development and installation.

OPERATIONS

Location and Facilities

Rose's Colored Glass is located in a newly renovated, two–story, 2,500–square–foot brick commercial building in downtown Lansing Hills (a busy tourist area) with off–street parking. Originally a small town grocery store, the lower–level was most recently a combination drugstore/gift shop. We have devoted 1,250 square feet of the first level to retail sales. The former pharmacy area will serve as a 400–square foot classroom space. In addition, the first level includes a 100–square–foot office and a 750–square–foot workshop area with overhead door access from the rear alley. The second story includes two, two–bedroom apartments that presently are occupied by long–term tenants. The building includes many upgrades, such as new electrical service and wiring, heating, plumbing, windows, as well as a new roof.

Hours of Operation

Rose's Colored Glass will operate Monday through Sunday from Memorial Day through October 31st, which is Lansing Hills' peak tourist season. We will be open on weekends during most of the off–season, but are closed on major holidays and during the months of January and February, at which time we will focus on stained glass production and planning for the next tourist season. Our hours of operation generally are 10:00 a.m. to 7:00 p.m.

Suppliers

Our business will purchase materials at wholesale from a number of leading suppliers, including:

- ABC Glass Supplies
- Worthington International
- Glassworks
- ColorArt LLC
- Delphi International
- Wexford Supply

Equipment

Because the Maxwells have been engaged in stained glass production on a part–time/hobby basis for some time now, they have all of the equipment needed to begin their business. A partial list of the assets they will contribute to the business in this category include:

- Glass cutter
- Steel wheel cutter
- Circle cutter
- Tungsten carbide cutter
- Pliers (breaking, running, lead–cutting, grozing)
- Lead knife
- Copper foil
- Carborundum file
- Soldering iron
- Sharpening stone
- Lead vice

- Lead came

- Fids

- Flux

- Small wire brush

- Straight edge

- Light table box

- Bench brush

- Pattern knife

- Glass marking pen

- Safety glasses

MANAGEMENT SUMMARY

For more than 15 years, Rose and Stanley Maxwell have been making and selling stained glass items on a part–time basis while maintaining full–time jobs. Rose has worked as an office manager and book-keeper for Gustafson Fastener Manufacturing Co. since 1995. She became interested in stained glass when she received a Tiffany lamp as a gift from her grandmother. To learn more, she and Stanley attended a stained glass course at a local community college and began making stained glass items for their home, as well as for sale at craft fairs, bazaars, and festivals.

Stanley, a career carpenter, has worked for Golden Hammer Construction Company since 1999. During that time he has developed a reputation for quality workmanship with builders and contractors in the Lansing Hills area. Combined with his ability to work with stained glass, Stanley's construction knowledge allows him to perform both residential and commercial window installation jobs.

The Maxwells are ready to transition to a new stage of their lives. Rose plans to continue performing bookkeeping work for Gustafson Fastener Manufacturing as a part–time employee, but will relinquish her office manager responsibilities. Gustafson Fastener Manufacturing has agreed to let her work a flexible schedule, which will be compatible with the hours she must maintain for the new stained glass business. Likewise, Stanley plans to scale back his work as a full–time carpenter. He will now work quarter–time (e.g., as needed) for Golden Hammer.

MARKETING & SALES

We have developed a marketing plan for Rose's Colored Glass that includes the following tactics:

- **Word–of–Mouth Advertising**—In speaking with stained glass merchants in other U.S. tourist towns, we have learned that word–of–mouth advertising is very powerful. To this end, we are confident that customers who have purchased our stained glass items at craft fairs and other events over the years will visit our store and purchase something from the wider selection of items we can now offer with a dedicated location. To encourage word–of–mouth referrals, we will provide customers with 10 percent discount "refer a friend" coupons.

- **Web Site**—We will develop a simple Web site describing our business, hours of operation, specials, and products offered.

- *Print Advertising*—The Lansing Hills Chamber of Commerce, to which we belong, profiles area businesses in a free tourist publication that is distributed at most local business locations. Members also are profiled on the chamber's Web site.

- *Promotional Brochure*—We have developed a colorful brochure that showcases the beauty of our stained glass work and entices prospective customers to visit our store with a 10 percent discount coupon. We will distribute this brochure to area hotels and B&Bs.

- *Direct Marketing*—To raise awareness about our contract services, Stanley Maxwell will send a direct mail letter to architects, real estate developers, home builders, unions, and churches through-out our primary service area.

FINANCIAL ANALYSIS

Following are estimated revenues and expenses for our first year of operation. To cover the purchase price of the building ($158,500), the owners are seeking a mortgage (term of 15 years at 5.471% APR). The owners plan to put 15 percent down on the property ($23,775), and will contribute $20,000 from personal savings for general operating purposes.

Revenues

Gift sales	$ 58,000
Contract services	$ 28,000
Classes	$ 12,500
Apartment rental	$ 20,400
Gross sales	$118,900

Expenses

Supplies	$ 18,000
Maintenance	$ 750
Advertising	$ 1,000
Mileage	$ 850
Accounting & legal	$ 700
Mortgage	$ 13,212
Salaries	$ 45,000
Property taxes	$ 1,704
Telephone	$ 1,000
Utilities	$ 2,900
Insurance	$ 1,850
Loan payment	$ 8,760
Total	**$ 95,726**
Net profit	$ 23,574

Web Design
Web Wizards

6678 Ardmore
St. Clair Shores, MI 48081

Heidi Denler

Web Wizards is being formed as a partnership that will be owned and operated by brothers Frank and Mike Jestar. The company will be a home–based business in St. Clair Shores, Michigan, a middle–class suburb of Detroit, with many small businesses and no shortage of home–based businesses.

INTRODUCTION

Web Wizards is being formed as a partnership that will be owned and operated by brothers Frank and Mike Jestar. The company will be a home–based business in St. Clair Shores, Michigan, a middle–class suburb of Detroit, with many small businesses and no shortage of home–based businesses.

MANAGEMENT SUMMARY

Frank and Mike Jestar are determined to follow their grandfather's admonition to "Find something you really enjoy doing and figure out a way to get paid for it." They are self–proclaimed computer geeks, having excelled in every computer programming and skills class they took beginning in middle school. Before they even started high school, teachers, family members, neighbors, and friends were asking for their assistance with programming, web site design, set–up, and repair of their computers. Their reputation in the area has continued to grow and their services have been in demand, leading them to decide to start Web Wizards.

MISSION STATEMENT

Web Wizards will offer fast, reliable quality programming, web site design, and technical assistance to individuals, small businesses, and home offices for set–up and repair of personal computers.

VISION STATEMENT

The future of Web Wizards will be based on referrals from current and future clients, as well as through media advertising. Client satisfaction will play a part in growth as it will lead to additional referrals from returning clients. Quick response, expertise, and high quality will create stability in a customer base and lead to expansion of that base.

VALUES STATEMENT

The Jestar brothers are committed to providing timely, quality service and practical solutions to the clients' computer issues, upgrades, and programming at a reasonable, competitive rate. This will encourage customer loyalty in the form of repeat business and recommendations.

BUSINESS PHILOSOPHY

Clients of Web Wizards will experience friendly, on–time, quality service along with customer education, reliability, and availability for all their computer needs, from set–up to trouble–shooting technology problems.

GOALS AND OBJECTIVES

Frank and Mike Jestar have set financial goals based on past and current experience helping friends, neighbors, and teachers. They project that they will generate adequate profit to build their fledgling enterprise and finance growth in capital furnishings.

Customer relation goals are equally clear and based on experience. Providing friendly, high–quality, timely service and assistance will generate relationships with customers that will benefit both the owners and the customers.

At the outset, promotion and advertising will be low–key, including flyers distributed to neighbors and posted on college campuses. The brothers will talk with managers of local office supply stores to encourage sending customers their way. Their high school and middle school technology teachers have already offered to send customers to them when asked by students or parents for assistance.

ORGANIZATION STRUCTURE

Web Wizards will be run as a partnership between brothers Frank and Mike Jestar. They will share equally in the responsibility, workload, and profits of the company. They expect to be profitable immediately because they will be using their home as their base of operations and have the majority of equipment needed since they are expanding what has been a hobby that has generated some income into a for–profit service.

The Jestar brothers' philosophy is to avoid debt and plan to start their company with as little expense as possible, following the concept that this type of enterprise is ideal for entrepreneurs. Start–up expenses will be minimal and will be completely financed from the Jestar brothers' savings. Those expenses include typical start–up paperwork and filing (legal, accounting, state/federal/local licensing, etc.), cash reserve of at least one month's rent, and cost of equipment (all–in–one printer, fax, voice mail, paper, and printing for flyers, brochures, etc.).

ADVERTISING AND PROMOTION

Web Wizards will initially create a logo that incorporates a stylized computer theme. That logo will serve as a watermark for their stationery, and will be included on flyers, brochures, business cards, and car magnets that they will place on their personal cars. A friend who is a graphic artist is working with the brothers to design a unique, recognizable logo.

The company will use the logo on its brochure and flyers, and incorporate it into the software template used. The logo will also be on every web page designed by Web Wizards, with a link to the company's own web site.

The Jestar brothers will network with local computer and office supply stores, as well as with such business organizations as the SBDC and Chamber of Commerce, to form alliances for promotion. The stores and organizations may also become clients of Web Wizards while they are providing leads for new clients.

The brothers will share brochures with current customers announcing their new venture. They are considering leaving flyers at neighbors' homes. A website is being built to promote Web Wizards.

CUSTOMER BASE

The partners expect to broaden the customer base by word of mouth referrals from friends and neighboring businesses, as well as through flyers, advertising, and e–mail contact. Seniors will be offered a 10 percent discount on all services. The brothers expect customer, store, and organization referrals to build their customer base.

Customers will include individuals with home computers, owners of home–based businesses, small businesses with under 100 employees, and medium-sized businesses with up to 500 employees all using computers that will require set–up, software and hardware upgrades, networking, trouble–shooting, data recovery, data storage, and repairs.

PRODUCTS AND SERVICES

Frank and Mike Jestar will provide all services for their clients. They are committed to staying up–to–date with cutting edge technology to remain competitive.

Web Wizards will provide timely, reliable, quality technical assistance for individuals, small businesses, and home office workers at a competitive, reasonable price. The main services offered will be technical (billed by the hour), retainer (contract work for specific skills, web site design and maintenance), and consulting.

Technical services will be billed hourly. They will provide the client with immediate solutions to a software or hardware problem, whether it is emergency or non–emergency. These services are typically short–term responses to find solutions for immediate problems.

Specific skills will include set–up and consulting (for purchases), system optimization, network administration, education, repair, data recovery and storage, and data protection. Retainer services will include traditional consulting, system maintenance, including upgrades to the clients' systems, and network administration. This area will also serve for web site design and maintenance.

Consulting services will be billed by project or by retainer, depending on the client's individual requirements. Frank and Mike Jestar will be available to consult on hardware and software purchases, system installation and troubleshooting.

LOCATION

The Jestar brothers will operate from their home in a spare room. They will expand slightly on materials they currently have that has been collected over the last several years. Each has a computer, which they will link so they can use them to chat while on service calls if necessary.

They will invest in a portable wi–fi through Verizon wireless USB modems that will allow them to stay connected to the Internet regardless of their location when working at a client's home or business.

EQUIPMENT

Web Wizards will make use of two laptop computers, one desktop computer, LAN, Verizon mobile broadband, miscellaneous screwdrivers, wiring tools, soldering iron, etc.

The office area of their work space will hold a desk with chair, filing cabinet, all–in–one printer/copier/scanner, fax, and shelving for holding paper, brochures, flyers, and such office supplies as pencils, pens, binders, and printer cartridges.

The owners' personal cars will be enlisted as traveling advertisements with magnetic ads on each side and rear end.

FINANCIAL

Start-up costs will include standard licensing and registration fees required by federal, state, and local governments. The Jestar brothers will incur federal, state, and local self–employment taxes, key man insurance, property and liability insurance geared specifically for home–based businesses, cellular phone and linked wi–fi access, an upgraded alarm system, and advertising. As noted, specific insurance for home–based businesses include loss of business equipment due to theft, damage, or natural disaster; property liability, such as a client being injured on the Jestars' property; and loss of business income due to any number of reasons.

PROFESSIONAL AND ADVISORY SUPPORT

Legal matters will be handled initially by the family's personal attorney, who is a general practice attorney and is familiar with the legalities of small businesses. A local CPA will manage financial matters.

The Jestars will work with Mike Rowe, their personal financial consultant to ensure life, health, and dental insurance coverage. They have an established relationship with Charter One Bank that they will continue for business use.

BUSINESS AND GROWTH STRATEGY

The owners of Web Wizards will remain up–to–date on technological developments in the industry. They will also keep their equipment upgraded to meet the demand of their clients.

Client growth will be separated according to type and size. The Jestar brothers will continue to work with individuals who need their services to set up a home computer, load software, install hardware upgrades, and/or troubleshoot problems with the clients' system. This segment will be phased out, however, replaced with home office and small businesses.

Home offices will become an increasingly important segment of Web Wizards' business. According to market research, this is the largest and fastest growing segment in the U.S. economy. The Jestar brothers will be able to easily identify with these customers, as well as provide optimal, reliable service for them.

Medium-sized businesses (with up to 499 employees) will be a small segment of Web Wizards clients, as will large businesses. Within two years, the Jestars project that these two segments will grow to become at least 50 percent of their business.

Strategies for growth for Web Wizards include networking, referrals, and web site promotion. The brothers will use current contacts and clients to increase their network and identify new clients through referrals. They will promote the company web site, which will be a platform for the owners' skills and expertise. It will serve as an e–brochure and point of contact for potential clients to ask questions. In addition, Web Wizards will have a presence in the Yellow Pages, classified ads, display ads, and such local media outlets as newspapers, magazines, and local cable TV.

The Jestars will work with a local PR guru to prepare and send an announcement of Web Wizards to current clients and contacts, as well as press releases to local media. They will concentrate on current relationships, networking for referrals. Customer satisfaction will be the final key in the growth strategy for Web Wizards.

The demand for computer repair is driven by computer issues and crashes, rather than by client demand, which the Jestars recognize. However, they seek to be the first call when computer disasters strike. System and software upgrades will offer Web Wizards the opportunity to provide quality service so they will, in fact, be the first responder to computer emergencies.

Web Wizards will focus on the few businesses not yet using computers, or underutilizing them; small businesses looking to upgrade to multiple computers for their employees that will be linked; trouble shooting specific problems; and custom computer programming and analysis.

COMPETITION

Big box office supply stores, such as Staples and Office Depot, and stores that specialize in computer sales will offer the greatest competition to Web Wizards. However, the Jestars are confident that their personal service, which will be quick and reliable, as well as in home at no extra charge, will give them a competitive edge over the big box stores that require in–store drop–off and lengthy service time because of shipping to outside sources.

Industry research indicates customer loyalty in this field, which continues to grow and has not yet reached a saturation point.

Web Wizards will set its price scale based on prices charged by the competition, charging less whenever possible, and never charging more. They will have hourly, retainer, and project pricing in keeping with local computer repair and consulting companies.

WEB SITE

Web Wizards is developing a web page that will serve as an e–brochure and be a contact point for interested clients. The web page will also serve as a source of information about services offered and the Jestars themselves. It will highlight their experience and expertise.

CONCLUSION

Client satisfaction, Web Wizards' reliable, timely service and expertise, and competitive pricing will enable the Jestar brothers to retain current clients and gain new ones across the local business and home computer users. Continued growth in the use of computers for home and business use will serve to help Web Wizards grow as well.

Through marketing and networking, in addition to quick response, quality service, and outstanding client relations, Frank and Mike Jestar project that Web Wizards will be profitable immediately.

Business Plan Template

USING THIS TEMPLATE

A business plan carefully spells out a company's projected course of action over a period of time, usually the first two to three years after the start-up. In addition, banks, lenders, and other investors examine the information and financial documentation before deciding whether or not to finance a new business venture. Therefore, a business plan is an essential tool in obtaining financing and should describe the business itself in detail as well as all important factors influencing the company, including the market, industry, competition, operations and management policies, problem solving strategies, financial resources and needs, and other vital information. The plan enables the business owner to anticipate costs, plan for difficulties, and take advantage of opportunities, as well as design and implement strategies that keep the company running as smoothly as possible.

This template has been provided as a model to help you construct your own business plan. Please keep in mind that there is no single acceptable format for a business plan, and that this template is in no way comprehensive, but serves as an example.

The business plans provided in this section are fictional and have been used by small business agencies as models for clients to use in compiling their own business plans.

GENERIC BUSINESS PLAN

Main headings included below are topics that should be covered in a comprehensive business plan. They include:

Business Summary

Purpose
Provides a brief overview of your business, succinctly highlighting the main ideas of your plan.

Includes

- Name and Type of Business
- Description of Product/Service
- Business History and Development
- Location
- Market
- Competition
- Management
- Financial Information
- Business Strengths and Weaknesses
- Business Growth

Table of Contents

Purpose
Organized in an Outline Format, the Table of Contents illustrates the selection and arrangement of information contained in your plan.

Includes

- Topic Headings and Subheadings
- Page Number References

Business History and Industry Outlook

Purpose

Examines the conception and subsequent development of your business within an industry specific context.

Includes

- Start-up Information
- Owner/Key Personnel Experience
- Location
- Development Problems and Solutions
- Investment/Funding Information
- Future Plans and Goals
- Market Trends and Statistics
- Major Competitors
- Product/Service Advantages
- National, Regional, and Local Economic Impact

Product/Service

Purpose

Introduces, defines, and details the product and/or service that inspired the information of your business.

Includes

- Unique Features
- Niche Served
- Market Comparison
- Stage of Product/Service Development
- Production
- Facilities, Equipment, and Labor
- Financial Requirements
- Product/Service Life Cycle
- Future Growth

Market Examination

Purpose

Assessment of product/service applications in relation to consumer buying cycles.

Includes

- Target Market
- Consumer Buying Habits
- Product/Service Applications
- Consumer Reactions
- Market Factors and Trends
- Penetration of the Market
- Market Share
- Research and Studies
- Cost
- Sales Volume and Goals

Competition

Purpose

Analysis of Competitors in the Marketplace.

Includes

- Competitor Information
- Product/Service Comparison
- Market Niche
- Product/Service Strengths and Weaknesses
- Future Product/Service Development

Marketing

Purpose

Identifies promotion and sales strategies for your product/service.

Includes

- Product/Service Sales Appeal
- Special and Unique Features
- Identification of Customers
- Sales and Marketing Staff
- Sales Cycles
- Type of Advertising/ Promotion
- Pricing
- Competition
- Customer Services

Operations

Purpose

Traces product/service development from production/inception to the market environment.

Includes

- Cost Effective Production Methods
- Facility
- Location
- Equipment
- Labor
- Future Expansion

Administration and Management

Purpose

Offers a statement of your management philosophy with an in-depth focus on processes and procedures.

Includes

- Management Philosophy
- Structure of Organization
- Reporting System
- Methods of Communication
- Employee Skills and Training
- Employee Needs and Compensation
- Work Environment
- Management Policies and Procedures
- Roles and Responsibilities

Key Personnel

Purpose

Describes the unique backgrounds of principle employees involved in business.

Includes

- Owner(s)/Employee Education and Experience
- Positions and Roles
- Benefits and Salary
- Duties and Responsibilities
- Objectives and Goals

Potential Problems and Solutions

Purpose

Discussion of problem solving strategies that change issues into opportunities.

Includes

- Risks
- Litigation
- Future Competition
- Economic Impact
- Problem Solving Skills

Financial Information

Purpose

Secures needed funding and assistance through worksheets and projections detailing financial plans, methods of repayment, and future growth opportunities.

Includes

- Financial Statements
- Bank Loans
- Methods of Repayment
- Tax Returns
- Start-up Costs
- Projected Income (3 years)
- Projected Cash Flow (3 Years)
- Projected Balance Statements (3 years)

Appendices

Purpose

Supporting documents used to enhance your business proposal.

Includes

- Photographs of product, equipment, facilities, etc.
- Copyright/Trademark Documents
- Legal Agreements
- Marketing Materials
- Research and or Studies
- Operation Schedules
- Organizational Charts
- Job Descriptions
- Resumes
- Additional Financial Documentation

Fictional Food Distributor

Commercial Foods, Inc.

3003 Avondale Ave.
Knoxville, TN 37920

This plan demonstrates how a partnership can have a positive impact on a new business. It demonstrates how two individuals can carve a niche in the specialty foods market by offering gourmet foods to upscale restaurants and fine hotels. This plan is fictional and has not been used to gain funding from a bank or other lending institution.

STATEMENT OF PURPOSE

Commercial Foods, Inc. seeks a loan of $75,000 to establish a new business. This sum, together with $5,000 equity investment by the principals, will be used as follows:

- Merchandise inventory $25,000

- Office fixture/equipment $12,000

- Warehouse equipment $14,000

- One delivery truck $10,000

- Working capital $39,000

- Total $100,000

DESCRIPTION OF THE BUSINESS

Commercial Foods, Inc. will be a distributor of specialty food service products to hotels and upscale restaurants in the geographical area of a 50 mile radius of Knoxville. Richard Roberts will direct the sales effort and John Williams will manage the warehouse operation and the office. One delivery truck will be used initially with a second truck added in the third year. We expect to begin operation of the business within 30 days after securing the requested financing.

MANAGEMENT

A. Richard Roberts is a native of Memphis, Tennessee. He is a graduate of Memphis State University with a Bachelor's degree from the School of Business. After graduation, he worked for a major manufacturer of specialty food service products as a detail sales person for five years, and, for the past three years, he has served as a product sales manager for this firm.

B. John Williams is a native of Nashville, Tennessee. He holds a B.S. Degree in Food Technology from the University of Tennessee. His career includes five years as a product development chemist in gourmet food products and five years as operations manager for a food service distributor.

Both men are healthy and energetic. Their backgrounds complement each other, which will ensure the success of Commercial Foods, Inc. They will set policies together and personnel decisions will be made jointly. Initial salaries for the owners will be $1,000 per month for the first few years. The spouses of both principals are successful in the business world and earn enough to support the families.

They have engaged the services of Foster Jones, CPA, and William Hale, Attorney, to assist them in an advisory capacity.

PERSONNEL

The firm will employ one delivery truck driver at a wage of $8.00 per hour. One office worker will be employed at $7.50 per hour. One part-time employee will be used in the office at $5.00 per hour. The driver will load and unload his own trucks. Mr. Williams will assist in the warehouse operation as needed to assist one stock person at $7.00 per hour. An additional delivery truck and driver will be added the third year.

LOCATION

The firm will lease a 20,000 square foot building at 3003 Avondale Ave., in Knoxville, which contains warehouse and office areas equipped with two-door truck docks. The annual rental is $9,000. The building was previously used as a food service warehouse and very little modification to the building will be required.

PRODUCTS AND SERVICES

The firm will offer specialty food service products such as soup bases, dessert mixes, sauce bases, pastry mixes, spices, and flavors, normally used by upscale restaurants and nice hotels. We are going after a niche in the market with high quality gourmet products. There is much less competition in this market than in standard run of the mill food service products. Through their work experiences, the principals have contacts with supply sources and with local chefs.

THE MARKET

We know from our market survey that there are over 200 hotels and upscale restaurants in the area we plan to serve. Customers will be attracted by a direct sales approach. We will offer samples of our products and product application data on use of our products in the finished prepared foods. We will cultivate the chefs in these establishments. The technical background of John Williams will be especially useful here.

COMPETITION

We find that we will be only distributor in the area offering a full line of gourmet food service products. Other foodservice distributors offer only a few such items in conjunction with their standard product line. Our survey shows that many of the chefs are ordering products from Atlanta and Memphis because of a lack of adequate local supply.

SUMMARY

Commercial Foods, Inc. will be established as a foodservice distributor of specialty food in Knoxville. The principals, with excellent experience in the industry, are seeking a $75,000 loan to establish the business. The principals are investing $25,000 as equity capital.

The business will be set up as an S Corporation with each principal owning 50% of the common stock in the corporation.

Fictional Hardware Store

Oshkosh Hardware, Inc.

123 Main St.
Oshkosh, WI 54901

The following plan outlines how a small hardware store can survive competition from large discount chains by offering products and providing expert advice in the use of any product it sells. This plan is fictional and has not been used to gain funding from a bank or other lending institution.

EXECUTIVE SUMMARY

Oshkosh Hardware, Inc. is a new corporation that is going to establish a retail hardware store in a strip mall in Oshkosh, Wisconsin. The store will sell hardware of all kinds, quality tools, paint, and housewares. The business will make revenue and a profit by servicing its customers not only with needed hardware but also with expert advice in the use of any product it sells.

Oshkosh Hardware, Inc. will be operated by its sole shareholder, James Smith. The company will have a total of four employees. It will sell its products in the local market. Customers will buy our products because we will provide free advice on the use of all of our products and will also furnish a full refund warranty.

Oshkosh Hardware, Inc. will sell its products in the Oshkosh store staffed by three sales representatives. No additional employees will be needed to achieve its short and long range goals. The primary short range goal is to open the store by October 1, 1994. In order to achieve this goal a lease must be signed by July 1, 1994 and the complete inventory ordered by August 1, 1994.

Mr. James Smith will invest $30,000 in the business. In addition, the company will have to borrow $150,000 during the first year to cover the investment in inventory, accounts receivable, and furniture and equipment. The company will be profitable after six months of operation and should be able to start repayment of the loan in the second year.

THE BUSINESS

The business will sell hardware of all kinds, quality tools, paint, and housewares. We will purchase our products from three large wholesale buying groups.

In general our customers are homeowners who do their own repair and maintenance, hobbyists, and housewives. Our business is unique in that we will have a complete line of all hardware items and will be able to get special orders by overnight delivery. The business makes revenue and profits by servicing our customers not only with needed hardware but also with expert advice in the use of any product we sell. Our major costs for bringing our products to market are cost of merchandise of 36%, salaries of $45,000, and occupancy costs of $60,000.

Oshkosh Hardware, Inc.'s retail outlet will be located at 1524 Frontage Road, which is in a newly developed retail center of Oshkosh. Our location helps facilitate accessibility from all parts of town and reduces our delivery costs. The store will occupy 7500 square feet of space. The major equipment involved in our business is counters and shelving, a computer, a paint mixing machine, and a truck.

THE MARKET

Oshkosh Hardware, Inc. will operate in the local market. There are 15,000 potential customers in this market area. We have three competitors who control approximately 98% of the market at present. We feel we can capture 25% of the market within the next four years. Our major reason for believing this is that our staff is technically competent to advise our customers in the correct use of all products we sell.

After a careful market analysis, we have determined that approximately 60% of our customers are men and 40% are women. The percentage of customers that fall into the following age categories are:

Under 16: 0%
17-21: 5%
22-30: 30%
31-40: 30%
41-50: 20%
51-60: 10%
61-70: 5%
Over 70: 0%

The reasons our customers prefer our products is our complete knowledge of their use and our full refund warranty.

We get our information about what products our customers want by talking to existing customers. There seems to be an increasing demand for our product. The demand for our product is increasing in size based on the change in population characteristics.

SALES

At Oshkosh Hardware, Inc. we will employ three sales people and will not need any additional personnel to achieve our sales goals. These salespeople will need several years experience in home repair and power tool usage. We expect to attract 30% of our customers from newspaper ads, 5% of our customers from local directories, 5% of our customers from the yellow pages, 10% of our customers from family and friends, and 50% of our customers from current customers. The most cost effect source will be current customers. In general our industry is growing.

MANAGEMENT

We would evaluate the quality of our management staff as being excellent. Our manager is experienced and very motivated to achieve the various sales and quality assurance objectives we have set. We will use a management information system that produces key inventory, quality assurance, and sales data on a weekly basis. All data is compared to previously established goals for that week, and deviations are the primary focus of the management staff.

GOALS IMPLEMENTATION

The short term goals of our business are:

1. Open the store by October 1, 1994
2. Reach our breakeven point in two months
3. Have sales of $100,000 in the first six months

In order to achieve our first short term goal we must:

1. Sign the lease by July 1, 1994
2. Order a complete inventory by August 1, 1994

In order to achieve our second short term goal we must:

1. Advertise extensively in Sept. and Oct.
2. Keep expenses to a minimum

In order to achieve our third short term goal we must:

1. Promote power tool sales for the Christmas season
2. Keep good customer traffic in Jan. and Feb.

The long term goals for our business are:

1. Obtain sales volume of $600,000 in three years
2. Become the largest hardware dealer in the city
3. Open a second store in Fond du Lac

The most important thing we must do in order to achieve the long term goals for our business is to develop a highly profitable business with excellent cash flow.

FINANCE

Oshkosh Hardware, Inc. Faces some potential threats or risks to our business. They are discount house competition. We believe we can avoid or compensate for this by providing quality products complimented by quality advice on the use of every product we sell. The financial projections we have prepared are located at the end of this document.

JOB DESCRIPTION-GENERAL MANAGER

The General Manager of the business of the corporation will be the president of the corporation. He will be responsible for the complete operation of the retail hardware store which is owned by the corporation. A detailed description of his duties and responsibilities is as follows.

Sales

Train and supervise the three sales people. Develop programs to motivate and compensate these employees. Coordinate advertising and sales promotion effects to achieve sales totals as outlined in budget. Oversee purchasing function and inventory control procedures to insure adequate merchandise at all times at a reasonable cost.

Finance

Prepare monthly and annual budgets. Secure adequate line of credit from local banks. Supervise office personnel to insure timely preparation of records, statements, all government reports, control of receivables and payables, and monthly financial statements.

Administration

Perform duties as required in the areas of personnel, building leasing and maintenance, licenses and permits, and public relations.

Organizations, Agencies, & Consultants

A listing of Associations and Consultants of interest to entrepreneurs, followed by the ten Small Business Administration Regional Offices, Small Business Development Centers, Service Corps of Retired Executives offices, and Venture Capital and Finance Companies.

Associations

This section contains a listing of associations and other agencies of interest to the small business owner. Entries are listed alphabetically by organization name.

American Business Women's Association
9100 Ward Pkwy.
PO Box 8728
Kansas City, MO 64114-0728
(800)228-0007
E-mail: abwa@abwa.org
Website: http://www.abwa.org
Jeanne Banks, National President

American Franchisee Association
53 W Jackson Blvd., Ste. 1157
Chicago, IL 60604
(312)431-0545
E-mail: info@franchisee.org
Website: http://www.franchisee.org
Susan P. Kezios, President

American Independent Business Alliance
222 S Black Ave.
Bozeman, MT 59715
(406)582-1255
E-mail: info@amiba.net
Website: http://www.amiba.net
Jennifer Rockne, Director

American Small Businesses Association
206 E College St., Ste. 201
Grapevine, TX 76051
800-942-2722
E-mail: info@asbaonline.org
Website: http://www.asbaonline.org/

American Women's Economic Development Corporation
216 East 45th St., 10th Floor
New York, NY 10017
(917)368-6100

Fax: (212)986-7114
E-mail: info@awed.org
Website: http://www.awed.org
Roseanne Antonucci, Exec. Dir.

Association for Enterprise Opportunity
1601 N Kent St., Ste. 1101
Arlington, VA 22209
(703)841-7760
Fax: (703)841-7748
E-mail: aeo@assoceo.org
Website: http://www.micro
enterpriseworks.org
Bill Edwards, Exec.Dir.

Association of Small Business Development Centers
c/o Don Wilson
8990 Burke Lake Rd.
Burke, VA 22015
(703)764-9850
Fax: (703)764-1234
E-mail: info@asbdc-us.org
Website: http://www.asbdc-us.org
Don Wilson, Pres./CEO

BEST Employers Association
2505 McCabe Way
Irvine, CA 92614
(949)253-4080
800-433-0088
Fax: (714)553-0883
E-mail: info@bestlife.com
Website: http://www.bestlife.com
Donald R. Lawrenz, CEO

Center for Family Business
PO Box 24219
Cleveland, OH 44124
(440)460-5409
E-mail: grummi@aol.com
Dr. Leon A. Danco, Chm.

Coalition for Government Procurement
1990 M St. NW, Ste. 400
Washington, DC 20036
(202)331-0975
E-mail: info@thecgp.org
Website: http://www.coalgovpro.org
Paul Caggiano, Pres.

Employers of America
PO Box 1874
Mason City, IA 50402-1874
(641)424-3187
800-728-3187
Fax: (641)424-1673
E-mail: employer@employerhelp.org
Website: http://www.employerhelp.org
Jim Collison, Pres.

Family Firm Institute
200 Lincoln St., Ste. 201
Boston, MA 02111
(617)482-3045
Fax: (617)482-3049
E-mail: ffi@ffi.org
Website: http://www.ffi.org
Judy L. Green, Ph.D., Exec.Dir.

Independent Visually Impaired Enterprisers
500 S 3rd St., Apt. H
Burbank, CA 91502
(818)238-9321
E-mail: abazyn@bazyn
communications.com
http://www.acb.org/affiliates
Adris Bazyn, Pres.

International Association for Business Organizations
3 Woodthorn Ct., Ste. 12
Owings Mills, MD 21117
(410)581-1373
E-mail: nahbb@msn.com
Rudolph Lewis, Exec. Officer

International Council for Small Business
The George Washington University
School of Business and Public
Management
2115 G St. NW, Ste. 403
Washington, DC 20052
(202)994-0704
Fax: (202)994-4930
E-mail: icsb@gwu.edu
Website: http://www.icsb.org
Susan G. Duffy. Admin.

International Small Business Consortium
3309 Windjammer St.
Norman, OK 73072
E-mail: sb@isbc.com
Website: http://www.isbc.com

Kauffman Center for Entrepreneurial Leadership
4801 Rockhill Rd.
Kansas City, MO 64110-2046
(816)932-1000
E-mail: info@kauffman.org
Website: http://www.entreworld.org

National Alliance for Fair Competition
3 Bethesda Metro Center, Ste. 1100
Bethesda, MD 20814
(410)235-7116
Fax: (410)235-7116
E-mail: ampesq@aol.com
Tony Ponticelli, Exec.Dir.

National Association for the Self-Employed
PO Box 612067
DFW Airport
Dallas, TX 75261-2067
(800)232-6273
E-mail: mpetron@nase.org
Website: http://www.nase.org
Robert Hughes, Pres.

National Association of Business Leaders
4132 Shoreline Dr., Ste. J & H
Earth City, MO 63045
Fax: (314)298-9110
E-mail: nabl@nabl.com
Website: http://www.nabl.com/
Gene Blumenthal, Contact

National Association of Private Enterprise
PO Box 15550
Long Beach, CA 90815
888-224-0953

Fax: (714)844-4942
Website: http://www.napeonline.net
Laura Squiers, Exec.Dir.

National Association of Small Business Investment Companies
666 11th St. NW, Ste. 750
Washington, DC 20001
(202)628-5055
Fax: (202)628-5080
E-mail: nasbic@nasbic.org
Website: http://www.nasbic.org
Lee W. Mercer, Pres.

National Business Association
PO Box 700728
5151 Beltline Rd., Ste. 1150
Dallas, TX 75370
(972)458-0900
800-456-0440
Fax: (972)960-9149
E-mail: info@nationalbusiness.org
Website: http://www.national
business.org
Raj Nisankarao, Pres.

National Business Owners Association
PO Box 111
Stuart, VA 24171
(276)251-7500
(866)251-7505
Fax: (276)251-2217
E-mail: membershipservices@nboa.org
Website: http://www.rvmdb.com.nboa
Paul LaBarr, Pres.

National Center for Fair Competition
PO Box 220
Annandale, VA 22003
(703)280-4622
Fax: (703)280-0942
E-mail: kentonp1@aol.com
Kenton Pattie, Pres.

National Family Business Council
1640 W. Kennedy Rd.
Lake Forest, IL 60045
(847)295-1040
Fax: (847)295-1898
E-mail: lmsnfbc@email.msn.com
Jogn E. Messervey, Pres.

National Federation of Independent Business
53 Century Blvd., Ste. 250
Nashville, TN 37214
(615)872-5800
800-NFIBNOW
Fax: (615)872-5353
Website: http://www.nfib.org
Jack Faris, Pres. and CEO

National Small Business Association
1156 15th St. NW, Ste. 1100
Washington, DC 20005
(202)293-8830
800-345-6728
Fax: (202)872-8543
E-mail: press@nsba.biz
Website: http://www.nsba.biz
Rob Yunich, Dir. of Communications

PUSH Commercial Division
930 E 50th St.
Chicago, IL 60615-2702
(773)373-3366
Fax: (773)373-3571
E-mail: info@rainbowpush.org
Website: http://www.rainbowpush.org
Rev. Willie T. Barrow, Co-Chm.

Research Institute for Small and Emerging Business
722 12th St. NW
Washington, DC 20005
(202)628-8382
Fax: (202)628-8392
E-mail: info@riseb.org
Website: http://www.riseb.org
Allan Neece, Jr., Chm.

Sales Professionals USA
PO Box 149
Arvada, CO 80001
(303)534-4937
888-736-7767
E-mail: salespro@salesprofessionals-usa.com
Website: http://www.salesprofessionals-usa.com
Sharon Herbert, Natl. Pres.

Score Association - Service Corps of Retired Executives
409 3rd St. SW, 6th Fl.
Washington, DC 20024
(202)205-6762
800-634-0245
Fax: (202)205-7636
E-mail: media@score.org
Website: http://www.score.org
W. Kenneth Yancey, Jr., CEO

Small Business and Entrepreneurship Council
1920 L St. NW, Ste. 200
Washington, DC 20036
(202)785-0238
Fax: (202)822-8118
E-mail: membership@sbec.org
Website: http://www.sbecouncil.org
Karen Kerrigan, Pres./CEO

Small Business in Telecommunications
1331 H St. NW, Ste. 500
Washington, DC 20005
(202)347-4511
Fax: (202)347-8607
E-mail: sbt@sbthome.org
Website: http://www.sbthome.org
Lonnie Danchik, Chm.

Small Business Legislative Council
1010 Massachusetts Ave. NW, Ste. 540
Washington, DC 20005
(202)639-8500
Fax: (202)296-5333
E-mail: email@sblc.org
Website: http://www.sblc.org
John Satagaj, Pres.

Small Business Service Bureau
554 Main St.
PO Box 15014
Worcester, MA 01615-0014
(508)756-3513
800-343-0939
Fax: (508)770-0528
E-mail: membership@sbsb.com
Website: http://www.sbsb.com
Francis R. Carroll, Pres.

Small Publishers Association of North America
1618 W COlorado Ave.
Colorado Springs, CO 80904
(719)475-1726
Fax: (719)471-2182
E-mail: span@spannet.org
Website: http://www.spannet.org
Scott Flora, Exec. Dir.

SOHO America
PO Box 941
Hurst, TX 76053-0941
800-495-SOHO
E-mail: soho@1sas.com
Website: http://www.soho.org

Structured Employment Economic Development Corporation
915 Broadway, 17th Fl.
New York, NY 10010
(212)473-0255
Fax: (212)473-0357
E-mail: info@seedco.org
Website: http://www.seedco.org
William Grinker, CEO

Support Services Alliance
107 Prospect St.
Schoharie, NY 12157
800-836-4772

E-mail: info@ssamembers.com
Website: http://www.ssainfo.com
Steve COle, Pres.

United States Association for Small Business and Entrepreneurship
975 University Ave., No. 3260
Madison, WI 53706
(608)262-9982
Fax: (608)263-0818
E-mail: jgillman@wisc.edu
Website: http://www.ususbe.org
Joan Gillman, Exec. Dir.

Consultants

This section contains a listing of consultants specializing in small business development. It is arranged alphabetically by country, then by state or province, then by city, then by firm name.

Canada

Alberta

Common Sense Solutions
3405 16A Ave.
Edmonton, AB, Canada
(403)465-7330
Fax: (403)465-7380
E-mail: gcoulson@comsense solutions.com
Website: http://www.comsense solutions.com

Varsity Consulting Group
School of Business
University of Alberta
Edmonton, AB, Canada T6G 2R6
(780)492-2994
Fax: (780)492-5400
Website: http://www.bus.ualberta.ca/vcg

Viro Hospital Consulting
42 Commonwealth Bldg., 9912 - 106 St. NW
Edmonton, AB, Canada T5K 1C5
(403)425-3871
Fax: (403)425-3871
E-mail: rpb@freenet.edmonton.ab.ca

British Columbia

SRI Strategic Resources Inc.
4330 Kingsway, Ste. 1600
Burnaby, BC, Canada V5H 4G7
(604)435-0627
Fax: (604)435-2782

E-mail: inquiry@sri.bc.ca
Website: http://www.sri.com

Andrew R. De Boda Consulting
1523 Milford Ave.
Coquitlam, BC, Canada V3J 2V9
(604)936-4527
Fax: (604)936-4527
E-mail: deboda@intergate.bc.ca
Website: http://www.ourworld.
compuserve.com/homepages/deboda

The Sage Group Ltd.
980 - 355 Burrard St.
744 W Haistings, Ste. 410
Vancouver, BC, Canada V6C 1A5
(604)669-9269
Fax: (604)669-6622

Tikkanen-Bradley
1345 Nelson St., Ste. 202
Vancouver, BC, Canada V6E 1J8
(604)669-0583
E-mail: webmaster@tikkanen
bradley.com
Website: http://www.tikkanenbradley.com

Ontario

The Cynton Co.
17 Massey St.
Brampton, ON, Canada L6S 2V6
(905)792-7769
Fax: (905)792-8116
E-mail: cynton@home.com
Website: http://www.cynton.com

Begley & Associates
RR 6
Cambridge, ON, Canada N1R 5S7
(519)740-3629
Fax: (519)740-3629
E-mail: begley@in.on.ca
Website: http://www.in.on.ca/~begley/index.htm

CRO Engineering Ltd.
1895 William Hodgins Ln.
Carp, ON, Canada K0A 1L0
(613)839-1108
Fax: (613)839-1406
E-mail: J.Grefford@ieee.ca
Website: http://www.geocities.com/WallStreet/District/7401/

Task Enterprises
Box 69, RR 2 Hamilton
Flamborough, ON, Canada L8N 2Z7
(905)659-0153
Fax: (905)659-0861

HST Group Ltd.
430 Gilmour St.
Ottawa, ON, Canada K2P 0R8
(613)236-7303
Fax: (613)236-9893

Harrison Associates
BCE Pl.
181 Bay St., Ste. 3740
PO Box 798
Toronto, ON, Canada M5J 2T3
(416)364-5441
Fax: (416)364-2875

TCI Convergence Ltd. Management Consultants
99 Crown's Ln.
Toronto, ON, Canada M5R 3P4
(416)515-4146
Fax: (416)515-2097
E-mail: tci@inforamp.net
Website: http://tciconverge.com/index.1.html

Ken Wyman & Associates Inc.
64B Shuter St., Ste. 200
Toronto, ON, Canada M5B 1B1
(416)362-2926
Fax: (416)362-3039
E-mail: kenwyman@compuserve.com

JPL Business Consultants
82705 Metter Rd.
Wellandport, ON, Canada L0R 2J0
(905)386-7450
Fax: (905)386-7450
E-mail: plamarch@freenet.npiec.on.ca

Quebec

The Zimmar Consulting Partnership Inc.
Westmount
PO Box 98
Montreal, QC, Canada H3Z 2T1
(514)484-1459
Fax: (514)484-3063

Saskatchewan

Trimension Group
No. 104-110 Research Dr.
Innovation Place, SK, Canada S7N 3R3
(306)668-2560
Fax: (306)975-1156
E-mail: trimension@trimension.ca
Website: http://www.trimension.ca

Corporate Management Consultants
40 Government Road - PO Box 185
Prud Homme, SK, Canada, S0K 3K0
(306)654-4569
Fax: (650)618-2742

E-mail: cmccorporatemanagement@shaw.ca
Website: http://www.Corporatemanagementconsultants.com
Gerald Rekve

United States

Alabama

Business Planning Inc.
300 Office Park Dr.
Birmingham, AL 35223-2474
(205)870-7090
Fax: (205)870-7103

Tradebank of Eastern Alabama
546 Broad St., Ste. 3
Gadsden, AL 35901
(205)547-8700
Fax: (205)547-8718
E-mail: mansion@webex.com
Website: http://www.webex.com/~tea

Alaska

AK Business Development Center
3335 Arctic Blvd., Ste. 203
Anchorage, AK 99503
(907)562-0335
Free: 800-478-3474
Fax: (907)562-6988
E-mail: abdc@gci.net
Website: http://www.abdc.org

Business Matters
PO Box 287
Fairbanks, AK 99707
(907)452-5650

Arizona

Carefree Direct Marketing Corp.
8001 E Serene St.
PO Box 3737
Carefree, AZ 85377-3737
(480)488-4227
Fax: (480)488-2841

Trans Energy Corp.
1739 W 7th Ave.
Mesa, AZ 85202
(480)827-7915
Fax: (480)967-6601
E-mail: aha@clean-air.org
Website: http://www.clean-air.org

CMAS
5125 N 16th St.
Phoenix, AZ 85016

(602)395-1001
Fax: (602)604-8180

Comgate Telemanagement Ltd.
706 E Bell Rd., Ste. 105
Phoenix, AZ 85022
(602)485-5708
Fax: (602)485-5709
E-mail: comgate@netzone.com
Website: http://www.comgate.com

Moneysoft Inc.
1 E Camelback Rd. #550
Phoenix, AZ 85012
Free: 800-966-7797
E-mail: mbray@moneysoft.com

Harvey C. Skoog
PO Box 26439
Prescott Valley, AZ 86312
(520)772-1714
Fax: (520)772-2814

LMC Services
8711 E Pinnacle Peak Rd., No. 340
Scottsdale, AZ 85255-3555
(602)585-7177
Fax: (602)585-5880
E-mail: louws@earthlink.com

Sauerbrun Technology Group Ltd.
7979 E Princess Dr., Ste. 5
Scottsdale, AZ 85255-5878
(602)502-4950
Fax: (602)502-4292
E-mail: info@sauerbrun.com
Website: http://www.sauerbrun.com

Gary L. McLeod
PO Box 230
Sonoita, AZ 85637
Fax: (602)455-5661

Van Cleve Associates
6932 E 2nd St.
Tucson, AZ 85710
(520)296-2587
Fax: (520)296-3358

California

Acumen Group Inc.
(650)949-9349
Fax: (650)949-4845
E-mail: acumen-g@ix.netcom.com
Website: http://pw2.netcom.com/~janed/acumen.html

On-line Career and Management Consulting
420 Central Ave., No. 314
Alameda, CA 94501

(510)864-0336
Fax: (510)864-0336
E-mail: career@dnai.com
Website: http://www.dnai.com/~career

Career Paths-Thomas E. Church & Associates Inc.
PO Box 2439
Aptos, CA 95001
(408)662-7950
Fax: (408)662-7955
E-mail: church@ix.netcom.com
Website: http://www.careerpaths-tom.com

Keck & Co. Business Consultants
410 Walsh Rd.
Atherton, CA 94027
(650)854-9588
Fax: (650)854-7240
E-mail: info@keckco.com
Website: http://www.keckco.com

Ben W. Laverty III, PhD, REA, CEI
4909 Stockdale Hwy., Ste. 132
Bakersfield, CA 93309
(661)283-8300
Free: 800-833-0373
Fax: (661)283-8313
E-mail: cstc@cstcsafety.com
Website: http://www.cstcsafety.com/cstc

Lindquist Consultants-Venture Planning
225 Arlington Ave.
Berkeley, CA 94707
(510)524-6685
Fax: (510)527-6604

Larson Associates
PO Box 9005
Brea, CA 92822
(714)529-4121
Fax: (714)572-3606
E-mail: ray@consultlarson.com
Website: http://www.consultlarson.com

Kremer Management Consulting
PO Box 500
Carmel, CA 93921
(408)626-8311
Fax: (408)624-2663
E-mail: ddkremer@aol.com

W and J PARTNERSHIP
PO Box 2499
18876 Edwin Markham Dr.
Castro Valley, CA 94546
(510)583-7751
Fax: (510)583-7645
E-mail: wamorgan@wjpartnership.com
Website: http://www.wjpartnership.com

JB Associates
21118 Gardena Dr.
Cupertino, CA 95014
(408)257-0214
Fax: (408)257-0216
E-mail: semarang@sirius.com

House Agricultural Consultants
PO Box 1615
Davis, CA 95617-1615
(916)753-3361
Fax: (916)753-0464
E-mail: infoag@houseag.com
Website: http://www.houseag.com/

3C Systems Co.
16161 Ventura Blvd., Ste. 815
Encino, CA 91436
(818)907-1302
Fax: (818)907-1357
E-mail: mark@3CSysCo.com
Website: http://www.3CSysCo.com

Technical Management Consultants
3624 Westfall Dr.
Encino, CA 91436-4154
(818)784-0626
Fax: (818)501-5575
E-mail: tmcrs@aol.com

RAINWATER-GISH & Associates, Business Finance & Development
317 3rd St., Ste. 3
Eureka, CA 95501
(707)443-0030
Fax: (707)443-5683

Global Tradelinks
451 Pebble Beach Pl.
Fullerton, CA 92835
(714)441-2280
Fax: (714)441-2281
E-mail: info@globaltradelinks.com
Website: http://www.globaltradelinks.com

Strategic Business Group
800 Cienaga Dr.
Fullerton, CA 92835-1248
(714)449-1040
Fax: (714)525-1631

Burnes Consulting
20537 Wolf Creek Rd.
Grass Valley, CA 95949
(530)346-8188
Free: 800-949-9021
Fax: (530)346-7704
E-mail: kent@burnesconsulting.com
Website: http://www.burnesconsulting.com

Pioneer Business Consultants
9042 Garfield Ave., Ste. 312
Huntington Beach, CA 92646
(714)964-7600

Beblie, Brandt & Jacobs Inc.
16 Technology, Ste. 164
Irvine, CA 92618
(714)450-8790
Fax: (714)450-8799
E-mail: darcy@bbjinc.com
Website: http://198.147.90.26

Fluor Daniel Inc.
3353 Michelson Dr.
Irvine, CA 92612-0650
(949)975-2000
Fax: (949)975-5271
E-mail: sales.consulting@fluordaniel.com
Website: http://www.fluordaniel
consulting.com

MCS Associates
18300 Von Karman, Ste. 710
Irvine, CA 92612
(949)263-8700
Fax: (949)263-0770
E-mail: info@mcsassociates.com
Website: http://www.mcsassociates.com

Inspired Arts Inc.
4225 Executive Sq., Ste. 1160
La Jolla, CA 92037
(619)623-3525
Free: 800-851-4394
Fax: (619)623-3534
E-mail: info@inspiredarts.com
Website: http://www.inspiredarts.com

The Laresis Companies
PO Box 3284
La Jolla, CA 92038
(619)452-2720
Fax: (619)452-8744

RCL & Co.
PO Box 1143
737 Pearl St., Ste. 201
La Jolla, CA 92038
(619)454-8883
Fax: (619)454-8880

Comprehensive Business Services
3201 Lucas Cir.
Lafayette, CA 94549
(925)283-8272
Fax: (925)283-8272

The Ribble Group
27601 Forbes Rd., Ste. 52
Laguna Niguel, CA 92677

(714)582-1085
Fax: (714)582-6420
E-mail: ribble@deltanet.com

Norris Bernstein, CMC
9309 Marina Pacifica Dr. N
Long Beach, CA 90803
(562)493-5458
Fax: (562)493-5459
E-mail: norris@ctecomputer.com
Website: http://foodconsultants.com/
bernstein/

Horizon Consulting Services
1315 Garthwick Dr.
Los Altos, CA 94024
(415)967-0906
Fax: (415)967-0906

Brincko Associates Inc.
1801 Avenue of the Stars, Ste. 1054
Los Angeles, CA 90067
(310)553-4523
Fax: (310)553-6782

**Rubenstein/Justman Management
Consultants**
2049 Century Park E, 24th Fl.
Los Angeles, CA 90067
(310)282-0800
Fax: (310)282-0400
E-mail: info@rjmc.net
Website: http://www.rjmc.net

F.J. Schroeder & Associates
1926 Westholme Ave.
Los Angeles, CA 90025
(310)470-2655
Fax: (310)470-6378
E-mail: fjsacons@aol.com
Website: http://www.mcninet.com/
GlobalLook/Fjschroe.html

Western Management Associates
5959 W Century Blvd., Ste. 565
Los Angeles, CA 90045-6506
(310)645-1091
Free: (888)788-6534
Fax: (310)645-1092
E-mail: gene@cfoforrent.com
Website: http://www.cfoforrent.com

Darrell Sell and Associates
Los Gatos, CA 95030
(408)354-7794
E-mail: darrell@netcom.com

Leslie J. Zambo
3355 Michael Dr.
Marina, CA 93933
(408)384-7086

Fax: (408)647-4199
E-mail: 104776.1552@compuserve.com

Marketing Services Management
PO Box 1377
Martinez, CA 94553
(510)370-8527
Fax: (510)370-8527
E-mail: markserve@biotechnet.com

William M. Shine Consulting Service
PO Box 127
Moraga, CA 94556-0127
(510)376-6516

Palo Alto Management Group Inc.
2672 Bayshore Pky., Ste. 701
Mountain View, CA 94043
(415)968-4374
Fax: (415)968-4245
E-mail: mburwen@pamg.com

BizplanSource
1048 Irvine Ave., Ste. 621
Newport Beach, CA 92660
Free: 888-253-0974
Fax: 800-859-8254
E-mail: info@bizplansource.com
Website: http://www.bizplansource.com
Adam Greengrass, President

The Market Connection
4020 Birch St., Ste. 203
Newport Beach, CA 92660
(714)731-6273
Fax: (714)833-0253

Muller Associates
PO Box 7264
Newport Beach, CA 92658
(714)646-1169
Fax: (714)646-1169

International Health Resources
PO Box 329
North San Juan, CA 95960-0329
(530)292-1266
Fax: (530)292-1243
Website: http://www.futureof
healthcare.com

NEXUS - Consultants to Management
PO Box 1531
Novato, CA 94948
(415)897-4400
Fax: (415)898-2252
E-mail: jimnexus@aol.com

Aerospcace.Org
PO Box 28831
Oakland, CA 94604-8831

(510)530-9169
Fax: (510)530-3411
Website: http://www.aerospace.org

Intelequest Corp.
722 Gailen Ave.
Palo Alto, CA 94303
(415)968-3443
Fax: (415)493-6954
E-mail: frits@iqix.com

McLaughlin & Associates
66 San Marino Cir.
Rancho Mirage, CA 92270
(760)321-2932
Fax: (760)328-2474
E-mail: jackmcla@msn.com

**Carrera Consulting Group, a division
of Maximus**
2110 21st St., Ste. 400
Sacramento, CA 95818
(916)456-3300
Fax: (916)456-3306
E-mail: central@carreraconsulting.com
Website: http://www.carreraconsulting.com

**Bay Area Tax Consultants and Bayhill
Financial Consultants**
1150 Bayhill Dr., Ste. 1150
San Bruno, CA 94066-3004
(415)952-8786
Fax: (415)588-4524
E-mail: baytax@compuserve.com
Website: http://www.baytax.com/

AdCon Services, LLC
8871 Hillery Dr.
Dan Diego, CA 92126
(858)433-1411
E-mail: adam@adconservices.com
Website: http://www.adconservices.com
Adam Greengrass

California Business Incubation Network
101 W Broadway, No. 480
San Diego, CA 92101
(619)237-0559
Fax: (619)237-0521

G.R. Gordetsky Consultants Inc.
11414 Windy Summit Pl.
San Diego, CA 92127
(619)487-4939
Fax: (619)487-5587
E-mail: gordet@pacbell.net

Freeman, Sullivan & Co.
131 Steuart St., Ste. 500
San Francisco, CA 94105
(415)777-0707

Free: 800-777-0737
Fax: (415)777-2420
Website: http://www.fsc-research.com

Ideas Unlimited
2151 California St., Ste. 7
San Francisco, CA 94115
(415)931-0641
Fax: (415)931-0880

Russell Miller Inc.
300 Montgomery St., Ste. 900
San Francisco, CA 94104
(415)956-7474
Fax: (415)398-0620
E-mail: rmi@pacbell.net
Website: http://www.rmisf.com

PKF Consulting
425 California St., Ste. 1650
San Francisco, CA 94104
(415)421-5378
Fax: (415)956-7708
E-mail: callahan@pkfc.com
Website: http://www.pkfonline.com

Welling & Woodard Inc.
1067 Broadway
San Francisco, CA 94133
(415)776-4500
Fax: (415)776-5067

Highland Associates
16174 Highland Dr.
San Jose, CA 95127
(408)272-7008
Fax: (408)272-4040

ORDIS Inc.
6815 Trinidad Dr.
San Jose, CA 95120-2056
(408)268-3321
Free: 800-446-7347
Fax: (408)268-3582
E-mail: ordis@ordis.com
Website: http://www.ordis.com

Stanford Resources Inc.
20 Great Oaks Blvd., Ste. 200
San Jose, CA 95119
(408)360-8400
Fax: (408)360-8410
E-mail: sales@stanfordsources.com
Website: http://www.stanfordresources.com

Technology Properties Ltd. Inc.
PO Box 20250
San Jose, CA 95160
(408)243-9898
Fax: (408)296-6637
E-mail: sanjose@tplnet.com

Helfert Associates
1777 Borel Pl., Ste. 508
San Mateo, CA 94402-3514
(650)377-0540
Fax: (650)377-0472

Mykytyn Consulting Group Inc.
185 N Redwood Dr., Ste. 200
San Rafael, CA 94903
(415)491-1770
Fax: (415)491-1251
E-mail: info@mcgi.com
Website: http://www.mcgi.com

Omega Management Systems Inc.
3 Mount Darwin Ct.
San Rafael, CA 94903-1109
(415)499-1300
Fax: (415)492-9490
E-mail: omegamgt@ix.netcom.com

The Information Group Inc.
4675 Stevens Creek Blvd., Ste. 100
Santa Clara, CA 95051
(408)985-7877
Fax: (408)985-2945
E-mail: dvincent@tig-usa.com
Website: http://www.tig-usa.com

Cast Management Consultants
1620 26th St., Ste. 2040N
Santa Monica, CA 90404
(310)828-7511
Fax: (310)453-6831

Cuma Consulting Management
Box 724
Santa Rosa, CA 95402
(707)785-2477
Fax: (707)785-2478

The E-Myth Academy
131B Stony Cir., Ste. 2000
Santa Rosa, CA 95401
(707)569-5600
Free: 800-221-0266
Fax: (707)569-5700
E-mail: info@e-myth.com
Website: http://www.e-myth.com

Reilly, Connors & Ray
1743 Canyon Rd.
Spring Valley, CA 91977
(619)698-4808
Fax: (619)460-3892
E-mail: davidray@adnc.com

Management Consultants
Sunnyvale, CA 94087-4700
(408)773-0321

RJR Associates
1639 Lewiston Dr.
Sunnyvale, CA 94087
(408)737-7720
E-mail: bobroy@rjrassoc.com
Website: http://www.rjrassoc.com

Schwafel Associates
333 Cobalt Way, Ste. 21
Sunnyvale, CA 94085
(408)720-0649
Fax: (408)720-1796
E-mail: schwafel@ricochet.net
Website: http://www.patca.org

Staubs Business Services
23320 S Vermont Ave.
Torrance, CA 90502-2940
(310)830-9128
Fax: (310)830-9128
E-mail: Harry_L_Staubs@Lamg.com

Out of Your Mind . . . and Into the Marketplace
13381 White Sands Dr.
Tustin, CA 92780-4565
(714)544-0248
Free: 800-419-1513
Fax: (714)730-1414
E-mail: lpinson@aol.com
Website: http://www.business-plan.com

Independent Research Services
PO Box 2426
Van Nuys, CA 91404-2426
(818)993-3622

Ingman Company Inc.
7949 Woodley Ave., Ste. 120
Van Nuys, CA 91406-1232
(818)375-5027
Fax: (818)894-5001

Innovative Technology Associates
3639 E Harbor Blvd., Ste. 203E
Ventura, CA 93001
(805)650-9353

Grid Technology Associates
20404 Tufts Cir.
Walnut, CA 91789
(909)444-0922
Fax: (909)444-0922
E-mail: grid_technology@msn.com

Ridge Consultants Inc.
100 Pringle Ave., Ste. 580
Walnut Creek, CA 94596
(925)274-1990
Fax: (510)274-1956
E-mail: info@ridgecon.com
Website: http://www.ridgecon.com

Bell Springs Publishing
PO Box 1240
Willits, CA 95490
(707)459-6372
E-mail: bellsprings@sabernet
Website: http://www.bellsprings.com

Hutchinson Consulting and Appraisal
23245 Sylvan St., Ste. 103
Woodland Hills, CA 91367
(818)888-8175
Free: 800-977-7548
Fax: (818)888-8220
E-mail: r.f.hutchinson-cpa@worldnet.
att.net

Colorado

Sam Boyer & Associates
4255 S Buckley Rd., No. 136
Aurora, CO 80013
Free: 800-785-0485
Fax: (303)766-8740
E-mail: samboyer@samboyer.com
Website: http://www.samboyer.com/

Ameriwest Business Consultants Inc.
PO Box 26266
Colorado Springs, CO 80936
(719)380-7096
Fax: (719)380-7096
E-mail: email@abchelp.com
Website: http://www.abchelp.com

GVNW Consulting Inc.
2270 La Montana Way
Colorado Springs, CO 80936
(719)594-5800
Fax: (719)594-5803
Website: http://www.gvnw.com

M-Squared Inc.
755 San Gabriel Pl.
Colorado Springs, CO 80906
(719)576-2554
Fax: (719)576-2554

Thornton Financial FNIC
1024 Centre Ave., Bldg. E
Fort Collins, CO 80526-1849
(970)221-2089
Fax: (970)484-5206

TenEyck Associates
1760 Cherryville Rd.
Greenwood Village, CO 80121-1503
(303)758-6129
Fax: (303)761-8286

Associated Enterprises Ltd.
13050 W Ceder Dr., Unit 11
Lakewood, CO 80228

(303)988-6695
Fax: (303)988-6739
E-mail: ael1@classic.msn.com

The Vincent Company Inc.
200 Union Blvd., Ste. 210
Lakewood, CO 80228
(303)989-7271
Free: 800-274-0733
Fax: (303)989-7570
E-mail: vincent@vincentco.com
Website: http://www.vincentco.com

Johnson & West Management Consultants Inc.
7612 S Logan Dr.
Littleton, CO 80122
(303)730-2810
Fax: (303)730-3219

Western Capital Holdings Inc.
10050 E Applwood Dr.
Parker, CO 80138
(303)841-1022
Fax: (303)770-1945

Connecticut

Stratman Group Inc.
40 Tower Ln.
Avon, CT 06001-4222
(860)677-2898
Free: 800-551-0499
Fax: (860)677-8210

Cowherd Consulting Group Inc.
106 Stephen Mather Rd.
Darien, CT 06820
(203)655-2150
Fax: (203)655-6427

Greenwich Associates
8 Greenwich Office Park
Greenwich, CT 06831-5149
(203)629-1200
Fax: (203)629-1229
E-mail: lisa@greenwich.com
Website: http://www.greenwich.com

Follow-up News
185 Pine St., Ste. 818
Manchester, CT 06040
(860)647-7542
Free: 800-708-0696
Fax: (860)646-6544
E-mail: Followupnews@aol.com

Lovins & Associates Consulting
309 Edwards St.
New Haven, CT 06511
(203)787-3367

Fax: (203)624-7599
E-mail: Alovinsphd@aol.com
Website: http://www.lovinsgroup.com

JC Ventures Inc.
4 Arnold St.
Old Greenwich, CT 06870-1203
(203)698-1990
Free: 800-698-1997
Fax: (203)698-2638

Charles L. Hornung Associates
52 Ned's Mountain Rd.
Ridgefield, CT 06877
(203)431-0297

Manus
100 Prospect St., S Tower
Stamford, CT 06901
(203)326-3880
Free: 800-445-0942
Fax: (203)326-3890
E-mail: manus1@aol.com
Website: http://www.RightManus.com

RealBusinessPlans.com
156 Westport Rd.
Wilton, CT 06897
(914)837-2886
E-mail: ct@realbusinessplans.com
Website: http://www.RealBusinessPlans.com
Tony Tecce

Delaware

Focus Marketing
61-7 Habor Dr.
Claymont, DE 19703
(302)793-3064

Daedalus Ventures Ltd.
PO Box 1474
Hockessin, DE 19707
(302)239-6758
Fax: (302)239-9991
E-mail: daedalus@mail.del.net

The Formula Group
PO Box 866
Hockessin, DE 19707
(302)456-0952
Fax: (302)456-1354
E-mail: formula@netaxs.com

Selden Enterprises Inc.
2502 Silverside Rd., Ste. 1
Wilmington, DE 19810-3740
(302)529-7113
Fax: (302)529-7442
E-mail: selden2@bellatlantic.net
Website: http://www.seldenenterprises.com

District of Columbia

Bruce W. McGee and Associates
7826 Eastern Ave. NW, Ste. 30
Washington, DC 20012
(202)726-7272
Fax: (202)726-2946

McManis Associates Inc.
1900 K St. NW, Ste. 700
Washington, DC 20006
(202)466-7680
Fax: (202)872-1898
Website: http://www.mcmanis-mmi.com

Smith, Dawson & Andrews Inc.
1000 Connecticut Ave., Ste. 302
Washington, DC 20036
(202)835-0740
Fax: (202)775-8526
E-mail: webmaster@sda-inc.com
Website: http://www.sda-inc.com

Florida

BackBone, Inc.
20404 Hacienda Court
Boca Raton, FL 33498
(561)470-0965
Fax: 516-908-4038
E-mail: BPlans@backboneinc.com
Website: http://www.backboneinc.com
Charles Epstein, President

Whalen & Associates Inc.
4255 Northwest 26 Ct.
Boca Raton, FL 33434
(561)241-5950
Fax: (561)241-7414
E-mail: drwhalen@ix.netcom.com

E.N. Rysso & Associates
180 Bermuda Petrel Ct.
Daytona Beach, FL 32119
(386)760-3028
E-mail: erysso@aol.com

Virtual Technocrats LLC
560 Lavers Circle, #146
Delray Beach, FL 33444
(561)265-3509
E-mail: josh@virtualtechnocrats.com;
info@virtualtechnocrats.com
Website: http://www.virtualtechno
crats.com
Josh Eikov, Managing Director

Eric Sands Consulting Services
6193 Rock Island Rd., Ste. 412
Fort Lauderdale, FL 33319
(954)721-4767

Fax: (954)720-2815
E-mail: easands@aol.com
Website: http://www.ericsandsconsultig.com

Professional Planning Associates, Inc.
1975 E. Sunrise Blvd. Suite 607
Fort Lauderdale, FL 33304
(954)764-5204
Fax: 954-463-4172
E-mail: Mgoldstein@proplana.com
Website: http://proplana.com
Michael Goldstein, President

Host Media Corp.
3948 S 3rd St., Ste. 191
Jacksonville Beach, FL 32250
(904)285-3239
Fax: (904)285-5618
E-mail: msconsulting@compuserve.com
Website: http://www.media
servicesgroup.com

William V. Hall
1925 Brickell, Ste. D-701
Miami, FL 33129
(305)856-9622
Fax: (305)856-4113
E-mail: williamvhall@compuserve.com

F.A. McGee Inc.
800 Claughton Island Dr., Ste. 401
Miami, FL 33131
(305)377-9123

Taxplan Inc.
Mirasol International Ctr.
2699 Collins Ave.
Miami Beach, FL 33140
(305)538-3303

T.C. Brown & Associates
8415 Excalibur Cir., Apt. B1
Naples, FL 34108
(941)594-1949
Fax: (941)594-0611
E-mail: tcater@naples.net.com

RLA International Consulting
713 Lagoon Dr.
North Palm Beach, FL 33408
(407)626-4258
Fax: (407)626-5772

Comprehensive Franchising Inc.
2465 Ridgecrest Ave.
Orange Park, FL 32065
(904)272-6567
Free: 800-321-6567
Fax: (904)272-6750
E-mail: theimp@cris.com
Website: http://www.franchise411.com

Hunter G. Jackson Jr. - Consulting Environmental Physicist
PO Box 618272
Orlando, FL 32861-8272
(407)295-4188
E-mail: hunterjackson@juno.com

F. Newton Parks
210 El Brillo Way
Palm Beach, FL 33480
(561)833-1727
Fax: (561)833-4541

Avery Business Development Services
2506 St. Michel Ct.
Ponte Vedra Beach, FL 32082
(904)285-6033
Fax: (904)285-6033

Strategic Business Planning Co.
PO Box 821006
South Florida, FL 33082-1006
(954)704-9100
Fax: (954)438-7333
E-mail: info@bizplan.com
Website: http://www.bizplan.com

Dufresne Consulting Group Inc.
10014 N Dale Mabry, Ste. 101
Tampa, FL 33618-4426
(813)264-4775
Fax: (813)264-9300
Website: http://www.dcgconsult.com

Agrippa Enterprises Inc.
PO Box 175
Venice, FL 34284-0175
(941)355-7876
E-mail: webservices@agrippa.com
Website: http://www.agrippa.com

Center for Simplified Strategic Planning Inc.
PO Box 3324
Vero Beach, FL 32964-3324
(561)231-3636
Fax: (561)231-1099
Website: http://www.cssp.com

Georgia

Marketing Spectrum Inc.
115 Perimeter Pl., Ste. 440
Atlanta, GA 30346
(770)395-7244
Fax: (770)393-4071

Business Ventures Corp.
1650 Oakbrook Dr., Ste. 405
Norcross, GA 30093
(770)729-8000
Fax: (770)729-8028

Informed Decisions Inc.
100 Falling Cheek
Sautee Nacoochee, GA 30571
(706)878-1905
Fax: (706)878-1802
E-mail: skylake@compuserve.com

Tom C. Davis & Associates, P.C.
3189 Perimeter Rd.
Valdosta, GA 31602
(912)247-9801
Fax: (912)244-7704
E-mail: mail@tcdcpa.com
Website: http://www.tcdcpa.com/

Illinois

TWD and Associates
431 S Patton
Arlington Heights, IL 60005
(847)398-6410
Fax: (847)255-5095
E-mail: tdoo@aol.com

Management Planning Associates Inc.
2275 Half Day Rd., Ste. 350
Bannockburn, IL 60015-1277
(847)945-2421
Fax: (847)945-2425

Phil Faris Associates
86 Old Mill Ct.
Barrington, IL 60010
(847)382-4888
Fax: (847)382-4890
E-mail: pfaris@meginsnet.net

Seven Continents Technology
787 Stonebridge
Buffalo Grove, IL 60089
(708)577-9653
Fax: (708)870-1220

Grubb & Blue Inc.
2404 Windsor Pl.
Champaign, IL 61820
(217)366-0052
Fax: (217)356-0117

ACE Accounting Service Inc.
3128 N Bernard St.
Chicago, IL 60618
(773)463-7854
Fax: (773)463-7854

AON Consulting Worldwide
200 E Randolph St., 10th Fl.
Chicago, IL 60601
(312)381-4800
Free: 800-438-6487
Fax: (312)381-0240
Website: http://www.aon.com

FMS Consultants
5801 N Sheridan Rd., Ste. 3D
Chicago, IL 60660
(773)561-7362
Fax: (773)561-6274

Grant Thornton
800 1 Prudential Plz.
130 E Randolph St.
Chicago, IL 60601
(312)856-0001
Fax: (312)861-1340
E-mail: gtinfo@gt.com
Website: http://www.grantthornton.com

Kingsbury International Ltd.
5341 N Glenwood Ave.
Chicago, IL 60640
(773)271-3030
Fax: (773)728-7080
E-mail: jetlag@mcs.com
Website: http://www.kingbiz.com

MacDougall & Blake Inc.
1414 N Wells St., Ste. 311
Chicago, IL 60610-1306
(312)587-3330
Fax: (312)587-3699
E-mail: jblake@compuserve.com

James C. Osburn Ltd.
6445 N. Western Ave., Ste. 304
Chicago, IL 60645
(773)262-4428
Fax: (773)262-6755
E-mail: osburnltd@aol.com

Tarifero & Tazewell Inc.
211 S Clark
Chicago, IL 60690
(312)665-9714
Fax: (312)665-9716

Human Energy Design Systems
620 Roosevelt Dr.
Edwardsville, IL 62025
(618)692-0258
Fax: (618)692-0819

China Business Consultants Group
931 Dakota Cir.
Naperville, IL 60563
(630)778-7992
Fax: (630)778-7915
E-mail: cbcq@aol.com

Center for Workforce Effectiveness
500 Skokie Blvd., Ste. 222
Northbrook, IL 60062
(847)559-8777
Fax: (847)559-8778

E-mail: office@cwelink.com
Website: http://www.cwelink.com

Smith Associates
1320 White Mountain Dr.
Northbrook, IL 60062
(847)480-7200
Fax: (847)480-9828

Francorp Inc.
20200 Governors Dr.
Olympia Fields, IL 60461
(708)481-2900
Free: 800-372-6244
Fax: (708)481-5885
E-mail: francorp@aol.com
Website: http://www.francorpinc.com

Camber Business Strategy Consultants
1010 S Plum Tree Ct
Palatine, IL 60078-0986
(847)202-0101
Fax: (847)705-7510
E-mail: camber@ameritech.net

Partec Enterprise Group
5202 Keith Dr.
Richton Park, IL 60471
(708)503-4047
Fax: (708)503-9468

Rockford Consulting Group Ltd.
Century Plz., Ste. 206
7210 E State St.
Rockford, IL 61108
(815)229-2900
Free: 800-667-7495
Fax: (815)229-2612
E-mail: rligus@RockfordConsulting.com
Website: http://www.Rockford
Consulting.com

RSM McGladrey Inc.
1699 E Woodfield Rd., Ste. 300
Schaumburg, IL 60173-4969
(847)413-6900
Fax: (847)517-7067
Website: http://www.rsmmcgladrey.com

A.D. Star Consulting
320 Euclid
Winnetka, IL 60093
(847)446-7827
Fax: (847)446-7827
E-mail: startwo@worldnet.att.net

Indiana

Modular Consultants Inc.
3109 Crabtree Ln.
Elkhart, IN 46514

(219)264-5761
Fax: (219)264-5761
E-mail: sasabo5313@aol.com

Midwest Marketing Research
PO Box 1077
Goshen, IN 46527
(219)533-0548
Fax: (219)533-0540
E-mail: 103365.654@compuserve

Ketchum Consulting Group
8021 Knue Rd., Ste. 112
Indianapolis, IN 46250
(317)845-5411
Fax: (317)842-9941

MDI Management Consulting
1519 Park Dr.
Munster, IN 46321
(219)838-7909
Fax: (219)838-7909

Iowa

McCord Consulting Group Inc.
4533 Pine View Dr. NE
PO Box 11024
Cedar Rapids, IA 52410
(319)378-0077
Fax: (319)378-1577
E-mail: smmccord@hom.com
Website: http://www.mccordgroup.com

Management Solutions L.C.
3815 Lincoln Pl. Dr.
Des Moines, IA 50312
(515)277-6408
Fax: (515)277-3506
E-mail: wasunimers@uswest.net

Grandview Marketing
15 Red Bridge Dr.
Sioux City, IA 51104
(712)239-3122
Fax: (712)258-7578
E-mail: eandrews@pionet.net

Kansas

Assessments in Action
513A N Mur-Len
Olathe, KS 66062
(913)764-6270
Free: (888)548-1504
Fax: (913)764-6495
E-mail: lowdene@qni.com
Website: http://www.assessments-in-action.com

Maine

Edgemont Enterprises
PO Box 8354
Portland, ME 04104
(207)871-8964
Fax: (207)871-8964

Pan Atlantic Consultants
5 Milk St.
Portland, ME 04101
(207)871-8622
Fax: (207)772-4842
E-mail: pmurphy@maine.rr.com
Website: http://www.panatlantic.net

Maryland

Clemons & Associates Inc.
5024-R Campbell Blvd.
Baltimore, MD 21236
(410)931-8100
Fax: (410)931-8111
E-mail: info@clemonsmgmt.com
Website: http://www.clemonsmgmt.com

Imperial Group Ltd.
305 Washington Ave., Ste. 204
Baltimore, MD 21204-6009
(410)337-8500
Fax: (410)337-7641

Leadership Institute
3831 Yolando Rd.
Baltimore, MD 21218
(410)366-9111
Fax: (410)243-8478
E-mail: behconsult@aol.com

Burdeshaw Associates Ltd.
4701 Sangamore Rd.
Bethesda, MD 20816-2508
(301)229-5800
Fax: (301)229-5045
E-mail: jstacy@burdeshaw.com
Website: http://www.burdeshaw.com

Michael E. Cohen
5225 Pooks Hill Rd., Ste. 1119 S
Bethesda, MD 20814
(301)530-5738
Fax: (301)530-2988
E-mail: mecohen@crosslink.net

World Development Group Inc.
5272 River Rd., Ste. 650
Bethesda, MD 20816-1405
(301)652-1818
Fax: (301)652-1250
E-mail: wdg@has.com
Website: http://www.worlddg.com

Swartz Consulting
PO Box 4301
Crofton, MD 21114-4301
(301)262-6728

Software Solutions International Inc.
9633 Duffer Way
Gaithersburg, MD 20886
(301)330-4136
Fax: (301)330-4136

Strategies Inc.
8 Park Center Ct., Ste. 200
Owings Mills, MD 21117
(410)363-6669
Fax: (410)363-1231
E-mail: strategies@strat1.com
Website: http://www.strat1.com

Hammer Marketing Resources
179 Inverness Rd.
Severna Park, MD 21146
(410)544-9191
Fax: (305)675-3277
E-mail: info@gohammer.com
Website: http://www.gohammer.com

Andrew Sussman & Associates
13731 Kretsinger
Smithsburg, MD 21783
(301)824-2943
Fax: (301)824-2943

Massachusetts

Geibel Marketing and Public Relations
PO Box 611
Belmont, MA 02478-0005
(617)484-8285
Fax: (617)489-3567
E-mail: jgeibel@geibelpr.com
Website: http://www.geibelpr.com

Bain & Co.
2 Copley Pl.
Boston, MA 02116
(617)572-2000
Fax: (617)572-2427
E-mail: corporate.inquiries@bain.com
Website: http://www.bain.com

Mehr & Co.
62 Kinnaird St.
Cambridge, MA 02139
(617)876-3311
Fax: (617)876-3023
E-mail: mehrco@aol.com

Monitor Company Inc.
2 Canal Park
Cambridge, MA 02141

(617)252-2000
Fax: (617)252-2100
Website: http://www.monitor.com

Information & Research Associates
PO Box 3121
Framingham, MA 01701
(508)788-0784

Walden Consultants Ltd.
252 Pond St.
Hopkinton, MA 01748
(508)435-4882
Fax: (508)435-3971
Website: http://www.waldencon
sultants.com

Jeffrey D. Marshall
102 Mitchell Rd.
Ipswich, MA 01938-1219
(508)356-1113
Fax: (508)356-2989

Consulting Resources Corp.
6 Northbrook Park
Lexington, MA 02420
(781)863-1222
Fax: (781)863-1441
E-mail: res@consultingresources.net
Website: http://www.consulting
resources.net

Planning Technologies Group L.L.C.
92 Hayden Ave.
Lexington, MA 02421
(781)778-4678
Fax: (781)861-1099
E-mail: ptg@plantech.com
Website: http://www.plantech.com

Kalba International Inc.
23 Sandy Pond Rd.
Lincoln, MA 01773
(781)259-9589
Fax: (781)259-1460
E-mail: info@kalbainternational.com
Website: http://www.kalbainter
national.com

VMB Associates Inc.
115 Ashland St.
Melrose, MA 02176
(781)665-0623
Fax: (425)732-7142
E-mail: vmbinc@aol.com

The Company Doctor
14 Pudding Stone Ln.
Mendon, MA 01756
(508)478-1747
Fax: (508)478-0520

Data and Strategies Group Inc.
190 N Main St.
Natick, MA 01760
(508)653-9990
Fax: (508)653-7799
E-mail: dsginc@dsggroup.com
Website: http://www.dsggroup.com

The Enterprise Group
73 Parker Rd.
Needham, MA 02494
(617)444-6631
Fax: (617)433-9991
E-mail: lsacco@world.std.com
Website: http://www.enterprise-group.com

PSMJ Resources Inc.
10 Midland Ave.
Newton, MA 02458
(617)965-0055
Free: 800-537-7765
Fax: (617)965-5152
E-mail: psmj@tiac.net
Website: http://www.psmj.com

Scheur Management Group Inc.
255 Washington St., Ste. 100
Newton, MA 02458-1611
(617)969-7500
Fax: (617)969-7508
E-mail: smgnow@scheur.com
Website: http://www.scheur.com

I.E.E.E., Boston Section
240 Bear Hill Rd., 202B
Waltham, MA 02451-1017
(781)890-5294
Fax: (781)890-5290

Business Planning and Consulting Services
20 Beechwood Ter.
Wellesley, MA 02482
(617)237-9151
Fax: (617)237-9151

Michigan

Walter Frederick Consulting
1719 South Blvd.
Ann Arbor, MI 48104
(313)662-4336
Fax: (313)769-7505

Fox Enterprises
6220 W Freeland Rd.
Freeland, MI 48623
(517)695-9170
Fax: (517)695-9174
E-mail: foxjw@concentric.net
Website: http://www.cris.com/~foxjw

G.G.W. and Associates
1213 Hampton
Jackson, MI 49203
(517)782-2255
Fax: (517)782-2255

Altamar Group Ltd.
6810 S Cedar, Ste. 2-B
Lansing, MI 48911
(517)694-0910
Free: 800-443-2627
Fax: (517)694-1377

Sheffieck Consultants Inc.
23610 Greening Dr.
Novi, MI 48375-3130
(248)347-3545
Fax: (248)347-3530
E-mail: cfsheff@concentric.net

Rehmann, Robson PC
5800 Gratiot
Saginaw, MI 48605
(517)799-9580
Fax: (517)799-0227
Website: http://www.rrpc.com

Francis & Co.
17200 W 10 Mile Rd., Ste. 207
Southfield, MI 48075
(248)559-7600
Fax: (248)559-5249

Private Ventures Inc.
16000 W 9 Mile Rd., Ste. 504
Southfield, MI 48075
(248)569-1977
Free: 800-448-7614
Fax: (248)569-1838
E-mail: pventuresi@aol.com

JGK Associates
14464 Kerner Dr.
Sterling Heights, MI 48313
(810)247-9055
Fax: (248)822-4977
E-mail: kozlowski@home.com

Minnesota

Health Fitness Corp.
3500 W 80th St., Ste. 130
Bloomington, MN 55431
(612)831-6830
Fax: (612)831-7264

Consatech Inc.
PO Box 1047
Burnsville, MN 55337
(612)953-1088
Fax: (612)435-2966

Robert F. Knotek
14960 Ironwood Ct.
Eden Prairie, MN 55346
(612)949-2875

DRI Consulting
7715 Stonewood Ct.
Edina, MN 55439
(612)941-9656
Fax: (612)941-2693
E-mail: dric@dric.com
Website: http://www.dric.com

Markin Consulting
12072 87th Pl. N
Maple Grove, MN 55369
(612)493-3568
Fax: (612)493-5744
E-mail: markin@markinconsulting.com
Website: http://www.markin
consulting.com

**Minnesota Cooperation Office for
Small Business & Job Creation Inc.**
5001 W 80th St., Ste. 825
Minneapolis, MN 55437
(612)830-1230
Fax: (612)830-1232
E-mail: mncoop@msn.com
Website: http://www.mnco.org

Enterprise Consulting Inc.
PO Box 1111
Minnetonka, MN 55345
(612)949-5909
Fax: (612)906-3965

Amdahl International
724 1st Ave. SW
Rochester, MN 55902
(507)252-0402
Fax: (507)252-0402
E-mail: amdahl@best-service.com
Website: http://www.wp.com/amdahl_int

Power Systems Research
1365 Corporate Center Curve, 2nd Fl.
St. Paul, MN 55121
(612)905-8400
Free: (888)625-8612
Fax: (612)454-0760
E-mail: Barb@Powersys.com
Website: http://www.powersys.com

Missouri

**Business Planning and Development
Corp.**
4030 Charlotte St.
Kansas City, MO 64110
(816)753-0495

E-mail: humph@bpdev.demon.co.uk
Website: http://www.bpdev.demon.co.uk

CFO Service
10336 Donoho
St. Louis, MO 63131
(314)750-2940
E-mail: jskae@cfoservice.com
Website: http://www.cfoservice.com

Nebraska

**International Management Consulting
Group Inc.**
1309 Harlan Dr., Ste. 205
Bellevue, NE 68005
(402)291-4545
Free: 800-665-IMCG
Fax: (402)291-4343
E-mail: imcg@neonramp.com
Website: http://www.mgtcon
sulting.com

**Heartland Management Consulting
Group**
1904 Barrington Pky.
Papillion, NE 68046
(402)339-2387
Fax: (402)339-1319

Nevada

The DuBois Group
865 Tahoe Blvd., Ste. 108
Incline Village, NV 89451
(775)832-0550
Free: 800-375-2935
Fax: (775)832-0556
E-mail: DuBoisGrp@aol.com

New Hampshire

Wolff Consultants
10 Buck Rd.
Hanover, NH 03755
(603)643-6015

BPT Consulting Associates Ltd.
12 Parmenter Rd., Ste. B-6
Londonderry, NH 03053
(603)437-8484
Free: (888)278-0030
Fax: (603)434-5388
E-mail: bptcons@tiac.net
Website: http://www.bptconsulting.com

New Jersey

Bedminster Group Inc.
1170 Rte. 22 E
Bridgewater, NJ 08807

(908)500-4155
Fax: (908)766-0780
E-mail: info@bedminstergroup.com
Website: http://www.bedminster
group.com
Fax: (202)806-1777
Terry Strong, Acting Regional Dir.

Delta Planning Inc.
PO Box 425
Denville, NJ 07834
(913)625-1742
Free: 800-672-0762
Fax: (973)625-3531
E-mail: DeltaP@worldnet.att.net
Website: http://deltaplanning.com

Kumar Associates Inc.
1004 Cumbermeade Rd.
Fort Lee, NJ 07024
(201)224-9480
Fax: (201)585-2343
E-mail: mail@kumarassociates.com
Website: http://kumarassociates.com

John Hall & Company Inc.
PO Box 187
Glen Ridge, NJ 07028
(973)680-4449
Fax: (973)680-4581
E-mail: jhcompany@aol.com

Market Focus
PO Box 402
Maplewood, NJ 07040
(973)378-2470
Fax: (973)378-2470
E-mail: mcss66@marketfocus.com

Vanguard Communications Corp.
100 American Rd.
Morris Plains, NJ 07950
(973)605-8000
Fax: (973)605-8329
Website: http://www.vanguard.net/

ConMar International Ltd.
1901 US Hwy. 130
North Brunswick, NJ 08902
(732)940-8347
Fax: (732)274-1199

KLW New Products
156 Cedar Dr.
Old Tappan, NJ 07675
(201)358-1300
Fax: (201)664-2594
E-mail: lrlarsen@usa.net
Website: http://www.klwnew
products.com

PA Consulting Group
315A Enterprise Dr.
Plainsboro, NJ 08536
(609)936-8300
Fax: (609)936-8811
E-mail: info@paconsulting.com
Website: http://www.pa-consulting.com

Aurora Marketing Management Inc.
66 Witherspoon St., Ste. 600
Princeton, NJ 08542
(908)904-1125
Fax: (908)359-1108
E-mail: aurora2@voicenet.com
Website: http://www.auroramarketing.net

Smart Business Supersite
88 Orchard Rd., CN-5219
Princeton, NJ 08543
(908)321-1924
Fax: (908)321-5156
E-mail: irv@smartbiz.com
Website: http://www.smartbiz.com

Tracelin Associates
1171 Main St., Ste. 6K
Rahway, NJ 07065
(732)381-3288

Schkeeper Inc.
130-6 Bodman Pl.
Red Bank, NJ 07701
(732)219-1965
Fax: (732)530-3703

Henry Branch Associates
2502 Harmon Cove Twr.
Secaucus, NJ 07094
(201)866-2008
Fax: (201)601-0101
E-mail: hbranch161@home.com

Robert Gibbons & Company Inc.
46 Knoll Rd.
Tenafly, NJ 07670-1050
(201)871-3933
Fax: (201)871-2173
E-mail: crisisbob@aol.com

PMC Management Consultants Inc.
6 Thistle Ln.
Three Bridges, NJ 08887-0332
(908)788-1014
Free: 800-PMC-0250
Fax: (908)806-7287
E-mail: int@pmc-management.com
Website: http://www.pmc-management.com

R.W. Bankart & Associates
20 Valley Ave., Ste. D-2
Westwood, NJ 07675-3607
(201)664-7672

New Mexico

Vondle & Associates Inc.
4926 Calle de Tierra, NE
Albuquerque, NM 87111
(505)292-8961
Fax: (505)296-2790
E-mail: vondle@aol.com

InfoNewMexico
2207 Black Hills Rd., NE
Rio Rancho, NM 87124
(505)891-2462
Fax: (505)896-8971

New York

Powers Research and Training Institute
PO Box 78
Bayville, NY 11709
(516)628-2250
Fax: (516)628-2252
E-mail: powercocch@compuserve.com
Website: http://www.nancypowers.com

Consortium House
296 Wittenberg Rd.
Bearsville, NY 12409
(845)679-8867
Fax: (845)679-9248
E-mail: eugenegs@aol.com
Website: http://www.chpub.com

Progressive Finance Corp.
3549 Tiemann Ave.
Bronx, NY 10469
(718)405-9029
Free: 800-225-8381
Fax: (718)405-1170

Wave Hill Associates Inc.
2621 Palisade Ave., Ste. 15-C
Bronx, NY 10463
(718)549-7368
Fax: (718)601-9670
E-mail: pepper@compuserve.com

Management Insight
96 Arlington Rd.
Buffalo, NY 14221
(716)631-3319
Fax: (716)631-0203
E-mail: michalski@foodservice insight.com
Website: http://www.foodservice insight.com

Samani International Enterprises, Marions Panyaught Consultancy
2028 Parsons
Flushing, NY 11357-3436
(917)287-8087
Fax: 800-873-8939
E-mail: vjp2@biostrategist.com
Website: http://www.biostrategist.com

Marketing Resources Group
71-58 Austin St.
Forest Hills, NY 11375
(718)261-8882

Mangabay Business Plans & Development Subsidiary of Innis Asset Allocation
125-10 Queens Blvd., Ste. 2202
Kew Gardens, NY 11415
(905)527-1947
Fax: 509-472-1935
E-mail: mangabay@mangabay.com
Website: http://www.mangabay.com
Lee Toh, Managing Partner

ComputerEase Co.
1301 Monmouth Ave.
Lakewood, NY 08701
(212)406-9464
Fax: (914)277-5317
E-mail: crawfordc@juno.com

Boice Dunham Group
30 W 13th St.
New York, NY 10011
(212)924-2200
Fax: (212)924-1108

Elizabeth Capen
27 E 95th St.
New York, NY 10128
(212)427-7654
Fax: (212)876-3190

Haver Analytics
60 E 42nd St., Ste. 2424
New York, NY 10017
(212)986-9300
Fax: (212)986-5857
E-mail: data@haver.com
Website: http://www.haver.com

The Jordan, Edmiston Group Inc.
150 E 52nd Ave., 18th Fl.
New York, NY 10022
(212)754-0710
Fax: (212)754-0337

KPMG International
345 Park Ave.
New York, NY 10154-0102
(212)758-9700

Fax: (212)758-9819
Website: http://www.kpmg.com

Mahoney Cohen Consulting Corp.
111 W 40th St., 12th Fl.
New York, NY 10018
(212)490-8000
Fax: (212)790-5913

Management Practice Inc.
342 Madison Ave.
New York, NY 10173-1230
(212)867-7948
Fax: (212)972-5188
Website: http://www.mpiweb.com

Moseley Associates Inc.
342 Madison Ave., Ste. 1414
New York, NY 10016
(212)213-6673
Fax: (212)687-1520

Practice Development Counsel
60 Sutton Pl. S
New York, NY 10022
(212)593-1549
Fax: (212)980-7940
E-mail: pwhaserot@pdcounsel.com
Website: http://www.pdcounsel.com

Unique Value International Inc.
575 Madison Ave., 10th Fl.
New York, NY 10022-1304
(212)605-0590
Fax: (212)605-0589

The Van Tulleken Co.
126 E 56th St.
New York, NY 10022
(212)355-1390
Fax: (212)755-3061
E-mail: newyork@vantulleken.com

Vencon Management Inc.
301 W 53rd St.
New York, NY 10019
(212)581-8787
Fax: (212)397-4126
Website: http://www.venconinc.com

Werner International Inc.
55 E 52nd, 29th Fl.
New York, NY 10055
(212)909-1260
Fax: (212)909-1273
E-mail: richard.downing@rgh.com
Website: http://www.wernertex.com

Zimmerman Business Consulting Inc.
44 E 92nd St., Ste. 5-B
New York, NY 10128

(212)860-3107
Fax: (212)860-7730
E-mail: ljzzbci@aol.com
Website: http://www.zbcinc.com

Overton Financial
7 Allen Rd.
Peekskill, NY 10566
(914)737-4649
Fax: (914)737-4696

Stromberg Consulting
2500 Westchester Ave.
Purchase, NY 10577
(914)251-1515
Fax: (914)251-1562
E-mail: strategy@stromberg_consul
ting.com
Website: http://www.stromberg_
consulting.com

Innovation Management Consulting Inc.
209 Dewitt Rd.
Syracuse, NY 13214-2006
(315)425-5144
Fax: (315)445-8989
E-mail: missonneb@axess.net

M. Clifford Agress
891 Fulton St.
Valley Stream, NY 11580
(516)825-8955
Fax: (516)825-8955

Destiny Kinal Marketing Consultancy
105 Chemung St.
Waverly, NY 14892
(607)565-8317
Fax: (607)565-4083

Valutis Consulting Inc.
5350 Main St., Ste. 7
Williamsville, NY 14221-5338
(716)634-2553
Fax: (716)634-2554
E-mail: valutis@localnet.com
Website: http://www.valutisconsulting.com

North Carolina

Best Practices L.L.C.
6320 Quadrangle Dr., Ste. 200
Chapel Hill, NC 27514
(919)403-0251
Fax: (919)403-0144
E-mail: best@best:in/class
Website: http://www.best-in-class.com

Norelli & Co.
Bank of America Corporate Ctr.
100 N Tyron St., Ste. 5160

Charlotte, NC 28202-4000
(704)376-5484
Fax: (704)376-5485
E-mail: consult@norelli.com
Website: http://www.norelli.com

North Dakota

Center for Innovation
4300 Dartmouth Dr.
PO Box 8372
Grand Forks, ND 58202
(701)777-3132
Fax: (701)777-2339
E-mail: bruce@innovators.net
Website: http://www.innovators.net

Ohio

Transportation Technology Services
208 Harmon Rd.
Aurora, OH 44202
(330)562-3596

Empro Systems Inc.
4777 Red Bank Expy., Ste. 1
Cincinnati, OH 45227-1542
(513)271-2042
Fax: (513)271-2042

Alliance Management International Ltd.
1440 Windrow Ln.
Cleveland, OH 44147-3200
(440)838-1922
Fax: (440)838-0979
E-mail: bgruss@amiltd.com
Website: http://www.amiltd.com

Bozell Kamstra Public Relations
1301 E 9th St., Ste. 3400
Cleveland, OH 44114
(216)623-1511
Fax: (216)623-1501
E-mail: jfeniger@cleveland.bozellk
amstra.com
Website: http://www.bozellk
amstra.com

Cory Dillon Associates
111 Schreyer Pl. E
Columbus, OH 43214
(614)262-8211
Fax: (614)262-3806

Holcomb Gallagher Adams
300 Marconi, Ste. 303
Columbus, OH 43215
(614)221-3343
Fax: (614)221-3367
E-mail: riadams@acme.freenet.oh.us

Young & Associates
PO Box 711
Kent, OH 44240
(330)678-0524
Free: 800-525-9775
Fax: (330)678-6219
E-mail: online@younginc.com
Website: http://www.younginc.com

Robert A. Westman & Associates
8981 Inversary Dr. SE
Warren, OH 44484-2551
(330)856-4149
Fax: (330)856-2564

Oklahoma

Innovative Partners L.L.C.
4900 Richmond Sq., Ste. 100
Oklahoma City, OK 73118
(405)840-0033
Fax: (405)843-8359
E-mail: ipartners@juno.com

Oregon

INTERCON - The International Converting Institute
5200 Badger Rd.
Crooked River Ranch, OR 97760
(541)548-1447
Fax: (541)548-1618
E-mail: johnbowler@
crookedriverranch.com

Talbott ARM
HC 60, Box 5620
Lakeview, OR 97630
(541)635-8587
Fax: (503)947-3482

Management Technology Associates Ltd.
2768 SW Sherwood Dr, Ste. 105
Portland, OR 97201-2251
(503)224-5220
Fax: (503)224-5334
E-mail: lcuster@mta-ltd.com
Website: http://www.mgmt-tech.com

Pennsylvania

Healthscope Inc.
400 Lancaster Ave.
Devon, PA 19333
(610)687-6199
Fax: (610)687-6376
E-mail: health@voicenet.com
Website: http://www.healthscope.net/

Elayne Howard & Associates Inc.
3501 Masons Mill Rd., Ste. 501

Huntingdon Valley, PA 19006-3509
(215)657-9550

GRA Inc.
115 West Ave., Ste. 201
Jenkintown, PA 19046
(215)884-7500
Fax: (215)884-1385
E-mail: gramail@gra-inc.com
Website: http://www.gra-inc.com

Mifflin County Industrial Development Corp.
Mifflin County Industrial Plz.
6395 SR 103 N
Bldg. 50
Lewistown, PA 17044
(717)242-0393
Fax: (717)242-1842
E-mail: mcide@acsworld.net

Autech Products
1289 Revere Rd.
Morrisville, PA 19067
(215)493-3759
Fax: (215)493-9791
E-mail: autech4@yahoo.com

Advantage Associates
434 Avon Dr.
Pittsburgh, PA 15228
(412)343-1558
Fax: (412)362-1684
E-mail: ecocba1@aol.com

Regis J. Sheehan & Associates
Pittsburgh, PA 15220
(412)279-1207

James W. Davidson Company Inc.
23 Forest View Rd.
Wallingford, PA 19086
(610)566-1462

Puerto Rico

Diego Chevere & Co.
Metro Parque 7, Ste. 204
Metro Office
Caparra Heights, PR 00920
(787)774-9595
Fax: (787)774-9566
E-mail: dcco@coqui.net

Manuel L. Porrata and Associates
898 Munoz Rivera Ave., Ste. 201
San Juan, PR 00927
(787)765-2140
Fax: (787)754-3285
E-mail: m_porrata@manuelporrata.com
Website: http://manualporrata.com

South Carolina

Aquafood Business Associates
PO Box 13267
Charleston, SC 29422
(843)795-9506
Fax: (843)795-9477
E-mail: rraba@aol.com

Profit Associates Inc.
PO Box 38026
Charleston, SC 29414
(803)763-5718
Fax: (803)763-5719
E-mail: bobrog@awod.com
Website: http://www.awod.com/gallery/
business/proasc

Strategic Innovations International
12 Executive Ct.
Lake Wylie, SC 29710
(803)831-1225
Fax: (803)831-1177
E-mail: stratinnov@aol.com
Website: http://www.
strategicinnovations.com

Minus Stage
Box 4436
Rock Hill, SC 29731
(803)328-0705
Fax: (803)329-9948

Tennessee

Daniel Petchers & Associates
8820 Fernwood CV
Germantown, TN 38138
(901)755-9896

Business Choices
1114 Forest Harbor, Ste. 300
Hendersonville, TN 37075-9646
(615)822-8692
Free: 800-737-8382
Fax: (615)822-8692
E-mail: bz-ch@juno.com

RCFA Healthcare Management Services L.L.C.
9648 Kingston Pke., Ste. 8
Knoxville, TN 37922
(865)531-0176
Free: 800-635-4040
Fax: (865)531-0722
E-mail: info@rcfa.com
Website: http://www.rcfa.com

Growth Consultants of America
3917 Trimble Rd.
Nashville, TN 37215

(615)383-0550
Fax: (615)269-8940
E-mail: 70244.451@compuserve.com

Texas

**Integrated Cost Management
Systems Inc.**
2261 Brookhollow Plz. Dr., Ste. 104
Arlington, TX 76006
(817)633-2873
Fax: (817)633-3781
E-mail: abm@icms.net
Website: http://www.icms.net

Lori Williams
1000 Leslie Ct.
Arlington, TX 76012
(817)459-3934
Fax: (817)459-3934

Business Resource Software Inc.
2013 Wells Branch Pky., Ste. 305
Austin, TX 78728
Free: 800-423-1228
Fax: (512)251-4401
E-mail: info@brs-inc.com
Website: http://www.brs-inc.com

Erisa Adminstrative Services Inc.
12325 Hymeadow Dr., Bldg. 4
Austin, TX 78750-1847
(512)250-9020
Fax: (512)250-9487
Website: http://www.cserisa.com

R. Miller Hicks & Co.
1011 W 11th St.
Austin, TX 78703
(512)477-7000
Fax: (512)477-9697
E-mail: millerhicks@rmhicks.com
Website: http://www.rmhicks.com

Pragmatic Tactics Inc.
3303 Westchester Ave.
College Station, TX 77845
(409)696-5294
Free: 800-570-5294
Fax: (409)696-4994
E-mail: ptactics@aol.com
Website: http://www.ptatics.com

Perot Systems
12404 Park Central Dr.
Dallas, TX 75251
(972)340-5000
Free: 800-688-4333
Fax: (972)455-4100
E-mail: corp.comm@ps.net
Website: http://www.perotsystems.com

ReGENERATION Partners
3838 Oak Lawn Ave.
Dallas, TX 75219
(214)559-3999
Free: 800-406-1112
E-mail: info@regeneration-partner.com
Website: http://www.regeneration-
partners.com

**High Technology Associates - Division
of Global Technologies Inc.**
1775 St. James Pl., Ste. 105
Houston, TX 77056
(713)963-9300
Fax: (713)963-8341
E-mail: hta@infohwy.com

MasterCOM
103 Thunder Rd.
Kerrville, TX 78028
(830)895-7990
Fax: (830)443-3428
E-mail: jmstubblefield@master
training.com
Website: http://www.mastertraining.com

PROTEC
4607 Linden Pl.
Pearland, TX 77584
(281)997-9872
Fax: (281)997-9895
E-mail: p.oman@ix.netcom.com

Alpha Quadrant Inc.
10618 Auldine
San Antonio, TX 78230
(210)344-3330
Fax: (210)344-8151
E-mail: mbussone@sbcglobal.net
Website:http://www.a-quadrant.com
Michele Bussone

Bastian Public Relations
614 San Dizier
San Antonio, TX 78232
(210)404-1839
E-mail: lisa@bastianpr.com
Website: http://www.bastianpr.com
Lisa Bastian CBC

**Business Strategy Development
Consultants**
PO Box 690365
San Antonio, TX 78269
(210)696-8000
Free: 800-927-BSDC
Fax: (210)696-8000

Tom Welch, CPC
6900 San Pedro Ave., Ste. 147
San Antonio, TX 78216-6207

(210)737-7022
Fax: (210)737-7022
E-mail: bplan@iamerica.net
Website: http://www.moneywords.com

Utah

Business Management Resource
PO Box 521125
Salt Lake City, UT 84152-1125
(801)272-4668
Fax: (801)277-3290
E-mail: pingfong@worldnet.att.net

Virginia

Tindell Associates
209 Oxford Ave.
Alexandria, VA 22301
(703)683-0109
Fax: 703-783-0219
E-mail: scott@tindell.net
Website: http://www.tindell.net
Scott Lockett, President

Elliott B. Jaffa
2530-B S Walter Reed Dr.
Arlington, VA 22206
(703)931-0040
E-mail: thetrainingdoctor@excite.com
Website: http://www.tregistry.com/
jaffa.htm

Koach Enterprises - USA
5529 N 18th St.
Arlington, VA 22205
(703)241-8361
Fax: (703)241-8623

Federal Market Development
5650 Chapel Run Ct.
Centreville, VA 20120-3601
(703)502-8930
Free: 800-821-5003
Fax: (703)502-8929

Huff, Stuart & Carlton
2107 Graves Mills Rd., Ste. C
Forest, VA 24551
(804)316-9356
Free: (888)316-9356
Fax: (804)316-9357
Website: http://www.wealthmgt.net

AMX International Inc.
1420 Spring Hill Rd. , Ste. 600
McLean, VA 22102-3006
(703)690-4100
Fax: (703)643-1279
E-mail: amxmail@amxi.com
Website: http://www.amxi.com

Charles Scott Pugh (Investor)
4101 Pittaway Dr.
Richmond, VA 23235-1022
(804)560-0979
Fax: (804)560-4670

John C. Randall and Associates Inc.
PO Box 15127
Richmond, VA 23227
(804)746-4450
Fax: (804)730-8933
E-mail: randalljcx@aol.com
Website: http://www.johncrandall.com

McLeod & Co.
410 1st St.
Roanoke, VA 24011
(540)342-6911
Fax: (540)344-6367
Website: http://www.mcleodco.com/

Salzinger & Company Inc.
8000 Towers Crescent Dr., Ste. 1350
Vienna, VA 22182
(703)442-5200
Fax: (703)442-5205
E-mail: info@salzinger.com
Website: http://www.salzinger.com

The Small Business Counselor
12423 Hedges Run Dr., Ste. 153
Woodbridge, VA 22192
(703)490-6755
Fax: (703)490-1356

Washington

Burlington Consultants
10900 NE 8th St., Ste. 900
Bellevue, WA 98004
(425)688-3060
Fax: (425)454-4383
E-mail: partners@burlington
consultants.com
Website: http://www.burlington
consultants.com

Perry L. Smith Consulting
800 Bellevue Way NE, Ste. 400
Bellevue, WA 98004-4208
(425)462-2072
Fax: (425)462-5638

St. Charles Consulting Group
1420 NW Gilman Blvd.
Issaquah, WA 98027
(425)557-8708
Fax: (425)557-8731
E-mail: info@stcharlesconsulting.com
Website: http://www.stcharlescon
sulting.com

Independent Automotive Training Services
PO Box 334
Kirkland, WA 98083
(425)822-5715
E-mail: ltunney@autosvccon.com
Website: http://www.autosvccon.com

Kahle Associate Inc.
6203 204th Dr. NE
Redmond, WA 98053
(425)836-8763
Fax: (425)868-3770
E-mail: randykahle@kahleassociates.com
Website: http://www.kahleassociates.com

Dan Collin
3419 Wallingord Ave N, No. 2
Seattle, WA 98103
(206)634-9469
E-mail: dc@dancollin.com
Website: http://members.home.net/
dcollin/

ECG Management Consultants Inc.
1111 3rd Ave., Ste. 2700
Seattle, WA 98101-3201
(206)689-2200
Fax: (206)689-2209
E-mail: ecg@ecgmc.com
Website: http://www.ecgmc.com

Northwest Trade Adjustment Assistance Center
900 4th Ave., Ste. 2430
Seattle, WA 98164-1001
(206)622-2730
Free: 800-667-8087
Fax: (206)622-1105
E-mail: matchingfunds@nwtaac.org
Website: http://www.taacenters.org

Business Planning Consultants
S 3510 Ridgeview Dr.
Spokane, WA 99206
(509)928-0332
Fax: (509)921-0842
E-mail: bpci@nextdim.com

West Virginia

**Stanley & Associates Inc./
BusinessandMarketingPlans.com**
1687 Robert C. Byrd Dr.
Beckley, WV 25801
(304)252-0324
Free: 888-752-6720
Fax: (304)252-0470
E-mail: cclay@charterinternet.com

Website: http://www.Businessand
MarketingPlans.com
Christopher Clay

Wisconsin

White & Associates Inc.
5349 Somerset Ln. S
Greenfield, WI 53221
(414)281-7373
Fax: (414)281-7006
E-mail: wnaconsult@aol.com

Small business administration regional offices

This section contains a listing of Small Business Administration offices arranged numerically by region. Service areas are provided. Contact the appropriate office for a referral to the nearest field office, or visit the Small Business Administration online at www.sba.gov.

Region 1

U.S. Small Business Administration
Region I Office
10 Causeway St., Ste. 812
Boston, MA 02222-1093
Phone: (617)565-8415
Fax: (617)565-8420
Serves Connecticut, Maine, Massachusetts, New Hampshire, Rhode Island, and Vermont.

Region 2

U.S. Small Business Administration
Region II Office
26 Federal Plaza, Ste. 3108
New York, NY 10278
Phone: (212)264-1450
Fax: (212)264-0038
Serves New Jersey, New York, Puerto Rico, and the Virgin Islands.

Region 3

U.S. Small Business Administration
Region III Office
Robert N C Nix Sr. Federal Building
900 Market St., 5th Fl.
Philadelphia, PA 19107
(215)580-2807
Serves Delaware, the District of Columbia, Maryland, Pennsylvania, Virginia, and West Virginia.

Region 4

U.S. Small Business Administration
Region IV Office
233 Peachtree St. NE
Harris Tower 1800
Atlanta, GA 30303
Phone: (404)331-4999
Fax: (404)331-2354
Serves Alabama, Florida, Georgia, Kentucky, Mississippi, North Carolina, South Carolina, and Tennessee.

Region 5

U.S. Small Business Administration
Region V Office
500 W. Madison St.
Citicorp Center, Ste. 1240
Chicago, IL 60661-2511
Phone: (312)353-0357
Fax: (312)353-3426
Serves Illinois, Indiana, Michigan, Minnesota, Ohio, and Wisconsin.

Region 6

U.S. Small Business Administration
Region VI Office
4300 Amon Carter Blvd., Ste. 108
Fort Worth, TX 76155
Phone: (817)684-5581
Fax: (817)684-5588
Serves Arkansas, Louisiana, New Mexico, Oklahoma, and Texas.

Region 7

U.S. Small Business Administration
Region VII Office
323 W. 8th St., Ste. 307
Kansas City, MO 64105-1500
Phone: (816)374-6380
Fax: (816)374-6339
Serves Iowa, Kansas, Missouri, and Nebraska.

Region 8

U.S. Small Business Administration
Region VIII Office
721 19th St., Ste. 400
Denver, CO 80202
Phone: (303)844-0500
Fax: (303)844-0506
Serves Colorado, Montana, North Dakota, South Dakota, Utah, and Wyoming.

Region 9

U.S. Small Business Administration
Region IX Office
330 N Brand Blvd., Ste. 1270
Glendale, CA 91203-2304
Phone: (818)552-3434
Fax: (818)552-3440
Serves American Samoa, Arizona, California, Guam, Hawaii, Nevada, and the Trust Territory of the Pacific Islands.

Region 10

U.S. Small Business Administration
Region X Office
2401 Fourth Ave., Ste. 400
Seattle, WA 98121
Phone: (206)553-5676
Fax: (206)553-4155
Serves Alaska, Idaho, Oregon, and Washington.

Small business development centers

This section contains a listing of all Small Business Development Centers, organized alphabetically by state/U.S. territory, then by city, then by agency name.

Alabama

Alabama SBDC
UNIVERSITY OF ALABAMA
2800 Milan Court Suite 124
Birmingham, AL 35211-6908
Phone: 205-943-6750
Fax: 205-943-6752
E-Mail: wcampbell@provost.uab.edu
Website: http://www.asbdc.org
Mr. William Campbell Jr, State Director

Alaska

Alaska SBDC
UNIVERSITY OF ALASKA - ANCHORAGE
430 West Seventh Avenue, Suite 110
Anchorage, AK 99501
Phone: 907-274 -7232
Fax: 907-274-9524
E-Mail: anerw@uaa.alaska.edu
Website: http://www.aksbdc.org
Ms. Jean R. Wall, State Director

American Samoa

American Samoa SBDC
AMERICAN SAMOA COMMUNITY COLLEGE
P.O. Box 2609
Pago Pago, American Samoa 96799
Phone: 011-684-699-4830
Fax: 011-684-699-6132
E-Mail: htalex@att.net
Mr. Herbert Thweatt, Director

Arizona

Arizona SBDC
MARICOPA COUNTY COMMUNITY COLLEGE
2411 West 14th Street, Suite 132
Tempe, AZ 85281
Phone: 480-731-8720
Fax: 480-731-8729
E-Mail: mike.york@domail.maricopa.edu
Website: http://www.dist.maricopa.edu.sbdc
Mr. Michael York, State Director

Arkansas

Arkansas SBDC
UNIVERSITY OF ARKANSAS
2801 South University Avenue
Little Rock, AR 72204
Phone: 501-324-9043
Fax: 501-324-9049
E-Mail: jmroderick@ualr.edu
Website: http://asbdc.ualr.edu
Ms. Janet M. Roderick, State Director

California

California - San Francisco SBDC
Northern California SBDC Lead Center
HUMBOLDT STATE UNIVERSITY
Office of Economic Development
1 Harpst Street 2006A, Siemens Hall
Arcata, CA, 95521
Phone: 707-826-3922
Fax: 707-826-3206
E-Mail: gainer@humboldt.edu
Ms. Margaret A. Gainer, Regional Director

California - Sacramento SBDC
CALIFORNIA STATE UNIVERSITY - CHICO
Chico, CA 95929-0765
Phone: 530-898-4598
Fax: 530-898-4734

E-Mail: dripke@csuchico.edu
Website: http://gsbdc.csuchico.edu
Mr. Dan Ripke, Interim Regional Director

California - San Diego SBDC
SOUTHWESTERN COMMUNITY
COLLEGE DISTRICT
900 Otey Lakes Road
Chula Vista, CA 91910
Phone: 619-482-6388
Fax: 619-482-6402
E-Mail: dtrujillo@swc.cc.ca.us
Website: http://www.sbditc.org
Ms. Debbie P. Trujillo, Regional Director

California - Fresno SBDC
UC Merced Lead Center
UNIVERSITY OF CALIFORNIA -
MERCED
550 East Shaw, Suite 105A
Fresno, CA 93710
Phone: 559-241-6590
Fax: 559-241-7422
E-Mail: crosander@ucmerced.edu
Website: http://sbdc.ucmerced.edu
Mr. Chris Rosander, State Director

California - Santa Ana SBDC
Tri-County Lead SBDC
CALIFORNIA STATE UNIVERSITY -
FULLERTON
800 North State College Boulevard, LH640
Fullerton, CA 92834
Phone: 714-278-2719
Fax: 714-278-7858
E-Mail: vpham@fullerton.edu
Website: http://www.leadsbdc.org
Ms. Vi Pham, Lead Center Director

California - Los Angeles Region SBDC
LONG BEACH COMMUNITY
COLLEGE DISTRICT
3950 Paramount Boulevard, Ste 101
Lakewood, CA 90712
Phone: 562-938-5004
Fax: 562-938-5030
E-Mail: ssloan@lbcc.edu
Ms. Sheneui Sloan, Interim Lead Center
Director

Colorado

Colorado SBDC
OFFICE OF ECONOMIC
DEVELOPMENT
1625 Broadway, Suite 170
Denver, CO 80202
Phone: 303-892-3864
Fax: 303-892-3848
E-Mail: Kelly.Manning@state.co.us

Website: http://www.state.co.us/oed/sbdc
Ms. Kelly Manning, State Director

Connecticut

Connecticut SBDC
UNIVERSITY OF CONNECTICUT
1376 Storrs Road, Unit 4094
Storrs, CT 06269-1094
Phone: 860-870-6370
Fax: 860-870-6374
E-Mail: richard.cheney@uconn.edu
Website: http://www.sbdc.uconn.edu
Mr. Richard Cheney, Interim State Director

Delaware

Delaware SBDC
DELAWARE TECHNOLOGY PARK
1 Innovation Way, Suite 301
Newark, DE 19711
Phone: 302-831-2747
Fax: 302-831-1423
E-Mail: Clinton.tymes@mvs.udel.edu
Website: http://www.delawaresbdc.org
Mr. Clinton Tymes, State Director

District of Columbia

District of Columbia SBDC
HOWARD UNIVERSITY
2600 6th Street, NW Room 128
Washington, DC 20059
Phone: 202-806-1550
Fax: 202-806-1777
E-Mail: hturner@howard.edu
Website: http://www.dcsbdc.com/
Mr. Henry Turner, Executive Director

Florida

Florida SBDC
UNIVERSITY OF WEST FLORIDA
401 East Chase Street, Suite 100
Pensacola, FL 32502
Phone: 850-473-7800
Fax: 850-473-7813
E-Mail: jcartwri@uwf.edu
Website: http://www.floridasbdc.com
Mr. Jerry Cartwright, State Director

Georgia

Georgia SBDC
UNIVERSITY OF GEORGIA
1180 East Broad Street
Athens, GA 30602
Phone: 706-542-6762
Fax: 706-542-6776
E-mail: aadams@sbdc.uga.edu

Website: http://www.sbdc.uga.edu
Mr. Allan Adams, Interim State Director

Guam

Guam Small Business Development
Center
UNIVERSITY OF GUAM
Pacific Islands SBDC
P.O. Box 5014 - U.O.G. Station
Mangilao, GU 96923
Phone: 671-735-2590
Fax: 671-734-2002
E-mail: casey@pacificsbdc.com
Website: http://www.uog.edu/sbdc
Mr. Casey Jeszenka, Director

Hawaii

Hawaii SBDC
UNIVERSITY OF HAWAII - HILO
308 Kamehameha Avenue, Suite 201
Hilo, HI 96720
Phone: 808-974-7515
Fax: 808-974-7683
E-Mail: darrylm@interpac.net
Website: http://www.hawaii-sbdc.org
Mr. Darryl Mleynek, State Director

Idaho

Idaho SBDC
BOISE STATE UNIVERSITY
1910 University Drive
Boise, ID 83725
Phone: 208-426-3799
Fax: 208-426-3877
E-mail: jhogge@boisestate.edu
Website: http://www.idahosbdc.org
Mr. Jim Hogge, State Director

Illinois

Illinois SBDC
DEPARTMENT OF COMMERCE
AND ECONOMIC OPPORTUNITY
620 E. Adams, S-4
Springfield, IL 62701
Phone: 217-524-5700
Fax: 217-524-0171
E-mail: mpatrilli@ildceo.net
Website: http://www.ilsbdc.biz
Mr. Mark Petrilli, State Director

Indiana

Indiana SBDC
INDIANA ECONOMIC
DEVELOPMENT CORPORATION
One North Capitol, Suite 900
Indianapolis, IN 46204

Organizations, Agencies, & Consultants

Phone: 317-234-8872
Fax: 317-232-8874
E-mail: dtrocha@isbdc.org
Website: http://www.isbdc.org
Ms. Debbie Bishop Trocha, State
Director

Iowa

Iowa SBDC
IOWA STATE UNIVERSITY
340 Gerdin Business Bldg.
Ames, IA 50011-1350
Phone: 515-294-2037
Fax: 515-294-6522
E-mail: jonryan@iastate.edu
Website: http://www.iabusnet.org
Mr. Jon Ryan, State Director

Kansas

Kansas SBDC
FORT HAYS STATE UNIVERSITY
214 SW Sixth Street, Suite 301
Topeka, KS 66603
Phone: 785-296-6514
Fax: 785-291-3261
E-mail: ksbdc.wkearns@fhsu.edu
Website: http://www.fhsu.edu/ksbdc
Mr. Wally Kearns, State Director

Kentucky

Kentucky SBDC
UNIVERSITY OF KENTUCKY
225 Gatton College of Business
Economics Building
Lexington, KY 40506-0034
Phone: 859-257-7668
Fax: 859-323-1907
E-mail: lrnaug0@pop.uky.edu
Website: http://www.ksbdc.org
Ms. Becky Naugle, State Director

Louisiana

Louisiana SBDC
**UNIVERSITY OF LOUISIANA -
MONROE**
College of Business Administration
700 University Avenue
Monroe, LA 71209
Phone: 318-342-5506
Fax: 318-342-5510
E-mail: wilkerson@ulm.edu
Website: http://www.lsbdc.org
Ms. Mary Lynn Wilkerson, State
Director

Maine

Maine SBDC
**UNIVERSITY OF SOUTHERN
MAINE**
96 Falmouth Street P.O. Box 9300
Portland, ME 04103
Phone: 207-780-4420
Fax: 207-780-4810
E-mail: jrmassaua@maine.edu
Website: http://www.mainesbdc.org
Mr. John Massaua, State Director

Maryland

Maryland SBDC
UNIVERSITY OF MARYLAND
7100 Baltimore Avenue, Suite 401
College Park, MD 20742
Phone: 301-403-8300
Fax: 301-403-8303
E-mail: rsprow@mdsbdc.umd.edu
Website: http://www.mdsbdc.umd.edu
Ms. Renee Sprow, State Director

Massachusetts

Massachusetts SBDC
UNIVERSITY OF MASSACHUSETTS
School of Management, Room 205
Amherst, MA 01003-4935
Phone: 413-545-6301
Fax: 413-545-1273
E-mail: gep@msbdc.umass.edu
Website: http://msbdc.som.umass.edu
Ms. Georgianna Parkin, State Director

Michigan

Michigan SBTDC
**GRAND VALLEY STATE
UNIVERSITY**
510 West Fulton Avenue
Grand Rapids, MI 49504
Phone: 616-331-7485
Fax: 616-331-7389
E-mail: lopuckic@gvsu.edu
Website: http://www.misbtdc.org
Ms. Carol Lopucki, State Director

Minnesota

Minnesota SBDC
**MINNESOTA SMALL BUSINESS
DEVELOPMENT CENTER**
1st National Bank Building
332 Minnesota Street, Suite E200
St. Paul, MN 55101-1351
Phone: 651-297-5773
Fax: 651-296-5287

E-mail: michael.myhre@state.mn.us
Website: http://www.mnsbdc.com
Mr. Michael Myhre, State Director

Mississippi

Mississippi SBDC
UNIVERSITY OF MISSISSIPPI
B-19 Jeanette Phillips Drive
P.O. Box 1848
University, MS 38677
Phone: 662-915-5001
Fax: 662-915-5650
E-mail: wgurley@olemiss.edu
Website: http://www.olemiss.edu/depts/
mssbdc
Mr. Doug Gurley, Jr., State Director

Missouri

Missouri SBDC
UNIVERSITY OF MISSOURI
1205 University Avenue, Suite 300
Columbia, MO 65211
Phone: 573-882-1348
Fax: 573-884-4297
E-mail: summersm@missouri.edu
Website: http://www.mo-sbdc.org/
index.shtml
Mr. Max Summers, State Director

Montana

Montana SBDC
DEPARTMENT OF COMMERCE
301 South Park Avenue, Room 114 /
P.O. Box 200505
Helena, MT 59620
Phone: 406-841-2746
Fax: 406-444-1872
E-mail: adesch@state.mt.us
Website: http://commerce.state.mt.us/
brd/BRD_SBDC.html
Ms. Ann Desch, State Director

Nebraska

Nebraska SBDC
**UNIVERSITY OF NEBRASKA -
OMAHA**
60th & Dodge Street, CBA Room 407
Omaha, NE 68182
Phone: 402-554-2521
Fax: 402-554-3473
E-mail: rbernier@unomaha.edu
Website: http://nbdc.unomaha.edu
Mr. Robert Bernier, State Director

Nevada

Nevada SBDC
UNIVERSITY OF NEVADA - RENO
Reno College of Business
Administration, Room 411
Reno, NV 89557-0100
Phone: 775-784-1717
Fax: 775-784-4337
E-mail: males@unr.edu
Website: http://www.nsbdc.org
Mr. Sam Males, State Director

New Hampshire

New Hampshire SBDC
UNIVERSITY OF NEW HAMPSHIRE
108 McConnell Hall
Durham, NH 03824-3593
Phone: 603-862-4879
Fax: 603-862-4876
E-mail: Mary.Collins@unh.edu
Website: http://www.nhsbdc.org
Ms. Mary Collins, State Director

New Jersey

New Jersey SBDC
RUTGERS UNIVERSITY
49 Bleeker Street
Newark, NJ 07102-1993
Phone: 973-353-5950
Fax: 973-353-1110
E-mail: bhopper@njsbdc.com
Website: http://www.njsbdc.com/home
Ms. Brenda Hopper, State Director

New Mexico

New Mexico SBDC
SANTA FE COMMUNITY COLLEGE
6401 Richards Avenue
Santa Fe, NM 87505
Phone: 505-428-1362
Fax: 505-471-9469
E-mail: rmiller@santa-fe.cc.nm.us
Website: http://www.nmsbdc.org
Mr. Roy Miller, State Director

New York

New York SBDC
STATE UNIVERSITY OF NEW YORK
SUNY Plaza, S-523
Albany, NY 12246
Phone: 518-443-5398
Fax: 518-443-5275
E-mail: j.king@nyssbdc.org
Website: http://www.nyssbdc.org
Mr. Jim King, State Director

North Carolina

North Carolina SBDTC
UNIVERSITY OF NORTH CAROLINA
5 West Hargett Street, Suite 600
Raleigh, NC 27601
Phone: 919-715-7272
Fax: 919-715-7777
E-mail: sdaugherty@sbtdc.org
Website: http://www.sbtdc.org
Mr. Scott Daugherty, State Director

North Dakota

North Dakota SBDC
UNIVERSITY OF NORTH DAKOTA
1600 E. Century Avenue, Suite 2
Bismarck, ND 58503
Phone: 701-328-5375
Fax: 701-328-5320
E-mail: christine.martin@und.nodak.edu
Website: http://www.ndsbdc.org
Ms. Christine Martin-Goldman, State
Director

Ohio

Ohio SBDC
**OHIO DEPARTMENT
OF DEVELOPMENT**
77 South High Street
Columbus, OH 43216
Phone: 614-466-5102
Fax: 614-466-0829
E-mail: mabraham@odod.state.oh.us
Website: http://www.ohiosbdc.org
Ms. Michele Abraham, State Director

Oklahoma

Oklahoma SBDC
**SOUTHEAST OKLAHOMA STATE
UNIVERSITY**
517 University, Box 2584, Station A
Durant, OK 74701
Phone: 580-745-7577
Fax: 580-745-7471
E-mail: gpennington@sosu.edu
Website: http://www.osbdc.org
Mr. Grady Pennington, State Director

Oregon

Oregon SBDC
LANE COMMUNITY COLLEGE
99 West Tenth Avenue, Suite 390
Eugene, OR 97401-3021
Phone: 541-463-5250
Fax: 541-345-6006
E-mail: carterb@lanecc.edu

Website: http://www.bizcenter.org
Mr. William Carter, State Director

Pennsylvania

Pennsylvania SBDC
UNIVERSITY OF PENNSYLVANIA
The Wharton School
3733 Spruce Street
Philadelphia, PA 19104-6374
Phone: 215-898-1219
Fax: 215-573-2135
E-mail: ghiggins@wharton.upenn.edu
Website: http://pasbdc.org
Mr. Gregory Higgins, State Director

Puerto Rico

Puerto Rico SBDC
**INTER-AMERICAN UNIVERSITY
OF PUERTO RICO**
416 Ponce de Leon Avenue, Union Plaza,
Seventh Floor
Hato Rey, PR 00918
Phone: 787-763-6811
Fax: 787-763-4629
E-mail: cmarti@prsbdc.org
Website: http://www.prsbdc.org
Ms. Carmen Marti, Executive Director

Rhode Island

Rhode Island SBDC
BRYANT UNIVERSITY
1150 Douglas Pike
Smithfield, RI 02917
Phone: 401-232-6923
Fax: 401-232-6933
E-mail: adawson@bryant.edu
Website: http://www.risbdc.org
Ms. Diane Fournaris, Interim State Director

South Carolina

South Carolina SBDC
UNIVERSITY OF SOUTH CAROLINA
College of Business Administration
1710 College Street
Columbia, SC 29208
Phone: 803-777-4907
Fax: 803-777-4403
E-mail: lenti@moore.sc.edu
Website: http://scsbdc.moore.sc.edu
Mr. John Lenti, State Director

South Dakota

South Dakota SBDC
UNIVERSITY OF SOUTH DAKOTA
414 East Clark Street, Patterson Hall
Vermillion, SD 57069

Phone: 605-677-6256
Fax: 605-677-5427
E-mail: jshemmin@usd.edu
Website: http://www.sdsbdc.org
Mr. John S. Hemmingstad, State
Director

Tennessee

Tennessee SBDC
TENNESSEE BOARD OF REGENTS
1415 Murfressboro Road, Suite 540
Nashville, TN 37217-2833
Phone: 615-898-2745
Fax: 615-893-7089
E-mail: pgeho@mail.tsbdc.org
Website: http://www.tsbdc.org
Mr. Patrick Geho, State Director

Texas

Texas-North SBDC
DALLAS COUNTY COMMUNITY COLLEGE
1402 Corinth Street
Dallas, TX 75215
Phone: 214-860-5835
Fax: 214-860-5813
E-mail: emk9402@dcccd.edu
Website: http://www.ntsbdc.org
Ms. Liz Klimback, Region Director

Texas-Houston SBDC
UNIVERSITY OF HOUSTON
2302 Fannin, Suite 200
Houston, TX 77002
Phone: 713-752-8425
Fax: 713-756-1500
E-mail: fyoung@uh.edu
Website: http://sbdcnetwork.uh.edu
Mr. Mike Young, Executive Director

Texas-NW SBDC
TEXAS TECH UNIVERSITY
2579 South Loop 289, Suite 114
Lubbock, TX 79423
Phone: 806-745-3973
Fax: 806-745-6207
E-mail: c.bean@nwtsbdc.org
Website: http://www.nwtsbdc.org
Mr. Craig Bean, Executive Director

Texas-South-West Texas Border Region SBDC
UNIVERSITY OF TEXAS - SAN ANTONIO
501 West Durango Boulevard
San Antonio, TX 78207-4415
Phone: 210-458-2742
Fax: 210-458-2464

E-mail: albert.salgado@utsa.edu
Website: http://www.iedtexas.org
Mr. Alberto Salgado, Region Director

Utah

Utah SBDC
SALT LAKE COMMUNITY COLLEGE
9750 South 300 West
Sandy, UT 84070
Phone: 801-957-3493
Fax: 801-957-3488
E-mail: Greg.Panichello@slcc.edu
Website:http://www.slcc.edu/sbdc
Mr. Greg Panichello, State Director

Vermont

Vermont SBDC
VERMONT TECHNICAL COLLEGE
PO Box 188, 1 Main Street
Randolph Center, VT 05061-0188
Phone: 802-728-9101
Fax: 802-728-3026
E-mail: lquillen@vtc.edu
Website: http://www.vtsbdc.org
Ms. Lenae Quillen-Blume, State Director

Virgin Islands

Virgin Islands SBDC
UNIVERSITY OF THE VIRGIN ISLANDS
8000 Nisky Center, Suite 720
St. Thomas, VI 00802-5804
Phone: 340-776-3206
Fax: 340-775-3756
E-mail: wbush@webmail.uvi.edu
Website: http://rps.uvi.edu/SBDC
Mr. Warren Bush, State Director

Virginia

Virginia SBDC
GEORGE MASON UNIVERSITY
4031 University Drive, Suite 200
Fairfax, VA 22030-3409
Phone: 703-277-7727
Fax: 703-352-8515
E-mail: jkeenan@gmu.edu
Website: http://www.virginiasbdc.org
Ms. Jody Keenan, Director

Washington

Washington SBDC
WASHINGTON STATE UNIVERSITY
534 E. Trent Avenue
P.O. Box 1495
Spokane, WA 99210-1495

Phone: 509-358-7765
Fax: 509-358-7764
E-mail: barogers@wsu.edu
Website: http://www.wsbdc.org
Mr. Brett Rogers, State Director

West Virginia

West Virginia SBDC
WEST VIRGINIA DEVELOPMENT OFFICE
Capital Complex, Building 6, Room 652
Charleston, WV 25301
Phone: 304-558-2960
Fax: 304-558-0127
E-mail: csalyer@wvsbdc.org
Website: http://www.wvsbdc.org
Mr. Conley Salyor, State Director

Wisconsin

Wisconsin SBDC
UNIVERSITY OF WISCONSIN
432 North Lake Street, Room 423
Madison, WI 53706
Phone: 608-263-7794
Fax: 608-263-7830
E-mail: erica.kauten@uwex.edu
Website: http://www.wisconsinsbdc.org
Ms. Erica Kauten, State Director

Wyoming

Wyoming SBDC
UNIVERSITY OF WYOMING
P.O. Box 3922
Laramie, WY 82071-3922
Phone: 307-766-3505
Fax: 307-766-3406
E-mail: DDW@uwyo.edu
Website: http://www.uwyo.edu/sbdc
Ms. Debbie Popp, Acting State Director

Service corps of retired executives (score) offices

This section contains a listing of all SCORE offices organized alphabetically by state/U.S. territory, then by city, then by agency name.

Alabama

SCORE Office (Northeast Alabama)
1330 Quintard Ave.
Anniston, AL 36202
(256)237-3536

SCORE Office (North Alabama)
901 South 15th St, Rm. 201
Birmingham, AL 35294-2060
(205)934-6868
Fax: (205)934-0538

SCORE Office (Baldwin County)
29750 Larry Dee Cawyer Dr.
Daphne, AL 36526
(334)928-5838

SCORE Office (Shoals)
612 S. COurt
Florence, AL 35630
(256)764-4661
Fax: (256)766-9017
E-mail: shoals@shoalschamber.com

SCORE Office (Mobile)
600 S Court St.
Mobile, AL 36104
(334)240-6868
Fax: (334)240-6869

SCORE Office (Alabama Capitol City)
600 S. Court St.
Montgomery, AL 36104
(334)240-6868
Fax: (334)240-6869

SCORE Office (East Alabama)
601 Ave. A
Opelika, AL 36801
(334)745-4861
E-mail: score636@hotmail.com
Website: http://www.angelfire.com/sc/
score636/

SCORE Office (Tuscaloosa)
2200 University Blvd.
Tuscaloosa, AL 35402
(205)758-7588

Alaska

SCORE Office (Anchorage)
510 L St., Ste. 310
Anchorage, AK 99501
(907)271-4022
Fax: (907)271-4545

Arizona

SCORE Office (Lake Havasu)
10 S. Acoma Blvd.
Lake Havasu City, AZ 86403
(520)453-5951
E-mail: SCORE@ctaz.com
Website: http://www.scorearizona.org/
lake_havasu/

SCORE Office (East Valley)
Federal Bldg., Rm. 104
26 N. MacDonald St.
Mesa, AZ 85201
(602)379-3100
Fax: (602)379-3143
E-mail: 402@aol.com
Website: http://www.scorearizona.
org/mesa/

SCORE Office (Phoenix)
2828 N. Central Ave., Ste. 800
Central & One Thomas
Phoenix, AZ 85004
(602)640-2329
Fax: (602)640-2360
E-mail: e-mail@SCORE-phoenix.org
Website: http://www.score-phoenix.org/

SCORE Office (Prescott Arizona)
1228 Willow Creek Rd., Ste. 2
Prescott, AZ 86301
(520)778-7438
Fax: (520)778-0812
E-mail: score@northlink.com
Website: http://www.scorearizona.org/
prescott/

SCORE Office (Tucson)
110 E. Pennington St.
Tucson, AZ 85702
(520)670-5008
Fax: (520)670-5011
E-mail: score@azstarnet.com
Website: http://www.scorearizona.org/
tucson/

SCORE Office (Yuma)
281 W. 24th St., Ste. 116
Yuma, AZ 85364
(520)314-0480
E-mail: score@C2i2.com
Website: http://www.scorearizona.org/
yuma

Arkansas

SCORE Office (South Central)
201 N. Jackson Ave.
El Dorado, AR 71730-5803
(870)863-6113
Fax: (870)863-6115

SCORE Office (Ozark)
Fayetteville, AR 72701
(501)442-7619

SCORE Office (Northwest Arkansas)
Glenn Haven Dr., No. 4
Ft. Smith, AR 72901
(501)783-3556

SCORE Office (Garland County)
Grand & Ouachita
PO Box 6012
Hot Springs Village, AR 71902
(501)321-1700

SCORE Office (Little Rock)
2120 Riverfront Dr., Rm. 100
Little Rock, AR 72202-1747
(501)324-5893
Fax: (501)324-5199

SCORE Office (Southeast Arkansas)
121 W. 6th
Pine Bluff, AR 71601
(870)535-7189
Fax: (870)535-1643

California

SCORE Office (Golden Empire)
1706 Chester Ave., No. 200
Bakersfield, CA 93301
(805)322-5881
Fax: (805)322-5663

SCORE Office (Greater Chico Area)
1324 Mangrove St., Ste. 114
Chico, CA 95926
(916)342-8932
Fax: (916)342-8932

SCORE Office (Concord)
2151-A Salvio St., Ste. B
Concord, CA 94520
(510)685-1181
Fax: (510)685-5623

SCORE Office (Covina)
935 W. Badillo St.
Covina, CA 91723
(818)967-4191
Fax: (818)966-9660

SCORE Office (Rancho Cucamonga)
8280 Utica, Ste. 160
Cucamonga, CA 91730
(909)987-1012
Fax: (909)987-5917

SCORE Office (Culver City)
PO Box 707
Culver City, CA 90232-0707
(310)287-3850
Fax: (310)287-1350

SCORE Office (Danville)
380 Diablo Rd., Ste. 103
Danville, CA 94526
(510)837-4400

SCORE Office (Downey)
11131 Brookshire Ave.
Downey, CA 90241
(310)923-2191
Fax: (310)864-0461

SCORE Office (El Cajon)
109 Rea Ave.
El Cajon, CA 92020
(619)444-1327
Fax: (619)440-6164

SCORE Office (El Centro)
1100 Main St.
El Centro, CA 92243
(619)352-3681
Fax: (619)352-3246

SCORE Office (Escondido)
720 N. Broadway
Escondido, CA 92025
(619)745-2125
Fax: (619)745-1183

SCORE Office (Fairfield)
1111 Webster St.
Fairfield, CA 94533
(707)425-4625
Fax: (707)425-0826

SCORE Office (Fontana)
17009 Valley Blvd., Ste. B
Fontana, CA 92335
(909)822-4433
Fax: (909)822-6238

SCORE Office (Foster City)
1125 E. Hillsdale Blvd.
Foster City, CA 94404
(415)573-7600
Fax: (415)573-5201

SCORE Office (Fremont)
2201 Walnut Ave., Ste. 110
Fremont, CA 94538
(510)795-2244
Fax: (510)795-2240

SCORE Office (Central California)
2719 N. Air Fresno Dr., Ste. 200
Fresno, CA 93727-1547
(559)487-5605
Fax: (559)487-5636

SCORE Office (Gardena)
1204 W. Gardena Blvd.
Gardena, CA 90247
(310)532-9905
Fax: (310)515-4893

SCORE Office (Lompoc)
330 N. Brand Blvd., Ste. 190
Glendale, CA 91203-2304

(818)552-3206
Fax: (818)552-3323

SCORE Office (Los Angeles)
330 N. Brand Blvd., Ste. 190
Glendale, CA 91203-2304
(818)552-3206
Fax: (818)552-3323

SCORE Office (Glendora)
131 E. Foothill Blvd.
Glendora, CA 91740
(818)963-4128
Fax: (818)914-4822

SCORE Office (Grover Beach)
177 S. 8th St.
Grover Beach, CA 93433
(805)489-9091
Fax: (805)489-9091

SCORE Office (Hawthorne)
12477 Hawthorne Blvd.
Hawthorne, CA 90250
(310)676-1163
Fax: (310)676-7661

SCORE Office (Hayward)
22300 Foothill Blvd., Ste. 303
Hayward, CA 94541
(510)537-2424

SCORE Office (Hemet)
1700 E. Florida Ave.
Hemet, CA 92544-4679
(909)652-4390
Fax: (909)929-8543

SCORE Office (Hesperia)
16367 Main St.
PO Box 403656
Hesperia, CA 92340
(619)244-2135

SCORE Office (Holloster)
321 San Felipe Rd., No. 11
Hollister, CA 95023

SCORE Office (Hollywood)
7018 Hollywood Blvd.
Hollywood, CA 90028
(213)469-8311
Fax: (213)469-2805

SCORE Office (Indio)
82503 Hwy. 111
PO Drawer TTT
Indio, CA 92202
(619)347-0676

SCORE Office (Inglewood)
330 Queen St.

Inglewood, CA 90301
(818)552-3206

SCORE Office (La Puente)
218 N. Grendanda St. D.
La Puente, CA 91744
(818)330-3216
Fax: (818)330-9524

SCORE Office (La Verne)
2078 Bonita Ave.
La Verne, CA 91750
(909)593-5265
Fax: (714)929-8475

SCORE Office (Lake Elsinore)
132 W. Graham Ave.
Lake Elsinore, CA 92530
(909)674-2577

SCORE Office (Lakeport)
PO Box 295
Lakeport, CA 95453
(707)263-5092

SCORE Office (Lakewood)
5445 E. Del Amo Blvd., Ste. 2
Lakewood, CA 90714
(213)920-7737

SCORE Office (Long Beach)
1 World Trade Center
Long Beach, CA 90831

SCORE Office (Los Alamitos)
901 W. Civic Center Dr., Ste. 160
Los Alamitos, CA 90720

SCORE Office (Los Altos)
321 University Ave.
Los Altos, CA 94022
(415)948-1455

SCORE Office (Manhattan Beach)
PO Box 3007
Manhattan Beach, CA 90266
(310)545-5313
Fax: (310)545-7203

SCORE Office (Merced)
1632 N. St.
Merced, CA 95340
(209)725-3800
Fax: (209)383-4959

SCORE Office (Milpitas)
75 S. Milpitas Blvd., Ste. 205
Milpitas, CA 95035
(408)262-2613
Fax: (408)262-2823

SCORE Office (Yosemite)
1012 11th St., Ste. 300
Modesto, CA 95354
(209)521-9333

SCORE Office (Montclair)
5220 Benito Ave.
Montclair, CA 91763

SCORE Office (Monterey Bay)
380 Alvarado St.
PO Box 1770
Monterey, CA 93940-1770
(408)649-1770

SCORE Office (Moreno Valley)
25480 Alessandro
Moreno Valley, CA 92553

SCORE Office (Morgan Hill)
25 W. 1st St.
PO Box 786
Morgan Hill, CA 95038
(408)779-9444
Fax: (408)778-1786

SCORE Office (Morro Bay)
880 Main St.
Morro Bay, CA 93442
(805)772-4467

SCORE Office (Mountain View)
580 Castro St.
Mountain View, CA 94041
(415)968-8378
Fax: (415)968-5668

SCORE Office (Napa)
1556 1st St.
Napa, CA 94559
(707)226-7455
Fax: (707)226-1171

SCORE Office (North Hollywood)
5019 Lankershim Blvd.
North Hollywood, CA 91601
(818)552-3206

SCORE Office (Northridge)
8801 Reseda Blvd.
Northridge, CA 91324
(818)349-5676

SCORE Office (Novato)
807 De Long Ave.
Novato, CA 94945
(415)897-1164
Fax: (415)898-9097

SCORE Office (East Bay)
519 17th St.
Oakland, CA 94612

(510)273-6611
Fax: (510)273-6015
E-mail: webmaster@eastbayscore.org
Website: http://www.eastbayscore.org

SCORE Office (Oceanside)
928 N. Coast Hwy.
Oceanside, CA 92054
(619)722-1534

SCORE Office (Ontario)
121 West B. St.
Ontario, CA 91762
Fax: (714)984-6439

SCORE Office (Oxnard)
PO Box 867
Oxnard, CA 93032
(805)385-8860
Fax: (805)487-1763

SCORE Office (Pacifica)
450 Dundee Way, Ste. 2
Pacifica, CA 94044
(415)355-4122

SCORE Office (Palm Desert)
72990 Hwy. 111
Palm Desert, CA 92260
(619)346-6111
Fax: (619)346-3463

SCORE Office (Palm Springs)
650 E. Tahquitz Canyon Way Ste. D
Palm Springs, CA 92262-6706
(760)320-6682
Fax: (760)323-9426

SCORE Office (Lakeside)
2150 Low Tree
Palmdale, CA 93551
(805)948-4518
Fax: (805)949-1212

SCORE Office (Palo Alto)
325 Forest Ave.
Palo Alto, CA 94301
(415)324-3121
Fax: (415)324-1215

SCORE Office (Pasadena)
117 E. Colorado Blvd., Ste. 100
Pasadena, CA 91105
(818)795-3355
Fax: (818)795-5663

SCORE Office (Paso Robles)
1225 Park St.
Paso Robles, CA 93446-2234
(805)238-0506
Fax: (805)238-0527

SCORE Office (Petaluma)
799 Baywood Dr., Ste. 3
Petaluma, CA 94954
(707)762-2785
Fax: (707)762-4721

SCORE Office (Pico Rivera)
9122 E. Washington Blvd.
Pico Rivera, CA 90660

SCORE Office (Pittsburg)
2700 E. Leland Rd.
Pittsburg, CA 94565
(510)439-2181
Fax: (510)427-1599

SCORE Office (Pleasanton)
777 Peters Ave.
Pleasanton, CA 94566
(510)846-9697

SCORE Office (Monterey Park)
485 N. Garey
Pomona, CA 91769

SCORE Office (Pomona)
485 N. Garey Ave.
Pomona, CA 91766
(909)622-1256

SCORE Office (Antelope Valley)
4511 West Ave. M-4
Quartz Hill, CA 93536
(805)272-0087
E-mail: avscore@ptw.com
Website: http://www.score.av.org/

SCORE Office (Shasta)
737 Auditorium Dr.
Redding, CA 96099
(916)225-2770

SCORE Office (Redwood City)
1675 Broadway
Redwood City, CA 94063
(415)364-1722
Fax: (415)364-1729

SCORE Office (Richmond)
3925 MacDonald Ave.
Richmond, CA 94805

SCORE Office (Ridgecrest)
PO Box 771
Ridgecrest, CA 93555
(619)375-8331
Fax: (619)375-0365

SCORE Office (Riverside)
3685 Main St., Ste. 350
Riverside, CA 92501
(909)683-7100

SCORE Office (Sacramento)
9845 Horn Rd., 260-B
Sacramento, CA 95827
(916)361-2322
Fax: (916)361-2164
E-mail: sacchapter@directcon.net

SCORE Office (Salinas)
PO Box 1170
Salinas, CA 93902
(408)424-7611
Fax: (408)424-8639

SCORE Office (Inland Empire)
777 E. Rialto Ave.
Purchasing
San Bernardino, CA 92415-0760
(909)386-8278

SCORE Office (San Carlos)
San Carlos Chamber of Commerce
PO Box 1086
San Carlos, CA 94070
(415)593-1068
Fax: (415)593-9108

SCORE Office (Encinitas)
550 W. C St., Ste. 550
San Diego, CA 92101-3540
(619)557-7272
Fax: (619)557-5894

SCORE Office (San Diego)
550 West C. St., Ste. 550
San Diego, CA 92101-3540
(619)557-7272
Fax: (619)557-5894
Website: http://www.score-sandiego.org

SCORE Office (Menlo Park)
1100 Merrill St.
San Francisco, CA 94105
(415)325-2818
Fax: (415)325-0920

SCORE Office (San Francisco)
455 Market St., 6th Fl.
San Francisco, CA 94105
(415)744-6827
Fax: (415)744-6750
E-mail: sfscore@sfscore.
Website: http://www.sfscore.com

SCORE Office (San Gabriel)
401 W. Las Tunas Dr.
San Gabriel, CA 91776
(818)576-2525
Fax: (818)289-2901

SCORE Office (San Jose)
Deanza College
208 S. 1st. St., Ste. 137
San Jose, CA 95113
(408)288-8479
Fax: (408)535-5541

SCORE Office (Silicon Valley)
84 W. Santa Clara St., Ste. 100
San Jose, CA 95113
(408)288-8479
Fax: (408)535-5541
E-mail: info@svscore.org
Website: http://www.svscore.org

SCORE Office (San Luis Obispo)
3566 S. Hiquera, No. 104
San Luis Obispo, CA 93401
(805)547-0779

SCORE Office (San Mateo)
1021 S. El Camino, 2nd Fl.
San Mateo, CA 94402
(415)341-5679

SCORE Office (San Pedro)
390 W. 7th St.
San Pedro, CA 90731
(310)832-7272

SCORE Office (Orange County)
200 W. Santa Anna Blvd., Ste. 700
Santa Ana, CA 92701
(714)550-7369
Fax: (714)550-0191
Website: http://www.score114.org

SCORE Office (Santa Barbara)
3227 State St.
Santa Barbara, CA 93130
(805)563-0084

SCORE Office (Central Coast)
509 W. Morrison Ave.
Santa Maria, CA 93454
(805)347-7755

SCORE Office (Santa Maria)
614 S. Broadway
Santa Maria, CA 93454-5111
(805)925-2403
Fax: (805)928-7559

SCORE Office (Santa Monica)
501 Colorado, Ste. 150
Santa Monica, CA 90401
(310)393-9825
Fax: (310)394-1868

SCORE Office (Santa Rosa)
777 Sonoma Ave., Rm. 115E
Santa Rosa, CA 95404

(707)571-8342
Fax: (707)541-0331
Website: http://www.pressdemo.com/community/score/score.html

SCORE Office (Scotts Valley)
4 Camp Evers Ln.
Scotts Valley, CA 95066
(408)438-1010
Fax: (408)438-6544

SCORE Office (Simi Valley)
40 W. Cochran St., Ste. 100
Simi Valley, CA 93065
(805)526-3900
Fax: (805)526-6234

SCORE Office (Sonoma)
453 1st St. E
Sonoma, CA 95476
(707)996-1033

SCORE Office (Los Banos)
222 S. Shepard St.
Sonora, CA 95370
(209)532-4212

SCORE Office (Tuolumne County)
39 North Washington St.
Sonora, CA 95370
(209)588-0128
E-mail: score@mlode.com

SCORE Office (South San Francisco)
445 Market St., Ste. 6th Fl.
South San Francisco, CA 94105
(415)744-6827
Fax: (415)744-6812

SCORE Office (Stockton)
401 N. San Joaquin St., Rm. 215
Stockton, CA 95202
(209)946-6293

SCORE Office (Taft)
314 4th St.
Taft, CA 93268
(805)765-2165
Fax: (805)765-6639

SCORE Office (Conejo Valley)
625 W. Hillcrest Dr.
Thousand Oaks, CA 91360
(805)499-1993
Fax: (805)498-7264

SCORE Office (Torrance)
3400 Torrance Blvd., Ste. 100
Torrance, CA 90503
(310)540-5858
Fax: (310)540-7662

SCORE Office (Truckee)
PO Box 2757
Truckee, CA 96160
(916)587-2757
Fax: (916)587-2439

SCORE Office (Visalia)
113 S. M St,
Tulare, CA 93274
(209)627-0766
Fax: (209)627-8149

SCORE Office (Upland)
433 N. 2nd Ave.
Upland, CA 91786
(909)931-4108

SCORE Office (Vallejo)
2 Florida St.
Vallejo, CA 94590
(707)644-5551
Fax: (707)644-5590

SCORE Office (Van Nuys)
14540 Victory Blvd.
Van Nuys, CA 91411
(818)989-0300
Fax: (818)989-3836

SCORE Office (Ventura)
5700 Ralston St., Ste. 310
Ventura, CA 93001
(805)658-2688
Fax: (805)658-2252
E-mail: scoreven@jps.net
Website: http://www.jps.net/scoreven

SCORE Office (Vista)
201 E. Washington St.
Vista, CA 92084
(619)726-1122
Fax: (619)226-8654

SCORE Office (Watsonville)
PO Box 1748
Watsonville, CA 95077
(408)724-3849
Fax: (408)728-5300

SCORE Office (West Covina)
811 S. Sunset Ave.
West Covina, CA 91790
(818)338-8496
Fax: (818)960-0511

SCORE Office (Westlake)
30893 Thousand Oaks Blvd.
Westlake Village, CA 91362
(805)496-5630
Fax: (818)991-1754

Colorado

SCORE Office (Colorado Springs)
2 N. Cascade Ave., Ste. 110
Colorado Springs, CO 80903
(719)636-3074
Website: http://www.cscc.org/score02/index.html

SCORE Office (Denver)
US Custom's House, 4th Fl.
721 19th St.
Denver, CO 80201-0660
(303)844-3985
Fax: (303)844-6490
E-mail: score62@csn.net
Website: http://www.sni.net/score62

SCORE Office (Tri-River)
1102 Grand Ave.
Glenwood Springs, CO 81601
(970)945-6589

SCORE Office (Grand Junction)
2591 B & 3/4 Rd.
Grand Junction, CO 81503
(970)243-5242

SCORE Office (Gunnison)
608 N. 11th
Gunnison, CO 81230
(303)641-4422

SCORE Office (Montrose)
1214 Peppertree Dr.
Montrose, CO 81401
(970)249-6080

SCORE Office (Pagosa Springs)
PO Box 4381
Pagosa Springs, CO 81157
(970)731-4890

SCORE Office (Rifle)
0854 W. Battlement Pky., Apt. C106
Parachute, CO 81635
(970)285-9390

SCORE Office (Pueblo)
302 N. Santa Fe
Pueblo, CO 81003
(719)542-1704
Fax: (719)542-1624
E-mail: mackey@iex.net
Website: http://www.pueblo.org/score

SCORE Office (Ridgway)
143 Poplar Pl.
Ridgway, CO 81432

SCORE Office (Silverton)
PO Box 480

Silverton, CO 81433
(303)387-5430

SCORE Office (Minturn)
PO Box 2066
Vail, CO 81658
(970)476-1224

Connecticut

SCORE Office (Greater Bridgeport)
230 Park Ave.
Bridgeport, CT 06601-0999
(203)576-4369
Fax: (203)576-4388

SCORE Office (Bristol)
10 Main St. 1st. Fl.
Bristol, CT 06010
(203)584-4718
Fax: (203)584-4722

SCORE office (Greater Danbury)
246 Federal Rd.
Unit LL2, Ste. 7
Brookfield, CT 06804
(203)775-1151

SCORE Office (Greater Danbury)
246 Federal Rd., Unit LL2, Ste. 7
Brookfield, CT 06804
(203)775-1151

SCORE Office (Eastern Connecticut)
Administration Bldg., Rm. 313
PO 625
61 Main St. (Chapter 579)
Groton, CT 06475
(203)388-9508

SCORE Office (Greater Hartford County)
330 Main St.
Hartford, CT 06106
(860)548-1749
Fax: (860)240-4659
Website: http://www.score56.org

SCORE Office (Manchester)
20 Hartford Rd.
Manchester, CT 06040
(203)646-2223
Fax: (203)646-5871

SCORE Office (New Britain)
185 Main St., Ste. 431
New Britain, CT 06051
(203)827-4492
Fax: (203)827-4480

SCORE Office (New Haven)
25 Science Pk., Bldg. 25, Rm. 366

New Haven, CT 06511
(203)865-7645

SCORE Office (Fairfield County)
24 Beldon Ave., 5th Fl.
Norwalk, CT 06850
(203)847-7348
Fax: (203)849-9308

SCORE Office (Old Saybrook)
146 Main St.
Old Saybrook, CT 06475
(860)388-9508

SCORE Office (Simsbury)
Box 244
Simsbury, CT 06070
(203)651-7307
Fax: (203)651-1933

SCORE Office (Torrington)
23 North Rd.
Torrington, CT 06791
(203)482-6586

Delaware

SCORE Office (Dover)
Treadway Towers
PO Box 576
Dover, DE 19903
(302)678-0892
Fax: (302)678-0189

SCORE Office (Lewes)
PO Box 1
Lewes, DE 19958
(302)645-8073
Fax: (302)645-8412

SCORE Office (Milford)
204 NE Front St.
Milford, DE 19963
(302)422-3301

SCORE Office (Wilmington)
824 Market St., Ste. 610
Wilmington, DE 19801
(302)573-6652
Fax: (302)573-6092
Website: http://www.scoredelaware.com

District of Columbia

SCORE Office (George Mason University)
409 3rd St. SW, 4th Fl.
Washington, DC 20024
800-634-0245

SCORE Office (Washington DC)
1110 Vermont Ave. NW, 9th Fl.

Washington, DC 20043
(202)606-4000
Fax: (202)606-4225
E-mail: dcscore@hotmail.com
Website: http://www.scoredc.org/

Florida

SCORE Office (Desota County Chamber of Commerce)
16 South Velucia Ave.
Arcadia, FL 34266
(941)494-4033

SCORE Office (Suncoast/Pinellas)
Airport Business Ctr.
4707 - 140th Ave. N, No. 311
Clearwater, FL 33755
(813)532-6800
Fax: (813)532-6800

SCORE Office (DeLand)
336 N. Woodland Blvd.
DeLand, FL 32720
(904)734-4331
Fax: (904)734-4333

SCORE Office (South Palm Beach)
1050 S. Federal Hwy., Ste. 132
Delray Beach, FL 33483
(561)278-7752
Fax: (561)278-0288

SCORE Office (Ft. Lauderdale)
Federal Bldg., Ste. 123
299 E. Broward Blvd.
Ft. Lauderdale, FL 33301
(954)356-7263
Fax: (954)356-7145

SCORE Office (Southwest Florida)
The Renaissance
8695 College Pky., Ste. 345 & 346
Ft. Myers, FL 33919
(941)489-2935
Fax: (941)489-1170

SCORE Office (Treasure Coast)
Professional Center, Ste. 2
3220 S. US, No. 1
Ft. Pierce, FL 34982
(561)489-0548

SCORE Office (Gainesville)
101 SE 2nd Pl., Ste. 104
Gainesville, FL 32601
(904)375-8278

SCORE Office (Hialeah Dade Chamber)
59 W. 5th St.
Hialeah, FL 33010

(305)887-1515
Fax: (305)887-2453

SCORE Office (Daytona Beach)
921 Nova Rd., Ste. A
Holly Hills, FL 32117
(904)255-6889
Fax: (904)255-0229
E-mail: score87@dbeach.com

SCORE Office (South Broward)
3475 Sheridan St., Ste. 203
Hollywood, FL 33021
(305)966-8415

SCORE Office (Citrus County)
5 Poplar Ct.
Homosassa, FL 34446
(352)382-1037

SCORE Office (Jacksonville)
7825 Baymeadows Way, Ste. 100-B
Jacksonville, FL 32256
(904)443-1911
Fax: (904)443-1980
E-mail: scorejax@juno.com
Website: http://www.scorejax.org/

SCORE Office (Jacksonville Satellite)
3 Independent Dr.
Jacksonville, FL 32256
(904)366-6600
Fax: (904)632-0617

SCORE Office (Central Florida)
5410 S. Florida Ave., No. 3
Lakeland, FL 33801
(941)687-5783
Fax: (941)687-6225

SCORE Office (Lakeland)
100 Lake Morton Dr.
Lakeland, FL 33801
(941)686-2168

SCORE Office (St. Petersburg)
800 W. Bay Dr., Ste. 505
Largo, FL 33712
(813)585-4571

SCORE Office (Leesburg)
9501 US Hwy. 441
Leesburg, FL 34788-8751
(352)365-3556
Fax: (352)365-3501

SCORE Office (Cocoa)
1600 Farno Rd., Unit 205
Melbourne, FL 32935
(407)254-2288

SCORE Office (Melbourne)
Melbourne Professional Complex
1600 Sarno, Ste. 205
Melbourne, FL 32935
(407)254-2288
Fax: (407)245-2288

SCORE Office (Merritt Island)
1600 Sarno Rd., Ste. 205
Melbourne, FL 32935
(407)254-2288
Fax: (407)254-2288

SCORE Office (Space Coast)
Melbourn Professional Complex
1600 Sarno, Ste. 205
Melbourne, FL 32935
(407)254-2288
Fax: (407)254-2288

SCORE Office (Dade)
49 NW 5th St.
Miami, FL 33128
(305)371-6889
Fax: (305)374-1882
E-mail: score@netrox.net
Website: http://www.netrox.net/~score/

SCORE Office (Naples of Collier)
International College
2654 Tamiami Trl. E
Naples, FL 34112
(941)417-1280
Fax: (941)417-1281
E-mail: score@naples.net
Website: http://www.naples.net/clubs/
score/index.htm

SCORE Office (Pasco County)
6014 US Hwy. 19, Ste. 302
New Port Richey, FL 34652
(813)842-4638

SCORE Office (Southeast Volusia)
115 Canal St.
New Smyrna Beach, FL 32168
(904)428-2449
Fax: (904)423-3512

SCORE Office (Ocala)
110 E. Silver Springs Blvd.
Ocala, FL 34470
(352)629-5959

Clay County SCORE Office
Clay County Chamber of Commerce
1734 Kingsdey Ave.
PO Box 1441
Orange Park, FL 32073
(904)264-2651
Fax: (904)269-0363

SCORE Office (Orlando)
80 N. Hughey Ave.
Rm. 445 Federal Bldg.
Orlando, FL 32801
(407)648-6476
Fax: (407)648-6425

SCORE Office (Emerald Coast)
19 W. Garden St., No. 325
Pensacola, FL 32501
(904)444-2060
Fax: (904)444-2070

SCORE Office (Charlotte County)
201 W. Marion Ave., Ste. 211
Punta Gorda, FL 33950
(941)575-1818
E-mail: score@gls3c.com
Website: http://www.charlotte-
florida.com/business/scorepg01.htm

SCORE Office (St. Augustine)
1 Riberia St.
St. Augustine, FL 32084
(904)829-5681
Fax: (904)829-6477

SCORE Office (Bradenton)
2801 Fruitville, Ste. 280
Sarasota, FL 34237
(813)955-1029

SCORE Office (Manasota)
2801 Fruitville Rd., Ste. 280
Sarasota, FL 34237
(941)955-1029
Fax: (941)955-5581
E-mail: score116@gte.net
Website: http://www.score-suncoast.org/

SCORE Office (Tallahassee)
200 W. Park Ave.
Tallahassee, FL 32302
(850)487-2665

SCORE Office (Hillsborough)
4732 Dale Mabry Hwy. N, Ste. 400
Tampa, FL 33614-6509
(813)870-0125

SCORE Office (Lake Sumter)
122 E. Main St.
Tavares, FL 32778-3810
(352)365-3556

SCORE Office (Titusville)
2000 S. Washington Ave.
Titusville, FL 32780
(407)267-3036
Fax: (407)264-0127

SCORE Office (Venice)
257 N. Tamiami Trl.
Venice, FL 34285
(941)488-2236
Fax: (941)484-5903

SCORE Office (Palm Beach)
500 Australian Ave. S, Ste. 100
West Palm Beach, FL 33401
(561)833-1672
Fax: (561)833-1712

SCORE Office (Wildwood)
103 N. Webster St.
Wildwood, FL 34785

Georgia

SCORE Office (Atlanta)
Harris Tower, Suite 1900
233 Peachtree Rd., NE
Atlanta, GA 30309
(404)347-2442
Fax: (404)347-1227

SCORE Office (Augusta)
3126 Oxford Rd.
Augusta, GA 30909
(706)869-9100

SCORE Office (Columbus)
School Bldg.
PO Box 40
Columbus, GA 31901
(706)327-3654

SCORE Office (Dalton-Whitfield)
305 S. Thorton Ave.
Dalton, GA 30720
(706)279-3383

SCORE Office (Gainesville)
PO Box 374
Gainesville, GA 30503
(770)532-6206
Fax: (770)535-8419

SCORE Office (Macon)
711 Grand Bldg.
Macon, GA 31201
(912)751-6160

SCORE Office (Brunswick)
4 Glen Ave.
St. Simons Island, GA 31520
(912)265-0620
Fax: (912)265-0629

SCORE Office (Savannah)
111 E. Liberty St., Ste. 103
Savannah, GA 31401
(912)652-4335

Fax: (912)652-4184
E-mail: info@scoresav.org
Website: http://www.coastalempire.com/
score/index.htm

Guam

SCORE Office (Guam)
Pacific News Bldg., Rm. 103
238 Archbishop Flores St.
Agana, GU 96910-5100
(671)472-7308

Hawaii

SCORE Office (Hawaii, Inc.)
1111 Bishop St., Ste. 204
PO Box 50207
Honolulu, HI 96813
(808)522-8132
Fax: (808)522-8135
E-mail: hnlscore@juno.com

SCORE Office (Kahului)
250 Alamaha, Unit N16A
Kahului, HI 96732
(808)871-7711

SCORE Office (Maui, Inc.)
590 E. Lipoa Pkwy., Ste. 227
Kihei, HI 96753
(808)875-2380

Idaho

SCORE Office (Treasure Valley)
1020 Main St., No. 290
Boise, ID 83702
(208)334-1696
Fax: (208)334-9353

SCORE Office (Eastern Idaho)
2300 N. Yellowstone, Ste. 119
Idaho Falls, ID 83401
(208)523-1022
Fax: (208)528-7127

Illinois

SCORE Office (Fox Valley)
40 W. Downer Pl.
PO Box 277
Aurora, IL 60506
(630)897-9214
Fax: (630)897-7002

SCORE Office (Greater Belvidere)
419 S. State St.
Belvidere, IL 61008
(815)544-4357
Fax: (815)547-7654

SCORE Office (Bensenville)
1050 Busse Hwy. Suite 100
Bensenville, IL 60106
(708)350-2944
Fax: (708)350-2979

SCORE Office (Central Illinois)
402 N. Hershey Rd.
Bloomington, IL 61704
(309)644-0549
Fax: (309)663-8270
E-mail: webmaster@central-illinois-
score.org
Website: http://www.central-illinois-
score.org/

SCORE Office (Southern Illinois)
150 E. Pleasant Hill Rd.
Box 1
Carbondale, IL 62901
(618)453-6654
Fax: (618)453-5040

SCORE Office (Chicago)
Northwest Atrium Ctr.
500 W. Madison St., No. 1250
Chicago, IL 60661
(312)353-7724
Fax: (312)886-5688
Website: http://www.mcs.net/~bic/

SCORE Office (Chicago–Oliver Harvey College)
Pullman Bldg.
1000 E. 11th St., 7th Fl.
Chicago, IL 60628
Fax: (312)468-8086

SCORE Office (Danville)
28 W. N. Street
Danville, IL 61832
(217)442-7232
Fax: (217)442-6228

SCORE Office (Decatur)
Milliken University
1184 W. Main St.
Decatur, IL 62522
(217)424-6297
Fax: (217)424-3993
E-mail: charding@mail.millikin.edu
Website: http://www.millikin.edu/
academics/Tabor/score.html

SCORE Office (Downers Grove)
925 Curtis
Downers Grove, IL 60515
(708)968-4050
Fax: (708)968-8368

SCORE Office (Elgin)
24 E. Chicago, 3rd Fl.
PO Box 648
Elgin, IL 60120
(847)741-5660
Fax: (847)741-5677

SCORE Office (Freeport Area)
26 S. Galena Ave.
Freeport, IL 61032
(815)233-1350
Fax: (815)235-4038

SCORE Office (Galesburg)
292 E. Simmons St.
PO Box 749
Galesburg, IL 61401
(309)343-1194
Fax: (309)343-1195

SCORE Office (Glen Ellyn)
500 Pennsylvania
Glen Ellyn, IL 60137
(708)469-0907
Fax: (708)469-0426

SCORE Office (Greater Alton)
Alden Hall
5800 Godfrey Rd.
Godfrey, IL 62035-2466
(618)467-2280
Fax: (618)466-8289
Website: http://www.altonweb.com/
score/

SCORE Office (Grayslake)
19351 W. Washington St.
Grayslake, IL 60030
(708)223-3633
Fax: (708)223-9371

SCORE Office (Harrisburg)
303 S. Commercial
Harrisburg, IL 62946-1528
(618)252-8528
Fax: (618)252-0210

SCORE Office (Joliet)
100 N. Chicago
Joliet, IL 60432
(815)727-5371
Fax: (815)727-5374

SCORE Office (Kankakee)
101 S. Schuyler Ave.
Kankakee, IL 60901
(815)933-0376
Fax: (815)933-0380

SCORE Office (Macomb)
216 Seal Hall, Rm. 214

Macomb, IL 61455
(309)298-1128
Fax: (309)298-2520

SCORE Office (Matteson)
210 Lincoln Mall
Matteson, IL 60443
(708)709-3750
Fax: (708)503-9322

SCORE Office (Mattoon)
1701 Wabash Ave.
Mattoon, IL 61938
(217)235-5661
Fax: (217)234-6544

SCORE Office (Quad Cities)
622 19th St.
Moline, IL 61265
(309)797-0082
Fax: (309)757-5435
E-mail: score@qconline.com
Website: http://www.qconline.com/
business/score/

SCORE Office (Naperville)
131 W. Jefferson Ave.
Naperville, IL 60540
(708)355-4141
Fax: (708)355-8355

SCORE Office (Northbrook)
2002 Walters Ave.
Northbrook, IL 60062
(847)498-5555
Fax: (847)498-5510

SCORE Office (Palos Hills)
10900 S. 88th Ave.
Palos Hills, IL 60465
(847)974-5468
Fax: (847)974-0078

SCORE Office (Peoria)
124 SW Adams, Ste. 300
Peoria, IL 61602
(309)676-0755
Fax: (309)676-7534

SCORE Office (Prospect Heights)
1375 Wolf Rd.
Prospect Heights, IL 60070
(847)537-8660
Fax: (847)537-7138

SCORE Office (Quincy Tri-State)
300 Civic Center Plz., Ste. 245
Quincy, IL 62301
(217)222-8093
Fax: (217)222-3033

SCORE Office (River Grove)
2000 5th Ave.
River Grove, IL 60171
(708)456-0300
Fax: (708)583-3121

SCORE Office (Northern Illinois)
515 N. Court St.
Rockford, IL 61103
(815)962-0122
Fax: (815)962-0122

SCORE Office (St. Charles)
103 N. 1st Ave.
St. Charles, IL 60174-1982
(847)584-8384
Fax: (847)584-6065

SCORE Office (Springfield)
511 W. Capitol Ave., Ste. 302
Springfield, IL 62704
(217)492-4416
Fax: (217)492-4867

SCORE Office (Sycamore)
112 Somunak St.
Sycamore, IL 60178
(815)895-3456
Fax: (815)895-0125

SCORE Office (University)
Hwy. 50 & Stuenkel Rd. Ste. C3305
University Park, IL 60466
(708)534-5000
Fax: (708)534-8457

Indiana

SCORE Office (Anderson)
205 W. 11th St.
Anderson, IN 46015
(317)642-0264

SCORE Office (Bloomington)
Star Center
216 W. Allen
Bloomington, IN 47403
(812)335-7334
E-mail: wtfische@indiana.edu
Website: http://www.brainfreezemedia.
com/score527/

SCORE Office (South East Indiana)
500 Franklin St.
Box 29
Columbus, IN 47201
(812)379-4457

SCORE Office (Corydon)
310 N. Elm St.
Corydon, IN 47112

(812)738-2137
Fax: (812)738-6438

SCORE Office (Crown Point)
Old Courthouse Sq. Ste. 206
PO Box 43
Crown Point, IN 46307
(219)663-1800

SCORE Office (Elkhart)
418 S. Main St.
Elkhart, IN 46515
(219)293-1531
Fax: (219)294-1859

SCORE Office (Evansville)
1100 W. Lloyd Expy., Ste. 105
Evansville, IN 47708
(812)426-6144

SCORE Office (Fort Wayne)
1300 S. Harrison St.
Ft. Wayne, IN 46802
(219)422-2601
Fax: (219)422-2601

SCORE Office (Gary)
973 W. 6th Ave., Rm. 326
Gary, IN 46402
(219)882-3918

SCORE Office (Hammond)
7034 Indianapolis Blvd.
Hammond, IN 46324
(219)931-1000
Fax: (219)845-9548

SCORE Office (Indianapolis)
429 N. Pennsylvania St., Ste. 100
Indianapolis, IN 46204-1873
(317)226-7264
Fax: (317)226-7259
E-mail: inscore@indy.net
Website: http://www.score-
indianapolis.org/

SCORE Office (Jasper)
PO Box 307
Jasper, IN 47547-0307
(812)482-6866

**SCORE Office (Kokomo/Howard
Counties)**
106 N. Washington St.
Kokomo, IN 46901
(765)457-5301
Fax: (765)452-4564

SCORE Office (Logansport)
300 E. Broadway, Ste. 103
Logansport, IN 46947
(219)753-6388

SCORE Office (Madison)
301 E. Main St.
Madison, IN 47250
(812)265-3135
Fax: (812)265-2923

SCORE Office (Marengo)
Rt. 1 Box 224D
Marengo, IN 47140
Fax: (812)365-2793

SCORE Office (Marion/Grant Counties)
215 S. Adams
Marion, IN 46952
(765)664-5107

SCORE Office (Merrillville)
255 W. 80th Pl.
Merrillville, IN 46410
(219)769-8180
Fax: (219)736-6223

SCORE Office (Michigan City)
200 E. Michigan Blvd.
Michigan City, IN 46360
(219)874-6221
Fax: (219)873-1204

SCORE Office (South Central Indiana)
4100 Charleston Rd.
New Albany, IN 47150-9538
(812)945-0066

SCORE Office (Rensselaer)
104 W. Washington
Rensselaer, IN 47978

SCORE Office (Salem)
210 N. Main St.
Salem, IN 47167
(812)883-4303
Fax: (812)883-1467

SCORE Office (South Bend)
300 N. Michigan St.
South Bend, IN 46601
(219)282-4350
E-mail: chair@southbend-score.org
Website: http://www.southbend-score.org/

SCORE Office (Valparaiso)
150 Lincolnway
Valparaiso, IN 46383
(219)462-1105
Fax: (219)469-5710

SCORE Office (Vincennes)
27 N. 3rd
PO Box 553
Vincennes, IN 47591
(812)882-6440
Fax: (812)882-6441

SCORE Office (Wabash)
PO Box 371
Wabash, IN 46992
(219)563-1168
Fax: (219)563-6920

Iowa

SCORE Office (Burlington)
Federal Bldg.
300 N. Main St.
Burlington, IA 52601
(319)752-2967

SCORE Office (Cedar Rapids)
2750 1st Ave. NE, Ste 350
Cedar Rapids, IA 52401-1806
(319)362-6405
Fax: (319)362-7861
E:mail: score@scorecr.org
Website: http://www.scorecr.org

SCORE Office (Illowa)
333 4th Ave. S
Clinton, IA 52732
(319)242-5702

SCORE Office (Council Bluffs)
7 N. 6th St.
Council Bluffs, IA 51502
(712)325-1000

SCORE Office (Northeast Iowa)
3404 285th St.
Cresco, IA 52136
(319)547-3377

SCORE Office (Des Moines)
Federal Bldg., Rm. 749
210 Walnut St.
Des Moines, IA 50309-2186
(515)284-4760

SCORE Office (Ft. Dodge)
Federal Bldg., Rm. 436
205 S. 8th St.
Ft. Dodge, IA 50501
(515)955-2622

SCORE Office (Independence)
110 1st. St. east
Independence, IA 50644
(319)334-7178
Fax: (319)334-7179

SCORE Office (Iowa City)
210 Federal Bldg.
PO Box 1853
Iowa City, IA 52240-1853
(319)338-1662

SCORE Office (Keokuk)
401 Main St.
Pierce Bldg., No. 1
Keokuk, IA 52632
(319)524-5055

SCORE Office (Central Iowa)
Fisher Community College
709 S. Center
Marshalltown, IA 50158
(515)753-6645

SCORE Office (River City)
15 West State St.
Mason City, IA 50401
(515)423-5724

SCORE Office (South Central)
SBDC, Indian Hills Community College
525 Grandview Ave.
Ottumwa, IA 52501
(515)683-5127
Fax: (515)683-5263

SCORE Office (Dubuque)
10250 Sundown Rd.
Peosta, IA 52068
(319)556-5110

SCORE Office (Southwest Iowa)
614 W. Sheridan
Shenandoah, IA 51601
(712)246-3260

SCORE Office (Sioux City)
Federal Bldg.
320 6th St.
Sioux City, IA 51101
(712)277-2324
Fax: (712)277-2325

SCORE Office (Iowa Lakes)
122 W. 5th St.
Spencer, IA 51301
(712)262-3059

SCORE Office (Vista)
119 W. 6th St.
Storm Lake, IA 50588
(712)732-3780

SCORE Office (Waterloo)
215 E. 4th
Waterloo, IA 50703
(319)233-8431

Kansas

SCORE Office (Southwest Kansas)
501 W. Spruce
Dodge City, KS 67801
(316)227-3119

SCORE Office (Emporia)
811 Homewood
Emporia, KS 66801
(316)342-1600

SCORE Office (Golden Belt)
1307 Williams
Great Bend, KS 67530
(316)792-2401

SCORE Office (Hays)
PO Box 400
Hays, KS 67601
(913)625-6595

SCORE Office (Hutchinson)
1 E. 9th St.
Hutchinson, KS 67501
(316)665-8468
Fax: (316)665-7619

SCORE Office (Southeast Kansas)
404 Westminster Pl.
PO Box 886
Independence, KS 67301
(316)331-4741

SCORE Office (McPherson)
306 N. Main
PO Box 616
McPherson, KS 67460
(316)241-3303

SCORE Office (Salina)
120 Ash St.
Salina, KS 67401
(785)243-4290
Fax: (785)243-1833

SCORE Office (Topeka)
1700 College
Topeka, KS 66621
(785)231-1010

SCORE Office (Wichita)
100 E. English, Ste. 510
Wichita, KS 67202
(316)269-6273
Fax: (316)269-6499

SCORE Office (Ark Valley)
205 E. 9th St.
Winfield, KS 67156
(316)221-1617

Kentucky

SCORE Office (Ashland)
PO Box 830
Ashland, KY 41105
(606)329-8011
Fax: (606)325-4607

SCORE Office (Bowling Green)
812 State St.
PO Box 51
Bowling Green, KY 42101
(502)781-3200
Fax: (502)843-0458

SCORE Office (Tri-Lakes)
508 Barbee Way
Danville, KY 40422-1548
(606)231-9902

SCORE Office (Glasgow)
301 W. Main St.
Glasgow, KY 42141
(502)651-3161
Fax: (502)651-3122

SCORE Office (Hazard)
B & I Technical Center
100 Airport Gardens Rd.
Hazard, KY 41701
(606)439-5856
Fax: (606)439-1808

SCORE Office (Lexington)
410 W. Vine St., Ste. 290, Civic C
Lexington, KY 40507
(606)231-9902
Fax: (606)253-3190
E-mail: scorelex@uky.campus.mci.net

SCORE Office (Louisville)
188 Federal Office Bldg.
600 Dr. Martin L. King Jr. Pl.
Louisville, KY 40202
(502)582-5976

SCORE Office (Madisonville)
257 N. Main
Madisonville, KY 42431
(502)825-1399
Fax: (502)825-1396

SCORE Office (Paducah)
Federal Office Bldg.
501 Broadway, Rm. B-36
Paducah, KY 42001
(502)442-5685

Louisiana

SCORE Office (Central Louisiana)
802 3rd St.
Alexandria, LA 71309
(318)442-6671

SCORE Office (Baton Rouge)
564 Laurel St.
PO Box 3217
Baton Rouge, LA 70801

(504)381-7130
Fax: (504)336-4306

SCORE Office (North Shore)
2 W. Thomas
Hammond, LA 70401
(504)345-4457
Fax: (504)345-4749

SCORE Office (Lafayette)
804 St. Mary Blvd.
Lafayette, LA 70505-1307
(318)233-2705
Fax: (318)234-8671
E-mail: score302@aol.com

SCORE Office (Lake Charles)
120 W. Pujo St.
Lake Charles, LA 70601
(318)433-3632

SCORE Office (New Orleans)
365 Canal St., Ste. 3100
New Orleans, LA 70130
(504)589-2356
Fax: (504)589-2339

SCORE Office (Shreveport)
400 Edwards St.
Shreveport, LA 71101
(318)677-2536
Fax: (318)677-2541

Maine

SCORE Office (Augusta)
40 Western Ave.
Augusta, ME 04330
(207)622-8509

SCORE Office (Bangor)
Peabody Hall, Rm. 229
One College Cir.
Bangor, ME 04401
(207)941-9707

SCORE Office (Central & Northern Arroostock)
111 High St.
Caribou, ME 04736
(207)492-8010
Fax: (207)492-8010

SCORE Office (Penquis)
South St.
Dover Foxcroft, ME 04426
(207)564-7021

SCORE Office (Maine Coastal)
Mill Mall
Box 1105
Ellsworth, ME 04605-1105

(207)667-5800
E-mail: score@arcadia.net

SCORE Office (Lewiston-Auburn)
BIC of Maine-Bates Mill Complex
35 Canal St.
Lewiston, ME 04240-7764
(207)782-3708
Fax: (207)783-7745

SCORE Office (Portland)
66 Pearl St., Rm. 210
Portland, ME 04101
(207)772-1147
Fax: (207)772-5581
E-mail: Score53@score.maine.org
Website: http://www.score.maine.org/
chapter53/

SCORE Office (Western Mountains)
255 River St.
PO Box 252
Rumford, ME 04257-0252
(207)369-9976

SCORE Office (Oxford Hills)
166 Main St.
South Paris, ME 04281
(207)743-0499

Maryland

SCORE Office (Southern Maryland)
2525 Riva Rd., Ste. 110
Annapolis, MD 21401
(410)266-9553
Fax: (410)573-0981
E-mail: score390@aol.com
Website: http://members.aol.com/
score390/index.htm

SCORE Office (Baltimore)
The City Crescent Bldg., 6th Fl.
10 S. Howard St.
Baltimore, MD 21201
(410)962-2233
Fax: (410)962-1805

SCORE Office (Bel Air)
108 S. Bond St.
Bel Air, MD 21014
(410)838-2020
Fax: (410)893-4715

SCORE Office (Bethesda)
7910 Woodmont Ave., Ste. 1204
Bethesda, MD 20814
(301)652-4900
Fax: (301)657-1973

SCORE Office (Bowie)
6670 Race Track Rd.
Bowie, MD 20715
(301)262-0920
Fax: (301)262-0921

SCORE Office (Dorchester County)
203 Sunburst Hwy.
Cambridge, MD 21613
(410)228-3575

SCORE Office (Upper Shore)
210 Marlboro Ave.
Easton, MD 21601
(410)822-4606
Fax: (410)822-7922

SCORE Office (Frederick County)
43A S. Market St.
Frederick, MD 21701
(301)662-8723
Fax: (301)846-4427

SCORE Office (Gaithersburg)
9 Park Ave.
Gaithersburg, MD 20877
(301)840-1400
Fax: (301)963-3918

SCORE Office (Glen Burnie)
103 Crain Hwy. SE
Glen Burnie, MD 21061
(410)766-8282
Fax: (410)766-9722

SCORE Office (Hagerstown)
111 W. Washington St.
Hagerstown, MD 21740
(301)739-2015
Fax: (301)739-1278

SCORE Office (Laurel)
7901 Sandy Spring Rd. Ste. 501
Laurel, MD 20707
(301)725-4000
Fax: (301)725-0776

SCORE Office (Salisbury)
300 E. Main St.
Salisbury, MD 21801
(410)749-0185
Fax: (410)860-9925

Massachusetts

SCORE Office (NE Massachusetts)
100 Cummings Ctr., Ste. 101 K
Beverly, MA 01923
(978)922-9441
Website: http://www1.shore.net/~score/

SCORE Office (Boston)
10 Causeway St., Rm. 265
Boston, MA 02222-1093
(617)565-5591
Fax: (617)565-5598
E-mail: boston-score-20@worldnet.att.net
Website: http://www.scoreboston.org/

SCORE office (Bristol/Plymouth County)
53 N. 6th St., Federal Bldg.
Bristol, MA 02740
(508)994-5093

SCORE Office (SE Massachusetts)
60 School St.
Brockton, MA 02401
(508)587-2673
Fax: (508)587-1340
Website: http://www.metrosouth
chamber.com/score.html

SCORE Office (North Adams)
820 N. State Rd.
Cheshire, MA 01225
(413)743-5100

SCORE Office (Clinton Satellite)
1 Green St.
Clinton, MA 01510
Fax: (508)368-7689

SCORE Office (Greenfield)
PO Box 898
Greenfield, MA 01302
(413)773-5463
Fax: (413)773-7008

SCORE Office (Haverhill)
87 Winter St.
Haverhill, MA 01830
(508)373-5663
Fax: (508)373-8060

SCORE Office (Hudson Satellite)
PO Box 578
Hudson, MA 01749
(508)568-0360
Fax: (508)568-0360

SCORE Office (Cape Cod)
Independence Pk., Ste. 5B
270 Communications Way
Hyannis, MA 02601
(508)775-4884
Fax: (508)790-2540

SCORE Office (Lawrence)
264 Essex St.
Lawrence, MA 01840
(508)686-0900
Fax: (508)794-9953

SCORE Office (Leominster Satellite)
110 Erdman Way
Leominster, MA 01453
(508)840-4300
Fax: (508)840-4896

SCORE Office (Bristol/Plymouth Counties)
53 N. 6th St., Federal Bldg.
New Bedford, MA 02740
(508)994-5093

SCORE Office (Newburyport)
29 State St.
Newburyport, MA 01950
(617)462-6680

SCORE Office (Pittsfield)
66 West St.
Pittsfield, MA 01201
(413)499-2485

SCORE Office (Haverhill-Salem)
32 Derby Sq.
Salem, MA 01970
(508)745-0330
Fax: (508)745-3855

SCORE Office (Springfield)
1350 Main St.
Federal Bldg.
Springfield, MA 01103
(413)785-0314

SCORE Office (Carver)
12 Taunton Green, Ste. 201
Taunton, MA 02780
(508)824-4068
Fax: (508)824-4069

SCORE Office (Worcester)
33 Waldo St.
Worcester, MA 01608
(508)753-2929
Fax: (508)754-8560

Michigan

SCORE Office (Allegan)
PO Box 338
Allegan, MI 49010
(616)673-2479

SCORE Office (Ann Arbor)
425 S. Main St., Ste. 103
Ann Arbor, MI 48104
(313)665-4433

SCORE Office (Battle Creek)
34 W. Jackson Ste. 4A
Battle Creek, MI 49017-3505

(616)962-4076
Fax: (616)962-6309

SCORE Office (Cadillac)
222 Lake St.
Cadillac, MI 49601
(616)775-9776
Fax: (616)768-4255

SCORE Office (Detroit)
477 Michigan Ave., Rm. 515
Detroit, MI 48226
(313)226-7947
Fax: (313)226-3448

SCORE Office (Flint)
708 Root Rd., Rm. 308
Flint, MI 48503
(810)233-6846

SCORE Office (Grand Rapids)
111 Pearl St. NW
Grand Rapids, MI 49503-2831
(616)771-0305
Fax: (616)771-0328
E-mail: scoreone@iserv.net
Website: http://www.iserv.net/
~scoreone/

SCORE Office (Holland)
480 State St.
Holland, MI 49423
(616)396-9472

SCORE Office (Jackson)
209 East Washington
PO Box 80
Jackson, MI 49204
(517)782-8221
Fax: (517)782-0061

SCORE Office (Kalamazoo)
345 W. Michigan Ave.
Kalamazoo, MI 49007
(616)381-5382
Fax: (616)384-0096
E-mail: score@nucleus.net

SCORE Office (Lansing)
117 E. Allegan
PO Box 14030
Lansing, MI 48901
(517)487-6340
Fax: (517)484-6910

SCORE Office (Livonia)
15401 Farmington Rd.
Livonia, MI 48154
(313)427-2122
Fax: (313)427-6055

SCORE Office (Madison Heights)
26345 John R
Madison Heights, MI 48071
(810)542-5010
Fax: (810)542-6821

SCORE Office (Monroe)
111 E. 1st
Monroe, MI 48161
(313)242-3366
Fax: (313)242-7253

SCORE Office (Mt. Clemens)
58 S/B Gratiot
Mt. Clemens, MI 48043
(810)463-1528
Fax: (810)463-6541

SCORE Office (Muskegon)
PO Box 1087
230 Terrace Plz.
Muskegon, MI 49443
(616)722-3751
Fax: (616)728-7251

SCORE Office (Petoskey)
401 E. Mitchell St.
Petoskey, MI 49770
(616)347-4150

SCORE Office (Pontiac)
Executive Office Bldg.
1200 N. Telegraph Rd.
Pontiac, MI 48341
(810)975-9555

SCORE Office (Pontiac)
PO Box 430025
Pontiac, MI 48343
(810)335-9600

SCORE Office (Port Huron)
920 Pinegrove Ave.
Port Huron, MI 48060
(810)985-7101

SCORE Office (Rochester)
71 Walnut Ste. 110
Rochester, MI 48307
(810)651-6700
Fax: (810)651-5270

SCORE Office (Saginaw)
901 S. Washington Ave.
Saginaw, MI 48601
(517)752-7161
Fax: (517)752-9055

SCORE Office (Upper Peninsula)
2581 I-75 Business Spur
Sault Ste. Marie, MI 49783
(906)632-3301

SCORE Office (Southfield)
21000 W. 10 Mile Rd.
Southfield, MI 48075
(810)204-3050
Fax: (810)204-3099

SCORE Office (Traverse City)
202 E. Grandview Pkwy.
PO Box 387
Traverse City, MI 49685
(616)947-5075
Fax: (616)946-2565

SCORE Office (Warren)
30500 Van Dyke, Ste. 118
Warren, MI 48093
(810)751-3939

Minnesota

SCORE Office (Aitkin)
Aitkin, MN 56431
(218)741-3906

SCORE Office (Albert Lea)
202 N. Broadway Ave.
Albert Lea, MN 56007
(507)373-7487

SCORE Office (Austin)
PO Box 864
Austin, MN 55912
(507)437-4561
Fax: (507)437-4869

SCORE Office (South Metro)
Ames Business Ctr.
2500 W. County Rd., No. 42
Burnsville, MN 55337
(612)898-5645
Fax: (612)435-6972
E-mail: southmetro@scoreminn.org
Website: http://www.scoreminn.org/
southmetro/

SCORE Office (Duluth)
1717 Minnesota Ave.
Duluth, MN 55802
(218)727-8286
Fax: (218)727-3113
E-mail: duluth@scoreminn.org
Website: http://www.scoreminn.org

SCORE Office (Fairmont)
PO Box 826
Fairmont, MN 56031
(507)235-5547
Fax: (507)235-8411

SCORE Office (Southwest Minnesota)
112 Riverfront St.

Box 999
Mankato, MN 56001
(507)345-4519
Fax: (507)345-4451
Website: http://www.scoreminn.org/

SCORE Office (Minneapolis)
North Plaza Bldg., Ste. 51
5217 Wayzata Blvd.
Minneapolis, MN 55416
(612)591-0539
Fax: (612)544-0436
Website: http://www.scoreminn.org/

SCORE Office (Owatonna)
PO Box 331
Owatonna, MN 55060
(507)451-7970
Fax: (507)451-7972

SCORE Office (Red Wing)
2000 W. Main St., Ste. 324
Red Wing, MN 55066
(612)388-4079

SCORE Office (Southeastern Minnesota)
220 S. Broadway, Ste. 100
Rochester, MN 55901
(507)288-1122
Fax: (507)282-8960
Website: http://www.scoreminn.org/

SCORE Office (Brainerd)
St. Cloud, MN 56301

SCORE Office (Central Area)
1527 Northway Dr.
St. Cloud, MN 56301
(320)240-1332
Fax: (320)255-9050
Website: http://www.scoreminn.org/

SCORE Office (St. Paul)
350 St. Peter St., No. 295
Lowry Professional Bldg.
St. Paul, MN 55102
(651)223-5010
Fax: (651)223-5048
Website: http://www.scoreminn.org/

SCORE Office (Winona)
Box 870
Winona, MN 55987
(507)452-2272
Fax: (507)454-8814

SCORE Office (Worthington)
1121 3rd Ave.
Worthington, MN 56187
(507)372-2919
Fax: (507)372-2827

Mississippi

SCORE Office (Delta)
915 Washington Ave.
PO Box 933
Greenville, MS 38701
(601)378-3141

SCORE Office (Gulfcoast)
1 Government Plaza
2909 13th St., Ste. 203
Gulfport, MS 39501
(228)863-0054

SCORE Office (Jackson)
1st Jackson Center, Ste. 400
101 W. Capitol St.
Jackson, MS 39201
(601)965-5533

SCORE Office (Meridian)
5220 16th Ave.
Meridian, MS 39305
(601)482-4412

Missouri

SCORE Office (Lake of the Ozark)
University Extension
113 Kansas St.
PO Box 1405
Camdenton, MO 65020
(573)346-2644
Fax: (573)346-2694
E-mail: score@cdoc.net
Website: http://sites.cdoc.net/score/

Chamber of Commerce (Cape Girardeau)
PO Box 98
Cape Girardeau, MO 63702-0098
(314)335-3312

SCORE Office (Mid-Missouri)
1705 Halstead Ct.
Columbia, MO 65203
(573)874-1132

SCORE Office (Ozark-Gateway)
1486 Glassy Rd.
Cuba, MO 65453-1640
(573)885-4954

SCORE Office (Kansas City)
323 W. 8th St., Ste. 104
Kansas City, MO 64105
(816)374-6675
Fax: (816)374-6692
E-mail: SCOREBIC@AOL.COM
Website: http://www.crn.org/score/

SCORE Office (Sedalia)
Lucas Place
323 W. 8th St., Ste.104
Kansas City, MO 64105
(816)374-6675

SCORE office (Tri-Lakes)
PO Box 1148
Kimberling, MO 65686
(417)739-3041

SCORE Office (Tri-Lakes)
HCRI Box 85
Lampe, MO 65681
(417)858-6798

SCORE Office (Mexico)
111 N. Washington St.
Mexico, MO 65265
(314)581-2765

SCORE Office (Southeast Missouri)
Rte. 1, Box 280
Neelyville, MO 63954
(573)989-3577

SCORE office (Poplar Bluff Area)
806 Emma St.
Poplar Bluff, MO 63901
(573)686-8892

SCORE Office (St. Joseph)
3003 Frederick Ave.
St. Joseph, MO 64506
(816)232-4461

SCORE Office (St. Louis)
815 Olive St., Rm. 242
St. Louis, MO 63101-1569
(314)539-6970
Fax: (314)539-3785
E-mail: info@stlscore.org
Website: http://www.stlscore.org/

SCORE Office (Lewis & Clark)
425 Spencer Rd.
St. Peters, MO 63376
(314)928-2900
Fax: (314)928-2900
E-mail: score01@mail.win.org

SCORE Office (Springfield)
620 S. Glenstone, Ste. 110
Springfield, MO 65802-3200
(417)864-7670
Fax: (417)864-4108

SCORE office (Southeast Kansas)
1206 W. First St.
Webb City, MO 64870
(417)673-3984

Montana

SCORE Office (Billings)
815 S. 27th St.
Billings, MT 59101
(406)245-4111

SCORE Office (Bozeman)
1205 E. Main St.
Bozeman, MT 59715
(406)586-5421

SCORE Office (Butte)
1000 George St.
Butte, MT 59701
(406)723-3177

SCORE Office (Great Falls)
710 First Ave. N
Great Falls, MT 59401
(406)761-4434
E-mail: scoregtf@in.tch.com

SCORE Office (Havre, Montana)
518 First St.
Havre, MT 59501
(406)265-4383

SCORE Office (Helena)
Federal Bldg.
301 S. Park
Helena, MT 59626-0054
(406)441-1081

SCORE Office (Kalispell)
2 Main St.
Kalispell, MT 59901
(406)756-5271
Fax: (406)752-6665

SCORE Office (Missoula)
723 Ronan
Missoula, MT 59806
(406)327-8806
E-mail: score@safeshop.com
Website: http://missoula.bigsky.net/
score/

Nebraska

SCORE Office (Columbus)
Columbus, NE 68601
(402)564-2769

SCORE Office (Fremont)
92 W. 5th St.
Fremont, NE 68025
(402)721-2641

SCORE Office (Hastings)
Hastings, NE 68901
(402)463-3447

SCORE Office (Lincoln)
8800 O St.
Lincoln, NE 68520
(402)437-2409

SCORE Office (Panhandle)
150549 CR 30
Minatare, NE 69356
(308)632-2133
Website: http://www.tandt.com/
SCORE

SCORE Office (Norfolk)
3209 S. 48th Ave.
Norfolk, NE 68106
(402)564-2769

SCORE Office (North Platte)
3301 W. 2nd St.
North Platte, NE 69101
(308)532-4466

SCORE Office (Omaha)
11145 Mill Valley Rd.
Omaha, NE 68154
(402)221-3606
Fax: (402)221-3680
E-mail: infoctr@ne.uswest.net
Website: http://www.tandt.com/score/

Nevada

SCORE Office (Incline Village)
969 Tahoe Blvd.
Incline Village, NV 89451
(702)831-7327
Fax: (702)832-1605

SCORE Office (Carson City)
301 E. Stewart
PO Box 7527
Las Vegas, NV 89125
(702)388-6104

SCORE Office (Las Vegas)
300 Las Vegas Blvd. S, Ste. 1100
Las Vegas, NV 89101
(702)388-6104

SCORE Office (Northern Nevada)
SBDC, College of Business
Administration
Univ. of Nevada
Reno, NV 89557-0100
(702)784-4436
Fax: (702)784-4337

New Hampshire

SCORE Office (North Country)
PO Box 34

Berlin, NH 03570
(603)752-1090

SCORE Office (Concord)
143 N. Main St., Rm. 202A
PO Box 1258
Concord, NH 03301
(603)225-1400
Fax: (603)225-1409

SCORE Office (Dover)
299 Central Ave.
Dover, NH 03820
(603)742-2218
Fax: (603)749-6317

SCORE Office (Monadnock)
34 Mechanic St.
Keene, NH 03431-3421
(603)352-0320

SCORE Office (Lakes Region)
67 Water St., Ste. 105
Laconia, NH 03246
(603)524-9168

SCORE Office (Upper Valley)
Citizens Bank Bldg., Rm. 310
20 W. Park St.
Lebanon, NH 03766
(603)448-3491
Fax: (603)448-1908
E-mail: billt@valley.net
Website: http://www.valley.net/~score/

SCORE Office (Merrimack Valley)
275 Chestnut St., Rm. 618
Manchester, NH 03103
(603)666-7561
Fax: (603)666-7925

SCORE Office (Mt. Washington Valley)
PO Box 1066
North Conway, NH 03818
(603)383-0800

SCORE Office (Seacoast)
195 Commerce Way, Unit-A
Portsmouth, NH 03801-3251
(603)433-0575

New Jersey

SCORE Office (Somerset)
Paritan Valley Community College,
Rte. 28
Branchburg, NJ 08807
(908)218-8874
E-mail: nj-score@grizbiz.com.
Website: http://www.nj-score.org/

SCORE Office (Chester)
5 Old Mill Rd.
Chester, NJ 07930
(908)879-7080

**SCORE Office
(Greater Princeton)**
4 A George Washington Dr.
Cranbury, NJ 08512
(609)520-1776

SCORE Office (Freehold)
36 W. Main St.
Freehold, NJ 07728
(908)462-3030
Fax: (908)462-2123

SCORE Office (North West)
Picantinny Innovation Ctr.
3159 Schrader Rd.
Hamburg, NJ 07419
(973)209-8525
Fax: (973)209-7252
E-mail: nj-score@grizbiz.com
Website: http://www.nj-score.org/

SCORE Office (Monmouth)
765 Newman Springs Rd.
Lincroft, NJ 07738
(908)224-2573
E-mail: nj-score@grizbiz.com
Website: http://www.nj-score.org/

SCORE Office (Manalapan)
125 Symmes Dr.
Manalapan, NJ 07726
(908)431-7220

SCORE Office (Jersey City)
2 Gateway Ctr., 4th Fl.
Newark, NJ 07102
(973)645-3982
Fax: (973)645-2375

SCORE Office (Newark)
2 Gateway Center, 15th Fl.
Newark, NJ 07102-5553
(973)645-3982
Fax: (973)645-2375
E-mail: nj-score@grizbiz.com
Website: http://www.nj-score.org

SCORE Office (Bergen County)
327 E. Ridgewood Ave.
Paramus, NJ 07652
(201)599-6090
E-mail: nj-score@grizbiz.com
Website: http://www.nj-score.org/

SCORE Office (Pennsauken)
4900 Rte. 70

Pennsauken, NJ 08109
(609)486-3421

SCORE Office (Southern New Jersey)
4900 Rte. 70
Pennsauken, NJ 08109
(609)486-3421
E-mail: nj-score@grizbiz.com
Website: http://www.nj-score.org/

SCORE Office (Greater Princeton)
216 Rockingham Row
Princeton Forrestal Village
Princeton, NJ 08540
(609)520-1776
Fax: (609)520-9107
E-mail: nj-score@grizbiz.com
Website: http://www.nj-score.org/

SCORE Office (Shrewsbury)
Hwy. 35
Shrewsbury, NJ 07702
(908)842-5995
Fax: (908)219-6140

SCORE Office (Ocean County)
33 Washington St.
Toms River, NJ 08754
(732)505-6033
E-mail: nj-score@grizbiz.com
Website: http://www.nj-score.org/

SCORE Office (Wall)
2700 Allaire Rd.
Wall, NJ 07719
(908)449-8877

SCORE Office (Wayne)
2055 Hamburg Tpke.
Wayne, NJ 07470
(201)831-7788
Fax: (201)831-9112

New Mexico

SCORE Office (Albuquerque)
525 Buena Vista, SE
Albuquerque, NM 87106
(505)272-7999
Fax: (505)272-7963

SCORE Office (Las Cruces)
Loretto Towne Center
505 S. Main St., Ste. 125
Las Cruces, NM 88001
(505)523-5627
Fax: (505)524-2101
E-mail: score.397@zianet.com

SCORE Office (Roswell)
Federal Bldg., Rm. 237

Roswell, NM 88201
(505)625-2112
Fax: (505)623-2545

SCORE Office (Santa Fe)
Montoya Federal Bldg.
120 Federal Place, Rm. 307
Santa Fe, NM 87501
(505)988-6302
Fax: (505)988-6300

New York

SCORE Office (Northeast)
1 Computer Dr. S
Albany, NY 12205
(518)446-1118
Fax: (518)446-1228

SCORE Office (Auburn)
30 South St.
PO Box 675
Auburn, NY 13021
(315)252-7291

SCORE Office (South Tier Binghamton)
Metro Center, 2nd Fl.
49 Court St.
PO Box 995
Binghamton, NY 13902
(607)772-8860

SCORE Office (Queens County City)
12055 Queens Blvd., Rm. 333
Borough Hall, NY 11424
(718)263-8961

SCORE Office (Buffalo)
Federal Bldg., Rm. 1311
111 W. Huron St.
Buffalo, NY 14202
(716)551-4301
Website: http://www2.pcom.net/score/
buf45.html

SCORE Office (Canandaigua)
Chamber of Commerce Bldg.
113 S. Main St.
Canandaigua, NY 14424
(716)394-4400
Fax: (716)394-4546

SCORE Office (Chemung)
333 E. Water St., 4th Fl.
Elmira, NY 14901
(607)734-3358

SCORE Office (Geneva)
Chamber of Commerce Bldg.
PO Box 587

Geneva, NY 14456
(315)789-1776
Fax: (315)789-3993

SCORE Office (Glens Falls)
84 Broad St.
Glens Falls, NY 12801
(518)798-8463
Fax: (518)745-1433

SCORE Office (Orange County)
40 Matthews St.
Goshen, NY 10924
(914)294-8080
Fax: (914)294-6121

SCORE Office (Huntington Area)
151 W. Carver St.
Huntington, NY 11743
(516)423-6100

SCORE Office (Tompkins County)
904 E. Shore Dr.
Ithaca, NY 14850
(607)273-7080

SCORE Office (Long Island City)
120-55 Queens Blvd.
Jamaica, NY 11424
(718)263-8961
Fax: (718)263-9032

SCORE Office (Chatauqua)
101 W. 5th St.
Jamestown, NY 14701
(716)484-1103

SCORE Office (Westchester)
2 Caradon Ln.
Katonah, NY 10536
(914)948-3907
Fax: (914)948-4645
E-mail: score@w-w-w.com
Website: http://w-w-w.com/score/

SCORE Office (Queens County)
Queens Borough Hall
120-55 Queens Blvd. Rm. 333
Kew Gardens, NY 11424
(718)263-8961
Fax: (718)263-9032

SCORE Office (Brookhaven)
3233 Rte. 112
Medford, NY 11763
(516)451-6563
Fax: (516)451-6925

SCORE Office (Melville)
35 Pinelawn Rd., Rm. 207-W
Melville, NY 11747
(516)454-0771

SCORE Office (Nassau County)
400 County Seat Dr., No. 140
Mineola, NY 11501
(516)571-3303
E-mail: Counse1998@aol.com
Website: http://members.aol.com/
Counse1998/Default.htm

SCORE Office (Mt. Vernon)
4 N. 7th Ave.
Mt. Vernon, NY 10550
(914)667-7500

SCORE Office (New York)
26 Federal Plz., Rm. 3100
New York, NY 10278
(212)264-4507
Fax: (212)264-4963
E-mail: score1000@erols.com
Website: http://users.erols.com/
score-nyc/

SCORE Office (Newburgh)
47 Grand St.
Newburgh, NY 12550
(914)562-5100

SCORE Office (Owego)
188 Front St.
Owego, NY 13827
(607)687-2020

SCORE Office (Peekskill)
1 S. Division St.
Peekskill, NY 10566
(914)737-3600
Fax: (914)737-0541

SCORE Office (Penn Yan)
2375 Rte. 14A
Penn Yan, NY 14527
(315)536-3111

SCORE Office (Dutchess)
110 Main St.
Poughkeepsie, NY 12601
(914)454-1700

SCORE Office (Rochester)
601 Keating Federal Bldg., Rm. 410
100 State St.
Rochester, NY 14614
(716)263-6473
Fax: (716)263-3146
Website: http://www.ggw.org/score/

SCORE Office (Saranac Lake)
30 Main St.
Saranac Lake, NY 12983
(315)448-0415

SCORE Office (Suffolk)
286 Main St.
Setauket, NY 11733
(516)751-3886

SCORE Office (Staten Island)
130 Bay St.
Staten Island, NY 10301
(718)727-1221

SCORE Office (Ulster)
Clinton Bldg., Rm. 107
Stone Ridge, NY 12484
(914)687-5035
Fax: (914)687-5015
Website: http://www.scoreulster.org/

SCORE Office (Syracuse)
401 S. Salina, 5th Fl.
Syracuse, NY 13202
(315)471-9393

SCORE Office (Utica)
SUNY Institute of Technology, Route 12
Utica, NY 13504-3050
(315)792-7553

SCORE Office (Watertown)
518 Davidson St.
Watertown, NY 13601
(315)788-1200
Fax: (315)788-8251

North Carolina

SCORE office (Asheboro)
317 E. Dixie Dr.
Asheboro, NC 27203
(336)626-2626
Fax: (336)626-7077

SCORE Office (Asheville)
Federal Bldg., Rm. 259
151 Patton
Asheville, NC 28801-5770
(828)271-4786
Fax: (828)271-4009

SCORE Office (Chapel Hill)
104 S. Estes Dr.
PO Box 2897
Chapel Hill, NC 27514
(919)967-7075

SCORE Office (Coastal Plains)
PO Box 2897
Chapel Hill, NC 27515
(919)967-7075
Fax: (919)968-6874

SCORE Office (Charlotte)
200 N. College St., Ste. A-2015

Charlotte, NC 28202
(704)344-6576
Fax: (704)344-6769
E-mail: CharlotteSCORE47@AOL.com
Website: http://www.charweb.org/
business/score/

SCORE Office (Durham)
411 W. Chapel Hill St.
Durham, NC 27707
(919)541-2171

SCORE Office (Gastonia)
PO Box 2168
Gastonia, NC 28053
(704)864-2621
Fax: (704)854-8723

SCORE Office (Greensboro)
400 W. Market St., Ste. 103
Greensboro, NC 27401-2241
(910)333-5399

SCORE Office (Henderson)
PO Box 917
Henderson, NC 27536
(919)492-2061
Fax: (919)430-0460

SCORE Office (Hendersonville)
Federal Bldg., Rm. 108
W. 4th Ave. & Church St.
Hendersonville, NC 28792
(828)693-8702
E-mail: score@circle.net
Website: http://www.wncguide.com/
score/Welcome.html

SCORE Office (Unifour)
PO Box 1828
Hickory, NC 28603
(704)328-6111

SCORE Office (High Point)
1101 N. Main St.
High Point, NC 27262
(336)882-8625
Fax: (336)889-9499

SCORE Office (Outer Banks)
Collington Rd. and Mustain
Kill Devil Hills, NC 27948
(252)441-8144

SCORE Office (Down East)
312 S. Front St., Ste. 6
New Bern, NC 28560
(252)633-6688
Fax: (252)633-9608

SCORE Office (Kinston)
PO Box 95

New Bern, NC 28561
(919)633-6688

SCORE Office (Raleigh)
Century Post Office Bldg., Ste. 306
300 Federal St. Mall
Raleigh, NC 27601
(919)856-4739
E-mail: jendres@ibm.net
Website: http://www.intrex.net/score96/
score96.htm

SCORE Office (Sanford)
1801 Nash St.
Sanford, NC 27330
(919)774-6442
Fax: (919)776-8739

SCORE Office (Sandhills Area)
1480 Hwy. 15-501
PO Box 458
Southern Pines, NC 28387
(910)692-3926

SCORE Office (Wilmington)
Corps of Engineers Bldg.
96 Darlington Ave., Ste. 207
Wilmington, NC 28403
(910)815-4576
Fax: (910)815-4658

North Dakota

SCORE Office
(Bismarck-Mandan)
700 E. Main Ave., 2nd Fl.
PO Box 5509
Bismarck, ND 58506-5509
(701)250-4303

SCORE Office (Fargo)
657 2nd Ave., Rm. 225
Fargo, ND 58108-3083
(701)239-5677

SCORE Office (Upper Red River)
4275 Technology Dr., Rm. 156
Grand Forks, ND 58202-8372
(701)777-3051

SCORE Office (Minot)
100 1st St. SW
Minot, ND 58701-3846
(701)852-6883
Fax: (701)852-6905

Ohio

SCORE Office (Akron)
1 Cascade Plz., 7th Fl.
Akron, OH 44308

(330)379-3163
Fax: (330)379-3164

SCORE Office (Ashland)
Gill Center
47 W. Main St.
Ashland, OH 44805
(419)281-4584

SCORE Office (Canton)
116 Cleveland Ave. NW, Ste. 601
Canton, OH 44702-1720
(330)453-6047

SCORE Office (Chillicothe)
165 S. Paint St.
Chillicothe, OH 45601
(614)772-4530

SCORE Office (Cincinnati)
Ameritrust Bldg., Rm. 850
525 Vine St.
Cincinnati, OH 45202
(513)684-2812
Fax: (513)684-3251
Website: http://www.score.
chapter34.org/

SCORE Office (Cleveland)
Eaton Center, Ste. 620
1100 Superior Ave.
Cleveland, OH 44114-2507
(216)522-4194
Fax: (216)522-4844

SCORE Office (Columbus)
2 Nationwide Plz., Ste. 1400
Columbus, OH 43215-2542
(614)469-2357
Fax: (614)469-2391
E-mail: info@scorecolumbus.org
Website: http://www.scorecolumbus.org/

SCORE Office (Dayton)
Dayton Federal Bldg., Rm. 505
200 W. Second St.
Dayton, OH 45402-1430
(513)225-2887
Fax: (513)225-7667

SCORE Office (Defiance)
615 W. 3rd St.
PO Box 130
Defiance, OH 43512
(419)782-7946

SCORE Office (Findlay)
123 E. Main Cross St.
PO Box 923
Findlay, OH 45840
(419)422-3314

SCORE Office (Lima)
147 N. Main St.
Lima, OH 45801
(419)222-6045
Fax: (419)229-0266

SCORE Office (Mansfield)
55 N. Mulberry St.
Mansfield, OH 44902
(419)522-3211

SCORE Office (Marietta)
Thomas Hall
Marietta, OH 45750
(614)373-0268

SCORE Office (Medina)
County Administrative Bldg.
144 N. Broadway
Medina, OH 44256
(216)764-8650

SCORE Office (Licking County)
50 W. Locust St.
Newark, OH 43055
(614)345-7458

SCORE Office (Salem)
2491 State Rte. 45 S
Salem, OH 44460
(216)332-0361

SCORE Office (Tiffin)
62 S. Washington St.
Tiffin, OH 44883
(419)447-4141
Fax: (419)447-5141

SCORE Office (Toledo)
608 Madison Ave, Ste. 910
Toledo, OH 43624
(419)259-7598
Fax: (419)259-6460

SCORE Office (Heart of Ohio)
377 W. Liberty St.
Wooster, OH 44691
(330)262-5735
Fax: (330)262-5745

SCORE Office (Youngstown)
306 Williamson Hall
Youngstown, OH 44555
(330)746-2687

Oklahoma

SCORE Office (Anadarko)
PO Box 366
Anadarko, OK 73005
(405)247-6651

SCORE Office (Ardmore)
410 W. Main
Ardmore, OK 73401
(580)226-2620

SCORE Office (Northeast Oklahoma)
210 S. Main
Grove, OK 74344
(918)787-2796
Fax: (918)787-2796
E-mail: Score595@greencis.net

SCORE Office (Lawton)
4500 W. Lee Blvd., Bldg. 100, Ste. 107
Lawton, OK 73505
(580)353-8727
Fax: (580)250-5677

SCORE Office (Oklahoma City)
210 Park Ave., No. 1300
Oklahoma City, OK 73102
(405)231-5163
Fax: (405)231-4876
E-mail: score212@usa.net

SCORE Office (Stillwater)
439 S. Main
Stillwater, OK 74074
(405)372-5573
Fax: (405)372-4316

SCORE Office (Tulsa)
616 S. Boston, Ste. 406
Tulsa, OK 74119
(918)581-7462
Fax: (918)581-6908
Website: http://www.ionet.net/~tulscore/

Oregon

SCORE Office (Bend)
63085 N. Hwy. 97
Bend, OR 97701
(541)923-2849
Fax: (541)330-6900

SCORE Office (Willamette)
1401 Willamette St.
PO Box 1107
Eugene, OR 97401-4003
(541)465-6600
Fax: (541)484-4942

SCORE Office (Florence)
3149 Oak St.
Florence, OR 97439
(503)997-8444
Fax: (503)997-8448

SCORE Office (Southern Oregon)
33 N. Central Ave., Ste. 216

Medford, OR 97501
(541)776-4220
E-mail: pgr134f@prodigy.com

SCORE Office (Portland)
1515 SW 5th Ave., Ste. 1050
Portland, OR 97201
(503)326-3441
Fax: (503)326-2808
E-mail: gr134@prodigy.com

SCORE Office (Salem)
416 State St. (corner of Liberty)
Salem, OR 97301
(503)370-2896

Pennsylvania

SCORE Office (Altoona-Blair)
1212 12th Ave.
Altoona, PA 16601-3493
(814)943-8151

SCORE Office (Lehigh Valley)
Rauch Bldg. 37
Lehigh University
621 Taylor St.
Bethlehem, PA 18015
(610)758-4496
Fax: (610)758-5205

SCORE Office (Butler County)
100 N. Main St.
PO Box 1082
Butler, PA 16003
(412)283-2222
Fax: (412)283-0224

SCORE Office (Harrisburg)
4211 Trindle Rd.
Camp Hill, PA 17011
(717)761-4304
Fax: (717)761-4315

SCORE Office (Cumberland Valley)
75 S. 2nd St.
Chambersburg, PA 17201
(717)264-2935

SCORE Office (Monroe County-Stroudsburg)
556 Main St.
East Stroudsburg, PA 18301
(717)421-4433

SCORE Office (Erie)
120 W. 9th St.
Erie, PA 16501
(814)871-5650
Fax: (814)871-7530

SCORE Office (Bucks County)
409 Hood Blvd.
Fairless Hills, PA 19030
(215)943-8850
Fax: (215)943-7404

SCORE Office (Hanover)
146 Broadway
Hanover, PA 17331
(717)637-6130
Fax: (717)637-9127

SCORE Office (Harrisburg)
100 Chestnut, Ste. 309
Harrisburg, PA 17101
(717)782-3874

SCORE Office (East Montgomery County)
Baederwood Shopping Center
1653 The Fairways, Ste. 204
Jenkintown, PA 19046
(215)885-3027

SCORE Office (Kittanning)
2 Butler Rd.
Kittanning, PA 16201
(412)543-1305
Fax: (412)543-6206

SCORE Office (Lancaster)
118 W. Chestnut St.
Lancaster, PA 17603
(717)397-3092

SCORE Office (Westmoreland County)
300 Fraser Purchase Rd.
Latrobe, PA 15650-2690
(412)539-7505
Fax: (412)539-1850

SCORE Office (Lebanon)
252 N. 8th St.
PO Box 899
Lebanon, PA 17042-0899
(717)273-3727
Fax: (717)273-7940

SCORE Office (Lewistown)
3 W. Monument Sq., Ste. 204
Lewistown, PA 17044
(717)248-6713
Fax: (717)248-6714

SCORE Office (Delaware County)
602 E. Baltimore Pike
Media, PA 19063
(610)565-3677
Fax: (610)565-1606

SCORE Office (Milton Area)
112 S. Front St.
Milton, PA 17847

(717)742-7341
Fax: (717)792-2008

SCORE Office (Mon-Valley)
435 Donner Ave.
Monessen, PA 15062
(412)684-4277
Fax: (412)684-7688

SCORE Office (Monroeville)
William Penn Plaza
2790 Mosside Blvd., Ste. 295
Monroeville, PA 15146
(412)856-0622
Fax: (412)856-1030

SCORE Office (Airport Area)
986 Brodhead Rd.
Moon Township, PA 15108-2398
(412)264-6270
Fax: (412)264-1575

SCORE Office (Northeast)
8601 E. Roosevelt Blvd.
Philadelphia, PA 19152
(215)332-3400
Fax: (215)332-6050

SCORE Office (Philadelphia)
1315 Walnut St., Ste. 500
Philadelphia, PA 19107
(215)790-5050
Fax: (215)790-5057
E-mail: score46@bellatlantic.net
Website: http://www.pgweb.net/score46/

SCORE Office (Pittsburgh)
1000 Liberty Ave., Rm. 1122
Pittsburgh, PA 15222
(412)395-6560
Fax: (412)395-6562

SCORE Office (Tri-County)
801 N. Charlotte St.
Pottstown, PA 19464
(610)327-2673

SCORE Office (Reading)
601 Penn St.
Reading, PA 19601
(610)376-3497

SCORE Office (Scranton)
Oppenheim Bldg.
116 N. Washington Ave., Ste. 650
Scranton, PA 18503
(717)347-4611
Fax: (717)347-4611

SCORE Office (Central Pennsylvania)
200 Innovation Blvd., Ste. 242-B
State College, PA 16803

(814)234-9415
Fax: (814)238-9686
Website: http://countrystore.org/
business/score.htm

SCORE Office (Monroe-Stroudsburg)
556 Main St.
Stroudsburg, PA 18360
(717)421-4433

SCORE Office (Uniontown)
Federal Bldg.
Pittsburg St.
PO Box 2065 DTS
Uniontown, PA 15401
(412)437-4222
E-mail: uniontownscore@lcsys.net

SCORE Office (Warren County)
315 2nd Ave.
Warren, PA 16365
(814)723-9017

SCORE Office (Waynesboro)
323 E. Main St.
Waynesboro, PA 17268
(717)762-7123
Fax: (717)962-7124

SCORE Office (Chester County)
Government Service Center, Ste. 281
601 Westtown Rd.
West Chester, PA 19382-4538
(610)344-6910
Fax: (610)344-6919
E-mail: score@locke.ccil.org

SCORE Office (Wilkes-Barre)
7 N. Wilkes-Barre Blvd.
Wilkes Barre, PA 18702-5241
(717)826-6502
Fax: (717)826-6287

SCORE Office (North Central Pennsylvania)
240 W. 3rd St., Rm. 227
PO Box 725
Williamsport, PA 17703
(717)322-3720
Fax: (717)322-1607
E-mail: score234@mail.csrlink.net
Website: http://www.lycoming.org/
score/

SCORE Office (York)
Cyber Center
2101 Pennsylvania Ave.
York, PA 17404
(717)845-8830
Fax: (717)854-9333

Puerto Rico

SCORE Office (Puerto Rico & Virgin Islands)
PO Box 12383-96
San Juan, PR 00914-0383
(787)726-8040
Fax: (787)726-8135

Rhode Island

SCORE Office (Barrington)
281 County Rd.
Barrington, RI 02806
(401)247-1920
Fax: (401)247-3763

SCORE Office (Woonsocket)
640 Washington Hwy.
Lincoln, RI 02865
(401)334-1000
Fax: (401)334-1009

SCORE Office (Wickford)
8045 Post Rd.
North Kingstown, RI 02852
(401)295-5566
Fax: (401)295-8987

SCORE Office (J.G.E. Knight)
380 Westminster St.
Providence, RI 02903
(401)528-4571
Fax: (401)528-4539
Website: http://www.riscore.org

SCORE Office (Warwick)
3288 Post Rd.
Warwick, RI 02886
(401)732-1100
Fax: (401)732-1101

SCORE Office (Westerly)
74 Post Rd.
Westerly, RI 02891
(401)596-7761
800-732-7636
Fax: (401)596-2190

South Carolina

SCORE Office (Aiken)
PO Box 892
Aiken, SC 29802
(803)641-1111
800-542-4536
Fax: (803)641-4174

SCORE Office (Anderson)
Anderson Mall
3130 N. Main St.

Anderson, SC 29621
(864)224-0453

SCORE Office (Coastal)
284 King St.
Charleston, SC 29401
(803)727-4778
Fax: (803)853-2529

SCORE Office (Midlands)
Strom Thurmond Bldg., Rm. 358
1835 Assembly St., Rm 358
Columbia, SC 29201
(803)765-5131
Fax: (803)765-5962
Website: http://www.scoremid
lands.org/

SCORE Office (Piedmont)
Federal Bldg., Rm. B-02
300 E. Washington St.
Greenville, SC 29601
(864)271-3638

SCORE Office (Greenwood)
PO Drawer 1467
Greenwood, SC 29648
(864)223-8357

SCORE Office (Hilton Head Island)
52 Savannah Trail
Hilton Head, SC 29926
(803)785-7107
Fax: (803)785-7110

SCORE Office (Grand Strand)
937 Broadway
Myrtle Beach, SC 29577
(803)918-1079
Fax: (803)918-1083
E-mail: score381@aol.com

SCORE Office (Spartanburg)
PO Box 1636
Spartanburg, SC 29304
(864)594-5000
Fax: (864)594-5055

South Dakota

SCORE Office (West River)
Rushmore Plz. Civic Ctr.
444 Mount Rushmore Rd., No. 209
Rapid City, SD 57701
(605)394-5311
E-mail: score@gwtc.net

SCORE Office (Sioux Falls)
First Financial Center
110 S. Phillips Ave., Ste. 200
Sioux Falls, SD 57104-6727

(605)330-4231
Fax: (605)330-4231

Tennessee

SCORE Office (Chattanooga)
Federal Bldg., Rm. 26
900 Georgia Ave.
Chattanooga, TN 37402
(423)752-5190
Fax: (423)752-5335

SCORE Office (Cleveland)
PO Box 2275
Cleveland, TN 37320
(423)472-6587
Fax: (423)472-2019

SCORE Office (Upper Cumberland Center)
1225 S. Willow Ave.
Cookeville, TN 38501
(615)432-4111
Fax: (615)432-6010

SCORE Office (Unicoi County)
PO Box 713
Erwin, TN 37650
(423)743-3000
Fax: (423)743-0942

SCORE Office (Greeneville)
115 Academy St.
Greeneville, TN 37743
(423)638-4111
Fax: (423)638-5345

SCORE Office (Jackson)
194 Auditorium St.
Jackson, TN 38301
(901)423-2200

SCORE Office (Northeast Tennessee)
1st Tennessee Bank Bldg.
2710 S. Roan St., Ste. 584
Johnson City, TN 37601
(423)929-7686
Fax: (423)461-8052

SCORE Office (Kingsport)
151 E. Main St.
Kingsport, TN 37662
(423)392-8805

SCORE Office (Greater Knoxville)
Farragot Bldg., Ste. 224
530 S. Gay St.
Knoxville, TN 37902
(423)545-4203
E-mail: scoreknox@ntown.com
Website: http://www.scoreknox.org/

SCORE Office (Maryville)
201 S. Washington St.
Maryville, TN 37804-5728
(423)983-2241
800-525-6834
Fax: (423)984-1386

SCORE Office (Memphis)
Federal Bldg., Ste. 390
167 N. Main St.
Memphis, TN 38103
(901)544-3588

SCORE Office (Nashville)
50 Vantage Way, Ste. 201
Nashville, TN 37228-1500
(615)736-7621

Texas

SCORE Office (Abilene)
2106 Federal Post Office and Court Bldg.
Abilene, TX 79601
(915)677-1857

SCORE Office (Austin)
2501 S. Congress
Austin, TX 78701
(512)442-7235
Fax: (512)442-7528

SCORE Office (Golden Triangle)
450 Boyd St.
Beaumont, TX 77704
(409)838-6581
Fax: (409)833-6718

SCORE Office (Brownsville)
3505 Boca Chica Blvd., Ste. 305
Brownsville, TX 78521
(210)541-4508

SCORE Office (Brazos Valley)
3000 Briarcrest, Ste. 302
Bryan, TX 77802
(409)776-8876
E-mail: 102633.2612@compuserve.com

SCORE Office (Cleburne)
Watergarden Pl., 9th Fl., Ste. 400
Cleburne, TX 76031
(817)871-6002

SCORE Office (Corpus Christi)
651 Upper North Broadway, Ste. 654
Corpus Christi, TX 78477
(512)888-4322
Fax: (512)888-3418

SCORE Office (Dallas)
6260 E. Mockingbird
Dallas, TX 75214-2619

(214)828-2471
Fax: (214)821-8033

SCORE Office (El Paso)
10 Civic Center Plaza
El Paso, TX 79901
(915)534-0541
Fax: (915)534-0513

SCORE Office (Bedford)
100 E. 15th St., Ste. 400
Ft. Worth, TX 76102
(817)871-6002

SCORE Office (Ft. Worth)
100 E. 15th St., No. 24
Ft. Worth, TX 76102
(817)871-6002
Fax: (817)871-6031
E-mail: fwbac@onramp.net

SCORE Office (Garland)
2734 W. Kingsley Rd.
Garland, TX 75041
(214)271-9224

SCORE Office (Granbury Chamber of Commerce)
416 S. Morgan
Granbury, TX 76048
(817)573-1622
Fax: (817)573-0805

SCORE Office (Lower Rio Grande Valley)
222 E. Van Buren, Ste. 500
Harlingen, TX 78550
(956)427-8533
Fax: (956)427-8537

SCORE Office (Houston)
9301 Southwest Fwy., Ste. 550
Houston, TX 77074
(713)773-6565
Fax: (713)773-6550

SCORE Office (Irving)
3333 N. MacArthur Blvd., Ste. 100
Irving, TX 75062
(214)252-8484
Fax: (214)252-6710

SCORE Office (Lubbock)
1205 Texas Ave., Rm. 411D
Lubbock, TX 79401
(806)472-7462
Fax: (806)472-7487

SCORE Office (Midland)
Post Office Annex
200 E. Wall St., Rm. P121
Midland, TX 79701
(915)687-2649

SCORE Office (Orange)
1012 Green Ave.
Orange, TX 77630-5620
(409)883-3536
800-528-4906
Fax: (409)886-3247

SCORE Office (Plano)
1200 E. 15th St.
PO Drawer 940287
Plano, TX 75094-0287
(214)424-7547
Fax: (214)422-5182

SCORE Office (Port Arthur)
4749 Twin City Hwy., Ste. 300
Port Arthur, TX 77642
(409)963-1107
Fax: (409)963-3322

SCORE Office (Richardson)
411 Belle Grove
Richardson, TX 75080
(214)234-4141
800-777-8001
Fax: (214)680-9103

SCORE Office (San Antonio)
Federal Bldg., Rm. A527
727 E. Durango
San Antonio, TX 78206
(210)472-5931
Fax: (210)472-5935

SCORE Office (Texarkana State College)
819 State Line Ave.
Texarkana, TX 75501
(903)792-7191
Fax: (903)793-4304

SCORE Office (East Texas)
RTDC
1530 SSW Loop 323, Ste. 100
Tyler, TX 75701
(903)510-2975
Fax: (903)510-2978

SCORE Office (Waco)
401 Franklin Ave.
Waco, TX 76701
(817)754-8898
Fax: (817)756-0776
Website: http://www.brc-waco.com/

SCORE Office (Wichita Falls)
Hamilton Bldg.
900 8th St.
Wichita Falls, TX 76307
(940)723-2741
Fax: (940)723-8773

Utah

SCORE Office (Northern Utah)
160 N. Main
Logan, UT 84321
(435)746-2269

SCORE Office (Ogden)
1701 E. Windsor Dr.
Ogden, UT 84604
(801)629-8613
E-mail: score158@netscape.net

SCORE Office (Central Utah)
1071 E. Windsor Dr.
Provo, UT 84604
(801)373-8660

SCORE Office (Southern Utah)
225 South 700 East
St. George, UT 84770
(435)652-7751

SCORE Office (Salt Lake)
310 S Main St.
Salt Lake City, UT 84101
(801)746-2269
Fax: (801)746-2273

Vermont

SCORE Office (Champlain Valley)
Winston Prouty Federal Bldg.
11 Lincoln St., Rm. 106
Essex Junction, VT 05452
(802)951-6762

SCORE Office (Montpelier)
87 State St., Rm. 205
PO Box 605
Montpelier, VT 05601
(802)828-4422
Fax: (802)828-4485

SCORE Office (Marble Valley)
256 N. Main St.
Rutland, VT 05701-2413
(802)773-9147

SCORE Office (Northeast Kingdom)
20 Main St.
PO Box 904
St. Johnsbury, VT 05819
(802)748-5101

Virgin Islands

SCORE Office (St. Croix)
United Plaza Shopping Center
PO Box 4010, Christiansted
St. Croix, VI 00822
(809)778-5380

SCORE Office (St. Thomas-St. John)
Federal Bldg., Rm. 21
Veterans Dr.
St. Thomas, VI 00801
(809)774-8530

Virginia

SCORE Office (Arlington)
2009 N. 14th St., Ste. 111
Arlington, VA 22201
(703)525-2400

SCORE Office (Blacksburg)
141 Jackson St.
Blacksburg, VA 24060
(540)552-4061

SCORE Office (Bristol
20 Volunteer Pkwy.
Bristol, VA 24203
(540)989-4850

SCORE Office (Central Virginia)
1001 E. Market St., Ste. 101
Charlottesville, VA 22902
(804)295-6712
Fax: (804)295-7066

SCORE Office (Alleghany Satellite)
241 W. Main St.
Covington, VA 24426
(540)962-2178
Fax: (540)962-2179

SCORE Office (Central Fairfax)
3975 University Dr., Ste. 350
Fairfax, VA 22030
(703)591-2450

SCORE Office (Falls Church)
PO Box 491
Falls Church, VA 22040
(703)532-1050
Fax: (703)237-7904

SCORE Office (Glenns)
Glenns Campus
Box 287
Glenns, VA 23149
(804)693-9650

SCORE Office (Peninsula)
6 Manhattan Sq.
PO Box 7269
Hampton, VA 23666
(757)766-2000
Fax: (757)865-0339
E-mail: score100@seva.net

SCORE Office (Tri-Cities)
108 N. Main St.

Hopewell, VA 23860
(804)458-5536

SCORE Office (Lynchburg)
Federal Bldg.
1100 Main St.
Lynchburg, VA 24504-1714
(804)846-3235

SCORE Office (Greater Prince William)
8963 Center St
Manassas, VA 20110
(703)368-4813
Fax: (703)368-4733

SCORE Office (Martinsvile)
115 Broad St.
Martinsville, VA 24112-0709
(540)632-6401
Fax: (540)632-5059

SCORE Office (Hampton Roads)
Federal Bldg., Rm. 737
200 Grandby St.
Norfolk, VA 23510
(757)441-3733
Fax: (757)441-3733
E-mail: scorehr60@juno.com

SCORE Office (Norfolk)
Federal Bldg., Rm. 737
200 Granby St.
Norfolk, VA 23510
(757)441-3733
Fax: (757)441-3733

SCORE Office (Virginia Beach)
Chamber of Commerce
200 Grandby St., Rm 737
Norfolk, VA 23510
(804)441-3733

SCORE Office (Radford)
1126 Norwood St.
Radford, VA 24141
(540)639-2202

SCORE Office (Richmond)
Federal Bldg.
400 N. 8th St., Ste. 1150
PO Box 10126
Richmond, VA 23240-0126
(804)771-2400
Fax: (804)771-8018
E-mail: scorechapter12@yahoo.com
Website: http://www.cvco.org/score/

SCORE Office (Roanoke)
Federal Bldg., Rm. 716
250 Franklin Rd.
Roanoke, VA 24011

(540)857-2834
Fax: (540)857-2043
E-mail: scorerva@juno.com
Website: http://hometown.aol.com/
scorerv/Index.html

SCORE Office (Fairfax)
8391 Old Courthouse Rd., Ste. 300
Vienna, VA 22182
(703)749-0400

SCORE Office (Greater Vienna)
513 Maple Ave. West
Vienna, VA 22180
(703)281-1333
Fax: (703)242-1482

SCORE Office (Shenandoah Valley)
301 W. Main St.
Waynesboro, VA 22980
(540)949-8203
Fax: (540)949-7740
E-mail: score427@intelos.net

SCORE Office (Williamsburg)
201 Penniman Rd.
Williamsburg, VA 23185
(757)229-6511
E-mail: wacc@williamsburgcc.com

SCORE Office (Northern Virginia)
1360 S. Pleasant Valley Rd.
Winchester, VA 22601
(540)662-4118

Washington

SCORE Office (Gray's Harbor)
506 Duffy St.
Aberdeen, WA 98520
(360)532-1924
Fax: (360)533-7945

SCORE Office (Bellingham)
101 E. Holly St.
Bellingham, WA 98225
(360)676-3307

SCORE Office (Everett)
2702 Hoyt Ave.
Everett, WA 98201-3556
(206)259-8000

SCORE Office (Gig Harbor)
3125 Judson St.
Gig Harbor, WA 98335
(206)851-6865

SCORE Office (Kennewick)
PO Box 6986
Kennewick, WA 99336
(509)736-0510

SCORE Office (Puyallup)
322 2nd St. SW
PO Box 1298
Puyallup, WA 98371
(206)845-6755
Fax: (206)848-6164

SCORE Office (Seattle)
1200 6th Ave., Ste. 1700
Seattle, WA 98101
(206)553-7320
Fax: (206)553-7044
E-mail: score55@aol.com
Website: http://www.scn.org/civic/score-online/index55.html

SCORE Office (Spokane)
801 W. Riverside Ave., No. 240
Spokane, WA 99201
(509)353-2820
Fax: (509)353-2600
E-mail: score@dmi.net
Website: http://www.dmi.net/score/

SCORE Office (Clover Park)
PO Box 1933
Tacoma, WA 98401-1933
(206)627-2175

SCORE Office (Tacoma)
1101 Pacific Ave.
Tacoma, WA 98402
(253)274-1288
Fax: (253)274-1289

SCORE Office (Fort Vancouver)
1701 Broadway, S-1
Vancouver, WA 98663
(360)699-1079

SCORE Office (Walla Walla)
500 Tausick Way
Walla Walla, WA 99362
(509)527-4681

SCORE Office (Mid-Columbia)
1113 S. 14th Ave.
Yakima, WA 98907
(509)574-4944
Fax: (509)574-2943
Website: http://www.ellensburg.com/
~score/

West Virginia

SCORE Office (Charleston)
1116 Smith St.
Charleston, WV 25301
(304)347-5463
E-mail: score256@juno.com

SCORE Office (Virginia Street)
1116 Smith St., Ste. 302
Charleston, WV 25301
(304)347-5463

SCORE Office (Marion County)
PO Box 208
Fairmont, WV 26555-0208
(304)363-0486

SCORE Office (Upper Monongahela Valley)
1000 Technology Dr., Ste. 1111
Fairmont, WV 26555
(304)363-0486
E-mail: score537@hotmail.com

SCORE Office (Huntington)
1101 6th Ave., Ste. 220
Huntington, WV 25701-2309
(304)523-4092

SCORE Office (Wheeling)
1310 Market St.
Wheeling, WV 26003
(304)233-2575
Fax: (304)233-1320

Wisconsin

SCORE Office (Fox Cities)
227 S. Walnut St.
Appleton, WI 54913
(920)734-7101
Fax: (920)734-7161

SCORE Office (Beloit)
136 W. Grand Ave., Ste. 100
PO Box 717
Beloit, WI 53511
(608)365-8835
Fax: (608)365-9170

SCORE Office (Eau Claire)
Federal Bldg., Rm. B11
510 S. Barstow St.
Eau Claire, WI 54701
(715)834-1573
E-mail: score@ecol.net
Website: http://www.ecol.net/~score/

SCORE Office (Fond du Lac)
207 N. Main St.
Fond du Lac, WI 54935
(414)921-9500
Fax: (414)921-9559

SCORE Office (Green Bay)
835 Potts Ave.
Green Bay, WI 54304
(414)496-8930
Fax: (414)496-6009

SCORE Office (Janesville)
20 S. Main St., Ste. 11
PO Box 8008
Janesville, WI 53547
(608)757-3160
Fax: (608)757-3170

SCORE Office (La Crosse)
712 Main St.
La Crosse, WI 54602-0219
(608)784-4880

SCORE Office (Madison)
505 S. Rosa Rd.
Madison, WI 53719
(608)441-2820

SCORE Office (Manitowoc)
1515 Memorial Dr.
PO Box 903
Manitowoc, WI 54221-0903
(414)684-5575
Fax: (414)684-1915

SCORE Office (Milwaukee)
310 W. Wisconsin Ave., Ste. 425
Milwaukee, WI 53203
(414)297-3942
Fax: (414)297-1377

SCORE Office (Central Wisconsin)
1224 Lindbergh Ave.
Stevens Point, WI 54481
(715)344-7729

SCORE Office (Superior)
Superior Business Center Inc.
1423 N. 8th St.
Superior, WI 54880
(715)394-7388
Fax: (715)393-7414

SCORE Office (Waukesha)
223 Wisconsin Ave.
Waukesha, WI 53186-4926
(414)542-4249

SCORE Office (Wausau)
300 3rd St., Ste. 200
Wausau, WI 54402-6190
(715)845-6231

SCORE Office (Wisconsin Rapids)
2240 Kingston Rd.
Wisconsin Rapids, WI 54494
(715)423-1830

Wyoming

SCORE Office (Casper)
Federal Bldg., No. 2215
100 East B St.

Casper, WY 82602
(307)261-6529
Fax: (307)261-6530

Venture capital & financing companies

This section contains a listing of financing and loan companies in the United States and Canada. These listing are arranged alphabetically by country, then by state or province, then by city, then by organization name.

Canada

Alberta

Launchworks Inc.
1902J 11th St., S.E.
Calgary, AB, Canada T2G 3G2
(403)269-1119
Fax: (403)269-1141
Website: http://www.launchworks.com

Native Venture Capital Company, Inc.
21 Artist View Point, Box 7
Site 25, RR 12
Calgary, AB, Canada T3E 6W3
(903)208-5380

Miralta Capital Inc.
4445 Calgary Trail South
888 Terrace Plaza Alberta
Edmonton, AB, Canada T6H 5R7
(780)438-3535
Fax: (780)438-3129

Vencap Equities Alberta Ltd.
10180-101st St., Ste. 1980
Edmonton, AB, Canada T5J 3S4
(403)420-1171
Fax: (403)429-2541

British Columbia

Discovery Capital
5th Fl., 1199 West Hastings
Vancouver, BC, Canada V6E 3T5
(604)683-3000
Fax: (604)662-3457
E-mail: info@discoverycapital.com
Website: http://www.discoverycapital.com

Greenstone Venture Partners
1177 West Hastings St.
Ste. 400
Vancouver, BC, Canada V6E 2K3
(604)717-1977
Fax: (604)717-1976
Website: http://www.greenstonevc.com

Growthworks Capital
2600-1055 West Georgia St.
Box 11170 Royal Centre
Vancouver, BC, Canada V6E 3R5
(604)895-7259
Fax: (604)669-7605
Website: http://www.wofund.com

MDS Discovery Venture Management, Inc.
555 W. Eighth Ave., Ste. 305
Vancouver, BC, Canada V5Z 1C6
(604)872-8464
Fax: (604)872-2977
E-mail: info@mds-ventures.com

Ventures West Management Inc.
1285 W. Pender St., Ste. 280
Vancouver, BC, Canada V6E 4B1
(604)688-9495
Fax: (604)687-2145
Website: http://www.ventureswest.com

Nova Scotia

ACF Equity Atlantic Inc.
Purdy's Wharf Tower II
Ste. 2106
Halifax, NS, Canada B3J 3R7
(902)421-1965
Fax: (902)421-1808

Montgomerie, Huck & Co.
146 Bluenose Dr.
PO Box 538
Lunenburg, NS, Canada B0J 2C0
(902)634-7125
Fax: (902)634-7130

Ontario

IPS Industrial Promotion Services Ltd.
60 Columbia Way, Ste. 720
Markham, ON, Canada L3R 0C9
(905)475-9400
Fax: (905)475-5003

Betwin Investments Inc.
Box 23110
Sault Ste. Marie, ON, Canada P6A 6W6
(705)253-0744
Fax: (705)253-0744

Bailey & Company, Inc.
594 Spadina Ave.
Toronto, ON, Canada M5S 2H4
(416)921-6930
Fax: (416)925-4670

BCE Capital
200 Bay St.

South Tower, Ste. 3120
Toronto, ON, Canada M5J 2J2
(416)815-0078
Fax: (416)941-1073
Website: http://www.bcecapital.com

Castlehill Ventures
55 University Ave., Ste. 500
Toronto, ON, Canada M5J 2H7
(416)862-8574
Fax: (416)862-8875

CCFL Mezzanine Partners of Canada
70 University Ave.
Ste. 1450
Toronto, ON, Canada M5J 2M4
(416)977-1450
Fax: (416)977-6764
E-mail: info@ccfl.com
Website: http://www.ccfl.com

Celtic House International
100 Simcoe St., Ste. 100
Toronto, ON, Canada M5H 3G2
(416)542-2436
Fax: (416)542-2435
Website: http://www.celtic-house.com

Clairvest Group Inc.
22 St. Clair Ave. East
Ste. 1700
Toronto, ON, Canada M4T 2S3
(416)925-9270
Fax: (416)925-5753

Crosbie & Co., Inc.
One First Canadian Place
9th Fl.
PO Box 116
Toronto, ON, Canada M5X 1A4
(416)362-7726
Fax: (416)362-3447
E-mail: info@crosbieco.com
Website: http://www.crosbieco.com

Drug Royalty Corp.
Eight King St. East
Ste. 202
Toronto, ON, Canada M5C 1B5
(416)863-1865
Fax: (416)863-5161

Grieve, Horner, Brown & Asculai
8 King St. E, Ste. 1704
Toronto, ON, Canada M5C 1B5
(416)362-7668
Fax: (416)362-7660

Jefferson Partners
77 King St. West
Ste. 4010

PO Box 136
Toronto, ON, Canada M5K 1H1
(416)367-1533
Fax: (416)367-5827
Website: http://www.jefferson.com

J.L. Albright Venture Partners
Canada Trust Tower, 161 Bay St.
Ste. 4440
PO Box 215
Toronto, ON, Canada M5J 2S1
(416)367-2440
Fax: (416)367-4604
Website: http://www.jlaventures.com

McLean Watson Capital Inc.
One First Canadian Place
Ste. 1410
PO Box 129
Toronto, ON, Canada M5X 1A4
(416)363-2000
Fax: (416)363-2010
Website: http://www.mcleanwatson.com

Middlefield Capital Fund
One First Canadian Place
85th Fl.
PO Box 192
Toronto, ON, Canada M5X 1A6
(416)362-0714
Fax: (416)362-7925
Website: http://www.middlefield.com

Mosaic Venture Partners
24 Duncan St.
Ste. 300
Toronto, ON, Canada M5V 3M6
(416)597-8889
Fax: (416)597-2345

Onex Corp.
161 Bay St.
PO Box 700
Toronto, ON, Canada M5J 2S1
(416)362-7711
Fax: (416)362-5765

Penfund Partners Inc.
145 King St. West
Ste. 1920
Toronto, ON, Canada M5H 1J8
(416)865-0300
Fax: (416)364-6912
Website: http://www.penfund.com

Primaxis Technology Ventures Inc.
1 Richmond St. West, 8th Fl.
Toronto, ON, Canada M5H 3W4
(416)313-5210
Fax: (416)313-5218
Website: http://www.primaxis.com

Priveq Capital Funds
240 Duncan Mill Rd., Ste. 602
Toronto, ON, Canada M3B 3P1
(416)447-3330
Fax: (416)447-3331
E-mail: priveq@sympatico.ca

Roynat Ventures
40 King St. West, 26th Fl.
Toronto, ON, Canada M5H 1H1
(416)933-2667
Fax: (416)933-2783
Website: http://www.roynatcapital.com

Tera Capital Corp.
366 Adelaide St. East, Ste. 337
Toronto, ON, Canada M5A 3X9
(416)368-1024
Fax: (416)368-1427

Working Ventures Canadian Fund Inc.
250 Bloor St. East, Ste. 1600
Toronto, ON, Canada M4W 1E6
(416)934-7718
Fax: (416)929-0901
Website: http://www.workingventures.ca

Quebec

Altamira Capital Corp.
202 University
Niveau de Maisoneuve, Bur. 201
Montreal, QC, Canada H3A 2A5
(514)499-1656
Fax: (514)499-9570

Federal Business Development Bank
Venture Capital Division
Five Place Ville Marie, Ste. 600
Montreal, QC, Canada H3B 5E7
(514)283-1896
Fax: (514)283-5455

Hydro-Quebec Capitech Inc.
75 Boul, Rene Levesque Quest
Montreal, QC, Canada H2Z 1A4
(514)289-4783
Fax: (514)289-5420
Website: http://www.hqcapitech.com

Investissement Desjardins
2 complexe Desjardins
C.P. 760
Montreal, QC, Canada H5B 1B8
(514)281-7131
Fax: (514)281-7808
Website: http://www.desjardins.com/id

Marleau Lemire Inc.
One Place Ville-Marie, Ste. 3601
Montreal, QC, Canada H3B 3P2

(514)877-3800
Fax: (514)875-6415

Speirs Consultants Inc.
365 Stanstead
Montreal, QC, Canada H3R 1X5
(514)342-3858
Fax: (514)342-1977

Tecnocap Inc.
4028 Marlowe
Montreal, QC, Canada H4A 3M2
(514)483-6009
Fax: (514)483-6045
Website: http://www.technocap.com

Telsoft Ventures
1000, Rue de la Gauchetiere
Quest, 25eme Etage
Montreal, QC, Canada H3B 4W5
(514)397-8450
Fax: (514)397-8451

Saskatchewan

Saskatchewan Government Growth Fund
1801 Hamilton St., Ste. 1210
Canada Trust Tower
Regina, SK, Canada S4P 4B4
(306)787-2994
Fax: (306)787-2086

United states

Alabama

FHL Capital Corp.
600 20th Street North
Suite 350
Birmingham, AL 35203
(205)328-3098
Fax: (205)323-0001

Harbert Management Corp.
One Riverchase Pkwy. South
Birmingham, AL 35244
(205)987-5500
Fax: (205)987-5707
Website: http://www.harbert.net

Jefferson Capital Fund
PO Box 13129
Birmingham, AL 35213
(205)324-7709

Private Capital Corp.
100 Brookwood Pl., 4th Fl.
Birmingham, AL 35209
(205)879-2722
Fax: (205)879-5121

21st Century Health Ventures
One Health South Pkwy.
Birmingham, AL 35243
(256)268-6250
Fax: (256)970-8928

FJC Growth Capital Corp.
200 W. Side Sq., Ste. 340
Huntsville, AL 35801
(256)922-2918
Fax: (256)922-2909

Hickory Venture Capital Corp.
301 Washington St. NW
Suite 301
Huntsville, AL 35801
(256)539-1931
Fax: (256)539-5130
E-mail: hvcc@hvcc.com
Website: http://www.hvcc.com

Southeastern Technology Fund
7910 South Memorial Pkwy., Ste. F
Huntsville, AL 35802
(256)883-8711
Fax: (256)883-8558

Cordova Ventures
4121 Carmichael Rd., Ste. 301
Montgomery, AL 36106
(334)271-6011
Fax: (334)260-0120
Website: http://www.cordova
ventures.com

**Small Business Clinic of Alabama/AG
Bartholomew & Associates**
PO Box 231074
Montgomery, AL 36123-1074
(334)284-3640

Arizona

Miller Capital Corp.
4909 E. McDowell Rd.
Phoenix, AZ 85008
(602)225-0504
Fax: (602)225-9024
Website: http://www.themiller
group.com

The Columbine Venture Funds
9449 North 90th St., Ste. 200
Scottsdale, AZ 85258
(602)661-9222
Fax: (602)661-6262

Koch Ventures
17767 N. Perimeter Dr., Ste. 101
Scottsdale, AZ 85255
(480)419-3600

Fax: (480)419-3606
Website: http://www.kochventures.com

McKee & Co.
7702 E. Doubletree Ranch Rd.
Suite 230
Scottsdale, AZ 85258
(480)368-0333
Fax: (480)607-7446

Merita Capital Ltd.
7350 E. Stetson Dr., Ste. 108-A
Scottsdale, AZ 85251
(480)947-8700
Fax: (480)947-8766

Valley Ventures / Arizona Growth Partners L.P.
6720 N. Scottsdale Rd., Ste. 208
Scottsdale, AZ 85253
(480)661-6600
Fax: (480)661-6262

Estreetcapital.com
660 South Mill Ave., Ste. 315
Tempe, AZ 85281
(480)968-8400
Fax: (480)968-8480
Website: http://www.estreetcapital.com

Coronado Venture Fund
PO Box 65420
Tucson, AZ 85728-5420
(520)577-3764
Fax: (520)299-8491

Arkansas

Arkansas Capital Corp.
225 South Pulaski St.
Little Rock, AR 72201
(501)374-9247
Fax: (501)374-9425
Website: http://www.arcapital.com

California

Sundance Venture Partners, L.P.
100 Clocktower Place, Ste. 130
Carmel, CA 93923
(831)625-6500
Fax: (831)625-6590

Westar Capital (Costa Mesa)
949 South Coast Dr., Ste. 650
Costa Mesa, CA 92626
(714)481-5160
Fax: (714)481-5166
E-mail: mailbox@westarcapital.com
Website: http://www.westarcapital.com

Alpine Technology Ventures
20300 Stevens Creek Boulevard, Ste. 495
Cupertino, CA 95014
(408)725-1810
Fax: (408)725-1207
Website: http://www.alpineventures.com

Bay Partners
10600 N. De Anza Blvd.
Cupertino, CA 95014-2031
(408)725-2444
Fax: (408)446-4502
Website: http://www.baypartners.com

Novus Ventures
20111 Stevens Creek Blvd., Ste. 130
Cupertino, CA 95014
(408)252-3900
Fax: (408)252-1713
Website: http://www.novusventures.com

Triune Capital
19925 Stevens Creek Blvd., Ste. 200
Cupertino, CA 95014
(310)284-6800
Fax: (310)284-3290

Acorn Ventures
268 Bush St., Ste. 2829
Daly City, CA 94014
(650)994-7801
Fax: (650)994-3305
Website: http://www.acornventures.com

Digital Media Campus
2221 Park Place
El Segundo, CA 90245
(310)426-8000
Fax: (310)426-8010
E-mail: info@thecampus.com
Website: http://www.digital
mediacampus.com

BankAmerica Ventures / BA Venture Partners
950 Tower Ln., Ste. 700
Foster City, CA 94404
(650)378-6000
Fax: (650)378-6040
Website: http://
www.baventurepartners.com

Starting Point Partners
666 Portofino Lane
Foster City, CA 94404
(650)722-1035
Website: http://www.startingpoint
partners.com

Opportunity Capital Partners
2201 Walnut Ave., Ste. 210

Fremont, CA 94538
(510)795-7000
Fax: (510)494-5439
Website: http://www.ocpcapital.com

Imperial Ventures Inc.
9920 S. La Cienega Boulevar, 14th Fl.
Inglewood, CA 90301
(310)417-5409
Fax: (310)338-6115

Ventana Global (Irvine)
18881 Von Karman Ave., Ste. 1150
Irvine, CA 92612
(949)476-2204
Fax: (949)752-0223
Website: http://www.ventanaglobal.com

Integrated Consortium Inc.
50 Ridgecrest Rd.
Kentfield, CA 94904
(415)925-0386
Fax: (415)461-2726

Enterprise Partners
979 Ivanhoe Ave., Ste. 550
La Jolla, CA 92037
(858)454-8833
Fax: (858)454-2489
Website: http://www.epvc.com

Domain Associates
28202 Cabot Rd., Ste. 200
Laguna Niguel, CA 92677
(949)347-2446
Fax: (949)347-9720
Website: http://www.domainvc.com

Cascade Communications Ventures
60 E. Sir Francis Drake Blvd., Ste. 300
Larkspur, CA 94939
(415)925-6500
Fax: (415)925-6501

Allegis Capital
One First St., Ste. Two
Los Altos, CA 94022
(650)917-5900
Fax: (650)917-5901
Website: http://www.allegiscapital.com

Aspen Ventures
1000 Fremont Ave., Ste. 200
Los Altos, CA 94024
(650)917-5670
Fax: (650)917-5677
Website: http://www.aspenventures.com

AVI Capital L.P.
1 First St., Ste. 2
Los Altos, CA 94022

(650)949-9862
Fax: (650)949-8510
Website: http://www.avicapital.com

Bastion Capital Corp.
1999 Avenue of the Stars, Ste. 2960
Los Angeles, CA 90067
(310)788-5700
Fax: (310)277-7582
E-mail: ga@bastioncapital.com
Website: http://www.bastioncapital.com

Davis Group
PO Box 69953
Los Angeles, CA 90069-0953
(310)659-6327
Fax: (310)659-6337

Developers Equity Corp.
1880 Century Park East, Ste. 211
Los Angeles, CA 90067
(213)277-0300

Far East Capital Corp.
350 S. Grand Ave., Ste. 4100
Los Angeles, CA 90071
(213)687-1361
Fax: (213)617-7939
E-mail: free@fareastnationalbank.com

Kline Hawkes & Co.
11726 San Vicente Blvd., Ste. 300
Los Angeles, CA 90049
(310)442-4700
Fax: (310)442-4707
Website: http://www.klinehawkes.com

Lawrence Financial Group
701 Teakwood
PO Box 491773
Los Angeles, CA 90049
(310)471-4060
Fax: (310)472-3155

Riordan Lewis & Haden
300 S. Grand Ave., 29th Fl.
Los Angeles, CA 90071
(213)229-8500
Fax: (213)229-8597

Union Venture Corp.
445 S. Figueroa St., 9th Fl.
Los Angeles, CA 90071
(213)236-4092
Fax: (213)236-6329

Wedbush Capital Partners
1000 Wilshire Blvd.
Los Angeles, CA 90017
(213)688-4545
Fax: (213)688-6642
Website: http://www.wedbush.com

Advent International Corp.
2180 Sand Hill Rd., Ste. 420
Menlo Park, CA 94025
(650)233-7500
Fax: (650)233-7515
Website: http://www.adventinter
national.com

Altos Ventures
2882 Sand Hill Rd., Ste. 100
Menlo Park, CA 94025
(650)234-9771
Fax: (650)233-9821
Website: http://www.altosvc.com

Applied Technology
1010 El Camino Real, Ste. 300
Menlo Park, CA 94025
(415)326-8622
Fax: (415)326-8163

APV Technology Partners
535 Middlefield, Ste. 150
Menlo Park, CA 94025
(650)327-7871
Fax: (650)327-7631
Website: http://www.apvtp.com

August Capital Management
2480 Sand Hill Rd., Ste. 101
Menlo Park, CA 94025
(650)234-9900
Fax: (650)234-9910
Website: http://www.augustcap.com

Baccharis Capital Inc.
2420 Sand Hill Rd., Ste. 100
Menlo Park, CA 94025
(650)324-6844
Fax: (650)854-3025

Benchmark Capital
2480 Sand Hill Rd., Ste. 200
Menlo Park, CA 94025
(650)854-8180
Fax: (650)854-8183
E-mail: info@benchmark.com
Website: http://www.benchmark.com

Bessemer Venture Partners (Menlo Park)
535 Middlefield Rd., Ste. 245
Menlo Park, CA 94025
(650)853-7000
Fax: (650)853-7001
Website: http://www.bvp.com

The Cambria Group
1600 El Camino Real Rd., Ste. 155
Menlo Park, CA 94025
(650)329-8600

Fax: (650)329-8601
Website: http://www.cambriagroup.com

Canaan Partners
2884 Sand Hill Rd., Ste. 115
Menlo Park, CA 94025
(650)854-8092
Fax: (650)854-8127
Website: http://www.canaan.com

Capstone Ventures
3000 Sand Hill Rd., Bldg. One, Ste. 290
Menlo Park, CA 94025
(650)854-2523
Fax: (650)854-9010
Website: http://www.capstonevc.com

Comdisco Venture Group (Silicon Valley)
3000 Sand Hill Rd., Bldg. 1, Ste. 155
Menlo Park, CA 94025
(650)854-9484
Fax: (650)854-4026

Commtech International
535 Middlefield Rd., Ste. 200
Menlo Park, CA 94025
(650)328-0190
Fax: (650)328-6442

Compass Technology Partners
1550 El Camino Real, Ste. 275
Menlo Park, CA 94025-4111
(650)322-7595
Fax: (650)322-0588
Website: http://www.compass
techpartners.com

Convergence Partners
3000 Sand Hill Rd., Ste. 235
Menlo Park, CA 94025
(650)854-3010
Fax: (650)854-3015
Website: http://www.conver
gencepartners.com

The Dakota Group
PO Box 1025
Menlo Park, CA 94025
(650)853-0600
Fax: (650)851-4899
E-mail: info@dakota.com

Delphi Ventures
3000 Sand Hill Rd.
Bldg. One, Ste. 135
Menlo Park, CA 94025
(650)854-9650
Fax: (650)854-2961
Website: http://www.delphiventures.com

El Dorado Ventures
2884 Sand Hill Rd., Ste. 121
Menlo Park, CA 94025
(650)854-1200
Fax: (650)854-1202
Website: http://www.eldorado
ventures.com

Glynn Ventures
3000 Sand Hill Rd., Bldg. 4, Ste. 235
Menlo Park, CA 94025
(650)854-2215

Indosuez Ventures
2180 Sand Hill Rd., Ste. 450
Menlo Park, CA 94025
(650)854-0587
Fax: (650)323-5561
Website: http://www.indosuez
ventures.com

Institutional Venture Partners
3000 Sand Hill Rd., Bldg. 2, Ste. 290
Menlo Park, CA 94025
(650)854-0132
Fax: (650)854-5762
Website: http://www.ivp.com

Interwest Partners (Menlo Park)
3000 Sand Hill Rd., Bldg. 3, Ste. 255
Menlo Park, CA 94025-7112
(650)854-8585
Fax: (650)854-4706
Website: http://www.interwest.com

**Kleiner Perkins Caufield & Byers
(Menlo Park)**
2750 Sand Hill Rd.
Menlo Park, CA 94025
(650)233-2750
Fax: (650)233-0300
Website: http://www.kpcb.com

Magic Venture Capital LLC
1010 El Camino Real, Ste. 300
Menlo Park, CA 94025
(650)325-4149

Matrix Partners
2500 Sand Hill Rd., Ste. 113
Menlo Park, CA 94025
(650)854-3131
Fax: (650)854-3296
Website: http://www.matrixpartners.com

Mayfield Fund
2800 Sand Hill Rd.
Menlo Park, CA 94025
(650)854-5560
Fax: (650)854-5712
Website: http://www.mayfield.com

**McCown De Leeuw and Co. (Menlo
Park)**
3000 Sand Hill Rd., Bldg. 3, Ste. 290
Menlo Park, CA 94025-7111
(650)854-6000
Fax: (650)854-0853
Website: http://www.mdcpartners.com

Menlo Ventures
3000 Sand Hill Rd., Bldg. 4, Ste. 100
Menlo Park, CA 94025
(650)854-8540
Fax: (650)854-7059
Website: http://www.menloventures.com

Merrill Pickard Anderson & Eyre
2480 Sand Hill Rd., Ste. 200
Menlo Park, CA 94025
(650)854-8600
Fax: (650)854-0345

**New Enterprise Associates (Menlo
Park)**
2490 Sand Hill Rd.
Menlo Park, CA 94025
(650)854-9499
Fax: (650)854-9397
Website: http://www.nea.com

Onset Ventures
2400 Sand Hill Rd., Ste. 150
Menlo Park, CA 94025
(650)529-0700
Fax: (650)529-0777
Website: http://www.onset.com

Paragon Venture Partners
3000 Sand Hill Rd., Bldg. 1, Ste. 275
Menlo Park, CA 94025
(650)854-8000
Fax: (650)854-7260

**Pathfinder Venture Capital Funds
(Menlo Park)**
3000 Sand Hill Rd., Bldg. 3, Ste. 255
Menlo Park, CA 94025
(650)854-0650
Fax: (650)854-4706

Rocket Ventures
3000 Sandhill Rd., Bldg. 1, Ste. 170
Menlo Park, CA 94025
(650)561-9100
Fax: (650)561-9183
Website: http://www.rocketventures.com

Sequoia Capital
3000 Sand Hill Rd., Bldg. 4, Ste. 280
Menlo Park, CA 94025
(650)854-3927
Fax: (650)854-2977

E-mail: sequoia@sequoiacap.com
Website: http://www.sequoiacap.com

Sierra Ventures
3000 Sand Hill Rd., Bldg. 4, Ste. 210
Menlo Park, CA 94025
(650)854-1000
Fax: (650)854-5593
Website: http://www.sierraventures.com

Sigma Partners
2884 Sand Hill Rd., Ste. 121
Menlo Park, CA 94025-7022
(650)853-1700
Fax: (650)853-1717
E-mail: info@sigmapartners.com
Website: http://www.sigmapartners.com

Sprout Group (Menlo Park)
3000 Sand Hill Rd.
Bldg. 3, Ste. 170
Menlo Park, CA 94025
(650)234-2700
Fax: (650)234-2779
Website: http://www.sproutgroup.com

TA Associates (Menlo Park)
70 Willow Rd., Ste. 100
Menlo Park, CA 94025
(650)328-1210
Fax: (650)326-4933
Website: http://www.ta.com

Thompson Clive & Partners Ltd.
3000 Sand Hill Rd., Bldg. 1, Ste. 185
Menlo Park, CA 94025-7102
(650)854-0314
Fax: (650)854-0670
E-mail: mail@tcvc.com
Website: http://www.tcvc.com

Trinity Ventures Ltd.
3000 Sand Hill Rd., Bldg. 1, Ste. 240
Menlo Park, CA 94025
(650)854-9500
Fax: (650)854-9501
Website: http://www.trinityventures.com

U.S. Venture Partners
2180 Sand Hill Rd., Ste. 300
Menlo Park, CA 94025
(650)854-9080
Fax: (650)854-3018
Website: http://www.usvp.com

USVP-Schlein Marketing Fund
2180 Sand Hill Rd., Ste. 300
Menlo Park, CA 94025
(415)854-9080
Fax: (415)854-3018
Website: http://www.usvp.com

Venrock Associates
2494 Sand Hill Rd., Ste. 200
Menlo Park, CA 94025
(650)561-9580
Fax: (650)561-9180
Website: http://www.venrock.com

Brad Peery Capital Inc.
145 Chapel Pkwy.
Mill Valley, CA 94941
(415)389-0625
Fax: (415)389-1336

Dot Edu Ventures
650 Castro St., Ste. 270
Mountain View, CA 94041
(650)575-5638
Fax: (650)325-5247
Website: http://www.dotedu
ventures.com

Forrest, Binkley & Brown
840 Newport Ctr. Dr., Ste. 480
Newport Beach, CA 92660
(949)729-3222
Fax: (949)729-3226
Website: http://www.fbbvc.com

Marwit Capital LLC
180 Newport Center Dr., Ste. 200
Newport Beach, CA 92660
(949)640-6234
Fax: (949)720-8077
Website: http://www.marwit.com

Kaiser Permanente / National Venture Development
1800 Harrison St., 22nd Fl.
Oakland, CA 94612
(510)267-4010
Fax: (510)267-4036
Website: http://www.kpventures.com

Nu Capital Access Group, Ltd.
7677 Oakport St., Ste. 105
Oakland, CA 94621
(510)635-7345
Fax: (510)635-7068

Inman and Bowman
4 Orinda Way, Bldg. D, Ste. 150
Orinda, CA 94563
(510)253-1611
Fax: (510)253-9037

Accel Partners (San Francisco)
428 University Ave.
Palo Alto, CA 94301
(650)614-4800
Fax: (650)614-4880
Website: http://www.accel.com

Advanced Technology Ventures
485 Ramona St., Ste. 200
Palo Alto, CA 94301
(650)321-8601
Fax: (650)321-0934
Website: http://www.atvcapital.com

Anila Fund
400 Channing Ave.
Palo Alto, CA 94301
(650)833-5790
Fax: (650)833-0590
Website: http://www.anila.com

Asset Management Company Venture Capital
2275 E. Bayshore, Ste. 150
Palo Alto, CA 94303
(650)494-7400
Fax: (650)856-1826
E-mail: postmaster@assetman.com
Website: http://www.assetman.com

BancBoston Capital / BancBoston Ventures
435 Tasso St., Ste. 250
Palo Alto, CA 94305
(650)470-4100
Fax: (650)853-1425
Website: http://www.bancboston
capital.com

Charter Ventures
525 University Ave., Ste. 1400
Palo Alto, CA 94301
(650)325-6953
Fax: (650)325-4762
Website: http://www.charterventures.com

Communications Ventures
505 Hamilton Avenue, Ste. 305
Palo Alto, CA 94301
(650)325-9600
Fax: (650)325-9608
Website: http://www.comven.com

HMS Group
2468 Embarcadero Way
Palo Alto, CA 94303-3313
(650)856-9862
Fax: (650)856-9864

Jafco America Ventures, Inc.
505 Hamilton Ste. 310
Palto Alto, CA 94301
(650)463-8800
Fax: (650)463-8801
Website: http://www.jafco.com

New Vista Capital
540 Cowper St., Ste. 200

Palo Alto, CA 94301
(650)329-9333
Fax: (650)328-9434
E-mail: fgreene@nvcap.com
Website: http://www.nvcap.com

Norwest Equity Partners (Palo Alto)
245 Lytton Ave., Ste. 250
Palo Alto, CA 94301-1426
(650)321-8000
Fax: (650)321-8010
Website: http://www.norwestvp.com

Oak Investment Partners
525 University Ave., Ste. 1300
Palo Alto, CA 94301
(650)614-3700
Fax: (650)328-6345
Website: http://www.oakinv.com

Patricof & Co. Ventures, Inc. (Palo Alto)
2100 Geng Rd., Ste. 150
Palo Alto, CA 94303
(650)494-9944
Fax: (650)494-6751
Website: http://www.patricof.com

RWI Group
835 Page Mill Rd.
Palo Alto, CA 94304
(650)251-1800
Fax: (650)213-8660
Website: http://www.rwigroup.com

Summit Partners (Palo Alto)
499 Hamilton Ave., Ste. 200
Palo Alto, CA 94301
(650)321-1166
Fax: (650)321-1188
Website: http://www.summit
partners.com

Sutter Hill Ventures
755 Page Mill Rd., Ste. A-200
Palo Alto, CA 94304
(650)493-5600
Fax: (650)858-1854
E-mail: shv@shv.com

Vanguard Venture Partners
525 University Ave., Ste. 600
Palo Alto, CA 94301
(650)321-2900
Fax: (650)321-2902
Website: http://www.vanguard
ventures.com

Venture Growth Associates
2479 East Bayshore St., Ste. 710
Palo Alto, CA 94303

(650)855-9100
Fax: (650)855-9104

Worldview Technology Partners
435 Tasso St., Ste. 120
Palo Alto, CA 94301
(650)322-3800
Fax: (650)322-3880
Website: http://www.worldview.com

Draper, Fisher, Jurvetson / Draper Associates
400 Seaport Ct., Ste.250
Redwood City, CA 94063
(415)599-9000
Fax: (415)599-9726
Website: http://www.dfj.com

Gabriel Venture Partners
350 Marine Pkwy., Ste. 200
Redwood Shores, CA 94065
(650)551-5000
Fax: (650)551-5001
Website: http://www.gabrielvp.com

Hallador Venture Partners, L.L.C.
740 University Ave., Ste. 110
Sacramento, CA 95825-6710
(916)920-0191
Fax: (916)920-5188
E-mail: chris@hallador.com

Emerald Venture Group
12396 World Trade Dr., Ste. 116
San Diego, CA 92128
(858)451-1001
Fax: (858)451-1003
Website: http://www.emerald
venture.com

Forward Ventures
9255 Towne Centre Dr.
San Diego, CA 92121
(858)677-6077
Fax: (858)452-8799
E-mail: info@forwardventure.com
Website: http://www.forward
venture.com

Idanta Partners Ltd.
4660 La Jolla Village Dr., Ste. 850
San Diego, CA 92122
(619)452-9690
Fax: (619)452-2013
Website: http://www.idanta.com

Kingsbury Associates
3655 Nobel Dr., Ste. 490
San Diego, CA 92122
(858)677-0600
Fax: (858)677-0800

Kyocera International Inc.
Corporate Development
8611 Balboa Ave.
San Diego, CA 92123
(858)576-2600
Fax: (858)492-1456

Sorrento Associates, Inc.
4370 LaJolla Village Dr., Ste. 1040
San Diego, CA 92122
(619)452-3100
Fax: (619)452-7607
Website: http://www.sorrento
ventures.com

Western States Investment Group
9191 Towne Ctr. Dr., Ste. 310
San Diego, CA 92122
(619)678-0800
Fax: (619)678-0900

Aberdare Ventures
One Embarcadero Center, Ste. 4000
San Francisco, CA 94111
(415)392-7442
Fax: (415)392-4264
Website: http://www.aberdare.com

Acacia Venture Partners
101 California St., Ste. 3160
San Francisco, CA 94111
(415)433-4200
Fax: (415)433-4250
Website: http://www.acaciavp.com

Access Venture Partners
319 Laidley St.
San Francisco, CA 94131
(415)586-0132
Fax: (415)392-6310
Website: http://www.access
venturepartners.com

Alta Partners
One Embarcadero Center, Ste. 4050
San Francisco, CA 94111
(415)362-4022
Fax: (415)362-6178
E-mail: alta@altapartners.com
Website: http://www.altapartners.com

Bangert Dawes Reade Davis & Thom
220 Montgomery St., Ste. 424
San Francisco, CA 94104
(415)954-9900
Fax: (415)954-9901
E-mail: bdrdt@pacbell.net

Berkeley International Capital Corp.
650 California St., Ste. 2800
San Francisco, CA 94108-2609

(415)249-0450
Fax: (415)392-3929
Website: http://www.berkeleyvc.com

Blueprint Ventures LLC
456 Montgomery St., 22nd Fl.
San Francisco, CA 94104
(415)901-4000
Fax: (415)901-4035
Website: http://www.blue
printventures.com

Blumberg Capital Ventures
580 Howard St., Ste. 401
San Francisco, CA 94105
(415)905-5007
Fax: (415)357-5027
Website: http://www.blumberg-
capital.com

Burr, Egan, Deleage, and Co. (San Francisco)
1 Embarcadero Center, Ste. 4050
San Francisco, CA 94111
(415)362-4022
Fax: (415)362-6178

Burrill & Company
120 Montgomery St., Ste. 1370
San Francisco, CA 94104
(415)743-3160
Fax: (415)743-3161
Website: http://www.burrillandco.com

CMEA Ventures
235 Montgomery St., Ste. 920
San Francisco, CA 94401
(415)352-1520
Fax: (415)352-1524
Website: http://www.cmeaventures.com

Crocker Capital
1 Post St., Ste. 2500
San Francisco, CA 94101
(415)956-5250
Fax: (415)959-5710

Dominion Ventures, Inc.
44 Montgomery St., Ste. 4200
San Francisco, CA 94104
(415)362-4890
Fax: (415)394-9245

Dorset Capital
Pier 1
Bay 2
San Francisco, CA 94111
(415)398-7101
Fax: (415)398-7141
Website: http://www.dorsetcapital.com

Gatx Capital
Four Embarcadero Center, Ste. 2200
San Francisco, CA 94904
(415)955-3200
Fax: (415)955-3449

IMinds
135 Main St., Ste. 1350
San Francisco, CA 94105
(415)547-0000
Fax: (415)227-0300
Website: http://www.iminds.com

LF International Inc.
360 Post St., Ste. 705
San Francisco, CA 94108
(415)399-0110
Fax: (415)399-9222
Website: http://www.lfvc.com

Newbury Ventures
535 Pacific Ave., 2nd Fl.
San Francisco, CA 94133
(415)296-7408
Fax: (415)296-7416
Website: http://www.newburyven.com

Quest Ventures (San Francisco)
333 Bush St., Ste. 1750
San Francisco, CA 94104
(415)782-1414
Fax: (415)782-1415

Robertson-Stephens Co.
555 California St., Ste. 2600
San Francisco, CA 94104
(415)781-9700
Fax: (415)781-2556
Website: http://www.omegaad
ventures.com

Rosewood Capital, L.P.
One Maritime Plaza, Ste. 1330
San Francisco, CA 94111-3503
(415)362-5526
Fax: (415)362-1192
Website: http://www.rosewoodvc.com

Ticonderoga Capital Inc.
555 California St., No. 4950
San Francisco, CA 94104
(415)296-7900
Fax: (415)296-8956

21st Century Internet Venture Partners
Two South Park
2nd Floor
San Francisco, CA 94107
(415)512-1221
Fax: (415)512-2650
Website: http://www.21vc.com

VK Ventures
600 California St., Ste.1700
San Francisco, CA 94111
(415)391-5600
Fax: (415)397-2744

Walden Group of Venture Capital Funds
750 Battery St., Seventh Floor
San Francisco, CA 94111
(415)391-7225
Fax: (415)391-7262

Acer Technology Ventures
2641 Orchard Pkwy.
San Jose, CA 95134
(408)433-4945
Fax: (408)433-5230

Authosis
226 Airport Pkwy., Ste. 405
San Jose, CA 95110
(650)814-3603
Website: http://www.authosis.com

Western Technology Investment
2010 N. First St., Ste. 310
San Jose, CA 95131
(408)436-8577
Fax: (408)436-8625
E-mail: mktg@westerntech.com

Drysdale Enterprises
177 Bovet Rd., Ste. 600
San Mateo, CA 94402
(650)341-6336
Fax: (650)341-1329
E-mail: drysdale@aol.com

Greylock
2929 Campus Dr., Ste. 400
San Mateo, CA 94401
(650)493-5525
Fax: (650)493-5575
Website: http://www.greylock.com

Technology Funding
2000 Alameda de las Pulgas, Ste. 250
San Mateo, CA 94403
(415)345-2200
Fax: (415)345-1797

2M Invest Inc.
1875 S. Grant St.
Suite 750
San Mateo, CA 94402
(650)655-3765
Fax: (650)372-9107
E-mail: 2minfo@2minvest.com
Website: http://www.2minvest.com

Phoenix Growth Capital Corp.
2401 Kerner Blvd.
San Rafael, CA 94901
(415)485-4569
Fax: (415)485-4663

NextGen Partners LLC
1705 East Valley Rd.
Santa Barbara, CA 93108
(805)969-8540
Fax: (805)969-8542
Website: http://www.nextgen
partners.com

Denali Venture Capital
1925 Woodland Ave.
Santa Clara, CA 95050
(408)690-4838
Fax: (408)247-6979
E-mail: wael@denaliventurecapital.com
Website: http://www.denali
venturecapital.com

Dotcom Ventures LP
3945 Freedom Circle, Ste. 740
Santa Clara, CA 95045
(408)919-9855
Fax: (408)919-9857
Website: http://www.dotcom
venturesatl.com

Silicon Valley Bank
3003 Tasman
Santa Clara, CA 95054
(408)654-7400
Fax: (408)727-8728

Al Shugart International
920 41st Ave.
Santa Cruz, CA 95062
(831)479-7852
Fax: (831)479-7852
Website: http://www.alshugart.com

Leonard Mautner Associates
1434 Sixth St.
Santa Monica, CA 90401
(213)393-9788
Fax: (310)459-9918

Palomar Ventures
100 Wilshire Blvd., Ste. 450
Santa Monica, CA 90401
(310)260-6050
Fax: (310)656-4150
Website: http://www.palomar
ventures.com

Medicus Venture Partners
12930 Saratoga Ave., Ste. D8
Saratoga, CA 95070

(408)447-8600
Fax: (408)447-8599
Website: http://www.medicusvc.com

Redleaf Venture Management
14395 Saratoga Ave., Ste. 130
Saratoga, CA 95070
(408)868-0800
Fax: (408)868-0810
E-mail: nancy@redleaf.com
Website: http://www.redleaf.com

Artemis Ventures
207 Second St., Ste. E
3rd Fl.
Sausalito, CA 94965
(415)289-2500
Fax: (415)289-1789
Website: http://www.artemisventures.com

Deucalion Venture Partners
19501 Brooklime
Sonoma, CA 95476
(707)938-4974
Fax: (707)938-8921

Windward Ventures
PO Box 7688
Thousand Oaks, CA 91359-7688
(805)497-3332
Fax: (805)497-9331

National Investment Management, Inc.
2601 Airport Dr., Ste.210
Torrance, CA 90505
(310)784-7600
Fax: (310)784-7605

Southern California Ventures
406 Amapola Ave. Ste. 125
Torrance, CA 90501
(310)787-4381
Fax: (310)787-4382

Sandton Financial Group
21550 Oxnard St., Ste. 300
Woodland Hills, CA 91367
(818)702-9283

Woodside Fund
850 Woodside Dr.
Woodside, CA 94062
(650)368-5545
Fax: (650)368-2416
Website: http://www.woodsidefund.com

Colorado

Colorado Venture Management
Ste. 300
Boulder, CO 80301

(303)440-4055
Fax: (303)440-4636

Dean & Associates
4362 Apple Way
Boulder, CO 80301
Fax: (303)473-9900

Roser Ventures LLC
1105 Spruce St.
Boulder, CO 80302
(303)443-6436
Fax: (303)443-1885
Website: http://www.roserventures.com

Sequel Venture Partners
4430 Arapahoe Ave., Ste. 220
Boulder, CO 80303
(303)546-0400
Fax: (303)546-9728
E-mail: tom@sequelvc.com
Website: http://www.sequelvc.com

New Venture Resources
445C E. Cheyenne Mtn. Blvd.
Colorado Springs, CO 80906-4570
(719)598-9272
Fax: (719)598-9272

The Centennial Funds
1428 15th St.
Denver, CO 80202-1318
(303)405-7500
Fax: (303)405-7575
Website: http://www.centennial.com

Rocky Mountain Capital Partners
1125 17th St., Ste. 2260
Denver, CO 80202
(303)291-5200
Fax: (303)291-5327

Sandlot Capital LLC
600 South Cherry St., Ste. 525
Denver, CO 80246
(303)893-3400
Fax: (303)893-3403
Website: http://www.sandlotcapital.com

Wolf Ventures
50 South Steele St., Ste. 777
Denver, CO 80209
(303)321-4800
Fax: (303)321-4848
E-mail: businessplan@wolf
ventures.com
Website: http://www.wolfventures.com

The Columbine Venture Funds
5460 S. Quebec St., Ste. 270
Englewood, CO 80111

(303)694-3222
Fax: (303)694-9007

Investment Securities of Colorado, Inc.
4605 Denice Dr.
Englewood, CO 80111
(303)796-9192

Kinship Partners
6300 S. Syracuse Way, Ste. 484
Englewood, CO 80111
(303)694-0268
Fax: (303)694-1707
E-mail: block@vailsys.com

Boranco Management, L.L.C.
1528 Hillside Dr.
Fort Collins, CO 80524-1969
(970)221-2297
Fax: (970)221-4787

Aweida Ventures
890 West Cherry St., Ste. 220
Louisville, CO 80027
(303)664-9520
Fax: (303)664-9530
Website: http://www.aweida.com

Access Venture Partners
8787 Turnpike Dr., Ste. 260
Westminster, CO 80030
(303)426-8899
Fax: (303)426-8828

Medmax Ventures LP
1 Northwestern Dr., Ste. 203
Bloomfield, CT 06002
(860)286-2960
Fax: (860)286-9960

James B. Kobak & Co.
Four Mansfield Place
Darien, CT 06820
(203)656-3471
Fax: (203)655-2905

Orien Ventures
1 Post Rd.
Fairfield, CT 06430
(203)259-9933
Fax: (203)259-5288

ABP Acquisition Corporation
115 Maple Ave.
Greenwich, CT 06830
(203)625-8287
Fax: (203)447-6187

Catterton Partners
9 Greenwich Office Park
Greenwich, CT 06830
(203)629-4901

Fax: (203)629-4903
Website: http://www.cpequity.com

Consumer Venture Partners
3 Pickwick Plz.
Greenwich, CT 06830
(203)629-8800
Fax: (203)629-2019

Insurance Venture Partners
31 Brookside Dr., Ste. 211
Greenwich, CT 06830
(203)861-0030
Fax: (203)861-2745

The NTC Group
Three Pickwick Plaza
Ste. 200
Greenwich, CT 06830
(203)862-2800
Fax: (203)622-6538

Regulus International Capital Co., Inc.
140 Greenwich Ave.
Greenwich, CT 06830
(203)625-9700
Fax: (203)625-9706

Axiom Venture Partners
City Place II
185 Asylum St., 17th Fl.
Hartford, CT 06103
(860)548-7799
Fax: (860)548-7797
Website: http://www.axiomventures.com

Conning Capital Partners
City Place II
185 Asylum St.
Hartford, CT 06103-4105
(860)520-1289
Fax: (860)520-1299
E-mail: pe@conning.com
Website: http://www.conning.com

First New England Capital L.P.
100 Pearl St.
Hartford, CT 06103
(860)293-3333
Fax: (860)293-3338
E-mail: info@firstnewenglandcapital.com
Website: http://www.firstnewengland
capital.com

Northeast Ventures
One State St., Ste. 1720
Hartford, CT 06103
(860)547-1414
Fax: (860)246-8755

Windward Holdings
38 Sylvan Rd.
Madison, CT 06443
(203)245-6870
Fax: (203)245-6865

Advanced Materials Partners, Inc.
45 Pine St.
PO Box 1022
New Canaan, CT 06840
(203)966-6415
Fax: (203)966-8448
E-mail: wkb@amplink.com

RFE Investment Partners
36 Grove St.
New Canaan, CT 06840
(203)966-2800
Fax: (203)966-3109
Website: http://www.rfeip.com

Connecticut Innovations, Inc.
999 West St.
Rocky Hill, CT 06067
(860)563-5851
Fax: (860)563-4877
E-mail: pamela.hartley@ctin
novations.com
Website: http://www.ctinnovations.com

Canaan Partners
105 Rowayton Ave.
Rowayton, CT 06853
(203)855-0400
Fax: (203)854-9117
Website: http://www.canaan.com

Landmark Partners, Inc.
10 Mill Pond Ln.
Simsbury, CT 06070
(860)651-9760
Fax: (860)651-8890
Website: http://
www.landmarkpartners.com

Sweeney & Company
PO Box 567
Southport, CT 06490
(203)255-0220
Fax: (203)255-0220
E-mail: sweeney@connix.com

Baxter Associates, Inc.
PO Box 1333
Stamford, CT 06904
(203)323-3143
Fax: (203)348-0622

Beacon Partners Inc.
6 Landmark Sq., 4th Fl.
Stamford, CT 06901-2792

(203)359-5776
Fax: (203)359-5876

Collinson, Howe, and Lennox, LLC
1055 Washington Blvd., 5th Fl.
Stamford, CT 06901
(203)324-7700
Fax: (203)324-3636
E-mail: info@chlmedical.com
Website: http://www.chlmedical.com

Prime Capital Management Co.
550 West Ave.
Stamford, CT 06902
(203)964-0642
Fax: (203)964-0862

Saugatuck Capital Co.
1 Canterbury Green
Stamford, CT 06901
(203)348-6669
Fax: (203)324-6995
Website: http://www.sauga
tuckcapital.com

Soundview Financial Group Inc.
22 Gatehouse Rd.
Stamford, CT 06902
(203)462-7200
Fax: (203)462-7350
Website: http://www.sndv.com

TSG Ventures, L.L.C.
177 Broad St., 12th Fl.
Stamford, CT 06901
(203)406-1500
Fax: (203)406-1590

Whitney & Company
177 Broad St.
Stamford, CT 06901
(203)973-1400
Fax: (203)973-1422
Website: http://www.jhwhitney.com

Cullinane & Donnelly Venture Partners L.P.
970 Farmington Ave.
West Hartford, CT 06107
(860)521-7811

The Crestview Investment and Financial Group
431 Post Rd. E, Ste. 1
Westport, CT 06880-4403
(203)222-0333
Fax: (203)222-0000

Marketcorp Venture Associates, L.P. (MCV)
274 Riverside Ave.
Westport, CT 06880

(203)222-3030
Fax: (203)222-3033

Oak Investment Partners (Westport)
1 Gorham Island
Westport, CT 06880
(203)226-8346
Fax: (203)227-0372
Website: http://www.oakinv.com

Oxford Bioscience Partners
315 Post Rd. W
Westport, CT 06880-5200
(203)341-3300
Fax: (203)341-3309
Website: http://www.oxbio.com

Prince Ventures (Westport)
25 Ford Rd.
Westport, CT 06880
(203)227-8332
Fax: (203)226-5302

LTI Venture Leasing Corp.
221 Danbury Rd.
Wilton, CT 06897
(203)563-1100
Fax: (203)563-1111
Website: http://www.ltileasing.com

Delaware

Blue Rock Capital
5803 Kennett Pike, Ste. A
Wilmington, DE 19807
(302)426-0981
Fax: (302)426-0982
Website: http://www.bluerockcapital.com

District of Columbia

Allied Capital Corp.
1919 Pennsylvania Ave. NW
Washington, DC 20006-3434
(202)331-2444
Fax: (202)659-2053
Website: http://www.alliedcapital.com

Atlantic Coastal Ventures, L.P.
3101 South St. NW
Washington, DC 20007
(202)293-1166
Fax: (202)293-1181
Website: http://www.atlanticcv.com

Columbia Capital Group, Inc.
1660 L St. NW, Ste. 308
Washington, DC 20036
(202)775-8815
Fax: (202)223-0544

Core Capital Partners
901 15th St., NW
9th Fl.
Washington, DC 20005
(202)589-0090
Fax: (202)589-0091
Website: http://www.core-capital.com

Next Point Partners
701 Pennsylvania Ave. NW, Ste. 900
Washington, DC 20004
(202)661-8703
Fax: (202)434-7400
E-mail: mf@nextpoint.vc
Website: http://www.nextpointvc.com

Telecommunications Development Fund
2020 K. St. NW
Ste. 375
Washington, DC 20006
(202)293-8840
Fax: (202)293-8850
Website: http://www.tdfund.com

Wachtel & Co., Inc.
1101 4th St. NW
Washington, DC 20005-5680
(202)898-1144

Winslow Partners LLC
1300 Connecticut Ave. NW
Washington, DC 20036-1703
(202)530-5000
Fax: (202)530-5010
E-mail: winslow@winslowpartners.com

Women's Growth Capital Fund
1054 31st St., NW
Ste. 110
Washington, DC 20007
(202)342-1431
Fax: (202)341-1203
Website: http://www.wgcf.com

Sigma Capital Corp.
22668 Caravelle Circle
Boca Raton, FL 33433
(561)368-9783

North American Business Development Co., L.L.C.
111 East Las Olas Blvd.
Ft. Lauderdale, FL 33301
(305)463-0681
Fax: (305)527-0904
Website: http://
www.northamericanfund.com

Chartwell Capital Management Co. Inc.
1 Independent Dr., Ste. 3120

Jacksonville, FL 32202
(904)355-3519
Fax: (904)353-5833
E-mail: info@chartwellcap.com

CEO Advisors
1061 Maitland Center Commons
Ste. 209
Maitland, FL 32751
(407)660-9327
Fax: (407)660-2109

Henry & Co.
8201 Peters Rd., Ste. 1000
Plantation, FL 33324
(954)797-7400

Avery Business Development Services
2506 St. Michel Ct.
Ponte Vedra, FL 32082
(904)285-6033

New South Ventures
5053 Ocean Blvd.
Sarasota, FL 34242
(941)358-6000
Fax: (941)358-6078
Website: http://www.newsouth
ventures.com

Venture Capital Management Corp.
PO Box 2626
Satellite Beach, FL 32937
(407)777-1969

Florida Capital Venture Ltd.
325 Florida Bank Plaza
100 W. Kennedy Blvd.
Tampa, FL 33602
(813)229-2294
Fax: (813)229-2028

Quantum Capital Partners
339 South Plant Ave.
Tampa, FL 33606
(813)250-1999
Fax: (813)250-1998
Website: http://www.quantum
capitalpartners.com

South Atlantic Venture Fund
614 W. Bay St.
Tampa, FL 33606-2704
(813)253-2500
Fax: (813)253-2360
E-mail: venture@southatlantic.com
Website: http://www.southatlantic.com

LM Capital Corp.
120 S. Olive, Ste. 400
West Palm Beach, FL 33401

(561)833-9700
Fax: (561)655-6587
Website: http://www.lmcapital
securities.com

Georgia

Venture First Associates
4811 Thornwood Dr.
Acworth, GA 30102
(770)928-3733
Fax: (770)928-6455

Alliance Technology Ventures
8995 Westside Pkwy., Ste. 200
Alpharetta, GA 30004
(678)336-2000
Fax: (678)336-2001
E-mail: info@atv.com
Website: http://www.atv.com

Cordova Ventures
2500 North Winds Pkwy., Ste. 475
Alpharetta, GA 30004
(678)942-0300
Fax: (678)942-0301
Website: http://www.cordovaventures.
com

**Advanced Technology Development
Fund**
1000 Abernathy, Ste. 1420
Atlanta, GA 30328-5614
(404)668-2333
Fax: (404)668-2333

CGW Southeast Partners
12 Piedmont Center, Ste. 210
Atlanta, GA 30305
(404)816-3255
Fax: (404)816-3258
Website: http://www.cgwlp.com

Cyberstarts
1900 Emery St., NW
3rd Fl.
Atlanta, GA 30318
(404)267-5000
Fax: (404)267-5200
Website: http://www.cyberstarts.com

EGL Holdings, Inc.
10 Piedmont Center, Ste. 412
Atlanta, GA 30305
(404)949-8300
Fax: (404)949-8311

Equity South
1790 The Lenox Bldg.
3399 Peachtree Rd. NE
Atlanta, GA 30326

(404)237-6222
Fax: (404)261-1578

Five Paces
3400 Peachtree Rd., Ste. 200
Atlanta, GA 30326
(404)439-8300
Fax: (404)439-8301
Website: http://www.fivepaces.com

Frontline Capital, Inc.
3475 Lenox Rd., Ste. 400
Atlanta, GA 30326
(404)240-7280
Fax: (404)240-7281

Fuqua Ventures LLC
1201 W. Peachtree St. NW, Ste. 5000
Atlanta, GA 30309
(404)815-4500
Fax: (404)815-4528
Website: http://www.fuquaventures.com

Noro-Moseley Partners
4200 Northside Pkwy., Bldg. 9
Atlanta, GA 30327
(404)233-1966
Fax: (404)239-9280
Website: http://www.noro-moseley.com

Renaissance Capital Corp.
34 Peachtree St. NW, Ste. 2230
Atlanta, GA 30303
(404)658-9061
Fax: (404)658-9064

River Capital, Inc.
Two Midtown Plaza
1360 Peachtree St. NE, Ste. 1430
Atlanta, GA 30309
(404)873-2166
Fax: (404)873-2158

State Street Bank & Trust Co.
3414 Peachtree Rd. NE, Ste. 1010
Atlanta, GA 30326
(404)364-9500
Fax: (404)261-4469

UPS Strategic Enterprise Fund
55 Glenlake Pkwy. NE
Atlanta, GA 30328
(404)828-8814
Fax: (404)828-8088
E-mail: jcacyce@ups.com
Website: http://www.ups.com/sef/
sef_home

Wachovia
191 Peachtree St. NE, 26th Fl.
Atlanta, GA 30303

(404)332-1000
Fax: (404)332-1392
Website: http://www.wachovia.com/wca

Brainworks Ventures
4243 Dunwoody Club Dr.
Chamblee, GA 30341
(770)239-7447

First Growth Capital Inc.
Best Western Plaza, Ste. 105
PO Box 815
Forsyth, GA 31029
(912)781-7131

Financial Capital Resources, Inc.
21 Eastbrook Bend, Ste. 116
Peachtree City, GA 30269
(404)487-6650

Hawaii

HMS Hawaii Management Partners
Davies Pacific Center
841 Bishop St., Ste. 860
Honolulu, HI 96813
(808)545-3755
Fax: (808)531-2611

Idaho

Sun Valley Ventures
160 Second St.
Ketchum, ID 83340
(208)726-5005
Fax: (208)726-5094

Illinois

Open Prairie Ventures
115 N. Neil St., Ste. 209
Champaign, IL 61820
(217)351-7000
Fax: (217)351-7051
E-mail: inquire@openprairie.com
Website: http://www.openprairie.com

ABN AMRO Private Equity
208 S. La Salle St., 10th Fl.
Chicago, IL 60604
(312)855-7079
Fax: (312)553-6648
Website: http://www.abnequity.com

Alpha Capital Partners, Ltd.
122 S. Michigan Ave., Ste. 1700
Chicago, IL 60603
(312)322-9800
Fax: (312)322-9808
E-mail: acp@alphacapital.com

Ameritech Development Corp.
30 S. Wacker Dr., 37th Fl.
Chicago, IL 60606
(312)750-5083
Fax: (312)609-0244

Apex Investment Partners
225 W. Washington, Ste. 1450
Chicago, IL 60606
(312)857-2800
Fax: (312)857-1800
E-mail: apex@apexvc.com
Website: http://www.apexvc.com

Arch Venture Partners
8725 W. Higgins Rd., Ste. 290
Chicago, IL 60631
(773)380-6600
Fax: (773)380-6606
Website: http://www.archventure.com

The Bank Funds
208 South LaSalle St., Ste. 1680
Chicago, IL 60604
(312)855-6020
Fax: (312)855-8910

Batterson Venture Partners
303 W. Madison St., Ste. 1110
Chicago, IL 60606-3309
(312)269-0300
Fax: (312)269-0021
Website: http://www.battersonvp.com

William Blair Capital Partners, L.L.C.
222 W. Adams St., Ste. 1300
Chicago, IL 60606
(312)364-8250
Fax: (312)236-1042
E-mail: privateequity@wmblair.com
Website: http://www.wmblair.com

Bluestar Ventures
208 South LaSalle St., Ste. 1020
Chicago, IL 60604
(312)384-5000
Fax: (312)384-5005
Website: http://www.bluestarventures.com

The Capital Strategy Management Co.
233 S. Wacker Dr.
Box 06334
Chicago, IL 60606
(312)444-1170

DN Partners
77 West Wacker Dr., Ste. 4550
Chicago, IL 60601
(312)332-7960
Fax: (312)332-7979

Dresner Capital Inc.
29 South LaSalle St., Ste. 310
Chicago, IL 60603
(312)726-3600
Fax: (312)726-7448

Eblast Ventures LLC
11 South LaSalle St., 5th Fl.
Chicago, IL 60603
(312)372-2600
Fax: (312)372-5621
Website: http://www.eblastventures.com

Essex Woodlands Health Ventures, L.P.
190 S. LaSalle St., Ste. 2800
Chicago, IL 60603
(312)444-6040
Fax: (312)444-6034
Website: http://www.essexwood
lands.com

First Analysis Venture Capital
233 S. Wacker Dr., Ste. 9500
Chicago, IL 60606
(312)258-1400
Fax: (312)258-0334
Website: http://www.firstanalysis.com

Frontenac Co.
135 S. LaSalle St., Ste.3800
Chicago, IL 60603
(312)368-0044
Fax: (312)368-9520
Website: http://www.frontenac.com

GTCR Golder Rauner, LLC
6100 Sears Tower
Chicago, IL 60606
(312)382-2200
Fax: (312)382-2201
Website: http://www.gtcr.com

High Street Capital LLC
311 South Wacker Dr., Ste. 4550
Chicago, IL 60606
(312)697-4990
Fax: (312)697-4994
Website: http://www.highstr.com

IEG Venture Management, Inc.
70 West Madison
Chicago, IL 60602
(312)644-0890
Fax: (312)454-0369
Website: http://www.iegventure.com

JK&B Capital
180 North Stetson, Ste. 4500
Chicago, IL 60601
(312)946-1200
Fax: (312)946-1103

E-mail: gspencer@jkbcapital.com
Website: http://www.jkbcapital.com

Kettle Partners L.P.
350 W. Hubbard, Ste. 350
Chicago, IL 60610
(312)329-9300
Fax: (312)527-4519
Website: http://www.kettlevc.com

Lake Shore Capital Partners
20 N. Wacker Dr., Ste. 2807
Chicago, IL 60606
(312)803-3536
Fax: (312)803-3534

LaSalle Capital Group Inc.
70 W. Madison St., Ste. 5710
Chicago, IL 60602
(312)236-7041
Fax: (312)236-0720

Linc Capital, Inc.
303 E. Wacker Pkwy., Ste. 1000
Chicago, IL 60601
(312)946-2670
Fax: (312)938-4290
E-mail: bdemars@linccap.com

Madison Dearborn Partners, Inc.
3 First National Plz., Ste. 3800
Chicago, IL 60602
(312)895-1000
Fax: (312)895-1001
E-mail: invest@mdcp.com
Website: http://www.mdcp.com

Mesirow Private Equity Investments Inc.
350 N. Clark St.
Chicago, IL 60610
(312)595-6950
Fax: (312)595-6211
Website: http://www.meisrow
financial.com

Mosaix Ventures LLC
1822 North Mohawk
Chicago, IL 60614
(312)274-0988
Fax: (312)274-0989
Website: http://www.mosaix
ventures.com

Nesbitt Burns
111 West Monroe St.
Chicago, IL 60603
(312)416-3855
Fax: (312)765-8000
Website: http://www.harrisbank.com

Polestar Capital, Inc.
180 N. Michigan Ave., Ste. 1905
Chicago, IL 60601
(312)984-9090
Fax: (312)984-9877
E-mail: wl@polestarvc.com
Website: http://www.polestarvc.com

Prince Ventures (Chicago)
10 S. Wacker Dr., Ste. 2575
Chicago, IL 60606-7407
(312)454-1408
Fax: (312)454-9125

Prism Capital
444 N. Michigan Ave.
Chicago, IL 60611
(312)464-7900
Fax: (312)464-7915
Website: http://www.prismfund.com

Third Coast Capital
900 N. Franklin St., Ste. 700
Chicago, IL 60610
(312)337-3303
Fax: (312)337-2567
E-mail: manic@earthlink.com
Website: http://www.third
coastcapital.com

Thoma Cressey Equity Partners
4460 Sears Tower, 92nd Fl.
233 S. Wacker Dr.
Chicago, IL 60606
(312)777-4444
Fax: (312)777-4445
Website: http://www.thomacressey.com

Tribune Ventures
435 N. Michigan Ave., Ste. 600
Chicago, IL 60611
(312)527-8797
Fax: (312)222-5993
Website: http://www.tribuneventures.com

Wind Point Partners (Chicago)
676 N. Michigan Ave., Ste. 330
Chicago, IL 60611
(312)649-4000
Website: http://www.wppartners.com

Marquette Venture Partners
520 Lake Cook Rd., Ste. 450
Deerfield, IL 60015
(847)940-1700
Fax: (847)940-1724
Website: http://www.marquette
ventures.com

Duchossois Investments Limited, LLC
845 Larch Ave.
Elmhurst, IL 60126

(630)530-6105
Fax: (630)993-8644
Website: http://www.duchtec.com

Evanston Business Investment Corp.
1840 Oak Ave.
Evanston, IL 60201
(847)866-1840
Fax: (847)866-1808
E-mail: t-parkinson@nwu.com
Website: http://www.ebic.com

Inroads Capital Partners L.P.
1603 Orrington Ave., Ste. 2050
Evanston, IL 60201-3841
(847)864-2000
Fax: (847)864-9692

The Cerulean Fund/WGC Enterprises
1701 E. Lake Ave., Ste. 170
Glenview, IL 60025
(847)657-8002
Fax: (847)657-8168

Ventana Financial Resources, Inc.
249 Market Sq.
Lake Forest, IL 60045
(847)234-3434

Beecken, Petty & Co.
901 Warrenville Rd., Ste. 205
Lisle, IL 60532
(630)435-0300
Fax: (630)435-0370
E-mail: hep@bpcompany.com
Website: http://www.bpcompany.com

Allstate Private Equity
3075 Sanders Rd., Ste. G5D
Northbrook, IL 60062-7127
(847)402-8247
Fax: (847)402-0880

KB Partners
1101 Skokie Blvd., Ste. 260
Northbrook, IL 60062-2856
(847)714-0444
Fax: (847)714-0445
E-mail: keith@kbpartners.com
Website: http://www.kbpartners.com

Transcap Associates Inc.
900 Skokie Blvd., Ste. 210
Northbrook, IL 60062
(847)753-9600
Fax: (847)753-9090

**Graystone Venture Partners, L.L.C. /
Portage Venture Partners**
One Northfield Plaza, Ste. 530
Northfield, IL 60093

(847)446-9460
Fax: (847)446-9470
Website: http://www.portage
ventures.com

Motorola Inc.
1303 E. Algonquin Rd.
Schaumburg, IL 60196-1065
(847)576-4929
Fax: (847)538-2250
Website: http://www.mot.com/mne

Indiana

Irwin Ventures LLC
500 Washington St.
Columbus, IN 47202
(812)373-1434
Fax: (812)376-1709
Website: http://www.irwinventures.com

Cambridge Venture Partners
4181 East 96th St., Ste. 200
Indianapolis, IN 46240
(317)814-6192
Fax: (317)944-9815

CID Equity Partners
One American Square, Ste. 2850
Box 82074
Indianapolis, IN 46282
(317)269-2350
Fax: (317)269-2355
Website: http://www.cidequity.com

Gazelle Techventures
6325 Digital Way, Ste. 460
Indianapolis, IN 46278
(317)275-6800
Fax: (317)275-1101
Website: http://www.gazellevc.com

Monument Advisors Inc.
Bank One Center/Circle
111 Monument Circle, Ste. 600
Indianapolis, IN 46204-5172
(317)656-5065
Fax: (317)656-5060
Website: http://www.monumentadv.com

MWV Capital Partners
201 N. Illinois St., Ste. 300
Indianapolis, IN 46204
(317)237-2323
Fax: (317)237-2325
Website: http://www.mwvcapital.com

First Source Capital Corp.
100 North Michigan St.
PO Box 1602
South Bend, IN 46601

(219)235-2180
Fax: (219)235-2227

Iowa

Allsop Venture Partners
118 Third Ave. SE, Ste. 837
Cedar Rapids, IA 52401
(319)368-6675
Fax: (319)363-9515

InvestAmerica Investment Advisors, Inc.
101 2nd St. SE, Ste. 800
Cedar Rapids, IA 52401
(319)363-8249
Fax: (319)363-9683

Pappajohn Capital Resources
2116 Financial Center
Des Moines, IA 50309
(515)244-5746
Fax: (515)244-2346
Website: http://www.pappajohn.com

Berthel Fisher & Company Planning Inc.
701 Tama St.
PO Box 609
Marion, IA 52302
(319)497-5700
Fax: (319)497-4244

Kansas

Enterprise Merchant Bank
7400 West 110th St., Ste. 560
Overland Park, KS 66210
(913)327-8500
Fax: (913)327-8505

Kansas Venture Capital, Inc. (Overland Park)
6700 Antioch Plz., Ste. 460
Overland Park, KS 66204
(913)262-7117
Fax: (913)262-3509
E-mail: jdalton@kvci.com

Child Health Investment Corp.
6803 W. 64th St., Ste. 208
Shawnee Mission, KS 66202
(913)262-1436
Fax: (913)262-1575
Website: http://www.chca.com

Kansas Technology Enterprise Corp.
214 SW 6th, 1st Fl.
Topeka, KS 66603-3719
(785)296-5272
Fax: (785)296-1160

E-mail: ktec@ktec.com
Website: http://www.ktec.com

Kentucky

Kentucky Highlands Investment Corp.
362 Old Whitley Rd.
London, KY 40741
(606)864-5175
Fax: (606)864-5194
Website: http://www.khic.org

Chrysalis Ventures, L.L.C.
1850 National City Tower
Louisville, KY 40202
(502)583-7644
Fax: (502)583-7648
E-mail: bobsany@chrysalisventures.com
Website: http://www.chrysalis
ventures.com

Humana Venture Capital
500 West Main St.
Louisville, KY 40202
(502)580-3922
Fax: (502)580-2051
E-mail: gemont@humana.com
George Emont, Director

Summit Capital Group, Inc.
6510 Glenridge Park Pl., Ste. 8
Louisville, KY 40222
(502)332-2700

Louisiana

Bank One Equity Investors, Inc.
451 Florida St.
Baton Rouge, LA 70801
(504)332-4421
Fax: (504)332-7377

Advantage Capital Partners
LLE Tower
909 Poydras St., Ste. 2230
New Orleans, LA 70112
(504)522-4850
Fax: (504)522-4950
Website: http://www.advantagecap.com

Maine

CEI Ventures / Coastal Ventures LP
2 Portland Fish Pier, Ste. 201
Portland, ME 04101
(207)772-5356
Fax: (207)772-5503
Website: http://www.ceiventures.com

Commwealth Bioventures, Inc.
4 Milk St.
Portland, ME 04101

(207)780-0904
Fax: (207)780-0913

Maryland

Annapolis Ventures LLC
151 West St., Ste. 302
Annapolis, MD 21401
(443)482-9555
Fax: (443)482-9565
Website: http://www.annapolis
ventures.com

Delmag Ventures
220 Wardour Dr.
Annapolis, MD 21401
(410)267-8196
Fax: (410)267-8017
Website: http://www.delmag
ventures.com

Abell Venture Fund
111 S. Calvert St., Ste. 2300
Baltimore, MD 21202
(410)547-1300
Fax: (410)539-6579
Website: http://www.abell.org

ABS Ventures (Baltimore)
1 South St., Ste. 2150
Baltimore, MD 21202
(410)895-3895
Fax: (410)895-3899
Website: http://www.absventures.com

Anthem Capital, L.P.
16 S. Calvert St., Ste. 800
Baltimore, MD 21202-1305
(410)625-1510
Fax: (410)625-1735
Website: http://www.anthemcapital.com

Catalyst Ventures
1119 St. Paul St.
Baltimore, MD 21202
(410)244-0123
Fax: (410)752-7721

Maryland Venture Capital Trust
217 E. Redwood St., Ste. 2200
Baltimore, MD 21202
(410)767-6361
Fax: (410)333-6931

New Enterprise Associates (Baltimore)
1119 St. Paul St.
Baltimore, MD 21202
(410)244-0115
Fax: (410)752-7721
Website: http://www.nea.com

T. Rowe Price Threshold Partnerships
100 E. Pratt St., 8th Fl.
Baltimore, MD 21202
(410)345-2000
Fax: (410)345-2800

Spring Capital Partners
16 W. Madison St.
Baltimore, MD 21201
(410)685-8000
Fax: (410)727-1436
E-mail: mailbox@springcap.com

Arete Corporation
3 Bethesda Metro Ctr., Ste. 770
Bethesda, MD 20814
(301)657-6268
Fax: (301)657-6254
Website: http://www.arete-microgen.com

Embryon Capital
7903 Sleaford Place
Bethesda, MD 20814
(301)656-6837
Fax: (301)656-8056

Potomac Ventures
7920 Norfolk Ave., Ste. 1100
Bethesda, MD 20814
(301)215-9240
Website: http://www.potomacventures.com

Toucan Capital Corp.
3 Bethesda Metro Center, Ste. 700
Bethesda, MD 20814
(301)961-1970
Fax: (301)961-1969
Website: http://www.toucancapital.com

Kinetic Ventures LLC
2 Wisconsin Cir., Ste. 620
Chevy Chase, MD 20815
(301)652-8066
Fax: (301)652-8310
Website: http://www.kineticventures.com

Boulder Ventures Ltd.
4750 Owings Mills Blvd.
Owings Mills, MD 21117
(410)998-3114
Fax: (410)356-5492
Website: http://www.boulderventures.com

Grotech Capital Group
9690 Deereco Rd., Ste. 800
Timonium, MD 21093
(410)560-2000
Fax: (410)560-1910
Website: http://www.grotech.com

Massachusetts

Adams, Harkness & Hill, Inc.
60 State St.
Boston, MA 02109
(617)371-3900

Advent International
75 State St., 29th Fl.
Boston, MA 02109
(617)951-9400
Fax: (617)951-0566
Website: http://www.adventinternational.com

American Research and Development
30 Federal St.
Boston, MA 02110-2508
(617)423-7500
Fax: (617)423-9655

Ascent Venture Partners
255 State St., 5th Fl.
Boston, MA 02109
(617)270-9400
Fax: (617)270-9401
E-mail: info@ascentvp.com
Website: http://www.ascentvp.com

Atlas Venture
222 Berkeley St.
Boston, MA 02116
(617)488-2200
Fax: (617)859-9292
Website: http://www.atlasventure.com

Axxon Capital
28 State St., 37th Fl.
Boston, MA 02109
(617)722-0980
Fax: (617)557-6014
Website: http://www.axxoncapital.com

BancBoston Capital/BancBoston Ventures
175 Federal St., 10th Fl.
Boston, MA 02110
(617)434-2509
Fax: (617)434-6175
Website: http://www.bancbostoncapital.com

Boston Capital Ventures
Old City Hall
45 School St.
Boston, MA 02108
(617)227-6550
Fax: (617)227-3847
E-mail: info@bcv.com
Website: http://www.bcv.com

Boston Financial & Equity Corp.
20 Overland St.
PO Box 15071
Boston, MA 02215
(617)267-2900
Fax: (617)437-7601
E-mail: debbie@bfec.com

Boston Millennia Partners
30 Rowes Wharf
Boston, MA 02110
(617)428-5150
Fax: (617)428-5160
Website: http://www.millenniapartners.com

Bristol Investment Trust
842A Beacon St.
Boston, MA 02215-3199
(617)566-5212
Fax: (617)267-0932

Brook Venture Management LLC
50 Federal St., 5th Fl.
Boston, MA 02110
(617)451-8989
Fax: (617)451-2369
Website: http://www.brookventure.com

Burr, Egan, Deleage, and Co. (Boston)
200 Clarendon St., Ste. 3800
Boston, MA 02116
(617)262-7770
Fax: (617)262-9779

Cambridge/Samsung Partners
One Exeter Plaza
Ninth Fl.
Boston, MA 02116
(617)262-4440
Fax: (617)262-5562

Chestnut Street Partners, Inc.
75 State St., Ste. 2500
Boston, MA 02109
(617)345-7220
Fax: (617)345-7201
E-mail: chestnut@chestnutp.com

Claflin Capital Management, Inc.
10 Liberty Sq., Ste. 300
Boston, MA 02109
(617)426-6505
Fax: (617)482-0016
Website: http://www.claflincapital.com

Copley Venture Partners
99 Summer St., Ste. 1720
Boston, MA 02110
(617)737-1253
Fax: (617)439-0699

Corning Capital / Corning Technology Ventures
121 High Street, Ste. 400
Boston, MA 02110
(617)338-2656
Fax: (617)261-3864
Website: http://www.corningventures.com

Downer & Co.
211 Congress St.
Boston, MA 02110
(617)482-6200
Fax: (617)482-6201
E-mail: cdowner@downer.com
Website: http://www.downer.com

Fidelity Ventures
82 Devonshire St.
Boston, MA 02109
(617)563-6370
Fax: (617)476-9023
Website: http://www.fidelityventures.com

Greylock Management Corp. (Boston)
1 Federal St.
Boston, MA 02110-2065
(617)423-5525
Fax: (617)482-0059

Gryphon Ventures
222 Berkeley St., Ste.1600
Boston, MA 02116
(617)267-9191
Fax: (617)267-4293
E-mail: all@gryphoninc.com

Halpern, Denny & Co.
500 Boylston St.
Boston, MA 02116
(617)536-6602
Fax: (617)536-8535

Harbourvest Partners, LLC
1 Financial Center, 44th Fl.
Boston, MA 02111
(617)348-3707
Fax: (617)350-0305
Website: http://www.hvpllc.com

Highland Capital Partners
2 International Pl.
Boston, MA 02110
(617)981-1500
Fax: (617)531-1550
E-mail: info@hcp.com
Website: http://www.hcp.com

Lee Munder Venture Partners
John Hancock Tower T-53
200 Clarendon St.
Boston, MA 02103

(617)380-5600
Fax: (617)380-5601
Website: http://www.leemunder.com

M/C Venture Partners
75 State St., Ste. 2500
Boston, MA 02109
(617)345-7200
Fax: (617)345-7201
Website: http://www.mcventure
partners.com

Massachusetts Capital Resources Co.
420 Boylston St.
Boston, MA 02116
(617)536-3900
Fax: (617)536-7930

Massachusetts Technology Development Corp. (MTDC)
148 State St.
Boston, MA 02109
(617)723-4920
Fax: (617)723-5983
E-mail: jhodgman@mtdc.com
Website: http://www.mtdc.com

New England Partners
One Boston Place, Ste. 2100
Boston, MA 02108
(617)624-8400
Fax: (617)624-8999
Website: http://www.nepartners.com

North Hill Ventures
Ten Post Office Square
11th Fl.
Boston, MA 02109
(617)788-2112
Fax: (617)788-2152
Website: http://www.northhill
ventures.com

OneLiberty Ventures
150 Cambridge Park Dr.
Boston, MA 02140
(617)492-7280
Fax: (617)492-7290
Website: http://www.oneliberty.com

Schroder Ventures
Life Sciences
60 State St., Ste. 3650
Boston, MA 02109
(617)367-8100
Fax: (617)367-1590
Website: http://www.shroderventures.com

Shawmut Capital Partners
75 Federal St., 18th Fl.
Boston, MA 02110

(617)368-4900
Fax: (617)368-4910
Website: http://www.shawmutcapital.com

Solstice Capital LLC
15 Broad St., 3rd Fl.
Boston, MA 02109
(617)523-7733
Fax: (617)523-5827
E-mail: solticecapital@solcap.com

Spectrum Equity Investors
One International Pl., 29th Fl.
Boston, MA 02110
(617)464-4600
Fax: (617)464-4601
Website: http://www.spectrumequity.com

Spray Venture Partners
One Walnut St.
Boston, MA 02108
(617)305-4140
Fax: (617)305-4144
Website: http://www.sprayventure.com

The Still River Fund
100 Federal St., 29th Fl.
Boston, MA 02110
(617)348-2327
Fax: (617)348-2371
Website: http://www.stillriverfund.com

Summit Partners
600 Atlantic Ave., Ste. 2800
Boston, MA 02210-2227
(617)824-1000
Fax: (617)824-1159
Website: http://www.summitpartners.com

TA Associates, Inc. (Boston)
High Street Tower
125 High St., Ste. 2500
Boston, MA 02110
(617)574-6700
Fax: (617)574-6728
Website: http://www.ta.com

TVM Techno Venture Management
101 Arch St., Ste. 1950
Boston, MA 02110
(617)345-9320
Fax: (617)345-9377
E-mail: info@tvmvc.com
Website: http://www.tvmvc.com

UNC Ventures
64 Burough St.
Boston, MA 02130-4017
(617)482-7070
Fax: (617)522-2176

Venture Investment Management Company (VIMAC)
177 Milk St.
Boston, MA 02190-3410
(617)292-3300
Fax: (617)292-7979
E-mail: bzeisig@vimac.com
Website: http://www.vimac.com

MDT Advisers, Inc.
125 Cambridge Park Dr.
Cambridge, MA 02140-2314
(617)234-2200
Fax: (617)234-2210
Website: http://www.mdtai.com

TTC Ventures
One Main St., 6th Fl.
Cambridge, MA 02142
(617)528-3137
Fax: (617)577-1715
E-mail: info@ttcventures.com

Zero Stage Capital Co. Inc.
101 Main St., 17th Fl.
Cambridge, MA 02142
(617)876-5355
Fax: (617)876-1248
Website: http://www.zerostage.com

Atlantic Capital
164 Cushing Hwy.
Cohasset, MA 02025
(617)383-9449
Fax: (617)383-6040
E-mail: info@atlanticcap.com
Website: http://www.atlanticcap.com

Seacoast Capital Partners
55 Ferncroft Rd.
Danvers, MA 01923
(978)750-1300
Fax: (978)750-1301
E-mail: gdeli@seacoastcapital.com
Website: http://www.seacoast
capital.com

Sage Management Group
44 South Street
PO Box 2026
East Dennis, MA 02641
(508)385-7172
Fax: (508)385-7272
E-mail: sagemgt@capecod.net

Applied Technology
1 Cranberry Hill
Lexington, MA 02421-7397
(617)862-8622
Fax: (617)862-8367

Royalty Capital Management
5 Downing Rd.
Lexington, MA 02421-6918
(781)861-8490

Argo Global Capital
210 Broadway, Ste. 101
Lynnfield, MA 01940
(781)592-5250
Fax: (781)592-5230
Website: http://www.gsmcapital.com

Industry Ventures
6 Bayne Lane
Newburyport, MA 01950
(978)499-7606
Fax: (978)499-0686
Website: http://
www.industryventures.com

Softbank Capital Partners
10 Langley Rd., Ste. 202
Newton Center, MA 02459
(617)928-9300
Fax: (617)928-9305
E-mail: clax@bvc.com

Advanced Technology Ventures (Boston)
281 Winter St., Ste. 350
Waltham, MA 02451
(781)290-0707
Fax: (781)684-0045
E-mail: info@atvcapital.com
Website: http://www.atvcapital.com

Castile Ventures
890 Winter St., Ste. 140
Waltham, MA 02451
(781)890-0060
Fax: (781)890-0065
Website: http://www.castileventures.com

Charles River Ventures
1000 Winter St., Ste. 3300
Waltham, MA 02451
(781)487-7060
Fax: (781)487-7065
Website: http://www.crv.com

Comdisco Venture Group (Waltham)
Totton Pond Office Center
400-1 Totten Pond Rd.
Waltham, MA 02451
(617)672-0250
Fax: (617)398-8099

Marconi Ventures
890 Winter St., Ste. 310
Waltham, MA 02451
(781)839-7177

Fax: (781)522-7477
Website: http://www.marconi.com

Matrix Partners
Bay Colony Corporate Center
1000 Winter St., Ste.4500
Waltham, MA 02451
(781)890-2244
Fax: (781)890-2288
Website: http://www.matrix
partners.com

North Bridge Venture Partners
950 Winter St. Ste. 4600
Waltham, MA 02451
(781)290-0004
Fax: (781)290-0999
E-mail: eta@nbvp.com

Polaris Venture Partners
Bay Colony Corporate Ctr.
1000 Winter St., Ste. 3500
Waltham, MA 02451
(781)290-0770
Fax: (781)290-0880
E-mail: partners@polarisventures.com
Website: http://www.polar
isventures.com

Seaflower Ventures
Bay Colony Corporate Ctr.
1000 Winter St. Ste. 1000
Waltham, MA 02451
(781)466-9552
Fax: (781)466-9553
E-mail: moot@seaflower.com
Website: http://www.seaflower.com

Ampersand Ventures
55 William St., Ste. 240
Wellesley, MA 02481
(617)239-0700
Fax: (617)239-0824
E-mail: info@ampersandventures.com
Website: http://www.ampersand
ventures.com

Battery Ventures (Boston)
20 William St., Ste. 200
Wellesley, MA 02481
(781)577-1000
Fax: (781)577-1001
Website: http://www.battery.com

Commonwealth Capital Ventures, L.P.
20 William St., Ste.225
Wellesley, MA 02481
(781)237-7373
Fax: (781)235-8627
Website: http://www.ccvlp.com

Fowler, Anthony & Company
20 Walnut St.
Wellesley, MA 02481
(781)237-4201
Fax: (781)237-7718

Gemini Investors
20 William St.
Wellesley, MA 02481
(781)237-7001
Fax: (781)237-7233

Grove Street Advisors Inc.
20 William St., Ste. 230
Wellesley, MA 02481
(781)263-6100
Fax: (781)263-6101
Website: http://www.groves
treetadvisors.com

Mees Pierson Investeringsmaat B.V.
20 William St., Ste. 210
Wellesley, MA 02482
(781)239-7600
Fax: (781)239-0377

Norwest Equity Partners
40 William St., Ste. 305
Wellesley, MA 02481-3902
(781)237-5870
Fax: (781)237-6270
Website: http://www.norwestvp.com

Bessemer Venture Partners (Wellesley Hills)
83 Walnut St.
Wellesley Hills, MA 02481
(781)237-6050
Fax: (781)235-7576
E-mail: travis@bvpny.com
Website: http://www.bvp.com

Venture Capital Fund of New England
20 Walnut St., Ste. 120
Wellesley Hills, MA 02481-2175
(781)239-8262
Fax: (781)239-8263

Prism Venture Partners
100 Lowder Brook Dr., Ste. 2500
Westwood, MA 02090
(781)302-4000
Fax: (781)302-4040
E-mail: dwbaum@prismventure.com

Palmer Partners LP
200 Unicorn Park Dr.
Woburn, MA 01801
(781)933-5445
Fax: (781)933-0698

Michigan

Arbor Partners, L.L.C.
130 South First St.
Ann Arbor, MI 48104
(734)668-9000
Fax: (734)669-4195
Website: http://www.arborpartners.com

EDF Ventures
425 N. Main St.
Ann Arbor, MI 48104
(734)663-3213
Fax: (734)663-7358
E-mail: edf@edfvc.com
Website: http://www.edfvc.com

White Pines Management, L.L.C.
2401 Plymouth Rd., Ste. B
Ann Arbor, MI 48105
(734)747-9401
Fax: (734)747-9704
E-mail: ibund@whitepines.com
Website: http://www.whitepines.com

Wellmax, Inc.
3541 Bendway Blvd., Ste. 100
Bloomfield Hills, MI 48301
(248)646-3554
Fax: (248)646-6220

Venture Funding, Ltd.
Fisher Bldg.
3011 West Grand Blvd., Ste. 321
Detroit, MI 48202
(313)871-3606
Fax: (313)873-4935

Investcare Partners L.P. / GMA Capital LLC
32330 W. Twelve Mile Rd.
Farmington Hills, MI 48334
(248)489-9000
Fax: (248)489-8819
E-mail: gma@gmacapital.com
Website: http://www.gmacapital.com

Liberty Bidco Investment Corp.
30833 Northwestern Highway, Ste. 211
Farmington Hills, MI 48334
(248)626-6070
Fax: (248)626-6072

Seaflower Ventures
5170 Nicholson Rd.
PO Box 474
Fowlerville, MI 48836
(517)223-3335
Fax: (517)223-3337
E-mail: gibbons@seaflower.com
Website: http://www.seaflower.com

Ralph Wilson Equity Fund LLC
15400 E. Jefferson Ave.
Gross Pointe Park, MI 48230
(313)821-9122
Fax: (313)821-9101
Website: http://www.Ralph
WilsonEquityFund.com
J. Skip Simms, President

Minnesota

Development Corp. of Austin
1900 Eighth Ave., NW
Austin, MN 55912
(507)433-0346
Fax: (507)433-0361
E-mail: dca@smig.net
Website: http://www.spamtownusa.com

Northeast Ventures Corp.
802 Alworth Bldg.
Duluth, MN 55802
(218)722-9915
Fax: (218)722-9871

Medical Innovation Partners, Inc.
6450 City West Pkwy.
Eden Prairie, MN 55344-3245
(612)828-9616
Fax: (612)828-9596

St. Paul Venture Capital, Inc.
10400 Vicking Dr., Ste. 550
Eden Prairie, MN 55344
(612)995-7474
Fax: (612)995-7475
Website: http://www.stpaulvc.com

Cherry Tree Investments, Inc.
7601 France Ave. S, Ste. 150
Edina, MN 55435
(612)893-9012
Fax: (612)893-9036
Website: http://www.cherrytree.com

Shared Ventures, Inc.
6550 York Ave. S
Edina, MN 55435
(612)925-3411

Sherpa Partners LLC
5050 Lincoln Dr., Ste. 490
Edina, MN 55436
(952)942-1070
Fax: (952)942-1071
Website: http://www.sherpapartners.com

Affinity Capital Management
901 Marquette Ave., Ste. 1810
Minneapolis, MN 55402
(612)252-9900

Fax: (612)252-9911
Website: http://www.affinitycapital.com

Artesian Capital
1700 Foshay Tower
821 Marquette Ave.
Minneapolis, MN 55402
(612)334-5600
Fax: (612)334-5601
E-mail: artesian@artesian.com

Coral Ventures
60 S. 6th St., Ste. 3510
Minneapolis, MN 55402
(612)335-8666
Fax: (612)335-8668
Website: http://www.coralventures.com

Crescendo Venture Management, L.L.C.
800 LaSalle Ave., Ste. 2250
Minneapolis, MN 55402
(612)607-2800
Fax: (612)607-2801
Website: http://www.crescendo
ventures.com

Gideon Hixon Venture
1900 Foshay Tower
821 Marquette Ave.
Minneapolis, MN 55402
(612)904-2314
Fax: (612)204-0913

Norwest Equity Partners
3600 IDS Center
80 S. 8th St.
Minneapolis, MN 55402
(612)215-1600
Fax: (612)215-1601
Website: http://www.norwestvp.com

Oak Investment Partners (Minneapolis)
4550 Norwest Center
90 S. 7th St.
Minneapolis, MN 55402
(612)339-9322
Fax: (612)337-8017
Website: http://www.oakinv.com

Pathfinder Venture Capital Funds (Minneapolis)
7300 Metro Blvd., Ste. 585
Minneapolis, MN 55439
(612)835-1121
Fax: (612)835-8389
E-mail: jahrens620@aol.com

U.S. Bancorp Piper Jaffray Ventures, Inc.
800 Nicollet Mall, Ste. 800
Minneapolis, MN 55402

(612)303-5686
Fax: (612)303-1350
Website: http://www.paperjaffrey
ventures.com

The Food Fund, Ltd. Partnership
5720 Smatana Dr., Ste. 300
Minnetonka, MN 55343
(612)939-3950
Fax: (612)939-8106

Mayo Medical Ventures
200 First St. SW
Rochester, MN 55905
(507)266-4586
Fax: (507)284-5410
Website: http://www.mayo.edu

Missouri

Bankers Capital Corp.
3100 Gillham Rd.
Kansas City, MO 64109
(816)531-1600
Fax: (816)531-1334

Capital for Business, Inc. (Kansas City)
1000 Walnut St., 18th Fl.
Kansas City, MO 64106
(816)234-2357
Fax: (816)234-2952
Website: http://
www.capitalforbusiness.com

De Vries & Co. Inc.
800 West 47th St.
Kansas City, MO 64112
(816)756-0055
Fax: (816)756-0061

InvestAmerica Venture Group Inc. (Kansas City)
Commerce Tower
911 Main St., Ste. 2424
Kansas City, MO 64105
(816)842-0114
Fax: (816)471-7339

Kansas City Equity Partners
233 W. 47th St.
Kansas City, MO 64112
(816)960-1771
Fax: (816)960-1777
Website: http://www.kcep.com

Bome Investors, Inc.
8000 Maryland Ave., Ste. 1190
St. Louis, MO 63105
(314)721-5707
Fax: (314)721-5135

Website: http://www.gateway
ventures.com

Capital for Business, Inc. (St. Louis)
11 S. Meramac St., Ste. 1430
St. Louis, MO 63105
(314)746-7427
Fax: (314)746-8739
Website: http://www.capitalfor
business.com

Crown Capital Corp.
540 Maryville Centre Dr., Ste. 120
Saint Louis, MO 63141
(314)576-1201
Fax: (314)576-1525
Website: http://www.crown-
cap.com

Gateway Associates L.P.
8000 Maryland Ave., Ste. 1190
St. Louis, MO 63105
(314)721-5707
Fax: (314)721-5135

Harbison Corp.
8112 Maryland Ave., Ste. 250
Saint Louis, MO 63105
(314)727-8200
Fax: (314)727-0249

Heartland Capital Fund, Ltd.
PO Box 642117
Omaha, NE 68154
(402)778-5124
Fax: (402)445-2370
Website: http://www.heartland
capitalfund.com

Odin Capital Group
1625 Farnam St., Ste. 700
Omaha, NE 68102
(402)346-6200
Fax: (402)342-9311
Website: http://www.odincapital.com

Nevada

Edge Capital Investment Co. LLC
1350 E. Flamingo Rd., Ste. 3000
Las Vegas, NV 89119
(702)438-3343
E-mail: info@edgecapital.net
Website: http://www.edgecapital.net

The Benefit Capital Companies Inc.
PO Box 542
Logandale, NV 89021
(702)398-3222
Fax: (702)398-3700

Millennium Three Venture Group LLC
6880 South McCarran Blvd., Ste. A-11
Reno, NV 89509
(775)954-2020
Fax: (775)954-2023
Website: http://www.m3vg.com

New Jersey

Alan I. Goldman & Associates
497 Ridgewood Ave.
Glen Ridge, NJ 07028
(973)857-5680
Fax: (973)509-8856

CS Capital Partners LLC
328 Second St., Ste. 200
Lakewood, NJ 08701
(732)901-1111
Fax: (212)202-5071
Website: http://www.cs-capital.com

Edison Venture Fund
1009 Lenox Dr., Ste. 4
Lawrenceville, NJ 08648
(609)896-1900
Fax: (609)896-0066
E-mail: info@edisonventure.com
Website: http://www.edisonventure.com

Tappan Zee Capital Corp. (New Jersey)
201 Lower Notch Rd.
PO Box 416
Little Falls, NJ 07424
(973)256-8280
Fax: (973)256-2841

The CIT Group/Venture Capital, Inc.
650 CIT Dr.
Livingston, NJ 07039
(973)740-5429
Fax: (973)740-5555
Website: http://www.cit.com

Capital Express, L.L.C.
1100 Valleybrook Ave.
Lyndhurst, NJ 07071
(201)438-8228
Fax: (201)438-5131
E-mail: niles@capitalexpress.com
Website: http://www.capitalexpress.com

Westford Technology Ventures, L.P.
17 Academy St.
Newark, NJ 07102
(973)624-2131
Fax: (973)624-2008

Accel Partners
1 Palmer Sq.
Princeton, NJ 08542
(609)683-4500
Fax: (609)683-4880
Website: http://www.accel.com

Cardinal Partners
221 Nassau St.
Princeton, NJ 08542
(609)924-6452
Fax: (609)683-0174
Website: http://www.cardinal
healthpartners.com

Domain Associates L.L.C.
One Palmer Sq., Ste. 515
Princeton, NJ 08542
(609)683-5656
Fax: (609)683-9789
Website: http://www.domainvc.com

Johnston Associates, Inc.
181 Cherry Valley Rd.
Princeton, NJ 08540
(609)924-3131
Fax: (609)683-7524
E-mail: jaincorp@aol.com

Kemper Ventures
Princeton Forrestal Village
155 Village Blvd.
Princeton, NJ 08540
(609)936-3035
Fax: (609)936-3051

Penny Lane Parnters
One Palmer Sq., Ste. 309
Princeton, NJ 08542
(609)497-4646
Fax: (609)497-0611

Early Stage Enterprises L.P.
995 Route 518
Skillman, NJ 08558
(609)921-8896
Fax: (609)921-8703
Website: http://www.esevc.com

MBW Management Inc.
1 Springfield Ave.
Summit, NJ 07901
(908)273-4060
Fax: (908)273-4430

BCI Advisors, Inc.
Glenpointe Center W.
Teaneck, NJ 07666
(201)836-3900
Fax: (201)836-6368
E-mail: info@bciadvisors.com
Website: http://www.bci
partners.com

Demuth, Folger & Wetherill / DFW Capital Partners
Glenpointe Center E., 5th Fl.
300 Frank W. Burr Blvd.
Teaneck, NJ 07666
(201)836-2233
Fax: (201)836-5666
Website: http://www.dfwcapital.com

First Princeton Capital Corp.
189 Berdan Ave., No. 131
Wayne, NJ 07470-3233
(973)278-3233
Fax: (973)278-4290
Website: http://www.lytellcatt.net

Edelson Technology Partners
300 Tice Blvd.
Woodcliff Lake, NJ 07675
(201)930-9898
Fax: (201)930-8899
Website: http://www.edelsontech.com

New Mexico

Bruce F. Glaspell & Associates
10400 Academy Rd. NE, Ste. 313
Albuquerque, NM 87111
(505)292-4505
Fax: (505)292-4258

High Desert Ventures, Inc.
6101 Imparata St. NE, Ste. 1721
Albuquerque, NM 87111
(505)797-3330
Fax: (505)338-5147

New Business Capital Fund, Ltd.
5805 Torreon NE
Albuquerque, NM 87109
(505)822-8445

SBC Ventures
10400 Academy Rd. NE, Ste. 313
Albuquerque, NM 87111
(505)292-4505
Fax: (505)292-4528

Technology Ventures Corp.
1155 University Blvd. SE
Albuquerque, NM 87106
(505)246-2882
Fax: (505)246-2891

New York

New York State Science & Technology Foundation
Small Business Technology Investment Fund
99 Washington Ave., Ste. 1731
Albany, NY 12210

Organizations, Agencies, & Consultants

ORGANIZATIONS, AGENCIES, & CONSULTANTS

(518)473-9741
Fax: (518)473-6876

Rand Capital Corp.
2200 Rand Bldg.
Buffalo, NY 14203
(716)853-0802
Fax: (716)854-8480
Website: http://www.randcapital.com

Seed Capital Partners
620 Main St.
Buffalo, NY 14202
(716)845-7520
Fax: (716)845-7539
Website: http://www.seedcp.com

Coleman Venture Group
5909 Northern Blvd.
PO Box 224
East Norwich, NY 11732
(516)626-3642
Fax: (516)626-9722

Vega Capital Corp.
45 Knollwood Rd.
Elmsford, NY 10523
(914)345-9500
Fax: (914)345-9505

Herbert Young Securities, Inc.
98 Cuttermill Rd.
Great Neck, NY 11021
(516)487-8300
Fax: (516)487-8319

Sterling/Carl Marks Capital, Inc.
175 Great Neck Rd., Ste. 408
Great Neck, NY 11021
(516)482-7374
Fax: (516)487-0781
E-mail: stercrlmar@aol.com
Website: http://www.serling
carlmarks.com

Impex Venture Management Co.
PO Box 1570
Green Island, NY 12183
(518)271-8008
Fax: (518)271-9101

Corporate Venture Partners L.P.
200 Sunset Park
Ithaca, NY 14850
(607)257-6323
Fax: (607)257-6128

Arthur P. Gould & Co.
One Wilshire Dr.
Lake Success, NY 11020
(516)773-3000
Fax: (516)773-3289

Dauphin Capital Partners
108 Forest Ave.
Locust Valley, NY 11560
(516)759-3339
Fax: (516)759-3322
Website: http://www.dauphincapital.com

550 Digital Media Ventures
555 Madison Ave., 10th Fl.
New York, NY 10022
Website: http://www.550dmv.com

Aberlyn Capital Management Co., Inc.
500 Fifth Ave.
New York, NY 10110
(212)391-7750
Fax: (212)391-7762

Adler & Company
342 Madison Ave., Ste. 807
New York, NY 10173
(212)599-2535
Fax: (212)599-2526

Alimansky Capital Group, Inc.
605 Madison Ave., Ste. 300
New York, NY 10022-1901
(212)832-7300
Fax: (212)832-7338

Allegra Partners
515 Madison Ave., 29th Fl.
New York, NY 10022
(212)826-9080
Fax: (212)759-2561

The Argentum Group
The Chyrsler Bldg.
405 Lexington Ave.
New York, NY 10174
(212)949-6262
Fax: (212)949-8294
Website: http://www.argentum
group.com

Axavision Inc.
14 Wall St., 26th Fl.
New York, NY 10005
(212)619-4000
Fax: (212)619-7202

Bedford Capital Corp.
18 East 48th St., Ste. 1800
New York, NY 10017
(212)688-5700
Fax: (212)754-4699
E-mail: info@bedfordnyc.com
Website: http://www.bedfordnyc.com

Bloom & Co.
950 Third Ave.

New York, NY 10022
(212)838-1858
Fax: (212)838-1843

Bristol Capital Management
300 Park Ave., 17th Fl.
New York, NY 10022
(212)572-6306
Fax: (212)705-4292

**Citicorp Venture Capital Ltd.
(New York City)**
399 Park Ave., 14th Fl.
Zone 4
New York, NY 10043
(212)559-1127
Fax: (212)888-2940

CM Equity Partners
135 E. 57th St.
New York, NY 10022
(212)909-8428
Fax: (212)980-2630

Cohen & Co., L.L.C.
800 Third Ave.
New York, NY 10022
(212)317-2250
Fax: (212)317-2255
E-mail: nlcohen@aol.com

Cornerstone Equity Investors, L.L.C.
717 5th Ave., Ste. 1100
New York, NY 10022
(212)753-0901
Fax: (212)826-6798
Website: http://www.cornerstone-
equity.com

CW Group, Inc.
1041 3rd Ave., 2nd fl.
New York, NY 10021
(212)308-5266
Fax: (212)644-0354
Website: http://www.cwventures.com

DH Blair Investment Banking Corp.
44 Wall St., 2nd Fl.
New York, NY 10005
(212)495-5000
Fax: (212)269-1438

Dresdner Kleinwort Capital
75 Wall St.
New York, NY 10005
(212)429-3131
Fax: (212)429-3139
Website: http://www.dresdnerkb.com

East River Ventures, L.P.
645 Madison Ave., 22nd Fl.

312   **BUSINESS PLANS HANDBOOK,** *Volume 19*

New York, NY 10022
(212)644-2322
Fax: (212)644-5498

Easton Hunt Capital Partners
641 Lexington Ave., 21st Fl.
New York, NY 10017
(212)702-0950
Fax: (212)702-0952
Website: http://www.eastoncapital.com

Elk Associates Funding Corp.
747 3rd Ave., Ste. 4C
New York, NY 10017
(212)355-2449
Fax: (212)759-3338

EOS Partners, L.P.
320 Park Ave., 22nd Fl.
New York, NY 10022
(212)832-5800
Fax: (212)832-5815
E-mail: mfirst@eospartners.com
Website: http://www.eospartners.com

Euclid Partners
45 Rockefeller Plaza, Ste. 3240
New York, NY 10111
(212)218-6880
Fax: (212)218-6877
E-mail: graham@euclidpartners.com
Website: http://www.euclidpartners.com

Evergreen Capital Partners, Inc.
150 East 58th St.
New York, NY 10155
(212)813-0758
Fax: (212)813-0754

Exeter Capital L.P.
10 E. 53rd St.
New York, NY 10022
(212)872-1172
Fax: (212)872-1198
E-mail: exeter@usa.net

Financial Technology Research Corp.
518 Broadway
Penthouse
New York, NY 10012
(212)625-9100
Fax: (212)431-0300
E-mail: fintek@financier.com

4C Ventures
237 Park Ave., Ste. 801
New York, NY 10017
(212)692-3680
Fax: (212)692-3685
Website: http://www.4cventures.com

Fusient Ventures
99 Park Ave., 20th Fl.
New York, NY 10016
(212)972-8999
Fax: (212)972-9876
E-mail: info@fusient.com
Website: http://www.fusient.com

Generation Capital Partners
551 Fifth Ave., Ste. 3100
New York, NY 10176
(212)450-8507
Fax: (212)450-8550
Website: http://www.genpartners.com

Golub Associates, Inc.
555 Madison Ave.
New York, NY 10022
(212)750-6060
Fax: (212)750-5505

Hambro America Biosciences Inc.
650 Madison Ave., 21st Floor
New York, NY 10022
(212)223-7400
Fax: (212)223-0305

Hanover Capital Corp.
505 Park Ave., 15th Fl.
New York, NY 10022
(212)755-1222
Fax: (212)935-1787

Harvest Partners, Inc.
280 Park Ave, 33rd Fl.
New York, NY 10017
(212)559-6300
Fax: (212)812-0100
Website: http://www.harvpart.com

Holding Capital Group, Inc.
10 E. 53rd St., 30th Fl.
New York, NY 10022
(212)486-6670
Fax: (212)486-0843

Hudson Venture Partners
660 Madison Ave., 14th Fl.
New York, NY 10021-8405
(212)644-9797
Fax: (212)644-7430
Website: http://www.hudsonptr.com

IBJS Capital Corp.
1 State St., 9th Fl.
New York, NY 10004
(212)858-2018
Fax: (212)858-2768

InterEquity Capital Partners, L.P.
220 5th Ave.
New York, NY 10001

(212)779-2022
Fax: (212)779-2103
Website: http://www.interequity-capital.com

The Jordan Edmiston Group Inc.
150 East 52nd St., 18th Fl.
New York, NY 10022
(212)754-0710
Fax: (212)754-0337

Josephberg, Grosz and Co., Inc.
633 3rd Ave., 13th Fl.
New York, NY 10017
(212)974-9926
Fax: (212)397-5832

J.P. Morgan Capital Corp.
60 Wall St.
New York, NY 10260-0060
(212)648-9000
Fax: (212)648-5002
Website: http://www.jpmorgan.com

The Lambda Funds
380 Lexington Ave., 54th Fl.
New York, NY 10168
(212)682-3454
Fax: (212)682-9231

Lepercq Capital Management Inc.
1675 Broadway
New York, NY 10019
(212)698-0795
Fax: (212)262-0155

Loeb Partners Corp.
61 Broadway, Ste. 2400
New York, NY 10006
(212)483-7000
Fax: (212)574-2001

Madison Investment Partners
660 Madison Ave.
New York, NY 10021
(212)223-2600
Fax: (212)223-8208

MC Capital Inc.
520 Madison Ave., 16th Fl.
New York, NY 10022
(212)644-0841
Fax: (212)644-2926

McCown, De Leeuw and Co. (New York)
65 E. 55th St., 36th Fl.
New York, NY 10022
(212)355-5500
Fax: (212)355-6283
Website: http://www.mdcpartners.com

Morgan Stanley Venture Partners
1221 Avenue of the Americas, 33rd Fl.
New York, NY 10020
(212)762-7900
Fax: (212)762-8424
E-mail: msventures@ms.com
Website: http://www.msvp.com

Nazem and Co.
645 Madison Ave., 12th Fl.
New York, NY 10022
(212)371-7900
Fax: (212)371-2150

Needham Capital Management, L.L.C.
445 Park Ave.
New York, NY 10022
(212)371-8300
Fax: (212)705-0299
Website: http://www.needhamco.com

Norwood Venture Corp.
1430 Broadway, Ste. 1607
New York, NY 10018
(212)869-5075
Fax: (212)869-5331
E-mail: nvc@mail.idt.net
Website: http://www.norven.com

Noveltek Venture Corp.
521 Fifth Ave., Ste. 1700
New York, NY 10175
(212)286-1963

Paribas Principal, Inc.
787 7th Ave.
New York, NY 10019
(212)841-2005
Fax: (212)841-3558

Patricof & Co. Ventures, Inc. (New York)
445 Park Ave.
New York, NY 10022
(212)753-6300
Fax: (212)319-6155
Website: http://www.patricof.com

The Platinum Group, Inc.
350 Fifth Ave, Ste. 7113
New York, NY 10118
(212)736-4300
Fax: (212)736-6086
Website: http://www.platinumgroup.com

Pomona Capital
780 Third Ave., 28th Fl.
New York, NY 10017
(212)593-3639
Fax: (212)593-3987
Website: http://www.pomonacapital.com

Prospect Street Ventures
10 East 40th St., 44th Fl.
New York, NY 10016
(212)448-0702
Fax: (212)448-9652
E-mail: wkohler@prospectstreet.com
Website: http://www.prospectstreet.com

Regent Capital Management
505 Park Ave., Ste. 1700
New York, NY 10022
(212)735-9900
Fax: (212)735-9908

Rothschild Ventures, Inc.
1251 Avenue of the Americas, 51st Fl.
New York, NY 10020
(212)403-3500
Fax: (212)403-3652
Website: http://www.nmrothschild.com

Sandler Capital Management
767 Fifth Ave., 45th Fl.
New York, NY 10153
(212)754-8100
Fax: (212)826-0280

Siguler Guff & Company
630 Fifth Ave., 16th Fl.
New York, NY 10111
(212)332-5100
Fax: (212)332-5120

Spencer Trask Ventures Inc.
535 Madison Ave.
New York, NY 10022
(212)355-5565
Fax: (212)751-3362
Website: http://www.spencertrask.com

Sprout Group (New York City)
277 Park Ave.
New York, NY 10172
(212)892-3600
Fax: (212)892-3444
E-mail: info@sproutgroup.com
Website: http://www.sproutgroup.com

US Trust Private Equity
114 W.47th St.
New York, NY 10036
(212)852-3949
Fax: (212)852-3759
Website: http://www.ustrust.com/privateequity

Vencon Management Inc.
301 West 53rd St., Ste. 10F
New York, NY 10019
(212)581-8787
Fax: (212)397-4126
Website: http://www.venconinc.com

Venrock Associates
30 Rockefeller Plaza, Ste. 5508
New York, NY 10112
(212)649-5600
Fax: (212)649-5788
Website: http://www.venrock.com

Venture Capital Fund of America, Inc.
509 Madison Ave., Ste. 812
New York, NY 10022
(212)838-5577
Fax: (212)838-7614
E-mail: mail@vcfa.com
Website: http://www.vcfa.com

Venture Opportunities Corp.
150 E. 58th St.
New York, NY 10155
(212)832-3737
Fax: (212)980-6603

Warburg Pincus Ventures, Inc.
466 Lexington Ave., 11th Fl.
New York, NY 10017
(212)878-9309
Fax: (212)878-9200
Website: http://www.warburgpincus.com

Wasserstein, Perella & Co. Inc.
31 W. 52nd St., 27th Fl.
New York, NY 10019
(212)702-5691
Fax: (212)969-7879

Welsh, Carson, Anderson, & Stowe
320 Park Ave., Ste. 2500
New York, NY 10022-6815
(212)893-9500
Fax: (212)893-9575

Whitney and Co. (New York)
630 Fifth Ave. Ste. 3225
New York, NY 10111
(212)332-2400
Fax: (212)332-2422
Website: http://www.jhwitney.com

Winthrop Ventures
74 Trinity Place, Ste. 600
New York, NY 10006
(212)422-0100

The Pittsford Group
8 Lodge Pole Rd.
Pittsford, NY 14534
(716)223-3523

Genesee Funding
70 Linden Oaks, 3rd Fl.
Rochester, NY 14625
(716)383-5550
Fax: (716)383-5305

Gabelli Multimedia Partners
One Corporate Center
Rye, NY 10580
(914)921-5395
Fax: (914)921-5031

Stamford Financial
108 Main St.
Stamford, NY 12167
(607)652-3311
Fax: (607)652-6301
Website: http://www.stamford
financial.com

Northwood Ventures LLC
485 Underhill Blvd., Ste. 205
Syosset, NY 11791
(516)364-5544
Fax: (516)364-0879
E-mail: northwood@northwood.com
Website: http://www.north
woodventures.com

Exponential Business Development Co.
216 Walton St.
Syracuse, NY 13202-1227
(315)474-4500
Fax: (315)474-4682
E-mail: dirksonn@aol.com
Website: http://www.exponential-ny.com

Onondaga Venture Capital Fund Inc.
714 State Tower Bldg.
Syracuse, NY 13202
(315)478-0157
Fax: (315)478-0158

Bessemer Venture Partners (Westbury)
1400 Old Country Rd., Ste. 109
Westbury, NY 11590
(516)997-2300
Fax: (516)997-2371
E-mail: bob@bvpny.com
Website: http://www.bvp.com

Ovation Capital Partners
120 Bloomingdale Rd., 4th Fl.
White Plains, NY 10605
(914)258-0011
Fax: (914)684-0848
Website: http://www.ovation
capital.com

North Carolina

Carolinas Capital Investment Corp.
1408 Biltmore Dr.
Charlotte, NC 28207
(704)375-3888
Fax: (704)375-6226

First Union Capital Partners
1st Union Center, 12th Fl.
301 S. College St.
Charlotte, NC 28288-0732
(704)383-0000
Fax: (704)374-6711
Website: http://www.fucp.com

Frontier Capital LLC
525 North Tryon St., Ste. 1700
Charlotte, NC 28202
(704)414-2880
Fax: (704)414-2881
Website: http://www.frontierfunds.com

Kitty Hawk Capital
2700 Coltsgate Rd., Ste. 202
Charlotte, NC 28211
(704)362-3909
Fax: (704)362-2774
Website: http://www.kittyhawk
capital.com

Piedmont Venture Partners
One Morrocroft Centre
6805 Morisson Blvd., Ste. 380
Charlotte, NC 28211
(704)731-5200
Fax: (704)365-9733
Website: http://www.piedmontvp.com

Ruddick Investment Co.
1800 Two First Union Center
Charlotte, NC 28282
(704)372-5404
Fax: (704)372-6409

The Shelton Companies Inc.
3600 One First Union Center
301 S. College St.
Charlotte, NC 28202
(704)348-2200
Fax: (704)348-2260

Wakefield Group
1110 E. Morehead St.
PO Box 36329
Charlotte, NC 28236
(704)372-0355
Fax: (704)372-8216
Website: http://www.wakefiel
dgroup.com

Aurora Funds, Inc.
2525 Meridian Pkwy., Ste. 220
Durham, NC 27713
(919)484-0400
Fax: (919)484-0444
Website: http://www.aurora
funds.com

Intersouth Partners
3211 Shannon Rd., Ste. 610
Durham, NC 27707
(919)493-6640
Fax: (919)493-6649
E-mail: info@intersouth.com
Website: http://www.intersouth.com

Geneva Merchant Banking Partners
PO Box 21962
Greensboro, NC 27420
(336)275-7002
Fax: (336)275-9155
Website: http://www.geneva
merchantbank.com

The North Carolina Enterprise Fund, L.P.
3600 Glenwood Ave., Ste. 107
Raleigh, NC 27612
(919)781-2691
Fax: (919)783-9195
Website: http://www.ncef.com

Ohio

Senmend Medical Ventures
4445 Lake Forest Dr., Ste. 600
Cincinnati, OH 45242
(513)563-3264
Fax: (513)563-3261

The Walnut Group
312 Walnut St., Ste. 1151
Cincinnati, OH 45202
(513)651-3300
Fax: (513)929-4441
Website: http://www.thewal
nutgroup.com

Brantley Venture Partners
20600 Chagrin Blvd., Ste. 1150
Cleveland, OH 44122
(216)283-4800
Fax: (216)283-5324

Clarion Capital Corp.
1801 E. 9th St., Ste. 1120
Cleveland, OH 44114
(216)687-1096
Fax: (216)694-3545

Crystal Internet Venture Fund, L.P.
1120 Chester Ave., Ste. 418
Cleveland, OH 44114
(216)263-5515
Fax: (216)263-5518
E-mail: jf@crystalventure.com
Website: http://www.crystal
venture.com

Key Equity Capital Corp.
127 Public Sq., 28th Fl.
Cleveland, OH 44114
(216)689-3000
Fax: (216)689-3204
Website: http://www.keybank.com

Morgenthaler Ventures
Terminal Tower
50 Public Square, Ste. 2700
Cleveland, OH 44113
(216)416-7500
Fax: (216)416-7501
Website: http://www.morgenthaler.com

National City Equity Partners Inc.
1965 E. 6th St.
Cleveland, OH 44114
(216)575-2491
Fax: (216)575-9965
E-mail: nccap@aol.com
Website: http://www.nccapital.com

Primus Venture Partners, Inc.
5900 LanderBrook Dr., Ste. 2000
Cleveland, OH 44124-4020
(440)684-7300
Fax: (440)684-7342
E-mail: info@primusventure.com
Website: http://www.primusventure.com

Banc One Capital Partners (Columbus)
150 East Gay St., 24th Fl.
Columbus, OH 43215
(614)217-1100
Fax: (614)217-1217

Battelle Venture Partners
505 King Ave.
Columbus, OH 43201
(614)424-7005
Fax: (614)424-4874

Ohio Partners
62 E. Board St., 3rd Fl.
Columbus, OH 43215
(614)621-1210
Fax: (614)621-1240

Capital Technology Group, L.L.C.
400 Metro Place North, Ste. 300
Dublin, OH 43017
(614)792-6066
Fax: (614)792-6036
E-mail: info@capitaltech.com
Website: http://www.capitaltech.com

Northwest Ohio Venture Fund
4159 Holland-Sylvania R., Ste. 202
Toledo, OH 43623
(419)824-8144

Fax: (419)882-2035
E-mail: bwalsh@novf.com

Oklahoma

Moore & Associates
1000 W. Wilshire Blvd., Ste. 370
Oklahoma City, OK 73116
(405)842-3660
Fax: (405)842-3763

Chisholm Private Capital Partners
100 West 5th St., Ste. 805
Tulsa, OK 74103
(918)584-0440
Fax: (918)584-0441
Website: http://www.chisholmvc.com

Davis, Tuttle Venture Partners (Tulsa)
320 S. Boston, Ste. 1000
Tulsa, OK 74103-3703
(918)584-7272
Fax: (918)582-3404
Website: http://www.davistuttle.com

RBC Ventures
2627 E. 21st St.
Tulsa, OK 74114
(918)744-5607
Fax: (918)743-8630

Oregon

Utah Ventures II LP
10700 SW Beaverton-Hillsdale Hwy.,
Ste. 548
Beaverton, OR 97005
(503)574-4125
E-mail: adishlip@uven.com
Website: http://www.uven.com

Orien Ventures
14523 SW Westlake Dr.
Lake Oswego, OR 97035
(503)699-1680
Fax: (503)699-1681

OVP Venture Partners (Lake Oswego)
340 Oswego Pointe Dr., Ste. 200
Lake Oswego, OR 97034
(503)697-8766
Fax: (503)697-8863
E-mail: info@ovp.com
Website: http://www.ovp.com

Oregon Resource and Technology Development Fund
4370 NE Halsey St., Ste. 233
Portland, OR 97213-1566
(503)282-4462
Fax: (503)282-2976

Shaw Venture Partners
400 SW 6th Ave., Ste. 1100
Portland, OR 97204-1636
(503)228-4884
Fax: (503)227-2471
Website: http://www.shawventures.com

Pennsylvania

Mid-Atlantic Venture Funds
125 Goodman Dr.
Bethlehem, PA 18015
(610)865-6550
Fax: (610)865-6427
Website: http://www.mavf.com

Newspring Ventures
100 W. Elm St., Ste. 101
Conshohocken, PA 19428
(610)567-2380
Fax: (610)567-2388
Website: http://www.news
printventures.com

Patricof & Co. Ventures, Inc.
455 S. Gulph Rd., Ste. 410
King of Prussia, PA 19406
(610)265-0286
Fax: (610)265-4959
Website: http://www.patricof.com

Loyalhanna Venture Fund
527 Cedar Way, Ste. 104
Oakmont, PA 15139
(412)820-7035
Fax: (412)820-7036

Innovest Group Inc.
2000 Market St., Ste. 1400
Philadelphia, PA 19103
(215)564-3960
Fax: (215)569-3272

Keystone Venture Capital Management Co.
1601 Market St., Ste. 2500
Philadelphia, PA 19103
(215)241-1200
Fax: (215)241-1211
Website: http://www.keystonevc.com

Liberty Venture Partners
2005 Market St., Ste. 200
Philadelphia, PA 19103
(215)282-4484
Fax: (215)282-4485
E-mail: info@libertyvp.com
Website: http://www.libertyvp.com

Penn Janney Fund, Inc.
1801 Market St., 11th Fl.
Philadelphia, PA 19103

(215)665-4447
Fax: (215)557-0820

Philadelphia Ventures, Inc.
The Bellevue
200 S. Broad St.
Philadelphia, PA 19102
(215)732-4445
Fax: (215)732-4644

Birchmere Ventures Inc.
2000 Technology Dr.
Pittsburgh, PA 15219-3109
(412)803-8000
Fax: (412)687-8139
Website: http://www.birchmerevc.com

CEO Venture Fund
2000 Technology Dr., Ste. 160
Pittsburgh, PA 15219-3109
(412)687-3451
Fax: (412)687-8139
E-mail: ceofund@aol.com
Website: http://www.ceoventure
fund.com

Innovation Works Inc.
2000 Technology Dr., Ste. 250
Pittsburgh, PA 15219
(412)681-1520
Fax: (412)681-2625
Website: http://www.innovation
works.org

Keystone Minority Capital Fund L.P.
1801 Centre Ave., Ste. 201
Williams Sq.
Pittsburgh, PA 15219
(412)338-2230
Fax: (412)338-2224

Mellon Ventures, Inc.
One Mellon Bank Ctr., Rm. 3500
Pittsburgh, PA 15258
(412)236-3594
Fax: (412)236-3593
Website: http://www.mellon
ventures.com

Pennsylvania Growth Fund
5850 Ellsworth Ave., Ste. 303
Pittsburgh, PA 15232
(412)661-1000
Fax: (412)361-0676

Point Venture Partners
The Century Bldg.
130 Seventh St., 7th Fl.
Pittsburgh, PA 15222
(412)261-1966
Fax: (412)261-1718

Cross Atlantic Capital Partners
5 Radnor Corporate Center, Ste. 555
Radnor, PA 19087
(610)995-2650
Fax: (610)971-2062
Website: http://www.xacp.com

Meridian Venture Partners (Radnor)
The Radnor Court Bldg., Ste. 140
259 Radnor-Chester Rd.
Radnor, PA 19087
(610)254-2999
Fax: (610)254-2996
E-mail: mvpart@ix.netcom.com

TDH
919 Conestoga Rd., Bldg. 1, Ste. 301
Rosemont, PA 19010
(610)526-9970
Fax: (610)526-9971

Adams Capital Management
500 Blackburn Ave.
Sewickley, PA 15143
(412)749-9454
Fax: (412)749-9459
Website: http://www.acm.com

S.R. One, Ltd.
Four Tower Bridge
200 Barr Harbor Dr., Ste. 250
W. Conshohocken, PA 19428
(610)567-1000
Fax: (610)567-1039

Greater Philadelphia Venture Capital Corp.
351 East Conestoga Rd.
Wayne, PA 19087
(610)688-6829
Fax: (610)254-8958

PA Early Stage
435 Devon Park Dr., Bldg. 500, Ste. 510
Wayne, PA 19087
(610)293-4075
Fax: (610)254-4240
Website: http://www.paearlystage.com

The Sandhurst Venture Fund, L.P.
351 E. Constoga Rd.
Wayne, PA 19087
(610)254-8900
Fax: (610)254-8958

TL Ventures
700 Bldg.
435 Devon Park Dr.
Wayne, PA 19087-1990
(610)975-3765
Fax: (610)254-4210
Website: http://www.tlventures.com

Rockhill Ventures, Inc.
100 Front St., Ste. 1350
West Conshohocken, PA 19428
(610)940-0300
Fax: (610)940-0301

Puerto Rico

Advent-Morro Equity Partners
Banco Popular Bldg.
206 Tetuan St., Ste. 903
San Juan, PR 00902
(787)725-5285
Fax: (787)721-1735

North America Investment Corp.
Mercantil Plaza, Ste. 813
PO Box 191831
San Juan, PR 00919
(787)754-6178
Fax: (787)754-6181

Rhode Island

Manchester Humphreys, Inc.
40 Westminster St., Ste. 900
Providence, RI 02903
(401)454-0400
Fax: (401)454-0403

Navis Partners
50 Kennedy Plaza, 12th Fl.
Providence, RI 02903
(401)278-6770
Fax: (401)278-6387
Website: http://www.navis
partners.com

South Carolina

Capital Insights, L.L.C.
PO Box 27162
Greenville, SC 29616-2162
(864)242-6832
Fax: (864)242-6755
E-mail: jwarner@capitalinsights.com
Website: http://www.capitalin
sights.com

Transamerica Mezzanine Financing
7 N. Laurens St., Ste. 603
Greenville, SC 29601
(864)232-6198
Fax: (864)241-4444

Tennessee

Valley Capital Corp.
Krystal Bldg.
100 W. Martin Luther King Blvd.,
Ste. 212

Chattanooga, TN 37402
(423)265-1557
Fax: (423)265-1588

Coleman Swenson Booth Inc.
237 2nd Ave. S
Franklin, TN 37064-2649
(615)791-9462
Fax: (615)791-9636
Website: http://
www.colemanswenson.com

Capital Services & Resources, Inc.
5159 Wheelis Dr., Ste. 106
Memphis, TN 38117
(901)761-2156
Fax: (907)767-0060

Paradigm Capital Partners LLC
6410 Poplar Ave., Ste. 395
Memphis, TN 38119
(901)682-6060
Fax: (901)328-3061

SSM Ventures
845 Crossover Ln., Ste. 140
Memphis, TN 38117
(901)767-1131
Fax: (901)767-1135
Website: http://www.ssm
ventures.com

Capital Across America L.P.
501 Union St., Ste. 201
Nashville, TN 37219
(615)254-1414
Fax: (615)254-1856
Website: http://
www.capitalacrossamerica.com

Equitas L.P.
2000 Glen Echo Rd., Ste. 101
PO Box 158838
Nashville, TN 37215-8838
(615)383-8673
Fax: (615)383-8693

Massey Burch Capital Corp.
One Burton Hills Blvd., Ste. 350
Nashville, TN 37215
(615)665-3221
Fax: (615)665-3240
E-mail: tcalton@masseyburch.com
Website: http://www.masseyburch.com

Nelson Capital Corp.
3401 West End Ave., Ste. 300
Nashville, TN 37203
(615)292-8787
Fax: (615)385-3150

Texas

Phillips-Smith Specialty Retail Group
5080 Spectrum Dr., Ste. 805 W
Addison, TX 75001
(972)387-0725
Fax: (972)458-2560
E-mail: pssrg@aol.com
Website: http://www.phillips-smith.com

Austin Ventures, L.P.
701 Brazos St., Ste. 1400
Austin, TX 78701
(512)485-1900
Fax: (512)476-3952
E-mail: info@ausven.com
Website: http://www.austinventures.com

The Capital Network
3925 West Braker Lane, Ste. 406
Austin, TX 78759-5321
(512)305-0826
Fax: (512)305-0836

Techxas Ventures LLC
5000 Plaza on the Lake
Austin, TX 78746
(512)343-0118
Fax: (512)343-1879
E-mail: bruce@techxas.com
Website: http://www.techxas.com

Alliance Financial of Houston
218 Heather Ln.
Conroe, TX 77385-9013
(936)447-3300
Fax: (936)447-4222

Amerimark Capital Corp.
1111 W. Mockingbird, Ste. 1111
Dallas, TX 75247
(214)638-7878
Fax: (214)638-7612
E-mail: amerimark@amcapital.com
Website: http://www.amcapital.com

AMT Venture Partners / AMT Capital Ltd.
5220 Spring Valley Rd., Ste. 600
Dallas, TX 75240
(214)905-9757
Fax: (214)905-9761
Website: http://www.amtcapital.com

Arkoma Venture Partners
5950 Berkshire Lane, Ste. 1400
Dallas, TX 75225
(214)739-3515
Fax: (214)739-3572
E-mail: joell@arkomavp.com

Capital Southwest Corp.
12900 Preston Rd., Ste. 700
Dallas, TX 75230
(972)233-8242
Fax: (972)233-7362
Website: http://
www.capitalsouthwest.com

Dali, Hook Partners
One Lincoln Center, Ste. 1550
5400 LBJ Freeway
Dallas, TX 75240
(972)991-5457
Fax: (972)991-5458
E-mail: dhook@hookpartners.com
Website: http://www.hookpartners.com

HO2 Partners
Two Galleria Tower
13455 Noel Rd., Ste. 1670
Dallas, TX 75240
(972)702-1144
Fax: (972)702-8234
Website: http://www.ho2.com

Interwest Partners (Dallas)
2 Galleria Tower
13455 Noel Rd., Ste. 1670
Dallas, TX 75240
(972)392-7279
Fax: (972)490-6348
Website: http://www.interwest.com

Kahala Investments, Inc.
8214 Westchester Dr., Ste. 715
Dallas, TX 75225
(214)987-0077
Fax: (214)987-2332

MESBIC Ventures Holding Co.
2435 North Central Expressway, Ste. 200
Dallas, TX 75080
(972)991-1597
Fax: (972)991-4770
Website: http://www.mvhc.com

North Texas MESBIC, Inc.
9500 Forest Lane, Ste. 430
Dallas, TX 75243
(214)221-3565
Fax: (214)221-3566

Richard Jaffe & Company, Inc,
7318 Royal Cir.
Dallas, TX 75230
(214)265-9397
Fax: (214)739-1845

Sevin Rosen Management Co.
13455 Noel Rd., Ste. 1670
Dallas, TX 75240

(972)702-1100
Fax: (972)702-1103
E-mail: info@srfunds.com
Website: http://www.srfunds.com

Stratford Capital Partners, L.P.
300 Crescent Ct., Ste. 500
Dallas, TX 75201
(214)740-7377
Fax: (214)720-7393
E-mail: stratcap@hmtf.com

Sunwestern Investment Group
12221 Merit Dr., Ste. 935
Dallas, TX 75251
(972)239-5650
Fax: (972)701-0024

Wingate Partners
750 N. St. Paul St., Ste. 1200
Dallas, TX 75201
(214)720-1313
Fax: (214)871-8799

Buena Venture Associates
201 Main St., 32nd Fl.
Fort Worth, TX 76102
(817)339-7400
Fax: (817)390-8408
Website: http://www.buenaventure.com

The Catalyst Group
3 Riverway, Ste. 770
Houston, TX 77056
(713)623-8133
Fax: (713)623-0473
E-mail: herman@thecatalystgroup.net
Website: http://www.thecatalyst
group.net

Cureton & Co., Inc.
1100 Louisiana, Ste. 3250
Houston, TX 77002
(713)658-9806
Fax: (713)658-0476

Davis, Tuttle Venture Partners (Dallas)
8 Greenway Plaza, Ste. 1020
Houston, TX 77046
(713)993-0440
Fax: (713)621-2297
Website: http://www.davistuttle.com

Houston Partners
401 Louisiana, 8th Fl.
Houston, TX 77002
(713)222-8600
Fax: (713)222-8932

Southwest Venture Group
10878 Westheimer, Ste. 178

Houston, TX 77042
(713)827-8947
(713)461-1470

AM Fund
4600 Post Oak Place, Ste. 100
Houston, TX 77027
(713)627-9111
Fax: (713)627-9119

Ventex Management, Inc.
3417 Milam St.
Houston, TX 77002-9531
(713)659-7870
Fax: (713)659-7855

MBA Venture Group
1004 Olde Town Rd., Ste. 102
Irving, TX 75061
(972)986-6703

First Capital Group Management Co.
750 East Mulberry St., Ste. 305
PO Box 15616
San Antonio, TX 78212
(210)736-4233
Fax: (210)736-5449

The Southwest Venture Partnerships
16414 San Pedro, Ste. 345
San Antonio, TX 78232
(210)402-1200
Fax: (210)402-1221
E-mail: swvp@aol.com

Medtech International Inc.
1742 Carriageway
Sugarland, TX 77478
(713)980-8474
Fax: (713)980-6343

Utah

First Security Business Investment Corp.
15 East 100 South, Ste. 100
Salt Lake City, UT 84111
(801)246-5737
Fax: (801)246-5740

Utah Ventures II, L.P.
423 Wakara Way, Ste. 206
Salt Lake City, UT 84108
(801)583-5922
Fax: (801)583-4105
Website: http://www.uven.com

Wasatch Venture Corp.
1 S. Main St., Ste. 1400
Salt Lake City, UT 84133
(801)524-8939

Fax: (801)524-8941
E-mail: mail@wasatchvc.com

Vermont

North Atlantic Capital Corp.
76 Saint Paul St., Ste. 600
Burlington, VT 05401
(802)658-7820
Fax: (802)658-5757
Website: http://www.north
atlanticcapital.com

Green Mountain Advisors Inc.
PO Box 1230
Quechee, VT 05059
(802)296-7800
Fax: (802)296-6012
Website: http://www.gmtcap.com

Virginia

Oxford Financial Services Corp.
Alexandria, VA 22314
(703)519-4900
Fax: (703)519-4910
E-mail: oxford133@aol.com

Continental SBIC
4141 N. Henderson Rd.
Arlington, VA 22203
(703)527-5200
Fax: (703)527-3700

Novak Biddle Venture Partners
1750 Tysons Blvd., Ste. 1190
McLean, VA 22102
(703)847-3770
Fax: (703)847-3771
E-mail: roger@novakbiddle.com
Website: http://www.novakbiddle.com

Spacevest
11911 Freedom Dr., Ste. 500
Reston, VA 20190
(703)904-9800
Fax: (703)904-0571
E-mail: spacevest@spacevest.com
Website: http://www.spacevest.com

Virginia Capital
1801 Libbie Ave., Ste. 201
Richmond, VA 23226
(804)648-4802
Fax: (804)648-4809
E-mail: webmaster@vacapital.com
Website: http://www.vacapital.com

Calvert Social Venture Partners
402 Maple Ave. W
Vienna, VA 22180

(703)255-4930
Fax: (703)255-4931
E-mail: calven2000@aol.com

Fairfax Partners
8000 Towers Crescent Dr., Ste. 940
Vienna, VA 22182
(703)847-9486
Fax: (703)847-0911

Global Internet Ventures
8150 Leesburg Pike, Ste. 1210
Vienna, VA 22182
(703)442-3300
Fax: (703)442-3388
Website: http://www.givinc.com

Walnut Capital Corp. (Vienna)
8000 Towers Crescent Dr., Ste. 1070
Vienna, VA 22182
(703)448-3771
Fax: (703)448-7751

Washington

Encompass Ventures
777 108th Ave. NE, Ste. 2300
Bellevue, WA 98004
(425)486-3900
Fax: (425)486-3901
E-mail: info@evpartners.com
Website: http://www.encom
passventures.com

Fluke Venture Partners
11400 SE Sixth St., Ste. 230
Bellevue, WA 98004
(425)453-4590
Fax: (425)453-4675
E-mail: gabelein@flukeventures.com
Website: http://www.flukeventures.com

Pacific Northwest Partners SBIC, L.P.
15352 SE 53rd St.
Bellevue, WA 98006
(425)455-9967
Fax: (425)455-9404

Materia Venture Associates, L.P.
3435 Carillon Pointe
Kirkland, WA 98033-7354
(425)822-4100
Fax: (425)827-4086

OVP Venture Partners (Kirkland)
2420 Carillon Pt.
Kirkland, WA 98033
(425)889-9192
Fax: (425)889-0152
E-mail: info@ovp.com
Website: http://www.ovp.com

Digital Partners
999 3rd Ave., Ste. 1610
Seattle, WA 98104
(206)405-3607
Fax: (206)405-3617
Website: http://www.digitalpartners.com

Frazier & Company
601 Union St., Ste. 3300
Seattle, WA 98101
(206)621-7200
Fax: (206)621-1848
E-mail: jon@frazierco.com

Kirlan Venture Capital, Inc.
221 First Ave. W, Ste. 108
Seattle, WA 98119-4223
(206)281-8610
Fax: (206)285-3451
Website: http://www.kirlanventure.com

Phoenix Partners
1000 2nd Ave., Ste. 3600
Seattle, WA 98104
(206)624-8968
Fax: (206)624-1907

Voyager Capital
800 5th St., Ste. 4100
Seattle, WA 98103
(206)470-1180
Fax: (206)470-1185
E-mail: info@voyagercap.com
Website: http://www.voyagercap.com

Northwest Venture Associates
221 N. Wall St., Ste. 628
Spokane, WA 99201
(509)747-0728
Fax: (509)747-0758
Website: http://www.nwva.com

Wisconsin

Venture Investors Management, L.L.C.
University Research Park
505 S. Rosa Rd.
Madison, WI 53719
(608)441-2700
Fax: (608)441-2727
E-mail: roger@ventureinvestors.com
Website: http://www.venture
investers.com

Capital Investments, Inc.
1009 West Glen Oaks Lane, Ste. 103
Mequon, WI 53092
(414)241-0303
Fax: (414)241-8451
Website: http://
www.capitalinvestmentsinc.com

Future Value Venture, Inc.
2745 N. Martin Luther King
Dr., Ste. 204
Milwaukee, WI 53212-2300
(414)264-2252
Fax: (414)264-2253
E-mail: fvvventures@aol.com
William Beckett, President

Lubar and Co., Inc.
700 N. Water St., Ste. 1200
Milwaukee, WI 53202
(414)291-9000
Fax: (414)291-9061

GCI
20875 Crossroads Cir., Ste. 100
Waukesha, WI 53186
(262)798-5080
Fax: (262)798-5087

Glossary of Small Business Terms

Absolute liability
Liability that is incurred due to product defects or negligent actions. Manufacturers or retail establishments are held responsible, even though the defect or action may not have been intentional or negligent.

ACE
See Active Corps of Executives

Accident and health benefits
Benefits offered to employees and their families in order to offset the costs associated with accidental death, accidental injury, or sickness.

Account statement
A record of transactions, including payments, new debt, and deposits, incurred during a defined period of time.

Accounting system
System capturing the costs of all employees and/or machinery included in business expenses.

Accounts payable
See Trade credit

Accounts receivable
Unpaid accounts which arise from unsettled claims and transactions from the sale of a company's products or services to its customers.

Active Corps of Executives (ACE)
A group of volunteers for a management assistance program of the U.S. Small Business Administration; volunteers provide one-on-one counseling and teach workshops and seminars for small firms.

ADA
See Americans with Disabilities Act

Adaptation
The process whereby an invention is modified to meet the needs of users.

Adaptive engineering
The process whereby an invention is modified to meet the manufacturing and commercial requirements of a targeted market.

Adverse selection
The tendency for higher-risk individuals to purchase health care and more comprehensive plans, resulting in increased costs.

Advertising
A marketing tool used to capture public attention and influence purchasing decisions for a product or service. Utilizes various forms of media to generate consumer response, such as flyers, magazines, newspapers, radio, and television.

Age discrimination
The denial of the rights and privileges of employment based solely on the age of an individual.

Agency costs
Costs incurred to insure that the lender or investor maintains control over assets while allowing the borrower or entrepreneur to use them. Monitoring and information costs are the two major types of agency costs.

Agribusiness
The production and sale of commodities and products from the commercial farming industry.

America Online
An online service which is accessible by computer modem. The service features Internet access, bulletin boards, online periodicals, electronic mail, and other services for subscribers.

Americans with Disabilities Act (ADA)
Law designed to ensure equal access and opportunity to handicapped persons.

Annual report
Yearly financial report prepared by a business that adheres to the requirements set forth by the Securities and Exchange Commission (SEC).

Antitrust immunity
Exemption from prosecution under antitrust laws. In the transportation industry, firms with antitrust immunity are permitted under certain conditions to set schedules and sometimes prices for the public benefit.

Applied research
Scientific study targeted for use in a product or process.

Asians
A minority category used by the U.S. Bureau of the Census to represent a diverse group that includes Aleuts, Eskimos, American Indians, Asian Indians, Chinese, Japanese, Koreans, Vietnamese, Filipinos, Hawaiians, and other Pacific Islanders.

Assets
Anything of value owned by a company.

Audit
The verification of accounting records and business procedures conducted by an outside accounting service.

Average cost
Total production costs divided by the quantity produced.

Balance Sheet
A financial statement listing the total assets and liabilities of a company at a given time.

Bankruptcy
The condition in which a business cannot meet its debt obligations and petitions a federal district court either for reorganization of its debts (Chapter 11) or for liquidation of its assets (Chapter 7).

Basic research
Theoretical scientific exploration not targeted to application.

Basket clause
A provision specifying the amount of public pension funds that may be placed in investments not included on a state's legal list (see separate citation).

BBS
See Bulletin Board Service

BDC
See Business development corporation

Benefit
Various services, such as health care, flextime, day care, insurance, and vacation, offered to employees as part of a hiring package. Typically subsidized in whole or in part by the business.

BIDCO
See Business and industrial development company

Billing cycle
A system designed to evenly distribute customer billing throughout the month, preventing clerical backlogs.

Birth
See Business birth

Blue chip security
A low-risk, low-yield security representing an interest in a very stable company.

Blue sky laws
A general term that denotes various states' laws regulating securities.

Bond
A written instrument executed by a bidder or contractor (the principal) and a second party (the surety or sureties) to assure fulfillment of the principal's obligations to a third party (the obligee or government) identified in the bond. If the principal's obligations are not met, the bond assures payment to the extent stipulated of any loss sustained by the obligee.

Bonding requirements
Terms contained in a bond (see separate citation).

Bonus
An amount of money paid to an employee as a reward for achieving certain business goals or objectives.

Brainstorming
A group session where employees contribute their ideas for solving a problem or meeting a company objective without fear of retribution or ridicule.

Brand name
The part of a brand, trademark, or service mark that can be spoken. It can be a word, letter, or group of words or letters.

Bridge financing
A short-term loan made in expectation of intermediateterm or long-term financing. Can be used when a company plans to go public in the near future.

Broker
One who matches resources available for innovation with those who need them.

Budget
An estimate of the spending necessary to complete a project or offer a service in comparison to cash-on-hand and expected earnings for the coming year, with an emphasis on cost control.

Bulletin Board Service (BBS)
An online service enabling users to communicate with each other about specific topics.

Business and industrial development company (BIDCO)
A private, for-profit financing corporation chartered by the state to provide both equity and long-term debt capital to small business owners (see separate citations for equity and debt capital).

Business birth
The formation of a new establishment or enterprise. The appearance of a new establishment or enterprise in the Small Business Data Base (see separate citation).

Business conditions
Outside factors that can affect the financial performance of a business.

Business contractions
The number of establishments that have decreased in employment during a specified time.

Business cycle
A period of economic recession and recovery. These cycles vary in duration.

Business death
The voluntary or involuntary closure of a firm or establishment. The disappearance of an establishment or enterprise from the Small Business Data Base (see separate citation).

Business development corporation (BDC)
A business financing agency, usually composed of the financial institutions in an area or state, organized to assist in financing businesses unable to obtain assistance through normal channels; the risk is spread among various members of the business development corporation, and interest rates may vary somewhat from those charged by member institutions. A venture capital firm in which shares of ownership are publicly held and to which the Investment Act of 1940 applies.

Business dissolution
For enumeration purposes, the absence of a business that was present in the prior time period from any current record.

Business entry
See Business birth

Business ethics
Moral values and principles espoused by members of the business community as a guide to fair and honest business practices.

Business exit
See Business death

Business expansions
The number of establishments that added employees during a specified time.

Business failure
Closure of a business causing a loss to at least one creditor.

Business format franchising
The purchase of the name, trademark, and an ongoing business plan of the parent corporation or franchisor by the franchisee.

Business license
A legal authorization issued by municipal and state governments and required for business operations.

Business name
Enterprises must register their business names with local governments usually on a "doing business as" (DBA) form. (This name is sometimes referred to as a "fictional name.") The procedure is part of the business licensing process and prevents any other business from using that same name for a similar business in the same locality.

Business norms
See Financial ratios

Business permit
See Business license

Business plan
A document that spells out a company's expected course of action for a specified period, usually including a detailed listing and analysis of risks and uncertainties. For the small business, it should examine the proposed products, the market, the industry, the management policies, the marketing policies, production needs, and financial needs. Frequently, it is used as a prospectus for potential investors and lenders.

Business proposal
See Business plan

Business service firm
An establishment primarily engaged in rendering services to other business organizations on a fee or contract basis.

Business start
For enumeration purposes, a business with a name or similar designation that did not exist in a prior time period.

Cafeteria plan
See Flexible benefit plan

Capacity
Level of a firm's, industry's, or nation's output corresponding to full practical utilization of available resources.

Capital
Assets less liabilities, representing the ownership interest in a business. A stock of accumulated goods, especially at a specified time and in contrast to income received during a specified time period. Accumulated goods devoted to production. Accumulated possessions calculated to bring income.

Capital expenditure
Expenses incurred by a business for improvements that will depreciate over time.

Capital gain
The monetary difference between the purchase price and the selling price of capital. Capital gains are taxed at a rate of 28% by the federal government.

Capital intensity
The relative importance of capital in the production process, usually expressed as the ratio of capital to labor but also sometimes as the ratio of capital to output.

Capital resource
The equipment, facilities and labor used to create products and services.

Caribbean Basin Initiative
An interdisciplinary program to support commerce among the businesses in the nations of the Caribbean Basin and the United States. Agencies involved include: the Agency for International Development, the U.S. Small Business Administration, the International Trade Administration of the U.S. Department of Commerce, and various private sector groups.

Catastrophic care
Medical and other services for acute and long-term illnesses that cost more than insurance coverage limits or that cost the amount most families may be expected to pay with their own resources.

CDC
See Certified development corporation

CD-ROM
Compact disc with read-only memory used to store large amounts of digitized data.

Certified development corporation (CDC)
A local area or statewide corporation or authority (for profit or nonprofit) that packages U.S. Small Business Administration (SBA), bank, state, and/or private money into financial assistance for existing business capital improvements. The SBA holds the second lien on its maximum share of 40 percent involvement. Each state has at least one certified development corporation. This program is called the SBA 504 Program.

Certified lenders
Banks that participate in the SBA guaranteed loan program (see separate citation). Such banks must have a good track record with the U.S. Small Business Administration (SBA) and must agree to certain conditions set forth by the agency. In return, the SBA agrees to process any guaranteed loan application within three business days.

Champion
An advocate for the development of an innovation.

Channel of distribution
The means used to transport merchandise from the manufacturer to the consumer.

Chapter 7 of the 1978 Bankruptcy Act
Provides for a court-appointed trustee who is responsible for liquidating a company's assets in order to settle outstanding debts.

Chapter 11 of the 1978 Bankruptcy Act
Allows the business owners to retain control of the company while working with their creditors to reorganize their finances and establish better business practices to prevent liquidation of assets.

Closely held corporation
A corporation in which the shares are held by a few persons, usually officers, employees, or others close to the management; these shares are rarely offered to the public.

Code of Federal Regulations
Codification of general and permanent rules of the federal government published in the Federal Register.

Code sharing
See Computer code sharing

Coinsurance
Upon meeting the deductible payment, health insurance participants may be required to make additional health care cost-sharing payments. Coinsurance is a payment of a fixed percentage of the cost of each service; copayment is usually a fixed amount to be paid with each service.

Collateral
Securities, evidence of deposit, or other property pledged by a borrower to secure repayment of a loan.

Collective ratemaking
The establishment of uniform charges for services by a group of businesses in the same industry.

Commercial insurance plan
See Underwriting

Commercial loans
Short-term renewable loans used to finance specific capital needs of a business.

Commercialization
The final stage of the innovation process, including production and distribution.

Common stock
The most frequently used instrument for purchasing ownership in private or public companies. Common stock generally carries the right to vote on certain corporate actions and may pay dividends, although it rarely does in venture investments. In liquidation, common stockholders are the last to share in the proceeds from the sale of a corporation's assets; bondholders and preferred shareholders have priority. Common stock is often used in firstround start-up financing.

Community development corporation
A corporation established to develop economic programs for a community and, in most cases, to provide financial support for such development.

Competitor
A business whose product or service is marketed for the same purpose/use and to the same consumer group as the product or service of another.

Computer code sharing
An arrangement whereby flights of a regional airline are identified by the two-letter code of a major carrier in the computer reservation system to help direct passengers to new regional carriers.

Consignment
A merchandising agreement, usually referring to secondhand shops, where the dealer pays the owner of an item a percentage of the profit when the item is sold.

Consortium
A coalition of organizations such as banks and corporations for ventures requiring large capital resources.

Consultant
An individual that is paid by a business to provide advice and expertise in a particular area.

Consumer price index
A measure of the fluctuation in prices between two points in time.

Consumer research
Research conducted by a business to obtain information about existing or potential consumer markets.

Continuation coverage
Health coverage offered for a specified period of time to employees who leave their jobs and to their widows, divorced spouses, or dependents.

Contractions
See Business contractions

Convertible preferred stock
A class of stock that pays a reasonable dividend and is convertible into common stock (see separate citation). Generally the convertible feature may only be exercised after being held for a stated period of time. This arrangement is usually considered second-round financing when a company needs equity to maintain its cash flow.

Convertible securities
A feature of certain bonds, debentures, or preferred stocks that allows them to be exchanged by the owner for another class of securities at a future date and in accordance with any other terms of the issue.

Copayment
See Coinsurance

Copyright
A legal form of protection available to creators and authors to safeguard their works from unlawful use or claim of ownership by others. Copyrights may be acquired for works of art, sculpture, music, and published or unpublished manuscripts. All copyrights should be registered at the Copyright Office of the Library of Congress.

Corporate financial ratios
The relationship between key figures found in a company's financial statement expressed as a numeric value. Used to evaluate risk and company performance. Also known as Financial averages, Operating ratios, and Business ratios.

Corporation
A legal entity, chartered by a state or the federal government, recognized as a separate entity having its own rights, privileges, and liabilities distinct from those of its members.

Cost containment
Actions taken by employers and insurers to curtail rising health care costs; for example, increasing

employee cost sharing (see separate citation), requiring second opinions, or preadmission screening.

Cost sharing
The requirement that health care consumers contribute to their own medical care costs through deductibles and coinsurance (see separate citations). Cost sharing does not include the amounts paid in premiums. It is used to control utilization of services; for example, requiring a fixed amount to be paid with each health care service.

Cottage industry
Businesses based in the home in which the family members are the labor force and family-owned equipment is used to process the goods.

Credit Rating
A letter or number calculated by an organization (such as Dun & Bradstreet) to represent the ability and disposition of a business to meet its financial obligations.

Customer service
Various techniques used to ensure the satisfaction of a customer.

Cyclical peak
The upper turning point in a business cycle.

Cyclical trough
The lower turning point in a business cycle.

DBA
See Business name

Death
See Business death

Debenture
A certificate given as acknowledgment of a debt (see separate citation) secured by the general credit of the issuing corporation. A bond, usually without security, issued by a corporation and sometimes convertible to common stock.

Debt
Something owed by one person to another. Financing in which a company receives capital that must be repaid; no ownership is transferred.

Debt capital
Business financing that normally requires periodic interest payments and repayment of the principal within a specified time.

Debt financing
See Debt capital

Debt securities
Loans such as bonds and notes that provide a specified rate of return for a specified period of time.

Deductible
A set amount that an individual must pay before any benefits are received.

Demand shock absorbers
A term used to describe the role that some small firms play by expanding their output levels to accommodate a transient surge in demand.

Demographics
Statistics on various markets, including age, income, and education, used to target specific products or services to appropriate consumer groups.

Demonstration
Showing that a product or process has been modified sufficiently to meet the needs of users.

Deregulation
The lifting of government restrictions; for example, the lifting of government restrictions on the entry of new businesses, the expansion of services, and the setting of prices in particular industries.

Desktop Publishing
Using personal computers and specialized software to produce camera-ready copy for publications.

Disaster loans
Various types of physical and economic assistance available to individuals and businesses through the U.S. Small Business Administration (SBA). This is the only SBA loan program available for residential purposes.

Discrimination
The denial of the rights and privileges of employment based on factors such as age, race, religion, or gender.

Diseconomies of scale
The condition in which the costs of production increase faster than the volume of production.

Dissolution
See Business dissolution

Distribution
Delivering a product or process to the user.

Distributor
One who delivers merchandise to the user.

Diversified company
A company whose products and services are used by several different markets.

Doing business as (DBA)
See Business name

Dow Jones
An information services company that publishes the Wall Street Journal and other sources of financial information.

Dow Jones Industrial Average
An indicator of stock market performance.

Earned income
A tax term that refers to wages and salaries earned by the recipient, as opposed to monies earned through interest and dividends.

Economic efficiency
The use of productive resources to the fullest practical extent in the provision of the set of goods and services that is most preferred by purchasers in the economy.

Economic indicators
Statistics used to express the state of the economy. These include the length of the average work week, the rate of unemployment, and stock prices.

Economically disadvantaged
See Socially and economically disadvantaged

Economies of scale
See Scale economies

EEOC
See Equal Employment Opportunity Commission

8(a) Program
A program authorized by the Small Business Act that directs federal contracts to small businesses owned and

operated by socially and economically disadvantaged individuals.

Electronic mail (e-mail)
The electronic transmission of mail via phone lines.

E-mail
See Electronic mail

Employee leasing
A contract by which employers arrange to have their workers hired by a leasing company and then leased back to them for a management fee. The leasing company typically assumes the administrative burden of payroll and provides a benefit package to the workers.

Employee tenure
The length of time an employee works for a particular employer.

Employer identification number
The business equivalent of a social security number. Assigned by the U.S. Internal Revenue Service.

Enterprise
An aggregation of all establishments owned by a parent company. An enterprise may consist of a single, independent establishment or include subsidiaries and other branches under the same ownership and control.

Enterprise zone
A designated area, usually found in inner cities and other areas with significant unemployment, where businesses receive tax credits and other incentives to entice them to establish operations there.

Entrepreneur
A person who takes the risk of organizing and operating a new business venture.

Entry
See Business entry

Equal Employment Opportunity Commission (EEOC)
A federal agency that ensures nondiscrimination in the hiring and firing practices of a business.

Equal opportunity employer
An employer who adheres to the standards set by the Equal Employment Opportunity Commission (see separate citation).

Equity
The ownership interest. Financing in which partial or total ownership of a company is surrendered in exchange for capital. An investor's financial return comes from dividend payments and from growth in the net worth of the business.

Equity capital
See Equity; Equity midrisk venture capital

Equity financing
See Equity; Equity midrisk venture capital

Equity midrisk venture capital
An unsecured investment in a company. Usually a purchase of ownership interest in a company that occurs in the later stages of a company's development.

Equity partnership
A limited partnership arrangement for providing start-up and seed capital to businesses.

Equity securities
See Equity

Equity-type
Debt financing subordinated to conventional debt.

Establishment
A single-location business unit that may be independent (a single-establishment enterprise) or owned by a parent enterprise.

Establishment and Enterprise Microdata File
See U.S. Establishment and Enterprise Microdata File

Establishment birth
See Business birth

Establishment Longitudinal Microdata File
See U.S. Establishment Longitudinal Microdata File

Ethics
See Business ethics

Evaluation
Determining the potential success of translating an invention into a product or process.

Exit
See Business exit

Experience rating
See Underwriting

Export
A product sold outside of the country.

Export license
A general or specific license granted by the U.S. Department of Commerce required of anyone wishing to export goods. Some restricted articles need approval from the U.S. Departments of State, Defense, or Energy.

Failure
See Business failure

Fair share agreement
An agreement reached between a franchisor and a minority business organization to extend business ownership to minorities by either reducing the amount of capital required or by setting aside certain marketing areas for minority business owners.

Feasibility study
A study to determine the likelihood that a proposed product or development will fulfill the objectives of a particular investor.

Federal Trade Commission (FTC)
Federal agency that promotes free enterprise and competition within the U.S.

Federal Trade Mark Act of 1946
See Lanham Act

Fictional name
See Business name

Fiduciary
An individual or group that hold assets in trust for a beneficiary.

Financial analysis
The techniques used to determine money needs in a business. Techniques include ratio analysis, calculation of return on investment, guides for measuring profitability, and break-even analysis to determine ultimate success.

Financial intermediary
A financial institution that acts as the intermediary between borrowers and lenders. Banks, savings and loan associations, finance companies, and venture capital companies are major financial intermediaries in the United States.

Financial ratios
See Corporate financial ratios; Industry financial ratios

Financial statement
A written record of business finances, including balance sheets and profit and loss statements.

Financing
See First-stage financing; Second-stage financing; Thirdstage financing

First-stage financing
Financing provided to companies that have expended their initial capital, and require funds to start full-scale manufacturing and sales. Also known as First-round financing.

Fiscal year
Any twelve-month period used by businesses for accounting purposes.

504 Program
See Certified development corporation

Flexible benefit plan
A plan that offers a choice among cash and/or qualified benefits such as group term life insurance, accident and health insurance, group legal services, dependent care assistance, and vacations.

FOB
See Free on board

Format franchising
See Business format franchising; Franchising

401(k) plan
A financial plan where employees contribute a percentage of their earnings to a fund that is invested in stocks, bonds, or money markets for the purpose of saving money for retirement.

Four Ps
Marketing terms referring to Product, Price, Place, and Promotion.

Franchising
A form of licensing by which the owner-the franchisor- distributes or markets a product, method, or service through affiliated dealers called franchisees. The product, method, or service being marketed is identified by a brand name, and the franchisor

maintains control over the marketing methods employed. The franchisee is often given exclusive access to a defined geographic area.

Free on board (FOB)
A pricing term indicating that the quoted price includes the cost of loading goods into transport vessels at a specified place.

Frictional unemployment
See Unemployment

FTC
See Federal Trade Commission

Fulfillment
The systems necessary for accurate delivery of an ordered item, including subscriptions and direct marketing.

Full-time workers
Generally, those who work a regular schedule of more than 35 hours per week.

Garment registration number
A number that must appear on every garment sold in the U.S. to indicate the manufacturer of the garment, which may or may not be the same as the label under which the garment is sold. The U.S. Federal Trade Commission assigns and regulates garment registration numbers.

Gatekeeper
A key contact point for entry into a network.

GDP
See Gross domestic product

General obligation bond
A municipal bond secured by the taxing power of the municipality. The Tax Reform Act of 1986 limits the purposes for which such bonds may be issued and establishes volume limits on the extent of their issuance.

GNP
See Gross national product

Good Housekeeping Seal
Seal appearing on products that signifies the fulfillment of the standards set by the Good Housekeeping Institute to protect consumer interests.

Goods sector
All businesses producing tangible goods, including agriculture, mining, construction, and manufacturing businesses.

GPO
See Gross product originating

Gross domestic product (GDP)
The part of the nation's gross national product (see separate citation) generated by private business using resources from within the country.

Gross national product (GNP)
The most comprehensive single measure of aggregate economic output. Represents the market value of the total output of goods and services produced by a nation's economy.

Gross product originating (GPO)
A measure of business output estimated from the income or production side using employee compensation, profit income, net interest, capital consumption, and indirect business taxes.

HAL
See Handicapped assistance loan program

Handicapped assistance loan program (HAL)
Low-interest direct loan program through the U.S. Small Business Administration (SBA) for handicapped persons. The SBA requires that these persons demonstrate that their disability is such that it is impossible for them to secure employment, thus making it necessary to go into their own business to make a living.

Health maintenance organization (HMO)
Organization of physicians and other health care professionals that provides health services to subscribers and their dependents on a prepaid basis.

Health provider
An individual or institution that gives medical care. Under Medicare, an institutional provider is a hospital, skilled nursing facility, home health agency, or provider of certain physical therapy services.

Hispanic
A person of Cuban, Mexican, Puerto Rican, Latin American (Central or South American), European Spanish, or other Spanish-speaking origin or ancestry.

HMO
See Health maintenance organization

Home-based business
A business with an operating address that is also a residential address (usually the residential address of the proprietor).

Hub-and-spoke system
A system in which flights of an airline from many different cities (the spokes) converge at a single airport (the hub). After allowing passengers sufficient time to make connections, planes then depart for different cities.

Human Resources Management
A business program designed to oversee recruiting, pay, benefits, and other issues related to the company's work force, including planning to determine the optimal use of labor to increase production, thereby increasing profit.

Idea
An original concept for a new product or process.

Import
Products produced outside the country in which they are consumed.

Income
Money or its equivalent, earned or accrued, resulting from the sale of goods and services.

Income statement
A financial statement that lists the profits and losses of a company at a given time.

Incorporation
The filing of a certificate of incorporation with a state's secretary of state, thereby limiting the business owner's liability.

Incubator
A facility designed to encourage entrepreneurship and minimize obstacles to new business formation and growth, particularly for high-technology firms, by housing a number of fledgling enterprises that share an array of services, such as meeting areas, secretarial services, accounting, research library, on-site financial and management counseling, and word processing facilities.

Independent contractor
An individual considered self-employed (see separate citation) and responsible for paying Social Security taxes and income taxes on earnings.

Indirect health coverage
Health insurance obtained through another individual's health care plan; for example, a spouse's employersponsored plan.

Industrial development authority
The financial arm of a state or other political subdivision established for the purpose of financing economic development in an area, usually through loans to nonprofit organizations, which in turn provide facilities for manufacturing and other industrial operations.

Industry financial ratios
Corporate financial ratios averaged for a specified industry. These are used for comparison purposes and reveal industry trends and identify differences between the performance of a specific company and the performance of its industry. Also known as Industrial averages, Industry ratios, Financial averages, and Business or Industrial norms.

Inflation
Increases in volume of currency and credit, generally resulting in a sharp and continuing rise in price levels.

Informal capital
Financing from informal, unorganized sources; includes informal debt capital such as trade credit or loans from friends and relatives and equity capital from informal investors.

Initial public offering (IPO)
A corporation's first offering of stock to the public.

Innovation
The introduction of a new idea into the marketplace in the form of a new product or service or an improvement in organization or process.

Intellectual property
Any idea or work that can be considered proprietary in nature and is thus protected from infringement by others.

Internal capital
Debt or equity financing obtained from the owner or through retained business earnings.

Internet
A government-designed computer network that contains large amounts of information and is accessible through various vendors for a fee.

Intrapreneurship
The state of employing entrepreneurial principles to nonentrepreneurial situations.

Invention
The tangible form of a technological idea, which could include a laboratory prototype, drawings, formulas, etc.

IPO
See Initial public offering

Job description
The duties and responsibilities required in a particular position.

Job tenure
A period of time during which an individual is continuously employed in the same job.

Joint marketing agreements
Agreements between regional and major airlines, often involving the coordination of flight schedules, fares, and baggage transfer. These agreements help regional carriers operate at lower cost.

Joint venture
Venture in which two or more people combine efforts in a particular business enterprise, usually a single transaction or a limited activity, and agree to share the profits and losses jointly or in proportion to their contributions.

Keogh plan
Designed for self-employed persons and unincorporated businesses as a tax-deferred pension account.

Labor force
Civilians considered eligible for employment who are also willing and able to work.

Labor force participation rate
The civilian labor force as a percentage of the civilian population.

Labor intensity
The relative importance of labor in the production process, usually measured as the capital-labor ratio; i.e., the ratio of units of capital (typically, dollars of tangible assets) to the number of employees. The higher the capital-labor ratio exhibited by a firm or industry, the lower the capital intensity of that firm or industry is said to be.

Labor surplus area
An area in which there exists a high unemployment rate. In procurement (see separate citation), extra points are given to firms in counties that are designated a labor surplus area; this information is requested on procurement bid sheets.

Labor union
An organization of similarly-skilled workers who collectively bargain with management over the conditions of employment.

Laboratory prototype
See Prototype

LAN
See Local Area Network

Lanham Act
Refers to the Federal Trade Mark Act of 1946. Protects registered trademarks, trade names, and other service marks used in commerce.

Large business-dominated industry
Industry in which a minimum of 60 percent of employment or sales is in firms with more than 500 workers.

LBO
See Leveraged buy-out

Leader pricing
A reduction in the price of a good or service in order to generate more sales of that good or service.

Legal list
A list of securities selected by a state in which certain institutions and fiduciaries (such as pension funds, insurance companies, and banks) may invest. Securities not on the list are not eligible for investment. Legal lists typically restrict investments to high quality securities meeting certain specifications. Generally, investment is

limited to U.S. securities and investment-grade blue chip securities (see separate citation).

Leveraged buy-out (LBO)
The purchase of a business or a division of a corporation through a highly leveraged financing package.

Liability
An obligation or duty to perform a service or an act. Also defined as money owed.

License
A legal agreement granting to another the right to use a technological innovation.

Limited partnerships
See Venture capital limited partnerships

Liquidity
The ability to convert a security into cash promptly.

Loans
See Commercial loans; Disaster loans; SBA direct loans; SBA guaranteed loans; SBA special lending institution categories Local Area Network (LAN) Computer networks contained within a single building or small area; used to facilitate the sharing of information.

Local development corporation
An organization, usually made up of local citizens of a community, designed to improve the economy of the area by inducing business and industry to locate and expand there. A local development corporation establishes a capability to finance local growth.

Long-haul rates
Rates charged by a transporter in which the distance traveled is more than 800 miles.

Long-term debt
An obligation that matures in a period that exceeds five years.

Low-grade bond
A corporate bond that is rated below investment grade by the major rating agencies (Standard and Poor's, Moody's).

Macro-efficiency
Efficiency as it pertains to the operation of markets and market systems.

Managed care
A cost-effective health care program initiated by employers whereby low-cost health care is made available to the employees in return for exclusive patronage to program doctors.

Management Assistance Programs
See SBA Management Assistance Programs

Management and technical assistance
A term used by many programs to mean business (as opposed to technological) assistance.

Mandated benefits
Specific treatments, providers, or individuals required by law to be included in commercial health plans.

Market evaluation
The use of market information to determine the sales potential of a specific product or process.

Market failure
The situation in which the workings of a competitive market do not produce the best results from the point of view of the entire society.

Market information
Data of any type that can be used for market evaluation, which could include demographic data, technology forecasting, regulatory changes, etc.

Market research
A systematic collection, analysis, and reporting of data about the market and its preferences, opinions, trends, and plans; used for corporate decision-making.

Market share
In a particular market, the percentage of sales of a specific product.

Marketing
Promotion of goods or services through various media.

Master Establishment List (MEL)
A list of firms in the United States developed by the U.S. Small Business Administration; firms can be selected by industry, region, state, standard metropolitan statistical area (see separate citation), county, and zip code.

Maturity
The date upon which the principal or stated value of a bond or other indebtedness becomes due and payable.

Medicaid (Title XIX)
A federally aided, state-operated and administered program that provides medical benefits for certain low income persons in need of health and medical care who are eligible for one of the government's welfare cash payment programs, including the aged, the blind, the disabled, and members of families with dependent children where one parent is absent, incapacitated, or unemployed.

Medicare (Title XVIII)
A nationwide health insurance program for disabled and aged persons. Health insurance is available to insured persons without regard to income. Monies from payroll taxes cover hospital insurance and monies from general revenues and beneficiary premiums pay for supplementary medical insurance.

MEL
See Master Establishment List

MESBIC
See Minority enterprise small business investment corporation

MET
See Multiple employer trust

Metropolitan statistical area (MSA)
A means used by the government to define large population centers that may transverse different governmental jurisdictions. For example, the Washington, D.C. MSA includes the District of Columbia and contiguous parts of Maryland and Virginia because all of these geopolitical areas comprise one population and economic operating unit.

Mezzanine financing
See Third-stage financing

Micro-efficiency
Efficiency as it pertains to the operation of individual firms.

Microdata
Information on the characteristics of an individual business firm.

Mid-term debt
An obligation that matures within one to five years.

Midrisk venture capital
See Equity midrisk venture capital

Minimum premium plan
A combination approach to funding an insurance plan aimed primarily at premium tax savings. The employer self-funds a fixed percentage of estimated monthly claims and the insurance company insures the excess.

Minimum wage
The lowest hourly wage allowed by the federal government.

Minority Business Development Agency
Contracts with private firms throughout the nation to sponsor Minority Business Development Centers which provide minority firms with advice and technical assistance on a fee basis.

Minority Enterprise Small Business Investment Corporation (MESBIC)
A federally funded private venture capital firm licensed by the U.S. Small Business Administration to provide capital to minority-owned businesses (see separate citation).

Minority-owned business
Businesses owned by those who are socially or economically disadvantaged (see separate citation).

Mom and Pop business
A small store or enterprise having limited capital, principally employing family members.

Moonlighter
A wage-and-salary worker with a side business.

MSA
See Metropolitan statistical area

Multi-employer plan
A health plan to which more than one employer is required to contribute and that may be maintained through a collective bargaining agreement and required to meet standards prescribed by the U.S. Department of Labor.

Multi-level marketing
A system of selling in which you sign up other people to assist you and they, in turn, recruit others to help them. Some entrepreneurs have built successful

companies on this concept because the main focus of their activities is their product and product sales.

Multimedia
The use of several types of media to promote a product or service. Also, refers to the use of several different types of media (sight, sound, pictures, text) in a CD-ROM (see separate citation) product.

Multiple employer trust (MET)
A self-funded benefit plan generally geared toward small employers sharing a common interest.

NAFTA
See North American Free Trade Agreement

NASDAQ
See National Association of Securities Dealers Automated Quotations

National Association of Securities Dealers Automated Quotations
Provides price quotes on over-the-counter securities as well as securities listed on the New York Stock Exchange.

National income
Aggregate earnings of labor and property arising from the production of goods and services in a nation's economy.

Net assets
See Net worth

Net income
The amount remaining from earnings and profits after all expenses and costs have been met or deducted. Also known as Net earnings.

Net profit
Money earned after production and overhead expenses (see separate citations) have been deducted.

Net worth
The difference between a company's total assets and its total liabilities.

Network
A chain of interconnected individuals or organizations sharing information and/or services.

New York Stock Exchange (NYSE)
The oldest stock exchange in the U.S. Allows for trading in stocks, bonds, warrants, options, and rights that meet listing requirements.

Niche
A career or business for which a person is well-suited. Also, a product which fulfills one need of a particular market segment, often with little or no competition.

Nodes
One workstation in a network, either local area or wide area (see separate citations).

Nonbank bank
A bank that either accepts deposits or makes loans, but not both. Used to create many new branch banks.

Noncompetitive awards
A method of contracting whereby the federal government negotiates with only one contractor to supply a product or service.

Nonmember bank
A state-regulated bank that does not belong to the federal bank system.

Nonprofit
An organization that has no shareholders, does not distribute profits, and is without federal and state tax liabilities.

Norms
See Financial ratios

North American Free Trade Agreement (NAFTA)
Passed in 1993, NAFTA eliminates trade barriers among businesses in the U.S., Canada, and Mexico.

NYSE
See New York Stock Exchange

Occupational Safety & Health Administration (OSHA)
Federal agency that regulates health and safety standards within the workplace.

Optimal firm size
The business size at which the production cost per unit of output (average cost) is, in the long run, at its minimum.

Organizational chart
A hierarchical chart tracking the chain of command within an organization.

OSHA
See Occupational Safety & Health Administration

Overhead
Expenses, such as employee benefits and building utilities, incurred by a business that are unrelated to the actual product or service sold.

Owner's capital
Debt or equity funds provided by the owner(s) of a business; sources of owner's capital are personal savings, sales of assets, or loans from financial institutions.

P & L
See Profit and loss statement

Part-time workers
Normally, those who work less than 35 hours per week. The Tax Reform Act indicated that part-time workers who work less than 17.5 hours per week may be excluded from health plans for purposes of complying with federal nondiscrimination rules.

Part-year workers
Those who work less than 50 weeks per year.

Partnership
Two or more parties who enter into a legal relationship to conduct business for profit. Defined by the U.S. Internal Revenue Code as joint ventures, syndicates, groups, pools, and other associations of two or more persons organized for profit that are not specifically classified in the IRS code as corporations or proprietorships.

Patent
A grant made by the government assuring an inventor the sole right to make, use, and sell an invention for a period of 17 years.

PC
See Professional corporation

Peak
See Cyclical peak

Pension
A series of payments made monthly, semiannually, annually, or at other specified intervals during the lifetime of the pensioner for distribution upon retirement. The term is sometimes used to denote the portion of the retirement allowance financed by the employer's contributions.

Pension fund
A fund established to provide for the payment of pension benefits; the collective contributions made by all of the parties to the pension plan.

Performance appraisal
An established set of objective criteria, based on job description and requirements, that is used to evaluate the performance of an employee in a specific job.

Permit
See Business license

Plan
See Business plan

Pooling
An arrangement for employers to achieve efficiencies and lower health costs by joining together to purchase group health insurance or self-insurance.

PPO
See Preferred provider organization

Preferred lenders program
See SBA special lending institution categories

Preferred provider organization (PPO)
A contractual arrangement with a health care services organization that agrees to discount its health care rates in return for faster payment and/or a patient base.

Premiums
The amount of money paid to an insurer for health insurance under a policy. The premium is generally paid periodically (e.g., monthly), and often is split between the employer and the employee. Unlike deductibles and coinsurance or copayments, premiums are paid for coverage whether or not benefits are actually used.

Prime-age workers
Employees 25 to 54 years of age.

Prime contract
A contract awarded directly by the U.S. Federal Government.

Private company
See Closely held corporation

Private placement
A method of raising capital by offering for sale an investment or business to a small group of investors (generally avoiding registration with the Securities and Exchange Commission or state securities registration agencies). Also known as Private financing or Private offering.

Pro forma
The use of hypothetical figures in financial statements to represent future expenditures, debts, and other potential financial expenses.

Proactive
Taking the initiative to solve problems and anticipate future events before they happen, instead of reacting to an already existing problem or waiting for a difficult situation to occur.

Procurement
A contract from an agency of the federal government for goods or services from a small business.

Prodigy
An online service which is accessible by computer modem. The service features Internet access, bulletin boards, online periodicals, electronic mail, and other services for subscribers.

Product development
The stage of the innovation process where research is translated into a product or process through evaluation, adaptation, and demonstration.

Product franchising
An arrangement for a franchisee to use the name and to produce the product line of the franchisor or parent corporation.

Production
The manufacture of a product.

Production prototype
See Prototype

Productivity
A measurement of the number of goods produced during a specific amount of time.

Professional corporation (PC)
Organized by members of a profession such as medicine, dentistry, or law for the purpose of conducting their professional activities as a corporation. Liability of a member or shareholder is limited in the same manner as in a business corporation.

Profit and loss statement (P & L)
The summary of the incomes (total revenues) and costs of a company's operation during a specific period of time. Also known as Income and expense statement.

Proposal
See Business plan

Proprietorship
The most common legal form of business ownership; about 85 percent of all small businesses are proprietorships. The liability of the owner is unlimited in this form of ownership.

Prospective payment system
A cost-containment measure included in the Social Security Amendments of 1983 whereby Medicare payments to hospitals are based on established prices, rather than on cost reimbursement.

Prototype
A model that demonstrates the validity of the concept of an invention (laboratory prototype); a model that meets the needs of the manufacturing process and the user (production prototype).

Prudent investor rule or standard
A legal doctrine that requires fiduciaries to make investments using the prudence, diligence, and intelligence that would be used by a prudent person in making similar investments. Because fiduciaries make investments on behalf of third-party beneficiaries, the standard results in very conservative investments. Until recently, most state regulations required the fiduciary to apply this standard to each investment. Newer, more progressive regulations permit fiduciaries to apply this standard to the portfolio taken as a whole, thereby allowing a fiduciary to balance a portfolio with higher-yield, higher-risk investments. In states with more progressive regulations, practically every type of security is eligible for inclusion in the portfolio of investments made by a fiduciary, provided

that the portfolio investments, in their totality, are those of a prudent person.

Public equity markets
Organized markets for trading in equity shares such as common stocks, preferred stocks, and warrants. Includes markets for both regularly traded and nonregularly traded securities.

Public offering
General solicitation for participation in an investment opportunity. Interstate public offerings are supervised by the U.S. Securities and Exchange Commission (see separate citation).

Quality control
The process by which a product is checked and tested to ensure consistent standards of high quality.

Rate of return
The yield obtained on a security or other investment based on its purchase price or its current market price. The total rate of return is current income plus or minus capital appreciation or depreciation.

Real property
Includes the land and all that is contained on it.

Realignment
See Resource realignment

Recession
Contraction of economic activity occurring between the peak and trough (see separate citations) of a business cycle.

Regulated market
A market in which the government controls the forces of supply and demand, such as who may enter and what price may be charged.

Regulation D
A vehicle by which small businesses make small offerings and private placements of securities with limited disclosure requirements. It was designed to ease the burdens imposed on small businesses utilizing this method of capital formation.

Regulatory Flexibility Act
An act requiring federal agencies to evaluate the impact of their regulations on small businesses before

the regulations are issued and to consider less burdensome alternatives.

Research
The initial stage of the innovation process, which includes idea generation and invention.

Research and development financing
A tax-advantaged partnership set up to finance product development for start-ups as well as more mature companies.

Resource mobility
The ease with which labor and capital move from firm to firm or from industry to industry.

Resource realignment
The adjustment of productive resources to interindustry changes in demand.

Resources
The sources of support or help in the innovation process, including sources of financing, technical evaluation, market evaluation, management and business assistance, etc.

Retained business earnings
Business profits that are retained by the business rather than being distributed to the shareholders as dividends.

Revolving credit
An agreement with a lending institution for an amount of money, which cannot exceed a set maximum, over a specified period of time. Each time the borrower repays a portion of the loan, the amount of the repayment may be borrowed yet again.

Risk capital
See Venture capital

Risk management
The act of identifying potential sources of financial loss and taking action to minimize their negative impact.

Routing
The sequence of steps necessary to complete a product during production.

S corporations
See Sub chapter S corporations

SBA
See Small Business Administration

SBA direct loans
Loans made directly by the U.S. Small Business Administration (SBA); monies come from funds appropriated specifically for this purpose. In general, SBA direct loans carry interest rates slightly lower than those in the private financial markets and are available only to applicants unable to secure private financing or an SBA guaranteed loan.

SBA 504 Program
See Certified development corporation

SBA guaranteed loans
Loans made by lending institutions in which the U.S. Small Business Administration (SBA) will pay a prior agreed-upon percentage of the outstanding principal in the event the borrower of the loan defaults. The terms of the loan and the interest rate are negotiated between theborrower and the lending institution, within set parameters.

SBA loans
See Disaster loans; SBA direct loans; SBA guaranteed loans; SBA special lending institution categories

SBA Management Assistance Programs
Classes, workshops, counseling, and publications offered by the U.S. Small Business Administration.

SBA special lending institution categories
U.S. Small Business Administration (SBA) loan program in which the SBA promises certified banks a 72-hour turnaround period in giving its approval for a loan, and in which preferred lenders in a pilot program are allowed to write SBA loans without seeking prior SBA approval.

SBDB
See Small Business Data Base

SBDC
See Small business development centers

SBI
See Small business institutes program

SBIC
See Small business investment corporation

SBIR Program
See Small Business Innovation Development Act of 1982

Scale economies
The decline of the production cost per unit of output (average cost) as the volume of output increases.

Scale efficiency
The reduction in unit cost available to a firm when producing at a higher output volume.

SCORE
See Service Corps of Retired Executives

SEC
See Securities and Exchange Commission

SECA
See Self-Employment Contributions Act

Second-stage financing
Working capital for the initial expansion of a company that is producing, shipping, and has growing accounts receivable and inventories. Also known as Second-round financing.

Secondary market
A market established for the purchase and sale of outstanding securities following their initial distribution.

Secondary worker
Any worker in a family other than the person who is the primary source of income for the family.

Secondhand capital
Previously used and subsequently resold capital equipment (e.g., buildings and machinery).

Securities and Exchange Commission (SEC)
Federal agency charged with regulating the trade of securities to prevent unethical practices in the investor market.

Securitized debt
A marketing technique that converts long-term loans to marketable securities.

Seed capital
Venture financing provided in the early stages of the innovation process, usually during product development.

Self-employed person
One who works for a profit or fees in his or her own business, profession, or trade, or who operates a farm.

Self-Employment Contributions Act (SECA)
Federal law that governs the self-employment tax (see separate citation).

Self-employment income
Income covered by Social Security if a business earns a net income of at least $400.00 during the year. Taxes are paid on earnings that exceed $400.00.

Self-employment retirement plan
See Keogh plan

Self-employment tax
Required tax imposed on self-employed individuals for the provision of Social Security and Medicare. The tax must be paid quarterly with estimated income tax statements.

Self-funding
A health benefit plan in which a firm uses its own funds to pay claims, rather than transferring the financial risks of paying claims to an outside insurer in exchange for premium payments.

Service Corps of Retired Executives (SCORE)
Volunteers for the SBA Management Assistance Program who provide one-on-one counseling and teach workshops and seminars for small firms.

Service firm
See Business service firm

Service sector
Broadly defined, all U.S. industries that produce intangibles, including the five major industry divisions of transportation, communications, and utilities; wholesale trade; retail trade; finance, insurance, and real estate; and services.

Set asides
See Small business set asides

Short-haul service
A type of transportation service in which the transporter supplies service between cities where the maximum distance is no more than 200 miles.

Short-term debt
An obligation that matures in one year.

SIC codes
See Standard Industrial Classification codes

Single-establishment enterprise
See Establishment

Small business
An enterprise that is independently owned and operated, is not dominant in its field, and employs fewer than 500 people. For SBA purposes, the U.S. Small Business Administration (SBA) considers various other factors (such as gross annual sales) in determining size of a business.

Small Business Administration (SBA)
An independent federal agency that provides assistance with loans, management, and advocating interests before other federal agencies.

Small Business Data Base
A collection of microdata (see separate citation) files on individual firms developed and maintained by the U.S. Small Business Administration.

Small business development centers (SBDC)
Centers that provide support services to small businesses, such as individual counseling, SBA advice, seminars and conferences, and other learning center activities. Most services are free of charge, or available at minimal cost.

Small business development corporation
See Certified development corporation

Small business-dominated industry
Industry in which a minimum of 60 percent of employment or sales is in firms with fewer than 500 employees.

Small Business Innovation Development Act of 1982
Federal statute requiring federal agencies with large extramural research and development budgets to allocate a certain percentage of these funds to small research and development firms. The program, called the Small Business Innovation Research (SBIR) Program, is designed to stimulate technological innovation and make greater use of small businesses in meeting national innovation needs.

Small business institutes (SBI) program
Cooperative arrangements made by U.S. Small Business Administration district offices and local colleges and

universities to provide small business firms with graduate students to counsel them without charge.

Small business investment corporation (SBIC)
A privately owned company licensed and funded through the U.S. Small Business Administration and private sector sources to provide equity or debt capital to small businesses.

Small business set asides
Procurement (see separate citation) opportunities required by law to be on all contracts under $10,000 or a certain percentage of an agency's total procurement expenditure.

Smaller firms
For U.S. Department of Commerce purposes, those firms not included in the Fortune 1000.

SMSA
See Metropolitan statistical area

Socially and economically disadvantaged
Individuals who have been subjected to racial or ethnic prejudice or cultural bias without regard to their qualities as individuals, and whose abilities to compete are impaired because of diminished opportunities to obtain capital and credit.

Sole proprietorship
An unincorporated, one-owner business, farm, or professional practice.

Special lending institution categories
See SBA special lending institution categories

Standard Industrial Classification (SIC) codes
Four-digit codes established by the U.S. Federal Government to categorize businesses by type of economic activity; the first two digits correspond to major groups such as construction and manufacturing, while the last two digits correspond to subgroups such as home construction or highway construction.

Standard metropolitan statistical area (SMSA)
See Metropolitan statistical area

Start-up
A new business, at the earliest stages of development and financing.

Start-up costs
Costs incurred before a business can commence operations.

Start-up financing
Financing provided to companies that have either completed product development and initial marketing or have been in business for less than one year but have not yet sold their product commercially.

Stock
A certificate of equity ownership in a business.

Stop-loss coverage
Insurance for a self-insured plan that reimburses the company for any losses it might incur in its health claims beyond a specified amount.

Strategic planning
Projected growth and development of a business to establish a guiding direction for the future. Also used to determine which market segments to explore for optimal sales of products or services.

Structural unemployment
See Unemployment

Sub chapter S corporations
Corporations that are considered noncorporate for tax purposes but legally remain corporations.

Subcontract
A contract between a prime contractor and a subcontractor, or between subcontractors, to furnish supplies or services for performance of a prime contract (see separate citation) or a subcontract.

Surety bonds
Bonds providing reimbursement to an individual, company, or the government if a firm fails to complete a contract. The U.S. Small Business Administration guarantees surety bonds in a program much like the SBA guaranteed loan program (see separate citation).

Swing loan
See Bridge financing

Target market
The clients or customers sought for a business' product or service.

Targeted Jobs Tax Credit
Federal legislation enacted in 1978 that provides a tax credit to an employer who hires structurally unemployed individuals.

Tax number
A number assigned to a business by a state revenue department that enables the business to buy goods without paying sales tax.

Taxable bonds
An interest-bearing certificate of public or private indebtedness. Bonds are issued by public agencies to finance economic development.

Technical assistance
See Management and technical assistance

Technical evaluation
Assessment of technological feasibility.

Technology
The method in which a firm combines and utilizes labor and capital resources to produce goods or services; the application of science for commercial or industrial purposes.

Technology transfer
The movement of information about a technology or intellectual property from one party to another for use.

Tenure
See Employee tenure

Term
The length of time for which a loan is made.

Terms of a note
The conditions or limits of a note; includes the interest rate per annum, the due date, and transferability and convertibility features, if any.

Third-party administrator
An outside company responsible for handling claims and performing administrative tasks associated with health insurance plan maintenance.

Third-stage financing
Financing provided for the major expansion of a company whose sales volume is increasing and that is breaking even or profitable. These funds are used for further plant expansion, marketing, working capital, or development of an improved product. Also known as Third-round or Mezzanine financing.

Time deposit
A bank deposit that cannot be withdrawn before a specified future time.

Time management
Skills and scheduling techniques used to maximize productivity.

Trade credit
Credit extended by suppliers of raw materials or finished products. In an accounting statement, trade credit is referred to as "accounts payable."

Trade name
The name under which a company conducts business, or by which its business, goods, or services are identified. It may or may not be registered as a trademark.

Trade periodical
A publication with a specific focus on one or more aspects of business and industry.

Trade secret
Competitive advantage gained by a business through the use of a unique manufacturing process or formula.

Trade show
An exhibition of goods or services used in a particular industry. Typically held in exhibition centers where exhibitors rent space to display their merchandise.

Trademark
A graphic symbol, device, or slogan that identifies a business. A business has property rights to its trademark from the inception of its use, but it is still prudent to register all trademarks with the Trademark Office of the U.S. Department of Commerce.

Translation
See Product development

Treasury bills
Investment tender issued by the Federal Reserve Bank in amounts of $10,000 that mature in 91 to 182 days.

Treasury bonds
Long-term notes with maturity dates of not less than seven and not more than twenty-five years.

Treasury notes
Short-term notes maturing in less than seven years.

Trend
A statistical measurement used to track changes that occur over time.

Trough
See Cyclical trough

UCC
See Uniform Commercial Code

UL
See Underwriters Laboratories

Underwriters Laboratories (UL)
One of several private firms that tests products and processes to determine their safety. Although various firms can provide this kind of testing service, many local and insurance codes specify UL certification.

Underwriting
A process by which an insurer determines whether or not and on what basis it will accept an application for insurance. In an experience-rated plan, premiums are based on a firm's or group's past claims; factors other than prior claims are used for community-rated or manually rated plans.

Unfair competition
Refers to business practices, usually unethical, such as using unlicensed products, pirating merchandise, or misleading the public through false advertising, which give the offending business an unequitable advantage over others.

Unfunded accrued liability
The excess of total liabilities, both present and prospective, over present and prospective assets.

Unemployment
The joblessness of individuals who are willing to work, who are legally and physically able to work, and who are seeking work. Unemployment may represent the temporary joblessness of a worker between jobs (frictional unemployment) or the joblessness of a worker whose skills are not suitable for jobs available in the labor market (structural unemployment).

Uniform Commercial Code (UCC)
A code of laws governing commercial transactions across the U.S., except Louisiana. Their purpose is to bring uniformity to financial transactions.

Uniform product code (UPC symbol)
A computer-readable label comprised of ten digits and stripes that encodes what a product is and how much it costs. The first five digits are assigned by the Uniform Product Code Council, and the last five digits by the individual manufacturer.

Unit cost
See Average cost

UPC symbol
See Uniform product code

U.S. Establishment and Enterprise Microdata (USEEM) File
A cross-sectional database containing information on employment, sales, and location for individual enterprises and establishments with employees that have a Dun & Bradstreet credit rating.

U.S. Establishment Longitudinal Microdata (USELM) File
A database containing longitudinally linked sample microdata on establishments drawn from the U.S. Establishment and Enterprise Microdata file (see separate citation).

U.S. Small Business Administration 504 Program
See Certified development corporation

USEEM
See U.S. Establishment and Enterprise Microdata File

USELM
See U.S. Establishment Longitudinal Microdata File

VCN
See Venture capital network

Venture capital
Money used to support new or unusual business ventures that exhibit above-average growth rates, significant potential for market expansion, and are in need of additional financing to sustain growth or further research and development; equity or equity-type financing traditionally provided at the

commercialization stage, increasingly available prior to commercialization.

Venture capital company

A company organized to provide seed capital to a business in its formation stage, or in its first or second stage of expansion. Funding is obtained through public or private pension funds, commercial banks and bank holding companies, small business investment corporations licensed by the U.S. Small Business Administration, private venture capital firms, insurance companies, investment management companies, bank trust departments, industrial companies seeking to diversify their investment, and investment bankers acting as intermediaries for other investors or directly investing on their own behalf.

Venture capital limited partnerships

Designed for business development, these partnerships are an institutional mechanism for providing capital for young, technology-oriented businesses. The investors' money is pooled and invested in money market assets until venture investments have been selected. The general partners are experienced investment managers who select and invest the equity and debt securities of firms with high growth potential and the ability to go public in the near future.

Venture capital network (VCN)

A computer database that matches investors with entrepreneurs.

WAN

See Wide Area Network

Wide Area Network (WAN)

Computer networks linking systems throughout a state or around the world in order to facilitate the sharing of information.

Withholding

Federal, state, social security, and unemployment taxes withheld by the employer from employees' wages; employers are liable for these taxes and the corporate umbrella and bankruptcy will not exonerate an employer from paying back payroll withholding. Employers should escrow these funds in a separate account and disperse them quarterly to withholding authorities.

Workers' compensation

A state-mandated form of insurance covering workers injured in job-related accidents. In some states, the state is the insurer; in other states, insurance must be acquired from commercial insurance firms. Insurance rates are based on a number of factors, including salaries, firm history, and risk of occupation.

Working capital

Refers to a firm's short-term investment of current assets, including cash, short-term securities, accounts receivable, and inventories.

Yield

The rate of income returned on an investment, expressed as a percentage. Income yield is obtained by dividing the current dollar income by the current market price of the security. Net yield or yield to maturity is the current income yield minus any premium above par or plus any discount from par in purchase price, with the adjustment spread over the period from the date of purchase to the date of maturity.

Index

Listings in this index are arranged alphabetically by business plan type, then alphabetically by business plan name. Users are provided with the volume number in which the plan appears.

Index